Lecture Notes in Computer Scie

Commenced Publication in 1973
Founding and Former Series Editors:
Gerhard Goos, Juris Hartmanis, and Jan van Leeuwen

Walter G. Kropatsch   Robert Sablatnig
Allan Hanbury (Eds.)

Pattern
Recognition

27th DAGM Symposium
Vienna, Austria, August 31 – September 2, 2005
Proceedings

 Springer

Volume Editors

Walter G. Kropatsch
Robert Sablatnig
Allan Hanbury
Vienna University of Technology
Institute of Computer-Aided Automation
Pattern Recognition and Image Processing Group
Favoritenstr. 9/1832, 1040 Vienna, Austria
E-mail: {krw, sab, hanbury}@prip.tuwien.ac.at

Library of Congress Control Number: 2005931332

CR Subject Classification (1998): I.5, I.4, I.3.5, I.2.10, I.2.6, F.2.2

ISSN   0302-9743
ISBN-10   3-540-28703-5 Springer Berlin Heidelberg New York
ISBN-13   978-3-540-28703-2 Springer Berlin Heidelberg New York

Springer is a part of Springer Science+Business Media

springeronline.com

© Springer-Verlag Berlin Heidelberg 2005
Printed in Germany

Typesetting: Camera-ready by author, data conversion by Scientific Publishing Services, Chennai, India
Printed on acid-free paper   SPIN: 11550518   06/3142   5 4 3 2 1 0

Preface

It is both an honor and a pleasure to hold the 27th Annual Meeting of the German Association for Pattern Recognition, DAGM 2005, at the Vienna University of Technology, Austria, organized by the Pattern Recognition and Image Processing (PRIP) Group. We received 122 contributions of which we were able to accept 29 as oral presentations and 31 as posters. Each paper received three reviews, upon which decisions were made based on correctness, presentation, technical depth, scientific significance and originality. The selection as oral or poster presentation does not signify a quality grading but reflects attractiveness to the audience which is also reflected in the order of appearance of papers in these proceedings. The papers are printed in the same order as presented at the symposium and posters are integrated in the corresponding thematic session.

In putting these proceedings together, many people played significant roles which we would like to acknowledge. First of all our thanks go to the authors who contributed their work to the symposium. Second, we are grateful for the dedicated work of the 38 members of the Program Committee for their effort in evaluating the submitted papers and in providing the necessary decision support information and the valuable feedback for the authors. Furthermore, the Program Committee awarded prizes for the best papers, and we want to sincerely thank the donors.

We were honored to have the following three invited speakers at the conference:

- *Jan P. Allebach (School of Electrical and Computer Engineering, Purdue University)*: Digital Printing – A Rich Domain for Image Analysis and Pattern Recognition.
- *Sven Dickinson (Department of Computer Science, University of Toronto)*: Object Categorization and the Need for Many-to-Many Matching.
- *Václav Hlaváč (Center for Machine Perception, Czech Technical University)*: Simple Solvers for Large Quadratic Programming Tasks.

We are grateful for economic support from the Austrian Computer Society, Microsoft Europe, IBM, Advanced Computer Vision, and the Vienna Convention Bureau. Many thanks to our local support team, Karin Hraby, Ernestine Zolda and Patrizia Schmidt-Simonsky, who made this symposium possible and took care of all practical tasks involved in planning DAGM 2005. Special thanks go to Martin Kampel, who wrote and maintained the symposium website and supported the organization of the review process. We hope that these proceedings, following the tradition of all DAGM symposiums, will not only impact on the current research of the readers but will also represent important archival material.

June 2005   Robert Sablatnig, Walter Kropatsch and Allan Hanbury

DAGM[1] 2005 Organization

General Chairs

Walter G. Kropatsch	TU Wien
Robert Sablatnig	TU Wien

Organizing Committee

Karin Hraby	TU Wien
Ernestine Zolda	TU Wien
Martin Kampel	TU Wien
Patrizia Schmidt-Simonsky	TU Wien

Since 1978 DAGM (German Association for Pattern Recognition) has organized annual scientific conferences at various venues. The goal of each DAGM symposium is to inspire conceptual thinking, support the dissemination of ideas and research results from different areas in the field of pattern recognition, stimulate discussions and the exchange of ideas among experts, and support and motivate the next generation of young researchers.

DAGM e.V. was founded as a registered research association in September 1999. Until that time, DAGM had been comprised of the following support organizations that have since become honorary members of DAGM e.V.:

1. DGaO, Deutsche Arbeitsgemeinschaft für angewandte Optik (German Society for Applied Optics)
2. GMDS, Deutsche Gesellschaft für Medizinische Informatik, Biometrie und Epidemiologie (German Society for Medical Informatics, Biometry, and Epidemiology)
3. GI, Gesellschaft für Informatik (German Informatics Society)
4. ITG, Informationstechnische Gesellschaft (Information Technology Society)
5. DGN, Deutsche Gesellschaft für Nuklearmedizin (German Society for Nuclear Medicine)
6. IEEE, Deutsche Sektion des IEEE (Institute of Electrical and Electronics Engineers, German Section)
7. DGPF, Deutsche Gesellschaft für Photogrammetrie und Fernerkundung (German Society for Photogrammetry, Remote Sensing and Geo-information)
8. VDMA, Fachabteilung industrielle Bildverarbeitung/Machine Vision (VDMA Robotics + Automation Division)
9. GNNS, German Chapter of the European Neural Network Society
10. DGR, Deutsche Gesellschaft fur Robotik (German Robotics Society)

---

[1] DAGM e.V.: Deutsche Arbeitsgemeinschaft für Mustererkennung (German Association for Pattern Recognition).

Prizes 2004

Olympus Prize

The Olympus Prize 2004 was awarded to:

Daniel Cremers
for his significant contributions in the research area of Image Segmentation.

DAGM Prizes

The main prize was awarded to:

Bastian Leibe and Bernt Schiele
Scale-Invariant Object Categorization Using a Scale-Adaptive Mean Shift Search.

Further DAGM prizes for 2004 were awarded to:

Volker Roth and Tilman Lange
Adaptive Feature Selection in Image Segmentation.

Michael Felsberg and Gösta Granlund
POI Detection Using Channel Clustering and the 2D Energy Tensor.

Daniel Keysers, Thomas Deselaers and Hermann Ney
Pixel-to-Pixel Matching for Image Recognition Using Hungarian Graph Matching.

DAGM 2005 Program Committee

Horst Bischof	TU Graz
Joachim Buhmann	ETH Zürich
Hans Burkhardt	Univ. Freiburg
Wolfgang Förstner	Univ. Bonn
Siegfried Fuchs	TU Dresden
Gerd Hirzinger	DLR-Oberpfaffenhofen
Joachim Hornegger	Univ. Erlangen
Xiaoyi Jiang	Univ. Münster
Martin Kampel	TU Wien
Dietrich Klakow	Univ. Saarland
Reinhard Koch	Univ. Kiel
Walter Kropatsch	TU Wien
Gernot Kubin	TU Graz
Aleš Leonardis	Univ. Ljubljana
Claus-Eberhard Liedtke	Univ. Hannover
Bärbel Mertsching	Univ. Hamburg
Rudolf Mester	Univ. Frankfurt
Bernd Michaelis	Univ. Magdeburg
Heiko Neumann	Univ. Ulm
Hermann Ney	RWTH Aachen
Heinrich Niemann	Univ. Erlangen
Elmar Nöth	Univ. Erlangen
Bernd Radig	TU München
Helge Ritter	Univ. Bielefeld
Robert Sablatnig	TU Wien
Gerhard Sagerer	Univ. Bielefeld
Otmar Scherzer	Univ. Innsbruck
Bernt Schiele	ETH Zürich
Werner Schneider	BOKU Wien
Christoph Schnörr	Univ. Mannheim
Bernhard Schölkopf	MPI Tübingen
Hans-Peter Seidel	MPI Saarbrücken
Gerald Sommer	Univ. Kiel
Thomas Vetter	Univ. Basel
Markus Vincze	TU Wien
Friedrich M. Wahl	Univ. Braunschweig
Joachim Weickert	Univ. Saarland

Table of Contents

Invited Paper

Segmentation and Grouping

Automatic Speech Understanding

3D View Registration and Surface Modeling

Motion and Tracking

Computational Learning

Applications

Uncertainity and Robustness

Invited Paper

On Determining the Color of the Illuminant Using the Dichromatic Reflection Model

Marc Ebner and Christian Herrmann

Universität Würzburg, Lehrstuhl für Informatik II,
Am Hubland, 97074 Würzburg, Germany
ebner@informatik.uni-wuerzburg.de,
http://www2.informatik.uni-wuerzburg.de/staff/ebner/welcome.html

Abstract. The human visual system is able to accurately determine the color of objects irrespective of the spectral power distribution used to illuminate the scene. This ability to compute color constant descriptors is called color constancy. Many different algorithms have been proposed to solve the problem of color constancy. Usually, some assumptions have to be made in order to solve this problem. Algorithms based on the dichromatic reflection model assume that the light reflected from an object results from a combined matte and specular reflection. This assumption is used to estimate the color of the illuminant. Once the color of the illuminant is known, one can compute a color corrected image as it would appear under a canonical, i.e. white illuminant. A number of different methods can be used to estimate the illuminant from the dichromatic reflection model. We evaluate several different methods on a standard set of images. Our results indicate that the median operator is particularly useful in estimating the color of the illuminant. We also found that it is not advantageous to assume that the illuminant can be approximated by the curve of the black-body radiator.

1 Motivation

A white wall illuminated by yellowish light reflects more light in the red and green part than in the blue part of the spectrum. If we use a camera to take an image of the wall, the sensor of the camera will measure the light reflected from the wall. Thus, a photograph of the wall will have a yellow cast. A human observer, however, is able to somehow discount the illuminant. He will perceive the wall as being white irrespective of the type of illuminant used. This ability to compute color constant descriptors is known as color constancy [1]. Developing algorithms for color constancy is obviously very important for consumer photography. Another area where color constancy algorithms may be used is machine based object recognition. In this paper, we will be looking at several different methods on how to estimate the color of the illuminant from a color image. Once the illuminant is known, it can be used to compute a color corrected image under a canonical, i.e. white illuminant. The different methods will be evaluated on a standard set of test images.

W. Kropatsch, R. Sablatnig, and A. Hanbury (Eds.): DAGM 2005, LNCS 3663, pp. 1–8, 2005.
© Springer-Verlag Berlin Heidelberg 2005

2   The Dichromatic Reflection Model

The dichromatic reflection model assumes that object color is a result of a matte reflection in combination with a specular reflective component [2,3,4]. The overall color of the object is determined by the matte reflection whereas specular highlights are caused by the specular reflection. These highlights occur whenever the light is reflected such that it directly enters the camera. Since the light from the light source is reflected directly into the camera it can be used to estimate the color of the illuminant.

Let $\mathbf{S}(\lambda)$ be the vector with the response functions of the sensor. For an RGB-sensor, we have $\mathbf{S} = [S_r(\lambda), S_g(\lambda), S_b(\lambda)]$ where the functions $S_i(\lambda)$ with $i \in \{r, g, b\}$ specify the sensor's response characteristics to light in the red, green, and blue part of the spectrum. Let $E(\lambda)$ be the light falling into the sensor, then the response of the sensor is given by

$$\mathbf{I} = \int_{-\infty}^{+\infty} E(\lambda)\mathbf{S}(\lambda)d\lambda.$$

Under the dichromatic reflection model, the response of the sensor is given by

$$\mathbf{I} = \int_{-\infty}^{+\infty} \left(s_M R_M(\lambda)E(\lambda) + s_S R_S(\lambda)E(\lambda) \right) \mathbf{S}(\lambda)d\lambda$$

where $R_M(\lambda)$ is the object reflectance with regard to the matte reflection, $R_S(\lambda)$ is the object reflectance with regard to the specular reflection, s_M and s_S are two scaling factors which depend on the object geometry and $E(\lambda)$ is the irradiance falling onto the object [4].

Let us now assume that the response functions are very narrow, i.e. they can be modeled by delta functions $S_i(\lambda) = \delta(\lambda - \lambda_i)$. Such ideal sensors only respond to a single wavelength λ_i with $i \in \{r, g, b\}$. This gives us

$$I_i = s_M R_{M,i} E_i + s_S R_{S,i} E_i.$$

Assuming that the specular reflection behaves like a perfect mirror, i.e. $R_{S,i} = 1$, we obtain

$$I_i = s_M R_{M,i} E_i + s_S E_i.$$

Let $\mathbf{C}_M = [R_{M,r}E_r, R_{M,g}E_g, R_{M,b}E_b]$ be the measured matte color of the object and let $\mathbf{C}_S = [E_r, E_g, E_b]$ be the color of the illuminant. We now see that the color measured by the sensor is restricted to the linear combination of the matte color of the object point $\mathbf{C}_M$ as seen under illuminant E and the color of the illuminant $\mathbf{C}_S$. The two vectors $\mathbf{C}_M$ and $\mathbf{C}_S$ define a plane inside the RGB color space [3].

By computing chromaticities, the three-dimensional data points are projected onto the plane $r + g + b = 1$. This gives us a line in chromaticity space. The two points which define the line are the chromaticities of the measured object color $[r_O, g_O]^T$ and the chromaticities of the color of the illuminant $[r_E, g_E]^T$

$$\begin{pmatrix} r \\ g \end{pmatrix} = s \begin{pmatrix} r_O \\ g_O \end{pmatrix} + (1 - s) \begin{pmatrix} r_E \\ g_E \end{pmatrix}$$

for some scaling factor s. The data points which belong to a uniformly colored surface will all be distributed along this, so called, dichromatic line. We now assume that the illuminant is uniform over the entire scene. In this case, all dichromatic lines will have one point in common, the color of the illuminant.

3   Natural Illuminants

If we know the correspondence between data points and surfaces, we can compute the dichromatic line for each surface. The dichromatic line can be found by doing a linear regression on the data. Alternatively we can also compute the covariance matrix and then locate the eigenvector which corresponds to the largest eigenvalue to determine the orientation of the dichromatic line. According to Finlayson and Schaefer [4] the algorithms based on the dichromatic reflection model perform well only under idealized conditions. The estimated illuminant turns out not to be very accurate. If small amounts of noise are present in the data then the computed intersection may be very different from the actual intersection. Finlayson and Schaefer note that the method works well for highly saturated surfaces under laboratory conditions but does not work well for real images. In their work, they assumed the images to be pre-segmented.

They suggest to compute the intersection of the dichromatic lines with the curve of the black-body radiator in order to make the method more robust. Many natural light sources can be approximated by a black-body radiator. The power spectrum $E(\lambda, T)$ of a black-body radiator depends on the temperature T. It can be described by the following equation [5,6]

$$E(\lambda, T) = \frac{2hc^2}{\lambda^5} \frac{1}{\left(e^{\frac{hc}{k_B T \lambda}} - 1\right)}$$

where T is the temperature of the black-body measured in Kelvin, $h = 6.626176 \cdot 10^{-34} Js$ is Planck's constant, $k_B = 1.3806 \cdot 10^{-23} \frac{J}{K}$ is Boltzmann's constant, and $c = 2.9979 \cdot 10^8 \frac{m}{s}$ is the speed of light. Many natural light sources such as the flame of a candle, light from a light bulb or sunlight can be approximated by the power spectrum of the black-body radiator. The chromaticities of daylight also follows the curve of the black-body radiator closely [7]. Plotting the chromaticities of the black-body radiator in CIE XYZ color space, one obtains a curve which can be approximated by a quadratic equation.

Using this approximation, we can compute the intersection between the dichromatic line and the curve of the black-body radiator. As a result, one either obtains none, one or two points of intersection. If the dichromatic line does not intersect the curve of the black-body radiator, then one can locate the closest point between the line and the curve of the black-body radiator. If two intersections are found, one can use some heuristics to select one of the two as the correct intersection. Using the constraint that the illuminant can be approximated by the curve of the black-body radiator, in theory it is possible, to determine the color of the illuminant from a single surface. Algorithms based on the gray world assumption [8,9,10] in contrast, require that the scene be sufficiently diverse.

4 Estimating the Color of the Illuminant by Segmentation and Filtering

Risson [11] extended the algorithm of Finlayson and Schaefer by also addressing the segmentation problem. Risson proposed to determine the illuminant by first segmenting the image and then filtering out regions which are not in line with the dichromatic reflection model. As a first step, noise is removed by pre-filtering the image using a Gaussian or median filter. Then the image is segmented. Regions which do not agree with the dichromatic reflection model, such as achromatic regions or regions which belong to the sky, are removed. In order to compute the direction of the dichromatic line reliably, the region has to have a certain size. Risson [11] suggested to remove all regions with a saturation less than 12%. For each remaining region, the dichromatic line is computed.

The dichromatic line can be computed by performing a linear regression on the x- and y-coordinates in CIE XYZ chromaticity space. We can also compute the covariance matrix for the pixel colors which belong to a single region. Using singular value decomposition, the largest eigenvalue tells us the direction of the dichromatic line. Let $\mathbf{e}_i$ be the normalized eigenvector which corresponds to the largest eigenvalue obtained for region j. The dichromatic line $\mathcal{L}_j$ of region j is then given by

$$\mathcal{L}_j = \{\mathbf{a}_j + s\mathbf{e}_j | \text{with } s \in \mathbb{R}\}$$

where $\mathbf{a}_j$ is the average chromaticity of the region. In theory, the illuminant is located at the point where all dichromatic lines $\mathcal{L}_j$ intersect. In practice, however, the dichromatic lines do not intersect in a single point because of noise in the data. It may also be that some of the computed lines are not caused by pure matte reflections in combination with specular reflections.

It may be possible to develop a classifier to rule out lines which are not in agreement with the dichromatic reflection model. A simpler method is to use the large number of dichromatic lines obtained from the image and to gather statistical evidence for the actual point of intersection. The exact method on how to determine the location of the point of intersection is not specified by Risson [11]. In finding the point of intersection, the curve of the black-body radiator may or may not be used to constrain the set of possible illuminants.

A simple method with no constraints on the color of the illuminant would be to compute the intersection for all possible combinations between two dichromatic lines. This gives us a set of intersections [12]. Let n be the number of dichromatic lines of the image. This gives us $\frac{1}{2}n(n-1)$ points of intersection $\mathbf{p}_i = [x_i, y_i]$ where x_i and y_i are the chromaticities in CIE XYZ color space.

$$\{\mathbf{p}_i | \text{with } i \in [1, ..., \frac{1}{2}n(n-1)]\}$$

From this set we can estimate the actual point of intersection by computing the average of the points of intersection. In this case, the position of the illuminant $\mathbf{p}$ is given by

$$\mathbf{p} = \frac{2}{n(n-1)} \sum_i \mathbf{p}_i.$$

We could also compute the median independently for the x- and y-coordinates. Use of the median operator has the advantage that outliers are removed.

$$\mathbf{p} = [\text{Median}\{x_i\}, \text{Median}\{y_i\}]$$

where Median denotes the computation of the median.

Assuming that the illuminant can be approximated by the curve of the black-body radiator, we can use this curve to constrain the set of possible illuminants. Thus, for each dichromatic line we would first compute the intersection between each dichromatic line and the curve of the black-body radiator and then further process this data. Since the curve of the black-body radiator is a quadratic function of the single coordinate x we obtain either none, one or two points of intersection on the dichromatic line. We could take the average or the median value of all computed x coordinates and then compute the corresponding y coordinate. We could also compute a histogram for all intersection points and then select the bucket with the maximum count. Another possibility would be to determine the corresponding temperature of the black-body radiator for each intersection. Again we could then compute either the average or the median temperature of all intersections. Given the temperature we could compute the corresponding chromaticities in CIE XYZ color space.

Once the illuminant is known, it can be factored out of the image. As a result, we obtain a color image as it would appear under a canonical, e.g. white illuminant. Figure 1 shows the steps of the algorithm for a sample image.

5   Experimental Results

In order to evaluate which method of determining the most likely position of the illuminant works best, we have used a standard dataset for color constancy research, the datasets of Barnard et al. [13][1]. Five different sets were selected from the database. Set 1 contains only objects with minimal specularities, i.e. Lambertian reflectors. Set 2 contains objects with metallic specularities. Set 3 contains objects with non-negligible dielectric specularities. Set 4 contains objects with at least one fluorescent surface. Each object is imaged under up to 11 different illuminants. The objects remained stationary whenever the illuminant was changed. Set 5 can be used to evaluate the performance on object recognition tasks. Objects from set 5 were placed in a random position whenever the illuminant was changed. Sets 1, 2, 3, 4, and 5 contain 22, 14, 9, 6, and 20 different scenes, respectively.

The evaluation of the different methods described in the previous section was done as follows. The color constancy algorithm based on the dichromatic reflection model was applied to each image from the dataset. Then we randomly selected two images from the dataset for each object. This gave us two image sets. The first set of images contains the test images. The second set of images contains the model images. The histogram based object recognition, originally

---

[1] http://www.cs.sfu.ca/~colour/data/index.html

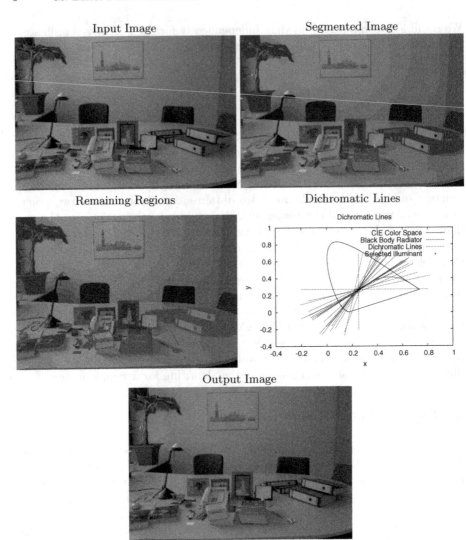

Input Image   Segmented Image

Remaining Regions   Dichromatic Lines

Output Image

Fig. 1. Steps of Risson's [11] algorithm. The input image is segmented into regions of uniform color. Regions which are not in line with the dichromatic reflection model are removed. Here, small regions and regions with low saturation are removed (marked in red). For each remaining region, the dichromatic line is computed. Only a subset of all lines are shown for clarity. The estimated illuminant is marked by a vertical and horizontal line. The last image shows the output image.

introduced by Swain and Ballard [14], was used to find a match for each test image. Since our goal is to evaluate the different estimation methods we have used only color histograms and did not include any other information, i.e. gradients. The χ^2 divergence measure [15,16] was used to find the best match. Let H_T be the color histogram of the test image and and let H_M be the color histogram of the model image. Let $H(\mathbf{c})$ be the probability that the color $\mathbf{c}$ occurs in the image then the χ^2 divergence measure is computed as

$$\chi^2(H_T, H_M) = \sum_{\mathbf{c}} \frac{(H_T(\mathbf{c}) - H_M(\mathbf{c}))^2}{H_T(\mathbf{c}) + H_M(\mathbf{c})}.$$

This process was repeated 100 times for each data set.

Table 1. Results for image sets 1 through 5. Histograms were computed in RGB chromaticity space. For each image set random performance is also shown.

Histogram-based Object Recognition, chromaticity space					
Estimation Method	1	2	3	4	5
Random Recognition Rate	0.045	0.071	0.111	0.167	0.050
Avg. Intersection	0.170	0.282	0.333	0.337	0.154
Median Intersection	**0.535**	**0.589**	**0.839**	**0.725**	**0.328**
Black-Body Average X	0.373	0.504	0.576	0.565	0.235
Black-Body Median X	0.359	0.461	0.580	0.580	0.243
Black-Body Histogram	0.339	0.429	0.608	0.533	0.251
Black-Body Avg. Temperature	0.325	0.434	0.584	0.540	0.228
Black-Body Med. Temperature	0.337	0.428	0.567	0.533	0.212

Table 1 shows the results for each data set and method of estimating the illuminant. The performance based on a random selection of matches is shown at the top of the table. Selecting the median intersection method clearly produced the best results. Since the dichromatic reflection model was developed for objects with specular surfaces it is of no surprise that best results were achieved for set 3. Recognition results for set 5 which presents a more realistic scenario for object recognition are much lower than the results for sets 1 through 4. Restricting the illuminant to be on the curve of the black-body radiator did not result in better performance compared to the median intersection. If we assume the illuminant to be caused by natural illumination such as sunlight or tungsten light then we automatically rule out a greenish or purple illuminant. The above results show that it makes sense not to make any assumptions on the color of the illuminant.

6   Conclusion

Algorithms based on the dichromatic reflection model are especially suited to achieve color constancy provided that specular objects are in the image. In theory, the color of the illuminant is located at the intersection of the dichromatic lines. In practice, however, the dichromatic lines do not intersect in a single point. Thus, one has to decide upon a method to estimate the color of the illuminant from the available data. We evaluated several different methods on how to estimate the color of the illuminant using histogram based object recognition. We found that selecting the median of the intersection of the dichromatic lines in

CIE chromaticity space gave best results. Also, it is not advantageous to make the assumption that the color of the illuminant can be approximated by the curve of the black-body radiator.

References

1. Zeki, S.: A Vision of the Brain. Blackwell Science, Oxford (1993)
2. Tominaga, S.: Surface identification using the dichromatic reflection model. IEEE Transactions on Pattern Analysis and Machine Intelligence **13**(7) (1991) 658–670
3. D'Zmura, M., Lennie, P.: Mechanisms of color constancy. In Healey, G.E., Shafer, S.A., Wolff, L.B., eds.: Color, Boston, Jones and Bartlett Publishers (1992) 224–234
4. Finlayson, G.D., Schaefer, G.: Solving for colour constancy using a constrained dichromatic reflection model. International Journal of Computer Vision **42**(3) (2001) 127–144
5. Haken, H., Wolf, H.C.: Atom- und Quantenphysik: Einführung in die experimentellen und theoretischen Grundlagen. Vierte edn. Springer-Verlag, Berlin, Heidelberg (1990)
6. Jähne, B.: Digitale Bildverarbeitung. Fifth edn. Springer-Verlag, Berlin (2002)
7. International Commission on Illumination: Colorimetry, 2nd edition, corrected reprint. Technical report, International Commission on Illumination (1996)
8. Buchsbaum, G.: A spatial processor model for object colour perception. Journal of the Franklin Institute **310**(1) (1980) 337–350
9. Gershon, R., Jepson, A.D., Tsotsos, J.K.: From [R,G,B] to surface reflectance: Computing color constant descriptors in images. In McDermott, J.P., ed.: Proceedings of the Tenth International Joint Conference on Artificial Intelligence, Milan, Italy. Volume 2., Morgan Kaufmann (1987) 755–758
10. Ebner, M.: A parallel algorithm for color constancy. Journal of Parallel and Distributed Computing **64**(1) (2004) 79–88
11. Risson, V.J.: Determination of an illuminant of digital color image by segmentation and filtering. United States Patent Application, Pub. No. US 2003/0095704 A1 (2003)
12. Herrmann, C.: Schätzung der Farbe einer Lichtquelle anhand eines digitalen Bildes durch Segmentierung und Filterung. Projektpraktikum, Universität Würzburg, Institut für Informatik, Lehrstuhl für Informatik II (2004)
13. Barnard, K., Martin, L., Funt, B., Coath, A.: A data set for color research. Color Research and Application **27**(3) (2002) 147–151
14. Swain, M.J., Ballard, D.H.: Color indexing. International Journal of Computer Vision **7** (1991) 11–32
15. Schiele, B., Crowley, J.L.: Object recognition using multidimensional receptive field histograms. In Buxton, B., Cipolla, R., eds.: Fourth European Conference On Computer Vision, Cambridge, UK, April 14-18, Berlin, Springer-Verlag (1996) 610–619
16. Schiele, B., Crowley, J.L.: Recognition without correspondence using multidimensional receptive field histograms. International Journal of Computer Vision **36**(1) (2000) 31–52

Probabilistic Color Optical Flow

Volker Willert[1], Julian Eggert[2], Sebastian Clever[1], and Edgar Körner[2]

[1] TU Darmstadt, Institute of Automatic Control, Control Theory and Robotics Lab,
Landgraf-Georg-Str.04, 64283 Darmstadt,
volker@rtr.tu-darmstadt.de, mail@sebastian-clever.de
[2] HRI Honda Research Institute GmbH,
Carl-Legien-Straße 30, 63073 Offenbach/Main,
{Julian.Eggert, Edgar.Koerner}@honda-ri.de

Abstract. Usually, optical flow computation is based on grayscale images and the brightness conservation assumption. Recently, some authors have investigated in transferring gradient-based grayscale optical flow methods to color images. These color optical flow methods are restricted to brightness and color conservation over time. In this paper, a correlation-based color optical flow method is presented that allows for brightness and color changes within an image sequence. Further on, the correlation results are used for a probabilistic evaluation that combines the velocity information gained from single color frames to a joint velocity estimate including all color frames. The resulting color optical flow is compared to other representative multi-frame color methods and standard single-frame grayscale methods.

1 Introduction

The optical flow is an approximation for a 2D motion field of the velocity vectors of each pixel of an image, with every vector being a projection of the real 3D velocity of a corresponding surface point [4]. In the literature, the term *optical flow* is usually related to image motion fields that are computed purely based on luminance information. To the contrary, *color optical flow* fields are image motion fields that are estimated based on color images which is also often termed multi-channel optical flow, image flow estimation and photometric invariant optical flow etc.

The usual way for motion estimation is using grayscale images and assuming constant brightness over time. The brightness constraint equation is a quite strong assumption which is only appropriate for high frame-rates with small changes between consecutive frames, so that it often does not hold for real world sequences. In fact, the luminance information is highly dependent on moving shadows, varying shading, moving specularities and fluctuations in the light source intensity [9]. To account for the luminance problem, some authors have extended standard optical flow estimation algorithms for the use of color images instead of grayscale ones. To do so, they replace the brightness assumption with a less restrictive constant chromaticity assumption, also called color invariance assumption, meaning that the color stays constant over time [6],[9]. Obviously, color images contain more scene information than grayscale images and therefore an improvement should be expected for color-based optical flow estimation. Nevertheless, the constant color assumption seems to be nearly as restrictive as the

W. Kropatsch, R. Sablatnig, and A. Hanbury (Eds.): DAGM 2005, LNCS 3663, pp. 9–16, 2005.

constant brightness assumption, since the problem of varying information over time is still present.

A simple experimental examination shown in Fig. 1 indicates that also color information varies to a large extent within consecutive images of a real world sequence. A person holding a yellow book in front of his body is moving towards the camera under a fluorescent tube illumination. Measuring the RGB/HSV values of two consecutive images $\mathbf{I}^t$ and $\mathbf{I}^{t+\Delta t}$ shows that the color information in the different color channels within the black circle is 1) not constant across different pixels within the circle, mainly because of chroma noise, and 2) also not constant for corresponding pixels within a color frame over time, mainly because of luminance and reflection changes. The variances for the different color channels within the circle and over the two consecutive images are listed in the table of Fig. 1.

$\mathbf{I}^t$  $\mathbf{I}^{t+\Delta t}$

		$\mathbf{I}^t$	$\mathbf{I}^t \to \mathbf{I}^{t+\Delta t}$
RGB		$\sigma_r = 13$ $\sigma_g = 14$ $\sigma_b = 21$	$\sigma_r = 12$ $\sigma_g = 7$ $\sigma_b = 3$
HSV		$\sigma_h = 5$ $\sigma_s = 22$ $\sigma_v = 6$	$\sigma_h = 8$ $\sigma_s = 13$ $\sigma_v = 4$

Fig. 1. Example showing the change of color over time because of independent changes of brightness and contrast within different color channels. The color components of an image pixel can change over time because of reflection and illumination changes.

Besides varying color information, it is not clear how existing correlations between the different color channels, mentioned by Madjidi and Negahdaripour in [7], can be used for optical flow computation and how to handle brightness and color assumptions concurrently. In spite of the many open questions regarding color optical flow, researches in that field are still quite sparse [6],[9],[1],[7],[3].

Looking at standard applications, the optical flow is usually gained by comparing brightness patterns of two consecutive images $\mathbf{I}^t$ and $\mathbf{I}^{t+\Delta t}$, where $\mathbf{I}^t$ is an image consisting of pixels at locations $\mathbf{x}$ at time t. Comparing brightness patterns often leads to assume brightness invariance of particular patterns under motion. Let $\hat{\mathbf{W}} \odot \mathbf{G}^{t,\mathbf{P}}$ be a weighted patch of gray values of image $\mathbf{I}^t$ centered and windowed about $\mathbf{p}$ (with $\odot$ symbolising the componentwise multiplication of two vectors). $\mathbf{G}^t$ denotes the vector of intensities linked to the particular image and $\hat{\mathbf{W}}$ defines a window function, which restricts the pattern size. Assuming brightness conservation the standard correlation-based optical flow equation can be formulated following [5] as:

$$\hat{\mathbf{W}} \odot \mathbf{G}^{t,\mathbf{P}} = \hat{\mathbf{W}} \odot \mathbf{G}^{t+\Delta t, \mathbf{p}+\Delta \mathbf{p}} \quad . \tag{1}$$

In order to obtain color optical flow Golland and Bruckstein [6] used a standard gradient-based approach with the same assumptions as in Eq. 1 and applied the resulting brightness constraint equation to each channel of the RGB color space. Then they solved the resulting overdetermined system of linear equations by a standard least-squares algorithm. In an alternative approach they propose that in pure color channels changes in brightness do not appear and the resulting color conservation assumption would be more appropriate. In this approach, they eliminate the brightness containing channel, e.g. the Value channel of the HSV color space, and applied the two pure color channels, e.g. the Hue and Saturation channel, to the mentioned constraint.

Starting from the dichromatic reflection model, van de Weijer and Gevers [9] derive photometric invariants to improve optical flow estimation that in their approach is independent of shadow-shading and specular reflectance changes. They propose the combination of a reliability measure that considers instabilities of the photometric invariants and optical flow estimation to increase robustness.

Based on Gollands and Brucksteins first proposal, Barron and Klette [2],[3] analysed different standard differential techniques for computing the optical flow, e.g. the Lucas and Kanade method or the Horn and Schunck regularization. For more details of standard methods see [4]. Furthermore, they recast the Horn and Schunck regularization adding a directional constraint that depends on one knowing whether the camera is panning or zooming in the standard minimization formula.

Andrews and Lovell [1] developed some faster algorithms for solving the color optical flow equations proposed by Golland, Bruckstein and Barron, Klette.

In this paper, we investigate the formulation of a local linear generative model that approximately describes the correlation between colored image patches within two consecutive multi-frame color images. This model is used to generate locally as well as channel independent measurements that are interpreted as discrete conditional probability density functions (pdfs) holding the probabilities for several motion hypotheses given two consecutive color patches. The advantage of these pdfs given a set of discrete velocities is that a number of velocity hypotheses can be tested concurrently. This means that the velocity information derived from the single color channels can be combined without loosing information. From these velocity distributions velocity vectors are extracted to estimate the optical flow of a color image sequence. The main assumptions are 1) that due to illumination and reflection changes, the color as well as the brightness and the contrast within an image patch can vary systematically over time, especially when there are moving objects in a scene and 2) the information in the color channels can be treated as statistically independent and so can be combined to one joint velocity distribution for each image location.

In Sec. 2 a short introduction to color spaces and a motivation why we treat the color channels as statistically independent is given. In Sec. 3 a model that allows for local value changes over time within the color channels is proposed and a correlation-based probabilistic interpretation is presented that leads to a contrast and brightness invariant color optical flow estimation. Finally some quantitative results are given in Sec. 4 followed by some short conclusion in Sec. 5.

2   Color Spaces

The representation of color in so called color spaces like the RGB, HSV or YCbCr follows the trichromatic theory of color, whereby every color can be specified by an additive composition of appropriate features like, e.g. the quota of red, green and blue in a particular color. Hence every color can be represented by a linear combination of those features each presenting a basis vector, since they are linearly independent and their span describes the whole space.

$$\mathbf{c}_i = x_i\mathbf{e}_x + y_i\mathbf{e}_y + z_i\mathbf{e}_z, \quad \text{with} \;\; 0 \leq x_i, y_i, z_i \leq 1 \;\; \text{and} \;\; i \in \{\text{RGB,HSV,YCbCr}\} \quad (2)$$

The vector $\mathbf{c}_i$ represents a particular color in space i, x_i, y_i, z_i are the corresponding values of the associated features and $\mathbf{e}_x$, $\mathbf{e}_y$, $\mathbf{e}_z$ are the standard basis vectors. Thus, the whole color picture is described by

$$\mathbf{C}_i = (\mathbf{X}_i; \mathbf{Y}_i; \mathbf{Z}_i)^T, \quad (3)$$

where $\mathbf{X}_i$, $\mathbf{Y}_i$, $\mathbf{Z}_i$ are the single color channels of the frame.

An example of a typical three channel HSV color frame is given in Fig. 2. Remarkable are the large differences according to contrastive and homogenous areas between the channels. Every color space is spanned by a 3D coordinate system which describes the color gamut of a particular device [8].

Hue   Saturation   Value

Fig. 2. Example of a three channel HSV color frame with remarkable differences between the channels

The spectral responsivity of the used sensors for measurement, e.g. of the red, green and blue component, will overlap in most cases. Thus the measured components will be correlated. Nevertheless we assume that the measured data of the different channels are statistical independent, since 1) the spectral overlapping appears only in subareas of the spectral responses and 2) the measured data is mostly preprocessed with device specific parameters that differs between the different sensor types meaning the dependence between the channels is unknown. The assumption of statistical independent spectral responses seems to be a good approximation, since in most cases knowing the spectral response of one channel does not allow to draw any conclusions regarding the responses of the other channels. Even if the value of one pixel in a particular channel is measured, this does not constrain the set of possible values of another channel.

3   Correlation-Based Color Optical Flow

Our approach for calculating color optical flow bases on a formulation for computing the optical flow of intensity images [5]. The used notation is illustrated and described in

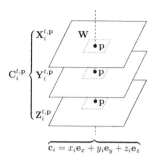

$$\mathbf{C}_i^{t,\mathbf{P}} \begin{cases} \mathbf{X}_i^{t,\mathbf{P}} \\ \mathbf{Y}_i^{t,\mathbf{P}} \\ \mathbf{Z}_i^{t,\mathbf{P}} \end{cases}$$

$$\mathbf{c}_i = x_i \mathbf{e}_x + y_i \mathbf{e}_y + z_i \mathbf{e}_z$$

Fig. 3. This figure shows the used notation. A color picture $\mathbf{C}_i^{t,\mathbf{P}}$ consists of three color channels $\mathbf{X}_i^{t,\mathbf{P}}, \mathbf{Y}_i^{t,\mathbf{P}}, \mathbf{Z}_i^{t,\mathbf{P}}$ with each channel containing a component, e.g. x_i, y_i or z_i (See Eq. 2), for each pixel $\mathbf{p}$. A particular weighted 3D-patch of an image at position $\mathbf{p}$ at time t is achieved with the $\odot$ operation of the window vector $\mathbf{W} := (\hat{\mathbf{W}}; \hat{\mathbf{W}}; \hat{\mathbf{W}})^T$ on the vector $\mathbf{C}_i^{t,\mathbf{P}}$ in the sense $\mathbf{W} \odot \mathbf{C}_i^{t,\mathbf{P}} = (\mathbf{W} \odot \mathbf{X}_i^{t,\mathbf{P}}; \mathbf{W} \odot \mathbf{Y}_i^{t,\mathbf{P}}; \mathbf{W} \odot \mathbf{Z}_i^{t,\mathbf{P}})^T$, denoting elementwise multiplication.

Fig. 3. Here, extending the brightness constancy assumption of Eq. 1, it is assumed that during motion the contributions of the single color channels are independently jittered by noise η and that brightness and contrast variations may occur over time, allowing for systematic brightness, contrast and in addition color changes. The assumed color changes imply e.g. changes of brightness or changes of the spectrum of the illumination. These color changes are accounted for by a scaling vector $\boldsymbol{\lambda}_i$ and a bias vector $\boldsymbol{\kappa}_i$. For the sake of simplicity, we now neglect index i for the different color spaces and arrive in analogy to Eq. 1 at

$$\mathbf{W} \odot \mathbf{C}^{t,\mathbf{P}} = \mathbf{W} \odot \left[\boldsymbol{\lambda} \odot \mathbf{C}^{t+\Delta t, \mathbf{p}+\Delta \mathbf{p}} + \boldsymbol{\kappa} \right] + \boldsymbol{\eta} \quad , \text{ with} \tag{4}$$

$$\boldsymbol{\lambda} := (\lambda_x \mathbf{1}; \lambda_y \mathbf{1}; \lambda_z \mathbf{1})^T, \quad \boldsymbol{\kappa} := (\kappa_x \mathbf{1}; \kappa_y \mathbf{1}; \kappa_z \mathbf{1})^T \quad \text{and} \quad \boldsymbol{\eta} := (\eta_x \mathbf{1}; \eta_y \mathbf{1}; \eta_z \mathbf{1})^T$$

In this expression the patch $\mathbf{W} \odot \mathbf{C}^{t,\mathbf{P}}$ contains in accordance to Eq. 3 for each pixel a vector.

Assuming that the image noise of each channel is zero mean Gaussian and statistically independent from the noise in the other channels, with variances $\sigma_{\eta x}$, $\sigma_{\eta y}$ and $\sigma_{\eta z}$, we get a covariance matrix $\boldsymbol{\Sigma}_\eta$, where only the elements of the leading diagonal are different from zero. Thus, the likelihood that $\mathbf{C}^{t,\mathbf{P}}$ is a match for $\mathbf{C}^{t+\Delta t, \mathbf{p}+\Delta \mathbf{p}}$, given a velocity $\mathbf{v} = \Delta \mathbf{p}/\Delta t$ and the parameter vectors $\boldsymbol{\lambda}, \boldsymbol{\kappa}$, the window function $\mathbf{W}$ and the covariance matrix $\boldsymbol{\Sigma}_\eta$, can be written down as:

$$\rho \left(\mathbf{C}^{t+\Delta t, \mathbf{p}+\Delta \mathbf{p}}, \mathbf{C}^{t,\mathbf{P}} \mid \mathbf{v} \right) \sim \tag{5}$$

$$\sim e^{-\frac{1}{2} \left(\mathbf{W} \odot (\boldsymbol{\lambda} \odot \mathbf{C}^{t,\mathbf{P}} + \boldsymbol{\kappa} - \mathbf{C}^{t+\Delta t, \mathbf{p}+\Delta \mathbf{p}}) \right) \boldsymbol{\Sigma}_\eta^{-1} \left(\mathbf{W} \odot (\boldsymbol{\lambda} \odot \mathbf{C}^{t,\mathbf{P}} + \boldsymbol{\kappa} - \mathbf{C}^{t+\Delta t, \mathbf{p}+\Delta \mathbf{p}}) \right)^T}$$

We now proceed to make Eq. 5 independent on $\boldsymbol{\lambda}$ and $\boldsymbol{\kappa}$. Thus we maximize Eq. 5 with respect to $\boldsymbol{\lambda}$ and $\boldsymbol{\kappa}$. This leads to a minimization of the exponent of Eq. 5:

$$\{\boldsymbol{\lambda}^*, \boldsymbol{\kappa}^*\} := \min_{\boldsymbol{\lambda}, \boldsymbol{\kappa}} F, \quad \text{with} \tag{6}$$

$$F := \left(\mathbf{W} \odot (\boldsymbol{\lambda} \odot \mathbf{C}^{t,\mathbf{P}} + \boldsymbol{\kappa} - \mathbf{C}^{t+\Delta t, \mathbf{p}+\Delta \mathbf{p}}) \right) \boldsymbol{\Sigma}_\eta^{-1} \left(\mathbf{W} \odot (\boldsymbol{\lambda} \odot \mathbf{C}^{t,\mathbf{P}} + \boldsymbol{\kappa} - \mathbf{C}^{t+\Delta t, \mathbf{p}+\Delta \mathbf{p}}) \right)^T.$$

This amounts to solve the homogeneous equation system which we get from setting the derivatives of Eq. 6 in direction of $(\boldsymbol{\lambda}, \boldsymbol{\kappa})$ to zero:

$$\frac{d}{d(\boldsymbol{\lambda}, \boldsymbol{\kappa})} F = 0 \quad , \quad \frac{d^2}{d(\boldsymbol{\lambda}, \boldsymbol{\kappa})^2} F > 0 \quad . \tag{7}$$

In the case that each color channel has an independent λ, this minimization leads to three independent equation systems each containing two constraints with two unknowns, which can be solved separately.

Let $\boldsymbol{\lambda}^* = \left(\lambda_x^*, \lambda_y^*, \lambda_z^*\right)^T$, $\boldsymbol{\kappa}^* = \left(\kappa_x^*, \kappa_y^*, \kappa_z^*\right)^T$ be the parameters which minimize Eq. 6. Substituting $\boldsymbol{\lambda} = \boldsymbol{\lambda}^*$ and $\boldsymbol{\kappa} = \boldsymbol{\kappa}^*$ into Eq. 5, the final likelihood reads:

$$\rho\left(\mathbf{C}^{t+\Delta t,\mathbf{p}+\Delta \mathbf{p}}, \mathbf{C}^{t,\mathbf{p}} \mid \mathbf{v}\right) \sim e^{-\frac{1}{2}\sum_{A=X,Y,Z}\left(\frac{\sigma_{A^{t,p}}}{\sigma_{\eta A}}\right)^2 \left(1-\varrho^2_{A^{t,p},A^{t+\Delta t,p+\Delta p}}\right)} \quad , \quad (8)$$

with $\sigma_{A^{t,p}}$ being the variance of the weighted patch of the momentary channel and $\varrho_{A^{t,p},A^{t+\Delta t,p+\Delta p}}$ being the correlation coefficient between two patches of two consecutive channels over time. From here on, for the sake of brevity, we now write $\rho^t(\mathbf{p}|\mathbf{v}) := \rho\left(\mathbf{C}^{t+\Delta t,\mathbf{p}+\Delta \mathbf{p}}, \mathbf{C}^{t,\mathbf{p}} \mid \mathbf{v}\right)$, which expresses the joint likelihood of the image data at location $\mathbf{p}$ at time t given discrete motion hypotheses $\mathbf{v}$ for all color channels. We see that $\rho^t(\mathbf{p}|\mathbf{v})$ factorizes, so that the corresponding probability for the whole image can be written as

$$\rho^t(\mathbf{p}|\mathbf{v}) = \rho_x^t(\mathbf{p}|\mathbf{v}) \cdot \rho_y^t(\mathbf{p}|\mathbf{v}) \cdot \rho_z^t(\mathbf{p}|\mathbf{v}) \quad , \quad (9)$$

meaning that they can be calculated separately, with $\rho_x^t(\mathbf{p}|\mathbf{v}), \rho_y^t(\mathbf{p}|\mathbf{v}), \rho_z^t(\mathbf{p}|\mathbf{v})$ being the likelihoods of each channel. The final optical flow field can directly be estimated from the joint likelihood $\rho^t(\mathbf{p}|\mathbf{v})$ and a given prior $\rho(\mathbf{v})$ using Bayes' rule and the maximum a posteriori estimator:

$$\rho^t(\mathbf{v}|\mathbf{p}) = \rho(\mathbf{v})\,\rho^t(\mathbf{p}|\mathbf{v}) , \quad \text{and} \quad \mathbf{v} = \max_{\mathbf{v}}\left(\rho^t(\mathbf{v}|\mathbf{p})\right) \quad . \quad (10)$$

In the following experiments the prior was chosen to be equally distributed.

4 Results

To give a quantitative analysis and a comparison to other existing color optical flow methods we used two pan and zoom synthetic image sequences generated by John Barron and Reinhard Klette and added our results to the results presented in [3]. The quantitative error measurements can be seen in Table 1 and the corresponding optical flows

Fig. 4. Panning and Zooming color optical flow for the RGB color image

Table 1. Error measurements reported in [3] including our results for comparison

Panning		$e_M \pm \sigma_{e_M}$	$e_\varphi \pm \sigma_{e_\varphi}$		Zooming		$e_M \pm \sigma_{e_M}$	$e_\varphi \pm \sigma_{e_\varphi}$
Horn-Schunk	RGB	$24.27\% \pm 23.62\%$	$4.56° \pm 6.19°$		Horn-Schunk	RGB	$13.72\% \pm 14.92\%$	$6.54° \pm 7.91°$
Lucas-Kanade	RGB	$4.90\% \pm 9.31\%$	$1.00° \pm 3.44°$		Lucas-Kanade	RGB	$8.17\% \pm 12.04\%$	$4.01° \pm 12.13°$
Barron-Klette	RGB	$26.21\% \pm 19.29\%$	$0.0°$		Barron-Klette	RGB	$15.48\% \pm 23.89\%$	$0.0°$
Golland-Bruckstein	RGB	$11.38\% \pm 17.36\%$	$5.04° \pm 11.80°$		Golland-Bruckstein	RGB	$14.74\% \pm 19.37\%$	$7.56° \pm 14.87°$
Otha	RGB	$12.38\% \pm 18.91\%$	$6.04° \pm 12.80°$		Otha	RGB	$18.69\% \pm 27.87\%$	$9.78° \pm 15.80°$
Willert-Eggert-Clever	RGB	0.0%	$0.0°$		Willert-Eggert-Clever	RGB	$22.17\% \pm 18.77\%$	$6.34° \pm 6.33°$
Willert-Eggert-Clever	HSV	$1.97\% \pm 13.9\%$	$0.001° \pm 0.41°$		Willert-Eggert-Clever	HSV	$26.20\% \pm 21.39\%$	$7.79° \pm 8.61°$
Willert-Eggert-Clever	YCbCr	0.0%	$0.0°$		Willert-Eggert-Clever	YCbCr	$22.43\% \pm 18.91\%$	$6.52° \pm 6.48°$
Horn-Schunk	S	$43.69\% \pm 28.94\%$	$10.48° \pm 11.61°$		Horn-Schunk	S	$22.83\% \pm 11.23\%$	$11.23° \pm 12.81°$
Lucas-Kanade	S	$6.54\% \pm 13.19\%$	$1.39° \pm 4.54°$		Lucas-Kanade	S	$10.21\% \pm 14.66\%$	$5.32° \pm 13.62°$
Barron-Klette	S	$32.59\% \pm 20.19\%$	$0.0°$		Barron-Klette	S	$26.43\% \pm 39.99\%$	$0.0°$
Golland-Bruckstein	S	$16.97\% \pm 22.41\%$	$9.34° \pm 20.80°$		Golland-Bruckstein	S	$20.08\% \pm 24.05\%$	$12.99° \pm 23.98°$
Willert-Eggert-Clever	S	$10.77\% \pm 31.00\%$	$0.002° \pm 0.70°$		Willert-Eggert-Clever	S	$37.69\% \pm 24.68\%$	$16.55° \pm 21.10°$
Horn-Schunk	Y	$22.90\% \pm 24.12\%$	$4.73° \pm 7.28°$		Horn-Schunk	Y	$21.47\% \pm 20.50\%$	$10.35° \pm 11.73°$
Lucas-Kanade	Y	$6.14\% \pm 11.95\%$	$1.63° \pm 5.23°$		Lucas-Kanade	Y	$9.46\% \pm 14.04\%$	$5.05° \pm 13.61°$
Barron-Klette	Y	$20.06\% \pm 20.67\%$	$0.0°$		Barron-Klette	Y	$23.67\% \pm 21.18\%$	$0.0°$
Golland-Bruckstein	Y	$21.08\% \pm 28.07\%$	$12.59° \pm 24.99°$		Golland-Bruckstein	Y	$18.91\% \pm 23.72\%$	$11.46° \pm 21.84°$
Willert-Eggert-Clever	Y	$0.005\% \pm 0.51\%$	$0.007° \pm 0.89°$		Willert-Eggert-Clever	Y	$23.01\% \pm 18.32\%$	$6.73° \pm 6.72°$

Fig. 5. Color optical flow for real-world sequences for a YCbCr and a RGB color sequence

are printed in Fig. 4. The same quantitative error measurements reported in [3], that is, the relative magnitude errors $e_M = 1/ij \sum_{ij} \|\mathbf{v}_{ij}^c - \mathbf{v}_{ij}^e\|^2 / \sum_{ij} \|\mathbf{v}_{ij}^c\|^2 \times 100\%$ and the angle errors $e_\varphi = 1/ij \sum_{ij} \arccos(\mathbf{v}_{ij}^c \cdot \mathbf{v}_{ij}^e)$ with their corresponding variances σ_{e_M} and σ_{e_φ}, are used. Although the test sequences are synthetic sequences with no illumination and reflection changes at all, which means the extension to a channelwise contrast and brightness invariant measurement is not necessary, our method compares quite favourably to the others. Especially for the panning sequence our method outperforms the existing ones. Since we use the maximum a posteriori estimator we cannot reach subpixel accuracy and our results for the zooming sequence are not that convincing. To give a first impression on how our method works on real world sequences we added two further example sequences shown in Fig. 5. The qualitative optical flow results for an YCbCr (left) color and a RGB (right) color sequence processing only two consecutive images of the sequence can be seen.

5   Conclusion

We have presented a probabilistic correlation-based color optical flow algorithm that allows for brightness, contrast and color changes over time. In the case of pixel accuracy it compares quite favourably to existing gradient-based approaches that assume brightness, contrast and color to be constant over time. Our generative model for color image formation can be extended straightforwardly to also allow for correlations between the color channels by adding crossterms to the scaling and bias parameters. To study the usefulness of such crossterms for optical flow estimation will be the topic of further research.

Acknowledgements. Special thanks to Prof. John L. Barron from the University of Western Ontario, Canada, and his college Prof. Dr. Reinhard Klette from the University of Auckland, New Zealand, who provided us with their test sequences.

References

1. J. Andrews and B.C. Lovell. Color optical flow. *Eds. Workshop on Digital Image Computing, Brisbane, Australia*, 1(1):135–139, 2003.
2. J. Barron and R. Klette. Experience with optical flow in colour video image sequences. *Image and Vision Computing'2001, Auckland University, New Zealand*, pages 195–200, 2001.
3. J. Barron and R. Klette. Quantitative color optical flow. *International Conference on Pattern Recognition, Vancouver, Canada*, pages 251–255, 2002.
4. S.S. Beauchemin and J.L. Barron. The computation of optical flow. *ACM Computing Surveys*, 27(3):433–467, 1995.
5. J. Eggert, V. Willert, and E. Körner. *LNCS 3175*, chapter Building a Motion Resolution Pyramid by Combining Velocity Distributions, pages 310–317. Springer, Berlin, Germany, 2004.
6. P. Golland and A.M. Bruckstein. Motion from color. *Computer Vision and Image Understanding*, 68(3):346–362, 1997.
7. H. Madjidi and S. Negahdaripour. On robustness and localization accuracy of optical flow computation from color imagery. *2nd International Symposium on 3D Data Processing, Visualization, and Transmission, Thessaloniki, Greece*, pages 317–324, 2004.
8. S. Süsstrunk, R. Buckley, and S. Swen. Standard rgb color spaces. In *Color Imaging Conference*, pages 127–134. IS&T - The Society for Imaging Science and Technology, 1999.
9. J. van de Weijer and Th. Gevers. Robust optical flow from photometric invariants. *IEEE International Conference on Image Processing, Singapore*, pages 251–255, 2004.

Illumination Invariant Color Texture Analysis Based on Sum- and Difference-Histograms

Christian Münzenmayer[1], Sylvia Wilharm[2],
Joachim Hornegger[2], and Thomas Wittenberg[1]

[1] Fraunhofer Institut für Integrierte Schaltungen,
Am Wolfsmantel 33, D-91058 Erlangen
{mzn, wbg}@iis.fraunhofer.de
[2] Lehrstuhl für Mustererkennung, Universität Erlangen-Nürnberg,
Martensstr. 3, D-91058 Erlangen
Joachim.Hornegger@informatik.uni-erlangen.de

Abstract. Color texture algorithms have been under investigation for quite a few years now. However, the results of these algorithms are still under considerable influence of the illumination conditions under which the images were captured. It is strongly desireable to reduce the influence of illumination as much as possible to obtain stable and satisfying classification results even under difficult imaging conditions, as they can occur e.g. in medical applications like endoscopy. In this paper we present the analysis of a well-known texture analysis algorithm, namely the sum- and difference-histogram features, with respect to illumination changes. Based on this analysis, we propose a novel set of features factoring out the illumination influence from the majority of the original features. We conclude our paper with a quantitative, experimental evaluation on artificial and real image samples.

1 Introduction

For many years the automatic analysis and classification of structured surfaces in color images has been an active field of reserach in the image processing and pattern recognition community. Currently, there exists a wide range of texture and color texture methods, and an ongoing development of new methods, even for pure gray level image material. Texture features may be divided into the categories *spectral, statistical* and *model-based* features [14]. The most common spectral features are based on spectral transforms whereas many statistical methods use so-called co-occurrence matrices or *sum- and difference-histograms* [16,10]. Color texture analysis has been of increasing interest in the last few years with important works of Tan and Kittler [15] proposing a parallel approach to 'color texture', i.e. color and texture features are extracted separately. Alternatively, integrated color and texture extraction techniques have been developed [7,2,9,12]. Basically, all of these expand concepts of gray level analysis to the color domain, whereas some of them emphasize on different color spaces as well [13,3]. Most of these techniques were developed and evaluated on more or less artificial sample images which were taken under laboratory conditions. Robustness

W. Kropatsch, R. Sablatnig, and A. Hanbury (Eds.): DAGM 2005, LNCS 3663, pp. 17–24, 2005.

against changing color temperature of light sources or inhomogeneous illumination conditions as required by practical applications is still not very common,
with only few new approaches recently known [4,6,21,20,11]. The present work
addresses exactly this problem assuming a global color temperature change of
the light source.

In the next section we will introduce the linear model of illumination change.
Section 3 summmarizes the definition of the *intra-* and *inter-plane* sum- and
difference-histograms published by Unser [16] and its color extension in [10].
These well known features will be analysed and a modification will be proposed
in Section 4 with an experimental evaluation following in Section 5. We will
conclude our contribution by a short discussion in Section 6.

2   Linear Model of Illumination Change

For image formation we assume a linear model which is widely known as state of
the art [19,8,18]. It models the linear sensor response $\rho^{(k)}$ for the k'th spectral
band as the result of the integration of spectral radiance of the light source $E(\lambda)$
with wavelength λ, the spectral reflectivity of the surface $s(\lambda)$ and the sensor's
sensitivities $R^{(k)}(\lambda)$:

$$\rho^{(k)} = \int_{\lambda} R^{(k)}(\lambda)E(\lambda)s(\lambda)d\lambda. \tag{1}$$

For simplicity of our analysis we omit any references to the surface, illumination
and viewing geometry, commonly expressed by the emitting light source vector
and the surface normal vector, and to camera parameters like integration time
or gamma correction non-linearities. In his fundamental work [19], Wandell uses
low-dimensional *linear models* for the representation of spectral reflectance and
illuminant functions. Using D_E and D_s basis functions $E_i(\lambda)$ and $s_j(\lambda)$, respectively, the illumination $E(\lambda)$ and surface reflectivity $s(\lambda)$ can be formulated as:

$$E(\lambda) = \sum_{i=0}^{D_E-1} \epsilon_i E_i(\lambda), \quad s(\lambda) = \sum_{j=0}^{D_s-1} \sigma_j s_j(\lambda). \tag{2}$$

There exist many possibilities to select basis functions, e.g. *Fourier* expansion, or
a basis derived from a *principal components analysis* of a representative spectral
reflectance set. Now, if the illuminant is known by its coefficients ϵ_i, the *linear
image formation model* (1) can be reduced to

$$\rho = \Lambda_E \sigma \tag{3}$$

where σ is a column vector of surface basis function coefficients σ_j and Λ_E is
the lighting matrix where the kjth entry is

$$\Lambda_{Ekj} = \sum_{i=0}^{D_E-1} \epsilon_i \int_{\lambda} R^{(k)}(\lambda)E_i(\lambda)s_j(\lambda)d\lambda. \tag{4}$$

Note that Λ_E depends only on the light source (ϵ_i and $E_i(\lambda)$), the surface basis functions $s_j(\lambda)$ and the sensor characteristics $R^{(k)}(\lambda)$ but not on the actual surface reflectance coefficients σ_j. Thus, in case of an illumination change, there will be alterations in Λ_E which affect each surface point equivalently. Following the work of Barnard [1], we assume a 3-dimensional surface reflection model ($D_s = 3$). Note, that there is no restriction on the dimensionality of the illumination spectrum (D_E). Thus, with $K = 3$ color sensors, we obtain a 3×3 lighting matrix Λ_E. Now, let $\rho^{E1} = \Lambda_E^{E1}\sigma$ be the sensor response under illumination E1 and $\rho^{E2} = \Lambda_E^{E2}\sigma$ the response under E2. Substituting the common term σ, it can be shown easily that

$$\rho^{E2} = \underbrace{\Lambda_E^{E2}(\Lambda_E^{E1})^{-1}}_{M}\rho^{E1}, \tag{5}$$

i.e. the illumination change induces a linear transform of the sensor responses by a 3×3 matrix M. Assuming narrow-band sensors, a diagonal transformation D can be used as an approximation which is known in color constancy literature as the von Kries coefficient rule [1].

3   Sum- and Difference-Histograms in Color Space

In this section we introduce the sum- and difference histogram features as proposed by Unser [16]. They are based on the so-called co-occurrence features introduced by Haralick [5] which are based on an estimate of the joint probability function of pixels in certain spatial relationships. Sum- and difference-histograms provide an efficient approximation for the joint probability by counting the frequencies of sums respectively differences of pixel pairs

$$\pi_{r\Theta} = [(x_1, y_1), (x_2 = x_1 + r\cos\Theta, y_2 = y_1 + r\sin\Theta)] \tag{6}$$

with the radial distance r and the angular displacement Θ. With G being the maximum intensity level these histograms are defined as:

$$h_S(i) = |\{\pi_{r\Theta}|I(x_1, y_1) + I(x_2, y_2) = i\}|, \tag{7}$$
$$h_D(j) = |\{\pi_{r\Theta}|I(x_1, y_1) - I(x_2, y_2) = j\}|, \tag{8}$$

with $i = 0, \ldots, 2(G - 1)$ and $j = -G + 1, \ldots, G - 1$. In general, it is sufficient to use $\Theta \in \{0, \pi/4, \pi/2, 3\pi/4\}$ and a small radius r, and calculate features on each of the histograms separately. The approximative probabilities are derived by normalization with the total number of pixels N in the considered image region of interest:

$$p_S(i) = \frac{h_S(i)}{N}, \quad p_D(j) = \frac{h_D(j)}{N}. \tag{9}$$

Integrated color texture extraction by *intra-* and *inter-plane* sum- and difference-histograms

$$h_{S,D}^{(pq)}(i) = \left|\left\{\pi_{r\Theta}|I^{(p)}(x_1, y_1) \pm I^{(q)}(x_2, y_2) = i\right\}\right| \tag{10}$$

was presented in [10] and will be reviewed shortly here. Here, joint probabilities over different color channels $p, q \in \{R, G, B\}$ are approximated and evaluated by the same features as in the gray level case. In the following *intra-plane* features are computed from pixel pairs within each plane $p = q$ and *inter-plane* features from distinct planes $p \neq q$. All features for differenct directions Θ and different *intra-* or *inter-plane* combinations are concatenated to the final feature vector which is used for classification.

4   Deriving Illumination Invariant Features

The next section is dedicated to the analysis of the sum- and difference-histograms and derived features in context of a *multiplicative* or *diagonal* illumination change. A multiplicative illumination change has influence only on the brightness of an image pixel and can be modeled by a multiplicative factor k. In consequence the sum- and difference-histograms change by:

$$
\begin{aligned}
\hat{h}_{S,D}{}^{(pq)}(i) &= \left| \left\{ \pi_{r\Theta} | k \cdot I^{(p)}(x_1, y_1) \pm k \cdot I^{(q)}(x_2, y_2) = i \right\} \right| \\
&= \left| \left\{ \pi_{r\Theta} | I^{(p)}(x_1, y_1) \pm I^{(q)}(x_2, y_2) = i/k \right\} \right| = h_{S,D}{}^{(pq)}(i/k).
\end{aligned}
\tag{11}
$$

This is true for *intra-plane* ($p = q$) and *inter-plane* ($p \neq q$) histograms, not counting quantization errors. For the *diagonal model*, the illumination change is equivalent to an independent scaling of each color channel by a separate factor k_p. *Intra-plane* histograms will therefore change similarly. Thus, in the following considerations we will restrict ourselves only to the *intra-plane* model with *multiplicative* and *diagonal* illumination change.

Unser [16] proposed a set of 15 features based on the normalized sum- and difference distributions $p_S(i)$ and $p_D(j)$ (see Table 1) which will be analysed with regard to the influence of illumination changes. Therefore, we try to express the value of a feature under illumination change $\hat{c}$ as a function of the feature c under unchanged illumination. As an example, we derive the following change for the feature *sum mean* c_0:

$$
\hat{c}_0 = \hat{\mu}_s = \sum_i \hat{p}_s(i) \cdot i = \sum_i p_s(i/k) \cdot i = \sum_{i'} p_s(i') \cdot ki' = k \cdot c_0 \tag{12}
$$

As can be seen, the feature c_0 is scaled by the factor of the multiplicative illumination change. Similarly, the feature *sum variance* c_1 can be considered and reformulated by variable substitution:

$$
\hat{c}_1 = \sum_i (i - \hat{\mu}_s)^2 \hat{p}_s(i) = \sum_i (i - k\mu_s)^2 p_s(i/k) = \sum_{i'} (ki' - k\mu_s)^2 p_s(i') = k^2 c_1 \tag{13}
$$

In this case the feature c_1 is scaled by the square of the illumination change. We conducted this analysis on all 15 features with the summary of results in Table 1. In total 6 of 15 features, namely sum energy c_2, sum entropy c_3, diff energy c_6

Table 1. Scalar texture features derived from sum- and difference-histograms with the original features by Unser [16] and the same features under illumination change with multiplicative and intra-plane model and modified features invariant against illumination changes

Features	Original Definition	Illumination Change $I'^{(p)} = k_p \cdot I^{(p)}$	New Definition
sum mean	$c_0 = \mu_s = \sum_i i p_s(i)$	$\hat{c}_0 = k \cdot c_0$	-
sum variance	$c_1 = \sum_i (i - \mu_s)^2 p_s(i)$	$\hat{c}_1 = k^2 \cdot c_1$	$\hat{c}_1' = \frac{\hat{c}_1}{\hat{\mu}_s^2} = \frac{c_1}{\mu_s^2}$
sum energy	$c_2 = \sum_i p_s^2(i)$	$\hat{c}_2 = c_2$	$\hat{c}_2' = \hat{c}_2 = c_2$
sum entropy	$c_3 = -\sum_i p_s(i) \log p_s(i)$	$\hat{c}_3 = c_3$	$\hat{c}_3' = \hat{c}_3 = c_3$
diff mean	$c_4 = \mu_d = \sum_j j p_d(j)$	$\hat{c}_4 = k \cdot c_4$	$\hat{c}_4' = \frac{\hat{c}_4}{\hat{\mu}_s} = \frac{c_4}{\mu_s}$
diff variance	$c_5 = \sum_j (j - \mu_d)^2 p_d(j)$	$\hat{c}_5 = k^2 \cdot c_5$	$\hat{c}_5' = \frac{\hat{c}_5}{\hat{\mu}_s^2} = \frac{c_5}{\mu_s^2}$
diff energy	$c_6 = \sum_j p_d^2(j)$	$\hat{c}_6 = c_6$	$\hat{c}_6' = \hat{c}_6 = c_6$
diff entropy	$c_7 = -\sum_j p_d(j) \log p_d(j)$	$\hat{c}_7 = c_7$	$\hat{c}_7' = \hat{c}_7 = c_7$
cluster shade	$c_8 = \sum_i (i - \mu_s)^3 p_s(i)$	$\hat{c}_8 = k^3 \cdot c_8$	$\hat{c}_8' = \frac{\hat{c}_8}{\hat{\mu}_s^3} = \frac{c_8}{\mu_s^3}$
cluster prominence	$c_9 = \sum_i (i - \mu_s)^4 p_s(i)$	$\hat{c}_9 = k^4 \cdot c_9$	$\hat{c}_9' = \frac{\hat{c}_9}{\hat{\mu}_s^4} = \frac{c_9}{\mu_s^4}$
contrast	$c_{10} = \sum_j j^2 p_d(j)$	$\hat{c}_{10} = k^2 \cdot c_{10}$	$\hat{c}_{10}' = \frac{\hat{c}_{10}}{\hat{\mu}_s^2} = \frac{c_{10}}{\mu_s^2}$
homogenity	$c_{11} = \sum_j \frac{1}{1+j^2} p_d(i)$	$\hat{c}_{11} = \sum_{j'} \frac{1}{1+(kj')^2} p_d(j')$	-
correlation	$c_{12} = c_1 - c_{10}$	$\hat{c}_{12} = k^2 \cdot c_{12}$	$\hat{c}_{12}' = \frac{\hat{c}_{12}}{\hat{\mu}_s^2} = \frac{c_{12}}{\mu_s^2}$
angular 2nd moment	$c_{13} = c_2 \cdot c_6$	$\hat{c}_{13} = c_{13}$	$\hat{c}_{13}' = \hat{c}_{13} = c_{13}$
entropy	$c_{14} = c_3 + c_7$	$\hat{c}_{14} = c_{14}$	$\hat{c}_{14}' = \hat{c}_{14} = c_{14}$

and diff entropy c_7 as well as the total entropy c_{14} and the angular second moment c_{13} are invariant under this model of illumination change. That means, that more than half of all features are affected by diagonal illumination changes, thus degrading classification performance. From Table 1 it is also obvious, that all other features except *homogenity* c_{11} contain a power of k as a multiplicative factor. Therefore, we propose to normalize these features except c_0 by a power of the sum mean $c_0 = \mu_s$, thus canceling out the factor k. Normalizing e.g. the *sum variance* c_1 yields

$$\hat{c}_1' = \frac{\hat{c}_1}{\hat{c}_0^2} = \frac{k^2 c_1}{k^2 c_0^2} = \frac{c_1}{c_0^2}. \qquad (14)$$

All modifications are summarized in Table 1 representing a new set of illumination invariant features c'.

5 Experiments and Results

To validate our newly defined texture features we used two different color image sets. The first one is taken from the *VisTex (Vision Texture)* database [17] published by the *MIT*. We selected 32 images showing different color textures (also used in [9,10]). We selected 10 disjoint 64×64 pixel regions of interest (ROI) in each image for training of a *k nearest neighbor* classifier and another set of 10 regions per image for validation of the classification performance. To simulate illumination changes complying with the diagonal model, we calculated diagonal transform matrices based on the $\mathbf{RGB}_{\mathrm{CIE}}$-system by linear least squares regression. As there is no illumination related information available about the origin of the VisTex images, we assumed transformations from *CIE* daylight illuminant D55 with 5500 K *CCT (correlated color temperature)* to six different color temperatures in the range of 4000 to 7000 K. This leads to a color shift from a reddish (4000 K) to a bluish (7000 K) tint. To avoid clipping artefacts by coefficients > 1, the gray level dynamic of the original images was compressed by the factor 0.8.

The second data set we used, originates from a medical application of color texture analysis for the classification of different types of mucous tissue inside the esophagus. All images were acquired by a high-resolution magnification endoscope[3] after application of acid solution to enhance mucous structures. For each tissue class, irregularly bounded ROI's were classified by clinical experts with histologic confirmation by conventional biopsy. The whole data set includes 390 images with a total of 482 ROI's.

All texture features were individually normalized to $\mu = 0$ and $\sigma = 1$ on the training data set to ensure equal weighting in the calculation of the classifier's distance function. Fig. 1(a) shows the classification accuracy of the original and the illumination invariant features with and without the variant feature c_{11} for different diagonal illumination changes. Note that at 5500 K no illumination change takes place as we have chosen to use this point as the reference illumination. For the endoscopic data set Fig. 1(b) summarizes the classification accuracy in a leaving-one-out setting. We gathered results for the original image resolution of 768 × 576 pixels and 3 further reduction steps of a Gaussian multiresolution pyramid which proved advantageous in previous experiments and is advantageous to reduce computation time. In every case the illumination invariant feature set is superior to the original definition. However, the variant feature c_{11} (homogenity) seems to have a strong contribution on the final result so that it should not be excluded despite its obvious dependency on the illumination.

6   Discussion

In this work we presented the analysis of the sum- and difference histogram color texture features [10,16] with respect to changes in the spectral characteristics of the illumination. We modeled illumination changes by a diagonal transformation matrix based on a linear image formation model and have shown how the sum- and difference-histograms change with the coefficients of this matrix. Based on this analysis, we have presented novel definitions for features which are invariant to the considered illumination change.

Experiments on artificial and real images have shown that improvements in classification accuracy can be obtained by such a normalization. However, the

---

[3] Olympus GIF Q160Z.

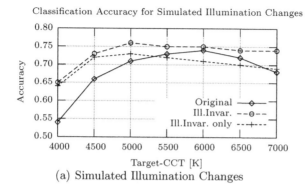

(a) Simulated Illumination Changes

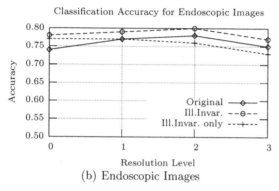

(b) Endoscopic Images

Fig. 1. Classification accuracy for sum- and difference-histogram features shown for the *original* features of Unser, our illumination invariant features including the variant feature c_{11} (*Ill.Invar.*) and without c_{11} (*Ill.Invar. only*). (a) Simulated diagonal illumination changes on VisTex images assuming $\mathbf{RGB}_{\mathrm{CIE}}$-system with transformations from 5500 K to a range of 4000 to 7000 K. (b) Classification of real endoscopic images of the esophagus for different resolutions in a multiresolution Gaussian pyramid.

amount of improvement naturally depends on the degree of change in the illumination, e.g. with 4000 K an improvement of 11% has been reached compared with only 2% in the reference cased (5500 K). For the endoscopic data set a maximum improvement of 4% for the original resolution and 2% for the reduced resolutions is a sign for the stability of the light source with respect to aging. Of course stronger improvements are expected for applications under natural light, e.g. in outdoor scenarios.

References

1. K. Barnard. Modeling scene illumination colour for computer vision and image reproduction: A survery of computational approaches. Technical report, Simon Fraser University, Vancouver, B.C., Canada, 1998.
2. G. V. de Wouwer, P. Scheunders, S. Livens, and D. V. Dyck. Wavelet correlation signatures for color texture characerization. *Pat. Rec.*, 32(3):443–451, 1999.

3. A. Drimbarean and P. Whelan. Experiments in colour texture analysis. *Pat. Rec. Letters*, 22:1161–1167, 2001.

4. G. Finlayson, S. Chatterjee, and B. Funt. Color angular indexing. In *ECCV (2)*, pages 16–27, 1996.

5. R. Haralick, K. Shanmugam, and I. Dinstein. Textural features for image classification. *IEEE Trans. Syst. Man Cyb.*, SMC-3(6):610–621, November 1973.

6. G. Healey and D. Slater. Computing illumination-invariant descriptors of spatially filtered color image regions. *IEEE Trans. Image Process.*, 6(7):1002–1013, July 1997.

7. A. Jain and G. Healey. A Multiscale Representation Including Opponent Color Features for Texture Recognition. *IEEE Trans. Image Process.*, 7(1):124–128, January 1998.

8. J.H., B. Funt, and M. Drew. Separating a color signal into illumination and surface reflectance components: Theory and applications. *IEEE Trans. Pattern Anal. Mach. Intell.*, 12(10):966–977, October 1990.

9. R. Lakmann. *Statistische Modellierung von Farbtexturen*. PhD thesis, Universität Koblenz-Landau, Koblenz, 1998.

10. C. Münzenmayer, H. Volk, C. Küblbeck, K. Spinnler, and T. Wittenberg. Multispectral Texture Analysis using Interplane Sum- and Difference-Histograms. In L. V. Gool, editor, *Pattern Recognition - Proceedings of the 24th DAGM Symposium Zurich, Switzerland, September 2002*, pages 25–31, Berlin, 2002. Springer.

11. T. Ojala, M. Pietikäinen, and T. Mäenpää. Multiresolution gray-scale and rotation invariant texture classification with local binary patterns. *IEEE Trans. Pattern Anal. Mach. Intell.*, 24(7):971–987, 2002.

12. C. Palm. *Integrative Auswertung von Farbe und Textur*. PhD thesis, RWTH Aachen, Osnabrück, 2003.

13. G. Paschos. Perceptually Uniform Color Spaces for Color Texture Analysis: An Empirical Evaluation. *IEEE Trans. Image Process.*, 10(6):932–937, June 2001.

14. T. Randen and J. H. Husoy. Filtering for texture classification: A comparative study. *IEEE Trans. Pattern Anal. Mach. Intell.*, 21(4):291–310, April 1999.

15. T. Tan and J. Kittler. Colour texture analysis using colour histogram. In *IEE Proc.-Vis. Image Signal Process.*, volume 141, pages 260–26, December 1994.

16. M. Unser. Sum and difference histograms for texture analysis. *IEEE Transactions on Pattern Analysis and Machine Intelligence*, 8(1):118–125, 1986.

17. M. M. L. Vision and M. group. Vistex vision texture database, http://www-white.media.mit.edu/vismod/imagery/visiontexture, 1995.

18. P. Vora, J. Farrell, J. Tietz, and D. Brainard. Linear models for digital cameras. In *Proc. of the 1997 IS&T 50th Annual Conference*, pages 377–382, Cambridge, MA, 1997.

19. B. Wandell. The synthesis and analysis of color images. *IEEE Trans. Pattern Anal. Mach. Intell.*, 9(1):2–13, January 1987.

20. J. F. C. Wanderley and M. H. Fisher. Multiscale color invariants based on the human visual system. *IEEE Trans. Image Process.*, 10(11):1630–1638, November 2001.

21. L. Wang and G. Healey. Using zernike moments for the illumination and geometry invariant classification of multispectral texture. *IEEE Trans. Image Process.*, 7(2):196–203, February 1998.

Color Image Compression: Early Vision and the Multiresolution Representations

Ahmed Nabil Belbachir and Peter Michael Goebel

Vienna University of Technology, Institute of Computer Aided Automation,
Pattern Recognition and Image Processing Group,
Favoritenstr. 9/183-2, A-1040, Vienna
{nabil, goe}@prip.tuwien.ac.at

Abstract. The efficiency of an image compression technique relies on the capability of finding sparse M-terms for best approximation with reduced visually significant quality loss. By "visually significant" it is meant the information to which human observer can perceive. The **H**uman **V**isual **S**ystem (HVS) is generally sensitive to the contrast, color, spatial frequency...etc. This paper is concerned with the compression of color images where the psycho-visual representation is an important strategy to define the best M-term approximation technique. Digital color images are usually stored using the RGB space, television broadcast uses YUV (YIQ) space while the psycho-visual representation relies on 3 components: one for the luminance and two for the chrominance. In this paper, an analysis of the wavelet and contourlet representation of the color image both in RGB and YUV spaces is performed. A approximation technique is performed in order to investigate the performance of image compression technique using one of those transforms.

1 Introduction

The question of why some abstract shapes are more attractive to human observers than others, may be answered, in that, we probably find pleasing those forms, most closely tuned to the properties of our human visual system (HVS) [11]. An example of differential tuning is the oblique effect[1] in orientation perception. Thus aesthetic pleasure is linked in some general way to neural activity. In [7] a theory of spatial vision is given, by integrating psychophysics, neurophysiology and linear systems. They carried out many electro-physiological experiments, showing the cells of the primary visual cortex be tuned to bands in spatial frequency and orientation, which was confirmed by other physiological experiments [6]. However, the orientation properties of color perception is still an open issue. In applications where lossy compression is needed, one has to consider subjective assessments, rather than – or besides – strict PSNR values for an optimal quality of the reconstruction.

As shown in a recent paper [3], considering anisotropy in luminance images in the compression stage, has led to better compression performance and better

---

[1] horizontal and vertical lines have privileged access.

W. Kropatsch, R. Sablatnig, and A. Hanbury (Eds.): DAGM 2005, LNCS 3663, pp. 25–32, 2005.

preservation of details, thus getting higher image quality. The question is: can the considerations in [3] be exploited for color images?

This paper analyzes a compression technique on color images. In the following subsections, the modeling of color in images as well as the performance of compression in color space are considered.

1.1 Psycho-Visual Representation of Color Images

The quantization of color perception in the HVS is a challenging process. There exist different theoretical studies [20,18] of the chromatic psycho-visual components that the HVS could perceive. The theories show that the HVS separates light information, received by the retina, into three distinct, non independent components. Thus, HVS color perception can be modeled in two steps [20]. In the first step, the received light is transformed into three bio-electrical signals (L,M,S) as received by the three types of cones on the retina [4]. In the second step, the resulting signals are combined into three psycho-visual components: one achromatic (A) and two color components (C1 and C2).

Using this model, the achromatic component A is calculated by $A = L + M$ [1]. The first color component $C1$ corresponds to the chromatic axis Red-Green $C1 = L - M$. The second color component C2 corresponds to the chromatic axis Blue-Yellow $C2 = S - 0.5(L + M)$. Note also that if $C1$ corresponds to the a axis from $L*ab$ space defined by the CIE-Lab [15], then $C2$ diverges from the b component of this space. An investigation has been made in [1] on the possible relationships between the three components A, C1 and C2. It was shown a strong interaction between A and C1, and C1 and C2, while C2 has a limited influence on the perception of A. Thus, efficient quantization process should take into account these relationships instead of handling the three components independently.

1.2 Color Compression Standards

Lossy compression mainly consists of de-correlation and quantization stages that reduce the image size by permanently eliminating certain information. The decorrelation stage of the image compression algorithm is usually done by a transformation from one space to another space to facilitate compaction of information. One approach is the use of the **D**iscrete **C**osine **T**ransform (DCT), which is used in the JPEG (baseline) industry standard [16].

The recent standard "JPEG 2000" [17] exploits the sparse approximation of the **D**iscrete **W**avelet **T**ransform (DWT) for image compression purpose, which is free from the blocking effect artifacts of DCT. DWT allows the decomposition of an image into a set of contributions at different frequency bands and resolution levels. The corresponding coefficients of the different decomposition levels are correlated and show characteristic trends for additional compression potential.

Many coding techniques of the DWT coefficients have been investigated, like the **E**mbedded **Z**ero-**T**ree **W**avelet (EZW), the **S**et **P**artitioning **I**n **H**ierarchical

Trees (SPIHT) and the **E**mbedded **B**lock **C**oding with **O**ptimized **T**runcation (EBCOT) [16,17].

1.3 Color Images Modeled in RGB and YUV

There exist many possible color space definitions [14] and this paper addresses those commonly required by image compression techniques. For digital still images, the **R**ed-**G**reen-**B**lue color space, known as RGB, is commonly used. RGB is an additive color model [15], which appropriately fits the physics of usual capturing and display devices. A RGB representation of an image is generated by spectral primary filtering an arbitrary color scene. Filters generate three channels by the spectral subbands red, green and blue, which usually overlap. Therefore the RGB model representation is a very redundant one.

The combining of these three channels of light produces a wide range of visible colors. All color spaces are three-dimensional orthogonal coordinate systems, meaning that there are three axes (in this case the red, green, and blue color intensities) that are perpendicular one to another. The luminance is given by $Y = 0.299R + 0.587G + 0.114B$ and is represented by the area of the triangle, spanned from the three RGB vectors. All three components must be tuned proportionally for changing the luminance, therefore, RGB is not optimal for compression purpose. Thus, a changeover to a color space with uncorrelated components is more convenient and provides better compression performance.

Television broadcast makes use of color spaces based on luminance and chrominance, which correspond to brightness and color respectively. These color spaces are denoted as YUV and YIQ [14]. The YUV space is used for the PAL broadcast television system standard in Europe and the YIQ color space is used for the NTSC broadcast standard in North America.

Chrominance carries only the differences R-Y and B-Y, which is the principle advantage of using YUV or YIQ for broadcast. Thus the amount of information is significantly reduced to define such a color television image. From the past, the compatibility with monochrome receivers should be noticed.

Based on psycho-visual properties of the human eye, luminance is more important for subjective good image quality than chrominance. Therefore chrominance components can be downsampled to achieve better compression performance. So the formats YUV:4:2:2 and YUV:4:1:1 were generated, especially for video compression applications.

1.4 Multiresolution Representations of Images

For compression purposes, sparse representation[2] of images is an important issue, where the compact approximation is mainly achieved by means of quantization,

---

[2] A general WVT series expansion by Φ_n for a given image I, such that $I = \sum_0^\infty C_n \Phi_n$, where C_n are the transform coefficients. The best M-term approximation, using this expansion, is defined as $I_M = \sum_{n \in G_M} C_n \Phi_n$, where G_M is the set of indexes of the M-largest C_n. The quality of the approximated function I_M relates to how sparse the WVT expansion by Φ_n is, or how well the expansion compacts the energy of I into few coefficients.

which also yields to a degradation of the images. Separable WVT [9] offers an acceptable tradeoff between visual quality and information sparsity. Thus, WVT has been adopted for gray-level and color image compression standards (i.e. JPEG2000) [12,16,17].

The quality of the approximation images strongly depends on the quantization noise. For gray-level images, this noise is uniform as one quantization procedure is used. However, three quantization procedures are used for the three image components that may yield a quantization noise localized on certain structures. The minimization of such noise depends on the capability of exploiting the interaction between the three components.

For the assessment of the reconstruction quality another important aspect is the relationship between the contrast sensitivity and the spatial frequency. This is described by the **C**ontrast **S**ensitivity **F**unction (CSF) [12]. For compression purposes, CSF is exploited to regulate the quantization step-size to minimize the visibility of artifacts. This approach can be used for luminance as well as for color images. For color perception three different CSFs describe the sensitivity for the respective color bands. Implemented in JPEG2000 compression standard on the WVT coefficients, CSF schemes provide visually more efficient image approximation than conventional hard thresholding.

2   The Contourlet Transform

Efficient image representations require that coefficients of functions, which represent the regions of interest, are sparse. Wavelets can pick up discontinuities of one dimensional piecewise smooth functions very efficiently and represent them as point discontinuities. 2D WVT obtained by a tensor product of one-dimensional wavelets are good to isolate discontinuities at edge points, but cannot recognize smoothness along contours. Numerous methods were developed to overcome this limitation by adaptive [13], Radon-based [5], or filter bank-based techniques [8].

2.1   Contourlets for Luminance Images

Inspired by Candes theory [5], Do and Vetterli [8] proposed the **P**yramidal **D**irectional **F**ilter-**B**ank (PDFB), which overcomes the curvelet in sparsity using a directional filter bank, applied on the whole scale, also known as CTT. Besides their parsimony, CTT offers the directionality and anisotropy to image representation that are not provided by separable WVT.

In [3], the potential of the CTT for image compression has been demonstrated on gray-level images. The advantage of CTT over WVT, is the sparse approximation of images with smooth contours. We did experiments with over 100 high resolution images, and it was shown, that the smoothness of the contours within an image is coupled with the spatial resolution of a desired scale. It is found, that below a spatial resolution around 2^8 pixels, the application of the CTT carries no advantage compared with WVT in terms of compaction of energy. By combining CTT and WVT as unique image transform, an interesting gain in image quality has been demonstrated. These results motivate the interest for extending this approach to color images.

2.2   Contourlets for Color Images

The proposed approach for color images approximation is very close to the one used in [3] for gray-level images. Consequently, the main idea is to combine CTT-WVT for the approximation of the three image components Y, and also U and V. The adopted procedure for image compression is as follows:

1. The used digital images are stored using RGB coordinates. In the first step, the RGB component of the color image are transformed into YUV space as defined in [15].
2. In case of image size of $\leq$ 512 x 512 pixels, four decomposition levels are used, where the two fine scales are CTT, (with l=8 directions) and the remaining two are obtained using WVT. However, in case of images with $\leq$ 2048 x 2048 pixels, five decomposition steps are using with three CTT levels (l=16 directions).
3. This decomposition is used to each component independently Y, U and V.
4. Simple thresholding of the coefficients from Y space is performed as in [3].
5. The same thresholding strategy, as in 4., is performed for the resulting coefficients from U image decomposition.
6. In the V decomposition, the coefficients located in the same position as the truncated Y coefficients as excluded from the thresholding. Other V coefficients follow the same thresholding strategy.

3   Experimental Results and Analysis

This analysis has been performed on more than 100 digital color images from a multimedia database. The WVT and combined CTT-WVT approach have been analyzed for compression purpose. A set of images have been selected for this paper that are depicted in Figure 1.

Most of those images have been used in [10]. The image A and C are the Lena and F16 color images respectively, with 512x512 pixels, which are usually used in standard image compression literate. In B, there is Zaza image with 512x512 pixels that has the property of containing smooth contours without a complex structure. The image in D is the Art image with 2048x2048 pixels that contains a diversity of colors.

Compression results using WVT and CTT-WVT on the four selected images, are reported in this Section. The evaluation between these approaches is performed using the PSNR criterion. The images have been reconstructed from the remaining significant coefficients and the reconstruction error (PSNR) has been derived. The normalized log energy entropy measures (Equation 1) indicate the potential of energy compaction for the desired transformation. The factor between the original image size and the non-zeros coefficients size is used to derive

Fig. 1. Example of color images used for the analysis: A. Lena(512x512), B. Zaza(512x512), C. F16(512x512) and D. Art image(2Mx2M).

the compression ratio. Note that state-of-the-art coders (e.g. EBCOT contextual coding [17]) also exploit high order statistics. Thus, the used measures (entropy) are an approximation that can only give a hint on the relative performance. The entropy measure is given over the whole YUV components as well as over the luminance component Y.

$$E(s) = \sum_i Log(s_i^2). \tag{1}$$

It can be noticed that the combination CTT-WVT provides higher reduction than that of WVT. However, the entropy measure of the resulting YUV space coefficients seems to be advantageous for WVT such that the remaining coefficients can be efficiently coded. The most significant improvement in the compression ratio can be noticed on the Art image. This gain is related to the high edge density in the image. However, this gain is less significant if the image has less discontinuities (zaza and F16). On the other hand, the entropy results of the Y space coefficients show that CTT-WVT provides a sparser representation for

Table 1. Compression results

Images	PSNR	Entropy YUV	Entropy Y	Compression Ratio
Lena (WVT)	30.1	0.054	0.054	21.8
Lena (CTT-WVT)	29.9	0.065	0.053	20.7
F16 (WVT)	26.8	0.035	0.033	31.4
F16 (CTT-WVT)	26.8	0.043	0.032	32
Zaza (WVT)	29.7	0.031	0.029	38.1
Zaza (CTT-WVT)	29.6	0.034	0.028	39.3
Art (WVT)	28.1	0.057	0.048	34.8
Art (CTT-WVT)	28.2	0.061	0.045	36.7

luminance than that with WVT while chromatic components seems to be compactly represented by WVT. Therefore, one possible alternative to investigate would be the combination of CTT and WVT for luminance and chrominance components respectively. In such a scheme, CTT can be used to code the Y channel while WVT can be applied for U and V components

4   Conclusions

This paper investigates the potential of the **C**on**T**ourlet **T**ransform (CTT) for compression of color images. In [3], it was demonstrated the potential of CTT, in providing a more compact representation of the energy, compared to that of the **W**a**V**elet **T**ransform (WVT), used in the compression standard JPEG2000, for gray-level images. CTT shows less information loss and artifacts in the reconstructed images after simple thresholding of the transformed coefficients. Indeed, WVT exhibits a large number of coefficients for representing smooth contours, which are usually present in high resolution images.

For this reason, this paper investigates the extension of the CTT-WVT approach to color images. Several color spaces has been discussed including the space with the psycho-visual perception of colors. The CTT potential has been investigated in YUV space, the one used in JPEG and JPEG2000 standards. After the quantization step, CTT provides a reduced size of coefficients, compared to WVT. Unfortunately, the log energy entropy measure indicates that the resulting WVT coefficients may be compacter coded. This is apart to the Y channel, which can be coded better by processing by CTT. However, as a perspective, it is recommended to determine different contrast sensitivity functions [12] for the chrominance channels as well as for the luminance. To tune the quantization process, one can estimate the receptor noise [19], as threshold, to detect a just noticeable difference (Weber-Fechner law), based on the Human Visual System sensitivity.

References

1. D. Barba. Codage avec Compression d'Images Couleur. Ecole du Printemps, Pau, France, 2001.
2. L. Bedat. Aspects Psychovisuels de la Perception des Couleurs. Application au Codage d'Images Couleur Fixes avec Compression de l'Information. PhD Thesis at University of Nantes, France, Oct. 1998.
3. A.N. Belbachir and P.M. Goebel. A Sparse Image Representation Using Contourlets. 10th Computer Vision Winter Workshop, Zell an der Pram, Austria, February 2005.
4. P. Le Callet and D. Barba. A Robust Quality Metric for Color Image Quality Assessment. Proceeding of the International Conference on Image Processing, Vol 1, pp. 437-440, Sep. 2003.
5. E.J. Candes and D.L. Donoho. Curvelets - A Surprisingly Effective Non-Adaptive Representation for Objects with Edges. in Curve and Surface Fitting, A. Cohen, C. Rabut, and L.L. Schumaker, Eds. Saint Malo: Vanderbilt University, 1999.
6. J. G. Daugman. Complete discrete 2D Gabor transforms by neural networks for image analysis and compression. IEEE Transactions on Acoustics, Speech, and Signal Processing, Vol. 36, No.7, pp. 1169-1179, 1988.
7. K. and R. De Valois. Spatial Vision. Oxford Psychology Series No. 14; Oxford University Press, 1990
8. M.N. Do and M. Vetterli. The Contourlet Transform: An Efficient Directional Multiresolution Image Representation. IEEE Transactions on Image Processing, Dec. 2004.
9. I. Daubechies. Ten Lectures on Wavelets. CBMS-NSF Lecture Notes Nr. 61, Seventh Printing SIAM, 2002.
10. D.M. Gomes, W.T.A. Filho and A.D.D. Neto. A Method for Selective Color Images Compression. Proceedings of the International Joint Conference on Neural Networks, Volume 2, 20-24 July 2003.
11. B. C. Hansen, J. K. DeFord, M. J. Sinai and E. A. Essock. Anisotropic processing of natural scenes depends on scene content. Journal of Vision, 2(7), 500a, http://journalofvision.org/2/7/500/, doi:10.1167/2.7.500, 2002.
12. M.J. Nadenau, J. Reichel and M. Kunt. Wavelet-Based Color Image Compression: Exploiting the Contrast Sensitivity Function. IEEE Transactions on Image Processing Vol.12, NO.1, January 2003.
13. E.L. Pennec and S. Mallat. Image Compression with Geometric Wavelets. IEEE International Conference on Image Processing, 2000.
14. C.A. Poynton. A Technical Introduction to Digital Video. John Wiley, NY, 1996.
15. M. Richter. Einfuehrung in die Farbmetrik. W..D Gruyter, Berlin-NY, 1981.
16. K. Sayood. Introduction to Data Compression. *Second Edition, Morgan Kaufmann, 2000.*
17. D. Taubman. High Performance Scalable Image Compression with EBCOT. IEEE Trans. on Image Processing, VOL. 9, NO. 7, July 2000.
18. K.K. De Valois, M.A. Webster and E. Switkes. Orientation and Spatial Frequency Discrimination for Luminance and Chromatic Gratings. JOSA, Vol. 7, N6, pp. 1034-1049, 1990.
19. M. Vorobyev and D. Osorio. Receptor Noise as a Determinant of Colour Thresholds. Pro. Royal Society, London 265, pp. 351-358, 1998.
20. D.R. Williams, J. Krauskopf and D.W. Heeley. Cardinal Direction of Color Space. Vision Research, Vol.22, pp. 1123-1131, 1982.

Optic Flow Goes Stereo:
A Variational Method for Estimating
Discontinuity-Preserving Dense Disparity Maps

Natalia Slesareva, Andrés Bruhn, and Joachim Weickert

Mathematical Image Analysis Group,
Faculty of Mathematics and Computer Science,
Saarland University, Building 27.1, 66041 Saarbrücken, Germany
{Slesareva, Bruhn, Weickert}@mia.uni-saarland.de

Abstract. We present a novel variational method for estimating dense disparity maps from stereo images. It integrates the epipolar constraint into the currently most accurate optic flow method (Brox *et al.* 2004). In this way, a new approach is obtained that offers several advantages compared to existing variational methods: (i) It preservers discontinuities very well due to the use of the total variation as solution-driven regulariser. (ii) It performs favourably under noise since it uses a robust function to penalise deviations from the data constraints. (iii) Its minimisation via a coarse-to-fine strategy can be theoretically justified. Experiments with both synthetic and real-world data show the excellent performance and the noise robustness of our approach.

Keywords: computer vision, variational methods, stereo reconstruction, differential techniques, partial differential equations.

1 Introduction

The reconstruction of 3-D information from two views is one of the key problems in computer vision. Since the prototypical approach of Marr and Poggio [11] three decades ago, a variety of algorithms have been proposed for this purpose. Depending on their strategy for solving the correspondence problem, these algorithms can be divided into four classes: *Feature-based* algorithms [3,6] that make use of characteristic image features such as corners or lines, *area-based* methods [8,15,16] that correlate image patches by aggregating local similarity measures, *phase-based* approaches [4,5,7] that estimate displacements via the phase in the Fourier domain, and *energy-based* techniques [1,9,10,12,14,15] that seek to minimise variational formulations, where deviations from data and smoothness constraints are penalised.

Variational methods offer one decisive advantage when compared to the other three strategies: They allow for an estimation of correspondences at those locations where no image information is available. Since they regularise the often non-unique solution of their data constraints by assuming (piecewise) smoothness of the result, neighbourhood information is propagated to locations where such information is missing. As a consequence, always 100% dense estimates are obtained. This so-called *filling-in effect* is one reason why variational techniques have become increasingly popular during the last few years.

W. Kropatsch, R. Sablatnig, and A. Hanbury (Eds.): DAGM 2005, LNCS 3663, pp. 33–40, 2005.
© Springer-Verlag Berlin Heidelberg 2005

A second reason is the fact that this regularisation can be adapted such that it respects discontinuities in the data (*image-driven*) or the solution (*solution-driven*). Thus, objects boundaries are preserved and the accuracy of the reconstruction increases. First approaches with image-driven regularisation go back to Mansouri *et al.* [10] who proposed an anisotropic method that smoothes along object boundaries but not across them. More recently, Kim and Sohn [9], presented a similar approach with non-convex regularisation that gives even sharper results. However, both techniques are restricted to the ortho-parallel case, where images have already been *rectified* and the correspondence problem reduces to a search along the x-axis. In Alvarez *et al.* [1] a more general variational method with image-driven regularisation is proposed: By using knowledge on the geometry of the scene this technique does not require an explicit rectification of the input images but still satisfies the so-called *epipolar constraint* that relates corresponding points in both views. A similar method, however with solution-driven regularisation was presented by Robert and Deriche [12]. Apart from using a different regularisation strategy, their approach was also the first one that considered constancy assumptions on higher order image derivatives such as the image gradient or the Laplacian. This, in general, yields a better performance under varying illumination.

While the previous methods already combine some successful concepts, recent progress in variational optic flow computation shows that there are even more useful strategies which should be integrated in the estimation. This problem is addressed in our paper: We propose a novel variational method for estimating dense disparity maps that is based on the currently most accurate optic flow technique: The optic flow method of Brox *et al.* [2]. By integrating knowledge on the geometry of the scene we obtain a general approach that introduces the following novelties to the field of variational stereo reconstruction: Firstly, a robust data term is used. Although this concept is quite common for area-based reconstruction methods (cf. [15]), it has not been considered for variational techniques so far. Secondly, we make use of the total variation (TV) [13]. During the last years this form of penalisation of both the smoothness and the data term has become very popular and achieved good results in various research fields such as deconvolution, image restoration and optic flow estimation. And finally, the proposed approach allows to extend the theoretical justification of the warping strategy given by Brox *et al.* [2] to the field of variational stereo reconstruction methods.

Our paper is organised as follows. In Section 2 we give a short review on the stereo problem and discuss how knowledge on the geometry of the scene can be integrated appropriately into the estimation of the correspondences. This motivates us to propose a novel variational approach in Section 3 that transfers successful concepts of the highly accurate optic flow method of Brox *et al.* [2] to the field of stereo reconstruction. In Section 4 the performance of our approach is evaluated on both synthetic and real-world data while a summary in Section 5 concludes this paper.

2   The Stereo Problem

Let us consider a stereo image pair $g_l^*(\mathbf{x})$ and $g_r^*(\mathbf{x})$, where the subscripts l and r stand for the left and the right camera, respectively, and $\mathbf{x} = (x, y)^\top$ denotes the location within a rectangular image domain Ω. Then, projective geometry tells us that we can recover the depth of a point $\mathbf{x}$ in the left image by finding its corresponding point $\mathbf{x}'$ in the right image. In other words: If we are able to compute the displacement field $\mathbf{d}(\mathbf{x}) = \mathbf{x}' - \mathbf{x}$ between the two images (*disparity*) we can reconstruct the original scene.

2.1 Epipolar Geometry

However, the displacement field $\mathbf{d}(\mathbf{x})$ cannot be arbitrary. Due to the geometry of the scene the so called *epipolar constraint* [3] must hold. It is given by

$$\hat{\mathbf{x}}'^{\top} F \hat{\mathbf{x}} = 0 \tag{1}$$

and relates the projective coordinates $\hat{\mathbf{x}} = (x, y, 1)^{\top}$ and $\hat{\mathbf{x}}' = (x', y', 1)^{\top}$ of corresponding points in both views via a 3×3 matrix of rank two – the so called *fundamental matrix F*. For a given point $\mathbf{x}$, this constraint describes a line in the right image on which $\mathbf{x}'$ must lie: The *epipolar line Φ*. Defining the following abbreviations

$$a(\mathbf{x}) := f_{11}x + f_{12}y + f_{13},$$
$$b(\mathbf{x}) := f_{21}x + f_{22}y + f_{23},$$
$$c(\mathbf{x}) := f_{31}x + f_{32}y + f_{33},$$

with f_{ij} being the entries of the fundamental matrix F, this epipolar line Φ can be written as

$$a(\mathbf{x})x' + b(\mathbf{x})y' + c(\mathbf{x}) = 0. \tag{2}$$

2.2 Integration of the Epipolar Constraint

In order to allow for an accurate estimation of the displacement field $\mathbf{d}(\mathbf{x})$, the epipolar constraint has to be integrated in the formulation of the correspondence problem. To this end, we follow the idea of Alvarez *et al.* [1] and perform an orthogonal decomposition of $\mathbf{d}(\mathbf{x})$ with respect to the direction of the epipolar line Φ. Thus, we obtain

$$\mathbf{d}(p(\mathbf{x})) = p(\mathbf{x}) \underbrace{\frac{1}{\sqrt{a^2(\mathbf{x})+b^2(\mathbf{x})}} \begin{pmatrix} -b(\mathbf{x}) \\ a(\mathbf{x}) \end{pmatrix}}_{\text{epipolar direction } e(\mathbf{x})} + q(\mathbf{x}) \underbrace{\frac{1}{\sqrt{a^2(\mathbf{x})+b^2(\mathbf{x})}} \begin{pmatrix} -a(\mathbf{x}) \\ -b(\mathbf{x}) \end{pmatrix}}_{\text{epipolar normal } e^{\perp}(\mathbf{x})}, \tag{3}$$

where $p(\mathbf{x})$ and $q(\mathbf{x})$ stand for the component of the projection of the displacement field $\mathbf{d}(\mathbf{x})$ in direction of and orthogonal to the epipolar line Φ, respectively. For a point $\mathbf{x}'$ on the epipolar line Φ, however, $q(\mathbf{x})$ is known. It is the distance of the point $\mathbf{x}$ to the epipolar line Φ and can be computed via

$$q(\mathbf{x}) = \left(\frac{a(\mathbf{x})x + b(\mathbf{x})y + c(\mathbf{x})}{\sqrt{a^2(\mathbf{x}) + b^2(\mathbf{x})}} \right). \tag{4}$$

Plugging this expression in equation (3) satisfies the epipolar constraint and restricts the correspondence problem to the search of one unknown function, namely $p(\mathbf{x})$.

3   From Optic Flow to Stereo

Recently, Brox *et al.* [2] proposed a highly accurate variational method for computing the displacement field between two images. However, their method was designed to be used in the context of *optic flow estimation*, where correspondences can be *arbitrary*. Since we have seen that the epipolar constraint can be satisfied if a suitable decomposition of the displacement field $\mathbf{d}(\mathbf{x})$ is performed, we can modify this approach such that it meets all requirements for a stereo reconstruction method. In the following, we present the new approach in detail.

3.1   The Variational Model

Let $g_r(\mathbf{x})$ and $g_l(\mathbf{x})$ be presmoothed versions of the original images $g_r^*(\mathbf{x})$ and $g_l^*(\mathbf{x})$ that have been obtained by convolution with a Gaussian kernel of standard deviation σ. Furthermore, let α and β be nonnegative weights. Then we propose to compute $p(\mathbf{x})$ as minimiser of the energy functional

$$E(p) = E_D(p) + \beta\, E_S(p), \tag{5}$$

where the data term is given by

$$E_D(p) = \int_\Omega \Psi_D\left(|g_r(\mathbf{x}+\mathbf{d}(p)) - g_l(\mathbf{x})|^2 + \alpha\,|\nabla g_r(\mathbf{x}+\mathbf{d}(p)) - \nabla g_l(\mathbf{x})|^2\right)\, dx\, dy, \tag{6}$$

and the smoothness term reads

$$E_S(s) = \int_\Omega \Psi_S\left(|\nabla p|^2\right)\, dx\, dy. \tag{7}$$

While the first part of the data term models the assumption of a constant grey value in both views, the second one renders the approach more robust against varying illumination. This is achieved by assuming constancy of the spatial image gradient $\nabla g = (g_x, g_y)^\top$. In accordance with equation (3) both assumptions are modified such that the epipolar constraint is satisfied. Moreover, no linearisation of the data term is performed to allow for a correct estimation of large displacements. Finally, in order to render the approach more robust with respect to outliers, a robust function Ψ_S is applied to the whole data term. As proposed in [2] we consider a regularised version of the total variation (TV) [13] for this purpose that is given by $\Psi(s^2) = \sqrt{s^2 + \epsilon^2}$ with $\epsilon := 10^{-3}$.

In the smoothness term we follow a different strategy: Instead of regularising the total displacement field $\mathbf{d}(p(\mathbf{x}))$ we penalise deviations from the unknown function $p(\mathbf{x})$ directly. Also in this case, the regularised version of the total variation with $\epsilon = 10^{-3}$ is used as non-quadratic function Ψ_S. This solution-driven regularisation models a piecewise smooth result and thus preserves discontinuities in the disparity map.

3.2   The Euler-Lagrange-Equation

Let us now derive the Euler-Lagrange equation that is a necessary condition for the minimiser of the proposed energy functional. For better readability we use the following abbreviations for derivatives and differences:

$$
\begin{aligned}
g &:= g_r\left(\mathbf{x}+\mathbf{d}(p)\right) & , && g_{xx} &:= \partial_{xx} g_r\left(\mathbf{x}+\mathbf{d}(p)\right), \\
g_x &:= \partial_x g_r\left(\mathbf{x}+\mathbf{d}(p)\right) & , && g_{xy} &:= \partial_{xy} g_r\left(\mathbf{x}+\mathbf{d}(p)\right), \\
g_y &:= \partial_y g_r\left(\mathbf{x}+\mathbf{d}(p)\right) & , && g_{yy} &:= \partial_{yy} g_r\left(\mathbf{x}+\mathbf{d}(p)\right), \\
g_z &:= g_r\left(\mathbf{x}+\mathbf{d}(p)\right) - g_l\left(\mathbf{x}\right) & , && g_{xz} &:= \partial_x g_r\left(\mathbf{x}+\mathbf{d}(p)\right) - \partial_x g_l\left(\mathbf{x}\right), \\
& & && g_{yz} &:= \partial_y g_r\left(\mathbf{x}+\mathbf{d}(p)\right) - \partial_y g_l\left(\mathbf{x}\right).
\end{aligned}
$$

Moreover, we define the components of the direction $\mathbf{e}$ of the epipolar line Φ by $\mathbf{e} = (e_1, e_2)^\top$. Then, the Euler-Lagrange-equation can be written as

$$
\begin{aligned}
& \Psi_D'\left(g_z^2 + \alpha\left(g_{xz}^2 + g_{yz}^2\right)\right)\left(g_z\left(g_x e_1 + g_y e_2\right)\right) \\
& + \alpha\, \Psi_D'\left(g_z^2 + \alpha\left(g_{xz}^2 + g_{yz}^2\right)\right)\left(g_{xz}\left(g_{xx} e_1 + g_{xy} e_2\right) + g_{yz}\left(g_{xy} e_1 + g_{yy} e_2\right)\right) \\
& - \beta\,\mathrm{div}\left(\Psi_S'\left(|\nabla p|^2\right) \nabla p\right) = 0
\end{aligned}
\tag{8}
$$

with reflecting boundary conditions.

As proposed in [2] this coupled system of PDEs is solved by means of two nested fixed point iterations. Thereby a coarse-to-fine warping strategy with downsampling factor η is used. As for the original optic flow method it can be theoretically justified as an approximation strategy to the continuous energy functional.

Fig. 1. *Corridor* stereo data set (http://www-dbv.cs.uni-bonn.de/stereo_data/). *(a) Top Left:* Left frame. *(b) Top Center:* Right frame. *(c) Top Right:* Ground truth disparity map. *(d) Bottom Left:* Correlation method. *(e) Bottom Center:* Method of Alvarez *et al.* [1]. *(f) Bottom Right:* Our method ($\sigma = 1.55$, $\alpha = 1.1$, $\beta = 5$, $\eta = 0.95$). Computing time on a standard PC with 3.06 GHz Pentium4 CPU: 21 seconds.

Table 1. Results for the *Corridor* scene. AADE = Average absolute disparity error.

(a) Overall performance

Technique	AADE
Correlation method [1]	0.4978
Alvarez *et al.* [1]	0.2639
Our method	**0.1731**

(b) Impact of noise

Technique	Noise level σ_n^2	AADE
Our method	1	0.1952
Our method	10	0.2519
Our method	100	0.3297

4   Experiments

The proposed algorithm has been evaluated on two commonly used stereo test pairs: The synthetic *Corridor* scene from the University of Bonn, and the areal photos of the *Pentagon* building from the CMU image data base. In the case of the *Corridor* scene the known ground truth allowed us to determine the estimation quality quantitatively. This was done by computing the *average absolute disparity error* via

$$\textbf{AADE} = \frac{1}{N} \sum_{i=1}^{N} |d_i^{\text{truth}} - d_i^{\text{estimate}}|. \tag{9}$$

where N is the number of pixels.

In our first experiment we have tested the proposed approach on the *Corridor* data set *without* noise. The achieved error is shown in Table 1(a), where it is compared to results from the variational approach of Alvarez *et al.* [1] and a correlation based technique with sub-pixel accuracy from the same authors. As one can see, our method outperforms both techniques significantly.

The reason for the good performance becomes obvious in the corresponding disparity maps that are presented in Figure 1: Connected areas such as ceiling, floor, walls and objects are estimated homogeneously while boundaries between them remain relatively sharp. This is a straight consequence of using the total variation in both the data and the smoothness term. In this context one should note that in accordance with Alvarez *et al.* [1] a boundary layer of 15 pixels was omitted when computing the disparity error. From the presented maps, however, one can see that this would not have been necessary for our method.

In our second experiment we have evaluated the performance of our approach with respect to noise. To this end, we used three variants of the *Corridor* scene, where Gaussian noise of zero mean and different variance σ_n^2 has been added. While Scharstein and Szeliski [15] claim that these data sets would be too difficult for a reasonable estimation, our results in Table 1(b) show that this is not the case. As one can see, they are still very accurate. In particular, one should note that our result for the version with $\sigma_n^2 = 10$ is still more precise than the results of the other two approaches for the original data set *without* noise.

In our third experiment we have reconstructed the *Pentagon* scene using the computed dense disparity map as hightfield. This is shown in Figure 2. Evidently, the whole scene looks very realistic: The discontinuities between the different sectors of the building are well preserved, the huge bridge in the upper right corner of the image is reconstructed accurately, and there are no outliers present that require the use of postprocessing steps.

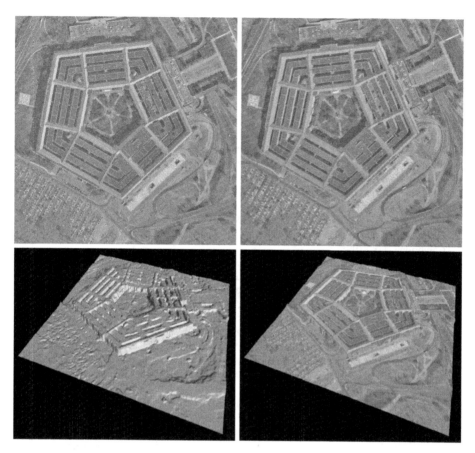

Fig. 2. *Pentagon* stereo data set (http://vasc.ri.cmu.edu/idb/html/stereo/). *(a) Top Left:* Left frame. *(b) Top Right:* Right frame. *(c) Bottom Left:* Computed disparity map height field with lighting ($\sigma = 1.05$, $\alpha = 1.1$, $\beta = 6$, $\eta = 0.95$). *(d) Bottom Right:* Computed Disparity map height field with texture. Computing time on a standard PC with 3.06 GHz Pentium4 CPU: 83 seconds.

5   Summary and Conclusions

In this paper we have demonstrated that variational stereo reconstruction methods can benefit from recent progress in optic flow computation. By embedding the currently most accurate optic flow method into epipolar geometry, we achieved dense disparity maps with high quality. They respect discontinuities and are very robust under noise.

It is our hope that this strategy serves only as a first step towards a generic and mathemetically well-founded variational framework for solving the entire class of correspondence problems with high accuracy. This is a topic of our ongoing work. Apart from improving the model, e.g. by the explicit consideration of occlusions, we will also investiagte highly efficient numerifcal methods for our framework. This in turn may allow to obtain dense deformation maps for matching problems in real-time.

Acknowledgements

Natalia Slesareva gratefully acknowledges funding by the International Max-Planck Research School. Moreover, the authors thank Oliver Vogel who developed the visualisation software.

References

1. L. Alvarez, R. Deriche, J. Sánchez, and J. Weickert. Dense disparity map estimation respecting image derivatives: a PDE and scale-space based approach. *Journal of Visual Communication and Image Representation*, 13(1/2):3–21, 2002.
2. T. Brox, A. Bruhn, N. Papenberg, and J. Weickert. High accuracy optic flow estimation based on a theory for warping. In T. Pajdla and J. Matas, editors, *Computer Vision – ECCV 2004*, volume 3024 of *Lecture Notes in Computer Science*, pages 25–36. Springer, Berlin, 2004.
3. O. Faugeras. *Three-Dimensional Computer Vision: A Geometric Viewpoint*. MIT Press, Cambridge, MA, 1993.
4. M. Felsberg. Disparity from monogenic phase. In L. Van Gool, editor, *Pattern Recognition*, volume 2449 of *Lecture Notes in Computer Science*, pages 248–256, Berlin, 2002. Springer.
5. T. Fröhlinghaus and J. M. Buhmann. Regularizing phase-based stereo. In *Proc. 13th International Conference on Pattern Recognition*, pages 451–455, Vienna, Austria, Aug. 1996.
6. W. E. L. Grimson. Computational experiments with a feature based stereo algorithm. *IEEE Transactions on Pattern Analysis and Machine Intelligence*, 7:17–34, 1985.
7. M. Hansen, K. Daniilidis, and G. Sommer. Optimization of stereo disparity estimation using the instantaneous frequency. M. Hansen, K. Daniilidis, and G. Sommer, *editors, Computer Analysis of Images and Patterns*, volume 1296 of *Lecture Notes in Computer Science*, pages 321–328, Berlin, 1997. Springer.
8. H. Hirschmüller, P. Innocent, and J. Garibaldi. Real-time correlation-based stereo vision with reduced border errors. *International Journal of Computer Vision*, 47(1-3):229–246, 2002.
9. H. Kim and K. Sohn. Hierarchical disparity estimation with energy based regularization. In *Proc. Tenth IEEE International Conference on Image Processing*, volume 1, pages 373–376, Barcelona, Spain, Sept. 2003.
10. A.-R. Mansouri, A. Mitchie, and J. Konrad. Selective image diffusion: application to disparity estimation. In *Proc. 1998 IEEE International Conference on Image Processing*, volume 3, pages 114–118, Chicago, IL, Oct. 1998. IEEE Computer Society Press.
11. D. Marr and T. Poggio. Cooperative computation of stereo disparity. *Science*, 194:283–287, 1976.
12. L. Robert and R. Deriche. Dense depth map reconstruction: A minimization and regularization approach which preserves discontinuities. In B. Buxton and R. Cipolla, editors, *Computer Vision – ECCV '96*, volume 1064 of *Lecture Notes in Computer Science*, pages 439–451. Springer, Berlin, 1996.
13. L. I. Rudin, S. Osher, and E. Fatemi. Nonlinear total variation based noise removal algorithms. *Physica D*, 60:259–268, 1992.
14. D. Scharstein and R. Szeliski. Stereo matching with non-linear diffusion. In *Proc. 1996 IEEE Computer Society Conference on Computer Vision and Pattern Recognition*, pages 343–350, San Francisco, CA, June 1996. IEEE Computer Society Press.
15. D. Scharstein and R. Szeliski. A taxonomy and evaluation of dense two-frame stereo correspondence algorithms. *International Journal of Computer Vision*, 47(1-3):7–42, 2002.
16. J. Wötzel and R. Koch. Multi-camera real-time depth estimation with discontinuity on PC graphics hardware. In *Proc. 17th International Conference on Pattern Recognition*, volume 1, pages 741–744, Cambridge, United Kingdom, August 2004.

Lens Model Selection for Visual Tracking

Birger Streckel and Reinhard Koch

Institute of Computer Science and Applied Mathematics,
Christian-Albrechts-UniversitÃt zu Kiel, 24098 Kiel, Germany

Abstract. A standard approach to generate a camera pose from images of a single moving camera is Structure From Motion (SfM). When aiming on a practical implementation of SfM often a camera is needed that is lightweight and small. This work analyses which is the best camera and lens for SfM, that is small in size and available on the market. Therefore we compare cameras with fisheye and perspective lenses. It is shown that pose estimation is improved by a fisheye lens. Also some methods are discussed, how the large Field of View can be further exploited to improve the pose estimation.

1   Introduction

Structure from Motion (SfM) is a well known approach for generating a camera pose from a single moving camera without the help of any markers [6]. A common application for SfM is the tracking of a persons head, i.e. in Augmented Reality where additional information has to be superimposed into the users view. Therefore the camera has to be attached to the users head and is possibly carried for a long time, hence a small and lightweight camera is inevitable.

This paper gives a detailed analysis on which is the best small and lightweight camera and lens configuration for SfM. Considered are cameras with fisheye and perspective lenses, it is shown that a camera with a fisheye lens is superior to a standard perspective camera. The presented results also apply to catadioptric cameras (perspective cameras looking into a convex mirror to get a hemispherical view), if they are designed to produce an image with constant angular resolution. These cameras are not suited for augmented reality, because the image center, commonly the users viewing direction, is blocked by the camera itself.

2   Previous Work

Over the last years there was already some research done on which camera is best suited for SfM [3][7] [2][5][1]. The most extensive theoretical approach is made by Neumann and Fermüller in [3] and [7]. They state, that from theoretical considerations a fisheye camera is more appropriate for SfM than a single perspective camera, with a drawback because of the low resolution. There is no analysis done on how much the resolution deficit impairs the overall SfM Quality, instead a multi-camera is proposed with many perspective cameras looking in different directions and thus combining a high resolution with a big FoV.

There are different approaches showing that a wide FoV stabilizes the pose estimation, i.e. Davison stated in [2] that for perspective cameras with small

W. Kropatsch, R. Sablatnig, and A. Hanbury (Eds.): DAGM 2005, LNCS 3663, pp. 41–48, 2005.
© Springer-Verlag Berlin Heidelberg 2005

FoV, the motion along the optical axis is always ill defined because the camera moves towards the focus of expansion (FOE) (or focus of contraction (FOC)). Only the motion perpendicular to the FOE/FOC can be estimated reliably. In a spherical image with a wide FoV, there will always be many features with vectors having a large angle to the cameras optical axis, hence the estimation of the camera motion is always reliable.

3   Robust Tracking from Camera Images

The implementation of the SfM approach [6] is divided into 2D feature tracking including initialization and robust 3D pose estimation.

Initialization and 2D Feature Tracking. In an initial step, salient 2D intensity corners are detected in the first image of the sequence. These 2D features are tracked throughout the image sequence by local feature matching, i.e. with the KLT operator [8]. Having corner correspondences between the first two images allows the computation of an Essential matrix between the views. With the Essential Matrix the relative pose of the cameras can be estimated and a 3D point can be triangulated for each 2D-2D pair.

3D Feature Tracking and Pose Estimation. After initialization each triangulated 3D feature point is assigned to a 2D feature track. From the third image on, the known 2D-3D correspondences can be used to determine the camera pose. Over time, new feature tracks are established and the 3D point positions are refined.

4   Lens Model Selection

In this section we will develop a simulation environment for the essential parts of SfM. This allows us to evaluate the effects of different lens models on point triangulation and camera pose errors.

Simulating Structure from Motion. The presented model implements the SfM approach for three images. As 3D scene a random 3D point cloud of 2000 points is generated, that is static for all experiments throughout this paper. The cloud is equally distributed in all directions around the camera center in a distance of 8-30 times the camera displacement length. Each camera can see parts of this cloud, these points are projected into the camera plane following the cameras projection model.

The only error source in SfM is the error in the feature position measurement of the 2D point tracker. If this tracker would return points with infinite accuracy and no wrong matches, the pose and scene estimation would also be perfect. According to [8] a good tracker is able to generate feature points with a standard deviation of $\sigma = 0.25$ pixel. To model the tracking error, Gaussian noise with a standard deviation of $\sigma = 0.25$ pixel is added to the points projection into the camera. With noise proportional to the pixel size, the tracking accuracy depends mainly on the camera resolution, which was fixed to $N = 1024$ in x- and y-direction. It is assumed, that all corner correspondences can be tracked independently of resolution and lens geometry and that no mismatches occur.

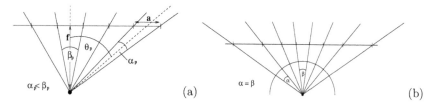

Fig. 1. Angular resolution of a perspective camera (a) and a fisheye camera (b)

With the knowledge about point correspondences for the first two cameras, the pose of the second camera relative to the first can be estimated from the Essential matrix and 3D points are triangulated up to scale. Knowing estimated 3D points and the corresponding 2D projection, the pose of the third camera relative to the first can also be evaluated.

Error Models for Perspective and Equidistant Projection. The difference between a perspective camera and a fisheye camera is the projection of a 3D point into the 2D image. The perspective camera performs a perspective projection, the ideal fisheye an equidistant projection [4]. These projections define the transformation of the modeled tracker noise into angular noise, which affects the triangulation quality.

An optimal fisheye lens gives a circular picture. The angle between the cameras optical axis and a ray through a 3D point (θ_p in fig. 1 (a)) is linear to the distance of the cameras focal point to the projection of the 3D point in the camera image. So for a fisheye the angular resolution is constant (see fig. 1(b)). In a perspective camera the angular resolution is higher for a greater angle θ_p, for points closer to the image border α_p is smaller than for points near the center (see fig. 1(a)).

To derive an error model for the perspective camera, it is necessary to calculate its angular resolution. From figure 1 (a) one can derive $\frac{f}{a} \sin(\alpha_p) + \sin(\frac{\alpha_p}{2}) = \cos^2 \theta_p$. With $f \gg a$ the term $\sin\frac{\alpha_p}{2}$ is negligible. It follows

$$\alpha_p \approx \operatorname{asin}(\frac{a}{f} \cos^2 \theta_p) = \operatorname{asin}(\frac{2\tan(\theta_{max})}{N} \cos^2 \theta_p), \tag{1}$$

where α_p is the angular resolution of the perspective camera, θ_p is the angle between the 3D point ray and cameras optical axis, f is the focal length, a is the size of a single CCD-Pixel, N is the full CCD-resolution and θ_{max} is the half FoV. With (1) we can compute the angular resolution of each pixel from its position on the chip.

The angular resolution of a fisheye camera is constant

$$\alpha_f = \frac{2\theta_{max}}{N}. \tag{2}$$

From (1) and (2) it is easy to see that the angular resolution of the fisheye camera is constant, while the angular resolution of the perspective camera is higher near the image borders. The functions for α_p and α_f are plotted in figure 2 for fisheye and perspective cameras with different FoVs. Figure 2(a) shows α_p and α_f at

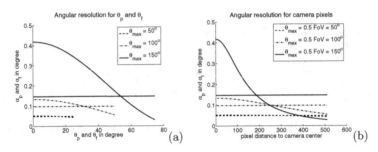

Fig. 2. Angular resolution for different FoVs

angular image positions θ_p and θ_f, in figure 2(b) the angular resolution is plotted against the pixel positions on the CCD. The angular resolution for the center pixels is very bad for a perspective camera with a wide FoV, while for small FoVs fisheye and perspective cameras have a similar characteristic.

This leads to the result, that from the same Gaussian error on the pixel position follow two different models for the angular errors, which directly affect the quality of the scene reconstruction.

Analysis of Reconstruction and Pose Errors. The camera FoV has the greatest effect on the reconstruction error. For a camera with a constant number of CCD-pixels the cameras angular resolution declines with an increasing FoV. On the other hand the wide FoV increases the number of trackable features and also the features in view have a better spatial distribution which improves the pose estimation.

As stated above, points perpendicular to the FOE or FOC can be estimated most reliably. To simulate the effects of a changing FoV a critical camera movement was chosen. The first camera displacement is directly in z-direction, the FOE is in the image center. The second camera movement is in y-direction, perpendicular to the first movement.

From the first two images the camera displacement and rotation is estimated up to scale and 3D points are triangulated. The errors of the triangulated points are shown in figure 3 (a) and (b). The curves give the mean of the relative triangulation error of 100 test runs on the same 3D point cloud with Gaussian noise applied for each projection. The triangulation results for x and y very similar and therefore represented by the same graph. They are better for a small FoV, because of the higher angular resolution of the camera. The z-coordinate estimation is always critical. The perspective camera z-error ascends fast with greater FoVs, because for a wide FoV perspective camera the angular resolution for center pixels gets very bad (see fig. 2(b)). The fisheye error characteristic is much better suited for triangulation at a wide FoV. The resolution degradation is compensated by the good estimation of points lying at the image borders, perpendicular to the FOE for the chosen movement. The z-error is therefore decreasing with increasing FoV.

The third cameras pose is reconstructed from the estimated points and their known projection. The pose error is given in figure 3 (c) to (f). The third cameras

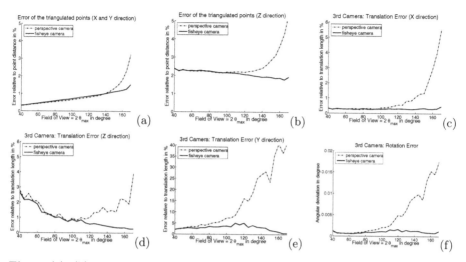

Fig. 3. (a), (b) Error of triangulated points from cameras 1 and 2 (z-displacement); (c)-(f) Error of predicted pose from camera 3 (y-displacement)

pose prediction quality depends very much on the triangulated points quality (figure 3 (a) and (b)). Also number and spatial distribution of the points used for the estimation have an impact on the quality. It is visible that the y coordinate error is much higher, this is due to the chosen movement. The first camera move in z-direction produces high covariances in the 3D points z-coordinate. By the cameras second move in y-direction these are projected onto the camera images y-axis and cause a higher error in this direction.

The pose estimation quality for the third fisheye camera rises with the FoV, the additional points perpendicular to the FOE are more than compensating the lower resolution. The pose estimation for the perspective camera degrades fast, analog to the triangulated points quality.

We have simulated different motion directions for the first motion as well. All simulations showed a similar trend, that in all cases the fisheye lens performs equal or better than the perspective lens. See section 5 for further analysis. For a small FoV both models are similar, for a FoV $> 100°$ the fisheye lens is superior to the perspective lens.

Lens Selection. From the preceding analysis follows that the precision of SfM is increased when using a fisheye lens with a large FoV. There are some further advantages of this lens that can hardly be modeled in this simulation but play an improtant part in a real system:

- The wide FoV covers a very large scene area and moving objects tend to be in a small part of the scene only. The hemispherical view will always see lots of static visual structures, even if the scene in front of the user may change dramatically.
- If fast rotations occur, a perspective camera will lose all tracked 2D features. This will not happen easily with a hemispherical view fisheye camera.

The drawback is, that the system is mainly designed for indoor use. In outdoor scenes the sun light falling directly onto the CCD sensor will cause problems. Also a cloudy sky would cause problems because a huge part of the scene is moving slowly enough to be still trackable. These problems can be facilitated by using CMOS sensors with logarithmic response and high dynamic range and a configuration where the fisheye camera is mostly looking to the ground.

5   Optimizing SfM for Spherical Images

For a perspective camera there are certain critical moves for pose estimation. These are moves along the optical axis where the FOE lies close to the focal point. Points perpendicular to the camera movement are well suited for pose estimation. For critical moves with a small FoV camera most point vectors have small angles to the camera movement vector and thus the points have large triangulation errors. A full spherical camera that is able to see in all directions has no critical moves, since always all feature points are in sight. For a fair comparison between perspective and fisheye lens in section 4 we defined the pole of the fisheye hemisphere to coincide with the perspective optical axis. Standard SfM was than computed on a tangent plane with the optical axis as normal.

For a true spherical camera, we can select a tangent plane with a normal perpendicular to the FOE to avoid uncertainties. Since we do not know the camera movement and have to estimate it, we need a two step process. For FOE estimation we use the approach from section 4. In a refinement step we define an undistortion plane with its normal perpendicular to the FOE and use this for SfM. This is equivalent to a rotation of the fisheye pole to the plane perpendicular to the FOE. The result of this modification is shown in figure 4 for the triangulated points from the first two cameras (a),(b) as well as for the error of the third camera pose estimation (c)-(f). The camera movement is equal to section 4, first z-displacement then y-displacement.

The "virtually rotated fisheye" performs much better for a camera FoV of less than 130 degree but then rapidly degrades. This is due to the fact that the rotated small FoV camera mostly sees points perpendicular to the FOE with a very good covariance. But as the FoV angle grows, more and more points lying near the FOE or FOC are used for pose estimation. Since those points have a very bad covariance they spoil the whole pose estimation. In section 4 this effect is compensated by the good angular resolution of a small FoV camera, there the points close to the FOC are predominantly in view when the FoV is still small. Here more and more uncertain points are added while the angular resolution is decreasing. From figure 4 one can see the great influence of using the correct point distribution for pose estimation. It would also be useful to weight the estimates depending on their uncertainty w.r.t. the FOE.

From the results of this section follows that a virtually rotated fisheye with a FoV of approximately 100° outperforms a full fisheye as presented in section 4. Knowing the FOE we could also perform a cylindrical rectification of the sphere aligned with the FOE direction. The cylinder would contain all tangent planes

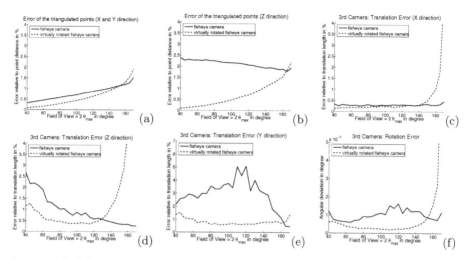

Fig. 4. (a), (b) Error of triangulated points from cameras 1 and 2 (z-displacement); (c)-(f) Error of predicted pose from camera 3 (y-displacement)

perpendicular to the FOE. This would further improve estimation quality, but was not done for this work.

6   Experiments

We have used perspective and fisheye sequences in an existing SfM system and evaluated the tracking results. To generate test sequences a high resolution (1600×1200 Pixel) fisheye camera with a FoV of 180° was used. Very accurate tracking on the full resolution images was performed, the results were taken as "ground truth" data. To compare the tracking performance on fisheye and

Table 1. Relative average translation and rotation error over 300 frames

	Translation Error	Rotation Error
Fisheye lens	3.3%	1.1%
Perspective lens	5%	1.4%

Fig. 5. (a) Original fisheye image, (b) and (c) video augmentation of a perspective cutout of the fisheye sequence from different view points

perspective sequences, the centers of the high resolution images were mapped artifact free to perspective images of 400×400 Pixel with a FoV of 60° and an angular resolution of $6 - 8\frac{pix}{\circ}$. To simulate a fisheye camera with identical resolution a FoV of 160° was subsampled to 400×400 Pixel, the angular resolution was $2.5\frac{pix}{\circ}$. The results of the experiments are shown in table 1. These results are only partially comparable to the presented analysis, because in the used SfM implementation there are many additional stabilization methods and tracking was performed over several hundred images.

We have also verified the fisheye tracking over very long image sequences and have optained very stable results. Figure 5 shows a video augmentation of virtual objects superimposed into the video stream in a complex environment.

7 Conclusions

The work shows that for SfM applications a fisheye lens is superior to a perspective lens, despite its lower average angular resolution. The lack of angular resolution is more than compensated by its linear characteristic. Also tracking is more robust because a greater part of the scene is in the cameras FoV.

There are still open issues to improve SfM with a fisheye camera. At first weighting of the 3D points w.r.t. the FOE for the camera pose estimation should be investigated. Points can be weighted according to their vectors angle to the cameras movement vector. Results from section 5 strongly imply that this is a promising approach. Furthermore real SfM on fisheye images without any projection has to be developed. The first step for this is already done in [9] where Svoboda et. al. evolved the epipolar geometry for fisheye images.

Acknowledgement. This work was supported by the Federal Ministry of Education and Research project ARTESAS (www.artesas.de).

References

1. P. Chang and M. Hebert. Omni-directional structure from motion. In *IEEE Workshop on Omnidirectional Vision 2000*, pages 153–160, 2000.
2. A. J. Davison, Y. González Cid, and N. Kita. Real-time 3D SLAM with wide-angle vision. In *Proc. IFAC Symp. on Intelligent Autonomous Vehicles, Lisbon*, July 2004.
3. Cornelia Fermüller, Yiannis Aloimonos, and Tomás Brodsky. New eyes for building models from video. *Computational Geom.: Theory and Applications*, 15:3–23, 2000.
4. M. Fleck. Perspective projection: the wrong imaging model. *Technical Report 95-01, Comp. Sci., U. Iowa*, 1995.
5. C. Geyer and K. Daniilidis. Catadioptric projective geometry. *Journal of Computer Vision*, 43:223–243, 2001.
6. R. Hartley and A. Zisserman. *Multiple View Geometry in Computer Vision*. Cambridge university press, 2000.
7. J. Neumann, C. Fermüller, and Y. Aloimonos. Eyes from eyes: New cameras for structure from motion. In *IEEE Workshop on Omnidir. Vision*, pages 19–26, 2002.
8. J. Shi and C. Tomasi. Good features to track. In *Conference on Computer Vision and Pattern Recognition*, pages 593–600, Seattle, June 1994. IEEE.
9. Tomás Svoboda, Tomás Pajdla, and Václav Hlavác. Epipolar geometry for panoramic cameras. *Lecture Notes in Computer Science*, 1406:218–??, 1998.

Omnidirectional Vision with Frontal Stereo*

W. Stürzl and M.V. Srinivasan

Centre for Visual Sciences, Research School of Biological Sciences,
Australian National University,
P.O. Box 475, Canberra, ACT 2601, Australia

Abstract. This study describes a novel imaging system that can be
used as a front end for a vision system for guidance of unmanned aerial
vehicles. A single camera and a combination of three specially designed
reflecting surfaces are used to provide (a) complete omnidirectional vision with no frontal blind zone and (b) stereo range within a frontal
field. Important features are (i) the use of a single camera, which, apart
from minimising cost, eliminates the need for alignment and calibration
of multiple cameras; and (ii) a novel approach to stereoscopic range computation that uses a single camera and a circular baseline to overcome
potential aperture problems.

1 Introduction

Over the past few years there has been a growing interest in the design and
development of vision systems for guidance of unmanned aerial vehicles (UAVs)
[1]. In military applications, guidance systems that use passive vision are preferred over active systems such as radar, sonar or laser-based systems, which emit
radiation that can be readily detected by the adversary. Vision based systems
offer the added advantage of low weight and cost, and are thus ideally suited
for guidance of micro UAVs. Visual information can be used to stabilise flight,
maintain a desired course and altitude, avoid obstacles, detect targets or objects
of interest, estimate distance flown, and guide autonomous landings.

Here we describe a system that uses a single camera and a set of three
reflective surfaces to achieve fully omnidirectional vision, as well as stereo vision
in a frontal field. Information on image motion (optic flow) in the panoramic
image can be used to guide many of the maneuvers described above, while stereo
vision can be used to estimate the distances to obstacles or targets in the frontal
visual field.

Previous studies have described reflective surfaces for panoramic imaging [2].
Such surfaces are designed to produce a constant vertical angular gain [3] or a
constant viewpoint [4]. Other studies have developed dual-surface systems for
achieving panoramic stereo [5,6]. All of these systems suffer from the drawback
of a blind zone that is created by the reflective surface itself, which occludes a

---

* Supported by the Deutsche Forschungsgemeinschaft (grant no. STU 413/1-1), and
  by the Army Research Office through MAV MURI program (grant no. ARMY-
  W911NF0410176) with technical monitor as Dr. Gary Anderson.

W. Kropatsch, R. Sablatnig, and A. Hanbury (Eds.): DAGM 2005, LNCS 3663, pp. 49–57, 2005.

part of the frontal field of the camera. Here we present a system that not only eliminates this blind zone, but also provides stereo (depth) information in the frontal field. We also introduce a novel approach to stereo imaging, which uses a single camera and a circular baseline to overcome potential aperture problems.

2   Design of the Vision System

Here we describe the design of the reflecting surfaces and the properties of the system with reference to Fig. 1.

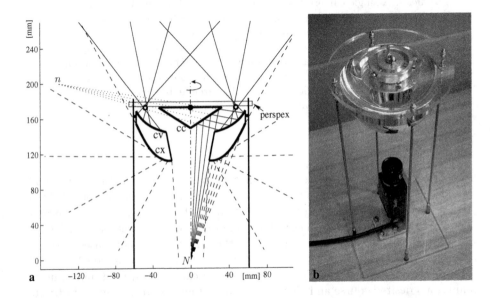

Fig. 1. Overview of the single camera vision system. **a:** Schematic drawing (axial section): The system consists of three reflective surfaces (shown as bold curves): The convex surface (labelled 'cx') with angular gain of $\alpha = 15$ yields a large field of view of about $150°$ (vertically) on either side. It reflects incoming light to the outer part of the camera image (see Fig. 3 a for an example). The concave surface (labelled 'cv') with angular gain of $\alpha = -10$ and the conic mirror (labelled 'cc') reflect light rays to the central part of the camera image. These provide a frontal stereo field. The small circles mark the location of the approximate "left" and "right" view points, which (in 3D) lie on a circle (orthogonal to the paper plane). The baseline of the frontal stereo is approx. 95 mm. N is the nodal point of the camera, and its mirror image with respect to the conic surface is n. The (vertical) field of view of the camera is approx $55°$. **b:** Picture of the vision system. The setup is about 35 cm high. The colour camera Marlin F046C offers a 780×580 pixel resolution at a frame rate of up to 50 Hz.

2.1   Mirrors with Constant Gain

The vision system consists of three reflective surfaces with constant (vertical) angular gain $\alpha := -\partial\theta/\partial\eta = \text{const.}$, where η is the camera angle and θ the angle between the z-axis and the incoming light ray.

Using the parameters γ (angle at the tip of the mirror) and r_0 (distance to the tip of the mirror along the optic axis) depicted in Fig. 2, the mirror surface can be described by (see [3] for derivation),

$$r(\eta) := r_0 \frac{\cos^k\gamma}{\cos(\eta/k + \gamma)^k} \; , \qquad k := \frac{2}{1+\alpha} \; , \tag{1}$$

where r is the distance of a point on the surface from the nodal point of the camera. The relation between the vertical angle θ and the camera angle is

$$\theta = \pi - \alpha\,\eta - 2\gamma \; . \tag{2}$$

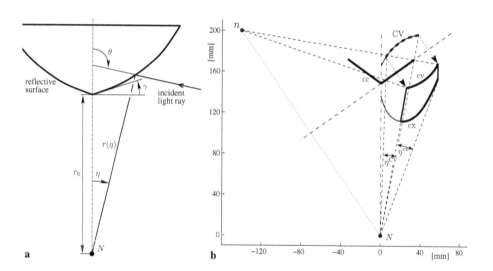

Fig. 2. a: Illustration of the parameters used in Eq. (1), which determine the shape of the reflective surface. **b:** Construction of the reflective surfaces using Eq. (1). The parameters for the convex surface are $\alpha^{cx} = 15$, $r_0^{cx} = 137\,\text{mm}$, $\gamma^{cx} = -77°$. The manufactured surface covers only the camera angle $10° < \eta^{cx} < 20.5°$. The concave surface is defined by $\alpha^{CV} = -10$, $r_0^{CV} = 166\,\text{mm}$, $\gamma^{CV} = 65.5°$, $1.5° < \eta^{CV} < 11°$.

2.2   Design and Realisation of the Reflective Surfaces

The vision system is designed to meet two important objectives. First, achieving true omnidirectional vision by avoiding the draw-back of most catadioptric systems where the view is partially restricted by the mirror. Secondly, providing range information within a restricted field of view.

While most catadioptric systems use only convex mirrors, we decided to use a concave surface for the stereo region since it allows a larger stereo base line and a more compact design: e.g. rays coming from nearby objects close to the axis of symmetry are reflected at the outer part of the concave surface, see Fig. 1 a.

In the following we use the labels 'cv' for the concave surface, 'cx' for the convex surface and 'cc' for the conic mirror, see Figs. 1 and 2 b. The distance of the nodal point to the tip of the conic mirror is $r_0^{cc} = 149$ mm, the diameter of the base is 67 mm and the apex angle is 110°. This can also be described by Eq. (1) using $\alpha^{cc} = 1$ and $\gamma^{cc} = 35°$. The angular gain of the concave mirror is $\alpha^{cv} = -10$. $|\alpha^{cv}|$ has been chosen smaller than the gain for the convex mirror $\alpha^{cx} = 15$ in order to obtain a higher image resolution for disparity calculation, see Sect. 4. Values for the other parameters are given in the caption of Fig. 2 b. As shown in Fig. 2 b the concave and convex surfaces span camera angles $1.5° < \eta^{CV} < 11°$ and $10° < \eta^{cx} < 20.5°$, respectively. To obtain the final position of the concave surface, the calculated curve has to be mirrored at the conic surface, $CV \rightarrow cv$ (according to the mirroring $N \rightarrow n$ of the nodal point). This is indicated by dotted lines.

Next, we can calculate the theoretical fields of view of the mirrors. For the concave surface we calculate from Eq. (2) that $\theta^{cv} = 61° - 10\eta$, which leads to $-39° < \theta^{cv} < 46°$ for the camera angle $\eta \in (1.5°, 10°)$. Because of the concave shape of the surface, larger excursions of θ are mapped to smaller camera angles. Therefore, we do not use the full angular range. The convex mirror spans the angular range $\theta^{cx} = 334° - 15\eta$, i.e. $184° < \theta^{cx} < 26.5°$ for $\eta \in (10°, 20.5°)$.

The mirrors were manufactured from aluminium using a computer controlled lathe. The reflective surfaces were polished and electro-plated with a nickel-silver coating. The conic mirror is mounted using a round perspex plate. The mirrors and perspex are supported by metal rods.

3   Creating an Omnidirectional Image

The outer part of the camera image (see Fig. 3), created by light reflected at the convex surface, will be called "panoramic image". The central part of the camera image (originating from reflections at the conic and concave surfaces) will be called "frontal image".

Since the angular ranges of the panoramic and the frontal image overlap, we can combine them to obtain a complete omnidirectional image, although not for a single view point. Currently we use the only outer part of the frontal image which corresponds to the angular range $0° \leq \theta < 40°$ in order to ensure that close objects in front of the vision system are displayed and to make use of the higher resolution there. This frontal image is combined with the panoramic image after correcting for the differences in gain of the two images, and comparing colour pixels in the overlap region to correct for any tinting imposed by the perspex. An example of a complete omnidirectional image is shown in Fig. 3 d-f.

Fig. 3. Creation of an omnidirectional image: **a:** Camera image of an outdoor scene; the area between the inner black circle and the white circle covers the angular range of $0° \leq \theta \lesssim 40°$, the area between the outer black circle and the white circle covers $30° \lesssim \theta \lesssim 180°$. The corresponding unwarped images are shown in b and c. **b:** Unwarped frontal image after applying the colour correction which is calculated from the overlapping area marked by the black rectangles in b and c. **c:** Unwarped panoramic image. The black rectangle marks the image area that is also visible in the frontal image shown in b. **d:** Complete omnidirectional image covering $0° \leq \theta \lesssim 180°$ (and $0° \leq \phi < 360°$), obtained by combining the images in b and c. The slightly blurry appearance is most likely caused by relatively poor camera resolution, which can be improved using a camera that provides more pixels. **e, f:** Two views of a sphere onto which the omnidirectional image has been mapped using OpenGL.

4   Stereo Algorithm

Here we give a short description of the disparity estimation for the frontal image.

Since the vision system is intended to be used on a small autonomous aerial vehicle, a fast and computationally inexpensive procedure is desirable. In recent years real-time disparity estimation has been achieved by a class of stereo algorithms which utilise a window-based "shift-and-match" approach with local minimum search, e.g. [7,8,9]. Global optimisation methods usually yield more accurate disparity maps but need significantly longer computation time [10,11]. Therefore we utilise a local (window-based) stereo algorithm, although the current implementation is not yet optimised for speed.

4.1   Matching Cost Function

To speed up the stereo computation, disparity estimation is performed after conversion of the frontal colour image to a monochrome image. Referring to the

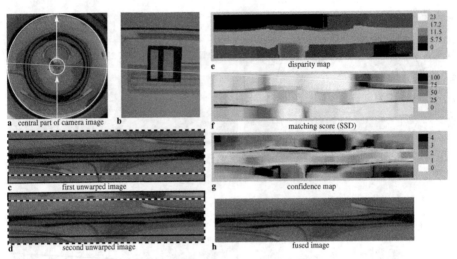

Fig. 4. Stereo computation for an indoor scene. **a:** Frontal stereo image: corresponding points lie on lines through the centre. **b:** Standard camera image of the scene, with nodal point positioned at the base of the conic mirror. The camera is looking upwards, a cardboard is placed a distance of 0.5 m. Distance to edge of the air-conditioning unit is approx. 1.2 m, distance to the light at the ceiling approx 1.6 m. **c, d:** The stereo matching algorithm is applied after unwarping the two annular segments of the frontal image, each spanning 180° azimuth. The dashed rectangles mark corresponding regions for zero disparity $d = 0$ pixels, the black rectangles mark corresponding regions for maximum disparity $d = 29$ pixels, see Eq. (4). **e:** Calculated disparity map, Eq.(7). **f:** Map of matching score, i.e. $E(d, x, y)$. **g:** Confidence map $s_d(x, y)$: dark regions correspond to low confidence. **h:** Image fused according to Eq. (9). (Parameter values of the current implementation: window size and penalty value: $w_0 = h_0 = 21$, $\Delta_0 = 0$; $w_1 = h_1 = 11$, $\Delta_1 = 50$; disparity range: 30 disparities, i.e. $d(x, y) \in \{0, 1, \ldots, 29\}$; "noise level": $\sigma_n^2 = 1$).

unwarped frontal images in Fig. 4 c,d, we denote the window patches centred at pixel x_0, y_0 by $U_k(x_0, y_0)$, i.e.

$$U_k(x_0, y_0) := \{(x, y)\,|\,|x - x_0| \leq (w_k - 1)/2, |y - y_0| \leq (h_k - 1)/2\} \quad (3)$$

We use matching windows of two different sizes $w_k \times h_k$, $k = 1, 2$, leading to a 4-dimensional cost function

$$E_1(d, k, x, y) := \frac{1}{w_k\,h_k} \sum_{(x', y') \in U_k(x, y)} \left(I^A(x', y' + \tfrac{1}{2}d) - I^B(x', y' - \tfrac{1}{2}d)\right)^2. \quad (4)$$

$I^A(x, y)$ and $I^B(x, y)$ are gray value pixels of the two unwarped frontal image parts, see Fig. 4. We use a symmetric stereo matching approach that enables us to compute a disparity map for a single view point located approximately at the centre of the base of the conic mirror. We also apply a shifting min-filter which has been shown to improve the stereo matching [10], i.e.

$$E_2(d, k, x, y) := \min_{(x_0, y_0) \in U_k(x,y)} E_1(d, k, x_0, y_0) \ . \tag{5}$$

In the next step, for each position and disparity the best match over all window sizes is determined. Since a larger support window usually yields more reliable disparity a constant Δ_k is added that decreases with increasing window size (see [12] for a similar approach):

$$E(d, x, y) := \min_k \left(E_2(d, k, x, y) + \Delta_k \right) \ . \tag{6}$$

Finally, the disparity at each position is estimated from the minimum matching error,

$$d(x, y) := \arg \min_{d'} E(d', x, y) \ . \tag{7}$$

4.2   Measure of Match Confidence

In addition to the matching score (Eq. (6)) we implemented, based on a Bayesian model, a second confidence measure for the estimated best match,

$$s_d^2(x, y) := \max_{d'} \left((d' - d(x, y))^2 \frac{2\sigma_n^2}{E(d', x, y) - E(d(x, y), x, y) + 2\sigma_n^2} \right) \ . \tag{8}$$

Disparities are regarded as more reliable, i.e. s_d^2 is small, if for all other disparities the difference in the matching error $E(d', x, y) - E(d(x, y), x, y)$ is large compared to some "noise level" σ_n^2 and if these alternative matches are close to the estimated one, i.e. for small $(d' - d(x, y))^2$.

4.3   Circular Baseline Stereo

The circular symmetry of the frontal stereo configuration implies that objects or features that are located on the optic axis of the system are viewed by an infinite number of stereo baselines with orientations all around the circle. It is therefore possible to combine disparity measurements and confidence estimates from all of the baselines to obtain a robust range estimate for such features. However, features located elsewhere in the frontal visual field may be susceptible to the aperture problem: Radially oriented edges or bars would yield low-confidence disparity estimates everywhere, because disparity is measured only in the local radial direction. On the other hand, a set of horizontal stripes, which would create severe aperture problems in a traditional twin-camera stereo system that uses a horizontal baseline, would yield high-confidence disparity estimates everywhere except along the stripe that runs through the centre of the visual field.

4.4   Reconstructed Frontal Views

Using the disparity map and the unwarped images in the stereo region, see Fig. 4 c-e, a frontal view can be computed as would be seen from a central view point located approximately at the base of the conic mirror. First, pixels in the two

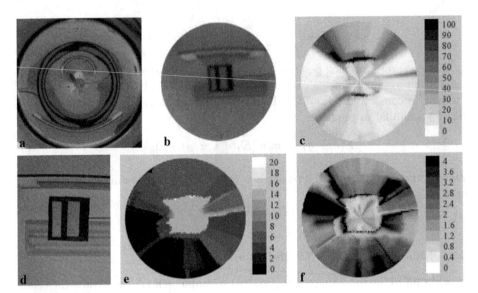

Fig. 5. Reconstructed frontal views. **a:** Central part of camera image of indoor scene (same as in Fig. 4). **b:** Reconstructed image for central view point corresponding to Fig. 4 h. Errors (visible in the area between cardboard and air-conditioning) are mainly due to occluded image parts for which no correct match exists, see Fig. 4 c,d. **c, e, f:** Frontal maps of matching score, disparity and confidence, corresponding to Fig. 4 f,e,g. **d:** Standard camera image of the scene for comparison with b.

images are shifted according to the estimated local disparities and a fused image is created (see Fig. 4 h) using the mean values of the shifted pixels, i.e.

$$\tilde{I}_c(x,y) := \frac{1}{2}(I_c^A(x, y + \tfrac{1}{2}d(x,y)) + I_c^B(x, y - \tfrac{1}{2}d(x,y)) \;, \quad c \in \{r, g, b\} \;. \quad (9)$$

Then the resulting image is transformed into the central frontal view using x and y as spherical coordinates $\phi \in [0°, 180°)$ and $\theta \in (-25°, 25°)$. The disparity and confidence maps are transformed similarly. An example is shown in Fig. 5.

5   Conclusions

We have described a front end for a vision system that provides full omnidirectional vision, and stereo within a restricted field of view. In an aircraft the device can be positioned with its optic axis oriented horizontally and looking forward, to obtain range information on obstacles and targets in the direction of flight. Alternatively the device can be configured with its optic axis pointing downward, to obtain information on height above the ground, for example during landing.

References

1. Peterson, A.I.: Launched to return. Unmanned Vehicles **8** (2003)

2. Ishiguro, H.: Development of low-cost compact omnidirectional vision sensors. In Benosman, R., Kang, S., eds.: Panoramic Vision. (2001) 23–38
3. Chahl, J., Srinivasan, M.: Reflective surfaces for panoramic imaging. Applied Optics **36** (1997) 8275–8285
4. Baker, S., Nayar, S.: Single viewpoint catadioptric cameras. In Benosman, R., Kang, S., eds.: Panoramic Vision. (2001) 39–70
5. Basu, A., Baldwin, J.: A real-time panoramic stereo imaging system and its applications. In Benosman, R., Kang, S., eds.: Panoramic Vision. (2001) 123–141
6. Stürzl, W., Dahmen, H.J., Mallot, H.: The quality of catadioptric imaging – application to omnidirectional stereo. In: ECCV. (2004) 614–627
7. Yang, R., Pollefeys, M.: Multi-resolution real-time stereo on commodity graphics hardware. In: CVPR Workshop on Real-time 3D Sensors and Their Use. (2004)
8. Hirschmüller, H.: Improvements in real-time correlation-based stereo vision. In: IEEE Workshop on Stereo and Multi-Baseline Vision. (2001) 141–148
9. Mühlmann, K., Maier, D., Hesser, J., Männer, R.: Calculating dense disparity maps from color stereo images, an efficient implementation. In: IJCV. (2002)
10. Scharstein, D., Szeliski, R.: A taxonomy and evaluation of dense two-frame stereo correspondence algorithms. Int. Journal of Computer Vision **47** (2002) 7–42
11. http://www.middlebury.edu/stereo: (Middlebury stereo vision page)
12. Veksler, O.: Fast variable window for stereo correspondence using integral images. In: CVPR. (2003) 556–564

Stereo Vision Based Reconstruction of Huge Urban Areas from an Airborne Pushbroom Camera (HRSC)

Heiko Hirschmüller[1], Frank Scholten[2], and Gerd Hirzinger[1]

[1] Institute of Robotics and Mechatronics, German Aerospace Center (DLR)
Oberpfaffenhofen
[2] Institute of Planetary Research, German Aerospace Center (DLR), Berlin,
Germany
heiko.hirschmueller@dlr.de

Abstract. This paper considers the application of capturing urban terrain by an airborne pushbroom camera (e.g. High Resolution Stereo Camera). The resulting images as well as disparity ranges are expected to be huge. A slightly non-linear flight path and small orientation changes are anticipated, which results in curved epipolar lines. These images cannot be geometrically corrected for matching purposes such that epipolar lines are exactly straight and parallel to each other. The proposed novel processing solution explicitly calculates epipolar lines for reducing the disparity search range to a minimum. This is a necessary prerequisite for using an accurate, but memory intensive semi global stereo matching method that is based on pixelwise matching. It is shown that the proposed approach performs accurate matching of urban terrain and is efficient on huge images.

1 Introduction

The High Resolution Stereo Camera (HRSC) has been developed by the Institute of Planetary Research (DLR)[1] for the exploration of the Marsian surface from orbit. The airborne version HRSC-AX is currently used for capturing earths landscape and cities from flight altitudes between 1500m to 5000m. The camera contains nine sensor arrays, which are arranged orthogonally to the flight direction in different angles. All arrays have a resolution of 12000 pixels. Five arrays are panchromatic. The other four capture red, green, blue and infrared light. The position and orientation of the camera is continuously measured by a sophisticated GPS/IMU system. Current post-processing [1,2,3] includes radiometric corrections as well as refinements of all camera positions, orientations and time offsets by means of photogrammetric methods based on HRSCs multi-stereo image information. A geometric correction step projects the pixels of each array at all camera positions onto an artificial plane, resulting in nine 2D images, in which effects caused by high and low frequent orientation variations are eliminated, while disparities caused by terrain and buildings still remain (Fig. 1).

W. Kropatsch, R. Sablatnig, and A. Hanbury (Eds.): DAGM 2005, LNCS 3663, pp. 58–66, 2005.

S2 (20.5°)   P2 (12.0°)   IR (4.6°)   Red (2.3°)   Nadir (0°) Gr. (−2.3°) Bl. (−4.6°) P1 (−12.0°) S1 (−20.5°)

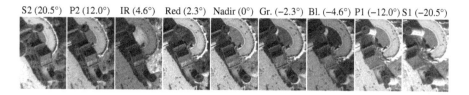

Fig. 1. Parts of corrected 2D pushbroom images with a resolution of 15cm/pixel

The current stereo method [1] performs hierarchical, correlation based stereo matching of these 2D images. Epipolar lines are assumed to be parallel to the overall flight direction. Violations of this assumption are handled by searching correspondences in a 2D area around suspected epipolar lines. The matching result is used for calculating Digital Elevation Models (DEM) and subsequently for the generation of true ortho images based on the DEM. This paper proposes the explicit calculation of epipolar lines in general, non-linear pushbroom images combined with a semi-global stereo matching method. The aim is to increase the accuracy in scenes of urban areas.

2   Related Literature

There are different possibilities for modeling the movement of pushbroom cameras. The *Linear Pushbroom Camera* model [4,5,6] assumes a movement with constant velocity and orientation in a straight line. This movement is not realistic for an airborne camera, which is exposed to wind. General movements may be approximated by polynomial functions [7] or explicitly represented by discrete positions and orientations [1,8,9].

Geometric corrections of the images as a pre-requisite for matching and subsequent 3D surface modeling are commonly done by projecting all pixels onto an artifical plane [1,8,9]. Straight lines and epipolar lines are *almost* straight in the corrected images, if the flight path is nearly linear. Thus, these corrected images can be treated as *almost* rectified [9]. However, a rectification that results in exactly straight epipolar lines is not possible, since epipolar lines are generally hyperbolas, even if the camera movement is exactly linear [4]. The complex shape of epipolar lines must be considered during stereo matching, either by searching in 2D around linearly approximated epipolar lines [1,8] or by explicitly calculating them [6] for reducing the search space to 1D. 2D search areas can also be reduced by ortho rectification implying rough terrain instead of simple geometric correction [2].

Stereo matching must be efficient, due to typically huge images and disparity ranges. Local, correlation based approaches are often applied, either by hierarchical matching [1] or by region growing [8,6], which starts at high confidence correspondences. However, correlation based methods are known to blur sharp object boundaries [10], which makes them less suitable for urban areas. Global cost minimization methods have been shown [11] to perform much better

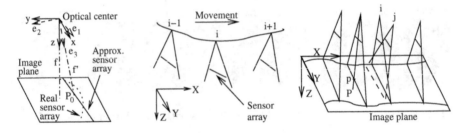

Fig. 2. Camera model and the creation of a corrected 2D image

at object boundaries. However, global methods are typically slow and memory intensive, which makes them unsuitable for huge images.

3   Reconstruction from Pushbroom Images

The following sections introduce the camera model (Section 3.1) as base for calculating epipolar lines (Section 3.2). Epipolar lines are required for limiting the correspondence search during stereo matching (Section 3.3). The matching result is finally used for calculating an orthographic projection of height and image information (Section 3.4).

3.1   Modeling Non-linear Pushbroom Cameras

Pushbroom cameras use an array of sensor elements that is arranged in a straight line on the image plane (Fig. 2a). Lens distortion is modeled by treating the sensor array as being curved. The intrinsic parameters are the focal length f (i.e. distance between optical center and image plane) and the positions x_k, y_k on the image plane for all pixels k. Thus, the 3D location of a pixel k is $S_k = \begin{pmatrix} x_k & y_k & f \end{pmatrix}^T$ in the camera coordinate system.

A 2D image is captured line by line, while the camera moves. A linear movement cannot always be guaranteed (e.g. while flying with an airplane). Therefore, it is assumed that the path is only roughly a straight line, the speed is not constant and the orientation is changing slightly (Fig. 2b). The lack of constraints requires to measure the orientations R_i and locations T_i at all capturing positions i with high accuracy. Since original GPS/IMU measurements describe the orientation of the IMU-axes, a photogrammetric reconstruction of the orientation of the camera axes is performed by means of photogrammetric methods [3]. This leads to the relationship $P = sR_iS_k + T_i$ between a world point P and the kth pixel of the ith capturing position. The reconstruction of the ray of light that ends in pixel k is, based on the previously described photogrammetric reconstruction, straight forward. However, the inverse (i.e. finding pixel k as projection of P) is difficult, because the list of pixel positions S is unsorted. The calculation is simplified by approximating the sensor array by the best fitting line, i.e.

$$P = sR_iS_k + T_i, \qquad\qquad S_k = kU + V + \epsilon_k. \tag{1}$$

This allows the definition of a new camera coordinate system e_1, e_2, e_3 (Fig. 2a) in which e_1 is parallel to the sensor line and $f'e_3$ intersects the line in the point P_0.

$$e_1 = \frac{U}{|U|} \qquad f'e_3 = P_0 = -\frac{UV}{UU}U + V \qquad e_2 = e_3 \times e_1 \tag{2}$$

The resulting closed form definition of the relationship becomes,

$$P = sR_iR_c\left(k'\ 0\ 1\right)^T + T_i, \qquad\qquad R_c = \left(e_1\ e_2\ e_3\right). \tag{3}$$

The relationship between the pixel k' and k can be derived easily as $k' = \frac{k|U|+e_1V}{f'}$. Corrected 2D images are obtained by projecting all pixel values onto a common image plane at $z = 0$ (Fig. 2c) using (1). The projection is generally irregular. The values at regular grid positions are calculated as linear interpolations of nearby pixels. Orientation changes that destroy the order of projected pixels (e.g. camera position j in Fig. 2c) are treated by removing disturbing camera positions and their projected pixels.

For 3D computer vision purposes it is important to have a projection model of the corrected 2D pushbroom images. The intrinsic parameters are the path of optical center positions T_i and corresponding viewing directions R_iR_c. The movement between discrete positions is assumed to be linear. Equation (3) can then be rewritten as,

$$P = sR_iR_c\left(k'\ 0\ 1\right)^T + T_i + s_i\frac{T_{i+1} - T_{i-1}}{2}. \tag{4}$$

The factor s_i controls the linear movement of the ith optical center for projecting P exactly on the sensor array (i.e. $y = 0$). Solving for s_i in dependence of P results in,

$$s_i(P) = 2\frac{r_2(P - T_i)}{r_2(T_{i+1} - T_{i-1})}, \text{ with } R_iR_c = \left(r_1\ r_2\ r_3\right). \tag{5}$$

The position $C(P)$ of the optical center is calculated from the closest base i, i.e.

$$C(P) = T_i + s_i(P)\frac{T_{i+1} - T_{i-1}}{2}, \text{ for } i \text{ such that } s_i(P) \text{ is a minium} \tag{6}$$

The closest base i can be found by a binary search in $O(\log_2 n)$ steps. Removing overlapping projections (e.g. j in Fig. 2c) ensures a sorted list. The sign of s_i determines the search direction. The determination of the optical center permits the projection of a world point P onto an image point p by calculating the intersection of P, $C(P)$ at $z = 0$.

$$p = f_{proj}(P) = \frac{C_z}{C_z - P_z}\left(\begin{matrix} P_x - C_x \\ P_y - C_y \end{matrix}\right) + \left(\begin{matrix} C_x \\ C_y \end{matrix}\right), \text{ with } C = C(P). \tag{7}$$

Similarly, the world point P is reconstructed from a given pixel p at the distance z.

$$P = f_{rec}(p, z) = \frac{C_z - z}{C_z}\left(\begin{matrix} p_x - C_x \\ p_y - C_y \\ -C_z \end{matrix}\right) + \left(\begin{matrix} C_x \\ C_y \\ C_z \end{matrix}\right), \text{ with } C = C((p_x\ p_y\ 0)^T) \tag{8}$$

3.2   Calculation of Epipolar Lines

A pixel $\boldsymbol{p}_1$ and the corresponding optical center $C_1(\boldsymbol{p}_1)$ define a line, which contains the world point $\boldsymbol{P}$ that is projected on $\boldsymbol{p}_1$. The projection of this line into a second image is called epipolar line. The projection of $\boldsymbol{P}$ in the second image must be on the epipolar line (Fig. 3a). This is formally defined as,

$$\boldsymbol{p}_2 = e_{12}(\boldsymbol{p}_1, d) = f_{proj,2}(f_{rec,1}(\boldsymbol{p}_1, -d\Delta z)). \tag{9}$$

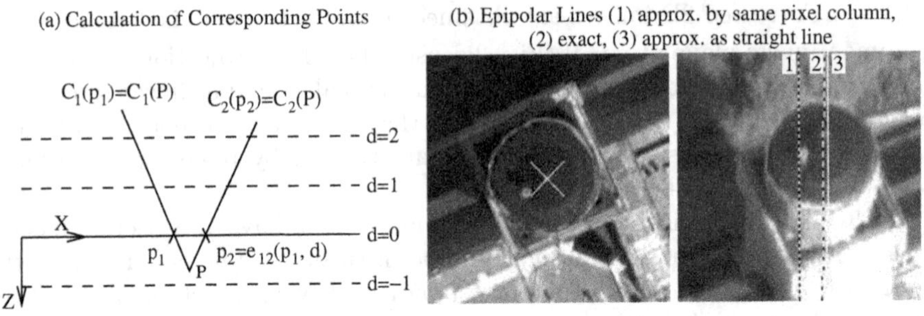

Fig. 3. Calculation of epipolar lines.

The disparity d controls the position on the epipolar line. The constant Δz is set such that a disparity step of 1 causes a mean translation of 1 pixel on the epipolar line. Figure 3b shows an example of an exactly calculated epipolar line and approximations by the same pixel column and as straight line. The overall flight path is vertical. The example shows that the approximated epipolar lines miss the correct correspondence by several pixel, which enforce a 2D search for finding correspondences. The exact point by point calculation of epipolar lines reduces the search range to a minimum. The efficiency of this approach is optimized by calculating only a few points on the line and assuming piecewise linearity in between.

3.3   Stereo Matching

Stereo matching is done with the Semi-Global Matching (SGM) method [12], which aims to determine the disparity image D, such that the cost $E(D)$ is a minimum.

$$E(D) = \sum_{\boldsymbol{p}} C(\boldsymbol{p}, D_{\boldsymbol{p}}) + \sum_{\boldsymbol{q} \in N_{\boldsymbol{p}}} P_1 T[|D_{\boldsymbol{p}} - D_{\boldsymbol{q}}| = 1] + \sum_{\boldsymbol{q} \in N_{\boldsymbol{p}}} P_2 T[|D_{\boldsymbol{p}} - D_{\boldsymbol{q}}| > 1] \tag{10}$$

The cost function evaluates pixelwise matching costs $C(\boldsymbol{p}, D_{\boldsymbol{p}})$ at the pixel $\boldsymbol{p}$ with the disparity $D_{\boldsymbol{p}}$. Piecewise smoothness of the disparity image is supported by adding a small cost P_1 for all small disparity changes and a higher cost P_2

for all higher disparity changes. Adding a *constant* cost for all higher disparity changes preserves discontinuities. Finding the minimum of equation (10) is an NP-complete problem. The SGM algorithm approximates the global minimization by pathwise minimizations from all directions. The complexity is only $O(ND)$, but the memory consumption is also proportional to ND (i.e. number of pixels times the disparity range). The pixelwise matching cost $C(\boldsymbol{p}, D_{\boldsymbol{p}})$ is based on hierarchically computing Mutual Information (MI) [12] instead of intensity differences. This makes it robust against recording differences and illumination changes, which can easily happen since pushbroom cameras capture corresponding points at different times on the flight path. Finally, the SGM method provides a multi-baseline extension [12] for reducing mismatches and increasing accuracy.

Applying the SGM method to HRSC images includes three adaptations. Firstly, multi-baseline matching uses the five panchromatic images of the HRSC (Sect. 1), weighted by their recording angle. Optionally, the red and green images are also matched against the panchromatic nadir image, which is possible with MI matching. Secondly, the huge images are split into manageable pieces (i.e. tiles) for matching. The tiles are defined slightly overlapping and pixels near image borders are rejected, because they receive support only from one side by the global cost function. Thirdly, the disparity range is determined automatically, by first processing downscaled images (e.g. factor 16) with a very large disparity range. A reduced range is determined from the result and used for higher resolutions. The disparity range determination is done during the hierarchical computation of MI.

3.4 Orthographic Projection

The resulting disparity image corresponds to the nadir image of the HRSC. The model of this image (Sect. 3.1) is complex due to low constraints on the flight path and a mixture of perspective and parallel projection models. The disparity image permits the conversion of the data into a simple orthographic model. Each pixel $\boldsymbol{p}$ of the disparity image D is reconstructed by $\boldsymbol{P} = f_{rec,D}(\boldsymbol{p}, -D_{\boldsymbol{p}}\Delta z)$. An orthographic projection is used, which stores each height value P_z at the pixel position P_x, P_y. Double mappings are resolved by using the height that is closest to the camera. This orthographic model also supports fusing results of different recordings, by taking the mean or median of heights, which decreases outliers. Finally, gaps are filled by interpolation. The result is a Digital Elevation Model (DEM) of the scene. The corresponding intensity or color value at P_x, P_y and the stored height value P_z is determined by bilinear interpolation in the image I at the position $\boldsymbol{q} = f_{proj,I}(\boldsymbol{P})$. The results is a true ortho-image.

4 Experimental Results

The first row of Fig. 4 shows small parts of three scenes. The DEMs of Neuschwanstein castle are the combination of 4 flights in cross directions over

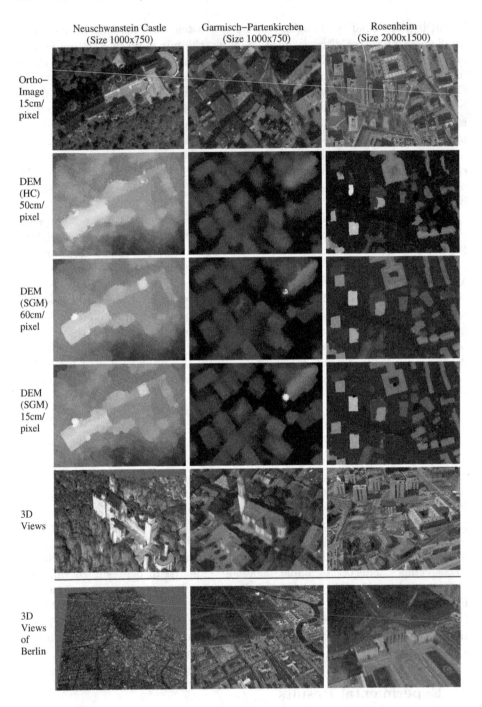

Fig. 4. Results of a hierarchical, correlation base method (HC) that finds correspondences within a 2D area and the SGM method that finds correspondences along calculated epipolar lines.

the castle. Similarly, the DEMs of Garmisch-Partenkirchen are the combination of 3 overlapping parallel flights. The DEMs of Rosenheim are the result of one flight only.

The second row shows DEMs that are produced by a hierarchical, correlation based method (HC) [1]. The method avoids the calculation of epipolar lines by searching correspondences in a 2D area. Matching is done in images that are sampled with 25cm/pixel. However, only every second pixel is calculated, which results in 50cm/pixel. It can be seen that the boundaries of houses are severely blurred and towers are unrecognized.

The third and fourth row of Fig. 4 present DEMs that have been produced by SGM with calculated epipolar lines with images at different resolutions. The boundaries of houses are much sharper and all towers are properly detected. The average processing time is one hour on a 2.8GHz Xeon computer for producing 11MPixel of the DEM by matching 5 images with an average disparity range of 400 pixel. The fifth row of Fig. 4 shows reconstructions, using the ortho image as well as the S1 and S2 images (e.g. Fig. 1) for top and side textures. The last row presents reconstructions of a $110km^2$ area of Berlin in a resolution of 20cm/pixel. The area has been captured by 6 parallel, partly overlapping flights. Each flight contributed approximately 1 billion height values to the DEM. The total processing time was 18 days on a 2.8GHz Xeon computer.

5 Conclusion

It has been shown that epipolar lines can be efficiently calculated in general non-linear pushbroom images. This permits the minimization of the correspondence search range for using the accurate, but memory intensive Semi-Global Matching method. Experiments confirmed that the proposed stereo processing solution performs accurate matching of urban terrain with sharp boundaries of buildings. The approach permits the efficient and fully automatic 3D reconstruction of whole cities. Future plans include the implementation of the approach on a processing cluster.

Acknowledgments

We would like to thank Klaus Gwinner, Johann Heindl, Frank Lehmann, Martin Oczipka, Sebastian Pless and Frank Trauthan for inspiring discussions.

References

1. Wewel, F., Scholten, F., Gwinner, K.: High resolution stereo camera (hrsc) - multispectral 3d-data acquisition and photogrammetric data processing. Canadian Journal of Remote Sensing **26** (2000) 466–474
2. Scholten, F., Gwinner, K., Wewel, F.: Angewandte digitale photogrammetrie mit der hrsc-a. In: Photogrammetrie, Fernerkundung, Geoinformation. Volume 5., Stuttgart, Germany, E. Schweizerbartsche Verlagsbuchhandlung (2002) 317–332

3. Scholten, F., Wewel, F., Sujew, S.: High resolution stereo camera airborne (hrsc-a): 4 years of experience in direct sensor orientation of a multi-line pushbroom scanner. In: ISPRS Proceedings Sensors and Mapping from Space, Hannover, Germany (2001)

4. Gupta, R., Hartley, R.I.: Linear pushbroom cameras. IEEE PAMI **19** (1997) 963–975

5. Morgan, M., Kim, K., Jeong, S., Habib, A.: Epipolar geometry of linear array scanners moving with constant velocity and constant attitude. In: ISPRS, Istanbul, Turkey (2004) 1024

6. Lee, H.Y., Park, W.K., Kim, T., Lee, H.K.: Accurate demlk extraction from sport stereo pairs: A stereo matching algorithm based on the geometry of the satellite. In: Asian Conference on Remote Sensing. (1999)

7. Lee, C., Theiss, H., Bethel, J., Mikhail, E.: Rigerous mathematical modeling of airborne pushbroom imaging systems. Journal of Photogrammetric Engineering and Remote Sensing **66** (2000) 385–392

8. Boerner, A.: Entwicklung und Test von Onboard-Algorithmen für die Landfern-erkundung. PhD thesis, Technical University of Berlin, Germany (1999)

9. Haala, N., Stallmann, D., Cramer, M.: Calibration of directly measured position and attitude by aerotriangulation of three-line airborne imagery. In: ISPRS, Object Recognition and Scene Classification from Multispectral and Multisensor Pixels, Columbus/Ohio, USA (1998) 23–30

10. Hirschmüller, H., Innocent, P.R., Garibaldi, J.M.: Real-time correlation-based stereo vision with reduced border errors. IJCV **47** (2002) 229–246

11. Scharstein, D., Szeliski, R.: A taxonomy and evaluation of dense two-frame stereo correspondence algorithms. IJCV **47** (2002) 7–42

12. Hirschmüller, H.: Accurate and efficient stereo processing by semi-global matching and mutual information. In: IEEE CVPR, San Diego, USA (2005)

Calibration–Free Hand–Eye Calibration: A Structure–from–Motion Approach

Jochen Schmidt*, Florian Vogt**, and Heinrich Niemann

Lehrstuhl für Mustererkennung, Universität Erlangen-Nürnberg,
Martensstr. 3, 91058 Erlangen, Germany
{jschmidt, vogt, niemann}@informatik.uni-erlangen.de

Abstract. The paper presents an extended hand-eye calibration approach that, in contrast to the standard method, does not require a calibration pattern for determining camera position and orientation. Instead, a structure-from-motion algorithm is applied for obtaining the eye-data that is necessary for computing the unknown hand-eye transformation. Different ways of extending the standard algorithm are presented, which mainly involves the estimation of a scale factor in addition to rotation and translation. The proposed methods are experimentally compared using data obtained from an optical tracking system that determines the pose of an endoscopic camera. The approach is of special interest in our clinical setup, as the usage of an unsterile calibration pattern is difficult in a sterile environment.

1 Introduction

Hand-eye calibration algorithms [9, 10, 7, 5] solve the following problem that originated in the robotics community: Given a robot arm and a camera mounted on that arm, compute the rigid transformation from arm to camera (hand-eye transformation). Knowledge of this transformation is necessary, because the pose of the robot arm is usually provided by the robot itself, while the pose of the camera is unknown but needed for visual guidance of the arm. However, if the hand-eye transformation is known the camera pose can be computed directly from the pose data provided by the robot.

Usually, the camera (*eye*) poses are computed using a calibration pattern and standard camera calibration techniques. In contrast to that, a method for hand-eye calibration is presented in this paper, where no calibration pattern is needed. Instead, the camera poses are obtained solely from an image sequence recorded using a hand-held camera by applying structure-from-motion methods.

Hand-eye calibration is also interesting for applications that are not directly related to robotics, but where similar problems arise. Instead of a robot we used an optical tracking system that provides hand data, and a camera, where the camera poses (*eye*) are computed using a calibration pattern for standard hand-eye calibration, and structure-from-motion for the extended hand-eye calibration described in this paper. The camera may in general be an arbitrary hand-held video camera. For our application—the reconstruction of high-quality medical light fields [11]—we used an endoscope with a rigidly

---

* This work was partially funded by the European Commission 5th IST Programme - Project VAMPIRE. Only the authors are responsible for the content.
** This work was partially funded by the Deutsche Forschungsgemeinschaft (DFG) under grant SFB 603/TP B6. Only the authors are responsible for the content.

W. Kropatsch, R. Sablatnig, and A. Hanbury (Eds.): DAGM 2005, LNCS 3663, pp. 67–74, 2005.

mounted CCD camera. The endoscope is moved by hand, its pose is determined by the optical tracking system. More details on this system will follow in the experiments section. The hand-eye transformation has to be estimated every time when the camera head is mounted anew on the endoscope optics, which is done before each operation because the endoscope has to be sterilized. This requires an algorithm that works automatically and fast with a minimum of human interaction.

The paper is structured as follows: After an introduction to hand-eye calibration in Sect. 2 the structure-from-motion algorithm will be described (Sect. 3). Section 4 shows the modifications to the hand-eye calibration equations that are necessary when using structure-from-motion instead of standard camera calibration. Experimental results are presented in Sect. 5.

2   Hand-Eye Calibration

The first hand-eye calibration methods were published by Tsai and Lenz [10], and Shiu and Ahmad [9], where the latter formulated the hand-eye calibration problem as a matrix equation of the form

$$T_{\mathrm{E}ij}T_{\mathrm{HE}} = T_{\mathrm{HE}}T_{\mathrm{H}ij}, \quad T_\chi = \begin{pmatrix} \boldsymbol{R}_\chi & \boldsymbol{t}_\chi \\ \boldsymbol{0}_3^\mathsf{T} & 1 \end{pmatrix}, \chi \in \{\mathrm{H}ij, \mathrm{E}ij, \mathrm{HE}\} \quad . \tag{1}$$

$T_{\mathrm{H}ij}$ is the robot arm (*hand*) movement from time step i to j, $T_{\mathrm{E}ij}$ the camera (*eye*) movement, and T_{HE} is the unknown hand-eye transformation, i.e. the transformation from gripper to camera. All transformations T_χ are described by a 3×3 rotation matrix $\boldsymbol{R}_\chi$ and a 3-D translation vector $\boldsymbol{t}_\chi$. Equation (1) can be directly derived from the following diagram:

$$
\begin{array}{ccc}
\boldsymbol{H}_j & \xrightarrow{\;T_{\mathrm{HE}}\;} & \boldsymbol{E}_j \\
{\scriptstyle T_{\mathrm{H}ij}}\uparrow & & \uparrow{\scriptstyle T_{\mathrm{E}ij}} \\
\boldsymbol{H}_i & \xrightarrow{\;T_{\mathrm{HE}}\;} & \boldsymbol{E}_i
\end{array}
\tag{2}
$$

$\boldsymbol{H}_i$ and $\boldsymbol{H}_j$ denote the gripper poses, $\boldsymbol{E}_i$ and $\boldsymbol{E}_j$ the camera poses at times i, j. The usual way to solve (1) is to split it into two separate equations, one that contains only rotation, and a second one that contains rotation and translation:

$$\boldsymbol{R}_{\mathrm{HE}}\boldsymbol{R}_{\mathrm{H}ij} = \boldsymbol{R}_{\mathrm{E}ij}\boldsymbol{R}_{\mathrm{HE}}, \quad (\boldsymbol{I}_{3\times3} - \boldsymbol{R}_{\mathrm{E}ij})\boldsymbol{t}_{\mathrm{HE}} = \boldsymbol{t}_{\mathrm{E}ij} - \boldsymbol{R}_{\mathrm{HE}}\boldsymbol{t}_{\mathrm{H}ij} \quad . \tag{3}$$

Thus, the rotational part of the hand-eye transformation can be determined first, and, after inserting it into the second equation, the translational part can be computed. This is the way hand-eye calibration is done, e. g., in [9, 10, 3]. Different parameterizations of rotation have been applied. The original works of [9, 10] use the axis/angle representation, quaternions were used by [3, 7], and dual quaternions were introduced by [5]. In contrast to the former approaches, it was suggested in [2] that rotation and translation should be solved for simultaneously and not separately. This approach is also followed in [7], where a non-linear optimization of rotation and translation is done.

3   Structure-from-Motion

The usual way to obtain the camera poses $\boldsymbol{E}_i$ is to capture images of a calibration pattern and apply standard camera calibration techniques [12]. In contrast to that our approach is capable of using an image sequence without a pattern and an uncalibrated camera. By applying a structure-from-motion approach, the camera motion (and therefore the eye poses E_i) can be computed for each recorded image. Basically, it is possible to use any algorithm that results in camera poses, as the following computation steps do not rely on the actual method used. The approach applied in this paper is based on the work of [6]; it will be outlined in the following.

The algorithm starts with establishing 2-D point correspondences between images. Each detected feature point has to be tracked over a sequence of images to allow a 3-D reconstruction. Here, a modified more robust and faster version of the Tomasi-Kanade-Shi tracker is used that can also deal with illumination changes [13].

After point features are tracked, the actual 3-D reconstruction step starts. First, an initial reconstruction is computed using the paraperspective factorization algorithm on a subset of the images, since all features have to be visible in all images. The reconstructed affine cameras are now converted to perspective ones by assuming a reasonable value for focal length and by choosing the center of the image as the principal point. These perspective cameras can be used as an initialization for a non-linear optimization step, where camera matrices and 3-D points are optimized alternatingly.

The initial sequence is now extended by performing the following steps for each frame that is to be added: First, 3-D scene points are triangulated from feature points that are visible in the new image using already reconstructed camera matrices. This way it is possible to use the triangulated points as calibration points and apply standard camera calibration techniques. In fact, since differences from one camera pose to the next will usually be small, it is sufficient in practice to skip the linear standard calibration methods and initialize the new camera pose with the parameters of the neighboring one. Non-linear optimization of this camera will yield the desired result. These two steps are repeated until all frames are processed. Optionally, the whole reconstruction can be optimized non-linearly by a final bundle-adjustment step.

The result is a reconstruction of the 3-D scene points as well as the extrinsic and intrinsic camera parameters for each recorded image. Note, however, that the reconstruction is only unique up to a similarity transformation, i. e., the world coordinate system can be chosen arbitrarily, and the scale of the reconstruction is unknown. While the choice of the world coordinate system is exactly the problem that is solved with standard hand-eye calibration, the unknown scale factor has to be estimated additionally. This topic will now be addressed.

4   Extended Hand-Eye Calibration

The drawback of using structure-from-motion instead of camera calibration is that the scaling factor mentioned above has to be estimated in addition to rotation and translation during hand-eye calibration; the modified method will be called *extended hand-eye calibration* in the following.

In [1] a structure-from-motion based hand-eye calibration approach was presented already, where the scaling factor has been integrated into the standard equations (3). The main drawback of that method is that the orthogonality of the rotation matrix R_{HE} is not guaranteed by the extended equations, but has to be enforced afterwards using the SVD.

4.1   Extension of Basic Equations

The straight-forward method is to extend (3) by a scaling factor s_{HE}, resulting in:

$$R_{HE}R_{Hij} = R_{Eij}R_{HE} \quad , \tag{4}$$

$$(I_{3\times3} - R_{Eij})t_{HE} = t_{Eij} - s_{HE}R_{HE}t_{Hij} \quad . \tag{5}$$

It can be observed that the rotational equation in (3) and eq. (4) are the same, i. e., the scale factor has no influence on the computation of rotation. Therefore, the rotation can be obtained by standard methods, e. g., using the quaternion representation of rotations [3,7], which guarantees that the resulting matrix actually is a rotation. Equation (5), however, contains translation and scale, and can be formulated as a linear system of equations as follows:

$$\left((I_{3\times3} - R_{Eij}) \; R_{HE}t_{Hij}\right) \begin{pmatrix} t_{HE} \\ s_{HE} \end{pmatrix} = t_{Eij} \quad . \tag{6}$$

This method of extended hand-eye calibration has the advantage that all equation systems are linear, but the disadvantage that one has to solve for rotation first, and then for translation and scale.

The equations (4) and (5) can be used to formulate an objective function $f(\cdot)$ for non-linear optimization, which is based on the objective function for standard hand-eye calibration proposed by [7]:

$$f(q_{HE}, t_{HE}, s_{HE}) = \sum_{i=1}^{N_{rel}} \|q_{Ei} - q_{HE}q_{Hi}q_{HE}^*\|^2 +$$
$$\sum_{i=1}^{N_{rel}} \|Q\left((I_{3\times3} - R_{Ei})\, t_{HE} - t_{Ei}\right) + q_{HE}Q(s_{HE}t_{Hi})q_{HE}^*\|^2 + \lambda\left(1 - q_{HE}q_{HE}^*\right)^2 . \tag{7}$$

where q_{HE} is the quaternion used for parameterization of the rotation matrix R_{HE} and λ is a regularization factor (e. g., $\lambda = 2 \cdot 10^6$) that penalizes deviations of the quaternion q_{HE} from norm one and thus implements the norm one constraint. The function $Q(\cdot)$ maps a 3-D vector to a purely imaginary quaternion: $Q(x) = 0 + x_1i + x_2j + x_3k$, where $x = \begin{pmatrix} x_1 & x_2 & x_3 \end{pmatrix}^T$. The single terms of (7) can be derived directly from the hand-eye equations (4) and (5): The first summand equals (4) in quaternion notation. The second one is derived from (5) by reformulating the multiplication of the rotation matrix R_{HE} and the translation vector of the relative movement of the left camera using quaternions.

4.2   Extension of the Dual Quaternion Algorithm

This section shows how the estimation of rotation, translation, and scale can be formulated using dual quaternions. As quaternions are a representation for 3-D rotations, dual quaternions treat rotations *and* translations in a unified way.

Dual numbers were proposed by Clifford in the 19th century [4]. They are defined by $\tilde{z} = a + \varepsilon b$, where $\varepsilon^2 = 0$. When using vectors for a and b instead of real numbers, the result is a dual vector.

A dual quaternion $\tilde{q}$ is defined as a quaternion, where the real and imaginary parts are dual numbers instead of real ones, or equivalently as a dual vector where the dual and the non-dual part are quaternions: $\widetilde{q} = q_{nd} + \varepsilon q_d$. Just as unit quaternions represent rotations, unit dual quaternions contain rotation and translation [5]. In the dual quaternion representation of R and t, the non-dual part q_{nd} is the well-known quaternion representation of R, and the dual part is given by

$$q_d = \frac{1}{2} t_q q_{nd}, \quad t_q = (0, t) \quad , \tag{8}$$

where t_q is a purely imaginary quaternion defined by the translation vector t. A dual quaternion formulation of hand-eye calibration was introduced by [5]. We will now show how to integrate scale into the dual quaternion formulation by using non-unit dual quaternions, which results in a unified representation of similarity transformations.

For this purpose a dual quaternion $\widetilde{q}_{sHE}$ containing all these parameters is introduced, which is defined by:

$$\widetilde{q}_{sHE} = q_{sHEnd} + \varepsilon q_{sHEd} = s_{HE} q_{HE} + \varepsilon \frac{1}{2} t_{HEq} q_{HE} \quad . \tag{9}$$

A dual quaternion has eight elements, but for rotation, translation, and scale only seven degrees of freedom are necessary. The norm of a dual quaternion is in general a *dual number* with non-negative real part given by:

$$|\widetilde{q}|^2 = \widetilde{q}\widetilde{q}^* = q_{nd} q_{nd}^* + \varepsilon (q_{nd} q_d^* + q_d q_{nd}^*) \quad . \tag{10}$$

When the dual quaternion as defined in (9) is used, the scale is actually modeled as the norm of $\widetilde{q}_{sHE}$:

$$|\widetilde{q}_{sHE}|^2 = s_{HE}^2 + \varepsilon 0 \quad \Leftrightarrow \quad |\widetilde{q}_{sHE}| = s_{HE} \quad . \tag{11}$$

Since the scale factor will always be a positive real number, the dual part of the norm has to be zero. Therefore, one degree of freedom is lost, and we get an additional constraint that is given by:

$$q_{sHEnd} q_{sHEd}^* + q_{sHEd} q_{sHEnd}^* = 0 \quad . \tag{12}$$

Using (9), the extended hand-eye calibration problem (cf. [5] for the standard formulation) solving for scale, rotation, and translation can be formulated as:

$$q_{End} q_{sHEnd} = q_{sHEnd} q_{Hnd} \quad , \tag{13}$$

$$q_{End} q_{sHEd} + \frac{1}{s_{HE}} q_{Ed} q_{sHEnd} = q_{sHEnd} q_{Hd} + q_{sHEd} q_{Hnd} \quad . \tag{14}$$

The indices ij that indicate a relative movement from frame i to frame j have been omitted for reasons of simplicity. Note that s_{HE} is not an additional independent parameter as in the previous section, but the norm of the dual quaternion $\widetilde{q}_{sHE}$ (cf. (11)).

It can be observed that (14) is a non-linear equation; an objective function $f'(\cdot)$ for non-linear optimization will look as follows:

$$f'(q_{sHEnd}, q_{sHEd}) = \sum_{i=1}^{N_{rel}} \left\| q_{Endi} q_{sHEnd} - q_{sHEnd} q_{Hndi} \right\|^2 +$$

$$\sum_{i=1}^{N_{rel}} \left\| q_{Endi} q_{sHEd} + \frac{1}{\sqrt{q_{sHEnd} q_{sHEnd}^*}} q_{Edi} q_{sHEnd} - q_{sHEnd} q_{Hdi} + q_{sHEd} q_{Hndi} \right\|^2 +$$

$$\lambda \left(q_{sHEnd} q_{sHEd}^* + q_{sHEd} q_{sHEnd}^* \right)^2 \quad . \tag{15}$$

Fig. 1. Optical tracking system (left) and one image of the sequences *ART1* (middle) and *ART2* (right) showing a silicon liver/gall-bladder model that were used for structure-from-motion based 3-D reconstruction

This objective function estimates rotation, translation, and scale, which are all encoded in the dual and non-dual parts of $\widetilde{q}_{sHE}$. The first summand is derived from (13), the second one from (14). As before, a regularization term enforces the constraint (12) on the norm of the dual quaternion $\widetilde{q}_{sHE}$, which has to be a real number. In this case, eight parameters with only seven degrees of freedom are optimized.

5   Experiments

In the following we present an experimental evaluation of the extended hand-eye calibration methods. The data were acquired using an endoscope with a camera mounted on it (the *eye*), which was moved by hand. An optical tracking system (cf. Fig. 1, left) provides pose data of a so-called target (the *hand*) that is fixed to the endoscope. The infrared optical tracking system smARTtrack1 by Advanced Realtime GmbH is employed. It is a typical optical tracking system consisting of two (or more) cameras and a target that is tracked. The target is built from markers that can easily be identified in the images captured by the cameras. In our case spheres with a retro-reflective surface are used. Infrared light simplifies marker identification. The 3-D position of each visible marker is calculated by the tracking system. The knowledge of the geometry of the target then allows to calculate its pose.

Instead of using consecutive movements for calibration, we applied the vector quantization based data selection method proposed in [8], which leads to more accurate results.

Since no ground truth is available when calibrating real data, we cannot give errors between the real hand-eye transformation and the computed one. It is desirable, however, that an error measure is available which rates the quality of the resulting transformation. Therefore, the following error measure is used: After applying the computed hand-eye transformation on the *hand* data, we get an estimate of the *eye* movements $\mathcal{E}'$. This estimated movement can now be compared to the original *eye* movement $\mathcal{E}$, which has been obtained by structure-from-motion: If the hand-eye transformation is correct, the relative movements between single camera positions are equal in $\mathcal{E}$ and $\mathcal{E}'$. The errors are computed by averaging over a set of randomly selected relative movements.

Table 1 shows residual errors in translation and rotation as well as the computation times for hand-eye calibration on a Linux PC (Athlon XP2600+) including data selection, but not feature tracking and 3-D reconstruction. The latter steps are the same for all methods, and take approximately 90 sec for tracking and 200 sec for 3-D reconstruction. The values shown are relative and absolute residuals for rotation, and relative errors for

Table 1. Mean errors in rotation and translation of relative *eye* movements computed with different hand-eye calibration methods using structure-from-motion as a basis

Data Set	Method	Translation	Rotation		Time
	DQ, scale sep.	22.3%	0.191°	3.75%	310 msec
	Hor., scale sep.	13.0%	0.179°	3.72%	2090 msec
ART1	non-lin., eq. (7)	17.8%	0.191°	3.75%	2350 msec
	non-lin., eq. (15)	44.6%	0.191°	3.75%	756 msec
	Andreff	13.2%	0.172°	3.60%	309 msec
	DQ, scale sep.	20.7%	0.290°	7.25%	433 msec
	Hor., scale sep.	18.7%	0.266°	7.00%	1590 msec
ART2	non-lin., eq. (7)	18.4%	0.290°	7.25%	1770 msec
	non-lin., eq. (15)	20.7%	0.290°	7.25%	482 msec
	Andreff	19.7%	0.272°	7.10%	434 msec

the norm of the translation vector of relative movements. Absolute errors for translation are not given, as these are highly dependent on the estimated scale factor and therefore cannot be compared directly, whereas absolute rotational residuals are independent of scale. We show the results for two data sets, namely *ART1* (190 images) and *ART2* (200 images). After feature tracking and 3-D reconstruction, different hand-eye calibration methods have been evaluated; in all cases the reconstructed camera movement has been used as eye-data. The results shown in Table 1 were computed as follows:

DQ, scale sep.: Here, the scale factor was estimated first by solving (4) and (5). After scaling the eye-reconstruction appropriately, rotation and translation were re-estimated using a standard hand-eye calibration method, namely the linear dual quaternion algorithm of [5].

Hor., scale sep.: The same as *DQ, scale sep.*, i. e., scale and rotation/translation were computed separately. Instead of dual quaternions the non-linear method proposed by [7] was used for hand-eye calibration.

non-lin., eq. (7)/(15): Here, the non-linear objective functions (7), (15) were used, which were initialized with the result of *DQ, scale sep.* After non-linear optimization of rotation, translation, and scale, rotation and translation were re-estimated using the linear dual quaternion method, which results in a more accurate hand-eye transformation compared to non-linear optimization alone.

Andreff: This is the result of the hand-eye calibration method proposed by [1].

The relative residual errors obtained using standard hand-eye calibration and a calibration pattern are 4.20% (transl.) and 0.725% (rot.) for the configuration similar to *ART2* and 5.39% (transl.) and 1.09% (rot.) for the configuration similar to *ART1*. The deviations to the hand-eye transformation computed this way compared to the extended approach using structure-from-motion (depending on the method) are 15% to 16% in rotation and about 35% for translation (*ART2*), and 9% to 11% in rotation and 26% to 32% in translation (*ART1*).

6 Conclusion

We presented methods for an extended hand-eye calibration, which allow to compute the hand-eye transformation without the necessity for using a calibration pattern in order to obtain the camera (eye) poses. Instead, these are computed using feature tracking and a structure-from-motion approach, which makes the extension of standard hand-eye calibration necessary since in addition to rotation and translation a scale factor has to be estimated. Different ways of extending these equations have been presented and compared. The main result is that the estimation of the hand-eye transformation is feasible without a calibration pattern. Of course, one could not expect to obtain results as accurate as with standard calibration; depending on the application, however, the advantages of the extended method may outweigh this drawback. This is especially true for the clinical setup that we have in mind, as hand-eye calibration has to be performed before each operation. The usage of an unsterile calibration pattern in combination with a sterile endoscope and a surgeon working under sterile conditions is difficult in practice, and can be completely circumvented when using the methods proposed here.

References

1. N. Andreff, R. Horaud, and B. Espiau. Robot Hand-Eye Calibration Using Structure from Motion. *Int. Journal of Robotics Research*, 20:228–248, 2001.
2. H. Chen. A Screw Motion Approach to Uniqueness Analysis of Head–Eye Geometry. In *Proc. of CVPR*, pages 145–151, Maui, Hawaii, 1991.
3. J. C. K. Chou and M. Kamel. Finding the Position and Orientation of a Sensor on a Robot Manipulator Using Quaternions. *Int. Journal of Robotics Research*, 10(3):240–254, 1991.
4. W. Clifford. Preliminary Sketch of Bi-quaternions. *Proc. of the London Mathematical Society*, 4:381–395, 1873.
5. K. Daniilidis. Hand-Eye Calibration Using Dual Quaternions. *Int. Journal of Robotics Research*, 18:286–298, 1999.
6. B. Heigl. *Plenoptic Scene Modeling from Uncalibrated Image Sequences*. ibidem-Verlag Stuttgart, 2004.
7. R. Horaud and F. Dornaika. Hand-Eye Calibration. *Int. Journal of Robotics Research*, 14(3):195–210, 1995.
8. J. Schmidt, F. Vogt, and H. Niemann. Vector Quantization Based Data Selection for Hand-Eye Calibration. In B. Girod, M. Magnor, and H.-P. Seidel, editors, *Vision, Modeling, and Visualization 2004*, pages 21–28, Stanford, USA, 2004. Aka / IOS Press, Berlin, Amsterdam.
9. Y. Shiu and S. Ahmad. Calibration of Wrist Mounted Robotic Sensors by Solving Homogeneous Transform Equations of the Form $AX = XB$. *IEEE Trans. on Robotics and Automation*, 5(1):16–29, 1989.
10. R. Y. Tsai and R. K. Lenz. A New Technique for Fully Autonomous and Efficient 3D Robotics Hand/Eye Calibration. *IEEE Trans. on Robotics and Automation*, 5(3):345–358, 1989.
11. F. Vogt, S. Krüger, J. Schmidt, D. Paulus, H. Niemann, W. Hohenberger, and C. H. Schick. Light Fields for Minimal Invasive Surgery Using an Endoscope Positioning Robot. *Methods of Information in Medicine*, 43(4):403–408, 2004.
12. Z. Zhang. A Flexible New Technique for Camera Calibration. *IEEE Trans. on Pattern Analysis and Machine Intelligence*, 22(11), 2000.
13. T. Zinßer, Ch. Gräßl, and H. Niemann. Efficient Feature Tracking for Long Video Sequences. In C. E. Rasmussen, H. H. Bülthoff, M. A. Giese, and B. Schölkopf, editors, *Pattern Recognition, 26th DAGM Symposium*, volume 3175 of *Lecture Notes in Computer Science*, pages 326–333. Springer-Verlag, Berlin, Heidelberg, New York, 2004.

Simple Solvers for Large Quadratic Programming Tasks

Vojtěch Franc and Václav Hlaváč

Center for Machine Perception, Department of Cybernetics,
Faculty of Electrical Engineering, Czech Technical University
{xfrancv, hlavac}@cmp.felk.cvut.cz
http://cmp.felk.cvut.cz

Abstract. This paper describes solvers for specific quadratic programming (QP) tasks. The QP tasks in question appear in numerous problems, e.g., classifier learning and probability density estimation. The QP task becomes challenging when large number of variables is to be optimized. This the case common in practice. We propose QP solvers which are simple to implement and still able to cope with problems having hundred thousands variables.

1 Introduction

A lot of problems in machine learning and pattern recognition lead to quadratic programming (QP) tasks. Although optimization of a general QP task have been studied at length, it is still a challenging problem when the number of variables is large. The large QP tasks are quite common in practice. In such cases it is necessary to derive specialized solvers which exploit all particular properties of the task at hand. In this paper, we propose solvers for special instances of QP tasks which can be applied to many problems. The proposed solvers are simple to implement and they allow to cope with QP tasks having hundred thousands of variables.

The quadratic programming (QP) task which we tackle in this paper is very related to two geometrical tasks. These task are the minimal norm problem (MNP) and the nearest point problem (NPP). The MNP aims to find the minimal norm vector from a convex hull defined by a finite set of vectors. The NPP searches for two nearest vectors from two different convex hulls defined again by finite sets of vectors. Algorithms to solve the MNP and the NPP first appeared in computational geometry and control engineering but later they were applied in pattern recognition. A simple algorithm for the MNP was published by Gilbert [4]. Kozinec [9] proposed a very similar method which he used for separation of two convex hulls given by finite vector sets. A different algorithm for the MNP was described by Mitchell, Demyanov and Malozemov [10]. Various modifications of the Kozinec's algorithm applied for analysis of linear discriminant functions were described in the book by Schlesinger and Hlaváč [11]. Keerthi et al. [7] proposed a new method to solve the NPP which was applied for training

W. Kropatsch, R. Sablatnig, and A. Hanbury (Eds.): DAGM 2005, LNCS 3663, pp. 75–84, 2005.

of binary Support Vector Machines (SVM) classifiers. Another method for the NPP was proposed by Kowalczyk [8] who also used it for training of the SVM's. A modification of the Kozinec's algorithm for training of the SVM's was further proposed by Franc and Hlaváč [2].

We concentrate on a slightly more general QP tasks the special cases of which are the MNP and the NPP. We denote this task as the generalized MNP and the generalized NPP problem. The generalization consists in adding a linear term to the QP criterion and assuming that the Hessian of the criterion is an arbitrary symmetric positive definite matrix. The original problems are recovered after the linear term is removed and the Hessian equals to a product of two matrices. The exact definitions of the generalized MNP and NPP are given in Section 2.

We claim that the above mentioned methods designed to solve the original MNP and NPP can be simply modified to solve the general problems. Moreover, we will introduce a general framework for sequential algorithms suitable to solve the generalized problems. The special instances of the general framework are the MNP and NPP methods. The introduced framework allows for their comparison and better understanding. We also derived a new method which proved to outperform the original ones. Due to a lack of space, we describe only the new method in Section 3. Detailed description and experimental evaluation can be found in [1].

While the original solvers were used mainly for training of binary SVM's their generalization proposed in this paper is applicable in many other problems. For example, training of multi-class SVM classifiers [3], Reduced Set Density Estimation [5], Support Vector Data Description [12], several modifications of SVM's for classification and regression introduced in [6].

The paper is organized as follows. The generalized MNP and NPP are defined in Section 2. The general framework and two particular algorithms are described in Section 3. Conclusions are drawn in Section 4.

2   Generalized Minimal Norm and Nearest Point Problems

Let a quadratic objective function

$$Q(\boldsymbol{\alpha}) = \frac{1}{2}\langle \boldsymbol{\alpha}, \mathbf{H}\boldsymbol{\alpha} \rangle + \langle \boldsymbol{c}, \boldsymbol{\alpha} \rangle \,, \tag{1}$$

be determined by a vector $\boldsymbol{c} \in \mathbb{R}^m$ and a symmetric positive definite matrix $\mathbf{H} \in \mathbb{R}^{m \times m}$. The symbol $\langle \cdot, \cdot \rangle$ stands for the dot product Let $\mathcal{A} \subseteq \mathbb{R}^m$ be a convex set of feasible solutions $\boldsymbol{\alpha} \in \mathcal{A}$. The goal is to solve the following task

$$\boldsymbol{\alpha}^* = \underset{\boldsymbol{\alpha} \in \mathcal{A}}{\operatorname{argmin}} \frac{1}{2}\langle \boldsymbol{\alpha}, \mathbf{H}\boldsymbol{\alpha} \rangle + \langle \boldsymbol{c}, \boldsymbol{\alpha} \rangle \,. \tag{2}$$

Let $\mathcal{I}_1$ and $\mathcal{I}_2$ be non-empty disjoint sets of indices such that $\mathcal{I}_1 \cup \mathcal{I}_2 = \mathcal{I} = \{1, 2, \ldots, m\}$. Let vectors $\boldsymbol{e}, \boldsymbol{e}_1, \boldsymbol{e}_2 \in \mathbb{R}^m$ be defined as follows

$$[\boldsymbol{e}]_i = 1 \,, i \in \mathcal{I} \,, \quad [\boldsymbol{e}_1]_i = \begin{cases} 1 \text{ for } i \in \mathcal{I}_1 \\ 0 \text{ for } i \in \mathcal{I}_2 \end{cases} , \quad [\boldsymbol{e}_2]_i = \begin{cases} 0 \text{ for } i \in \mathcal{I}_1 \\ 1 \text{ for } i \in \mathcal{I}_2 \end{cases} ,$$

where $[\cdot]_i$ denotes i-the coordinate of a vector. The optimization problems (2) with two distinct feasible sets $\mathcal{A}$ are assumed. In the first case, the *generalized Minimal Norm Problem* is the optimization problem (2) with the feasible set $\mathcal{A}$ determined by

$$\mathcal{A} = \{\boldsymbol{\alpha} \in \mathbb{R}^m \colon \langle \boldsymbol{\alpha}, \boldsymbol{e} \rangle = 1, \boldsymbol{\alpha} \geq \boldsymbol{0}\} \,. \tag{3}$$

In the second case, the *generalized Nearest Point Problem* is the optimization problem (2) with the feasible set $\mathcal{A}$ determined by

$$\mathcal{A} = \{\boldsymbol{\alpha} \in \mathbb{R}^m \colon \langle \boldsymbol{\alpha}, \boldsymbol{e}_1 \rangle = 1, \langle \boldsymbol{\alpha}, \boldsymbol{e}_2 \rangle = 1, \boldsymbol{\alpha} \geq \boldsymbol{0}\} \,, \tag{4}$$

where vectors $\boldsymbol{e}, \boldsymbol{e}_1, \boldsymbol{e}_2 \in \mathbb{R}^m$ are defined as follows

$$[\boldsymbol{e}]_i = 1 \,, i \in \mathcal{I} \,, \quad [\boldsymbol{e}_1]_i = \begin{cases} 1 \text{ for } i \in \mathcal{I}_1 \\ 0 \text{ for } i \in \mathcal{I}_2 \end{cases} , \quad [\boldsymbol{e}_2]_i = \begin{cases} 0 \text{ for } i \in \mathcal{I}_1 \\ 1 \text{ for } i \in \mathcal{I}_2 \end{cases} .$$

The generalized MNP and generalized NPP are convex optimization problems as both the objective functions (1) and the feasible sets (3) and (4), respectively, are convex.

3   Algorithms

3.1   Framework of Sequential Algorithms

The optimization problem (2) with the feasible set $\mathcal{A}$ can be transformed to a sequence of auxiliary optimization problems with the same objective function (1) but with much simpler auxiliary feasible sets $\mathcal{A}^{(0)}$, $\mathcal{A}^{(1)}, \ldots, \mathcal{A}^{(t)}$. Solving the problem (2) with respect to the auxiliary feasible sets yields a sequence of solutions $\boldsymbol{\alpha}^{(0)}, \boldsymbol{\alpha}^{(1)}, \ldots, \boldsymbol{\alpha}^{(t)}$. The sequence of feasible sets $\mathcal{A}^{(0)}$, $\mathcal{A}^{(1)}, \ldots, \mathcal{A}^{(t)}$ is assumed to be constructed such that (i) the sequence $Q(\boldsymbol{\alpha}^{(0)}) > Q(\boldsymbol{\alpha}^{(1)}) > \ldots > Q(\boldsymbol{\alpha}^{(t)})$ converges to the optimal solution $Q(\boldsymbol{\alpha}^*)$ and (ii) the auxiliary problems can be solved efficiently. The sequential algorithm solving the QP task which implements the idea mentioned above is summarized by Algorithm 1.

Algorithm 1: A Sequential Optimization Algorithm

1. Initialization. Select $\boldsymbol{\alpha}^{(0)} \in \mathcal{A}$.
2. Repeat until stopping condition is satisfied:
   (a) Select a feasible set $\mathcal{A}^{(t+1)}$ such that

$$Q(\boldsymbol{\alpha}^{(t)}) > \min_{\boldsymbol{\alpha} \in \mathcal{A}^{(t+1)}} Q(\boldsymbol{\alpha}) \,. \tag{5}$$

   (b) Solve the auxiliary task

$$\boldsymbol{\alpha}^{(t+1)} = \operatorname*{argmin}_{\boldsymbol{\alpha} \in \mathcal{A}^{(t+1)}} Q(\boldsymbol{\alpha}) \,. \tag{6}$$

The auxiliary feasible sets $\mathcal{A}^{(t+1)}$ is assumed to be a line segment

$$\mathcal{A}_L^{(t+1)} = \{\boldsymbol{\alpha} \in \mathbb{R}^m \colon \boldsymbol{\alpha} = (1-\tau)\boldsymbol{\alpha}^{(t)} + \tau\boldsymbol{\beta}^{(t)}, 0 \le \tau \le 1\}, \tag{7}$$

between the current solution $\boldsymbol{\alpha}^{(t)}$ and a vector $\boldsymbol{\beta}^{(t)} \in \mathcal{A}$. The optimization task (6) has an analytical solution in the case in which the feasible set is a line segment. Moreover, there exist simple rules to construct the vectors $\boldsymbol{\beta}^{(t)}$ which guarantee that condition (5) is satisfied.

3.2 Stopping Conditions

There is a need to stop the algorithm when it gets sufficiently close to the optimum. We assume the following two reasonable stopping conditions:

1. ε-optimal solution. The algorithm stops if

$$Q(\boldsymbol{\alpha}) - Q(\boldsymbol{\alpha}^*) \le \varepsilon. \tag{8}$$

2. Scale invariant ε-optimal solution. The algorithm stops if

$$Q(\boldsymbol{\alpha}) - Q(\boldsymbol{\alpha}^*) \le \varepsilon|Q(\boldsymbol{\alpha})|. \tag{9}$$

The prescribed $\varepsilon > 0$ controls the precision of the found solution. The stopping conditions (8) and (9) can be evaluated despite the unknown optimal value $Q(\boldsymbol{\alpha}^*)$ because a lower bound $Q_{LB}(\boldsymbol{\alpha})$ can be used instead. Let the inequality $Q(\boldsymbol{\alpha}^*) \ge Q_{LB}(\boldsymbol{\alpha})$ hold. Then the satisfaction of the condition $Q(\boldsymbol{\alpha}) - Q_{LB}(\boldsymbol{\alpha}) \le \varepsilon$ implies that condition (8) holds as well. Similarly, if the condition $Q(\boldsymbol{\alpha}) - Q_{LB}(\boldsymbol{\alpha}) \le \varepsilon|Q(\boldsymbol{\alpha})|$ holds then (9) is also satisfied.

The computation of the lower bound $Q_{LB}(\boldsymbol{\alpha})$ depends on the feasible set used. We give the lower bounds without derivation which can be found in [1]. In the case of the generalized MNP with the feasible set $\mathcal{A}$ defined by (3), the following lower bound $Q_{LB}(\boldsymbol{\alpha})$ can be used

$$Q_{LB}(\boldsymbol{\alpha}) = \min_{i \in \mathcal{I}} [\mathbf{H}\boldsymbol{\alpha} + \mathbf{c}]_i - \frac{1}{2}\langle \boldsymbol{\alpha}, \mathbf{H}\boldsymbol{\alpha} \rangle. \tag{10}$$

In the case of the generalized NPP with the feasible set $\mathcal{A}$ defined by (4), the lower bound Q_{LB} reads

$$Q_{LB}(\boldsymbol{\alpha}) = \min_{i \in \mathcal{I}_1} [\mathbf{H}\boldsymbol{\alpha} + \mathbf{c}]_i + \min_{i \in \mathcal{I}_2} [\mathbf{H}\boldsymbol{\alpha} + \mathbf{c}]_i - \frac{1}{2}\langle \boldsymbol{\alpha}, \mathbf{H}\boldsymbol{\alpha} \rangle. \tag{11}$$

3.3 Solution for a Line Segment

Let the feasible set $\mathcal{A}_L^{(t+1)}$ be a line segment (7) between the current solution $\boldsymbol{\alpha}^{(t)}$ and a vector $\boldsymbol{\beta}^{(t)} \in \mathcal{A}$. The quadratic objective function (1) defined over the line segment $\mathcal{A}_L^{(t+1)}$ reads

$$\begin{aligned}
Q_L^{(t+1)}(\tau) &= Q\left(\boldsymbol{\alpha}^{(t)}(1-\tau) + \tau\boldsymbol{\beta}^{(t)}\right) \\
&= \frac{1}{2}(1-\tau)^2\langle\boldsymbol{\alpha}^{(t)}, \mathbf{H}\boldsymbol{\alpha}^{(t)}\rangle + \tau(1-\tau)\langle\boldsymbol{\beta}^{(t)}, \mathbf{H}\boldsymbol{\alpha}^{(t)}\rangle \\
&\quad + \frac{1}{2}\tau^2\langle\boldsymbol{\beta}^{(t)}, \mathbf{H}\boldsymbol{\beta}^{(t)}\rangle + (1-\tau)\langle\mathbf{c}, \boldsymbol{\alpha}^{(t)}\rangle + \tau\langle\mathbf{c}, \boldsymbol{\beta}^{(t)}\rangle.
\end{aligned} \tag{12}$$

The objective function is now parameterized by a single variable $0 \leq \tau \leq 1$. It is obvious that $Q_L^{(t+1)}(0) = Q(\boldsymbol{\alpha}^{(t)})$ and $Q_L^{(t+1)}(1) = Q(\boldsymbol{\beta}^{(t)})$. The improvement gained from the optimization over the line segment $\mathcal{A}_L^{(t+1)}$ is

$$\Delta^{(t+1)} = Q(\boldsymbol{\alpha}^{(t)}) - Q(\boldsymbol{\alpha}^{(t+1)}) = Q(\boldsymbol{\alpha}^{(t)}) - \min_{0 \leq \tau \leq 1} Q_L^{(t+1)}(\tau) . \qquad (13)$$

A new vector $\boldsymbol{\alpha}^{(t+1)}$ is determined as

$$\boldsymbol{\alpha}^{(t+1)} = \boldsymbol{\alpha}^{(t)}(1 - \tau^*) + \tau^*\boldsymbol{\beta}^{(t)} \quad \text{where} \quad \tau^* = \operatorname*{argmin}_{0 \leq \tau \leq 1} Q_L^{(t+1)}(\tau) . \qquad (14)$$

The vector $\boldsymbol{\beta}^{(t)} \in \mathcal{A}$ must be selected such that the improvement (13) is positive. This occurs when the derivative of $Q_L^{(t+1)}(\tau)$ evaluated in zero is negative, i.e.,

$$\left. \frac{\partial Q_L^{(t+1)}(\tau)}{\partial \tau} \right|_{\tau=0} = \langle (\boldsymbol{\beta}^{(t)} - \boldsymbol{\alpha}^{(t)}), (\mathbf{H}\boldsymbol{\alpha}^{(t)} + \mathbf{c}) \rangle < 0 . \qquad (15)$$

The solution of (14) can be found analytically by setting the derivative of $Q_L^{(t+1)}(\tau)$ to zero and solving for τ. This yields

$$\tau^* = \min \left(1, \frac{\langle (\boldsymbol{\alpha}^{(t)} - \boldsymbol{\beta}^{(t)}), (\mathbf{H}\boldsymbol{\alpha}^{(t)} + \mathbf{c}) \rangle}{\langle \boldsymbol{\alpha}^{(t)}, \mathbf{H}\boldsymbol{\alpha}^{(t)} \rangle - 2\langle \boldsymbol{\beta}^{(t)}, \mathbf{H}\boldsymbol{\alpha}^{(t)} \rangle + \langle \boldsymbol{\beta}^{(t)}, \mathbf{H}\boldsymbol{\beta}^{(t)} \rangle} \right) , \qquad (16)$$

where the minimum $\min(1, \cdot)$ guarantees that the solution does not leave the feasible set $\mathcal{A}_L^{(t+1)}$. If $\tau^* = 1$ then $\boldsymbol{\alpha}^{(t+1)} = \boldsymbol{\beta}^{(t)}$ which implies that the value of improvement (13) equals to

$$\Delta^{(t+1)} = Q(\boldsymbol{\alpha}^{(t)}) - Q(\boldsymbol{\beta}^{(t)}) . \qquad (17)$$

If $\tau^* < 0$ then the value of improvement can be derived by substituting (12) and (16) to (13). After some manipulation we get

$$\Delta^{(t+1)} = \frac{\langle (\boldsymbol{\alpha}^{(t)} - \boldsymbol{\beta}^{(t)}), (\mathbf{H}\boldsymbol{\alpha}^{(t)} + \mathbf{c}) \rangle^2}{2(\langle \boldsymbol{\alpha}^{(t)}, \mathbf{H}\boldsymbol{\alpha}^{(t)} \rangle - 2\langle \boldsymbol{\alpha}^{(t)}, \mathbf{H}\boldsymbol{\beta}^{(t)} \rangle + \langle \boldsymbol{\beta}^{(t)}, \mathbf{H}\boldsymbol{\beta}^{(t)} \rangle)} . \qquad (18)$$

3.4 Algorithm for Generalized Minimal Norm Problem

The algorithm described in this section fulfills the general framework outlined by Algorithm 1. The particular algorithm is determined by a rule for selection of the line segment $\mathcal{A}_L^{(t+1)}$. The line segment is constructed between the current solution $\boldsymbol{\alpha}^{(t)}$ and a vector $\boldsymbol{\beta}^{(t)}$. In this case, we assume that all entries of the vector $\boldsymbol{\beta}^{(t)}$ equal to the current solution $\boldsymbol{\alpha}^{(t)}$ except for two entries u and v, i.e.,

$$[\boldsymbol{\beta}^{(t)}]_i = \begin{cases} [\boldsymbol{\alpha}^{(t)}]_u + [\boldsymbol{\alpha}^{(t)}]_v & \text{for } i = u , \\ 0 & \text{for } i = v , \\ [\boldsymbol{\alpha}^{(t)}]_i & \text{for } i \neq u \wedge i \neq v, \end{cases} \quad \forall i \in \mathcal{I} . \qquad (19)$$

If proper u and v are used then the optimization over the line segment between $\boldsymbol{\alpha}^{(t)}$ and $\boldsymbol{\beta}^{(t)}$ leads to the improvement $\Delta^{(t+1)}(u,v) = Q(\boldsymbol{\alpha}^{(t)}) - Q(\boldsymbol{\alpha}^{(t+1)})$. The exact value of the improvement can be derived by substituting (19) to (18) which for $\tau < 1$ gives

$$\Delta^{(t+1)}(u,v) = \frac{([\mathbf{H}\boldsymbol{\alpha}^{(t)} + \mathbf{c}]_v - [\mathbf{H}\boldsymbol{\alpha}^{(t)} + \mathbf{c}]_u)^2}{2([\mathbf{H}]_{u,u} - 2[\mathbf{H}]_{u,v} + [\mathbf{H}]_{v,v})}, \tag{20}$$

and substituting (19) to (17) which for $\tau = 1$ gives

$$\Delta^{(t+1)}(u,v) = [\boldsymbol{\alpha}^{(t)}]_v ([\mathbf{H}\boldsymbol{\alpha}^{(t)} + \mathbf{c}]_v - [\mathbf{H}\boldsymbol{\alpha}^{(t)} + \mathbf{c}]_u) - \frac{1}{2}[\boldsymbol{\alpha}^{(t)}]_v^2 ([\mathbf{H}]_{u,u} - 2[\mathbf{H}]_{u,v} + [\mathbf{H}]_{v,v}). \tag{21}$$

From (15) it follows that u and v must be selected such that $[\boldsymbol{\alpha}^{(t)}]_v > 0$ and the inequality

$$\kappa(u,v) = [\mathbf{H}\boldsymbol{\alpha}^{(t)} + \mathbf{c}]_v - [\mathbf{H}\boldsymbol{\alpha}^{(t)} + \mathbf{c}]_u > 0,$$

holds to guarantee a non-zero improvement. The computation of τ for $\boldsymbol{\beta}^{(t)}$ given by (19) simplifies to

$$\tau = \frac{[\mathbf{H}\boldsymbol{\alpha}^{(t)} + \mathbf{c}]_v - [\mathbf{H}\boldsymbol{\alpha}^{(t)} + \mathbf{c}]_u}{[\boldsymbol{\alpha}^{(t)}]_v ([\mathbf{H}]_{u,u} - 2[\mathbf{H}]_{u,v} + [\mathbf{H}]_{v,v})}. \tag{22}$$

It remains to select the indices u and v such that the improvement will be maximized. The algorithm proposed by Mitchell, Demyanov and Malozemov (MDM) selects the indices u and v so that $\kappa(u,v)$ is maximized. This is reasonable since the value of $\kappa(u,v)$ approximates the value of improvement $\Delta^{(t+1)}(u,v)$. A novel method proposed here is based on searching for the entries u and v which maximize the exact value of the improvement $\Delta^{(t+1)}(u,v)$ instead of its approximation $\kappa(u,v)$.

The computation of the improvement for given u and v requires evaluation of the (22) and, based on the value of τ, (20) or (21) is used. To select the optimal pair (u,v) one has to try $\frac{d(d+1)}{2}$ combinations where d is the number of non-zero entries of the current solution $\boldsymbol{\alpha}^{(t)}$. Notice that zero entries of $\boldsymbol{\alpha}^{(t)}$ can be disregarded as the corresponding vector $\boldsymbol{\beta}^{(t)}$ would be the same as $\boldsymbol{\alpha}^{(t)}$. The search for the optimal (u,v) would require to access d columns of the matrix $\mathbf{H}$ which would be too expensive . To overcome this difficulty, the following strategy of selecting (u,v) is proposed. The index u is selected such that

$$u \in \underset{i \in \mathcal{I}}{\operatorname{argmin}}[\mathbf{H}\boldsymbol{\alpha}^{(t)} + \mathbf{c}]_i.$$

The found u is fixed and the index v is computed as

$$v \in \underset{i \in \mathcal{I}_V}{\operatorname{argmax}} \Delta^{(t+1)}(u,i),$$

where the $\mathcal{I}_V = \{i \in \mathcal{I} : [\mathbf{H}\boldsymbol{\alpha}^{(t)} + \mathbf{c}]_i > [\mathbf{H}\boldsymbol{\alpha}^{(t)} + \mathbf{c}]_u \wedge [\boldsymbol{\alpha}^{(t)}]_i > 0\}$ is a set of admissible indices for v for which the improvement can be greater than zero.

A similar strategy would be to fix v and search for the optimal u or to apply both these searches together. All these three combinations were experimentally tested and the proposed strategy required on average the minimal access to the matrix $\mathbf{H}$. Algorithm 2 summarizes the proposed method:

Algorithm 2: Algorithm for generalized MNP

---

1. Initialization. Set $\boldsymbol{\alpha}^{(0)} \in \mathcal{A}$.
2. Repeat until stopping condition is satisfied:
   (a) Construct vector $\boldsymbol{\beta}^{(t)} \in \mathcal{A}$ such that

   $$[\boldsymbol{\beta}^{(t)}]_i = \begin{cases} [\boldsymbol{\alpha}^{(t)}]_u + [\boldsymbol{\alpha}^{(t)}]_v & \text{for } i = u, \\ 0 & \text{for } i = v, \\ [\boldsymbol{\alpha}^{(t)}]_i & \text{for } i \neq u \wedge i \neq v, \end{cases} \quad \forall i \in \mathcal{I},$$

   where

   $$u \in \operatorname*{argmin}_{i \in \mathcal{I}}[\mathbf{H}\boldsymbol{\alpha}^{(t)} + \mathbf{c}]_i, \quad \text{and} \quad v \in \operatorname*{argmax}_{i \in \mathcal{I}_V} \Delta^{(t+1)}(u, i).$$

   The improvement $\Delta^{(t+1)}(u, i)$ is computed using (22), (20) and (21).
   (b) Update
   $$\boldsymbol{\alpha}^{(t+1)} = \boldsymbol{\alpha}^{(t)}(1 - \tau) + \tau \boldsymbol{\beta}^{(t)},$$

   where

   $$\tau = \min\left(1, \frac{\langle(\boldsymbol{\alpha}^{(t)} - \boldsymbol{\beta}^{(t)}), (\mathbf{H}\boldsymbol{\alpha}^{(t)} + \mathbf{c})\rangle}{\langle \boldsymbol{\alpha}^{(t)}, \mathbf{H}\boldsymbol{\alpha}^{(t)}\rangle - 2\langle \boldsymbol{\beta}^{(t)}, \mathbf{H}\boldsymbol{\alpha}^{(t)}\rangle + \langle \boldsymbol{\beta}^{(t)}, \mathbf{H}\boldsymbol{\beta}^{(t)}\rangle}\right).$$

The number of iterations depends on used stopping condition. Let us assume that ε-optimality condition (8) is applied. We can prove that the number of iterations t can be bounded using the following quantities: the prescribed precision ε, the initial value $Q(\boldsymbol{\alpha}^{(0)})$, the optimal value $Q(\boldsymbol{\alpha}^*)$ and a diameter $D \in \mathbb{R}^+$ of the matrix $\mathbf{H}$ defined as

$$D^2 = \max_{\substack{\boldsymbol{\alpha} \in \mathcal{A} \\ \boldsymbol{\beta} \in \mathcal{A}}} (\langle \boldsymbol{\alpha}, \mathbf{H}\boldsymbol{\beta}\rangle - 2\langle \boldsymbol{\alpha}, \mathbf{H}\boldsymbol{\beta}\rangle + \langle \boldsymbol{\beta}, \mathbf{H}\boldsymbol{\beta}\rangle).$$

Theorem 1. *Algorithm 2 started from an arbitrary vector $\boldsymbol{\alpha}^{(0)} \in \mathcal{A}$ returns the vector $\boldsymbol{\alpha}$ satisfying for any $\varepsilon > 0$ the ε-optimality condition $Q(\boldsymbol{\alpha}) - Q(\boldsymbol{\alpha}^*) \leq \varepsilon$ after at most $t_{max} < \infty$ iterations, where*

$$t_{max} = \frac{2D^2(m-1)}{\varepsilon^2}(Q(\boldsymbol{\alpha}^{(0)}) - Q(\boldsymbol{\alpha}^*)).$$

For proof we refer to [1].

3.5   Algorithm for Generalized Nearest Point Problem

The algorithm to solve the generalized NPP is of the same nature as that solving the generalized MNP problem. Let $\mathcal{A}_1^{(t+1)} = \{\alpha \in \mathcal{A} \colon [\alpha]_i = [\alpha^{(t)}]_i, i \in \mathcal{I}_2\}$ denote a set of vectors from the feasible set $\mathcal{A}$ which have the entries $\mathcal{I}_2$ fixed to corresponding entries of the current solution $\alpha^{(t)}$. Similarly, let $\mathcal{A}_2^{(t+1)} = \{\alpha \in \mathcal{A} \colon [\alpha]_i = [\alpha^{(t)}]_i, i \in \mathcal{I}_1\}$ denote vectors with the entries $\mathcal{I}_1$ fixed. The algorithm for the generalized NPP constructs the vector $\beta^{(t)}$ such that it belongs either to $\mathcal{A}_1^{(t+1)}$ or to $\mathcal{A}_2^{(t+1)}$ which is only the difference compared to Algorithm 2.

Using the same reasoning as discussed in Section 3.4 we first find the indices

$$u_1 \in \operatorname*{argmin}_{i \in \mathcal{I}_1} [\mathbf{H}\alpha^{(t)} + c]_i \,, \qquad u_2 \in \operatorname*{argmin}_{i \in \mathcal{I}_2} [\mathbf{H}\alpha^{(t)} + c]_i \,. \tag{23}$$

Second, the optimal v_1 and v_2 are sought for so that

$$v_1 \in \operatorname*{argmin}_{i \in \mathcal{I}_{V1}} \Delta^{(t+1)}(u_1, i) \,, \qquad v_2 \in \operatorname*{argmin}_{i \in \mathcal{I}_{V2}} \Delta^{(t+1)}(u_2, i) \,, \tag{24}$$

where $\mathcal{I}_{V1} = \{i \in \mathcal{I}_1 \colon [\mathbf{H}\alpha^{(t)} + c]_i > [\mathbf{H}\alpha^{(t)} + c]_{u_1} \wedge [\alpha^{(t)}]_i > 0\}$ and $\mathcal{I}_{V2} = \{i \in \mathcal{I}_2 \colon [\mathbf{H}\alpha^{(t)} + c]_i > [\mathbf{H}\alpha^{(t)} + c]_{u_2} \wedge [\alpha^{(t)}]_i > 0\}$ are sets of admissible indices. Finally, the pair of indices (u_1, v_1) or (u_2, v_2) which yields the bigger improvement is used to construct the vector $\beta^{(t)}$. The formula for the improvement $\Delta^{(t+1)}(u, v)$ can be derived using the same way as in the the generalized MNP case. So that the improvement is computed by the formula (20) if $\tau < 1$ and (21) if $\tau = 1$. Algorithm 3 summarizes the proposed method:

Algorithm 3: Algorithm for generalized NPP

1. Initialization. Set $\alpha^{(0)} \in \mathcal{A}$.
2. Repeat until stopping condition is satisfied:
   (a) Construct vector $\beta^{(t)} \in \mathcal{A}$

   $$[\beta^{(t)}]_i = \begin{cases} [\alpha^{(t)}]_u + [\alpha^{(t)}]_v & \text{for } i = u \,, \\ 0 & \text{for } i = v \,, \\ [\alpha^{(t)}]_i & \text{for } i \neq u \wedge i \neq v, \end{cases}$$

   where the indices (u, v) are computed as follows. First, the pairs (u_1, v_1) and (u_2, v_2) are computed by (23) and (24). Second, the pair which yields the bigger improvement $\Delta^{(t+1)}(u, v)$ is taken for (u, v).
   (b) Update

   $$\alpha^{(t+1)} = \alpha^{(t)}(1 - \tau) + \tau \beta^{(t)} \,,$$

   where

   $$\tau = \min \left(1, \frac{\langle (\alpha^{(t)} - \beta^{(t)}), (\mathbf{H}\alpha^{(t)} + c) \rangle}{\langle \alpha^{(t)}, \mathbf{H}\alpha^{(t)} \rangle - 2\langle \beta^{(t)}, \mathbf{H}\alpha^{(t)} \rangle + \langle \beta^{(t)}, \mathbf{H}\beta^{(t)} \rangle} \right) \,.$$

Theorem 2. *Algorithm 3 started from an arbitrary vector $\alpha^{(0)} \in \mathcal{A}$ returns the vector α satisfying for any $\varepsilon > 0$ the ε-optimality condition $Q(\alpha) - Q(\alpha^*) \leq \varepsilon$ after at most $t_{max} < \infty$ iterations, where*

$$t_{max} = \frac{8D^2(m-2)}{\varepsilon^2}(Q(\alpha^{(0)}) - Q(\alpha^*)) \, .$$

The upper bound on the maximal number of iterations is defined by the same quantities as in Theorem 1 except for the diameter D. We refer to [1] for the definition of D and the proof of Theorem 2.

3.6 Efficient Implementation

The main requirement on the developed QP solvers is the ability to deal with large problems, i.e., problems where the matrix $\mathbf{H}$ in the definition of the QP task is large and cannot be stored in the memory. The aim is to minimize an access of the QP solver to the entries of the matrix $\mathbf{H}$. It is seen that the algorithms described in Sections 3.4 and 3.4 require only two columns of the matrix $\mathbf{H}$ in each iteration. Moreover, in many cases only a small subset of the columns is requested by the algorithms, i.e., those which corresponds to the non-zero entries $\mathcal{I}_\emptyset = \{i \in \mathcal{I} : [\alpha]_i > 0\}$ of the vector $\alpha^{(t)}$. This allows to use a cache for the most often requested columns without the need to store the whole matrix $\mathbf{H}$. For instance, the *First In First Out* (FIFO) turned out to be suitable.

The efficient implementation of the algorithms lies in maintaining a cache of key variables. In the case of the generalized MNP problem, these variables are

$$\delta_\alpha^{(t)} = \langle \alpha^{(t)}, \mathbf{H}\alpha^{(t)} \rangle \, , \quad \mathbf{h}_\alpha^{(t)} = \mathbf{H}\alpha^{(t)} \, , \quad \delta_\beta^{(t)} = \langle \beta^{(t)}, \mathbf{H}\alpha^{(t)} \rangle \, , \qquad (25)$$

where $\delta_\alpha^{(t)} \in \mathbb{R}$ is a scalar, $\mathbf{h}_\alpha^{(t)} \in \mathbb{R}^m$ is a vector and $\delta_\beta^{(t)} \in \mathbb{R}$ is a scalar. Having the variables (25), the number of computations scales with $O(m)$ in each iteration of any QP solver, i.e., it is linear with respect to the number of variables m. It is easy to show that the variables (25) can be updated in each iteration instead of computing them from a scratch. The updates of all variables also require $O(m)$ operations. The exact updating formulas can be simply derived by substituting rule (19) to (25).

The same idea is also applied for the generalized NPP. In this case, there are more key variables to be cached. However, the number of computations required for their updating is also $O(m)$. The overall number of computations required in each iteration is thus $O(m)$ for both described algorithms. We refer to [1] for a detailed description.

4   Conclusions

We introduced a general framework for sequential algorithms suitable to solve the generalized minimal norm problem (MNP) and generalized nearest point problem (NPP). The framework allows for comparison of existing methods designed to solve original MNP and NPP. The methods can be simply modified to solve the generalized formulations. We also derived a new algorithm with performance superior to other methods. The new algorithm is described in this paper while comparison to other methods was skipped due to a lack of space. We refer to [1] where all the methods are described in details and compared to each other in numerous synthetical and real-life problems.

Acknowledgments

The authors were supported by the projects IST-004176 COSPAL, CONEX GZ 45.535. The first author was also supported by MSM 6840770013. The second author was also supported by INTAS 04-77-7347 (PRINCESS).

References

1. V. Franc. Optimization algorithms for kernel methods. PhD Thesis, Center for Machine Perception, K13133 FEE Czech Technical University, Prague, Czech Republic, 2005. To be submitted in July 2005.
2. V. Franc and V. Hlaváč. A Simple Learning Algorithm for Maximal Margin Classifier. In *Kernel and Subspace Methods for Computer Vision, workshop adjoint to the Int. Conference on Neural Netwoks*, pages 1–11. TU Vienna, August 2001.
3. V. Franc and V. Hlaváč. Multi-class Support Vector Machine. In R. Kasturi, D. Laurendeau, and Suen C., editors, *16th International Conference on Pattern Recognition*, volume 2, pages 236–239, Los Alamitos, CA 90720-1314, August 2002. IEEE Computer Society.
4. E.G. Gilbert. Minimizing the quadratic form on a convex set. *SIAM journal on Control and Optimization*, 4:61–79, 1966.
5. M. Girolami and C. He. Probability density estimation from optimally condensed data sample. *IEEE PAMI*, 25(10), 2003.
6. L. Gonzales, C. Angulo, and A. Velasco, F. Catala. Unified dual for bi-class SVM approaches. *Patter Recognition*, 2005. Article in press.
7. S.S. Keerthi, S.K. Shevade, C. Bhattacharya, and K.R.K. Murthy. A Fast Iterative Nearest Point Algorithm for Support Vector Machine Classifier Design. *IEEE Transactions on Neural Networks*, 11(1):124–136, January 2000.
8. A. Kowalczyk. Maximal margin perceptron. In P.J. Bartlett, B. Schloköpf, D. Schuurmans, and A.J. Smola, editors, *Advances in Large-Margin Classifiers*, pages 75–113. The MIT Press, 2000.
9. B.N. Kozinec. Recurrent algorithm separating convex hulls of two sets. In V.N. Vapnik, editor, *Learning algorithms in pattern recognition*, pages 43–50. Sovetskoje radio, Moskva, 1973.
10. B.F. Mitchell, V.F. Demyanov, and V.N. Malozemov. Finding the point of a polyhedron closest to the origin. *SIAM journal on Control and Optimization*, 12:19–26, 1974.
11. M.I. Schlesinger and V. Hlaváč. *Ten lectures on statistical and structural pattern recognition*. Kluwer Academic Publishers, 2002.
12. D.M.J. Tax and R.P.W Duin. Data domain description by support vectors. In M. Verleysen, editor, *Proceedings ESANN*, pages 251–256, Brussels, 1999.

Voxel-Wise Gray Scale Invariants for Simultaneous Segmentation and Classification

Olaf Ronneberger, Janis Fehr, and Hans Burkhardt

Albert-Ludwigs-Universität Freiburg, Institut für Informatik,
Lehrstuhl für Mustererkennung und Bildverarbeitung,
Georges-Köhler-Allee Geb. 052, 79110 Freiburg, Deutschland
ronneber@informatik.uni-freiburg.de
http://lmb.informatik.uni-freiburg.de

Abstract. 3D volumetric microscopical techniques (e.g. confocal laser scanning microscopy) have become a standard tool in biomedical applications to record three-dimensional objects with highly anisotropic morphology. To analyze these data in high-throughput experiments, reliable, easy to use and generally applicable pattern recognition tools are required. The major problem of nearly all existing applications is their high specialization to exact one problem, and the their time-consuming adaption to new problems, that has to be done by pattern recognition experts. We therefore search for a tool that can be adapted to new problems just by an interactive training process. Our main idea is therefore to combine object segmentation and recognition into one step by computing voxel-wise gray scale invariants (using nonlinear kernel functions and Haar-integration) on the volumetric multi-channel data set and classify each voxel using support vector machines.

After the selection of an appropriate set of nonlinear kernel functions (which allows to integrate previous knowledge, but still needs some expertise), this approach allows a biologist to adapt the recognition system for his problem just by interactively selecting several voxels as training points for each class of objects. Based on these points the classification result is computed and the biologist may refine it by selecting additional training points until the result meets his needs. In this paper we present the theoretical background and a fast approximative algorithm using FFTs for computing Haar-integrals over the very rich class of nonlinear 3-point-kernel functions. The approximation still fulfils the invariance conditions. The experimental application for the recognition of different cell cores of the chorioallantoic membrane is presented in the accompanying paper [1] and in the technical report [2]

1 Introduction

Three-dimensional microscopical techniques, e.g., confocal laser scanning microscopy, has become a standard tool in biomedical applications within the last few years. Due to the increasing need of high throughput experiments, e.g. in the analysis of 3D gene expression patterns, the gap between the automated

W. Kropatsch, R. Sablatnig, and A. Hanbury (Eds.): DAGM 2005, LNCS 3663, pp. 85–92, 2005.
© Springer-Verlag Berlin Heidelberg 2005

recording of the data and the tedious and subjective manual evaluation becomes larger and larger.

Due to the rapidly changing requirements for an automatic evaluation, the traditional way of developing highly specialized model-based solutions for exactly one problem with dozens of manually selected morphological processing steps and thresholds does usually not meet the needs of the biologists.

A step towards a generally applicable and easy to use system is presented in this paper. Many of the problems can be reduced to a rotation and translation invariant recognition of certain 3D structures, that are trained by a manually labeled database (e.g., counting or localization of different cell cores). Therefore, we use gray scale invariants [3,4], that have already been successfully applied to the recognition of pollen grains in volumetric data sets [5]. The main limitation of this approach was its need for objects that are already segmented from the background. A good segmentation on the other hand needs already much information about the object to isolate it from the background.

To overcome this classical dilemma, we integrated the segmentation and recognition of the objects into one step by calculating voxel-wise gray scale invariants: For each voxel several rotation invariant features from its surrounding are extracted and the resulting feature vector is classified using support vector machines [6]. The result is a label for each voxel (or several probabilities per voxel). A simple connected component analysis in the next step then searches regions with the same label to segment the objects.

The main advantage of this approach is its direct operation on the raw data and the avoidance of manually selected thresholds. Instead it learns all necessary informations from a labeled training data set.

2   Theory

2.1   Construction of Gray Scale Invariants

The precondition for the use of gray scale invariants in recognizing n-dimensional structures in the real world are:

1. One or more reproducible measurement techniques, that are able to measure certain properties within the structure at definite positions independent from the orientation of the structure (e.g., to measure the fluorescence activity at a certain wavelength at the focal point of a confocal laser scanning microscope) resulting in an n-dimensional multi-channel data set
2. Knowledge of those mathematical transformations, which do not change the meaning of the structure (e.g. rotation and translation)

If these preconditions are fulfilled, we can find a feature extraction, that is able to map all representations of the same object (given by the transformation group) into one point of the feature space by using a nonlinear kernel function and a Haar-integration over the whole transformation group [5].

$$T[f](\mathbf{X}) := \int_G f(g\mathbf{X})\,dg$$

G : transformation group
g : one element of the transformation group
f : nonlinear kernel function   (1)
$\mathbf{X}$: n-dim, multi-channel data set
$g\mathbf{X}$: the transformed n-dim data set

For each nonlinear kernel function f this integral returns a scalar value that describes a certain feature of the n-dimensional data set invariant under the given transformations, as long as the integral exists and is finite.

Reduction to Kernel-Functions with sparse support. If the kernel function f only depends on a few points of the image or volume, i.e., if we can rewrite $f(\mathbf{X})$ as $f\left(\mathbf{X}(\boldsymbol{x}_1), \mathbf{X}(\boldsymbol{x}_2), \mathbf{X}(\boldsymbol{x}_3), \ldots\right)$, where $\mathbf{X}(\boldsymbol{x}_i)$ is the gray value[1] at position $\boldsymbol{x}_i$ we only need to transform the kernel points $\boldsymbol{x}_1, \boldsymbol{x}_2, \boldsymbol{x}_3, \ldots$ accordingly, instead of the whole data set $\mathbf{X}$. This transformation of the kernel points is denoted as $s_g(\boldsymbol{x}_i)$ such that

$$(g\mathbf{X})(\boldsymbol{x}_i) := \mathbf{X}(s_g(\boldsymbol{x}_i)) \quad \forall g, \boldsymbol{x}_i . \tag{2}$$

With this we can rewrite (1) as

$$T[f](\mathbf{X}) := \int_G f\left(\mathbf{X}(s_g(\boldsymbol{x}_1)), \mathbf{X}(s_g(\boldsymbol{x}_2)), \mathbf{X}(s_g(\boldsymbol{x}_3)), \ldots\right) dg . \tag{3}$$

This considerably speeds up the computation and results for a given kernel in linear complexity $O(N)$ of the algorithm, where N is the number of voxels in the data set.

Multi Scale Approach. In the general formulation of the gray scale invariants (1) appropriate kernel functions can be used in order to sense any features of the structures at any scales. Computable kernel functions (3) depend only on a few gray values at certain points. To use them for sensing also large-scale informations, a multi scale approach is applied [5]. In the continuous domain this is equivalent to applying a certain low-pass filter (e.g. convolution with a Gaussian) to the data set before evaluating the kernel functions (see Fig. 1)

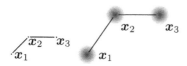

Fig. 1. Computable kernels rely on a small number of sampling points. To sense informations at multiple scales, the sampling points are "enlarged" with Gaussians of mutliple size

---

[1] We use the term "gray value" even for color or other multi-channel data. In this case one "gray value" has multiple components.

Voxel-Wise Gray Scale Invariants. For voxel-wise invariants the transformation group is just a rotation, where the origin of the coordinate system is shifted to a certain voxel in advance. The resulting features from the different kernel functions are collected in a feature vector, which then describes the surrounding of this voxel in a unique and rotation invariant way. This is done for all voxels in a volume.

2.2   Computation of Gray Scale Invariants

To compute the gray scale invariants from (3) we first have to select a parameterization $\boldsymbol{\lambda}$ of s_g so that (3) can be rewritten as

$$T[f](\mathbf{X}) := \int f\Big(\mathbf{X}(s_\lambda(\boldsymbol{x}_1)),\ \mathbf{X}(s_\lambda(\boldsymbol{x}_2)),\ \mathbf{X}(s_\lambda(\boldsymbol{x}_3)),\dots\Big)\,d\boldsymbol{\lambda}\ . \qquad (4)$$

For a given data set $\mathbf{X}$ and given kernel points $\boldsymbol{x}_1$, $\boldsymbol{x}_2$, $\boldsymbol{x}_3$, ... we can substitute $\mathbf{X}(s_\lambda(\boldsymbol{x}_i))$ with $v_i(\boldsymbol{\lambda})$, where $\mathbf{X}(s_\lambda(\boldsymbol{x}_i))$ are the gray values, that are touched by the i'th kernel point $\boldsymbol{x}_i$ during all transformations described by $\boldsymbol{\lambda}$, resulting in

$$T = \int f\Big(v_1(\boldsymbol{\lambda}),\ v_2(\boldsymbol{\lambda}),\ v_3(\boldsymbol{\lambda}),\dots\Big)\,d\boldsymbol{\lambda}\ . \qquad (5)$$

A simple example for the resulting one-dimensional curves $v_1(\varphi)$, $v_2(\varphi)$ and $v_3(\varphi)$ when using a 3-point kernel on a 2D image and the transformation group of rotations is given in Fig. 2.

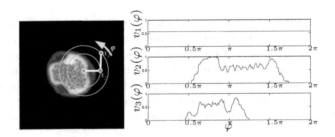

Fig. 2. When using a 3-point kernel on a continuous 2D image and the transformation group of rotations, the gray values, that are touched by the kernel points $\boldsymbol{x}_1$, $\boldsymbol{x}_2$ and $\boldsymbol{x}_3$, are one-dimensional functions $v_1(\varphi)$, $v_2(\varphi)$ and $v_3(\varphi)$

Two-Point Kernel Functions. The direct evaluation of the integral (3) is usually too slow for real applications. A fast calculation method (using FFTs) for a certain class of kernel-functions (so called separable two-point-kernel functions) of the form

$$f(\mathbf{X}) = f_a\Big(\mathbf{X}(\mathbf{0})\Big)\cdot f_b\Big(\mathbf{X}(\boldsymbol{q})\Big)$$

f_a, f_b : any nonlinear functions that
transform the gray values   (6)
$\boldsymbol{q}$: span of the kernel function

and for Euclidean transformations was presented in [5]: For this purpose we define $\mathbf{A}(\boldsymbol{x}) := f_a(\mathbf{X}(\boldsymbol{x}))$ and $\mathbf{B}(\boldsymbol{x}) := f_b(\mathbf{X}(\boldsymbol{x}))$ The resulting Haar integral (3) is

$$T[f](\mathbf{X}) = \int d\boldsymbol{x}\ \mathbf{A}(\boldsymbol{x}) \cdot (\mathbf{B} * \mathbf{S})(\boldsymbol{x}), \qquad \text{with } \mathbf{S}(\boldsymbol{x}) := \delta(|\boldsymbol{x}| - q) \qquad (7)$$

which is the convolution (denoted as '$*$') of $\mathbf{B}$ with $\mathbf{S}$ (which is a surface of a sphere in 3D or a circle in 2D) and the point-wise multiplication with $\mathbf{A}$. For the evaluation of voxel-wise gray scale invariants the final integration over $\boldsymbol{x}$ is omitted.

Three-Point-Kernel Functions Two-point kernel functions perform very well in Haar integrals over Euclidean motions. For the voxel-wise invariants, they are somewhat limited in their discrimination power, because the resulting invariants are not only invariant to rotation of the surrounding but also to any random permutation of the gray values at the same radius. In contrast to this, three-point kernel functions, where the first point is located at the rotation center[2]

$$f(\mathbf{X}) = f_a\Big(\mathbf{X}(\mathbf{0})\Big) \cdot f_b\Big(\mathbf{X}(\boldsymbol{q_2})\Big) \cdot f_c\Big(\mathbf{X}(\boldsymbol{q_3})\Big) \qquad (8)$$

are sensitive to such permutations but they cannot be computed directly with the above mentioned fast algorithm, because both factors in the product $f_b(\mathbf{X}(\boldsymbol{q_1})) \cdot f_c(\mathbf{X}(\boldsymbol{q_2}))$ change when rotating the kernel and therefore cannot be calculated by a simple convolution.

In the following we present an expansion into a series of simple coonvolutions with the nice property, that every truncated evaluation of this series still fulfills the invariance criterion.

For volumetric data the rotations must be parameterized by three angles $\boldsymbol{\lambda} = (\varphi_1, \varphi_2, \varphi_3)^T$ (see Fig. 3).

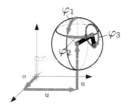

Fig. 3. Parameterization of the 3D rotation with $\boldsymbol{\lambda} = (\varphi_1, \varphi_2, \varphi_3)^T$

The first kernel point is always shifted to the rotation center, which results in $v_1(\boldsymbol{\lambda}) = v_1(\mathbf{0})$. Without changing the result we can rotate the kernel function, such that the second kernel point is located on the z-axis, which makes

---

[2] For Euclidean transformations, a translation of the kernel function does not change the integral. We use the same terminology for voxel-wise invariants. If you do not plan to integrate over translations in a later step, you could leave out the first kernel point.

$v_2(\boldsymbol{\lambda})$ insensitive to φ_3-rotations, resulting in $v_2(\boldsymbol{\lambda}) = v_2(\varphi_1, \varphi_2, 0)$. With this parameterization the Haar integral becomes

$$T = f_a\Big(v_1(\mathbf{0})\Big) \int_0^\pi d\varphi_1 \sin(\varphi_1) \int_{-\pi}^\pi d\varphi_2 \ f_b\Big(v_2(\varphi_1, \varphi_2, 0)\Big) \int_{-\pi}^\pi d\varphi_3 \ f_c\Big(v_3(\varphi_1, \varphi_2, \varphi_3)\Big) \, . \tag{9}$$

The integration in the last term can be rewritten as a convolution with a circle on the sphere surface,

$$\begin{aligned}
v_{cc}(\varphi_1, \varphi_2) &:= \int_{-\pi}^\pi d\varphi_3 \ f_c\Big(v_3(\varphi_1, \varphi_2, \varphi_3)\Big) \\
&= \int_0^\pi d\psi_1 \sin(\psi_1) \int_{-\pi}^\pi d\psi_2 \int_{-\pi}^\pi d\psi_3 \ f_c\Big(v_3(\psi_1, \psi_2, \psi_3)\Big) \\
&\qquad \cdot \delta\Big(\mathrm{dist}\left((\psi_1, \psi_2, \psi_3), (\varphi_1, \varphi_2, 0)\right) - r\Big) \ (10)
\end{aligned}$$

where "dist" is the distance between two points on a sphere surface and r the distance of the third kernel-point to the "north pole" of the sphere. This reduces the evaluation of the Haar integral to a pixel-wise multiplication and subsequent integration of two gray value data sets on the sphere surfaces. By defining $v_a = f_a\Big(v_1(\mathbf{0})\Big)$ and $v_b(\varphi_1, \varphi_2) = f_b\Big(v_2(\varphi_1, \varphi_2, 0)\Big)$, the Haar integral becomes

$$T = v_a \int_0^\pi d\varphi_1 \sin(\varphi_1) \int_{-\pi}^\pi d\varphi_2 \ v_b(\varphi_1, \varphi_2) \cdot v_{cc}(\varphi_1, \varphi_2) \tag{11}$$

Analogous to Fourier series in 2D, this can be approximated with spherical harmonics as basis functions. The coefficients are

$$W_{blm} = \int_0^\pi d\varphi_1 \sin(\varphi_1) \int_{-\pi}^\pi d\varphi_2 \ v_b(\varphi_1, \varphi_2) \ Y_m^{l\,*}(\varphi_1, \varphi_2) \tag{12}$$

(W_{cclm} if defined analogously) which allows to write the Haar integral as

$$\begin{aligned}
T = v_a \int_0^\pi d\varphi_1 \sin(\varphi_1) \int_{-\pi}^\pi d\varphi_2 \ &\left(\sum_{l_1=0}^\infty \sum_{m_1=-l_1}^{l_1} W_{bl_1 m_1} Y_{m_1}^{l_1}(\varphi_1, \varphi_2) \right) \\
\cdot &\left(\sum_{l_2=0}^\infty \sum_{m_2=-l_2}^{l_2} W_{ccl_2 m_2} Y_{m_2}^{l_2}(\varphi_1, \varphi_2) \right) \ (13)
\end{aligned}$$

Using the orthogonality relationships between the basis functions Y_m^l and the precondition, that our data is real-valued, allows to reduce this integral to a simple summation

$$T \sim v_a \sum_{l=0}^N \sum_{m=0}^l \Re\left(W_{blm} W_{cclm}^*\right) \tag{14}$$

where the series may be truncated after the N'th coefficient without violating the rotation invariance. The full operations are shown in the scheme in Fig. 4.

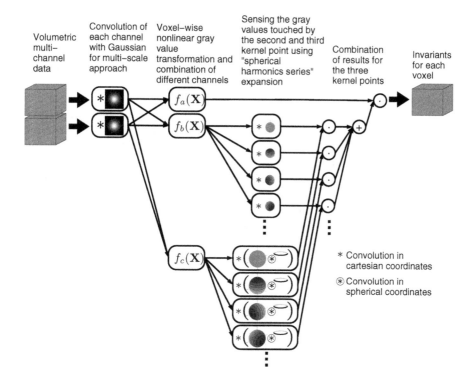

Fig. 4. Computation of three-point-kernel invariants $f(\mathbf{X}) = f_a(\mathbf{X}(0)) \cdot f_b(\mathbf{X}(q_2)) \cdot f_c(\mathbf{X}(q_3))$ on multi-channel volumetric data. For each kernel function this scheme simultaneously calculates the invariants for all voxels.

Voxel-Wise Classification After the extraction of multiple voxel-wise invariants, the feature vector for each voxel is classified with a SVM, that was trained on manually labeled data. A simple connected component analysis on these voxel-wise classification results is used to segment the different objects in the volume.

3 Experiments

Recognition of different cell cores on confocal recordings of the chicken embryo chorioallantoic membrane are promising and show good discrimination performance even for difficult constellations. For details see the accompanying paper [1] or technical report [2].

4 Conclusion and Outlook

Voxel-wise gray scale invariants allow to recognize objects in volumetric multi-channel data without prior segmentation. The presented fast computation algorithms allow to use them in real-world applications. Therefore they build an important step towards a reliable, generally applicable and easy to use pattern recognition system that can be adapted to new problems by a biologist just by an interactive point-and-click procedure.

The next obvious extension will be the use of the voxel-wise classification results (or probabilities) as additional synthetic data channels for additional feature extraction steps. This gives the biologist an easy possibility to integrate his previous knowledge just by decomposing the recognition task into single steps. E.g., in a first step he trains the system to recognize small low-level structures (like cell cores or cell walls) and then combines in the next steps these intermediate results for the recognition of higher level structures.

Present limitations of this framework are the need for manually selected kernel functions. Even though there are already some sets of kernel functions for several applications, our current research focusses on a completely automatic selection of the best kernel functions for a given training data set.

Another problem that cannot be solved with the current approach is segmentation of two neighboring objects of the same class, when there is no significant border between them, that can be trained and classified as an extra class or as background. One solution may be to train seeding points in the center of each object as an additional class. A seeded watershed on the classification results might then be used to crop the two objects at the correct position.

References

1. Fehr, J., Ronneberger, O., Kurz, H., Burkhardt, H.: Self-learning segmentation and classification of cell-nuclei in 3d volumetric data using voxel-wise gray scale invariants. In Kropatsch, W., Sablating, R., eds.: Pattern Recognition - Proc. of the 27th DAGM Symposium, Vienna, Austria, Springer, Berlin (2005)
2. Ronneberger, O., Fehr, J., Burkhardt, H.: Voxel-wise gray scale invariants for simultaneous segmentation and classification – theory and application to cell-nuclei in 3d volumetric data. Internal report 2/05, IIF-LMB, University Freiburg (2005)
3. Schulz-Mirbach, H.: Invariant features for gray scale images. In Sagerer, G., Posch, S., Kummert, F., eds.: 17. DAGM - Symposium "Mustererkennung", Bielefeld, Reihe Informatik aktuell, Springer (1995) 1–14
4. Burkhardt, H., Siggelkow, S.: Invariant features in pattern recognition – fundamentals and applications. In Kotropoulos, C., Pitas, I., eds.: Nonlinear Model-Based Image/Video Processing and Analysis, John Wiley & Sons (2001) 269–307
5. Ronneberger, O., Burkhardt, H., Schultz, E.: General-purpose Object Recognition in 3D Volume Data Sets using Gray-Scale Invariants – Classification of Airborne Pollen-Grains Recorded with a Confocal Laser Scanning Microscope. In: Proceedings of the International Conference on Pattern Recognition, Quebec, Canada (2002)
6. Vapnik, V.N.: The nature of statistical learning theory. Springer (1995)

Automatic Foreground Propagation in Image Sequences for 3D Reconstruction

Mario Sormann[1], Christopher Zach[1], Joachim Bauer[1], Konrad Karner[1], and Horst Bischof[2]

[1] VRVis Research Center, Inffeldgasse 16/II, A–8010 Graz, Austria
sormann@vrvis.at
[2] Institute for Computer Graphics and Vision, Graz University of Technology
bischof@icg.tu-graz.ac.at

Abstract. In this paper we introduce a novel method for automatic propagation of foreground objects in image sequences. Our method is based on a combination of the mean-shift operator with the well known intelligent scissors technique. It is effective due to the fact that the images are captured with high overlap, resulting in highly redundant scene information. The algorithm requires an initial segmentation of one image of the sequence as an input. In each consecutive image the segmentation of the previous image is taken as an initialization and the propagation procedure proceeds along four major steps. Each step refines the segmentation of the foreground object and the algorithm converges until all images of the sequence are processed. We demonstrate the effectiveness of our approach on several datasets.

1 Introduction

Efficient and interactive foreground/background separation of images have become a fundamental part of many applications in computer vision and 3D reconstruction [10]. Obviously manual segmentation is a tedious and time consuming process, especially when applied on a large number of images, as usual needed for a dense 3D reconstruction of complex objects. Therefore many segmentation algorithms have been developed recently [1,7].

This paper addresses the problem of automatic propagation of a foreground object in a complex environment for 3D reconstruction, whose background can not be removed in a simple way. The key idea of our approach is to take advantage of the high overlap of the images. Essentially we utilize redundant scene information to automate the segmentation procedure and propagate an initial segmentation through the image sequence. The goal of our approach is to achieve a fast, automatic and robust foreground segmentation. Moreover, our method minimizes the expenditure of time to achieve an accurate foreground segmentation. Its power can be derived from the fact that labelled image sequences simplify the correspondence problem dramatically and therefore, dense 3D reconstruction results of complex objects can be clearly improved.

W. Kropatsch, R. Sablatnig, and A. Hanbury (Eds.): DAGM 2005, LNCS 3663, pp. 93–100, 2005.

The main methods to accomplish the propagation procedure are the well known mean-shift technique and the intelligent scissors approach. Intelligent scissors, introduced by Mortenson and Barrett [7], also known as Live Wire or Magnetic Lasso, allows the user to define a precise contour with minimized human interaction, by roughly tracing the objects contour with the mouse. A user selects interactively optimal contour segments by immediately displaying the minimum cost path between the so called current seed point and the previous one, where the current seed point is represented as the position of the mouse cursor. The optimal path is computed via dynammic programming by applying Dijkstra's graph search algorithm [4] to find the optimal spanning tree. The second related technique is mean-shift analysis, which was originally invented by Fukunaga and Hostetler [5] and recently successfully applied to image segmentation and tracking by Comaniciu and Meer [2,3]. The mean-shift analysis approach is essentially defined as a gradient ascent search for maxima in a density function defined over a high dimensional feature space. The feature space include a combination of the spatial coordinates and all its associated attributes that are considered during the analysis. The main advantage of the mean-shift approach is based on the fact that it considers geometric coordinates and the associated attributes together at the same time.

The remainder of the paper is composed as follows. After a brief overview of our method we discuss the novel parts of the automatic foreground propagation algorithm in section 2. Experimental results and concluding remarks are presented in section 3 and 4.

2   The Automatic Foreground Propagation Algorithm

Our method is a multistage approach to separate a foreground object, for example a statue, from the background in all images of an image sequence. The algorithm requires as input an initial segmentation of one image, which can be obtained by utilizing intelligent scissors [7], GrabCut [9] or other interactive segmentation techniques. In this paper we focus on the propagation of this initial segmentation through all images of the sequence. The propagation task itself is mainly based on a region based matching algorithm. Therefore we segment the image into a certain number of regions. All these regions are classified into three different sets (foreground, background and uncertain regions), illustrated in Figure 2. The final contour can be extracted from these three sets. For dividing the image into regions we employ a mean-shift image segmentation proposed by Comaniciu and Meer [3].

Additionally, to improve the robustness of the propagation procedure, our algorithm requires the relative orientation of the images to be known. The orientation is determined based on methods described by Horn [6], and Nister [8] and provides both, an accurate orientation and a set of corresponding points.

The workflow of our proposed approach can be roughly seen as the composition of the following consecutive subtasks:

1. Extract an area of interest, which is called initial contour ring, with an inner boundary and an outer boundary.
2. Utilize information acquired from the contour ring and from the corresponding points to identify foreground and background regions.
3. Perform a region based matching algorithm based on mean-shift information to separate the remaining regions in the contour ring in foreground regions, background regions and uncertain regions.
4. Extract true contour segments from adjacent foreground and background regions and utilize intelligent scissors to close uncertain contour segments.

This procedure is repeated until all images of the sequence are processed.

2.1   Initial Contour Ring

The first step in our approach consists of extracting an initial contour ring, which represents an area of interest where we expect to find the true contour. Therefore, the initial contour of the first image is swept along the epipolar lines of the next image. For each position a support function can be formulated as

$$S_c = \sum_{i=1}^{n} g_i(x, y)$$

where $g_i(x, y)$ is the gradient of the contour i and n the number of sweep positions. The position with the highest support function is confirmed and represent the initial contour C_i in the next image. This initial contour C_i contains a set of continuous points and deviates in general slightly from the true contour of the current foreground object. Hence it is necessary to extract a contour ring where we expect to obtain the final contour of the object. Our next step includes an Euclidean distance transform on C_i to compute the contour ring. The scale of the distance transform, respectively the width of the contour ring can be directly derived from the relative orientation of the images, which guarantees that the true contour of the object is within the area of interest.

Such a contour ring, computed in the first step leads to several advantages. First, the following processing steps can concentrate on a smaller number of regions, which increases the performance of the algorithm dramatically. Moreover, the inner and outer boundary of the contour ring can be used to separate foreground regions and background regions with high confidence, which is described in more detail in the next section. Lastly, the reduction of the search area reduce the error propagation.

2.2   Prior Information

As previously outlined, different prior information is incorporated, to simplify the consecutive tasks and improve the robustness of our approach. We distinguish between two important types of information:

1. Information provided by the contour ring.
2. Information provided by the corresponding points.

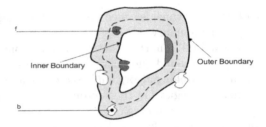

Fig. 1. Illustration of utilized information. Each region, which is adjacent to the inner boundary is labelled foreground (dark grey) and similar is applied for the outer boundary regions (white). Additionally **f** indicates a foreground correspondence, whereas **b** identifies a background correspondence, both acquired from the previous segmentation.

This information is used to label foreground regions and background regions with high confidence. In the former case the separation can be directly derived from the inner and outer boundary of the contour ring, which is illustrated in Figure 1.

Consequently we label all mean-shift regions which are directly connected to the inner boundary of the ring to foreground and those connected to outer boundary as background. A similar procedure is performed for the information which is provided by the corresponding points. Here we take advantage of the direct relationship of correspondences and simple separate foreground regions from background regions by comparing their location in the previous image against the already segmented contour.

2.3   Extended Region Matching

As mentioned before, we use the well known mean-shift algorithm to segment the image into a set of regions. So far we have already classified some of the mean-shift regions in our area of interest. For the remaining regions we perform an region based matching algorithm against the previous segmented image.

Basically our region matching algorithm works as follows: A matching between two regions r_i of the previous image and r_j of the current image is assigned with a similarity measure $S_{i,j}$. The similarity measure $S_{i,j}$ is based on the mean-shift parameters and the known relative orientation. Currently three different types of similarity measures are formulated. The first similarity measure S_{LUV} is represented by the LUV values of the mean-shift region, where L encodes luminance, and U and V encode color information. The other two similarity measures can be derived from the relative orientation. First, S_{Epi} encodes the distance of the epipolar line from region r_i to the center of gravity of region r_j. Second, the similarity measure S_{Corr} is composed from the distance of the nearest corresponding point to region r_i respectively to region r_j. The final distance function for two regions is formulated as:

$$d(r_i, r_j) = \omega_1 * S_{LUV} + \omega_2 * S_{Epi} + \omega_3 * S_{Corr}$$

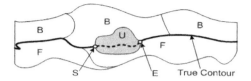

Fig. 2. Set of regions including foreground regions (F), background regions (B) and uncertain regions (U) and the highlighted true contour. Furthermore an illustration of start point (S) and end point (E) to automatically apply intelligent scissors.

where $\omega_1...\omega_3$ are weights to control the influence of the different similarity measures. We can distinguish between foreground regions, background regions and uncertain regions, by evaluating the introduced distance function for each remaining region against a user defined threshold. Uncertain regions are regions, which can be classified neither to foreground nor to background. In this case a further processing is necessary.

2.4 Foreground Extraction

The aim is to extract the final foreground object from previously labelled mean-shift regions. Obviously, the true contour lies between adjacent foreground regions and background regions or intersects an uncertain region. In the former case the final contour can be extracted with simple neighbourhood checks, whereas in the latter case the intelligent scissors algorithm is applied. Figure 2 illustrates the extraction of needed start and end points to initiate the intelligent scissors procedure.

Finally all obtained contour segments are combined to a closed continuous contour of the foreground object.

3 Experimental Results

All presented image sequences were taken with a calibrated high quality digital consumer camera with a 11.4 megapixels CMOS sensor. In a first evaluation we used an image sequence consisting of 12 images of a garden gnome which is approximately 23cm tall with a diameter of 10cm. Figure 3 shows the garden gnome with the overlayed segmentation, whereas Figure 4 demonstrates all intermediate results of our method.

Figure 5 illustrates a more complex dataset consisting of 12 images showing a statue of St. Barbara. The statue is 55cm tall with a diameter of 13cm at the pedestal. As shown in Figure 5, automatic approaches will sometimes lead to incorrect results. In our method, if the segmentation result is not satisfactory, a user has the possibility to correct a miss-segmentation, by manual assignment of the critical mean-shift regions or by an assisted intelligent scissors algorithm.

Finally, Figure 6 demonstrates the usability of our approach on a real-world dataset, which depicts a statue on the roof of the Austrian National Library.

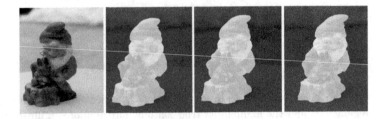

Fig. 3. Illustration of five images with overlayed segmentation of the garden gnome image sequence. The garden gnome is approximately 23cm tall with a diameter of 10cm. The last image illustrates the obtained 3D reconstruction.

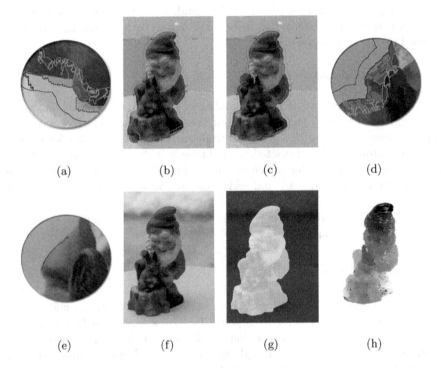

(a)   (b)   (c)   (d)

(e)   (f)   (g)   (h)

Fig. 4. Intermediate results of the automatic foreground propagation algorithm illustrating one image of the garden gnome image sequence. **(a)** Close-up from **(b)** showing labelled foreground (green) and background (blue) regions in the contour ring after incorporating prior information. **(d)** Close-up from **(c)** illustrating labelled foreground (green), background (blue) and uncertain regions (red) after applying extended region matching. **(e)** Close-up from **(f)** showing start and end point (red crosses) of intelligent scissors and the obtained true contour (blue) of a uncertain region. **(g)** Garden gnome image with the final segmentation overlayed. **(h)** Illustration of the achieved 3D reconstruction represented as depth map.

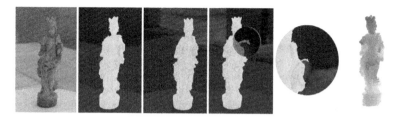

Fig. 5. Four images showing a statue of St. Barbara and achieved segmentation. The Barbara statue is approximately 55cm tall with a diameter of 13cm. One image of the sequence illustrates a small miss-segmentation, which can be corrected by human assisted intelligent scissors. The last images consists of our obtained 3D reconstruction result.

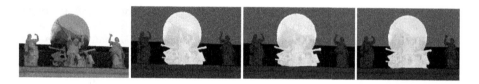

Fig. 6. Four images of a statue on the roof of the Austrian National Library and obtained propagation results. The first image illustrates the achieved mean-shift segmentation.

4 Conclusion and Future Work

We have developed an automatic foreground propagation method that performs well in terms of accuracy, robustness and efficiency. Our approach takes advantage of the redundant scene information, which is typically provided from image sequences for 3D reconstruction. The primary purpose of our method is the improvement of our 3D reconstruction results. Moreover, the tedious process of an interactive segmentation of all images is dramatically reduced, thus our method simply requires one initial segmentation.

Though the results are very promising, there are several improvements that can be made to our approach. In order to achieve more accurate results we are currently working on extending the similarity measures introduced by extended region matching. Another consideration is to utilize active contour models to extract foreground objects with sub-pixel accuracy.

Acknowledgements

This work is partly funded by the VRVis Research Center, Graz and Vienna/ Austria (http://www.vrvis.at) and the Vienna Science and Technology Fund (WWTF).

References

1. BOYKOV, Y., AND JOLLY, M. P. Interactive graph cuts for optimal boundary and region segmentation of objects in n-d images. In *International Conference of Computer Vision* (Vancouver, Canada, July 2001), vol. 1, pp. 105–112.

2. COMANICIU, D., AND MEER, P. Mean shift analysis and applications. In *International Conference of Computer Vision* (Corfu, Greece, June 1999), vol. 2, pp. 1197–1203.

3. COMANICIU, D., AND MEER, P. Mean shift: A robust approach toward feature space analysis. *IEEE Transactions on Pattern Analysis and Machine Intelligence 24*, 5 (May 2002), 603–619.

4. DIJKSTRA, E. W. A note on two problems in connexion with graphs. In *Numerische Mathematik*, vol. 1. Mathematical Centre, Amsterdam, The Netherlands, 1959, pp. 269–271.

5. FUKUNAGA, K., AND HOSTETLER, L. The estimation of the gradient of a density function, with applications in pattern recognition. *IEEE Transactions on Information Theory 21*, 1 (January 1975), 32–40.

6. HORN, B. Relative orientation. *International Journal of Computer Vision 4*, 1 (January 1990), 59–78.

7. MORTENSON, E. N., AND BARRETT, W. Intelligent scissors for image composition. *Graphical Models and Image Processing 60*, 5 (September 1998), 349–384.

8. NISTER, D. An efficient solution to the five-point relative pose problem. *IEEE Transactions on Pattern Analysis and Machine Intelligence 26*, 6 (June 2004), 756–777.

9. ROTHER, C., KOLMOGOROV, V., AND BLAKE, A. Grabcut - interactive foreground extraction using iterated graph cuts. *ACM Transactions on Graphics 23*, 3 (August 2004), 309–314.

10. ZIEGLER, R., MATUSIK, W., PFISTER, H., AND MCMILLAN, L. 3d reconstruction using labeled image regions. In *Eurographics/ACM SIGGRAPH symposium on Geometry processing* (Granada, Spain, September 2003), vol. 1, pp. 248–259.

Agglomerative Grouping of Observations by Bounding Entropy Variation

Christian Beder

Institute for Photogrammetry,
Bonn University, Germany
beder@ipb.uni-bonn.de

Abstract. An information theoretic framework for grouping observations is proposed. The entropy change incurred by new observations is analyzed using the Kalman filter update equations. It is found, that the entropy variation is caused by a positive similarity term and a negative proximity term. Bounding the similarity term in the spirit of the minimum description length principle and the proximity term in the spirit of maximum entropy inference a robust and efficient grouping procedure is devised. Some of its properties are demonstrated for the exemplary task of edgel grouping.

1 Introduction

Grouping observations has been identified as an important issue in many computer vision tasks and has been studied by many researchers (cf. [9], [10], [1], [11]). In this context the Gestalt laws of psychology have received much attention and the criterion of Prägnanz is considered extremely useful (cf. [13]). Its close connection to the information theoretic minimum description length criterion (cf. [14]) has been pointed out by [10] and [13].

In [12] the grouping is established based on local measures specially tailored for the task of edgel grouping. A similar approach is made in [3], but there the probability distributions of the observations are explicitly modeled and used to guide the grouping. An information theoretic approach is made in [13] by phrasing the various Gestalt principles in terms of energy functions and minimizing the overall free energy. Also the tensor voting approach of [5], [6] or [11] uses a global consistency measure based on local measures of similarity and proximity.

The problem with the minimum description length criterion of [14] in the context of an agglomerative grouping procedure is, that locally minimizing entropy contradicts the principle of maximum entropy inference (cf. [7]), since greedily grouping distant observations leads to the greatest entropy reduction. This effect is also known from robust statistics as leverage points (cf. [8]). To cope with this problem, the Kalman filter update equations (cf. [4]) will be reviewed, and the entropy change incurred by grouping a new observation is analyzed. It is found, that this entropy variation is caused by a positive observation dependent term, that measures similarity and a negative design dependent term, that measures proximity. A grouping algorithm based on bounding both influences on the

W. Kropatsch, R. Sablatnig, and A. Hanbury (Eds.): DAGM 2005, LNCS 3663, pp. 101–108, 2005.
© Springer-Verlag Berlin Heidelberg 2005

entropy variation is proposed, so that entropy reduction is caused by the observations in the spirit of minimum description length but the reduction through decisions by the algorithm is bounded from below in the spirit of maximum entropy inference. The algorithm and some of its properties will be demonstrated for the exemplary task of edgel grouping.

2   The Kalman Filter

Having two sets of independent observations l_1 and l_2 of size N_1 and N_2 with known covariance matrices C_{11} and C_{22} and a model depending on the parameter vector p of size U given by the two functions

$$g_1(p) = l_1 \quad \text{and} \quad g_2(p) = l_2$$

with the Jacobians

$$\frac{\partial g_1}{\partial p} = A_1 \quad \text{and} \quad \frac{\partial g_2}{\partial p} = A_2$$

the best linear unbiased estimation of the parameters $\hat{p}^{(-)}$ is found for the first set of observations using the expected covariance matrix (cf. [8])

$$C_{\hat{p}\hat{p}}^{(-)} = (A_1^T C_{11}^{-1} A_1)^{-1} \tag{1}$$

to be

$$\hat{p}^{(-)} = C_{\hat{p}\hat{p}}^{(-)} A_1^T C_{11}^{-1} l_1 \tag{2}$$

The redundancy of the estimation is given by

$$R_1 = N_1 - U \tag{3}$$

and in case $R_1 > 0$, using the residuals

$$\hat{v}_1 = A_1 \hat{p}^{(-)} - l_1$$

and their weighted squared sum

$$\Omega^{2(-)} = \hat{v}_1^T C_{11}^{-1} \hat{v}_1 \tag{4}$$

the covariance matrix of the estimated parameters can be obtained as

$$\hat{C}_{\hat{p}\hat{p}^{(-)}} = \frac{\Omega^{2(-)}}{R_1} C_{\hat{p}\hat{p}}^{(-)}$$

Thereafter it is possible to updated the estimation sequentially including the second set of observations. This is well known as Kalman filtering (cf. [4]) and using the prediction error and its covariance matrix

$$\hat{v}_2 = A_2 \hat{p}^{(-)} - l_2 \qquad\qquad C_{\hat{v}_2 \hat{v}_2} = C_{22} + A_2 C_{\hat{p}\hat{p}}^{(-)} A_2^T$$

and the Kalman filter gain matrix

$$F = C_{\hat{p}\hat{p}}^{(-)} A_2^T C_{\hat{v}_2 \hat{v}_2}^{-1} \tag{5}$$

the Kalman filter update equations are obtained as

$$C_{\hat{p}\hat{p}}^{(+)} = C_{\hat{p}\hat{p}}^{(-)} - FA_2 C_{\hat{p}\hat{p}}^{(-)} \quad (6) \qquad\qquad \Omega^{2(+)} = \Omega^{2(-)} + \Delta\Omega^2 \quad (9)$$

$$\hat{p}^{(+)} = \hat{p}^{(-)} + F\hat{v}_2 \quad (7) \qquad\qquad \Delta R = N_2 \quad (10)$$

$$\Delta\Omega^2 = \hat{v}_2^T C_{\hat{v}_2 \hat{v}_2}^{-1} \hat{v}_2 \quad (8) \qquad\qquad R_2 = R_1 + \Delta R \quad (11)$$

Finally the estimated covariance matrix of the parameters may be recomputed from the residuals using

$$\hat{C}_{\hat{p}\hat{p}}^{(+)} = \frac{\Omega^{2(+)}}{R_2} C_{\hat{p}\hat{p}}^{(+)}$$

3 Estimated Entropy Variation

The Kalman filter was used to sequentially estimate the first two moments $\hat{p}$ and $\hat{C}_{\hat{p}\hat{p}}$ of the distribution of the parameters. Knowing only those two moments, the maximum possible entropy of the estimation is (cf. [2])

$$\hat{h}(\hat{p}) = \frac{1}{2} \log \left| 2\pi e \hat{C}_{\hat{p}\hat{p}} \right| = \frac{1}{2} \log \left| 2\pi e \frac{\Omega^2}{R} C_{\hat{p}\hat{p}} \right|$$

$$= \frac{U}{2} \log \left(2\pi e \frac{\Omega^2}{R} \right) + \frac{1}{2} \log \left| C_{\hat{p}\hat{p}} \right|$$

Note that only the first term is caused by the randomness of the observations and the second term depends only on the geometry of the design of the estimation. Applying the results from Kalman filtering, the estimated entropy change by including the second set of observations is in case, that $R_1 > 0$

$$\Delta h = \hat{h}(\hat{p}^{(+)}) - \hat{h}(\hat{p}^{(-)}) = \frac{1}{2} \log \left| 2\pi e \hat{C}_{\hat{p}\hat{p}}^{(+)} \right| - \frac{1}{2} \log \left| 2\pi e \hat{C}_{\hat{p}\hat{p}}^{(-)} \right|$$

$$= \frac{U}{2} \log \frac{1 + \frac{\Delta\Omega^2}{\Omega^{2(-)}}}{1 + \frac{\Delta R}{R_1}} + \frac{1}{2} \log \frac{\left| C_{\hat{p}\hat{p}}^{(-)} - FA_2 C_{\hat{p}\hat{p}}^{(-)} \right|}{\left| C_{\hat{p}\hat{p}}^{(-)} \right|}$$

$$= \underbrace{\frac{U}{2} \log \frac{1 + \frac{\Delta\Omega^2}{\Omega^{2(-)}}}{1 + \frac{\Delta R}{R_1}}}_{\Delta h_o} + \underbrace{\frac{1}{2} \log |I - FA_2|}_{\Delta h_d} \quad (12)$$

Again the entropy change is constituted from a positive term Δh_o, that refelcts the increase in randomness due to the new observation, and a second negative term Δh_d, that reflects the decrease in randomness due to the decision of including the new observation into the estimation.

The first term Δh_o is closely related to the well known, and in case of Normal distributed observations Fisher distributed, test statistic

$$T = \frac{\frac{\Delta\Omega^2}{\Omega^{2(-)}}}{\frac{\Delta R}{R_1}} \propto \mathcal{F}(\Delta R, R_1)$$

that is frequently used to decide, if the second observation fits the model defined by the first. Given a significance level α, a threshold T_α is derived from the inverse of the Fisher distribution and the decision is made by comparing it with the test statistic T. The test is not rejected, if $T < T_\alpha$ or equivalent

$$\Delta h_o < \frac{U}{2} \log \left(T_\alpha \left(1 - \frac{1}{1+\frac{\Delta R}{R_1}} \right) + \frac{1}{1+\frac{\Delta R}{R_1}} \right) =: L_o \tag{13}$$

If $R_1 = 0$, the variance factor cannot be estimated from the observations and must therefore assumed to be known. Thus the entropy change incurred by including the new observation into the observation in case of $R_1 = 0$ is

$$\Delta h = \hat{h}(\hat{\boldsymbol{p}}^{(+)}) - h(\hat{\boldsymbol{p}}^{(-)}) = \frac{1}{2} \log \left| 2\pi e \hat{\boldsymbol{C}}_{\hat{\boldsymbol{p}}\hat{\boldsymbol{p}}}^{(+)} \right| - \frac{1}{2} \log \left| 2\pi e \boldsymbol{C}_{\hat{\boldsymbol{p}}\hat{\boldsymbol{p}}}^{(-)} \right|$$
$$= \underbrace{\frac{U}{2} \log \left(2\pi e \frac{\Delta \Omega^2}{\Delta R} \right)}_{\Delta h_o} + \underbrace{\frac{1}{2} \log |\boldsymbol{I} - \boldsymbol{F}\boldsymbol{A}_2|}_{\Delta h_d} \tag{14}$$

Again the first term Δh_o is related to a well known, and in case of Normal distributed observations χ^2-distributed, test statistic for the case, that the variance factor is known

$$T' = \frac{\Delta \Omega^2}{\Delta R} \propto \chi^2(\Delta R)$$

so that again a T'_α is derived from the inverse of the χ^2-distribution, and the hypothesis is not rejected, if

$$\Delta h_o < \frac{U}{2} \log \left(2\pi e T'_\alpha \right) =: L_o \tag{15}$$

This must be used to decide, if the new observation fits the model defined by the previous observation in case that $R_1 = 0$.

The above criterion measures the similarity between the new observation and the model estimated from the previous observations. The key idea here is, that also the entropy decrease Δh_d resulting from any decision made by the algorithm should be bounded, yielding a proximity criterion for the observations. To find this bound, the history of previous design matrices $\boldsymbol{A}_j$ and covariance matrices $\boldsymbol{C}_{jj}$ is analyzed, because the geometry of the previous observations defines the border, inside which the new observations may be encountered. Allowing new observations to be a bit outside the range of the previous observations by introducing a proximity factor $\lambda > 1$, the bound is found to be

$$\Delta h_d > \lambda \min_j \frac{1}{2} \log \left| \boldsymbol{I} - (\boldsymbol{C}_{\hat{\boldsymbol{p}}\hat{\boldsymbol{p}}}^{(-)} \boldsymbol{A}_j^T (\boldsymbol{C}_{jj} + \boldsymbol{A}_j \boldsymbol{C}_{\hat{\boldsymbol{p}}\hat{\boldsymbol{p}}}^{(-)} \boldsymbol{A}_j^T)^{-1} \boldsymbol{A}_j \right| =: L_d \tag{16}$$

4   The Grouping Algorithm

In the preceding section a similarity and a proximity criterion based on the information increase of including a new set of observations into an estimation were derived. Those two criteria could be used to decide, if a new set of observations could be grouped with an existing set of observations. Furthermore the Kalman filter update equations yield an efficient method to aggregate observations sequentially, thus enabling a very efficient agglomerative grouping strategy.

The greedy method proposed here starts from an arbitrary observation and sequentially aggregates new observations. In order to decide, which new observation is to be aggregated next, first the threshold on the design dependent entropy loss L_d is computed from all observations already aggregated. Then for every possible observation the observation dependent entropy increase Δh_o and the design dependent entropy loss $-\Delta h_d$ are computed and compared to the two thresholds. Among the qualifying observations, the grouping decision, that destroys fewest information, is chosen in the spirit of maximum entropy inference, i.e. the candidate observation is aggregated, for which the design dependent entropy loss $-\Delta h_d$ is minimal. This aggregation process is continued, until no more observations qualify according to the two criteria. Note that the criteria are efficiently computable due to the Kalman filter update equations. Finally the aggregated observations are removed and the whole process is repeated until all groups are found.

The complete grouping procedure is summarized in algorithm 1..

Algorithm 1. Grouping Algorithm

---

let the observations be $\mathcal{Y} = \{(l_i, C_{ii})\}$
while $\mathcal{Y} \neq \emptyset$ **do**
   pick initial $l_1 \in \mathcal{Y}$, compute the Jacobian A_1 of g_1
   start the group $\mathcal{G} = \{l_1\}$
   compute initial $C_{\hat{p}\hat{p}}^{(-)}$, $\hat{p}^{(-)}$, $\Omega^{2(-)}$ and R_1 according to (1), (2), (4) and (3)
   repeat
      compute the threshold L_d from $\mathcal{G}$ according to (16)
      determine the threshold L_o depending on R_1 according to (13) or (15)
      initialize the candidate set $\mathcal{C} = \emptyset$
      for all $l_i \in \mathcal{Y} \backslash \mathcal{G}$ **do**
         compute the Jacobian A_i of g_i at $\hat{p}^{(-)}$
         compute $F^{(i)}$, $\Delta\Omega^{2(i)}$ and $\Delta R^{(i)}$ for l_i according to (5), (8) and (10)
         compute $\Delta h_o{}^{(i)}$ depending on R_1 according to (12) or (14)
         compute $\Delta h_d{}^{(i)}$ according to (12)
         if $\Delta h_o{}^{(i)} < L_o \wedge \Delta h_d{}^{(i)} > L_d$ **then**
            include the candidate $\mathcal{C} = \mathcal{C} \cup \{l_i\}$
         end if
      end for
      pick $l_c \in \mathcal{C}$ with maximum $\Delta h_d{}^{(c)}$
      include it into the group $\mathcal{G} = \mathcal{G} \cup \{l_c\}$
      update $C_{\hat{p}\hat{p}}^{(-)}$, $\hat{p}^{(-)}$, $\Omega^{2(-)}$ and R_1 for l_c according to (6), (7), (9) and (11)
   until $\mathcal{C} = \emptyset$
   output group $\mathcal{G}$
   $\mathcal{Y} = \mathcal{Y} \backslash \mathcal{G}$
end while

---

5   Example: Edgel Grouping

The simple problem of grouping edgels in images to straight lines has been studied extensively and will be used here to demonstrate some properties of the presented grouping algorithm.

Using the measured image coordinates (r_i, c_i) together with the image gradients (n_{r_i}, n_{c_i}) the simple linear line model

$$\begin{pmatrix} c_i & 1 \\ 1 & 0 \end{pmatrix} \begin{pmatrix} m \\ b \end{pmatrix} = \begin{pmatrix} r_i \\ \frac{n_{r_i}}{n_{c_i}} \end{pmatrix}$$

can be used. Note that the coordinate system can be rotated for each group, so that the model can easily deal with vertical lines.

The 1000×1000 pixel patch depicted on the left hand side of figure 1 was cut out of an aerial image. The edge pixels were extracted using the Canny edge detector and for each edge pixel the gradient was computed using the Sobel operator. The resulting set of edgels and their gradients are shown on the right hand side of figure 1.

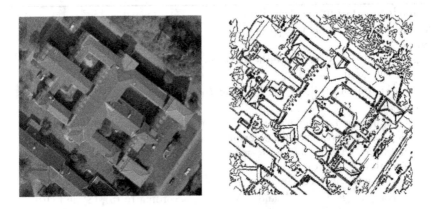

Fig. 1. 1000×1000 pixel patch cut out of an aerial image and the extracted edgels

The edgels were aggregated using the proposed grouping algorithm and two exemplary groups are shown in figure 2. Note that the two groups were not linked together, although they are on the same line and would be joined, if only the observation dependent similarity criterion had been used. Since no intermediate observation points are present, the proximity criterion imposed by the design of the estimation prevented further growth of the group.

The proximity factor was chosen as $\lambda = 1.5$, i.e. the grouping algorithm was allowed to decrease the entropy by $\frac{3}{2}$ the maximum number of bits, that any edgel lying between the other edgels would do. The resulting candidate sets of new observations for two stages of aggregation of the same exemplary group are shown in figure 3. The black dots are the qualifying observations according to the proximity criterion, the black crosses are the qualifying observations according to

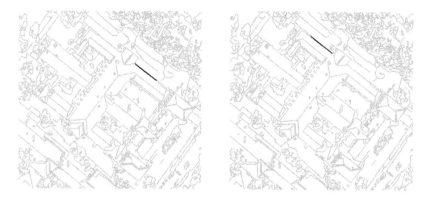

Fig. 2. Two exemplary groups of edgels.

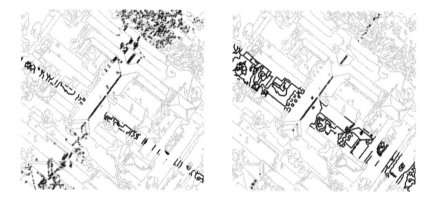

Fig. 3. Candidate sets of new observations at two stages of the same exemplary group. The black dots are the qualifying observations according to the proximity criterion, the black crosses according to the similarity criterion and the black asterisks are the intersection of both criteria.

the similarity criterion and the black asterisks at the intersection of both are the qualifying observations for the grouping. It can also be seen, that the two criteria are orthogonal. On the left hand side of figure 3 an early stage of aggregation is shown. The model line is still very uncertain especially far away from the few defining edgels. On the other hand, the range of qualifying observations on the line imposed by the proximity criterion is very narrow so that this effect is compensated and does not affect the grouping.

On the right hand side of figure 3 a latter stage of aggregation is shown. Observe that the model line has now become very narrow, reflecting the fact, that now many aggregated observations contribute to the estimation. The range of qualifying observations along the line has become wider, so that new observations can be collected.

6   Summary and Conclusions

An information theoretic framework for the grouping of observations was proposed. By analyzing the entropy change incurred by including a new observation into an estimation a similarity criterion, that minimizes description length, and a proximity criterion, that enforces maximum entropy decisions, was derived. Based on those two criteria a grouping algorithm was proposed, that, using the efficient Kalman filter update equations, greedily reduces description length and at the same time ensures robustness through maximum entropy inference.

The applicability of the presented method goes far beyond the presented edgel grouping example. Whenever similarity is defined by a known parametric object model, the presented method may be applied. This is the case for many important geometric grouping problems, like for example aggregating 3D-surface patches obtained from dense stereo matching or laser scanning to planes or conics, and will be subject to further investigation.

References

1. Kim L. Boyer and Sudeep Sarkar. Perceptual organization in computer vision: status, challenges, and potential. *Comput. Vis. Image Underst.*, 76(1):1–5, 1999.
2. T.M. Cover and J.A. Thomas. *Elements of Information Theory.* Wiley, 1991.
3. Daniel Crevier. A probabilistic method for extracting chains of collinear segments. *CVIU*, 76(1):36–53, 1999.
4. Wolfgang Förstner and Bernhard Wrobel. Mathematical concepts in photogrammetry. In J.C.McGlone, E.M.Mikhail, and J.Bethel, editors, *Manual of Photogrammetry.* ASPRS, 2004.
5. Gideon Guy and Gérard Medioni. Inferring global perceptual contours from local features. *Int. J. Comput. Vision*, 20(1-2):113–133, 1996.
6. Gideon Guy and Gérard G. Medioni. Inference of surfaces, 3d curves, and junctions from sparse, noisy, 3d data. *IEEE Trans. Pattern Anal. Mach. Intell.*, 19(11):1265–1277, 1997.
7. E.T. Jaynes. On the rationale of maximum entropy methods. *Proc. IEEE*, 70:939–952, 1982.
8. K.-R. Koch. *Parameter estimation and hypothesis testing in linear models.* Springer, 1988.
9. David G. Lowe. *Perceptual Organization and Visual Recognition.* Kluwer Academic Publishers, 1985.
10. J.D. McCafferty. *Human And Machine Vision.* Ellis Horwood, 1990.
11. Gerard Medioni, Chi-Keung Tang, and Mi-Suen Lee. *A Computational Framework for Segmentation and Grouping.* Elsevier, 2000.
12. Rakesh Mohan and Ramakant Nevatia. Perceptual organization for scene segmentation and description. *IEEE Trans. Pattern Anal. Mach. Intell.*, 14(6):616–635, 1992.
13. Björn Ommer and Joachim M. Buhmann. A compositionality architecture for perceptual feature grouping. In *Energy Minimization Methods in Computer Vision and Pattern Recognition*, number 2683 in LNCS, pages 275–290. Springer, 2003.
14. Jorma Rissanen. Minimum-Description-Length Principle. In S.Kotz and N.L.Johnson, editors, *Encyclopedia of Statistical Science*, volume 5, pages 523–527. John Wiley & Sons, 1985.

Three-Dimensional Shape Knowledge for Joint Image Segmentation and Pose Estimation *

Thomas Brox[1], Bodo Rosenhahn[2], and Joachim Weickert[1]

[1] Mathematical Image Analysis Group, Faculty of Mathematics and Computer Science, Saarland University, Building 27, 66041 Saarbrücken, Germany
{brox, weickert}@mia.uni-saarland.de

[2] Centre for Imaging Technology and Robotics (CITR), University of Auckland, New Zealand
bros028@cs.auckland.ac.nz

Abstract. This paper presents the integration of 3D shape knowledge into a variational model for level set based image segmentation and tracking. Having a 3D surface model of an object that is visible in the image of a calibrated camera, the object contour stemming from the segmentation is applied to estimate the 3D pose parameters, whereas the object model projected to the image plane helps in a top-down manner to improve the extraction of the contour and the region statistics. The present approach clearly states all model assumptions in a single energy functional. This keeps the model manageable and allows further extensions for the future. While common alternative segmentation approaches that integrate 2D shape knowledge face the problem that an object can look very different from various viewpoints, a 3D free form model ensures that for each view the model can perfectly fit the data in the image. Moreover, one solves the higher level problem of determining the object pose including its distance to the camera. Experiments demonstrate the performance of the method.

1 Introduction

Pose estimation and image segmentation are principal problems in computer and robot vision. The task of 2D-3D pose estimation is to estimate a rigid motion which fits a 3D object model to 2D image data [8]. In this context it is crucial which features are used for the object model as they must be fit to corresponding features in the image to determine the pose. One such feature is the object surface with the object silhouette as its 2D counterpart in the image. The task of pose estimation is to find a rigid motion that minimizes the error between the projected object surface and the region encircled by the contour in the image. As the common role of image segmentation is exactly to extract the contour of objects in the image, this shows the possible connection between 2D-3D pose estimation and image segmentation.

Image segmentation can become very difficult, as the image gray value or color alone are rarely good indicators for object boundaries due to noise, texture, shading, occlusion, or simply because the color of two objects is nearly the same. Recent segmentation approaches therefore integrate 2D shape information in order to employ additional

---

* We gratefully acknowledge funding by the DFG projects We2602/1-1, We2602/1-2, Ro2497/1-1, and Ro2497/1-2.

W. Kropatsch, R. Sablatnig, and A. Hanbury (Eds.): DAGM 2005, LNCS 3663, pp. 109–116, 2005.
© Springer-Verlag Berlin Heidelberg 2005

constraints that force the contour to more desirable solutions. An early example can be found in [9] where shape information influences the evolution of an active contour model. This basic concept has been extended and modified in [16,6,13,5] and provides a good framework for the sound integration of 2D shape prior in segmentation processes. However, the real world has three spatial dimensions. This fact is responsible for an inherent shortcoming of 2D shape models: they cannot exactly describe the image of an object from arbitrary views. This problem is solved when the 2D shape model is replaced by a 3D surface model, as is suggested in the present paper.

For the integration of 3D shape information, the object model has to be projected onto the image plane, and for this its pose in the scene has to be known. We realize again the connection between image segmentation and pose estimation, yet now the connection points into the other direction: a pose estimate is needed in order to integrate the surface model. Note that a pose estimation problem appears in the case of 2D shape knowledge as well. Also there, it is necessary to estimate the translation, rotation, and scaling of the shape knowledge, before it can constrain the contour in the image. This is either achieved by explicit estimation of the pose parameters [16], or by an appropriate normalization of the shapes [5]. Extensions to perspective transformations of 2D shapes have recently been proposed in [13]. However, all these approaches only aim on the use of shape knowledge in order to yield improved segmentations. The 2D pose estimates do not allow a location of the object in the real 3D world but only in the 2D projection of this world. In contrast, the 2D-3D pose estimation employed in our model allows the exact location of the object in the scene.

We now have a classical chicken-and-egg problem: a contour is needed for pose estimation, and the pose estimates are necessary to integrate the shape prior into the segmentation that determines the contour. Such situations are in general best handled by solving both problems simultaneously. We achieve this by formulating an energy minimization problem that contains both the image contour and the pose parameters as unknowns. The minimization is done by alternating both image segmentation and pose estimation in an iterative manner, see Fig. 1. For the experiments we concentrate on the segmentation and pose estimation of a rigid object. It is demonstrated that the model

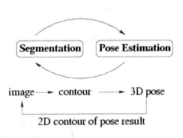

Fig. 1. Basic idea: Iterating segmentation and pose estimation. The projected pose result is used as a-priori knowledge for segmentation.

yields promising results both for the contour and the 3D pose parameters even in complex scenarios.

Paper Organization. The next section contains a brief review of the level set based image segmentation model used in our approach. Section 3, on the other side, explains the concept of 2D-3D pose estimation. In Section 4 we then introduce our idea to combine image segmentation and 3D pose estimation in a joint energy functional. Experiments in Section 5 show the performance of the proposed technique. The paper is concluded by a brief summary in Section 6.

2   Image Segmentation

2.1   Level Set Formulation

Our approach is based on image segmentation with level sets [7,11,3,12,4], in particular on the method described in [1]. A level set function $\Phi \in \Omega \mapsto \mathbb{R}$ splits the image domain Ω into two regions Ω_1 and Ω_2, with $\Phi(x) > 0$ if $x \in \Omega_1$ and $\Phi(x) < 0$ if $x \in \Omega_2$. The zero-level line thus marks the boundary between both regions.

The segmentation should maximize the total a-posteriori probability given the probability densities p_1 and p_2 of Ω_1 and Ω_2, i.e., pixels are assigned to the most probable region according to the Bayes rule. Further on, the boundary between both regions should be as small as possible. This can be expressed by the following energy functional:

$$E(\Phi) = - \int_\Omega \left(H(\Phi) \log p_1 + (1 - H(\Phi)) \log p_2 \right) dx + \nu \int_\Omega |\nabla H(\Phi)| \, dx \qquad (1)$$

where $\nu > 0$ is a weighting parameter and $H(s)$ is a regularized Heaviside function with $\lim_{s \to -\infty} H(s) = 0$, $\lim_{s \to \infty} H(s) = 1$, and $H(0) = 0.5$ (e.g. the error function). It indicates to which region a pixel belongs. Minimization with respect to the region boundary can be performed according to the gradient descent equation

$$\partial_t \Phi = H'(\Phi) \left(\log \frac{p_1}{p_2} + \nu \operatorname{div} \left(\frac{\nabla \Phi}{|\nabla \Phi|} \right) \right) \qquad (2)$$

where $H'(s)$ is the derivative of $H(s)$ with respect to its argument. The contour converges to a minimum for the numerical evolution parameter $t \to \infty$.

2.2   Region Statistics

For the curve evolution, still the probability densities p_1 and p_2 have to be determined. Our segmentation is driven by the texture feature space proposed in [2] which yields $M = 5$ feature channels I_j for gray scale images, and $M = 7$ channels if color is available. We assume that the probability densities of the feature channels are independent, thus $p_i = \prod_{j=1}^M p_{ij}(I_j)$.

The probability densities p_{ij} are estimated according to the *expectation-maximization principle*. Having the level set function initialized with some partitioning, the probability densities can be approximated by a Gaussian density estimate:

$$p_{ij}(s, x) \propto \frac{1}{\sqrt{2\pi}\sigma_{ij}(x)} \exp \left(\frac{(s - \mu_{ij}(x))^2}{2\sigma_{ij}(x)^2} \right). \qquad (3)$$

Note that these are *local* estimates of the probability densities. This can be useful particularly in complicated scenes where differences between regions are only locally visible. Consequently, the parameters $\mu_{ij}(x)$ and $\sigma_{ij}(x)$ are computed in a local neighborhood K_ρ of x by:

$$\mu_{ij}(x) = \frac{\int_{\Omega_i} K_\rho(\zeta - x) I_j(\zeta) \, d\zeta}{\int_{\Omega_i} K_\rho(\zeta - x) \, d\zeta} \qquad \sigma_{ij}(x) = \frac{\int_{\Omega_i} K_\rho(\zeta - x)(I_j(\zeta) - \mu_{ij}(x))^2 \, d\zeta}{\int_{\Omega_i} K_\rho(\zeta - x) \, d\zeta}. \qquad (4)$$

The densities are used for the level set evolution according to (2), leading to a further update of the probability densities, and so on. This iterative process converges to a local minimum, showing that the initialization matters. In order to attenuate this dependency on the initialization, it is recommendable to apply a coarse-to-fine strategy. Starting with a down-sampled image, there are less local minima, so the segmentation is more robust. The resulting segmentation can then be used as initialization for a finer scale, until the original segmentation problem is solved.

3   2D-3D Pose Estimation

2D-3D pose estimation [8] means to estimate a rigid body motion which maps a 3D surface model to an image of a calibrated camera. The scenario is visualized in Fig. 2.

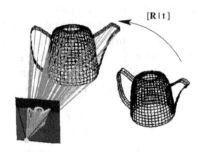

[R|t]

The core algorithm is based on a point-based constraint equation, which has been derived in the language of Clifford Algebras. We assume a set of point correspondences (X_i, x_i), with 4D (homogeneous) model points X_i and 3D (homogeneous) image points x_i. Each image point is

Fig. 2. The pose scenario: the aim is to estimate the pose R, t

reconstructed to a Plücker line $L_i = (n_i, m_i)$, with a (unit) direction n_i, and moment m_i [10]. The 3D rigid motion is represented as exponential form

$$M = \exp(\theta\hat{\xi}) = \exp\begin{pmatrix} \hat{\omega} & v \\ 0_{3\times1} & 0 \end{pmatrix} \tag{5}$$

where $\theta\hat{\xi}$ is the matrix representation of a twist $\xi = (\omega_1, \omega_2, \omega_3, v_1, v_2, v_3) \in se(3) = \{(v, \omega)|v \in \mathbf{R}^3, \hat{\omega} \in so(3)\}$, with $so(3) = \{A \in \mathbf{R}^{3\times3}|A = -A^T\}$. In fact, M is an element of the one-parametric Lie group $SE(3)$, known as the group of direct affine isometries. A main result of Lie theory is, that to each Lie group there exists a Lie algebra which can be found in its tangential space, by derivation and evaluation at its origin; see [10] for more details. The corresponding Lie algebra to $SE(3)$ is denoted as $se(3)$. A twist contains six parameters and can be scaled to $\theta\xi$ with a unit vector ω. The parameter $\theta \in \mathbf{R}$ corresponds to the motion velocity (i.e., the rotation velocity and pitch). For varying θ, the motion can be identified as screw motion around an axis in space. To reconstruct a group action $M \in SE(3)$ from a given twist, the exponential function $\exp(\theta\hat{\xi}) = M \in SE(3)$ must be computed. It can be calculated efficiently by using the Rodriguez formula [10],

$$\exp(\hat{\xi}\theta) = \begin{pmatrix} \exp(\theta\hat{\omega}) & (I - \exp(\hat{\omega}\theta))(\omega \times v) + \omega\omega^T v\theta \\ 0_{1\times3} & 1 \end{pmatrix} \quad \text{for } \omega \neq 0 \tag{6}$$

with $\exp(\theta\hat{\omega})$ computed by calculating

$$\exp(\theta\hat{\omega}) = I + \hat{\omega}\sin(\theta) + \hat{\omega}^2(1 - \cos(\theta)). \tag{7}$$

Note that only sine and cosine functions of real numbers need to be computed.

For pose estimation we combine the reconstructed Plücker lines with the screw representation for rigid motions and apply a gradient descent method: Incidence of the transformed 3D point X_i with the 3D ray $L_i = (n_i, m_i)$ can be expressed as

$$(\exp(\theta\hat{\xi})X_i)_{3\times1} \times n_i - m_i = 0. \tag{8}$$

Indeed, X_i is a homogeneous 4D vector, and after multiplication with the 4×4 matrix $\exp(\theta\hat{\xi})$ we neglect the homogeneous component (which is 1) to evaluate the cross product with n_i. Note, that this constraint equations expresses the perpendicular error vector between the Plücker line and the 3D point. The aim is to minimize this spatial error. Therefore we linearize the equation by using $\exp(\theta\hat{\xi}) = \sum_{k=0}^{\infty} \frac{(\theta\hat{\xi})^k}{k!} \approx I + \theta\hat{\xi}$, with I as identity matrix. This results in

$$((I + \theta\hat{\xi})X_i)_{3\times 1} \times n_i - m_i = 0 \qquad (9)$$

which can be reordered into an equation of the form $A\xi = b$. Collecting a set of such equations (each is of rank two) leads to an over-determined linear system of equations in ξ. The Rodriguez formula can be applied to reconstruct the group action M from the twist ξ. Then, the 3D points can be transformed and the process is iterated until the gradient descent approach converges. In recent years, this technique has been extended to higher order curves, free-form contours and free-form surfaces, see [14,15]. The surface based pose estimation procedure is basically an ICP-algorithm, which has the problem to get trapped in local minima. For this reason we use a sampling method with different (neighboring) start poses and use the resulting pose with minimum error. This can be seen as a simple particle filter during pose estimation. Note that the constraint equations express a spatial distance measure in 3D. In [14] we have shown that each equation can be rescaled individually to an equivalent 2D distance measure. For combining segmentation and pose estimation we make use of this property to get a single energy functional.

4   Coupling Image Segmentation and 2D-3D Pose Estimation

In order to couple pose estimation and image segmentation in a joint optimization problem, the energy functional for image segmentation in (1) is extended by an additional term that integrates the object model:

$$E(\Phi, \theta\xi) = -\int_{\Omega} \left(H(\Phi) \log p_1 + (1 - H(\Phi)) \log p_2\right) dx + \nu \int_{\Omega} |\nabla H(\Phi)| \, dx$$
$$+ \lambda \underbrace{\int_{\Omega} (\Phi - \Phi_0(\theta\xi))^2 \, dx}_{\text{Shape}} . \qquad (10)$$

The quadratic error measure in the shape term has been proposed in the context of 2D shape priors, e.g. in [16]. The prior $\Phi_0 \in \Omega \to \mathbb{R}$ is assumed to be represented by the signed distance function. This means in our case, $\Phi_0(x)$ yields the distance of x to the silhouette of the projected object surface.

In detail, Φ_0 is constructed as follows: let X_S denote the set of points X on the object surface. Projection of the transformed points $\exp(\theta\xi)X_S$ into the image plane yields the set x_S of all (homogeneously scaled) 2D points x on the image plane that correspond to a 3D point on the surface model

$$x = P \exp(\theta\xi)X, \qquad \forall X \in X_S \qquad (11)$$

Fig. 3. From left to right: (a) Initialization. (b) Segmentation result with object knowledge. (c) Pose result. (d) Segmentation result without object knowledge.

where P denotes a projection with known camera parameters. The level set function Φ_0 can then be constructed from x_S by setting $\Phi_0(x) = 1$ if $x \in x_S$, $\Phi_0(x) = -1$ otherwise, and applying the distance transform.

Note that the distance $(\Phi(x) - \Phi_0(x))^2$ is exactly the distance used in the pose estimation method. Given the contour Φ, the pose estimation method thus minimizes the shape term in (10). Minimizing (10) with respect to the contour Φ, on the other hand, leads to the gradient descent equation

$$\partial_t \Phi = H'(\Phi) \left(\log \frac{p_1}{p_2} + \nu \operatorname{div} \left(\frac{\nabla \Phi}{|\nabla \Phi|} \right) \right) + 2\lambda \left(\Phi - \Phi_0(\theta \xi) \right). \tag{12}$$

In order to minimize the total energy, an iterative approach is suggested: keeping the contour Φ fixed, the optimum pose parameters $\theta \xi$ are determined as described in Section 3 and yield the silhouette of the object model Φ_0. Retaining in the opposite way the pose parameters, (12) determines an update on the contour. Both iteration steps thereby minimize the distance between Φ and Φ_0. While the pose estimation method draws Φ_0 towards Φ, thereby respecting the constraint of a rigid motion, (12) in return draws the curve Φ towards Φ_0, thereby respecting the data in the image.

5 Experiments

Fig. 3 - 5 show tracking results with a tea box as object model and cluttered backgrounds. Fig. 3 demonstrates the advantage of integrating object knowledge into the segmentation process. Without object knowledge, parts of the tea box are neglected as they better fit to the background. The object prior can constrain the contour to the vicinity of the projected object model derived from those parts of the contour that can be extracted reliably.

In Fig. 4, the motion of the object causes severe reflections on the metallic surface of the tea box. Nevertheless, the results remain stable. Further note some smaller occlusions due to the fingers that do not disturb the pose estimation.

In Fig. 5 the amount of occlusion is far more eminent. This experiment also demonstrates the straightforward extension of the method to multiple cameras. The non-occluded parts of both views provide enough information for pose recognition of the object. However, we also do not want to conceal a decisive drawback of the method, this is the dependency of the result on the initialization. As the pose estimation of the object prior is based on the segmentation, the object model cannot help to initially find the object in the image. It can only improve the *tracking* of the object, once a good pose

Fig. 4. Top row: Initialization at the first frame. Frames 49, 50, and 117 of the sequence. **Bottom row:** Tracking results at frames 0, 49, 50, and 117. The tea box is moved in 3D, causing partially severe reflections on the box.

Fig. 5. Tracking result of a stereo sequence. In both views the object is partially occluded but the pose can be reconstructed from the remaining information (frame 98 from 210 frames).

initialization has been found. How to find such an initialization automatically, i.e. how to *detect* objects in cluttered scenes, is a topic on its own.

6   Conclusion

We presented a technique that integrates 3D shape knowledge into a variational model for level set based image segmentation. While the utilization of 2D shape knowledge has been investigated intensively in recent time, the presented approach accommodates the three-dimensional nature of the world. The technique is based on a powerful image-driven segmentation model on one side, and an elaborated method for 2D-3D pose estimation on the other side. The integration of both techniques improves the robustness of contour extraction and, consequently, also the robustness of pose estimation that relies on the contour. It allows for the tracking of three-dimensional objects in cluttered scenes with inconvenient illumination effects. The strategy to model the segmentation in the image plane, whereas the shape model is given in three-dimensional space, has the advantage that the image-driven part can operate on its natural domain as provided by the camera, while the 3D object model offers the full bandwidth of perspective views. Moreover, in contrast to 2D techniques, it gives the extracted object a position in space.

References

1. T. Brox, M. Rousson, R. Deriche, and J. Weickert. Unsupervised segmentation incorporating colour, texture, and motion. In N. Petkov and M. A. Westenberg, editors, *Computer Analysis of Images and Patterns*, volume 2756 of *Lecture Notes in Computer Science*, pages 353–360. Springer, Berlin, 2003.
2. T. Brox and J. Weickert. A TV flow based local scale measure for texture discrimination. In T. Pajdla and J. Matas, editors, *Proc. 8th European Conference on Computer Vision*, volume 3022 of *Lecture Notes in Computer Science*, pages 578–590. Springer, Berlin, May 2004.
3. V. Caselles, F. Catté, T. Coll, and F. Dibos. A geometric model for active contours in image processing. *Numerische Mathematik*, 66:1–31, 1993.
4. T. Chan and L. Vese. An active contour model without edges. In M. Nielsen, P. Johansen, O. F. Olsen, and J. Weickert, editors, *Scale-Space Theories in Computer Vision*, volume 1682 of *Lecture Notes in Computer Science*, pages 141–151. Springer, 1999.
5. D. Cremers, S. Osher, and S. Soatto. A multi-modal translation-invariant shape prior for level set segmentation. In C.-E. Rasmussen, H. Bülthoff, M. Giese, and B. Schölkopf, editors, *Pattern Recognition*, volume 3175 of *Lecture Notes in Computer Science*, pages 36–44. Springer, Berlin, Aug. 2004.
6. D. Cremers, F. Tischhäuser, J. Weickert, and C. Schnörr. Diffusion snakes: introducing statistical shape knowledge into the Mumford-Shah functional. *International Journal of Computer Vision*, 50(3):295–313, Dec. 2002.
7. A. Dervieux and F. Thomasset. A finite element method for the simulation of Rayleigh–Taylor instability. In R. Rautman, editor, *Approximation Methods for Navier–Stokes Problems*, volume 771 of *Lecture Notes in Mathematics*, pages 145–158. Springer, Berlin, 1979.
8. W. E. L. Grimson. *Object Recognition by Computer*. The MIT Press, Cambridge, MA, 1990.
9. M. E. Leventon, W. E. L. Grimson, and O. Faugeras. Statistical shape influence in geodesic active contours. In *Proc. 2000 IEEE Computer Society Conference on Computer Vision and Pattern Recognition*, volume 1, pages 316–323, Hilton Head, SC, June 2000. IEEE Computer Society Press.
10. R. Murray, Z. Li, and S. Sastry. *Mathematical Introduction to Robotic Manipulation*. CRC Press, Boca Raton, FL, 1994.
11. S. Osher and J. A. Sethian. Fronts propagating with curvature-dependent speed: Algorithms based on Hamilton–Jacobi formulations. *Journal of Computational Physics*, 79:12–49, 1988.
12. N. Paragios and R. Deriche. Unifying boundary and region-based information for geodesic active tracking. In *Proc. 1999 IEEE Computer Society Conference on Computer Vision and Pattern Recognition*, volume 2, pages 300–305, Forth Collins, Colorado, June 1999.
13. T. Riklin-Raviv, N. Kiryati, and N. Sochen. Unlevel-sets: geometry and prior-based segmentation. In T. Pajdla and J. Matas, editors, *Proc. 8th European Conference on Computer Vision*, volume 3024 of *Lecture Notes in Computer Science*, pages 50–61. Springer, Berlin, May 2004.
14. B. Rosenhahn. Pose estimation revisited. Technical Report TR-0308, Institute of Computer Science, University of Kiel, Germany, Oct. 2003.
15. B. Rosenhahn and G. Sommer. Pose estimation of free-form objects. In T. Pajdla and J. Matas, editors, *Proc. 8th European Conference on Computer Vision*, volume 3021 of *Lecture Notes in Computer Science*, pages 414–427, Prague, May 2004. Springer.
16. M. Rousson and N. Paragios. Shape priors for level set representations. In A. Heyden, G. Sparr, M. Nielsen, and P. Johansen, editors, *Computer Vision – ECCV 2002*, volume 2351 of *Lecture Notes in Computer Science*, pages 78–92. Springer, Berlin, 2002.

Goal-Directed Search with a Top-Down Modulated Computational Attention System

Simone Frintrop[1], Gerriet Backer[2], and Erich Rome[1]

[1] Fraunhofer Institut für Autonome Intelligente Systeme (AIS),
Schloss Birlinghoven, 53754 Sankt Augustin, Germany
[2] Krauss Software GmbH, Tiefe Str. 1, 38162 Cremlingen, Germany

Abstract. In this paper we present VOCUS: a robust computational attention system for goal-directed search. A standard bottom-up architecture is extended by a top-down component, enabling the weighting of features depending on previously learned weights. The weights are derived from both target (excitation) and background properties (inhibition). A single system is used for bottom-up saliency computations, learning of feature weights, and goal-directed search. Detailed performance results for artificial and real-world images are presented, showing that a target is typically among the first 3 focused regions. VOCUS represents a robust and time-saving front-end for object recognition since by selecting regions of interest it significantly reduces the amount of data to be processed by a recognition system.

1 Introduction and State of the Art

Suppose you are looking for your key. You know it to be somewhere on your desk but it still takes several fixations until your roaming view hits the key. If you have a salient key fob contrasting with the desk, you will detect the key with fewer fixations. This is according to the separation of visual processing into two subtasks as suggested by Neisser [9]: first, a fast parallel pre-selection of scene regions detects object candidates and second, complex recognition restricted to these regions verifies or falsifies the hypothesis. This dichotomy of fast localization processes and complex, robust, but slow identification processes is highly effective: expensive resources are guided towards the most promising and relevant candidates.

In computer vision, the efficient use of resources is equally important. Although an attention system generates a certain overhead in computation, it pays off since reliable object recognition is a complex vision task that is usually computationally expensive. The more general the recognizer – for different shapes, poses, scales, and illuminations – the more important is a pre-selection of regions of interest.

Concerning visual attention, most research has so far been done in the field of *bottom-up* processing (in psychology [13,15], neuro-biology [2,10] and computer vision [7,6,1,11]). Bottom-up attention is merely data-driven and finds regions that attract the attention automatically, e.g., a black sheep in a white

W. Kropatsch, R. Sablatnig, and A. Hanbury (Eds.): DAGM 2005, LNCS 3663, pp. 117–124, 2005.

flock. Koch & Ullman [7] described the first explicit computational architecture for bottom-up visual attention; it is strongly influenced by Treisman's *feature-integration theory* [13]. Many computational systems have been presented meanwhile [6,1,11,14], most restricted to bottom-up computations.

While much less analyzed, there is strong neurobiological and psychophysical evidence for top-down influences modifying early visual processing in the brain due to pre-knowledge, motivations, and goals [17,2,16]. However, only a few computational attention models integrate top-down information. The earliest approach is the *guided search* model by Wolfe [15], a result of his psychological investigations of human visual search. Tsotsos' system considers feature channels separately and uses inhibition for regions of a specified location or those that do not fit the target features [14]. Hamker performs visual search on selected images but without considering the target background [5]. The closest related work is presented by Navalpakkam et al. [8]; however, the region to learn is not determined automatically and exciting and inhibiting cues as well as bottom-up and top-down cues are not separated. Furthermore, quality and robustness of the system are not shown. To our knowledge, there exists no complete, well investigated system of top-down visual attention comparable to our approach.

In this paper, we present the attention system VOCUS that performs goal-directed search by extending a well-known bottom-up system [6] by a top-down part. The bottom-up part computes saliencies for the features intensity, orientation, and color independently, weights maps according to the uniqueness of the feature, and finally fuses the saliencies into a single map. The top-down part uses previously learned weights to enable the search for targets. The weighted features contribute to a top-down saliency map highlighting regions with target-relevant features. The relative strengths of bottom-up and top-down influences are adjustable according to the task. Cues from both maps are fused into a global saliency map and the focus of attention is directed to its most salient region. The system shows good performance on artificial as well as on real-world data: typically, one of the first 3 selected regions contains the target, in many cases it is the first region. In the future, we will integrate the system into a robot control architecture enabling the detection of salient regions and goal-directed search.

2   The Visual Attention System VOCUS

The computational attention system VOCUS (Visual Object detection with a CompUtational attention System) consists of a bottom-up part computing data-driven saliency and a top-down part enabling goal-directed search. Global saliency is determined from both cues (cf. Fig. 1).

2.1   Bottom-Up Saliency

VOCUS' bottom-up part detects salient image regions by using image contrasts and uniqueness of a feature, e.g., a red ball on green grass. It was inspired by Itti et al. [6] but differs in several aspects resulting in considerably improved performance (see [3]). The feature computations are performed on 3 different scales

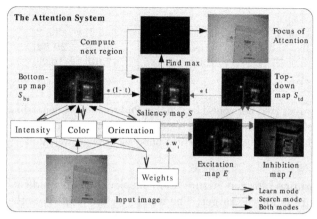

Feature	weights
intensity on/off	0.001
intensity off/on	9.616
orientation $0°$	4.839
orientation $45°$	9.226
orientation $90°$	2.986
orientation $135°$	8.374
color green	76.572
color blue	4.709
color red	0.009
color yellow	0.040
conspicuity I	6.038
conspicuity O	5.350
conspicuity C	12.312

Fig. 1. The goal-directed visual attention system with a bottom-up part (left) and a top-down part (right). In learning mode, target weights are learned (blue arrows). These are used in search mode (red arrows). Right: weights for target name plate.

using image pyramids. The feature intensity is computed by *center-surround mechanisms* extracting intensity differences between image regions and their surroundings, similar to cells in the human visual system [10]. In contrast to [6], we compute on-off and off-on contrasts separately [3,4]; after summing up the scales, this yields 2 intensity maps. Similar, 4 orientation maps $(0°, 45°, 90°, 135°)$ are computed by Gabor filters and 4 color maps (green, blue, red, yellow) by first converting the RGB image into the Lab color space, second determining the distance of the pixel color to the prototype color (the red map shows high activations for red regions and small ones for green regions) and third, applying center-surround mechanisms. Each feature map X is weighted with the uniqueness weight $\mathcal{W}(X) = X/\sqrt{m}$, where m is the number of local maxima that exceed a threshold t. This weighting is essential since it emphasizes important maps with few peaks, enabling the detection of *pop-outs* (outliers). After weighting, the maps are summed up to the bottom-up saliency map S_{bu}.

2.2 Top-Down Saliency

To perform visual search, VOCUS first computes target-specific weights (learning mode) and, second, uses these weights to adjust the saliency computations according to the target (search mode). We call this target-specific saliency *top-down saliency*.

In **learning mode**, VOCUS is provided with a training image and coordinates of a *region of interest (ROI)* that includes the target. The region might be the output of a classifier specifying the target or determined manually by the user. Then, the system computes the bottom-up saliency map and the *most salient region (MSR)* inside the ROI. So, VOCUS is able to decide autonomously what is important in a ROI, concentrating on parts that are most salient and disregarding the background or less salient parts. Note that this makes VOCUS also robust to small changes of the ROI coordinates.

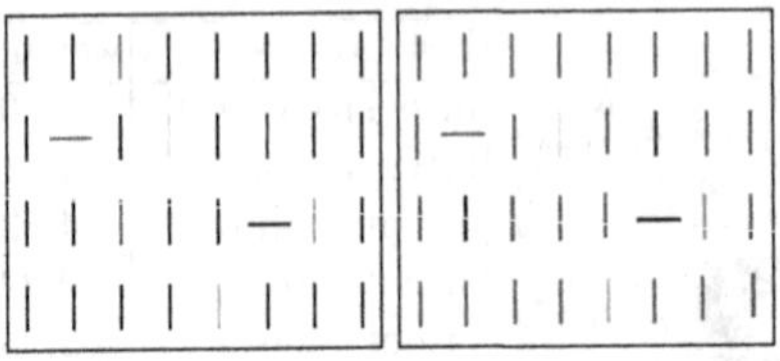

Feature	weights 1	weights 2
orientation 0°	20.64	**29.84**
color red	**47.60**	10.29

Fig. 2. The weights for the target (red horizontal bar, 2nd in 2nd row) differ depending on the environment: in the left image (black vertical bars) color is more important than orientation (weights 1), in the other image (red vertical bars) vice versa (weights 2).

Next, weights are determined for the feature and conspicuity maps, indicating how important a feature is for the target. The weight w_i for map X_i is the ratio of the mean saliency in the target region $m_{(MSR)}$ and in the background $m_{(image-MSR)}$: $w_i = m_{(MSR)}/m_{(image-MSR)}$ where $i \in \{1, ..., 13\}$. This computation does not only consider which features are the strongest in the target region, it also regards which features separate the region best from the rest of the image (cf. Fig. 2).

The learning of weights from one single training image yields good results if the target object occurs in all test images in a similar way, i.e., on a similar background and in a similar orientation. These conditions occur if the objects are fixed elements of the environment, e.g. fire extinguishers. Nevertheless, for movable objects it is necessary to learn from several training images which features are stable and which are not. This is done by determining the average weights from n training images using the geometric mean of the weights, i.e., $w_{i,(1..n)} = \sqrt[n]{\prod_{j=1}^{n} w_{i,j}}$. Instead of using all images from the training set, we choose the most suitable ones: first, the weights from one training image are applied to the training set, next, the image with the worst detection results is taken and the average weights from both images are computed. This procedure is repeated iteratively as long as the performance increases (details in [3,4]).

In **search mode**, we determine a top-down saliency map that is integrated with the bottom-up map to yield global saliency. The top-down map itself is composed of an excitation and an inhibition map. The excitation map E is the weighted sum of all feature and conspicuity maps X_i that are important for the learned region, i.e., $w_i > 1$. The inhibition map I shows the features more present in the background than in the target region, i.e., $w_i < 1$:

$$E = \sum_i (w_i * X_i) \qquad \forall i : w_i > 1$$
$$I = \sum_i ((1/w_i) * X_i) \qquad \forall i : w_i < 1 \tag{1}$$

The top-down saliency map S_{td} results from the difference of E and I and a clipping of negative values: $S_{td} = E - I$. To make S_{td} comparable to S_{bu}, it is normalized to the same range. I, E, and S_{td} are depicted in Fig. 3, showing that the excitation map as well as the inhibition map have an important influence.

The global saliency map S is the weighted sum of S_{bu} and S_{td}. The contribution of each map is adjusted by the top-down factor $t \in [0..1]$: $S = (1 - t) * S_{bu} + t * S_{td}$. For $t = 1$, VOCUS considers only target-relevant features (pure

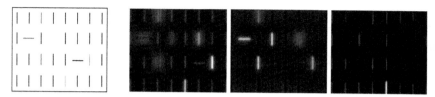

Fig. 3. Excitation and inhibition are both important: search target: cyan vertical bar (5th, last row). Left to right: test image, excitation map E, inhibition map I, top-down map S_{td}. E shows bright values for cyan, but brighter ones for the green bar (7th, 3rd row). Only the inhibition of the green bar enables the single peak for cyan in S_{td}.

top-down). For a lower t, salient bottom-up cues may divert the focus of attention, an important mechanism in human attention: a person suddenly entering a room immediately catches our attention. Also colored cues divert the search for non-colored objects as shown in [12]. Determining appropriate values for t depends on the system state, the environment and the current task; this is beyond the scope of this article and will be tackled when integrating our attention system into robotic applications.

After the computation of the global saliency map S, the most salient region is determined by *region growing* starting with the maximum of S. Finally, the focus of attention (FOA) is directed to this region. To compute the next FOA, this region is inhibited and the selection process is repeated.

3   Results

In this section, we present experimental results on artificial images to establish the link to human visual attention and on numerous real-world images. The quality of the search is given by the *hit number*, i.e., the number of the focus that hits the target (for several images the *average hit number*). Since we concentrate on computing the first n foci on a scene (usually $n = 10$), we additionally show the *detection rate*, i.e., the percentage of images in which the target was detected within the first n FOAs. Note that VOCUS works with the same parameters in all experiments; there is no target-specific adaptation.

Visual search in artificial images: first, VOCUS was trained on the image in Fig. 3 (left) to find different bars. Tab. 1 shows the hit number. The green, cyan, and yellow bar are not focused in bottom-up mode within the first 10 foci, since their saliency values are lower than those of the black vertical bars.

For $t = 1$, all targets are focused immediately with one exception (magenta vertical). Magenta has a lot of blue portions so the blue regions are also enhanced during search for magenta. This leads to focusing the blue before the magenta bar. Note that also black bars are found, considering the lack of color by inhibiting colored objects. For $t = 0.5$, bottom-up and top-down cues are both regarded. It shows that in most cases the hit number is the same as for $t = 1$, except for the red vertical bar. Here, the bottom-up saliency of the red horizontal bar diverts the focus. It looks as if the bottom-up cues have less influence than the top-down cues, but note that the saliency values in the bottom-up

Table 1. Search performance for different target bars for the training image of Fig. 3, left; test image is the horizontally flipped training image. The first 10 FOAs are computed. $t = 0$ is pure bottom-up search, $t = 1$ pure top-down search. The performance is given by the *hit number* on the target. The numbers in parentheses show the saliency value at the target region.

| | Hit number for several target bars (and saliency value) | | | | | | | | |
| | red | blue | black | magenta | red | black | green | cyan | yellow |
top-down factor	horiz	vert	horiz	vert	vert	vert	vert	vert	vert
$t = 0.0$	1 (24)	2 (23)	3 (21)	4 (18)	5 (17)	6 (15)	- (12)	- (8)	- (7)
$t = 0.5$	1	1	1	2	2	1	1	1	1
$t = 1.0$	1	1	1	2	1	1	1	1	1

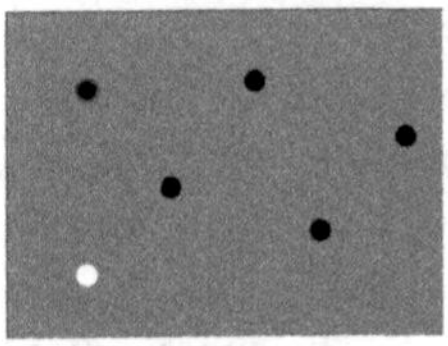

Intensity of background in %	10	20	30	40	50	60	70	80	90
Required t to override pop-out	0	0	0	0.3	0.4	0.5	0.6	0.9	-

Fig. 4. When searching for a black dot (left), the required value of the top-down factor t increases with rising background intensity (right)

saliency map (values in parentheses) do not differ a lot, so little influence by the top-down map is enough to change the order of the foci. In a *pop-out experiment* [15], the contrasts between target and distractor values are much larger.

To test the influence of the top-down factor t systematically, we use an image with one white and 5 black dots on a grey background (Fig. 4). We vary the intensity of the background between 10% (nearly white) and 90% (nearly black) and determine the top-down factor required to override the white pop-out and find a black dot. It shows that with increasing intensity, the value of t required to override the pop-out increases too, up to $t = 0.9$ for 80% intensity. For 90%, the pop-out is so strong that it cannot be overriden anymore.

Visual search in real-world images: In Tab. 2 and Fig. 5, we show some search results obtained from more than 1000 real-world images. We chose targets with high and with low bottom-up saliency, fixed at the wall as well as movable ones. The objects occupy about 1% of the image and occur in different contexts, with different distractors, and on differently colored and structured backgrounds.

We chose two kinds of targets fixed in an office environment: name plates and fire extinguishers. The largest test set was available for the name plates: we took 906 test and 54 training images of 3 different halls of our institute, showing about 50 different doors and name plates in different contexts due to differently colored and structured posters and photos at walls and doors. The movable objects are a key fob and a highlighter. The highlighter was placed on two different desks: a dark and a bright one. For each kind of target, one was highly salient by itself (fire extinguishers and highlighters are designed to attract attention), while the bottom-up saliency for the name plates and the key fob was much smaller.

Table 2. Search performance on real world data. Left: the targets and the extracted region for learning. Note that this is not the training data, training images contain a whole scene instead of an extracted object. The training images are chosen from training sets of 10 to 40 images with an algorithm described in [3]. For each target, 10 FOAs are computed. The table shows the average hit number for different top-down factors t and, in parentheses, the detection rate (d.r.) within 10 FOAs.

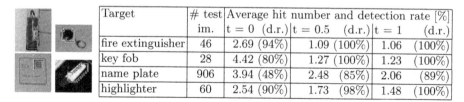

Target	# test im.	Average hit number and detection rate [%]		
		$t = 0$ (d.r.)	$t = 0.5$ (d.r.)	$t = 1$ (d.r.)
fire extinguisher	46	2.69 (94%)	1.09 (100%)	1.06 (100%)
key fob	28	4.42 (80%)	1.27 (100%)	1.23 (100%)
name plate	906	3.94 (48%)	2.48 (85%)	2.06 (89%)
highlighter	60	2.54 (90%)	1.73 (98%)	1.48 (100%)

Fig. 5. Some of the results from Tab. 2. Search for a a fire extinguisher, a key fob, a name plate, and a highlighter. The FOAs are depicted by red ellipses. All targets detected with 1st FOA, only in the 3rd image with the 6th FOA.

Tab. 2 shows that the performance depends on the kind of target and on its environment. We identified 3 scenarios: 1) The object is very salient and often detected at once in bottom-up mode, e.g., fire extinguisher and highlighter. Here, VOCUS is also very successful: the target is in average detected with the 1st or 2nd FOA. 2) The object is not very salient so the bottom-up value is low, but there are few regions in the scene with similar features. This enables VOCUS to separate the target well from the environment, resulting in a high detection rate (e.g. the key fob). 3) The target is not salient and there are a lot of similar regions in the environment that divert the focus. Even for humans, these are difficult conditions for visual search. An example is the name plate: in some of the test images, there are posters on walls or doors with colors similar to the logo of the name plate making the search difficult (cf. Fig. 5).

The results show convincingly that VOCUS is successful in finding targets. Salient objects are nearly always detected with the 1st or 2nd FOA, and even in difficult settings, the amount of regions to be investigated by a classifier is drastically reduced. The results also reveal that the system is highly robust: the images were taken under natural conditions, i.e., illumination and viewpoint of the target vary (details in [3]). Most difficult are images with several regions having nearly the same saliency values as the target; there, small variations of the image data may lead to a changed order of the foci. We also compared VOCUS to Itti's attention system NVT on the data presented in [8]; in [3] we showed that VOCUS clearly outperforms the NVT.

4   Conclusion

We introduced the new attention system VOCUS that uses previously learned target information to perform goal-directed search. During learning, it considers not only the properties of the target, but also of the background. In search mode, bottom-up and top-down influences compete for global saliency. The biologically plausible system has been thoroughly tested on artificial and real-world data and its suitability for detecting different targets was extensively demonstrated. In our examples, the target usually was among the first three selected regions.

In future work, we plan to utilize the system for robot control. Therefore, first the runtime (currently 1.7 sec on a 1.7 GHz Pentium IV for 300 × 300 pixel images) has to be improved to enable real-time performance. Then, VOCUS will determine salient regions in the robot's environment and search for previously learned objects. Directing the attention to regions of potential interest will be the basis for efficient object detection and manipulation.

References

1. Backer, G., Mertsching, B. and Bollmann, M. Data- and model-driven Gaze Control for an Active-Vision System. *IEEE Trans. on PAMI* **23(12)** (2001) 1415–1429.
2. Corbetta, M. and Shulman, G. L. Control of goal-directed and stimulus-driven attention in the brain. *Nature Reviews* **3** (3, 2002) 201–215.
3. Frintrop, S. VOCUS: A Visual Attention System for Object Detection and Goal-directed Search. PhD thesis University of Bonn Germany (to appear 2005).
4. Frintrop, S., Backer, G. and Rome, E. Selecting what is Important: Training Visual Attention. In: Proc. of KI (accepted), LNCS, Springer (2005).
5. Hamker, F. Modeling Attention: From computational neuroscience to computer vision. In: Proc. of WAPCV'04 (2004) 59–66.
6. Itti, L., Koch, C. and Niebur, E. A Model of Saliency-Based Visual Attention for Rapid Scene Analysis. *IEEE Trans. on PAMI* **20** (11, 1998) 1254–1259.
7. Koch, C. and Ullman, S. Shifts in selective visual attention: towards the underlying neural circuitry. *Human Neurobiology* **4** (4, 1985) 219–227.
8. Navalpakkam, V., Rebesco, J. and Itti, L. Modeling the influence of task on attention. *Vision Research* **45** (2, 2005) 205–231.
9. Neisser, U. *Cognitive Psychology* Appleton-Century-Crofts New York 1967.
10. Palmer, S. E. *Vision Science, Photons to Phenomenology* The MIT Press 1999.
11. Sun, Y. and Fisher, R. Object-based visual attention for computer vision. *Artificial Intelligence* **146** (1, 2003) 77–123.
12. Theeuwes, J. Top-down search strategies cannot override attentional capture. *Psychonomic Bulletin & Review* **11** (2004) 65–70.
13. Treisman, A. M. and Gelade, G. A feature integration theory of attention. *Cognitive Psychology* **12** (1980) 97–136.
14. Tsotsos, J. K., Culhane, S. M., Wai, W. Y. K., Lai, Y., Davis, N. and Nuflo, F. Modeling Visual Attention via Selective Tuning. *AI* **78** (1-2, 1995) 507–545.
15. Wolfe, J. Guided Search 2.0: A Revised Model of Visual Search. *Psychonomic Bulletin & Review* **1** (2, 1994) 202–238.
16. Wolfe, J. M., Horowitz, T., Kenner, N., Hyle, M. and Vasan, N. How fast can you change your mind? The speed of top-down guidance in visual search. *Vision Research* **44** (2004) 1411–1426.
17. Yarbus, A. L. *Eye Movements and Vision* Plenum Press (New York) 1969.

Telephone-Based Speech Dialog Systems

Jürgen Haas, Florian Gallwitz, Axel Horndasch, Richard Huber
and Volker Warnke

Sympalog Voice Solutions GmbH,
Karl-Zucker-Straße 10,
91052 Erlangen, Germany

Abstract. In this contribution we look back on the last years in the history of telephone-based speech dialog systems. We will start in 1993 when the world wide first natural language understanding dialog system using a mixed-initiative approach was made accessible for the public, the well-known EVAR system from the Chair for Pattern Recognition of the University of Erlangen-Nuremberg. Then we discuss certain requirements we consider necessary for the successful application of dialog systems. Finally we present trends and developments in the area of telephone-based dialog systems.

1 Introduction

Today people calling a company are more and more often confronted with automatic speech dialog systems. Those systems range from DTMF driven dialogs to natural language understanding systems with mixed-initiative dialog management - here we concentrate on the latter. Tasks provided by those systems also cover a wide range from simple call routing mechanisms(*"Press 1 for the CEO, 2 for sales department and 3 for financial administration."*) to complex transactions as e.g. bank transfers. Nowadays there is a common understanding that basic technology components like speech recognition, dialog management or speech synthesis are ready for use, but there still is a lack of good, i.e. highly usable applications with a wide user acceptance and visibility in general [3]. Therefore we look back in the research history and name certain milestones and important projects, like SunDial, ATIS or VERBMOBIL, on the way to todays systems. Afterwards, we present and discuss some guidelines for the implementation of dialog systems and finally we present current trends and developments.

2 Research History and Milestones

Looking back into the history of telephone-based dialog systems with natural language understanding capabilities and mixed-initiative dialog management, important milestones can be accentuated. One of them is January 1993: the Chair for Pattern Recognition from the University Erlangen-Nuremberg lead by Prof. Niemann connected the worldwide first conversational dialog system to the public telephone. The system was able to give information about the

W. Kropatsch, R. Sablatnig, and A. Hanbury (Eds.): DAGM 2005, LNCS 3663, pp. 125–132, 2005.

German train time table concerning IC and ICE connections. This demonstrator was developed during the SunDial project [8]. Only slightly later, Philips also presented a train time table information system to the public. Later, this system called TABA was deployed by Switzerland's Federal Railways (SBB).

The SunDial project[1] lasting from 1989 to 1993 was an EU-funded project, where besides the Chair for Pattern Recognition e.g. CSELT in Italy and CNET in France took part, but also companies like Siemens and Daimler-Benz. At several sites, natural language understanding dialog system using a mixed-initiative dialog management approach have been installed and evaluated [1]. But even before SunDial research in the area of spoken language dialog system was carried on at the Chair of Pattern Recognition which is described and documented e.g. in [5] or [6]. Starting from SunDial and the publically available EVAR system a lot of further research was done in Erlangen which is summarized in [2]. Besides the research, the work for and with EVAR, the experiences made with the capabilities of the system and the methodology of mixed-initiative dialog management in contrast to commercially available menu-driven dialog systems was one motivation for the founders to start with Sympalog.

Also in 1993 a world-wide well-known and highly respected research project funded by the BMBF[2] started: VERBMOBIL. In that project a system for the automatic translation of a telephone conversation between two people not speaking the other's language should be realized. In VERBMOBIL (see [4]), for which the project leader Prof. Wahlster was rewarded with the "2001 German Future Prize", a lot of new insights in speech and dialog processing were gained. From 1997 to 2000 there was a second phase for VERBMOBIL, followed by the SmartKom project which last until 2003 and finally followed by SmartWeb which is planed to end in 2007.

Apart from Europe, research on dialog systems was pursued also in the USA. There existed a framework for the proper evaluation of new ideas and developments in that area, called ATIS organized by DARPA (see e.g. [9]). The project provided a set of tasks from the domain of air travel information with which institutes and companies could benchmark their systems. Companies like AT&T and IBM took part in that evaluation, but also universities and research institutes.

A very important step for bringing speech understanding and dialog management capabilities into commercial use was made in 1995, when the German Bundesbahn deployed a natural language understanding system for train time table information. This system still is available under the cost free telephone number 0800-1507090 from the conversational telephone network and 01805-221100 from cell phones. Today there is a number of different telephone-based dialog systems in use, even in Germany. There are systems only giving information, others are used for call handling, routing and transfer, but there are also systems providing access to transactions, e.g. in the financial sector several banks have telephone-based dialog systems in use.

---

[1] for further information see http://www.sics.se/~scott/sundial.html

[2] The German Federal Ministry of Education and Research.

3   Requirements for Modern Speech Dialog Systems

In this section we discuss requirements we consider necessary implement and deploy a dialog system successfully. The experiences reported here have been made with different commercial spoken dialog systems implemented by Sympalog. We will focus on the following applications:

The **Sixt switchboard** application, handling the calls (approx. 1000 per day) to the Sixt AG's central phone number. 90% of the calls are transferred automatically to the correct person, the others are handed on to a human operator. The system knows the employee names, the departments, and a large variety of potential reasons why people call. In a number of cases, there is a clarification dialog to more precisely determine the contact person.

Berti, a football Bundesliga information system operated by a German media company. The system is an advanced version of the system evaluated in an independent Fraunhofer usability study, where it outperformed all other systems in the criteria "navigation/dialog" and "error management" [3].

Filmtips, the movie information system operated by a Cinema company in the Nuremberg region. Among other cinemas, it includes Germany's largest multiplex and IMAX cinema.

3.1   Conversational Systems will Prevail

One possibility to offer automatic services over the telephone is the *menu–driven approach*. Since many people are used to that kind of interaction, this approach seems obvious. But designing menus to be used on the telephone is a very difficult task: if there are too many alternatives presented in a system prompt, users tend to forget the choices offered at the beginning. Also the navigation within a hierarchical menu of a complex system can frustrate a caller, especially if something goes wrong and you have to go back to the "main menu" [3]. A more promising way to serve customers efficiently while creating high user–acceptance is the *conversational approach*. The prerequisites are a speech recognition engine that can handle spontaneous speech and an intelligent dialog management. Another important point is to tune both modules in terms of shared knowledge (e.g. the last system prompt). Conversational systems are characterized by human–like features when handling the input. The most important ones are mixed-initiative interaction, processing out–of–focus input, and the possibility to "over–answer" questions. The evaluation of users interacting with those systems shows, that callers appreciate this more human–like conversation and quickly adapt their way of communication.

It is essential that the system is prepared for users with different levels of experience: callers used to a menu–based system need to be led throughout the dialog, new users who never dealt with automatic systems need help, but intuitively they make use of the features offered by the conversational system, and "power–users" know the system very well and want to get the information very quickly. Another important characteristic is that the status of the back–end system is used for the dialog management. E.g. the result of a database request within the movie information system with "Munich" will be rather large so it is necessary to gather more information, e.g. the "time". However in a small town probably no more than three movies are shown on a certain day and so the system can produce a prompt containing information about all movies at once.

3.2   Building a Bridge

Telephone-based dialog systems could be seen as a middleware between a human and a data source with speech as interface. The problem when developing an application for a new domain is that it usually takes more than one iteration to build a system that will bridge the gap between the user and the information. Apart from getting speech data for adapting the recognizer, a thorough evaluation of test cases is necessary to get a feeling for what people actually say. Of course it is possible to recycle atomic knowledge from other domains, e.g. the way users refer to a point in time, but in general it is necessary to go through some iterations before the system can go online. A typical approach, where after each step the dialog system is optimized in all relevant aspects, is:

– build an initial system
– employees test the system (experienced, biased users)
– friends and family testing (semi–experienced, unbiased users)
– friendly user test(s) (unexperienced, unbiased, cooperative users)
– go online (all kinds of users)
– readjust the system if appropriate

Since this approach to building new conversational, mixed-initiative dialog systems is user–oriented and not database–oriented, there are new problems: because the user is not restricted to say certain things at a certain time, there will be questions or requests from the user that can not be covered, sometimes simply because the information is not in the database. It is however desirable to react in a sensible way, e.g. telling the user that some information is not included in the database as it is done with movie genres in **Filmtips** or scorers in **Berti**.

To improve the performance of an application, it is necessary to put work into the processing of different wordings referring to the same value, which is especially complex for names. The Sixt switchboard application knows approx. 350 employees. Customers however do not always use the correct names as they are stored in the database. So the system has to know that a "Robert" is also referred to as "Bob" or that "Maier" and "Meyer" are pronounced in the same way. Calls should also be routed to the "head of sales" or to "someone in marketing". As consequence the system understands about 1000 alternatives of the names and about 350 alternatives for the 40 Sixt departments.

3.3   Speech Output is What the User "Sees"

The importance of the text–to–speech component in a dialog system is often underestimated although it plays a crucial role for user–acceptance. For every application the decision if pre–recorded sound files or a speech synthesizer should be used has to be made. It is desirable to do use pre–recorded prompts if possible, although there are some obvious problems, for example, if the content of the data source, which is of interest to the user, changes quickly. In that case it makes sense to use an automatic speech synthesizer for the dynamic parts of the system prompt. Callers do accept a mixture of different voices as long as the dynamic content and the basic system prompts are sufficiently separate.

Another important point is the trade–off between the requirement for short prompts that contain a lot of information. A smart way to get around that problem is to make long pauses during prompts, to invite the user to barge in. Users who are still uncertain will wait and get more information. A very simple way to give the user a better idea of what the system can understand is to sometimes attach extra information to prompts: "What can I help you with? [attach:] You can for example ask me *What's the score in Dortmund right now?*"

Through proper prompting critical situations in a dialog can be avoided: Instructing the user explicitly on how to interact with the system can have a negative effect. E.g. telling the user to "speak loud and clearly" often results in user complaints about the system ("I AM speaking very clearly!") or even a hang–up. A better way is to react more subtle, almost human–like e.g. with: "Excuse me, I didn't hear you?", "What was that again?". To not annoy a caller by repeating a prompt over and over again there should be alternatives for prompts [1], especially general ones, e.g. when the system was not able to process the speech input in a meaningful way. For some applications it may even be useful (and fun) to create an atmosphere during the call playing sound files, like stadium noise or to use "earcons" (audio icons) indicating certain events.

3.4   Discover the Optimal Dialog Strategy

Experiences with **Berti** and **Filmtips** show that dialogs in different domains can look very different. Even if non–critical data is provided, it can be reasonable to get at least an implicit confirmation. That is the case in the movie information system, where up to four slots are necessary to retrieve the correct information. For transaction systems, which involve critical data like user names and PINs, explicit confirmation strategies may be inevitable, possibly even legally binding. Depending on the number of misunderstandings during a dialog the system should also apply relaxation strategies concerning confirmations. If an application is very complex and dialogs tend to get rather lengthy, it is helpful to restrict the flexibility of the dialog gradually. For example in an air travel reservation system, the dialog manager does not completely adhere to the concept of "say what you want at any time": after a flight was chosen, the first goal of the dialog has been reached. In a second part, the user provides his personal data. Switching between the two parts of the dialog is still possible with so called meta–utterances ("I want to change the date.").

During the first iterations of application development dialog strategies often need to be more robust due to the sub–optimal accuracy of the speech recognizer. During the later stages, when enough speech data has been collected for adapting the recognizer, the task becomes a lot easier in terms of dialog management and less restrictive dialog strategies can be applied.

3.5 Speed is Crucial

It is essential that a spoken dialog system reacts fast to any kind of user input, no matter how long the user utterance is. We found that a delay of two seconds or more is likely to confuse the user. This often misleads the users to repeat or to reformulate their utterance. This desynchronizes the interaction and may lead to a complete failure of the dialog. With today's speech recognition engines and hardware, faster than real–time performance of the recognizer can be achieved, even for 30 or more lines in parallel and vocabulary sizes of several thousand words. There exist commercial recognition engines adjusting the computational effort dynamically to the current system load, ensuring the availability of the recognition result fast enough after the turn end was detected. This may result in a minor decline in recognition accuracy under high system load, which is far less likely to confuse or annoy the user than a noticeable delay.

For the same reason, fast and reliable turn end detection is of extreme importance. Sympalog uses an algorithm which also incorporates prosodic information for this purpose. Only after the turn end has been detected, a semantic and pragmatic interpretation of the recognition result can be performed. The dialog management then creates a new system prompt, also taking into account the content of the back–end database. Finally, the speech signal is generated and sent to the caller. The whole course of action after the recognizer has produced its result needs to be finished within a very short time, preferably less than 0.15 seconds. Fast and reliable turn begin detection is equally important for the barge in feature, and a tight coupling of the turn begin detection with the speech output is required to immediately turn off the system voice in case the user takes the turn.

4   Trends and Developments

Finally, we discuss new developments and trends for telephone-based dialog systems. We focus on three issues: the ongoing standardization efforts, the detection of emotion in telephone speech and the challenge of multimodal systems.

4.1 Standards

The currently most obvious trend is the standardization for dialog systems. Apart from description languages like VoiceXML[3] or SALT[4], specialized markup languages for technology components like JSGF for speech recognizer grammars or SSML for speech synthesis tools have been developed. Also some standardization efforts on the protocol and API side are made with MRCP and SAPI. The

---

[3] see e.g. http://www.w3c.org/TR/voicexml20/ or http://www.voicexml.org/

[4] see e.g. http://www.saltforum.org/

idea behind those standards is to allow users of speech technology and speech systems to develop their applications along with the back–end integration independent from the underlying engines. In a way this is analogous to the emergence of HTML as the main description language for pages exchanged over the World Wide Web.

Therefore we think it is very important to support standards like VoiceXML, which currently is the most prominent one. We see its real power as an exchange format not as a tool for application development and dialog description. VoiceXML is great if you want to tell a synthesis tool what to say or a speech recognizer which words in which grammar it should recognize, but it is a poor description language if you want to build up a dialog system where the aim is high usability and user acceptance. Like with internet pages and HTML (almost no Web Site is written in HTML but designed using any web publishing tool or content management system), dialog systems should be implemented using an application development environment like SymMagic and SymDialog. Those tools are able to handle mixed-initiative dialogs where in each step a VoiceXML page is dynamically generated.

4.2 Emotion

Motivated by VERBMOBIL and the work presented in [7] the automatic detection of the user state on basis of the incoming speech signal is going to be implemented and evaluated in commercial pilot projects. Companies using dialog systems often face the challenge that e.g. due to recognizer errors the caller gets angry and as a consequence hangs up. Thus it is desirable that the system detects if the user gets angry and then tries to calm him down or transfers him to a human agent. This classification task can be accomplished using a set of phonetic and prosodic features derived from the energy and fundamental frequency contours and features describing e.g. the length of certain phones or phone classes. The acoustic processing is accompanied by a semantic processing step where the user utterance is examined for swear words and angry phrases.

4.3 Multimodality

Currently Voice over IP (VoIP) is becoming commonplace in the telecommunication market and making phone calls over an internet connection will soon be standard. If we consider that avatar technology has made great progress in the last years, one can claim that there is a chance to combine the two technology branches to generate new kinds of internet applications and web sites: you go to a web site and you have the possibility to send speech signals over the same connection (VoIP). Speech signals have to be processed by a recognition engine and the result is processed by a dialog manager, which also controls an avatar shown on the web site. That way it is possible to build an internet shop where the user can navigate with speech (e.g. *"Please show me the mobile phones you offer."*) and by clicking links.

The dialog management has to keep track of all interactions made by the user for every input modality, e.g. voice, mouse or keyboard. Such a system can pick the optimal output channel for the requested information: long lists or detailed descriptions are shown on a graphical display, short additional information or requests for further details are presented acoustically. Systems of that type have been or are investigated in the SmartKom and SmartWeb project, but so far no commercial relevant product has been released.

5 Conclusion

We have shown that the history of telephone-based dialog systems is long and sometimes spectacular but the promised breakthrough for speech recognition and dialog systems has not taken place yet. We believe that by following certain guidelines to build usable and well-performing dialog systems the visibility and acceptance of dialog systems will increase. Then one day, we will use our own voice to communicate with computers as easy as we do it with mouses and keyboards today.

References

1. W. Eckert. *Gesprochener Mensch-Maschine-Dialog.* PhD thesis, Universität Erlangen-Nürnberg, 1995.
2. F. Gallwitz, M. Aretoulaki, M. Boros, J. Haas, S. Harbeck, R. Huber, H. Niemann, and E. Nöth. The Erlangen Spoken Dialogue System EVAR: A State–of–the–art Information Retrieval System. In *Proc. of the 1998 Int. Symposium on Spoken Dialogue (ISSD 98)*, pages 19–26, Sydney, Australia, 1998.
3. M. Peissner, J. Biesterfeldt, and F. Heidmann. Akzeptanz und Usability von Sprachapplikationen in Deutschland. Technical report, Fraunhofer-Institut für Arbeitswirtschaft und Organisation (IAO), Stuttgart, 2004.
4. W. Wahlster, editor. *Verbmobil: Foundations of Speech-to-Speech Translation.* Springer, Berlin, 2000.
5. H. Niemann, A. Brietzmann, R. Mühlfeld, P. Regel and G. Schukat. The Speech Understanding and Dialog System EVAR. In *New Systems and Architectures for Automatic Speech Recognition and Synthesis*, Springer, NATO ASI Series, volume F16, pages 271–302, Berlin, Germany, 1985.
6. M. Mast, R. Kompe, F. Kummert, H. Niemann and E. Nöth. The Dialog Module of the Speech Recognition and Dialog System EVAR. In *Proc. Int. Conf. on Spoken Language Processing*, pages 1573–1576, volume 2, Banff, Canada, 1992.
7. R. Huber, A. Batliner, J. Buckow, E. Nöth, V. Warnke and H. Niemann Recognition of Emotion in a Realistic Dialogue Scenario. In *Proc. Int. Conf.on Spoken Language Processing*, pages 665-668, volume 1, Beijing, China, 2000.
8. A. Simpson and N. Fraser. Black Box and Glass Box Evaluation of the SUNDIAL System. In *Proc. European Conf. on Speech Communication and Technolgy*, volume 2, pages 1423–1426, Berlin, Germany, 1993.
9. P. Price. Evaluation of Spoken Language Systems: the ATIS Domain In *Proc. Speech and Natural Language Workshop*, pages 91–95, Morgan Kaufmann, San Mateo, California, USA, 1990.

Robust Parallel Speech Recognition in Multiple Energy Bands

Andreas Maier, Christian Hacker, Stefan Steidl, and Elmar Nöth
and Heinrich Niemann

Universität Erlangen-Nürnberg, Lehrstuhl für Mustererkennung, Germany
noeth@informatik.uni-erlangen.de
http://www5.informatik.uni-erlangen.de/

Abstract. In this paper we will investigate the performance of TRAP-features on clean and noisy data. Multiple feature sets are evaluated on a corpus which was recorded in clean and noisy environment. In addition, the clean version was reverberated artificially. The feature sets are assembled from selected energy bands. In this manner multiple recognizers are trained using different energy bands. The outputs of all recognizers are joined with ROVER in order to achieve a single recognition result. This system is compared to a baseline recognizer that uses Mel frequency cepstrum coefficients (MFCC). In this paper we will point out that the use of artificial reverberation leads to more robustness to noise in general. Furthermore most TRAP-based features excel in phone recognition. While MFCC features prove to be better in a matched training/test situation, TRAP-features clearly outperform them in a mismatched training/test situation: When we train on clean data and evaluate on noisy data the word accuracy (WA) can be raised by 173 % relative (from 12.0 % to 32.8 % WA).

1   Introduction

Noise and reverberation have a strong influence on automatic speech recognition systems. Even slight noise or reverberation can cause an enormous decrease of the recognition rate. Human beings are less affected by such disadvantageous effects. Unfortunately these disadvantageous sound situations are quite important in many application scenarios like driving a car or being in an "intelligent room" in which many appliances can be controlled by voice. The use of closetalk microphones is often not practical since they have to be attached very close to the speaker's head and the user acceptance of such a device is very low. This is the reason why robust automatic recognition systems with far distant microphones are desirable. To achieve this we look at two different aspects of automatic speech recognition: The use of features which are restricted to certain frequency bands but are calculated over a longer time span and the use of multiple recognizers.

Our features are based on the TRAP approach of Hynek Hermansky presented in [1]. In his investigations he especially pointed out the robustness of his features.

W. Kropatsch, R. Sablatnig, and A. Hanbury (Eds.): DAGM 2005, LNCS 3663, pp. 133–140, 2005.

The speech corpus used in this paper is available in three different levels of noise and reverberation. In addition to the recordings with a closetalk microphone the scenery was filmed by a video camera for documentary purposes. In this manner a second rather noisy version could be recorded. The third version was obtained by adding an artificial reverberation to the closetalk version.

Since the TRAP-features are computed for each band individually it is easy to train different independent recognizers. In case of a distortion of a single frequency band the other recognizers can still recognize the spoken utterance. In [2] it is shown that such a combination using the ROVER procedure can produce very promising results. A recognizer with a certain feature set is trained on every version of the corpus. Each feature set is created using different energy bands. Furthermore different types of TRAP-features are used as well. For the baseline system MFCCs are used.

After the training the recognizers are evaluated on a disjoint test set. We present results on phone and on word level. Furthermore outputs on word level are joined using ROVER included in the Speech Recognition Scoring Toolkit (SCTK) which can be downloaded from [3].

All recognizers trained on the closetalk and closetalk reverberated version of the corpus are evaluated on the test set of the room microphone version as well.

The next section gives a short literature overview. In chapter 3 a short description of the AIBO database follows. The experimental setup and the results are described in chapter 4. The paper ends with an outlook to future work and a summary.

2   Related Work

The feature extraction is primarily based on the work of Hynek Hermansky. In [1] the so called **Temporal Patterns** (TRAP) are introduced. Based on the assumption that the temporal context in each band is essential for the classification of phones each band is analyzed individually, first. Using a long context of up to one second a neural net is trained for each energy band. The outputs of the nets are scores for 29 phonetic classes. These scores are obtained for each band and used as input for a neural net merger. The merger's outputs are again scores for 29 phonetic classes. As Hermansky states these features can produce better results than perceptive linear prediction (PLP) features especially when the distortions occur only in certain bands.

Furthermore Hermansky points out the importance of the modulation spectrum in [4]. This spectrum can be obtained by a short-time analysis of each TRAP band. From this analysis a spectrum results whose both axes have frequency scales. One results from the filter bank analysis and displays the frequency of the signal. The other one displays the modulation frequency. As Hermansky states only modulations over 1 Hz and below 16 Hz are important for the perception of speech.

In [5] the importance of the modulation spectrum is highlighted even more. Greenberg proposes to use a so called modulation spectrogram. This kind of spectrogram does not display the strength of a certain frequency band anymore. It displays only the strength of the modulation around 4 Hz. In order to compute this, the spectrogram is processed for each frequency band and transformed into modulation frequency. It is processed in such a manner that in the end only a single coefficient is obtained for the modulation frequency between 2 and 8 Hz. These coefficients get arranged in a spectrographic layout to form the modulation spectrogram. Greenberg states that the modulation spectrogram is quite robust to noise and distortions.

In order to combine the recognizers the ROVER system is employed. [2] describes the algorithm as follows. The output of the recognizers on word level are aligned first and merged later on with the ROVER voting module. In order to do the alignment two hypotheses are processed iteratively by dynamic programming. To match the task the algorithm was extended by Fiscus et al. since the base hypothesis can hold more than one word at a time. Afterwards the best word for each alignment can be found. This is done with the voting module. It supports several modes which can even include the scores returned by the recognizer into the decision process. A reduction of up to 16 % of the word error rate was obtained.

In [6] it is shown, that reverberation can be created artificially if the characteristic spectral properties are known. Those properties can be acquired by recording a known signal from various positions in a room; for each position in the room attributes can be determined. The characteristics found can be applied to a clean signal by convoluting the signal with a finite-impulse-response (FIR) filter. In this manner reverberation can be added to any signal.

3 Corpus

As already mentioned in the introduction the AIBO database is available in three versions. The experimental setup of this database used a Sony AIBO robot [7]. The original design was intended to record emotional speech of children. The children were to accomplish several tasks with AIBO commanding it by voice. However, the robot was controlled by a wizard in a so called *wizard of Oz* experiment. The wizard was disguised as an audio technician. A complete description of the tasks can be found in [8]. The recordings were done with a closetalk microphone which was attached to the child's head. Thus a clean version of the data was recorded which is called closetalk (ct) later on.

For documentary purposes the whole experiment was filmed with a video camera as well. The sound track of the film contains a lot of reverberation and background noises, since the camera's microphone is designed to record the whole scenery in a room and since the camera was approximately 3 m away from the child. The fact that the distance between speaker and microphone was quite far and that the child was not facing the microphone emphasize the difficulty of this recognition task. This version is called room microphone (rm) in the following.

The third version of the corpus was created using artificial reverberation. To achieve this the data of the ct version were convoluted with different impulse

responses. The impulse responses were recored in a different room using multiple
speaker positions and echo durations T_{60} as shown in Fig. 1. With each of the
twelve responses 1/12 th of the corpus was reverberated. This corpus is called
closetalk reverberated (ct rv) later on.

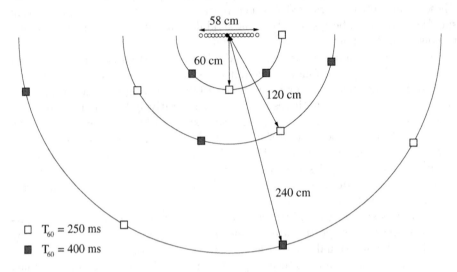

Fig. 1. Positions of the different impulse responses

The advantage of this procedure is that the data had to be transcribed only
once. So all versions have the same size in vocabulary (850 words and 350 word
fragments) and the same language models.

4   Experimental Setup

First, we give an overview of the used features, i.e. MFCCs, TRAPs, and filtered
TRAPs. Then a description of the recognizers and their combination follows.

4.1   Features

The baseline system which is compared to all results uses MFCC features. So
the signal is processed with a fast Hartley transform with a window size of 16 ms
computed every 10 ms. Then 22 filter banks are computed from the resulting
spectrum. After taking the logarithm the signal is processed with a discrete
Cosine transformation. In the end 11 Mel coefficients plus the signal's energy
are taken as static features and another 12 delta features are computed using a
regression line over 5 frames, i.e. 56 ms. Cepstrum mean abstraction is applied.

The TRAP features used in this paper are based on [1] but differ in several
details. They are computed from the logarithmic Mel spectrum. The Mel filter

bank consists of 18 banks. Using a context of ± 15 frames a TRAP with 31 entries is created for each band. In this phase n of 18 bands are chosen. The coefficients of these bands are concatenated and reduced to 24 dimensions using a linear discriminant analysis (LDA) instead of the neural nets used by Hermansky. The classes needed by the LDA are obtained by a forced alignment with the baseline hidden Markov recognizer. In total 47 German phonetic classes were used. In the following the TRAP-features are labeled with the letter T.

The modulation spectrum is computed in a similar manner. After the TRAP coefficients are found they are transformed with a fast Fourier transformation. This results in a complex spectrum which states the modulation of the different energy bands. So the filtered TRAP features can be computed using a band pass between 1 Hz and 16 Hz in modulation frequency. All coefficients of the spectrum outside these boundaries are set to 0. Then the modulation spectrum is transformed again into the TRAP domain. Fig. 2 shows the TRAP of the 8th band of a phone /i/ before and after the filtering on the different versions of the corpus. As can be seen the filtered curves are closer to each other, i.e. the filtering reduces the differences in the features caused by the different recording conditions. Again the desired bands are concatenated and reduced with a LDA transformation. This type of feature is called F in the following.

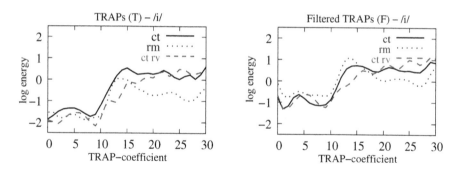

Fig. 2. TRAPs and Filtered TRAPs for the eighth band (from 1.1 kHz to 1.6 kHz) of a phone /i/ for different versions of the corpus

4.2 Recognizers

The hidden Markov models (HMM) which are employed here are trained with the ISADORA [9] system of the Chair for Pattern Recognition of the University of Erlangen–Nuremberg. This system has been developed since 1978 and has been employed on various tasks in the field of pattern recognition from speech recognition to genetic decoding and recognition of hand writing. The system provides all tools needed for the training of HMMs. For decoding the *lr_beam* recognizer is employed. In our experiments we used semi-continuous HMMs with full covariance matrices and polyphone models as elementary HMMs. The latest version of the system is described in [9]. Each recognizer provides a best recognized word chain. These word chains are used as input for ROVER. Using the output of multiple recognizers it can compute a single best word chain. To do this the word chains are aligned iteratively first. Then the best word for each position is chosen. This can be done using several algorithms. In our experiments we used voting and included confidence scores from the recognizers (method *avgconf*).

4.3 Results

In the following the presented features are evaluated. All of the recognizers trained here use only 6 of 18 critical bands in order to enable a majority decision with three recognizers. Tab. 1 gives an overview of the results obtained on phone level. As one can see the recognizers using every third band are far better than the baseline MFCC recognizer. However, if the bands are chosen consecutively like in the case of T_{1-6} the recognizers perform worse than the baseline. Therefore the results on word level focus only on the recognizers using every third band.

Table 1. Results of the different features on phone level; class wise averaged recognition rates in %.

Feature	Bands	Abbreviation	ct	ct rv	rm
MFCC			42.3	36.7	28.2
T	1,4,7,10,13,16	T_{3n+1}	**52.2**	**45.2**	**32.2**
T	1,2,3,4,5,6	T_{1-6}	41.2	33.4	22.0
F	1,4,7,10,13,16	F_{3n+1}	49.7	42.9	28.2

On word level the recognition rates of the individual recognizers can not compete with the baseline recognizers in most cases. Only if the training and the test data do not match like in the case of training on closetalk data and evaluation on room microphone data, some of the TRAP recognizers can obtain better results than the baseline system. Note, that the use of artificial reverberation during training always results in an improvement when evaluating on the room microphone test set. In order to focus on the performance of the acoustic models, Tab. 2 shows the recognition rates for a unigram language model.

When the recognizers are joined with ROVER better recognition rates can be achieved. The TRAP based recognizers can now obtain better results than the baseline in most cases. Nevertheless MFCC still return better results when training and test is done on closetalk microphone data. Tab. 3 gives 4-gram recognition rates, since such a language model is usually applied on a real task. Its perplexity on the test set is 50. Note that the consequence of the combination of the recognizers is an enormous improvement if training and test data do not match. Except for the ct/ct constellation the TRAP based recognizers give better results than the MFCC recognizers. Combining the TRAP-features with MFCC provides a small further improvement. When training is done on closetalk data and evaluation on room microphone data the recognition rate can be improved by 173 % relatively (from 12.0 % to 32.8 % WA).

Table 2. WAs of the individual recognizers with a unigram language model

Training	ct	ct rv	rm	ct	ct rv
Test	ct	ct rv	rm	rm	rm
MFCC	**69.3**	**63.1**	**35.2**	**4.9**	7.6
T_{3n+1}	55.0	50.5	27.6	-10.8	1.3
T_{3n+2}	53.2	48.8	27.0	-4.0	**9.4**
T_{3n}	55.1	49.1	29.1	-4.4	2.3
F_{3n+1}	57.3	**51.7**	29.1	-2.4	5.5
F_{3n+2}	55.8	50.5	28.5	**5.8**	**12.5**
F_{3n}	**57.6**	51.5	**29.5**	1.2	6.7

Table 3. Categorical 4-gram recognition rates of the combined recognizers

# of recognizers	Training	ct	ct rv	rm	ct	ct rv
	Test	ct	ct rv	rm	rm	rm
1	MFCC	**77.2**	63.1	46.9	12.0	18.8
1	F_{best}	66.1	61.1	39.0	15.8	23.0
3	T^{3n}	71.1	65.9	47.3	21.6	34.3
4	T^{3n}+MFCC	70.3	**66.7**	48.7	**32.8**	31.6
3	F^{3n}	72.1	63.4	48.9	27.2	34.3
4	F^{3n}+MFCC	73.4	64.5	**49.4**	30.9	**35.2**

5   Outlook and Summary

It could be shown that the TRAP features have the greatest advantage when training and test data are mismatched. We conclude that these features generalize better. Furthermore the use of TRAP features and artificial reverberation can improve the recognition rate on the room microphone test set from 12.0 % to 35.2 %. As the experiments show the upper limit (training and test on room microphone data) is 46.9 % in the baseline system. Fig. 3 gives an overview over the best achieved WAs. In our current research we adapt the ct rv recognizer with a small amount of "in task" data, i.e. rm data. We hope that this will close the gap between the currently best "mismatched" recognizer and the rm/rm baseline. Such a procedure will allow to use the vast amount of clean transcribed training data for the training of far distant microphone recognizers.

In this paper we presented the AIBO database in three versions. These versions are closetalk microphone, room microphone, and closetalk reverberated. Furthermore two TRAP based features were introduced. *T*-features are based on Hermansky's TRAP approach and *F*-features are created by filtering in the modulation frequency. Then a method to combine multiple recognizers was presented. In the results section the different recognition rates were given. The best improvement compared to an MFCC baseline system could be obtained on mismatched training and test data where a 173 % relative improvement was achieved (from 12.0 % to 32.8 % WA).

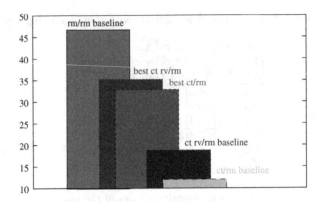

Fig. 3. Overview of the WAs on the room microphone test set

References

1. H. Hermansky and S. Sharma. TRAPs - Classifiers of Temporal Patterns. In *Proc. ICSLP '98*, volume 3, pages 1003–1006, Sydney, Australia, 1998.
2. J. Fiscus. A Post-processing System to Yield Reduced Word Error Rates: Recognizer Output Voting Error Reduction. In *Proc. IEEE ASRU Workshop*, pages 347–352, Santa Barbara, USA, 1997.
3. Speech Recognition Scoring Toolkit (SCTK). NIST Spoken Language Technology Evaluation and Utility. http://www.nist.gov/speech/tools/, last visited 28.03.2005.
4. H. Hermansky. The Modulation Spectrum in Automatic Recognition of Speech. In *IEEE Workshop on Automatic Speech Recognition and Understanding*, Santa Barbara, USA, 1997.
5. S. Greenberg and B. E. Kingsbury. The Modulation Spectrogram: In Pursuit of an Invariant Representation of Speech. In *Proc. ICASSP '97*, pages 1647–1650, Munich, Germany, 1997.
6. L. Couvreur and C. Couvreur. On the Use of Artificial Reverberation for ASR in Highly Reverberant Environments. In *Proc. of 2nd IEEE Benelux Signal Processing Symposium*, Hilvaranbeek, The Netherlands, 2000.
7. Sony Europe. AIBO Europe - Official Website, 2004. http://www.aibo-europe.com, last visited 19.12.2004.
8. A. Batliner, C. Hacker, S. Steidl, and E. Nöth. "You stupid tin box" - Children Interacting with the AIBO Robot: A Cross-linguistic Emotional Speech Corpus. In *Proc. of the 4th International Conference of Language Resources and Evaluation '04*, pages 171–174, Lisbon, Portugal, 2004.
9. G. Stemmer. *Modeling Variability in Speech Recognition*. PhD thesis, Universität Erlangen-Nürnberg, Lehrstuhl für Mustererkennung, Germany, 2005.

Pronunciation Feature Extraction

Christian Hacker[1,*], Tobias Cincarek[2,**], Rainer Gruhn[2,***], Stefan Steidl[1], Elmar Nöth[1], and Heinrich Niemann[1]

[1] Universität Erlangen-Nürnberg, Lehrstuhl für Mustererkennung, Martensstraße 3, D-91058 Erlangen, Germany
[2] ATR Spoken Language Translation Res. Labs., Kyoto, Japan
hacker@informatik.uni-erlangen.de

Abstract. Automatic pronunciation scoring makes novel applications for computer assisted language learning possible. In this paper we concentrate on the feature extraction. A relatively large feature vector with 28 sentence- and 33 word-level features has been designed. On the word-level correctly and mispronounced words are classified, on the sentence-level utterances are rated with 5 discrete marks. The features are evaluated on two databases with non-native adults' and children's speech, respectively. Up to 72 % class-wise-averaged recognition rate is achieved for 2 classes; the result of the 5-class problem can be interpreted as 80 % recognition rate.

1 Introduction

Pronunciation scoring is the automatic assessment of the pronunciation quality of phonemes, words, utterances, or larger units especially for non-native speakers. A possible application are systems for computer assisted pronunciation training (CAPT) to support the student of a foreign language to acquire correct pronunciation. In this paper a set of 28 sentence-level features is proposed which encodes a high amount of information that is important to grade the pronunciation of a sentence. A similar set of 33 features has been developed to reject mispronounced words. Some simple features that highly correlate with human marking are e.g. the word or phone recognition rate obtained by an automatic speech recognition system.

As reference two databases are applied and compared: The ATR/SLT NON-NATIVE-database, recorded at the Spoken Language Translation Research Laboratories (SLT) of ATR [5], contains speech of non-native adults from different countries reading English phrases. Secondly, the PF-STAR NON-NATIVE-database is applied. In the European project PF-STAR (http://pfstar.itc.it/)

---

* A part of this work was funded by the European Commission (IST programme) in the framework of PF-STAR (Grant IST-2001-37599) and by the German Federal Ministry of Education and Research (BMBF) in the frame of SmartWeb (Grant 01 IMD 01 F). The responsibility for the content lies with the authors.
** Now with Graduate School of Information Science, Nara Institute of Science and Technology, Japan; a part of this work was funded by the National Institute of Information and Communication Technology (NICT), Japan.
*** Now with Temic SDS, Ulm, Germany.

W. Kropatsch, R. Sablatnig, and A. Hanbury (Eds.): DAGM 2005, LNCS 3663, pp. 141–148, 2005.

native and non-native children's speech has been recorded from English, Italian, Swedish, and German partners. In this paper the data of German children reading English texts is investigated. For both databases human ratings are available for word- and sentence-level. Our feature set for automatic grading of the non-natives' English has been developed for the ATR/SLT NON-NATIVE data set. Although the age of the speakers, the recording conditions, the speakers' English proficiency, and the instruction of the labelers are different for both databases good classification results are achieved for the PF-STAR NON-NATIVE data, too.

2   Related Work

Neumeyer et al. [7] automatically score non-natives on the sentence- and speaker-level. The inter-rater open-correlation is 0.78 (sentence) and 0.87 (speaker). Correlations with different machine scores (likelihood, posterior scores, accuracy, duration and syllabic timing) are calculated. Different combination techniques for sentence based marks are investigated in [4]: with neural networks a correlation of 0.64 is achieved. Different aspects of human rating and different machine scores are compared in [2]. For phone-level scoring the liklihood based *Goodness of Pronunciation* measure is analyzed in [9,10]. In [6] a novel phonological representation of speech is used to grade the pronunciation.

3   Corpora

The pronunciation features will be evaluated on two different databases:

The part of the ATR/SLT NON-NATIVE-database [5] used in the following consists of 6.4 hours of speech: the 96 non-native speakers (81m, 15f, age 21 – 52) were reading 48 phonetically rich sentences from the TIMIT SX set with a vocabulary of 395 words. The first language of most speakers is Japanese, Chinese, German, French or Indonesian. Each speaker read each sentence usually only once. However, he was asked to repeat the recording of a sentence, when he completely misread or forgot to utter a word or made too long pauses between words. Further, a repetition was possible, if the speaker was not satisfied with the recorded utterance. 15 English teachers (native speakers) evaluated the data: Each utterance has been marked by 3 – 4 teachers, each teacher marked 24 speakers. They assigned a sentence-level rating from 1 (best) to 5 (worst) in terms of pronunciation and fluency and marked any mispronounced words.

The PF-STAR NON-NATIVE-database contains 3.4 hours of speech from 57 German children (26m, 31f, age 10 – 15) reading English texts, recorded by the University of Erlangen. Most children had been learning English for half a year only. They were reading known texts from their text book and some phrases and single words, which also have been recorded by our partners in the Pf-Star project. The recordings contain reading errors, repetitions of words, word fragments and nonverbals. The total size of the vocabulary is 940 words. A German student of English (graduate level) marked mispronounced words and rated the data on sentence-level. Further markings of mispronounced words by 12 teachers will be available soon.

To train speech recognizers, that are needed for the pronunciation feature extraction, further databases are applied. Read speech from the WALL STREET JOURNAL (WSJ)[1]-corpus is used to train an adults' recognizer for the ATR/SLT data; the PF-STAR NATIVE-database contains read speech from British English children [3] and is used to train the recognizer for the PF-STAR NON-NATIVE children. Some phone statistics are estimated from the TIMIT[2]-database.

4   Input Data for Pronunciation Feature Extraction

In our scenario the candidate who is practicing English is reading known texts. Classification of the candidate's pronunciation quality is performed in feature space. Our feature extraction requires several outputs of a speech recognizer and some statistics, which are explained in the following.

Word and phone recognition: The HTK toolkit is used for the estimation of monophone models and for the decoding. 39 features are extracted every 10 ms: 12 cepstral coefficients and the normalized log-energy with first and second derivatives. Cepstral mean subtraction is applied. The number of codebook mixtures was increased successively during training until 16 mixtures were reached. 44 3-state phoneme HMMs and silence models were retrained for four iterations after each mixture increment. The acoustic models for the non-native adults are built with native English data from the WSJ-corpus. The recognizer is evaluated on the Hub2 evaluation test set from WSJ. With a bigram language model (LM) 80.8 % word accuracy (WA) are achieved. The children's speech recognizer is trained with the PF-STAR NATIVE data. With a bigram LM 40.8 % WA are achieved on the native testing data-set.

Native phoneme language model: To compute prior probabilities of phone sequences obtained by unconstrained phoneme recognition, a bigram phoneme LM will be employed. The LM is estimated from the TIMIT-corpus.

Native phoneme duration statistic: In order to calculate the expected duration of words and phones or to estimate posterior probabilities of an observed length of time, the distribution of phoneme durations has to be modeled. They are estimated on the TIMIT-database after forced-alignment.

Phone confusion matrices: A Phone confusion occurs, if the reference phone and the recognized phone differ. Phone confusion matrices are estimated separately for both, the correctly pronounced and the mispronounced words. These matrices contain the probabilities $P(q|p)$, that phoneme p is recognized as q. The confusion matrices are estimated on the ATR/SLT NON-NATIVE-corpus. The reference sequence is obtained by forced-alignment and the recognized sequence is obtained with the phone-recognizer trained on WSJ.

5   Pronunciation Features

Next, a set of 28 sentence based pronunciation features is described, that is an extension of the features in [7]. After this 33 word-level features are proposed.

---
[1] http://www.ldc.upenn.edu/, catalog number LDC93S6
[2] http://www.ldc.upenn.edu/, catalog number LDC93S1

Table 1. *Correlation between each of the 28 sentence-features and the human rating (ATR/SLT data).*

R1	R2	R3	R4	R5	P1	P2	D1	D2	DS1	DS2	L1	L2	L3
−.34	−.37	+.37	+.39	−.32	+.33	+.32	+.30	+.28	−.45	−.46	−.24	−.34	−.28

L4	L5	L6	L7	L8	L9	LR1	LR2	LR3	A1	A2	PS1	PS2	PS3
−.41	−.42	−.37	−.35	−.41	−.43	−.48	−.50	−.52	−.45	−.38	−.22	−.28	−.40

5.1   Sentence-Level Features

First, some notations, that will be referred to in the following: Let t_i be the duration of phone number i in the utterance (pauses are not counted), and T_s the duration of the sentence. We introduce $T = \sum_{i=1}^{n} t_i \leq T_s$ as the sum of phone-durations per sentence without pauses. Assume further m to be the number of words and n the number of phones per sentence. Then the rate-of-speech is defined as

$$R^{(phon)} = n/T_s \quad \text{or} \quad R^{(word)} = m/T_s \tag{1}$$

To evaluate the features proposed in the following the correlation between automatic scores and human rating is analyzed for the ATR/SLT NON-NATIVE-database. The reference is the mean of the marks of the different human raters. An overview of features and correlation-values can be found in Tab. 1. Particularly since for the PF-STAR data only one rater is available, correlation coefficients would be clearly lower. Eight feature categories are built from the set of 33 sentence-level pronunciation features. Within such a feature-set elements differ mainly in the way of normalization.

Rate-Of-Speech (R): This category comprises 5 components: $R^{(word)}$ and $R^{(phon)}$ referred to as *R1* and *R2*, both reciprocals (*R3*, *R4*) and the phonation time ratio T/T_s. If we compare the features with the human annotation, absolute correlations between 0.32 and 0.39 are obtained. The best feature is *R4*.

Pauses (P): The total duration of between-word pauses (*P1*) is correlated with sentence-level ratings by 0.33. Normalization of the pause duration by the number of pauses did not lead to an increase of correlation. The number of between word pauses longer than 0.2 sec. (*P2*) correlates with 0.32.

DurationLUT (D): Elements of this category are computed from the duration statistics (look-up-table, LUT) introduced in Sect. 4. For all phonemes the expected duration d_i from the LUT is used to compute the deviation $|t_i - d_i|$. *D1* is the mean duration deviation, *D2* the scatter. The correlation with the human annotation is 0.30 and 0.28. In other feature groups d_i is used for normalization.

DurationScore (DS): Phoneme duration statistics have been estimated on native data (Sect. 4). To calculate *DS*-features for non-natives, we first normalize the observed phoneme duration (obtained by forced alignment) with the rate-of-speech; we achieve $\bar{t}_i$. Using natives' statistics we now calculate the probability $\log P(\bar{t}_i|p, \boldsymbol{x})$ given the phone p in the reference and the acoustic observation $\boldsymbol{x}$. Summing up these probabilities of an utterance *DS1* is achieved. After normalization with n (*DS2*) the correlation with the reference rating is -0.46.

Likelihood (L): This category contains 9 features based on log-likelihood scores $L(x) = \log P(x|\lambda_q)$ of the acoustic observation x given the HMM λ of the phone q the decoder has elected. The sentence likelihood $L1$ can be approximated by the sum of all phoneme log-likelihoods if independence of the phones is assumed. By normalizing with n or m we obtain $L2$ and $L3$. The global and local sentence likelihood as introduced in Neumeyer et al. [7] is additionally normalized by $R^{(phon)}$:

$$ L4 = \frac{1}{R^{(phon)}} \frac{\sum_{i=1}^{n} L(x)}{T} \qquad L5 = \frac{1}{nR^{(phon)}} \sum_{i=1}^{n} \frac{L(x)}{t_i} \qquad (2) $$

$L6$ and $L7$ are based on word-likelihoods. First, we normalize and then we average per sentence. By further replacing the observed phone duration t_i with d_i (from the duration statistic LUT) we get $L8$ and $L9$ from $L5$ and $L6$. Best correlation with the human reference is achieved with $L9$ (-0.43) and $L5$ (-0.42).

LikeliRatio (LR) comprises features that compare the likelihoods received from the forced alignment and the phone recognizer; in log-space for each frame both values are subtracted and summed up over the entire utterance. For $LR1$ we normalize with n, for $LR2$ with $T \cdot R^{(phon)}$ and for $LR3$ with $\sum_{i=1}^{n} d_i R^{(phon)}$. Correlation with human annotations is around 0.5.

Accuracy (A): Human ratings and the phoneme or word accuracy ($A1$ and $A2$) correlate with -0.45 and -0.38. Since a sentence contains only few words, the phone recognition rate can be calculated more robustly.

PhoneSeq (PS): With a phoneme bigram LM estimated on native-data (Sect. 4), the a priori probability $\log P(q|LM)$ of the observed phone sequence q can be computed ($PS1$). After normalization with n or the rate-of-speech $PS2$ and $PS3$ are obtained. The latter correlates -0.40 with human marks.

5.2   Word-Level Features

On word-level 33 features, partly similar to the sentence-features, are extracted from the data. *Pauses* and *LikeliRatio* are not considered. Here, *Rate-of-Speech*-features are based on the number of phonemes per word duration. The category *DurationLUT* contains amongst others the expected word duration, which is the sum of expected phone durations from the native duration statistic (Sect. 4). As for the *DurationScore*, the phone duration probabilities are now summed up for each word. The *Likelihood* group comprises features with similar normalizations as discussed above. Additionally minimum, maximum and scatter of frame-based log-likelihood values are taken into account. *Accuracy* only contains the phone accuracy. Given a phoneme bigram LM, the probability of the phone sequence corresponding to the current word is calculated in *PhoneSeq*. Additionally we compute the following features:

PhoneConfusion(PC). Instead of *LikeliRatio*-features PC-features are calculated on the word-level. Both groups compare forced alignment and phone-recognition. Phone-confusion occurs, if the reference phone p and the recognized phone q differ. From the two precalculated confusion matrices (Sect. 4), we get the probabilities $P(q|p)$ given either the class *wrongly pronounced* or the class

Table 2. *Word-/sentence-level classification with 1D-features. CL in %*

| | word (2 classes) | | sentence (3 cl.) | | sentence (5 cl.) | |
	PF-STAR	ATR/SLT	PF-STAR	ATR/SLT	PF-STAR	ATR/SLT
Rate-Of-Speech	59.5	65.9	41.2	54.5	28.6	32.2
Pauses	–	–	41.4	48.0	**29.1**	30.7
DurationLUT	58.3	64.5	40.0	54.7	23.7	35.0
DurationScore	62.1	**67.3**	**44.9**	**55.9**	28.5	**37.6**
Likelihood	62.6	**67.0**	41.1	**56.7**	26.4	**35.6**
LikeliRatio	–	–	**44.0**	**61.8**	27.0	**41.9**
PhoneConfusion	**65.5**	65.6	–	–	–	–
Accuracy	**64.6**	61.5	**47.8**	52.0	**29.1**	34.9
PhoneSeq	59.4	65.0	42.4	52.8	28.6	34.9
Confidence	61.5	**67.2**	–	–	–	–
Context	53.1	51.8	–	–	–	–

correctly pronounced. For each frame, the ratio of both probabilities is computed; the mean *(PC1)*, maximum *(PC2)*, minimum *(PC3)*, scatter *(PC4)*, and median *(PC5)* are used as features.

Confidence*(CF)***.** We measure with 3 *CF*-features the probability of words in the reference sequence, given a non-native's utterance. The assumption is: the better the pronunciation of a particular word, the higher is its posterior probability. The calculation of the word posteriors is based on n-best lists.

Context*(C)*-features are obtained by comparing word and sentence based likelihood scores or by calculating the fluctuation of either the local rate-of-speech or the local duration ratio between expected and observed word duration (7 features). Let $R_j^{(local)}$ be the number of phones per word duration of the *j*-th word, then the fluctuation *C2* is

$$C2 = \frac{2R_j^{(local)}}{R_{j-1}^{(local)} + R_{j+1}^{(local)}} \quad (3)$$

6   Results

To evaluate the pronunciation features we applied the leave-one-speaker-out cross-validation approach. We use the LDA-classifier and, additionally, for the experiments in the last paragraph the Gaussian classifier. For all experiments the class-wise averaged recognition rate (CL)[3] and in some cases additionally the overall recognition rate (RR) is given. Tab. 2 shows classification results for the individual feature components. For each feature category, the optimal result is shown as well for the word-level (2 classes: correctly pronounced / mispronounced) as for the sentence-level. On the sentence-level classes of neighboring marks overlap clearly, thus the classification results are rather low. For the 3-class

---

[3] Average of recalls (not weighted by prior probabilities). For unbalanced data robust recognition is required for both, classes with many and classes with few elements.

Table 3. *Results for 2 databases and 2 classification levels*

	word (CL in %) 2 classes	sentence (RR in %) 5 classes ±1 tolerance
PF-STAR cross-vali, all features	69.1	72.9
Training: ATR/SLT, test: PF-STAR	67.7	61.9
ATR/SLT cross-vali, feature selection	72.2	79.9

task we map mark $2 \rightarrow 1$ and $4 \rightarrow 3$. The reference rating is for the ATR/SLT NON-NATIVE data as follows: a word is considered to be mispronounced, if it is marked by at least 2 raters. On sentence-level, the discrete mean of the different teachers' marks is calculated. The PF-STAR data is on both levels marked by one rater, only. Consequently labels are less robust and the recognition results lower. Further reasons for the lower recognition rate on PF-STAR is, that the recognition of children's speech seems to be more difficult [8], that the utterances contain reading errors and word fragments, and that the overlap between training and test is smaller (the phone-confusion matrices are estimated from the ATR/SLT training-set; the ATR/SLT-speakers read TIMIT sentences as used for the phoneme LM and duration statistics). Best features on word-level are *Accuracy* and *PhoneConfusion* for the children's data and *DurationScore, Likelihood,* and *Confidence* for the adults. On sentence-level we obtained good results for PF-STAR with *Accuracy, DurationScore,* and *LikeliRatio,* for ATR/SLT in particular with *LikeliRatio*.

On the PF-STAR-corpus we investigate whether recognition rates increase if the entire feature-set is employed. Again we use the LDA-classifier. On word-level with 33 features 69.1 % CL (72.0 % RR, Tab. 3) are achieved. Features are highly correlated, nevertheless we gain 3.6 % points in comparison to the best single feature. On sentence-level best results are achieved after reduction of the 28 features to 14 principal-components, since otherwise not enough training data would be available. For the 3-class task CL is 50.2 % (52.6 % RR), for the 5-class task 33.4 % (28.7 % RR). If we allow confusion of neighboring marks, e.g. classifying mark 2 as 1, the recognition rate can be interpreted as 72.9 % RR (Tab. 3). Fortunately, the pronunciation features are transferable between different corpora: we train classifiers with the ATR/SLT-corpus and test them with PF-STAR children. On word-level 67.7 % CL are achieved; tolerating 1 mark deviation the sentence-level result can be interpreted as 61.9 % RR.

Further investigation were conducted with the Gaussian classifier and the floating search feature-selection algorithm using the ATR/SLT-corpus [1]. One optimal combination with five word-level features comprises features from the categories *Context*(2), *Confidence, Likelihood,* and *DurationScore*: 72.2 % CL are achieved (Tab. 3). On sentence-level 40.1 % CL for five classes is derived from *Accuracy, Likelihood* and *LikeliRatio*; with the best single feature (*LikeliRatio*) 36.7 % are achieved using Gauss and 41.9 % using LDA (cf. Tab. 2). If we allow the confusion of neighboring marks, the recognition rate can be interpreted as 79.9 % RR (Tab. 3). Further, assuming natives to have perfect pronunciation, they are recognized with 90.2 % RR using the 5-class recognizer.

7   Conclusion

In this paper two non-native speech databases with children's (PF-STAR) and adults' speech (ATR/SLT) are described. Raters marked correct and mispronounced words and graded the sentences with marks 1 – 5. For the adult's data ratings from 3 – 4 native teachers are available, for the children's data only one rating of a student of English. We described a set of 28 sentence-based pronunciation features and 35 word-level features. Best correlation with human ratings is obtained with the *LikeliRatio*-features, which compare the log-likelihood of forced-alignment and recognized phone-sequence. For classification experiments we employ leave-one-speaker-out cross-validation approach. With single features we get recognition rates up to 67 % (2 classes, word-level), 62 % (3 classes, sentence-level) and 42 % (5 classes, sentence-level). Due to the less precise rating, higher variability of children's speech, and the fact that the children's corpus contains reading errors and word fragments, worse results are achieved for the PF-STAR data. By combining features the recognition could be increased. With feature selection a combination of features could be found, that includes separately not well performing features like *Context*-features, that seem to contain additional information. Further could be shown that the features are transferable: After training with ATR/SLT data, we evaluated with PF-STAR data and obtained acceptable results. If we evaluate natives, in deed 90 % are recognized as very good speakers. For future work we expect further improvement from the combination of both classification levels.

References

1. T. Cincarek, R. Gruhn, C. Hacker, E. Nöth, and S. Nakamura. Pronunciation Scoring and Extraction of Mispronounced Words for Non-Native Speech. In *Proc. Acoustical Society of Japan*, pages 141–142, 2004.
2. C. Cucchiarini, H. Strik, and L. Boves. Different Aspects of Expert Pronunciation Quality Ratings and their Relation to Scores Produced by Speech Recognition Algorithms. *Speech Communication*, 30:109–119, 2000.
3. S.M. D'Arcy, L.P. Wong, and M.J. Russell. Recognition of Read and Spontaneous Children's Speech Using two New Corpora. In *Proc. ICSLP*, Korea, 2004.
4. H. Franco, L. Neumeyer, V. Digalakis, and O. Ronen. Combination of Machine Scores for Automatic Grading of Pronunciation Quality. *Speech Communication*, 30:121–130, 2000.
5. R. Gruhn, T. Cincarek, and S. Nakamura. A Multi-Accent Non-Native English Database. In *Proc. of the Acoustical Society of Japan*, 2004.
6. N. Minematsu. Pronunciation Assessment Based upon Phonological Distortions Observed in Language Learners' Utterances. In *Proc. ICSLP*, Korea, 2004.
7. L. Neumeyer, H. Franco, V. Digalakis, and M. Weintraub. Automatic Scoring of Pronunciation Quality. *Speech Communication*, 30:83–93, 2000.
8. G. Stemmer, C. Hacker, S. Steidl, and E. Nöth. Acoustic Normalization of Children's Speech. In *Proc. Eurospeech*, pages 1313–1316, Geneva, Switzerland, 2003.
9. S.M. Witt and S.J. Young. Language Learning Based on Non-Native Speech Recognition. In *Proc. Eurospeech*, pages 633 – 636, Rhodes, Greece, 1997.
10. S.M. Witt and S.J. Young. Phone-Level Pronunciation Scoring and Assessment for Interactive Language Learning. *Speech Communication*, 30:95–108, 2000.

Multi-lingual and Multi-modal Speech Processing and Applications

Jozef Ivanecky, Julia Fischer, Marion Mast, Siegfried Kunzmann, Thomas Ross, and Volker Fischer

IBM Deutschland Entwicklung, AIM Voice Technologies,
Schönaicher Str. 220, D-71072 Böblingen
{ivanecky, julifi, mmast, kunzmann, tross, vfischer}@de.ibm.com

Abstract. Over the last decade voice technologies for telephony and embedded solutions became much more mature, resulting in applications providing mobile access to digital information from anywhere. Both a growing demand for voice driven applications in many languages and the need for improved usability and user experience now drives the exploration of multi-lingual speech processing techniques for recognition, synthesis and conversational dialog management. In this overview article we discuss our recent activities on multi-lingual voice technologies and describe the benefits of multi-lingual modeling for the creation of multi-modal mobile and telephony applications.

1 Introduction

Since the mid 90's speech recognition technology made tremendous progress. At that time focus on research was mainly towards speaker dependent, very large vocabulary speech recognition to solve dictation type usage scenarios for a PC [1]. With the introduction of dictation products and their wide distribution to a broad audience research interest moved rapidly on towards speaker independent speech recognition technologies using mainly grammars and small to medium sized vocabularies. In addition, the convergence of mobile phones and embedded devices has driven progress in both research on noise robustness for telephone channels as well as in optimization techniques for very small footprint deployments.

Today, advances in voice technology development and the growing number of information access applications promise an easy and natural access to information in any environment. Imagine applications like tourist information, traffic jam information, stock quote query systems, and even more voice enabled Internet portals which must deal with content from multiple languages spoken by native, accented or non-native language speakers not only in stress and pronunciation handling, but at all levels of the system. Voice solutions might be deployed on small devices like PDA's and navigation systems with a variety of input and output modalities like voice, keyboard, stylus and display, whereas a telephone deals these days with voice input and output only. However, targeting all these rapidly growing solution scenarios requires not only research in the fields of the core technologies, but also on

W. Kropatsch, R. Sablatnig, and A. Hanbury (Eds.): DAGM 2005, LNCS 3663, pp. 149–159, 2005.
© Springer-Verlag Berlin Heidelberg 2005

technology standardization of voice user interfaces (VUI), programming languages covering multi-modal input & output, and research on conversational systems that can deal with natural dialogs [2]

Above considerations demonstrate that making multi-language information available anywhere via voice to a large user population requires extensive research in a wide range of multi-lingual voice technologies spanning speech recognition, speech synthesis and conversational dialog management. For efficiency and best system performance it is beneficial to systematically consider and exploit synergies between all employed voice technologies. Herein we will provide an overview on our recent multi-lingual activities which include the definition and use of common phone alphabets for speech recognition and synthesis, acoustic modeling for native and non-native multi-lingual speech recognition, and the development of systems capable of handling directed and conversational dialog in many languages. We also provide insight into functioning prototype development and system view introductions addressing standardization of voice user interface development for consumer devices and telephone systems.

The remainder of the paper is organised as follows: Section 2 provides a brief overview over progress on common phone alphabet definitions and Section 3 describes multi-lingual acoustic modelling experiments including results on non-native speaker recognition. Section 4 provides on overview on our initial activities on speech synthesis dealing with multi-lingual text and exploiting common phone alphabets. Section 5 introduces conversational dialog systems and adaptations for dealing with multi-language speech input. Section 6 focuses on voice user interface standardization and examples of prototypes for client and telephony systems. Finally Section 7 provides a conclusion and some prospect for further work.

2 Evolution of Common Phone Alphabets

The definition of a common phone alphabet for multilingual speech recognition has to deal with at least two conflicting goals: in speech recognition the phonetic inventory of each language should be covered as precise as possible in order to achieve high recognition accuracy, while at the same time as many phones as possible should be shared across languages. Maximizing the overlap will a) efficiently utilize the training data and b) lead to reasonably small acoustic models. A similar tradeoff can be observed for common phone alphabets defined for speech synthesis: while on the one hand the sounds of each language should be kept separate in order to enable high quality synthetic speech for all languages, a less detailed definition may result in a broader variety of individual synthesis units. In particular for small sized segment databases the latter may help to better match the targets requested by the synthesizers linguistic front end, cf. Section 4.

Starting from available, disjoint phonetic alphabets for seven languages (Arabic, British English, French, German, Italian, (Brazilian) Portuguese, and Spanish) which are used within our monolingual speech recognition research activities we have designed two common phonetic alphabets of different detail [3]. In a first step, language specific phone sets were simplified following available SAMPA transcription guidelines (see [4]) which affected each language's phone set to a different degree: While, for example the native French phone set remained unchanged, we gave up syllabic consonants for German, and at the same time introduced new diphthongs for British English. Then, language specific phones mapped to the same SAMPA symbol were merged into a common unit. This resulted in a common phonetic alphabet consisting of 121 phones (65 vowels, 56 consonants) for the seven languages. As can be seen in Table 1, this gave an overall reduction of 60 percent compared to the simplified language specific phonologies.

Table 1. Number for vowel and consonant phones for seven languages in the detailed common phone set. Languages are British English (En), French (Fr), German (Gr), Italian (It), Spanish (Es), Brazilian Portuguese (Pt), and Arabic (Ar).

	total	En	Fr	Gr	It	Es	Pt	Ar
vowels	65	20	17	23	14	10	20	14
consonants	56	24	19	26	32	30	22	29
Total	121	44	36	49	46	40	42	43

To increase the overlap we have defined a less detailed common phonetic alphabet, cf. Table 2. We achieved this in three steps: 1) we dropped the distinction between stressed and unstressed vowels for Spanish, Italian, and Portuguese 2) we represented all long vowels as a sequence of two (identical) short vowels and 3) we split diphthongs into their two vowel constituents. In doing so, the average number of languages that contribute to the training data for each of the 76 phones (the sharing factor) increased from 2.28 to 2.53. If we disregard Arabic, the sharing factor increased from 2.74 to 3.56. But this radical inventory reduction caused an increase of the average word error rate by about 7 percent measured on an in-house database if compared to the more detailed common phone alphabet.

Table 2. Number of vowels and consonants for seven languages in the reduced common phone set

	Total	En	Fr	Gr	It	Es	Pt	Ar
Vowels	31	13	15	17	7	5	12	11
Consonants	45	24	19	23	28	24	22	28
Total	76	37	34	40	35	29	34	39

A further benefit of the reduced phone inventory stems from the fact that additional languages can be covered with less new phones as with the detailed inventory. The integration of eight additional languages (Table 3) required only 2 additional vowels and 12 consonants which is a result that makes us believe that the slight degradation in accuracy is tolerable and likely to be adjustable by improved acoustic modelling techniques.

Table 3. Number of vowels and consonants for additional languages integrated into the reduced common phonetic alphabet: Czech (Cz), Japanese (Jp), Finnish (Fi), Greek (El), Dutch (Nl), Danish (Da), Norwegian (No), and Swedish (Sv).

	Cz	Jp	Fi	El	Nl	Da	No	Sv
vowels	5	5	8	5	14	14	17	17
consonants	27	23	19	25	22	20	23	24
total	32	28	27	30	36	34	40	41

3 Multilingual Acoustic Modeling

Multilingual acoustic modeling facilitates the development of speech recognizers for languages with only little available training data, and also allows reduced complexity of application development by the creation of acoustic models that can simultaneously recognize speech from several languages [5]. The use and combination of multilingual acoustic models has also proven advantageous for the recognition of accented speech produced by a wide variety of non-native speakers with different commands of the system's operating language [6].

Acoustic modeling for multilingual speech recognition to a large extend makes use of well established methods for (semi-)continuous Hidden-Markov-Model training. Methods that have been found of particular use in a multilingual setting include, but are not limited to, the use of *multilingual seed HMMs*, the use of *language questions* in phonetic decision tree growing, *polyphone decision tree specialization* for a better coverage of contexts from an unseen target language, and the determination of an appropriate *model complexity* by means of a Bayesian Information Criterion; see, for example, [5, 7] for an overview and further references.

Having now reached a certain maturity, the benefits of multilingual acoustic models are most evident in applications that require both robustness against foreign speakers and the recognition of foreign words. We have simultaneously explored both of these when creating a Finnish name dialer whose application directory consists of a mix of 6,000 Finnish and foreign names, and which is used by native and non-native speakers.

For that purpose, we created acoustic models with different proportions of speech data from Finnish (SpeechDat-II), US-English, UK-English, German, Italian and Spanish. The amount of training material used for the creation of various acoustic models ranges from a mono-lingual Finnish acoustic model created from 70,000 utterances to a multilingual model that was trained from up to 280,000 utterances (approx. 190 hours of speech). As expected, we found a decreasing word error rate when the amount of data increased. Word error rates on the 6,000 foreign names task were between 2.63 percent in case of the monolingual Finnish recognizers and 2.07 percent when the entire data was used for training. More interestingly, we obtained reduced word error rates also when performing digit recognition experiments in Spanish with the so created multilingual acoustic models. These results clearly demonstrate that the acoustic models learn from other languages data and thus provide robustness for native Spanish speakers.

4 Multilingual Speech Synthesis

Whereas multilingual modeling is an almost well established principle in speech recognition, it is an only emerging concept in the area of speech synthesis, although the need for a better utilization of synergies between both fields has been recently recognized [9]. Despite of some work towards system architectures and algorithms that can be used for the construction of synthesizers for a variety of languages [10,11], today's systems usually achieve speech output in multiple languages by use of two or more language dependent synthesizers (see, for example, [12]), which is frequently accompanied by switching to a different voice.

The IBM trainable text-to-speech system [13] serves as a test bed for our recent work on bilingual, unit selection based speech synthesis, which is briefly sketched in the following. While above mentioned deficiencies are addressed by the construction of a multilingual back end database, in contrast to [14] we do not provide any mixed-lingual text analysis, but employ a set of language specific linguistic front ends in conjunction with a recently developed transformation-based learning approach to language identification [15]. During synthesis, input text is annotated with a language identifier and passed to the corresponding front end that performs text normalization, text-to-phone conversion, and phrase boundary generation. Preprocessed phrases are passed to the back-end that employs a Viterbi beam-search to generate the synthetic speech. The cost function has been revised recently, and now tends to favor long contiguous segments which produces fewer splices and allows preservation of the natural prosody.

The construction of bilingual voices (German/English and Spanish/English) relies on a script of about 10.000 sentences (15 hours of speech, including silence) that include approximately 2000 phonetically balanced sentences as well as a variety of newspaper articles, emails about different topics, proper names, digits and natural numbers, and a number of prompts that are related to popular voice driven applications (e.g. air travel information). While the German or Spanish recording scripts already include some English words, for the construction of bilingual voices each script was augmented by 2000 phonetically balanced English sentences that were read by the same voice talents under the same recording conditions.

For the creation of bilingual Spanish/English and German/English voices, we have utilized common phonetic units to a different degree. For Spanish/English we followed a more conservative design and kept the vowels separate, while all of the consonant phonemes were merged. In contrast, a more aggressive strategy was followed for the construction of a bilingual German/English synthesizer, where we decided to share not only all consonants between the two languages, but also all vowels, nasal vowels and diphthongs. Multilingual Hidden Markov Models trained with approx. 50.000 utterances from five different languages (English, French, German, Spanish, and Italian) are used to construct the synthesizer's acoustic unit inventory. In order to obtain most accurate alignments, speaker-independent, time synchronous models are transformed into speaker-dependent, pitch synchronous models by running several iterations of the forward-backward algorithm during this process. Phonetic context clustering of the final, pitch-synchronous alignment is used to create a bilingual acoustic decision tree; each leaf of these trees holds a set of subphoneme-sized speech segments from which the output speech is generated.

During the construction of the system, we experienced several advantages from using multilingual models, ranging from the seamless alignment of both the native and the non-native part of the recorded corpus to a better agreement between the speaker's actual pronunciation of foreign words and the dictionary which helps to avoid segmental errors during synthesis. Additional benefits were seen when using bilingual decision trees for the creation of speaker dependent prosody targets. For that purpose, sets of features extracted from each language's front-end are mapped to pitch and duration targets for each syllable or phone, respectively. Training of a common decision tree from both the native and non-native part of the speech database turned out to be an efficient method to overcome data sparseness resulting from the fact that we have recorded only a small amount of non-native data so far. While informal listening tests unveiled no degradation for synthesis in any of the primary languages (German or Spanish) and showed improved synthesis quality for embedded English phrases, the construction of a fully bilingual synthesizer still requires the recording of a larger English corpus.

5   Multilingual Conversational Dialog Systems

The scale of multilinguality for a conversational system can reach from a set of monolingual systems for all languages, where the user chooses in the first utterance the language of choice to be used during the whole dialog, towards completely multilingual systems, where all system components are able to process multilingual input and output.

If built up from several separate monolingual systems, at the beginning of each dialog the system has to decide which language the user prefers. This can be done in different ways:

1.   the user can be asked in different languages to choose the preferred language by using touch tones,
2.   a language identification module utilizes the first user utterance to determine the language to be used for the remaining dialog,
3.   throughout the whole interaction the utterances can be processed in parallel in each language and the output with the best score determines the language.

The advantage of the latter approach is that a multilingual system can be built with minimal effort, in case systems for different languages exist.

An alternative approach is to combine a multilingual speech recognition system with several monolingual systems for the NLU and dialog that run in parallel. In this case the language of the dialog must be identified from the spoken utterance, either by employing a spoken language identification module, or – in case of grammar based speech recognition – by identifying the language from the grammar that scores best. Drawbacks of this approach are a potentially less accurate speech recognition component, and the possibility of incorrect language identification.

However, the most challenging approach is to create a conversational system in which all components can cope with multilingual input and output. Besides the multilingual speech recognition, multilingual NLU, dialog, answer generation and synthesis components are needed. The advantage is that a user can switch languages between utterances and even within an utterance. The system has to decide for each utterance, in which language the answer will be generated.

There are different aspects to keep in mind, when deciding for one approach or the other. As already discussed, accuracy and application maintenance issues can be an argument to decide for deploying several monolingual language components rather than full multilingual technologies. The parallel language component approach facilitates also the addition of further languages into the system. Another aspect is the practical usage of such a system. In the case of a telephony system, which provides communication in the users' mother tongue, it's rather unlikely that a user will switch between languages within an utterance or even between utterances. When deploying a kiosk system (e.g. at a train station or airport), the demands are quite different. It may be difficult for the system to determine the end of a dialog with one user, and the beginning of the next one. Thus, a system that allows switching of languages between utterances is a good compromise between flexibility and robust system performance.

An additional issue to consider is the nature of the backend database: If the backend content is available in only one language it needs translation, which is probably not a big deal for dates, prices and numbers, but can be a real challenge for content such as event information (for example the names of performers, venues, streets) which might be language specific and needs special handling during synthesis. In [8] results for two of the above approaches are presented: a system with parallel, monolingual components and a system where all components are bilingual. The developed application covers sport events of the Olympic Games in Athens in 2004. In many respects, the results showed the superiority of the multilingual architecture with parallel language-specific components. Furthermore, the maintenance of this approach turned out to be relatively easy: the system can be constructed from monolingual systems, and adding new languages requires only slight modifications in the overall system. However, the parallel approach is more expensive when it comes to processing power for all parallel components. Results from user tests with the parallel approach were promising and showed that multilingual systems can be built with rather small performance degradation. However, these were only first results, which will be further verified and extended e.g. by adding further languages and with other applications.

6 Multi-modal Voice User Interfaces

To enable the rapidly growing community of voice application designers to easily develop good voice applications it is required to implement programming models which allow hiding some of the complexity, especially when multiple modalities for input and output are available. When we started our activities there were no standards for Web-based multi-modal application development established. We thus explored several approaches to support both visual and oral input in a coordinated manner. The multi-modal techniques introduced in this section highlight one of the possible approaches. We picked this particular solution because it allowed natural extension of the VoiceXML model which provides already built-in dialog management capabilities.

In the design of a multi-modal system, one of the important architectural questions is how (and to what extend) user actions and respective application state changes are propagated from one modality to another (i.e. the *synchronization model*). The synchronization model implemented in our browser is a powerful approach to drive applications such as SMS dictation, yet quite compact, and straightforward to be implemented on commercially available PDA such as Compaq iPAQ, Loox and others. The synchronization framework is now introduced in some more detail.

The multi-modal capabilities of this newly developed browser are extensions to the standard VoiceXML input (DTMF and speech recognition) and output (pre-recorded audio or TTS) that support the rendering of HTML pages, and the use of HTML links and forms for user input. We support VoiceXML code to control loading of pages into the HTML component (page-level synchronization) and the HTML component to send specific user-related updates to the VoiceXML component (sub-page-level synchronization):

- Displaying HTML pages is implemented through extensions to the semantics of the VoiceXML <prompt> tag. HTML documents referenced from VoiceXML code are passed to the HTML viewer and treated as a page to be displayed. The page stays displayed until it is rewritten with a new content. Instead of referencing an URL, the designer has an option to construct HTML pages at runtime via ECMA script procedures included as part of the VoiceXML document. Runtime generation of HTML pages is beneficial for multi-modal applications with highly dynamic visual content, which is for example the case in SMS applications.

- The HTML pages displayed can also contain links and forms that can be used to provide explicit synchronization between HTML and VoiceXML components. For example, links with values are used as synchronization anchors that convey the information on user's clicking to the VoiceXML component. Similarly, the values of HTML form variables are propagated to the VoiceXML component upon form completion (on submit). Such sub-page-level synchronization is necessary to implement multi-modal applications that support dynamic filling of HTML forms via a GUI and / or voice.

We refined above mentioned techniques during the development of several multi-modal case study applications. While practical experience from these studies shows that the current set of multi-modal extensions is sufficient for efficient authoring of PDA-scale, multi-modal applications our recent voice user interface activities shifted towards multi-modal design leveraging XHTML and VoiceXML which are widely spread and starting to become a de facto standard.

Very often users have available more than one client (for example, a mobile phone, a PDA, and a notebook) which provide different modalities. Therefore, extending multi-modal concepts to cover multi-client aspects is a growing focus of interest. The techniques described constitute one of several possible approaches, and were selected because they allow easy extension of the application for a new client setup. Originally, we defined several requirements for the application behavior:

- The application has to cover different clients.
- The incorporation of a new client into the running application has to be maximally simplified.
- The executive code has to be separated from the data as well as dialog control description.

To achieve these requirements we decided to use XML, XSL and XSLT. The dialog flow is described within XSL files. For the different clients the different XSL files are defined wherever required. The dynamic data - like e.g. client side application data, grammars, etc. – is stored in XML files. Beside these two types of files there is also static data like audio files, graphical images, static grammars or other static data which can be used for improving the design for a certain client.

The server side application is waiting for clients' requests. Based on an incoming HTTP request and the type of the client, the executive code selects the appropriate XSL file (which holds the client dependent static data), an XML file (with client independent dynamic data), and additional static data files to generate the requested page (pages). The internal structure of the server side layout (as PHP environment) is depicted in Figure 1.

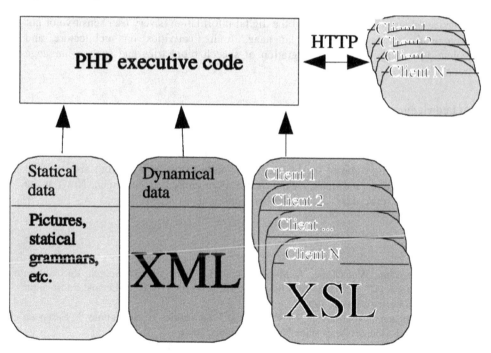

Fig. 1. Architecture of Server Side Layout

We refined the above mentioned techniques during the development of several simple multi-client case study applications. Initial experience during this development procedure indicates that this multi-client approach is powerful enough to cover efficiently several different clients.

Above overview on multi-modal design tasks as well as the ability to facilitate voice application development within multi-client scenarios will build the base for our ongoing activities to design multi-lingual applications which leverage recognition, synthesis and conversational understanding technologies.

7 Conclusion and Outlook

Within this article we provided an overview on our recent activities towards multi-lingual speech processing systems. Following a motivation for our overall scope of work we covered the definition and ongoing expansion of a common phone alphabet which builds the base for all our multi-lingual voice technology component activities. Exploiting the various versions of common phone sets we highlighted the progress for multi-lingual speech recognition and synthesis as well as the design and creation of differently architected conversational language understanding applications. To emphasize the importance of overall system and voice user interface needs we introduced the development of multi-modal and multi-client architectures and its design principles. This evolving infrastructure builds the base of integration of the multi-lingual voice technologies and will ultimately allow mobile access to digital information anywhere. As some of the digital information is very user sensitive or not even available in the user's language, future activities on architecture and technologies may cover the integration of speech biometrics and spoken language translation.

Acknowledgement. The authors wish to make explicit what is obvious to those at home in the community: At some point of our professional career all of us have been associated with the Chair for Pattern Recognition at Friedrich-Alexander-University Erlangen-Nürnberg, headed by Professor H. Niemann. It was Professor Niemann who not only taught us some of the basics of our daily technical work, but also sets the stage for excellence and quality we have been committed to since then. Now, at the occasion of his retirement, we want to say thank you.

References

1. S. Kunzmann, "VoiceType: A Multi-Lingual, Large vocabulary Speech Recognition System for a PC", Proceedings of the 2nd SQEL Workshop on Multi-Lingual Information Retrieval Dialogs, Pilsen, 1997.
2. S. Kunzmann, "Applied Speech Processing Technologies – our Journey", European Language Resources Association Newsletter, Paris, 2000.
3. S. Kunzmann, V. Fischer, J. Gonzalez, O. Emam, C. Günther, E. Janke, "Multilingual Acoustic Models for Speech Recognition and Synthesis", Proc. of the IEEE Int. Conf. on Acoustics, Speech, and Signal Processing, Montreal, 2004.
4. C.J. Wells, "Computer Coded Phonemic Notation of Individual Languages of the European Community", Journal of the International Phonetic Association, Vol. 19, pp. 32-54, 1989.

5. T. Schultz, A. Waibel, "Language Independent and Language Adaptive Acoustic Modeling for Speech Recognition", Speech Communications, Vol. 35, 2001.
6. V. Fischer, E. Janke, S. Kunzmann, "Likelihood Combination and Recognition Output Voting for the Decoding of Non-Native Speech with Multilingual HMMs, Proc. of the 7th Int. Conference on Spoken Language Processing, Denver, 2002.
7. V. Fischer, J. Gonzalez, E. Janke, M. Villani, C. Waast-Richard, "Towards Multilingual Acoustic Modeling for Large Vocabulary Speech Recognition", Proc. of the IEEE Workshop on Multilingual Speech Communications, Kyoto, 2000.
8. M. Mast, T. Roß, H. Schulz, H. Harrikari, "Different Approaches to Build Multilingual Conversational Systems", Proc. of the 5th International Conference on Text, Speech and Dialogue, Brno, Czech Republic, 2002.
9. M. Ostendorf, I. Bulyko, "The Impact of Speech Recognition on Speech Synthesis", Proc. of the IEEE 2002 Workshop on Speech Synthesis, Santa Monica, Ca., 2002.
10. R. Sproat, "Multilingual Text-to-Speech Synthesis. The Bell Labs Approach", Kluwer Academic Publishers, Dordrecht, Boston, London, 1998.
11. R. Hoffmann, O. Jokisch, D. Hirschfeld, H. Kruschke, U. Kordon, U. Koloska,"A Multilingual TTS System with less than 1 Mbyte Footprint fro Embedded Applications", Proc. of the IEEE Int. Conference on Acoustics, Speech, and Signal Processing, Hong Kong, 2003.
12. L. Mayfield Tomokiyo, A. Black, K.Lenzo, "Arabic in my Hand: Small-footprint Synthesis of Egyptian Arabic", Proc. of the   8th European Conf. on Speech Communication and Technology, Geneva, 2003.
13. E. Eide, A. Aaron, R. Bakis, P. Cohen, R. Donovan, W. Hamza, T. Mathes, M. Picheny, M. Polkosky, M. Smith, M. Viswanathan, "Recent Improvements to the IBM Trainable Speech Synthesos System", Proc. of the IEEE Int. Conf. on Acoustics, Speech, and Signal Processing, Hong Kong, 2003.
14. H. Romsdorfer, B. Pfister, "Multi-Context Rules for Phonological Processing in Polyglott TTS Synthesis", Proc. of the 8th Int. Conf. on Spoken Language Processing, Jeju Island, Korea, 2004.
15. J.C. Marcadet, V. Fischer, C. Waast-Richard, "A Transformation-Based Learning Approach To Language Identification For Mixed-Lingual Text-To-Speech Synthesis", Proc. of the   9th European Conf. on Speech Communication and Technology, Lisbon, 2005.

Cluster-Based Point Cloud Analysis for Rapid Scene Interpretation

Eric Wahl and Gerd Hirzinger

Institute of Robotics and Mechatronics,
German Aerospace Center (DLR)
eric.wahl@dlr.de

Abstract. A histogram-based method for the interpretation of three-dimensional (3D) point clouds is introduced, where point clouds represent the surface of a scene of multiple objects and background. The proposed approach relies on a pose-invariant object representation that describes the distribution of surface point-pair relations as a model histogram. The models of the used objects are previously trained and stored in a database. The paper introduces an algorithm that divides a large number of randomly drawn surface points, into sets of potential candidates for each object model. Then clusters are established in every model-specific point set. Each cluster contains a local subset of points, which is evaluated in six refinement steps. In the refinement steps point-pairs are built and the distribution of their relationships is used to select and merge reliable clusters or to delete them in the case of uncertainty. In the end, the algorithm provides local subsets of surface points, labeled as an object. In the experimental section the approach shows the capability for scene interpretation in terms of high classification rates and fast processing times for both synthetic and real data.

1 Introduction

Scene interpretation is an important basic step for several different applications. Therefore, it is most desirable to have a generic approach that fits to every kind of three-dimensional (3D) object and that minimizes application-specific adaption as much as possible.

Statistics of geometric feature distributions of shape are a generic description of free-form objects. Examples of representations for one and two-dimensional feature distributions are discussed in [1,2]. These approaches are capable of rapidly classifying objects with respect to large databases. However, the objects need to be isolated from background and suffer from moderate recognition accuracy, so that they are more suitable for only a coarse preliminary search.

An alternative line of research addresses local shape distributions that allow scenes of multiple objects and backgrounds. The *spin images* of Johnson and Hebert [3] as well as the *surface signatures* of Yamany and Farag [4] contributed a lot to local distribution analysis in cluttered scenes. To create their histograms, surface points are picked and a plane is rotated about their local surface normals. The surrounding points are accumulated in that plane. Thus, both approaches require dense surface meshes and relatively large memory consumption for object representation.

W. Kropatsch, R. Sablatnig, and A. Hanbury (Eds.): DAGM 2005, LNCS 3663, pp. 160–167, 2005.

This paper relies on a generic histogram-based description of shape as introduced in [5]. The object representation shows good performance with respect to recognition rate, processing time, memory consumption, and descriptive capacity. The contribution of this work is an expansion of the formerly isolated free-form objects to scenes that include several objects and background. A new cluster-based method is introduced, which iteratively separates object points from the point cloud with respect to the local distribution of point-pair relations.

2   Object Representation and Training Phase

This section summarizes the object representation (see [5] for details) and expands the former description with two additional parameters.

Free-form shapes that are composed of oriented surface points can be described by the statistical distribution of point-pair relations. An oriented point consists of its position $\mathbf{u}$ and its local surface normal $\mathbf{v}$ and is referred to as a *surflet* in the following.

The relationship of a surflet $\mathbf{p_1} = (\mathbf{u_1}, \mathbf{v_1})$ to another surflet $\mathbf{p_2} = (\mathbf{u_2}, \mathbf{v_2})$ is uniquely encoded by four parameters α, β, γ, and δ. The attributes α and β respectively represent $\mathbf{v_2}$ as an azimuthal angle and the cosine of a polar angle, with respect to $\mathbf{p_1}$. The parameters γ and δ represent the direction and length of the translation from $\mathbf{u_1}$ to $\mathbf{u_2}$, respectively. Furthermore, we refer to the relationships of a surflet-pair $\mathbf{s} = (\mathbf{p_1}, \mathbf{p_2})$ as a *feature* $\mathbf{f_s} = (\alpha, \beta, \gamma, \delta)$.

Taking all possible features into account leads to a characteristic distribution of an object surface. The feature distribution is quantized in a histogram H_M of normalized frequencies. For each dimension we use five quantization steps. This produces a number of $d = 5^4 = 625$ bins per histogram. The function $h_M : \mathbf{f_s} \mapsto \mathbf{b} \in \{1, 2, \ldots, \mathbf{d}\}$ maps a feature to the corresponding bin $H_M(b)$.

A model $M = (H_M, \delta_{M,\max}, \tilde{r}_M, r_{M,\max})$ consists of a normalized histogram of feature probabilities and three characteristic parameters. The first parameter is the maximum distance $\delta_{M,\max}$ between two object surflets. The last parameters are the mean distance $\tilde{r}_M$ and the maximum distance $r_{M,\max}$ of surface points to the centroid.

In the training phase, models are learned by uniformly drawing a large number of random surflet-pairs. The data source used for training can be either synthetical (e.g. from CAD models) or can be measurements from 3D-sensing. In the second case the measurements should contain no background surflets.

Experiments concerning the descriptive capacity of the object representation, i.e. recognition rates in the presence of noise, with partial visibility and variation of the surface point density, are discussed in [5].

3   Scene Interpretation

In this paper, we deal with 3D-scenes that consist of oriented surface points that build large point clouds.

Because we are representing an object as a distribution of its surflet-pair relations, the strategy of scene interpretation is to divide the point cloud into subsets and label them as an object or as background.

The structure of sensed data is often a point cloud with varying local densities, while objects are trained with randomly and uniformly drawn samples of the surface. The different conditions of surface density affects the probable location of a surflet and, therefore, lead to distorted feature histograms. To overcome this problem an initial reduction of data is necessary. A subdivision space (e.g. an octree or balanced binary tree, see [6] for details) is applied, which divides space into homogeneously-sized cells. Each cell contains the mean surflet value in its space. This preliminary step reduces the noise and size of data at once. Moreover, it guarantees an upper bound of surface density.

Since scenes consist of several objects and background, surflet-pairs are not necessary of one object only. Thus, the major problem the approach has to deal with, is to decide which surflet pairs can be trusted and which are *crosstalk*. Here, crosstalk is the relation of surflets that does not belong to the same source, e.g. a pair with one point being part of an object and one point being part of the background. The ratio of crosstalk to real object point-pairs contaminates the feature histograms and has to be kept as small as possible.

To reduce crosstalk resulting from background, two strategies are proposed. The first possibility is to *suppress* the background, in that case the position must be known and it must be the same for all measurements. A more flexible solution is to *identify and eliminate* the background. In this paper, we favor the second approach. To achieve this, the appearance of background features is trained like those of the objects.

In the following, an algorithm is proposed which cuts off local sets of points and classifies them with the label of an object. The processing is based on the previously reduced point cloud.

Step 1: Initialization of Cluster Seeds

As in the training phase, the algorithm starts with drawing a set $S = \{s_1, \ldots, s_n\}$ of n surflet-pairs s_i. With regard to the k models of the database $\Omega = \{M_1, \ldots, M_k\}$, the maximal diameter $\delta_{M_j,\max}$ of the largest model M_j limits the distance allowed in a surflet-pair.

Subsequently, the features $\mathbf{f_s}$ are calculated. At this stage it is not known whether both surflets are part of the same object or rather describe a false relation, that is crosstalk. Consequently, a second reduction step has to be applied which determines the sample set for each model M_i individually. The threshold significant surflets $\mathbf{p_s}$ of the model M_i.

$$S_{M_i}^* = \{\mathbf{p_s} \mid \exists \mathbf{s} \in S : \mathbf{p_s} \in \mathbf{s} \quad \wedge$$

$$H_{M_i}(h_{M_i}(\mathbf{f_s})) \geq \tilde{H}_{M_i} \quad \wedge \tag{1}$$

$$[H_{M_i}(h_{M_i}(\mathbf{f_s})) \geq H_{M_j}(h_{M_j}(\mathbf{f_s}))\forall j \neq i]\}, \tag{2}$$

$$\tilde{H}_M = \frac{\lambda_H}{m} \sum_{\forall \mathbf{f_s}} H_M(h_M(\mathbf{f_s})), \text{ where } m = \text{card}\{\mathbf{f_s} \mid H_M(h_M(\mathbf{f_s})) \neq 0\}, \tag{3}$$

It can be adjusted by a positive scalar[1] λ_H. The notation card is used for the cardinality of the set. Condition 2 limits the set to features, which respond most for the preferred

---

[1] We used $\lambda_H = 1.3$ in the tests.

model. Surflets collected by the background model need no further processing and affect classification no longer.

It is assumed that surflets in $\mathcal{S}_{M_i}^*$ build spatial clusters for objects represented by the model M_i. Accordingly, m random surflets are drawn therefrom. These surflets initialize the positions of a model-dependent set $\mathcal{C}_{M_i} \subseteq \mathcal{S}_{M_i}^*$ of *cluster seeds* **c**. The term "cluster seed" is used to emphasize the preliminary state as compared to a cluster.

Step 2: Cluster Seed Refinement

Each cluster seed $\mathbf{c} \in \mathcal{C}_{M_i}$ has a sphere of the radius $r_{M_i,\max}$ and initially contains the local subset

$$\mathcal{S}_{\mathbf{c},M_i}' = \{\mathbf{p_s} \in \mathcal{S}_{M_i}^* \mid r_{M_i,max} \geq \|\mathbf{p_s} - \mathbf{c}\|\} \subseteq \mathcal{S}_{M_i}^*. \qquad (4)$$

Not all of these surflets are reliable, so two alternating steps are iteratively applied for refinement.

Regrouping: Assuming that all surflets belong to the same object, a recombination of the surflets should produce acceptable features. On the other hand, false surflets that previously built also a valid feature by chance are now likely to cause crosstalk. The features of the recombined surflets are calculated and compared to the histogram H_{M_i} of the model. Impossible features that point to a zero value ($H_{M_i}(h_{M_i}(\mathbf{f_s})) = 0$) are labeled as crosstalk.

Crosstalk Elimination: A cluster seed is valid if it contains no crosstalk. All surflets that cause crosstalk are erased.

Both steps are applied until no crosstalk occurs or no surflets remain. Cluster seeds without surflets are deleted. The surflet sets of the remaining cluster seeds are referred to as $\mathcal{S}_{\mathbf{c},M_i}'' \subset \mathcal{S}_{\mathbf{c},M_i}'$.

Step 3: Cluster Seed Merging

Due to the large number of initial cluster seeds in relation to the number of expected objects, many cluster seeds belong to the same object. Cluster seeds of the same object share a large number of surflets. It is obvious that such cluster seeds should be merged into one large *cluster*.

To achieve good merging results it is advisable to start with the best cluster seeds. Therefore, a criterion is needed to rate the distribution quality of each cluster seed and its surflet set $\mathcal{S}_{\mathbf{c},M_i}''$. In [7] and [5] it is shown that the logarithmic likelihood outperforms other criteria like Kullback-Leibler divergence and χ^2-test in processing time and reliability. Accordingly, the criterion is applied.

$$\mathcal{L}(M_i|\mathcal{S}_{\mathbf{c},M_i}'') = \frac{1}{\operatorname{card}\mathcal{S}_{\mathbf{c},M_i}'} \sum_{\mathbf{p_s} \in \mathcal{S}_{\mathbf{c},M_i}'} \ln H_{M_i}(h(\mathbf{f_s})) \qquad (5)$$

Since higher votes $\mathcal{L}(M_i|\mathcal{S}_{\mathbf{c},M_i}'')$ refer to better model fits and a larger number of valid surflets, we can use $\mathcal{L}(M_i|\mathcal{S}_{\mathbf{c},M_i}'')$ to sort the cluster seeds by their quality.

Subsequently, the best ranked cluster seed is compared to all lower-ranked seeds. Each time the number of coincident surflets exceeds a certain threshold[2] λ_o, the common surflets are stored in a cluster $\hat{c}$. Restriction to surflets contained in both merging cluster seeds, reduces undetected crosstalk. Such crosstalk occurs when a cluster seed is placed in between two objects of the same model. Then, half of the set may point to one object and the other half to the second object.

Merged cluster seeds are deleted from the sorted list. If a cluster seed remains, the algorithm starts again at the top of the list. Otherwise, the merging process is finished.

Step 4: Distribution Checkup

After merging, the set of surflets has to be checked again. As previously done with the cluster seeds, the surflets of a cluster are regrouped and the features as well as their distribution histogram are calculated. Clusters of this state should contain nearly no crosstalk, thus we additionally demand the highest distribution response when applying (5) on the expected model. Otherwise the cluster is deleted.

Step 5: Cluster Similarity

Only few clusters $\hat{c} \in \hat{C}_M = \{\hat{c}_1, \ldots, \hat{c}_m\}$ reach this level. Misclassifications are rare but still possible, since similar parts of different objects may show similar distributions, e.g. the bottom of a cup and the bottom of a bottle. Nevertheless, the size of a cluster contains hints to the correctness of classification that could be described by two conditions. The first condition is that the cluster size has to exceed a minimum. Second condition is that all clusters of a model type should be of similar size. The size is measured in terms of the number $p_{\hat{c}}$ of contained surflets, where p_{max} is the surflet number of the largest cluster. The normalized surflet number $p_{\hat{c}}$ of each accepted cluster $\hat{c}$ must be in the interval $[\lambda_{\hat{c}}, 1]$, where $\lambda_{\hat{c}}$ is a threshold for the minimum number of surflets. Division by p_{max} is used for normalization.

Step 6: Cluster Competition

A last evaluation step prevents multiple classifications of an object. Therefore the centroid $\mathbf{u}_{\hat{c}_1}$ of a cluster $\hat{c}_1$ is calculated and compared to the centroids of all other clusters, e.g. the centroid $\mathbf{u}_{\hat{c}_2}$ of cluster $\hat{c}_2$. A collision occurs, if

$$\| \mathbf{u}_{\hat{c}_1} - \mathbf{u}_{\hat{c}_2} \| \leq \max(\tilde{r}_{M_i,\hat{c}_1}, \tilde{r}_{M_j,\hat{c}_2}), \tag{6}$$

holds, where $\tilde{r}_{M_i,\hat{c}_1}$ is the mean distance of the surflets to the centroid $\mathbf{u}_{M_j\hat{c}_1}$ (see Section 2). Two cases have to be distinguished. In the first case, both clusters are of the same model type ($M_i = M_j$) and then can be unified. In the second type, the clusters are of different model type ($M_i \neq M_j$). Thus, the cluster $\hat{c}_1$ of model M_i remains, if it fulfills at least two of the three following conditions:

$$p_{\hat{c}_1} > p_{\hat{c}_2}, \tag{7}$$

$$p_{\hat{c}_1}/n_{\hat{c}_1} > p_{\hat{c}_2}/n_{\hat{c}_2}, \tag{8}$$

$$\text{and} \quad n_{\hat{c}_1}/n_{max,\hat{c}_1} > n_{\hat{c}_2}/n_{max,\hat{c}_2}. \tag{9}$$

---

[2] 30% of co-occurrence shows good performance.

Condition 7 favors the cluster with the larger number of surflets with respect to its model-specific ranking, which was already calculated in Step 4. Condition 8 considers the number of surflets $p_{\hat{c}}$ in relation to the number $n_{\hat{c}}$ of merged cluster seeds per cluster. Finally, Condition 9 addresses the number of merged cluster seeds $n_{\hat{c}}$ in relation to the maximum number $n_{\max,\hat{c}}$ of merged cluster seeds per model.

4   Experiments

The experiment section is split into two parts. The first part discusses results achieved with synthetic data, while the second part takes a closer look at results from real data.

4.1   Synthetic Data

In the case of synthetic data, we use a database of eight entries, which is a sufficiently large number for most applications in robotics. The database contains models for the surface of the table, the bunny, the bottle, the carafe, the cup, the dragon, the horse, and the wine glass. All objects were randomly placed on the plain in an upright position. The minimal distance from one object to every other is always $r_{M,\max}$ of the smaller one. Fig. 2(a) shows one of a 1000 examples used in this experiment. The mean number of scene points was about 770,000 surface points, which the octree structure reduced to 77,000 points, leading to the generation of 232,000 features.

The algorithm performed at a rate of 97.2% correctly classified objects. The horse showed the weakest results. This effect derives from the disadvantageous point distribution. The thin but long legs widen the object size and therefore increment the possibility of non-object points without adding enough points themselves.

The accuracy in terms of included cluster points being part of the object achieved 96.1%, where clusters contained a mean number of 330 points. Processing times on an Intel Xeon 2.8GHz processor with 2GB RAM averaged 6.8 seconds.

4.2   Real Data

The DLR multi-sensory 3D-Modeler (see [8] for details) was used for real data acquisition. We used the laser-range scanner seven times and the laser-profiler two times in sampling the 3D-scenes. In contrast to the tests on synthetic data, the real scenes exhibit noise and incomplete surfaces (see Fig. 2(b)). The reasons for this clutter are surface parts that are unreachable for the sensor or regions that produce no valid information due to local reflectance behavior of the surface.

Here, a database of four objects is used: a toy phone, a wooden train, a bust of Zeus, and a bottle. The algorithm managed to correctly classify all objects in all nine scenes. Due to a better ratio of object points to background points the number of drawn samples can be reduced. Thus, the processing times on an Intel Xeon 2.8GHz processor with 2GB RAM for real data was only about 1.57 seconds. The separated clusters consisted of about 495 surflets. The algorithm showed no different performance between laser-range scans and laser-profile scans.

In addition to the fast classification results, the algorithm showed minor sensitivity to the threshold values. There was no need to re-parameterize them in the case of real data, so the settings of the synthetic data could be used.

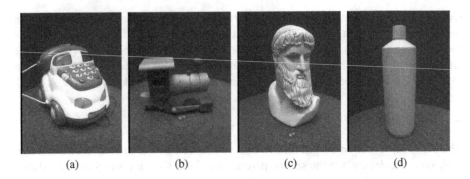

(a)   (b)   (c)   (d)

Fig. 1. The real objects database: (a) a toy phone, (b) a wooden train, (c) a bust of Zeus, and (d) a bottle

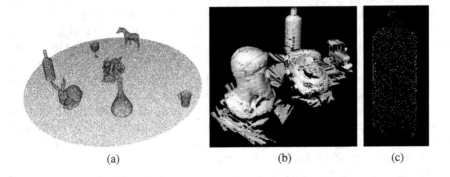

(a)   (b)   (c)

Fig. 2. (a) An example of all trained objects arbitrarily placed on a table. The scene shows the point cloud after the initial data reduction. (b) The surface mesh calculated from a 3D laser-scan of a scene. Holes on the surface result from unreachable regions or disadvantageous surface conditions (color, transparency, etc.). (c) The remaining surface points of the correctly classified bottle.

5   Conclusion

In this paper, we introduced a method for interpretation of 3D point cloud scenes using a previously trained database. A generic free-form description is used, which models the shape of an object by the statistical distribution histogram of parameterized four-dimensional relations of surface point-pairs.

Note that we are using a pose-invariant description. Only the point clouds can be extracted as input for an *iterative-closest-point algorithm (ICP)*, for example, to acquire object pose if necessary.

The proposed algorithm localizes objects in the scene by initially drawing a large number of random surface points and grouping them into pairs. Afterwards, the point-pair relations are calculated and the most likely origin for them are investigated. This is done in six evaluation steps by first establishing preliminary clusters that are later merged into final clusters if they are deemed trustworthy or that are deleted elsewhere.

Each cluster consists of a set of local points. Every evaluation step is a refinement of the sets, such that the result of the algorithm provides sets of surface points that are labeled with one of the trained objects.

In the experimental section we showed that our approach is capable of fast classification of objects in the presence of background. The experiments addressed classification results and processing times for both synthetic and real data. The generic free-form description, which allows training by CAD models or 3D-scans, combined with the high classification rates (above 97%) in less than 6.8 seconds for synthetic data and less than 2.1 seconds for real data, makes our algorithm an efficient tool for many applications in robotics.

References

1. Osada, R., Funkhouser, T., Chazelle, B., Dobkin, D.: Shape distributions. ACM Transcations on Graphics **21(4)** (2002) 807–832
2. Vandeborre, J.P., Couillet, V., Daoudi, M.: A practical aproach for 3D model indexing by combining local and global invariants. 3D Data Processing Visualization Transmission (3DPVT'02) (2002) 644–647
3. Johnson, A.E., Hebert, M.: Using spin images for efficient object recognition in cluttered 3D scenes. IEEE Transactions on Pattern Analysis and Machine Intelligence **21** (1999) 433–449
4. Yamany, S.M., Farag, A.A.: Surface signatures: An orientation indepentent free-form surface representation scheme for the purpose of objects registration and matching. IEEE Transactions on Pattern Analysis and Machine Intelligence **24** (2002) 1105–1120
5. Wahl, E., Hillenbrand, U., Hirzinger, G.: Surflet-pair-relation histograms: A statistical 3d-shape representation for rapid classification. International Conference on 3-D Digital Imaging and Modelling (2003)
6. Wahl, E., Hirzinger, G.: A method for fast search of variable regions on dynamic 3D point clouds. DAGM 2005 (27th Annual meeting of the German Association for Pattern Recognition) (2005)
7. Schiele, B., Crowley, J.L.: Recognition without correspondence using multidimensional receptive field histograms. International Journal of Computer Vision **36(1)** (2000) 31–52
8. Suppa, M., Hirzinger, G.: A novel system approach to multisensory data acquisition. The 8th Conference on Intelligent Autonomous Systems IAS-8 (2004)

A Novel Parameter Decomposition Approach to Faithful Fitting of Quadric Surfaces

Xiaoyi Jiang and Da-Chuan Cheng

Department of Computer Science, University of Münster, Germany
{xjiang, dacheng}@math.uni-muenster.de

Abstract. This paper addresses a common problem in dealing with range images. We propose a novel method to fit surfaces of known types via a parameter decomposition approach. This approach is faithful and it strongly reduces the possibilities of dropping into local minima in the process of iterative optimization. Therefore, it increases the tolerance in selecting the initializations. Moreover, it reduces the computation time and increases the fitting accuracy compared to former approaches. We present methods for fitting cylinders, cones, and tori to 3D data points. They share the fundamental idea of decomposing the set of parameters into two parts: one part has to be solved by some traditional optimization method and another part can be solved either analytically or directly. We experimentally compare our method with a fitting algorithm recently reported in the literature. The results demonstrate that our method has superior performance in accuracy and speed.

Keywords: parameter decomposition, cylinder fitting, cone fitting, torus fitting.

1 Introduction

Geometric fitting is a fundamental task in computer vision. Usually, a segmentation is carried out to group image points into sets, each corresponding to a different image feature [1]. Then, geometric fitting follows to compute the optimal mathematical representation of an appropriate type for each set of image points. This way we are able to generate a compact representation of image features.

In this work we investigate the fitting of cylinders, cones, and tori in 3D space. Since an analytic solution exists for spheres [2], we do not consider this type of quadric surfaces in this paper. Most of the related publications [3–5] are based on a straightforward parameterization with a high number of parameters to be optimized and a direct optimization of all parameters. It is our intention to carefully analyze the specific fitting problems at hand and to develop an optimization procedure with a substantially reduced number of parameters.

One recent work is presented by Marshall et al. [3]. They have proposed parameter representations for cylinders, cones, and tori. The advantage they have mentioned is of being robust in the sense that as the principal curvatures

W. Kropatsch, R. Sablatnig, and A. Hanbury (Eds.): DAGM 2005, LNCS 3663, pp. 168–175, 2005.
© Springer-Verlag Berlin Heidelberg 2005

of the surfaces being fitted decrease, the results naturally become closer and closer to the surfaces of fitted objects. They claim that using curvature instead of radius can avoid the divergence problem in the optimization. Their method is implemented and compared with our results in Section 6.

Typically, iterative techniques such as the Levenberg-Marquardt algorithm are used to compute the optimum of highly complex optimization functions. Here we are faced with two difficulties. First, any such iterative algorithm requires good initial estimate of the optimum which is then refined. It is not always easy to find reasonable initial estimates. Secondly, a large number of parameters results in a high-dimensional optimization space which may have a very complex topography and therefore brings a high risk of getting in local minima. In this case we often have troubles to analyze the optimization space, for instance by means of visualization. Consequently, it may even be impossible to specify maximal estimation errors of the initial parameter values such that the iterative process is guaranteed to reach the global minimum. This uncertainty is characteristic to high-dimensional non-linear optimization tasks.

In this work we apply a decomposition technique [6] to reduce the optimization space dimensions. A smaller number of parameters tends to ease the initial estimation of parameters. In addition, the reduction of parameters decreases the possibilities of dropping into local minima. In this case the optimization space may become simple enough to be analyzed to get an insight into its topography.

The paper is structured as follows. We first formulate the decomposition technique briefly in Section 2. Then the cylinder, cone, and torus fitting problem with the parameter decomposition construction are presented in Sections 3-5. Afterwards, the experimental results and comparisons are given in Section 6. Finally, some discussions conclude this paper.

2   Parameter Decomposition Technique

A novel method was proposed [6] for alleviating some difficulties in non-convex optimization problems. The traditional optimization treats the whole parameters simultaneously. Here the parameters are decomposed into two parts, one part of them can be solved by either an analytic or a direct method, and another part of parameters has to be solved by an iterative optimization process. Let $\mathbf{p}_i$, $i = 1, \cdots, n$, denote n data points to be fitted by a representation function $f(\mathbf{v}) = 0$, where $\mathbf{v} \in \Re^k$ is the parameter vector. We assume that the distance function of a point $\mathbf{p}_i$ to the fitted function $f(\mathbf{v})$ is $d(\mathbf{p}_i, f(\mathbf{v}))$. Thus, the geometric fitting problem can be formulated as:

$$\mathbf{v}_{opt} = \arg \min_{\mathbf{v} \in \Re^k} \sum_{i=1}^{n} d(\mathbf{p}_i, f(\mathbf{v}))$$

We decompose $\mathbf{v}$ into $\mathbf{v} = [\mathbf{v_1 v_2}]$, where $\mathbf{v_1} \in \Re^{k_1}$, $\mathbf{v_2} \in \Re^{k_2}$, and $k \equiv k_1 + k_2$. After some rearrangement of parameters $\mathbf{v}$, the optimization task is reorganized as:

$$\mathbf{v}_{opt} = \arg \min_{\mathbf{v_1} \in \Re^{k_1}} [\min_{\mathbf{v_2} \in \Re^{k_2}} \sum_{i=1}^{n} d(\mathbf{p}_i, f(\mathbf{v_1}, \mathbf{v_2}))] = \arg \min_{\mathbf{v_1} \in \Re^{k_1}} A(\mathbf{v_1})$$

where $A(\mathbf{v}_1)$ means the global minimum sum of the distance measures for a fixed $\mathbf{v}_1$ and all possibilities of $\mathbf{v}_2$. Assume that the optimal $\mathbf{v}_2$ for reaching $A(\mathbf{v}_1)$ can be solved analytically, the original optimization problem with a total of $k_1 + k_2$ parameters is transformed into an equivalent optimization problem with k_1 parameters only.

Intuitively, the parameter reduction decreases the number of local minima and thus reduces the possibilities of dropping into local minima, and increases the possibilities of reaching global minimum. Moreover, this scheme tends to reduce the computation time. Notably, it increases the probability of reaching global minima without the trade-off in increasing the computation time like genetic algorithms.

3   Cylinder Fitting

We now consider the 3D cylinder fitting problem. Let $\mathbf{a} = \mathbf{a}(\alpha, \beta)$ be the unit direction vector of the symmetry axis, where α is the angle between the projection of $\mathbf{a}$ onto the xy-plane and the x-axis, β is the angle between $\mathbf{a}$ and the z-axis. Thereafter, we can parameterize $\mathbf{a}$ by:

$$\mathbf{a} = (\cos\alpha\sin\beta, \sin\alpha\sin\beta, \cos\beta). \tag{1}$$

Once the angle set (α, β) is determined, the cylinder surface data can be orthogonally projected onto a plane $\mathbf{Q}_1$ passing through the origin whose normal vector is $\mathbf{a}$. If (α, β) is well selected, the mapped data on the plane should form a 2D circle with the same radius as the cylinder. Therefore, the 3D cylinder fitting problem is simplified to be a 2D circle fitting problem with $\mathbf{v} = (\alpha, \beta, \rho, \gamma, r)$:

$$\mathbf{v}_{opt} = \arg\min_{\alpha,\beta}[\min_{\rho,\gamma,r}\sum_{i=1}^{n} d(\mathbf{p}_i, f(\alpha, \beta, \rho, \gamma, r))] = \arg\min_{\alpha,\beta} A_1(\alpha, \beta) \tag{2}$$

where (ρ, γ, r) are the rest cylinder model parameters defined later, and (ρ, γ) are unnecessary to be computed during the iteration process. $A_1(\alpha, \beta)$ is the sum of distances between projected points $\hat{\mathbf{p}}_i$ of $\mathbf{p}_i$ and a fitted circle. Notably, the initial distance computation in 3D is reduced to one in 2D on the plane $\mathbf{Q}_1$. The optimization task is then interpreted as finding the best circle for the data points $\hat{\mathbf{p}}_i$ after the projection based on a given (α, β).

Many solutions exist for the simple 2D circle approximation problem. The methods proposed in [7,8] are applied. In [8], finding the best circle $(x - x_0)^2 + (y - y_0)^2 = r^2$ of n points (x_i, y_i), $i = 1, 2, \ldots, n$, is to minimize the term:

$$\sum_{i=1}^{n}[(x_i - x_0)^2 + (y_i - y_0)^2 - r^2]^2,$$

for which an analytical solution exists. In [7], one minimizes the term:

$$\sum_{i=1}^{n}[\frac{(x_i - x_0)^2 + (y_i - y_0)^2 - r^2}{r}]^2$$

by eigen computation. We may use either of the circle fitting methods to compute the circle center and radius (x_0, y_0, r). The results shown in Section 6 use Pratt's method [7]. However, the method [8] demonstrates similar results which are not reported in this paper.

Now we turn our attention to technical details. Let ρ be the orthogonal distance between the origin to the axis of the cylinder. We define $\mathbf{n}$ as the unit normal vector from the origin to the cylinder axis. Now we show that $\mathbf{n}$ can be represented by a single additional parameter γ. Differentiating $\mathbf{a}$ with respect to α and β, one obtains two orthogonal vectors which are orthogonal to $\mathbf{a}$:

$$\mathbf{a}_\alpha = (-\sin\alpha\sin\beta, \ \cos\alpha\sin\beta, \ 0) \tag{3}$$
$$\mathbf{a}_\beta = (\cos\alpha\cos\beta, \ \sin\alpha\cos\beta, \ -\sin\beta) \tag{4}$$

We let $\bar{\mathbf{a}}_\alpha = \mathbf{a}_\alpha / \sin\beta$ to be a unit vector, then $\mathbf{n}$ can be spanned by $\bar{\mathbf{a}}_\alpha$ and $\mathbf{a}_\beta$ as follows:

$$\mathbf{n} = \mathbf{a}_\beta\cos\gamma + \bar{\mathbf{a}}_\alpha\sin\gamma, \tag{5}$$

where γ is the angle between $\mathbf{n}$ and $\mathbf{a}_\beta$. Assuming r is the radius of the cylinder, then the cylinder is parameterized by: $(\alpha, \beta, \rho, \gamma, r)$.

For computing (x_0, y_0, r) for some fixed (α, β), the data points $\mathbf{p}_i$ are projected onto the plane $\mathbf{Q}_1$ spanned by $\bar{\mathbf{a}}_\alpha$ and $\mathbf{a}_\beta$. The projected points $\hat{\mathbf{p}}_i$ are obtained by:

$$\hat{\mathbf{p}}_i = (\mathbf{p}_i \cdot \bar{\mathbf{a}}_\alpha, \ \mathbf{p}_i \cdot \mathbf{a}_\beta).$$

The circle approximation is applied to $\hat{\mathbf{p}}_i$. After the analytical solution of the circle approximation, (x_0, y_0, r) are obtained.

For performance comparison purpose (see Section 6), we need to compute ρ and $\mathbf{n}$ after the fitting is done. A point on the cylinder axis can be calculated:

$$\mathbf{p}_c = \mathbf{M}^t\begin{bmatrix}x_0 & y_0 & 0\end{bmatrix}^t, \tag{6}$$

where $\mathbf{M} = \begin{bmatrix}\bar{\mathbf{a}}_\alpha & \mathbf{a}_\beta & \mathbf{a}\end{bmatrix}$. Then, the distance from the cylinder axis to the origin is $\rho = |\mathbf{a} \times \mathbf{p}_c|$. Furthermore, the point on the axis with the shortest distance to the origin is $\hat{\mathbf{p}}_c = \mathbf{p}_c - (\mathbf{p}_c \cdot \mathbf{a})\mathbf{a}$. Thus, the unit normal vector to the axis is $\mathbf{n} = \hat{\mathbf{p}}_c/|\hat{\mathbf{p}}_c|$.

4   Cone Fitting

Similar parameter decomposition technique can be utilized for cone fitting as well. Generally, a cone can be modeled by six parameters. In our approach, we denote the unit direction vector of the cone axis as $\mathbf{a}(\alpha, \beta)$, which is defined in Eq.(1). ρ and γ are the same as in Section 3. Therefore, the cone axis can be determined by four parameters and denoted by $\mathbf{a}^* = \mathbf{a}^*(\alpha, \beta, \rho, \gamma)$. Assuming $\hat{\mathbf{p}}_c$ is the point on $\mathbf{a}^*$ with the shortest distance to the origin, then we define l to be the distance between the cone tip to $\hat{\mathbf{p}}_c$. The last parameter w, $0 < w < \pi/2$, specifies the angle between the cone axis and cone surface. Thereafter, $(\alpha, \beta, \rho, \gamma, l, w)$ is the parameter set in our cone model.

Similarly, we decompose these parameters into two parts: $\mathbf{v}_1 = (\alpha, \beta, \rho, \gamma)$ and $\mathbf{v}_2 = (l, \omega)$. Then, the optimization problem can be formulated as:

$$\mathbf{v}_{opt} = \arg\min_{\mathbf{v}_1}[\min_{\mathbf{v}_2} \sum_{i=1}^{n} d(\mathbf{p}_i, f(\mathbf{v}_1, \mathbf{v}_2))] = \arg\min_{\alpha, \beta, \rho, \gamma} A_2(\alpha, \beta, \rho, \gamma). \qquad (7)$$

Once $\mathbf{v}_1$ is given, the cone axis is fixed. The orthogonal distance of every data point to the axis and their corresponding projecting coordinates on the axis of the cone can be determined. These two measurements ($\hat{\mathbf{p}}_i$) can be plotted on a two dimensional plane. If the axis is correctly chosen, then these measurements should form a straight line on the 2D plane. Therefore, $A_2(\alpha, \beta, \rho, \gamma)$ is simply a 2D line fitting problem, for which analytic solutions exist for different fitting error functions. The iterative algorithm is then only necessary for $\mathbf{v}_1$.

Considering technical details, $\mathbf{n}$ is defined in Eq. (5). Given $(\alpha, \beta, \rho, \gamma)$, the parametric form of the cone axis can be represented by: $\rho\mathbf{n} + t\mathbf{a}$, where $\mathbf{a}$ is defined in Eq. (1). According to the geometry, we obtain the parameter t_i which results in the shortest distance from the data point $\mathbf{p}_i$ to the cone axis:

$$t_i = \mathbf{a} \cdot (\mathbf{p}_i - \rho\mathbf{n}),$$

where t_i is the projection coordinate of point $\mathbf{p}_i$ on the cone axis. In addition, the distance between $\mathbf{p}_i$ and the axis is:

$$d_i = |\mathbf{a} \times (\rho\mathbf{n} - \mathbf{p}_i)|.$$

Therefore, for every $\mathbf{p}_i$ we obtain $\hat{\mathbf{p}}_i = (t_i, d_i)$, $i = 1, 2, 3, ..., n$. These points will be fitted by a 2D straight line and the least square error to the line is treated as the optimization error in fitting a cone. Normally, the 2D straight line fitting has two different forms of minimization: sum of vertical offsets or Euclidean distances. Here we show only the result of vertical offsets and the Euclidean distance has similar results. Note that in the latter case we actually perform a cone fitting based on the Euclidean distance in 3D. Let the fitting line be defined by:

$$d = b + mt.$$

The vertical offset error function is calculated in each iteration:

$$f(b, m) = \sum_{i=1}^{n} [d_i - (b + mt_i)]^2.$$

Once (b, m) is obtained, the shape of cone is fixed and the rest parameters are determined by $\omega = \arctan(m)$ and $l = -b/m$.

5   Torus Fitting

We now define our torus model and address the utilization of parameter decomposition technique in the torus fitting. Four parameters α, β, ρ, and γ as

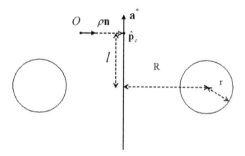

Fig. 1. The torus parameterization. $\mathbf{a}^*$ represents the torus axis. The half plane lies either on left or right side of $\mathbf{a}^*$.

defined before characterize the symmetry axis. r and R are the radii as shown in Fig. 1. l is the distance between point $\hat{\mathbf{p}}_c$ and the torus center. Thus, a torus can be parameterized by $(\alpha, \beta, \rho, \gamma, r, R, l)$. We decompose these parameters into $\mathbf{v}_1 = (\alpha, \beta, \rho, \gamma)$ and $\mathbf{v}_2 = (r, R, l)$. Similarly, the optimization task can be formulated as:

$$\mathbf{v}_{opt} = \arg\min_{\mathbf{v}_1}[\min_{\mathbf{v}_2} \sum_{i=1}^{n} d(\mathbf{p}_i, f(\mathbf{v}_1, \mathbf{v}_2))] = \arg\min_{\alpha, \beta, \rho, \gamma} A_3(\alpha, \beta, \rho, \gamma). \quad (8)$$

If $\mathbf{v}_1$ is given, the torus axis is determined. Then, the surface data can be transformed into a new 2D geometric space as follows. We consider an arbitrary half plane $\mathbf{Q}_2$ on which $\mathbf{a}^*$ lies. Then, each point is rotated using $\mathbf{a}^*$ as a rotation axis until it falls onto the plane $\mathbf{Q}_2$. If $\mathbf{v}_1$ is well selected, then all points on $\mathbf{Q}_2$ build a 2D circle. Therefore, $A_3(\alpha, \beta, \rho, \gamma)$ is simply a circle fitting problem.

Some technical details are given as follows. For a given $\mathbf{v}_1$, we rotate the coordinate system such that $\bar{\mathbf{a}}_\alpha/\mathbf{a}_\beta/\mathbf{a}$ becomes the new $x/y/z$ axis, respectively. Via this way $\mathbf{p}_i$ are mapped to $\mathbf{p}'_i$:

$$\mathbf{p}'_i = \mathbf{M}^t(\mathbf{p}_i - \rho\mathbf{n}).$$

where $\mathbf{M}$ is firstly appeared in Eq. (6). Since we are only interested in if the torus surface fits to a circle discarding the consideration of its ring position, the points $\mathbf{p}'_i$ are further rotated onto the $\mathbf{a}_\alpha\mathbf{a}$-plane around the $\mathbf{a}$-axis, i.e.:

$$\hat{\mathbf{p}}_i = \begin{bmatrix} \cos\theta & \sin\theta & 0 \\ 0 & 0 & 1 \end{bmatrix} \mathbf{p}'_i,$$

where θ is the angle between the projection of $\mathbf{p}'_i$ onto $\bar{\mathbf{a}}_\alpha\mathbf{a}_\beta$-plane and $\mathbf{a}_\alpha$. 2D circle fitting is now utilized on the projection $\hat{\mathbf{p}}_i$ and its cost function takes the place of the cost function in fitting torus. Again, we use Pratt's method and show results in Section 6. The method in [8] produces similar results which are not reported in this paper.

Table 1. Performance measurements for cylinder fitting

	Error	$\Delta\theta$(deg)	Δd	Δr	time(sec)
Our model	mean	0.0204	0.0032	0.0024	0.0273
	std	0.0146	0.0026	0.0020	0.0085
Marshall's model(a)	mean	0.3792	0.0547	3.9835	4.5997
	std	5.6646	1.2485	96.5737	4.5143
Marshall's model(b)	mean	0.0204	0.0032	0.0024	4.6117
	std	0.0146	0.0026	0.0020	4.5193

6   Results

We have performed simulations to evaluate our algorithms and to compare them with the one recently reported in [3]. One thousand cylinder, cone and torus data sets are randomly simulated, respectively. Only the visible part is selected to form data sets, and each set has less than 500 points. Several Gaussian noise levels are tested. We report here only noise level 0.3 and the other results are similar. Each data set has its own initial point for iteration. For the intention of comparison, we have the same initializations in all cases. For example, in the case of cylinder fitting we have randomly selected from $[-10, 10]$ degrees plus the ground truth of α and β, respectively.

In cylinder fitting, the radius range is between [50,100]. Table 1 shows the performance of two methods: our model and Marshall's model. Three averaged absolute errors are $\Delta\theta$, Δd and Δr. They denote the angle (in degree) difference of the estimated and ground truth cylinder axes, the distance of these two axes, and the cylinder radius difference. In Marshall's model(a), we found there are four results dropping into local minima, which results in extreme large errors. If these four results are removed, then their accuracy is similar to ours as shown in (b). In cone and torus fitting, we didn't find extreme large errors in both methods.

The performance for cone fitting is shown in Table 2. The definitions of $\Delta\theta$ and Δd have been mentioned before. $\Delta\omega$ and Δl are the absolute differences of angle ω and distance l defined in Section 4 between the fitting result and the ground truth, respectively.

Table 2. Performance measurements for cone fitting

	Error	$\Delta\theta$(deg)	Δd	$\Delta\omega$	Δl	time(sec)
Our model	mean	0.0133	0.0443	0.0076	0.0484	1.5322
	std	0.0098	0.0240	0.0078	0.0294	6.3357
Marshall's model	mean	0.1892	0.0649	0.2242	0.5862	72.6993
	std	0.5597	0.1575	0.6700	1.7312	281.4524

Table 3. Performance measurements for torus fitting

	Error	$\Delta\theta$(deg)	Δd	Δr	ΔR	Δl	time(sec)
Our model	mean	0.0027	0.0445	0.0023	0.0021	0.0440	0.2737
	std	0.0016	0.0247	0.0017	0.0017	0.0230	0.8969
Marshall's model	mean	0.0232	0.0690	0.0173	0.0217	0.0692	24.8774
	std	0.2243	0.1952	0.2037	0.1395	0.3261	100.8681

In torus fitting, the radii ranges are $10 \leq r \leq 40$ and $70 \leq R \leq 90$. With the same initializations, the comparison result is illustrated in Table 3.

The programs are written on Matlab (R14) platform. The matrices computations are used to shorten the computation time if possible. All of the three fitting results demonstrate that our model has superior performance than Marshall's model both in accuracy and in speed.

7   Conclusion

In this paper, we have proposed a novel method for cylinder, cone, and torus fitting based on the parameter decomposition approach. Through the experimental results, we observe our model showing superior performance to the Marshall's model both in accuracy and in speed. This approach can be easily extended to other fitting problems such as elliptic cylinder/torus, in which the 3D fitting task is reduced to a 2D elliptic fitting problem which can be directly solved [9]. Our contributions are not only proposing a better model for the three fitting tasks, but also pointing to a new aspect in solving an optimization problem. In addition to its practical relevance, the new insight given in this paper is a valuable contribution to understanding the fitting problem under consideration as well.

References

1. X. Jiang, "An adaptive contour closure algorithm and its experimental evaluation," *IEEE Trans. Pattern Analysis and Machine Intelligence*, vol. 22, no. 11, pp. 1252-1265, 2000.
2. B.B. Chaudhuri and P. Kundu, "Optimum circular fit to weighted data in multi-dimensional space," *Pattern Recognition Letter*, vol. 14, no. 1, pp. 1-6, 1993.
3. D. Marshall, G. Lukacs, and R. Martin, "Robust segmentation of primitives from range data in the presence of geometric degeneracy," *IEEE Trans. Pattern Analysis and Machine Intelligence*, vol. 23, no. 3, pp. 304-314, 2001.
4. N. Werghi, R. Fisher, C. Robertson, and A. Ashbrook, "Modelling objects having quadric surfaces incorporating geometric constraints," *ECCV 1998*, pp. 185-201, Freiburg, Germany, 1998.
5. P. J. Flynn and A. K. Jain, "Surface classification: hypothesis testing and parameter estimation," *In Computer Vision and Pattern Recognition*, pp. 261-267, Ann Arbor, Michigan, 1998.
6. X. Jiang, "A decomposition approach to geometric fitting," *Proc. of Int. Workshop on Machine Vision Applications*, pp. 467-470, 2000.
7. V. Pratt, "Direct least-squares fitting of algebraic surfaces," *Computer Graphics*, vol. 21 no. 4, pp. 145-152, 1987.
8. S.M. Thomas and Y.T. Chan, "A simple approach for the estimation of circular arc center and its radius," *CVGIP*, vol. 45, pp. 362-370, 1989.
9. A. Fitzgibbon, M. Pilu, and R.B. Fisher, "Direct least square fitting of ellipses," *IEEE Trans. Pattern Analysis and Machine Intelligence*, vol. 21, no. 5, pp. 476-480, 1999.

3D Surface Reconstruction by Combination of Photopolarimetry and Depth from Defocus

Pablo d'Angelo and Christian Wöhler

DaimlerChrysler AG Research and Technology, Machine Perception,
P. O. Box 2360, D-89013 Ulm, Germany
{pablo.d_angelo, christian.woehler}@daimlerchrysler.com

Abstract. In this paper we present a novel image-based 3D surface reconstruction technique that incorporates reflectance, polarisation, and defocus information into a variational framework. Our technique is especially suited for the difficult task of 3D reconstruction of rough metallic surfaces. An error functional composed of several error terms related to the measured reflectance and polarisation properties is minimised by means of an iterative scheme in order to obtain a 3D reconstruction of the surface. This iterative algorithm is initialised with the result of depth from defocus analysis. By evaluating the algorithm on synthetic ground truth data, we show that the combined approach strongly improves the accuracy of the surface reconstruction result compared to techniques based on either reflectance or polarisation alone. Furthermore, we report 3D reconstruction results for a raw forged iron surface. A comparison of our method to independently measured ground truth data yields an accuracy of about one third of the pixel resolution.

1 Introduction

A well-known image-based surface reconstruction method is *shape from shading*. This approach aims at deriving the orientation of the surface at each pixel by using a model of the reflectance properties of the surface and knowledge about the illumination conditions – for a detailed survey, cf. [2]. The integration of shadow information into the shape from shading formalism and applications of such methods in the context of industrial quality inspection have been demonstrated in [10].

A further approach to reveal the 3D shape of a surface is to utilise polarisation data. Most current literature concentrates on dielectric surfaces, as for smooth dielectric surfaces, the angle and degree of polarisation as a function of surface orientation are governed by elementary physical laws as detailed in [6]. There, information about the polarisation state of light reflected from the surface is utilised to reconstruct the 3D shape of transparent objects, involving multiple light sources equally distributed over a hemisphere and a large number of images acquired through a linear polarisation filter at many different orientations. This method is not straightforward to use in practice because it requires a somewhat elaborate setting of light sources. For smooth dielectric surfaces, in

W. Kropatsch, R. Sablatnig, and A. Hanbury (Eds.): DAGM 2005, LNCS 3663, pp. 176–183, 2005.

[7] a 3D surface reconstruction framework is proposed relying on the analysis
of the polarisation state of reflected light, the surface texture, and the locations
of specular reflections. In [11] reflectance and polarisation properties of metallic
surfaces are examined, but no physically motivated polarisation model is derived.
In [9] polarisation information is used to determine surface orientation.

The depth of a scene point can also be estimated by analysis of defocus
information (*depth from defocus*, cf. [1] for a detailed survey). This approach
makes use of the fact that the point spread function (PSF), i. e. the "blur"
at a certain image location, depends on the distance of the corresponding scene
point from the camera. It requires a calibration procedure which yields a relation
between PSF width and distance.

The three described image-based 3D surface reconstruction methods have in
common that corresponding applications to real-world scenarios are rarely described in the literature. A possible reason is the fact that each method alone
will not reveal the surface shape in an accurate and unique manner. Shape
from shading tends to produce ambiguous results for strongly specular non-
Lambertian surfaces even when several images are used. The shape from polarisation approach suffers from the same ambiguity problem and additionally
from the lack of a valid polarisation model for non-dielectric, especially metallic,
surfaces. Depth from defocus produces a dense solution for the surface shape,
which, however, tends to be very noisy.

Hence, we will present in this paper an image-based method for 3D surface reconstruction based on the simultaneous evaluation of reflectance, polarisation, and defocus data. All extracted information will be integrated into a
unified variational framework. This method is systematically evaluated based on
a synthetically generated surface to examine its accuracy and is applied to the
sophisticated real-world example of a raw forged iron surface.

2   Combination of Photopolarimetric and Defocus Information for 3D Surface Reconstruction

In our scenario, we will assume that the surface $z(x, y)$ to be reconstructed is
illuminated by a point light source and viewed by a camera, both situated at
infinite distance in the directions s and v, respectively. Parallel incident light and
an orthographic projection model can thus be assumed. For each pixel location
(u, v) of the image we intend to derive a depth value $z(u, v)$. The surface normal
is given in *gradient space* by the vector $n = (-p, -q, 1)^T$ with $p = \partial z/\partial x$ and
$q = \partial z/\partial y$. In an analogous manner, we set for the illumination direction $s =
(-p_s, -q_s, 1)^T$ and for the viewing direction $v = (-p_v, -q_v, 1)^T$. The *incidence
angle* θ_i is defined as the angle between n and s, the *emission angle* θ_e as the
angle between n and v, and the *phase angle* α as the (constant) angle between
the vectors s and v.

Estimation of depth from defocus relies on the fact that the image of a scene
point situated at a distance z from the camera becomes more and more blurred
with increasing depth offset $|z - z_0|$ between the scene point at distance z and

the plane at distance z_0 on which the camera is focussed. The blur is described by the *point spread function* (PSF) of the camera lens, which is assumed to be Gaussian with a width parameter σ.

The calibration procedure for estimating depth from defocus involves the determination of the lens-specific characteristic curve $\sigma(|z - z_0|)$ [1]. For this purpose we acquire two pixel-synchronous images of a rough, uniformly textured plane surface consisting of forged iron, inclined by 45° with respect to the optical axis. The image part in which the intensity displays maximum standard deviation (i. e. most pronounced high spatial frequencies) is sharp and thus situated at distance z_0. A given difference in pixel coordinates with respect to that image location directly yields the corresponding depth offset $|z - z_0|$. The first image is taken with small aperture, e. g. $f/16$, resulting in virtually absent image blur, while the second image is taken with the aperture that will be used later on for 3D reconstruction, e. g. $f/4$, resulting in a perceivable image blur that depends on the depth offset $|z - z_0|$. In practice, it is desirable but often unfeasible to use the sharp image acquired with small aperture for 3D reconstruction – the image brightness then tends to become too low for obtaining reasonably accurate polarisation data. Hence, the surface reconstruction algorithm must take into account the position-dependent PSF.

The images are partitioned into windows of $n_w \times n_w$ pixels size, for each of which the depth offset $|z - z_0|$ is known. After Tukey windowing, the PSF width parameter σ in frequency space is computed by fitting a Gaussian to the quotient of the amplitude spectra of the corresponding windows of the first and the second image, respectively. Only the range of intermediate spatial frequencies is regarded in order to reduce the influence of noise on the resulting value for σ. This technique and alternative methods are described in [1].

Once the characteristic curve $\sigma(|z - z_0|)$ is known, it is possible to extract a dense depth map from a pixel-synchronous pair of images of a surface of unknown shape, provided that the images are acquired at the same focus position and with the same apertures as the calibration images. The resulting depth map $z_{\text{dfd}}(u, v)$, however, tends to be very noisy. We therefore extract large-scale information about the surface orientation from it by fitting a plane of the form $\tilde{z}_{\text{dfd}}(u, v) = p_{\text{dfd}}u + q_{\text{dfd}}v + c$ to the data. The sign of either p_{dfd} or q_{dfd} must be provided a-priori.

The 3D surface reconstruction formalism we utilise throughout this paper is related to the shape from shading scheme described in detail in [2,3,4]. It relies on the global minimisation of an error function that consists of a weighted sum of several individual error terms. The observed image I is a convolution $G * I_0$ of the "true" image I_0 with the PSF G. The *intensity error* term

$$e_i = \sum_{u,v} [I(u, v) - G * R(\rho(u, v), p(u, v), q(u, v))]^2 \qquad (1)$$

describes the mean square deviation between the observed pixel intensity $I(u, v)$ and the modelled reflectance R convolved with the PSF G [5] extracted from the image as described above. It depends on the *surface albedo* $\rho(u, v)$ and the surface gradients $p(u, v)$ and $q(u, v)$, which in turn depend on the pixel coordinates (u, v).

The polarisation state of light reflected from the surface is determined based on several images of the surface acquired through a linear polarisation filter. The transmitted radiance of the reflected light oscillates sinusoidally with the orientation of the polarisation filter between a maximum I_{max} and a minimum I_{min}. The *polarisation angle* $\Phi \in [0°, 180°]$ describes the orientation under which maximum transmitted radiance I_{max} is observed. The *polarisation degree D* is given by $D = (I_{max} - I_{min})/(I_{max} + I_{min}) \in [0, 1]$. To integrate polarisation information into the 3D surface reconstruction framework we define the polarisation angle error term

$$e_\Phi = \sum_{u,v} [\Phi(u, v) - G * R_\Phi(p(u, v), q(u, v), \alpha)]^2 \qquad (2)$$

and the polarisation degree error term

$$e_D = \sum_{u,v} [D(u, v) - G * R_D(p(u, v), q(u, v), \alpha)]^2, \qquad (3)$$

describing the mean square deviation between the observations Φ and D and the corresponding modelled values R_Φ and R_D, respectively. Again the estimated PSF G is taken into account. As in this paper we will primarily examine rough metallic surfaces of industrial parts (cf. Sect. 4) in the context of industrial quality inspection, for which accurate physically motivated models are neither available for the surface reflectance nor for its polarisation properties, we will empirically determine R, R_Φ, and R_D as described in Sect. 3.

As the intensity and polarisation information alone is not necessarily sufficient to provide an unambiguous solution for the surface gradients $p(u, v)$ and $q(u, v)$, a regularisation constraint e_s is introduced as a further error term, requiring smoothness of the surface, for example small absolute values of the directional derivatives of the surface gradients. We will therefore make use of the error term (cf. also [2,4])

$$e_s = \sum_{u,v} [p_x^2 + p_y^2 + q_x^2 + q_y^2]. \qquad (4)$$

The smoothness constraint is acceptable for the surfaces regarded in this paper. For strongly wrinkled surfaces, too smooth results are yielded by (4); it might then be replaced by the *departure from integrability* error term discussed in detail in [3].

The surface gradients $p(u, v)$ and $q(u, v)$ are obtained by minimising the overall error functional $e = e_s + \lambda e_i + \mu e_\Phi + \nu e_D$, where the Lagrange parameters λ, μ, and ν denote the relative weights of the error terms. As described in detail in [4], setting the derivatives of e with respect to p and q to zero yields an iterative update rule for p,

$$p_{n+1} = \bar{p}_n + \lambda(I - G * R)G * \frac{\partial R}{\partial p} + \mu(\Phi - G * R_\Phi)G * \frac{\partial R_\Phi}{\partial p} +$$
$$\nu(D - G * R_D)G * \frac{\partial R_D}{\partial p}, \qquad (5)$$

with $\bar{p}$ as a local average. An analogous expression is obtained for q. Numerical integration of the gradient field, employing e. g. the algorithm described in [4], yields the surface profile $z(u, v)$.

Despite regularisation constraint (4) there is usually no unique solution for the surface gradients $p(u, v)$ and $q(u, v)$, especially for highly specular reflectance functions, such that the obtained solution tends to depend strongly on the initial values $p_0(u, v)$ and $q_0(u, v)$. As no a-priori information about the surface is available, we make use of the large-scale surface gradients obtained by depth from defocus analysis and set the initial values of the surface gradients to $p_0(u, v) = p_{\mathrm{dfd}}$ and $q_0(u, v) = q_{\mathrm{dfd}}$.

3   Determination of Empirical Photopolarimetric Models

For the purpose of determination of empirical reflectance and polarisation models for the surface material the surface normal n of a flat sample is adjusted by means of a goniometer, while the illumination direction s and the viewing direction v are constant over the image. Intensity I, polarisation angle Φ, and polarisation degree D are determined over a wide range of surface normals n.

According to [8], the reflectance of a typical rough metallic surface consists of three components: a diffuse (Lambertian) component, the *specular lobe*, and the *specular spike*. We model these components by the phenomenological approach

$$R(\theta_i, \theta_e, \alpha) = \rho \left[\cos\theta_i + \sum_{n=1}^{N} \sigma_n \cdot (2 \cos\theta_i \cos\theta_e - \cos\alpha)^{m_n} \right] \quad (6)$$

with $2 \cos\theta_i \cos\theta_e - \cos\alpha \equiv \cos\theta_r$ describing the angle between the specular direction r and the viewing direction v. For $\theta_r > 90°$ only the diffuse component proportional to $\cos\theta_i$ is considered. The albedo ρ is assumed to be constant over the image. The shapes of the two specular components are expressed by $N = 2$ terms proportional to powers of $\cos\theta_r$, where the coefficients $\{\sigma_n\}$ denote the strength of the specular components relative to the diffuse component and the parameters $\{m_n\}$ their widths.

The polarisation angle Φ is phenomenologically modelled by an incomplete third-degree polynomial in p and q according to

$$R_\Phi(p, q) = a_\Phi pq + b_\Phi q + c_\Phi p^2 q + d_\Phi q^3. \quad (7)$$

Without loss of generality we assume illumination from the right hand side ($p_s < 0$, $q_s = 0$) and view along the z axis ($p_v = q_v = 0$). Equation (7) is antisymmetric in q, and $R_\Phi(p, q) = 0$ for $q = 0$, i. e. coplanar vectors n, s, and v. These properties are required for geometrical symmetry reasons as long as an isotropic interaction between the incident light and the surface material can be assumed. The polarisation degree D is modelled by an incomplete second-degree polynomial in p and q according to

$$R_D(p, q) = a_D + b_D p + c_D p^2 + d_D q^2. \quad (8)$$

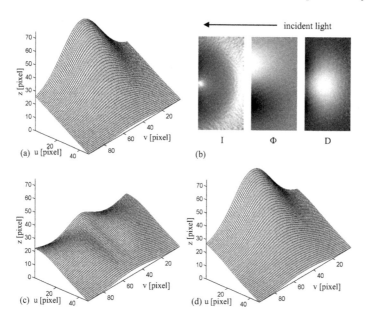

Fig. 1. 3D reconstruction of synthetic scene. (a) Ground truth. (b) Intensity I, polarisation angle Φ, and polarisation degree D images. The 3D reconstruction result was obtained based on photopolarimetric analysis (c) without and (d) with depth from defocus information. For details refer to Sect. 4.

For rough metallic surfaces, R_D is maximum near the direction of specular reflection. Symmetry in q is imposed to account for isotropic light-surface interaction.

4   Experimental Results

To examine the accuracy of 3D reconstruction we applied the algorithm described in Sect. 2 to the synthetically generated surface shown in Fig. 1a. For the PSF width parameter we assumed $\sigma \propto |z - z_0|^{-1}$ [1]. To generate a visible surface texture in the photopolarimetric images, we introduced random fluctuations of $z(u, v)$ of the order 0.1 pixels. We assumed a perpendicular view on the surface along the z axis with $v = (0, 0, 1)^T$. The scene was illuminated from the right hand side at a phase angle of $\alpha = 75°$. The surface albedo ρ was computed from (6) based on the specular reflections, which appear as regions of maximum intensity and for which we have $\theta_r = 0°$ and $\theta_i = \alpha/2$. We have set $p_0(u, v) = p_{\mathrm{dfd}}$ and $q_0(u, v) = q_{\mathrm{dfd}}$ in (5) when depth from defocus information was used, while otherwise, the PSF G was set to unity and the surface gradients were initialised with zero values due to the lack of prior information. We found that for the sort of surface regarded here, the influence of G on $z(u, v)$ is negligible and that the main benefit of depth from defocus analysis comes from the improved initialisation. The best results are obtained by utilising a combination of polarisation angle and degree, of reflectance and polarisation angle, or a combination of all three features. Detailed evaluation results are reported in Table 1.

Table 1. Evaluation results on synthetic ground truth data

Utilised information	RMS error (without dfd)			RMS error (with dfd)		
	z	p	q	z	p	q
Reflectance	11.6	0.620	0.514	9.62	0.551	0.514
Pol. angle	17.0	0.956	0.141	6.62	0.342	0.069
Pol. degree	4.72	0.138	0.514	4.73	0.135	0.514
Pol. angle and degree	1.83	0.121	0.057	1.71	0.119	0.056
Reflectance and pol. angle	12.0	0.528	0.099	2.52	0.280	0.055
Reflectance and pol. degree	10.9	0.575	0.514	8.46	0.418	0.517
Reflectance and polarisation (angle and degree)	10.2	0.277	0.072	0.91	0.091	0.050

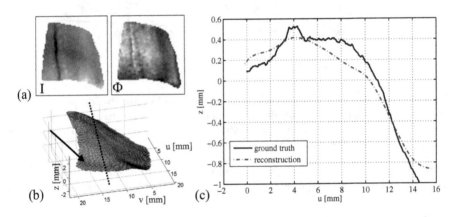

Fig. 2. 3D reconstruction of a forged iron surface. (a) Intensity and polarisation angle image. (b) 3D reconstruction result. The somewhat malformed, asymmetric surface shape is due to a fault caused during the forging process (arrow). The cross-section used in (c) is indicated by a dashed line. (c) Comparison to ground truth.

We furthermore applied our 3D surface reconstruction method to a raw forged iron part. According to Sect. 2 we empirically determined $\sigma \propto |z - z_0|^{-0.66}$ as the relation between PSF width parameter and depth offset. We found that the polarisation degree for specular reflection tends to vary over the surface by up to 20 percent, depending on the locally variable microscopic roughness. In contrast, the behaviour of the polarisation angle turned out to be very stable over the surface. We thus performed 3D reconstruction based on a combination of reflectance, polarisation angle, and depth from defocus (Fig. 2a and b). Image resolution was 0.30 mm per pixel. A cross-section of the same surface was measured with a laser focus profilometer at an accuracy of better than 1 μm (Fig. 2c), thus serving as ground truth. The RMS deviation between ground truth and the corresponding cross-section extracted from the 3D profile reconstructed with our approach amounts to 0.11 mm or about one third of the pixel resolution.

5   Summary and Conclusion

In this paper we have presented an image-based 3D surface reconstruction technique that incorporates reflectance, polarisation, and defocus information into a variational framework. Our method relies on an error functional composed of several error terms related to the measured reflectance and polarisation properties, which is minimised by means of an iterative scheme in order to obtain a 3D reconstruction of the surface. The iteration is initialised with the result of depth from defocus analysis. By evaluating the algorithm on synthetic ground truth data we show that the combined approach strongly increases the accuracy of the surface reconstruction result, compared to 3D reconstruction based on either reflectance or polarisation alone. Furthermore, we report 3D reconstruction results for a raw forged iron surface, demonstrating a reconstruction accuracy of our approach of about one third of the pixel resolution.

References

1. S. Chaudhuri, A. N. Rajagopalan. Depth From Defocus: A Real Aperture Imaging Approach. Springer-Verlag, New York, 1999.
2. B. K. P. Horn, M. J. Brooks. Shape from Shading. MIT Press, Cambridge, Massachusetts, 1989.
3. B. K. P. Horn. Height and Gradient from Shading. MIT technical report 1105A. http://people.csail.mit.edu/people/bkph/AIM/AIM-1105A-TEX.pdf
4. X. Jiang, H. Bunke. Dreidimensionales Computersehen. Springer-Verlag, Berlin, 1997.
5. M. V. Joshi, S. Chaudhuri. Photometric Stereo Under Blurred Observations. *Int. Conf. on Pattern Recognition*, Cambridge, UK, 2004.
6. D. Miyazaki, M. Kagesawa, K. Ikeuchi. Transparent Surface Modeling from a Pair of Polarization Images. *IEEE Trans. on Pattern Analysis and Machine Intelligence*, vol. 26, no. 1, pp. 73-82, 2004.
7. D. Miyazaki, R. T. Tan, K. Hara, K. Ikeuchi. Polarization-based Inverse Rendering from a Single View. *IEEE Int. Conf. on Computer Vision*, vol. II, pp. 982-987, Nice, France, 2003.
8. S. K. Nayar, K. Ikeuchi, T. Kanade. Surface Reflection: Physical and Geometrical Perspectives. *IEEE Trans. on Pattern Analysis and Machine Intelligence*, vol. 13, no. 7, 1991.
9. S. Rahmann, N. Canterakis. Reconstruction of Specular Surfaces using Polarization Imaging. *Int. Conf. on Computer Vision and Pattern Recogntion*, vol. I, pp. 149-155, Kauai, USA, 2001.
10. C. Wöhler, K. Hafezi. A general framework for three-dimensional surface reconstruction by self-consistent fusion of shading and shadow features. *Pattern Recognition*, vol. 38, no. 7, pp. 965-983, 2005.
11. L. B. Wolff. Constraining Object Features Using a Polarization Reflectance Model. *IEEE Trans. on Pattern Analysis and Machine Intelligence*, vol. 13, no. 7, 1991.

Vision-Based 3D Object Localization Using Probabilistic Models of Appearance

Christian Plagemann[1], Thomas Müller[2], and Wolfram Burgard[1]

[1] Department of Computer Science, University of Freiburg,
Georges-Koehler-Allee 79, 79110 Freiburg, Germany
{plagem, burgard}@informatik.uni-freiburg.de
[2] Fraunhofer Institute IITB, Fraunhoferstraße 1, 76131 Karlsruhe, Germany
mlt@iitb.fraunhofer.de

Abstract. The ability to accurately localize objects in an observed scene is regarded as an important precondition for many practical applications including automatic manufacturing, quality assurance, or human-robot interaction. A popular method to recognize three-dimensional objects in two-dimensional images is to apply so-called view-based approaches. In this paper, we present an approach that uses a probabilistic view-based object recognition technique for 3D localization of rigid objects. Our system generates a set of views for each object to learn an object model which is applied to identify the 6D pose of the object in the scene. In practical experiments carried out with real image data as well as rendered images, we demonstrate that our approach is robust against changing lighting conditions and high amounts of clutter.

1   Introduction

In this paper, we consider the problem of estimating the three-dimensional position and the orientation of rigid objects contained in images. This problem has been studied intensively in the computer vision community and its solution is regarded as a major precondition for many practical applications, like automatic manufacturing, quality assurance, or human-robot interaction. In this work, we are especially interested in view-based approaches, where objects are represented by 2-dimensional views. Such approaches allow to incorporate visual features directly and do not assume prior knowledge about the spatial structure of the objects. The limited localization accuracy caused by the view-based representation can be compensated for by a scene-based object tracking process, as will be demonstrated in Section 5.2.

Recently, Pope and Lowe [1] proposed the probabilistic alignment algorithm to identify two-dimensional views of objects in images. The goal of the work presented here is to investigate how this purely image-based approach can be utilized to achieve a robust estimate of the position and orientation of the object in the scene. The input to our system are either real images of an object or alternatively a volumetric model that is used to render the necessary views. We describe how the four parameters obtained from the 2D object recognition can

W. Kropatsch, R. Sablatnig, and A. Hanbury (Eds.): DAGM 2005, LNCS 3663, pp. 184–191, 2005.

be combined with the two parameters of the corresponding view to determine the pose of the object in the scene. We evaluate our approach on real images and perform simulation experiments to provide quantitative results for the localization accuracy. Experimental results carried out with free-form objects and objects with specular surfaces demonstrate the robustness of our approach.

2   Related Work

The problem of recognizing objects using two-dimensional views has been approached from many directions. Popular methods are based on eigenvector decomposition to represent and recognize 3D objects [2,3]. Alternative approaches learn networks of Gaussian basis functions [4] or build their models on wavelet-based features [5]. Several authors [6,7] apply support vector machines to object recognition. An additional approach is to train a neural network spanning the whole view sphere to classify single object views into orientation categories [8]. These methods, however, assume a segmented test image where the object instance is roughly isolated by a bounding box. The approach presented in this paper focuses on the case in which the object instance covers just a small part of the test image. To avoid the feature correspondence problem, Schiele and Pentland build position independent feature histograms [9]. To localize objects they apply a voting scheme similar to the Hough-transform. Several authors also combine view-based and model-based approaches to recognize and localize textured objects [10,11]. Finally, Lanser et al. [12] present a view-based localization system called MORAL. In their approach, the 3D object structure has to be known and is assumed to be polyhedral. The constructed object views are not clustered and generalized to achieve a more compact model.

3   View-Based Probabilistic Alignment

Pope and Lowe [1] introduced a visual object recognition approach based on probabilistic models of appearance. The appearance of an object is modeled by a relatively small set of 2-dimensional model views, each of which is assembled from discrete visual features, like edges, corners, joints, and complex combinations thereof. The features are associated with their uncertainty in presence and position as well as their distribution of attribute values. Hence, a single model view represents the appearance of an object from a whole range of view points. The scope of each model view is determined by an unsupervised learning process.

The recognition method, called probabilistic alignment, resembles Huttenlocher and Ullman's alignment approach [13] by gradually building feature pairings between model view and test image to align the view to the test image. The recognition process is guided by a probabilistic quality measure for possible alignment hypotheses.

$$g(E, T) \approx \log P(H \mid E, T) \tag{1}$$

In this equation, H denotes the hypothesis that the model view is contained in the image, E stands for the set of feature pairings contained in the hypothesized match, and T is the similarity transformation that aligns the model view with the test image. The typically large set of possible feature pairings is ordered using this measure to process likely hypotheses first.

The learning process for an unknown object starts with an empty set of model views and gradually incorporates all training views. If a new training view cannot be matched with a sufficient accuracy to an existing model view, a new model view is created. Otherwise, the training view and the matching model view are generalized to a combined model view. Therefore, the resulting view-based model is a set of generalized clusters of training views. The minimum description length principle is used to obtain the smallest model that sufficiently describes the visual appearance of the object.

4   3D Object Localization

In real world applications, it is generally not sufficient to identify an object within an image. Rather, one is often interested in its exact pose. The goal of this section is to embed the 2D recognition approach described above into a 3D object localization system, which covers object learning, view-based recognition and the calculation of the 3D pose.

4.1   Object Learning

A popular technique for the acquisition of training views for an object is to record images of the real object from different view points. This procedure requires an elaborate hardware setup to accurately measure the viewing angles and is quite time consuming. An alternative approach is to construct a 3D object model (e.g., by using photometric 3D scanning methods) and generate artificial training views. Using state of the art rendering techniques, like ray-tracing, a large training set of photo-realistic views covering different image resolutions and lighting conditions can be constructed. It may be favorable for specific applications to extract just the object silhouette, which can easily be achieved using rendering techniques. We generate photo-realistic views to keep the repertoire of visual features as wide as possible. Other systems that construct artificial views by just projecting 3D model features like lines and corners into the image plane limit themselves in that respect. As the experiments in Section 5 demonstrate, our recognition system achieves good results with real training images as well as generated ones.

The learning algorithm discussed in Section 3 clusters the training views to reflect the variance in visual appearance across the view sphere. It is therefore desirable to uniformly sample the view sphere. We achieve this by iteratively dividing a spherical triangular mesh. The individual training views are generated using ray-tracing. The optimal number of training views that have to be generated for a specific object can be determined as follows. As discussed in Section 3, the learning step builds a set of 2-dimensional model views by iteratively integrating training images. Assuming that the appearance of the object changes smoothly with small variations of the viewing angles and furthermore assuming

Fig. 1. One of the generated training images (left) and the recognition result (right) for a free-form object. It was sufficient for this object to learn and represent the silhouette.

that the views are uniformly distributed and presented in a coarse to fine order, the complete appearance of the object is covered after a certain number of training views. This number depends on the object and the learning parameters and is independent from the specific training views. In our current system, we define as the stopping criterion for generating new training views the point when the number of model views stops to increase. For example, 130 training views are sufficient to learn the 18 model views of the highly symmetric barbell object depicted in Figure 3.

4.2 Localization

For every 2-dimensional model view m, the alignment algorithm yields a 4D pose vector r (2D position (x, y), orientation α, and scale s) and a match quality measure. Assuming a calibrated camera, we can calculate the 6D pose vector of the object in the scene (3D position, 3D orientation) by utilizing information from the training step. In this section, we describe how a transformation T can be derived that maps object coordinates to scene coordinates. The localization result can be obtained directly from the transformation matrix. Let us decompose T^{-1} into four individual transformations $T^{-1} = T_4\, T_3\, T_2\, T_1$. In this equation, T_1 translates the center of the object to the origin of the scene coordinate system. It is therefore defined by the position vector $\mathbf{p}$ of the object. The distance of the object from the origin (the length of $\mathbf{p}$) can be derived from the scale factor s and the known object size from the training process. The direction of $\mathbf{p}$ is defined by the position (x, y) of the recognized view in the image plane and the camera calibration parameters. T_1 can be written as

$$T_1 = \begin{pmatrix} 1 & 0 & 0 & -p_x \\ 0 & 1 & 0 & -p_y \\ 0 & 0 & 1 & -p_z \\ 0 & 0 & 0 & 1 \end{pmatrix}, \qquad \mathbf{p} = \begin{pmatrix} p_x \\ p_y \\ p_z \end{pmatrix}. \tag{2}$$

The transformation T_2 rotates the vector $\mathbf{p}$ onto the z-axis. Vividly speaking, T_2 transforms the object into the same pose that its training counterpart was in

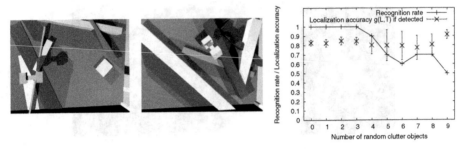

Fig. 2. Typical synthetic test data for quantitative performance analysis (left two images) and the localization results depending on the number of clutter objects (right)

when the training images for model view m were acquired. In the following, the vectors $\hat{\mathbf{x}}$, $\hat{\mathbf{y}}$, and $\hat{\mathbf{z}}$ denote the three unit vectors respectively. If we define $T_{\mathbf{a},\mathbf{b}}$ as the transformation that rotates the vector $\mathbf{a}$ onto a vector $\mathbf{b}$ around the axis perpendicular to $\mathbf{a}$ and $\mathbf{b}$ we have $T_2 = T_{\mathbf{p},\hat{\mathbf{z}}}$.

Furthermore, T_3 rotates the object within the image plane to account for the angle α that was part of the 2D recognition result. If we define $T_{\mathbf{a},\alpha}$ as the transformation that rotates around the axis $\mathbf{a}$ with angle α we obtain $T_3 = T_{\hat{\mathbf{z}},\alpha}$. Finally, T_4 rotates the object according to the viewing angles ϑ (azimuth angle) and φ (polar angle) associated with the recognized view during training, thus we obtain

$$T_4 = T_{4,2}\, T_{4,1} \qquad T_{4,1} = T_{\hat{\mathbf{x}},(180° - \varphi)} \qquad T_{4,2} = T_{\hat{\mathbf{z}},(\vartheta - 90°)} \qquad \acute{\mathbf{z}} = T_{4,1}\, \hat{\mathbf{z}}.$$

The 3D position vector of the object can be read directly from the last column of the transformation matrix of T. We refer to Shoemake [14] for details about the derivation of the 3D orientation vector in Euler's angular notation from the transformation matrix.

5   Experimental Results

5.1   Quantitative Evaluation

We conducted simulation experiments to evaluate the localization accuracy using the known ground truth. Figure 2 depicts typical examples of a series containing 100 test images. The task was to localize the barbell object among a varying number of random clutter objects using features like edges, corners, joints and complex groupings thereof. The used rectangular clutter structures made recognition harder than seemingly more realistic curved structures, because of their similarity to the barbell object. The test images were rendered to a size of 384×288 pixels using the freely available ray-tracer Povray. To compare the true object pose $\mathbf{T}$ with the localization result $\mathbf{L}$ we use the measure

$$g(\mathbf{L}, \mathbf{T}) := \max\left\{0, 1 - \left(f_z\, \delta_z^2 + f_{xy}\, \delta_{xy}^2 + f_\alpha\, \delta_\alpha^2\right)\right\} . \tag{3}$$

Fig. 3. View-based recognition result (left), the derived 3D pose (middle), and the 3D pose after refinement by a scene-based tracking process (right)

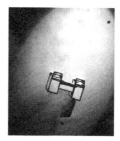

Fig. 4. Real training image (left) and recognition result (middle) for a highly specular object. Detected barbell (right) under extensive occlusion by fog.

In Equation 3, δ_z denotes the distance between the two poses along the z-axis (the viewing direction of the camera), δ_{xy} is the distance perpendicular to the z-axis, and δ_α is the difference in orientation. The weighting factors for the different dimensions have been set to $f_z = \frac{1}{250000}$, $f_{xy} = \frac{1}{50000}$, and $f_\alpha = \frac{1}{10000}$ to reflect the importance of the different dimensions given their scales. The quantities δ_z and δ_{xy} are measured in mm, δ_α in degrees. A typical value of $g = 0.80$ is reached for example with distances of $\delta_{xy} = 2.3$ cm, $\delta_z = 23$ cm, and $\delta_\alpha = 15°$. This displacement is small enough to initialize a scene-based tracking algorithm like the one described in the next section. The recognition rate for an increasing number of clutter objects as well as the achieved localization accuracy is plotted in Figure 2. The mean localization accuracy for recognized objects was $g = 0.82$ with a median of $g = 0.84$.

5.2 Recognizing Specular and Free-Form Objects and Refining the Estimated Object Pose

Specular and free-form objects are particularly hard to recognize visually. The appearance of a specular object varies greatly with changing lighting conditions or object movement. Therefore, feature-based recognition has to get by with only few robust feature pairings among many spurious ones. The rating of fea-

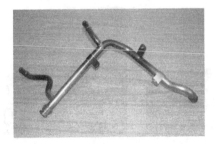

Fig. 5. Typical image containing the learned top view of a compound pipe object (left) and recognized object instance in a noticeably different pose (right)

ture pairings using statistics acquired during the training phase is especially important in such cases to reduce the amount of tested alignment hypotheses. Figure 4 shows a training image and recognition result for the highly specular coffee machine object. For this experiment, we used real training images rather than rendered ones to demonstrate that this is a viable option.

Objects of predominantly curved structure are harder to represent and recognize than purely polyhedral ones. To accurately represent views of non-polyhedral objects using curve-based features, higher order curves have to be fitted to the images. This not only increases the complexity in the feature extraction step, it also makes the feature-based representation less predictable. This points out the importance of the rating function for feature pairings to process useful pairings first.

Figure 1 shows a typical result of our experiments with a toy dinosaur. We used the optic 3D-Scanner DigiScan 2000 to obtain the 3D structure from the real object to generate the training set by simulation. A further experiment has been carried out with an object consisting of compound pipes (see Figure 5). Here, our system learned the view-based object model using only top-view images. Note that the test images contained object instances largely displaced from the image center which lead to perspectively distorted views that were not included in the training data. As shown on the right image of Figure 5, the object can still be localized.

We also applied our system to initialize a scene-based object tracking process [15]. In our experiments we found that the achieved localization accuracy was sufficient to robustly obtain a refined object pose after a few tracker iterations. Figure 3 shows the relationship between the 2D recognition result (the left image), the derived 3D pose (middle), and the refined pose after a few tracker iterations (on the right). Localization and pose refinement was also possible under extensive partial occlusion by fog as shown in the right image of Figure 4.

6   Conclusions

In this paper, we presented an approach to 3D object localization in single images using a probabilistic view-based alignment technique. Our system learns a view-based object model from a set of training views. During application, our system combines for the recognized view the four parameters of the 2D similarity transform with the orientation of the object in the corresponding training image to extract the 3D position and orientation of the object in the scene. The system has been implemented and validated on real images and images rendered from 3D-models. Experiments with free-form objects and objects with specular surfaces in cluttered scenes demonstrate the robustness of our approach. We furthermore presented an application of our approach for the initialization of a 3D scene-based tracking system.

Acknowledgments

We would like to thank Chen-Ko Sung, Fraunhofer Institute IITB, Karlsruhe, and the Benteler Group for providing valuable support.

References

1. Pope, A.R., Lowe, D.G.: Probabilistic models of appearance for 3-d object recognition. Int. Journ. of Computer Vision **40** (2000) 149–167
2. Murase, H., Nayar, S.K.: Visual learning and recognition of 3-d objects from appearance. Int. J. Comput. Vision **14** (1995) 5–24
3. Pentland, A., Moghaddam, B., Starner, T.: View-based and modular eigenspaces for face recognition. In: CVPR. (1994)
4. Pauli, J.: Learning to recognize and grasp objects. Machine Learning **31** (1998)
5. Reinhold, M., Paulus, D., Niemann, H.: Improved appearance-based 3-D object recognition using wavelet features. In: Vision, Modeling, and Visualization. (2001)
6. Schölkopf, B.: Support Vector Learning. PhD thesis, Universität Berlin (1997)
7. Blanz, V., Schölkopf, B., Bülthoff, H.H., Burges, C., Vapnik, V., Vetter, T.: Comparison of view-based object recognition algorithms using realistic 3d models. In: ICANN. (1996) 251–256
8. Wunsch, P., Winkler, S., Hirzinger, G.: Real-time pose estimation of 3-d objects from camera images using neural networks. In: ICRA. (1997) 3232–3237
9. Schiele, B., Pentland, A.: Probabilistic object recognition and localization. In: ICCV. (1999) 177–182
10. Allezard, N., Dhome, M., Jurie, F.: Recognition of 3d textured objects by mixing view-based and model-based representations. In: ICPR. (2000) 1960–1963
11. Rothganger, F., Lazebnik, S., Schmid, C., Ponce, J.: 3d object modeling and recognition using affine-invariant patches and multi-view spatial constraints. In: CVPR (2). (2003) 272–280
12. Lanser, S., Zierl, C., Munkelt, O., Radig, B.: Moral - a vision-based object recognition system for autonomous mobile systems. In: CAIP. (1997) 33–41
13. Huttenlocher, D.P., Ullman, S.: Recognizing solid objects by alignment with an image. Int. J. Comput. Vision **5** (1990) 195–212
14. Shoemake, K.: Euler angle conversion. In: Graphics gems IV. Academic Press Professional, Inc. (1994) 222–229
15. Plagemann, C.: Ansichtsbasierte Erkennung und Lokalisierung von Objekten zur Initialisierung eines Verfolgungsprozesses. Master's thesis, University of Karlsruhe (2004) in German.

Projective Model for Central Catadioptric Cameras Using Clifford Algebra*

Antti Tolvanen, Christian Perwass, and Gerald Sommer

Institut für Informatik und Praktische Mathematik,
Christian-Albrechts-Universität,
Christian-Albrechts-Platz 4, 24118 Kiel, Germany
{ant, chp, gs}@ks.informatik.uni-kiel.de

Abstract. A new method for describing the equivalence of catadioptric and stereographic projections is presented. This method produces a simple projection usable in all central catadioptric systems. A projective model for the sphere is constructed in such a way that it allows the effective use of Clifford algebra in the description of the geometrical entities on the spherical surface.

1 Introduction

Catadioptric cameras allow for a very large field of vision. This, in comparison to pinhole cameras, enables the system to perceive more visual information with one single image. The non-Euclidean geometry of the image enables more efficient self-calibration of the camera and reduces the complexity of algorithms needed to complete this task [5].

The mathematics used to model catadioptric cameras is slightly more complicated than for pinhole cameras. The main problem in the application of Clifford algebra to this modeling task is the local nature of the vector space structure on a curved manifold. This problem is solved in the following sections for central (single viewpoint) catadioptric systems, i.e. cameras with mirrors whose cross-sections are conic sections [1]. A projective model for parabolic, hyperbolic and elliptic mirrors is constructed taking the sphere as the unifying geometry. This model allows us to develop mathematical tools using Clifford algebra that are applicable to all these mirror geometries and works as a basis for our future research.

Clifford algebra has proven to be a powerfull tool in 2D-3D pose estimation (for example in [11],[12]). Using the model presented in this paper we hope these benefits gained in the Euclidean case of pinhole cameras will also be available in the omnidirectional vision using catadioptric cameras.

2 Unified Mirror Geometries

In [5] Geyer and Daniilidis present a unified model for single viewpoint catadioptric systems. In this model the world is first projected to the surface of a sphere

---

* This work has been supported by DFG grant So-320/2-3.

W. Kropatsch, R. Sablatnig, and A. Hanbury (Eds.): DAGM 2005, LNCS 3663, pp. 192–199, 2005.

with projective lines emerging from the center of the sphere. Stereographic projection from this spherical surface corresponds to the orthogonal projection from a parabolic mirror. Moving the projection point from the north pole of the sphere one may present perspective projections from the surfaces of elliptical and hyberbolical mirrors. Following the elegant description for the equivalence of the stereographic projection and orthogonal projection from a parabola by Penrose and Rindler [9], the unified model for single viewpoint catadioptric systems is reconstructed using a different mathematical method. This leads to simple projections for the different mirror geometries with a clear correspondence to the points on the sphere.

2.1   Modified Stereographic Projection

The stereographic projection is a one-to-one mapping between a sphere and a plane. Usually the sphere is defined along with the concept of ball:

Definition 1. *A n-ball of radius r centered at the origin is the set $B(0; r) = \{x \in \mathbb{R}^{n+1} \mid x^2 \le r^2\}$.*

The surface $\mathbb{S}^2 = \{x \in \mathbb{R}^{n+1} \mid x^2 = 1\}$ of the unit 2-ball, is called the sphere.

Instead of using this more common concept of sphere as a subset of $\mathbb{R}^3$ the sphere is now formed in the 4-dimensional Minkowski space $\mathbb{R}^{3,1}$, i.e. vector space with the signature $(-,+,+,+)$. This is done in order to stay consistent with the reference [9] and it offers the possibility to induce movement of points on the sphere by using Lorentz transformations which are known to be locally angle preserving.

The vectors $\mathbf{x} \in \mathbb{R}^{3,1}$ with $\mathbf{x}^2 = 0$ form a cone called the null cone. Let the vectors in $\mathbb{R}^{3,1}$ have the coordinates (t,x,y,z). The intersection of the null cone and the plane $t = 1$ forms a sphere. In stereographic projection a point $P(1, x, y, z)$ on this surface is projected to a plane T with $z = 0$ and $t = 1$ (see figure 1). The projective line is the line passing thru the north pole N and the point P. The intersection of this line and the plane T gives the coordinates of the projected point. To avoid inconsistencies in the projection of the point N the plane T has to be complex. This also enables the description of the projected point with just two parameters. Point A in figure 1 corresponds to the complex number $x + iy$. The x and y coordinates tell the position of the point P' in the complex plane and this is described by the complex number $\zeta = x' + iy'$. As the phase angle of the complex number $\zeta = x' + iy'$ is the azimuthal angle of the point (P' has the same direction from point C as point A) $P(1, x, y, z)$ on the sphere one has

$$A = hP' \quad \text{i.e} \quad x + iy = h\zeta, \tag{1}$$

where h is a real coefficient. The value of h is by geometric deduction (see figure 1)

$$h = \frac{CA}{CP'} = \frac{NP}{NP'} = \frac{NB}{NC} = 1 - z. \tag{2}$$

Using spherical coordinates ($0 \leq \phi \leq 2\pi, 0 < \theta, \pi$) to parameterise the sphere one gets

$$\zeta = \frac{x + iy}{1 - z} = e^{i\phi} \cot \frac{\theta}{2}. \tag{3}$$

As in the model by Geyer and Daniilidis the connection of different mirror geometries and the sphere is achieved by the movement of the projection point N. We start by moving the projection point N along the z direction which changes equation (2) to

$$h = \frac{CA}{CP'} = \frac{NP}{NP'} = \frac{NB}{NC} = \frac{\beta - z}{\beta} = 1 - \beta^{-1} z, \tag{4}$$

and equation (3) to

$$\zeta = \frac{x + iy}{1 - \alpha z} = e^{i\phi} \frac{\sin \theta}{1 - \alpha \cos \theta}, \quad \text{where } \alpha = \beta^{-1}. \tag{5}$$

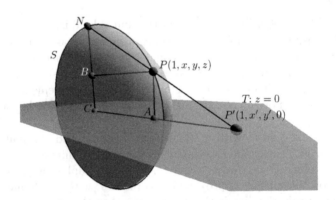

Fig. 1. Stereographic projection from sphere S to plane T. Only half of the Sphere S is drawn.

2.2   Connection to Conic Sections

This movement of the projection point is related to different conic sections in the following way. Let a null cone in $\mathbb{R}^{3,1}$ be intersected by the plane $t - z = 1$. This intersection forms a parabola. Let Q be a point of intersection of that plane and a line from the vertex of the cone to the point P given by $\mathbf{q} = u\mathbf{p}$, where $0 \leq u \leq 1$, $\mathbf{q}$ is the vector pointing at the point Q and $\mathbf{p}$ is the vector pointing at P (this is illustrated in the right part of figure 2). Solving the intersection of the line defined by $\mathbf{p}$ and the plane $t - z = 1$ gives $u = \frac{1}{1-z}$. Thus point Q has the coordinates

$$Q = \left(\frac{1}{1-z}, \frac{x}{1-z}, \frac{y}{1-z}, \frac{z}{1-z} \right), \tag{6}$$

from which the coordinates in the $x - y$-plane given by orthogonal projection are

$$P'(X', Y') = \left(\frac{x}{1-z}, \frac{y}{1-z} \right). \tag{7}$$

Labeling the points in the $(x - y)$-plane with complex numbers the point Q is projected to a point $\zeta = \frac{x+iy}{1-z}$ as in (3). This equivalency of the stereographic projection from a sphere and the orthogonal projection from a parabola can be shown by intersecting planes. Let plane $t = 1$ intersect the null cone with vertex O. This intersection is the spherical surface S^2. Let the north pole N of the sphere be at $(1, 0, 0, 1)$ and point Q be the intersection of the null line from O to P and the plane $t - z = 1$. The points O, Q, P, P' and N are coplanar and the points P, P' and N are collinear [9]. Thus the point P' is also the stereographic projection from the sphere S to the $(x - y)$-plane (see figure 2 representing the situation in one dimensional case).

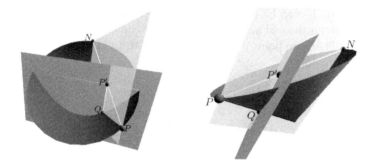

Fig. 2. Orthogonal projection from parabola and stereographic projection from circle. The parabola is formed by the intersection of the cone and the (non-transparent) $t - z = 1$ plane.

Tilting the $t - z = 1$ plane to the plane $t - \alpha z = 1$ changes the coordinates of Q to

$$Q = \left(\frac{1}{1-\alpha z}, \frac{x}{1-\alpha z}, \frac{y}{1-\alpha z}, \frac{z}{1-\alpha z} \right), \tag{8}$$

and the coordinates of the projected point to

$$P'(X', Y') = \left(\frac{x}{1-\alpha z}, \frac{y}{1-\alpha z} \right), \tag{9}$$

where α is the eccentricity of the conic section. Exactly as in (1) the projected point has the coordinates

$$\zeta = \frac{x+iy}{1-\alpha z}. \tag{10}$$

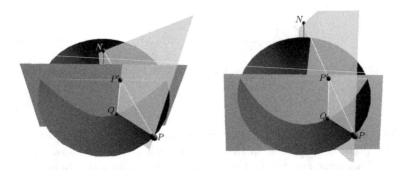

Fig. 3. Moving the point N keeps the points O, P, P', Q and N coplanar for different conic sections (center of the conic O not seen in image). The image on left shows the hyberbolic case and the image on right the elliptic case.

Moving the projection point N in the x direction in the stereographic projection corresponds to keeping the points O, P, P', Q and N coplanar. This is illustrated in figure 3.

In order to use the equation (10) in elliptic and hyperbolic cases the orthogonal projection has to be changed to a perspective projection [2]. Let c be the distance between the foci and d the distance of the image plane from the second focal point. Then the point ζ will be projected to the point

$$\zeta' = -\frac{d}{c}\zeta \tag{11}$$

in the hyperbolic case and

$$\zeta' = \frac{d}{c}\zeta \tag{12}$$

in the elliptic case.

With this construction the projections from different conic sections have simple equations which are easy to implement in applications.

3   Spherical Space and Clifford Algebra

In this section a projective model for the sphere is constructed in such a way that it allows the description of geometrical entities on the sphere with simple algebraic expressions. In contrast to the previous section the sphere is now embedded to $\mathbb{R}^3$ as usual. This means that we consider only the subspace $(1, x, y, z)$ of $\mathbb{M}^4$ and this subspace has the same structure as $\mathbb{R}^3$. In this subspace the sphere can be described with the set of vectors $\mathbf{r}(\theta, \phi) = \sin(\theta)\cos(\phi)\mathbf{e}_1 + \sin(\theta)\sin(\phi)\mathbf{e}_2 + \cos(\theta)\mathbf{e}_3$.

3.1   Clifford Algebra in Parameter Space

Let (V, g) be a vector space V equipped with a symmetric bilinear form (i.e. inner product) g. Algebra A over a ring R is compatible with the inner product space

(V, g) if V is a subspace of A and for each $x \in V$, $x^2 = g(x, x)$. Clifford algebra $\mathbb{G}_{p,q,r}$ is the compatible algebra for $\mathbb{R}^{p,q,r}$ [8], where p, q, r are the numbers of unit vectors with positive, negative and null signature.

Let $\{e_1, e_2, \ldots, e_n\}$ be an orthonormal basis for $\mathbb{R}^n$. Then the Clifford algebra $\mathbb{G}_n$ has dimension 2^n and basis $\{e_1^{\epsilon_1} e_2^{\epsilon_2} \ldots e_n^{\epsilon_n} | \epsilon_i = 0, 1\}$. For example the Clifford algebra $\mathbb{G}_3$ of $\mathbb{R}^3$ has the basis $\{1, e_1, e_2, e_3, e_1 e_2, e_1 e_3, e_2 e_3, e_1 e_2 e_3\}$

In practice it is useful to separate the *geometric product* of Clifford algebra in it's symmetric and antisymmetric parts: $xy = \frac{1}{2}(xy + yx) + \frac{1}{2}(xy - yx) = x \cdot y + x \wedge y$, where $(\cdot)$ is the inner product and $(\wedge)$ is the outer product ([6] contains a good introduction to the geometric product from a practical viewpoint).

Clifford algebra has proven to be a helpful tool in many applications with strong relation to geometry. Geometric transformations can be presented with simple geometric products and the inner and outer product null spaces are a simple way to present geometric entities of any dimension [10].

With the usual definition 1 of the sphere these benefits are lost as the inner and outer product null spaces describe the geometrical entities of the embedding space instead of the sphere itself. For example a line in $\mathbb{R}^n$ has at most two points common with the sphere. A conformal model for spherical geometry applying this kind of embedding can be found in [7]. Another possibility would be to use the Clifford algebra in the tangent spaces of $\mathbb{S}^2$, which is rather useless because it can only describe infinitesimal entities on the manifold.

A sphere can be parameterized in a number of ways. Parameterization with the least amount of ambiguities is the stereographic projection to the complex plane described in the previous section. In this projection the geodesic curves are mapped to curves in the complex plane, a fact which complicates their description with Clifford algebra. Instead, using the parameterization with azimuthal and polar angles $(\phi, \theta), 0 \le \phi < 2\pi, 0 < \theta < \pi$ the geodesic lines have a simple description. Rectangular objects in projection on to the sphere can be described with lines in the (ϕ, θ) space and thus retain the 'rectangularity'. Figure 4 shows how the image captured with a parabolic mirror is transformed to the $V(\theta, \phi)$ space using (3).

Fig. 4. Image captured with a parabolical mirror and its mapping to $V(\phi, \theta)$

To remove the periodicity in ϕ and θ on the image the following scaling is used:

$$\phi' = \frac{\phi}{2\pi - \phi} \quad \text{and} \quad \theta' = \frac{\theta}{\pi - \theta}. \tag{13}$$

The vector space $V(\theta', \phi')$ equipped with the Euclidean inner product is clearly isomorphic to $\mathbb{R}^2$. Using the Euclidean inner product in $V(\theta', \phi')$ areas calculated in parameter space differ from areas on the sphere. When needed a scaling between these areas can be calculated. Frequently used angular size $\Delta\alpha$ of an object is, for example, given by $\Delta\alpha = \sqrt{(\phi_2 - \phi_1)^2 + (\theta_2 - \theta_1)^2}$. Instead of using just the parameter space $V(\phi', \theta')$ a projective model is defined.

3.2 Clifford Algebra in the Projective Model

Definition 2. *The projective model of the sphere is the space* $\mathcal{S}_P = V(\phi', \theta') \times \{\mathbb{R}\backslash 0\}$ *equipped with the Euclidean inner product. The basis of* $\mathcal{S}_P$ *is* $\{\mathbf{e}_{\phi'}, \mathbf{e}_{\theta'}, \mathbf{e}_p\}$.

The corresponding Clifford algebra $\mathbb{G}(\mathcal{S}_P) \cong \mathbb{G}(\mathbb{R}^3)$ has the basis

$$\{1, \mathbf{e}_{\phi'}, \mathbf{e}_{\theta'}, \mathbf{e}_p, \mathbf{e}_{\phi'}\mathbf{e}_{\theta'}, \mathbf{e}_{\phi'}\mathbf{e}_p, \mathbf{e}_{\theta'}\mathbf{e}_p, \mathbf{e}_{\phi'}\mathbf{e}_{\theta'}\mathbf{e}_p\}. \tag{14}$$

A vector in $x \in V(\phi', \theta')$ is embedded in $\mathcal{S}_P$ with the mapping

$$\mathcal{P} : \mathbf{x} \in V(\phi', \theta') \mapsto \mathbf{x} + \mathbf{e}_p \in \mathcal{S}_P. \tag{15}$$

The inverse of $\mathcal{P}$ is

$$\mathcal{P}^{-1} : A \in \mathcal{S}_P \mapsto \frac{1}{A \cdot \mathbf{e}_p} [(A \cdot \mathbf{e}_{\phi'})\, \mathbf{e}_{\phi'} + (A \cdot \mathbf{e}_{\theta'})\, \mathbf{e}_{\theta'}] \tag{16}$$

In this projective model Euclidean inner and outer product null spaces, $\mathbb{NI}_E$ and $\mathbb{N}{\times}_E$, give a simple description for points, lines and planes on the parameter space $V(\phi', \theta')$. As an example let $A, B, C \in \mathcal{S}_P$. Now

$$\mathbb{NO}(A \wedge B) = \{C \in \mathcal{S}_P \mid A \wedge B \wedge C = 0\}. \tag{17}$$

As only the perpendicular component of C contributes to (17) one gets

$$\mathbb{NO}(A \wedge B) = \{C \in \mathcal{S}_P \mid A \wedge B \wedge C_\perp = 0\}, \tag{18}$$

i.e. C lies in the plane spanned by A and B. The corresponding euclidian outer product null space is given by the projection of the plane $A \wedge B$ to $V(\phi', \theta')$:

$$\begin{aligned}
\mathbb{NO}_E\,(A \wedge B) &= \mathcal{P}^{-1}\,(\mathbb{NO}(A \wedge B)) = \\
\mathcal{P}^{-1}\,(\alpha A + \beta B) &= \mathcal{P}^{-1}\,(\alpha A - \alpha B + \alpha B + \beta B) = \\
\mathcal{P}^{-1}\,[\alpha(A - B) + (\alpha + \beta)B] &= \mathbf{b} + \frac{\alpha}{\alpha + \beta}(\mathbf{a} - \mathbf{b}) \\
&= \mathbf{b} + t(\mathbf{a} - \mathbf{b}), t \in \mathbb{R},
\end{aligned} \tag{19}$$

which is a line in through points $\mathbf{a}$ and $\mathbf{b}$ in $V(\phi', \theta')$. In a similar manner $\mathbb{NO}_E(A) = \mathbf{a}$.

In order to consider also the radial position of objects in the enviroment of the camera one has to add also the radial dimension $\mathbf{e}_r$ to the model. This addition does not have any other effect on the model than the addition of one extra dimension.

4   Conclusion

In this paper a simple method for unifying central catadioptric systems was presented. Using Clifford algebra on the parameter space of the sphere allows an efficient method for describing rectangular objects that are also mapped to rectangular objects in the parameter space. This has not been possible in the previous models using Clifford algebra [3],[4].

Using the parameter space of the sphere the distance $\Delta\phi$ between points on the geodesics of the sphere have the simple form $\Delta\phi = \frac{2\pi\phi'_2}{\phi'_2+1} - \frac{2\pi\phi'_1}{\phi'_1+1} = \phi_2 - \phi_1$. One can also calculcate the distances between points on a line in the parameter space using basic algebra instead of using line integrals on the surface of the sphere (which lead in many cases to incomplete elliptic integrals).

In the parameter space the rotation of the sphere is achieved with the translation operator $T(\mathbf{x}) = \mathbf{x} + \mathbf{t}$. In order to linearise the translation operator the parameter space has to be embedded to a confromal space. This conformal model is included in our ongoing research as is the movement of the sensor in the enviroment. Using Clifford algebra on suitably embedded parameter space allows the description of the geometric entities and the camera movement.

References

1. Baker, S., Nayar, S. A theory of catadioptric image formation. Proc. Int. Conf on Computer Vision (1998) 35–42
2. Baker, S., Nayar, S. A theory of single view-point catadioptric image formation. International Journal of Computer Vision **35** (1999) 175–196
3. Bayro-Corrochano, E., López-Franco, C.: Omnidirectional vision: unified model using conformal geometry. ECCV 2004, Proceedings, Part I (2004) 536–548
4. Cameron, J.I.: Applications of Geometric Algebra, first year report. Signal Processing Laboratory, Department of Engineering, University of Cambridge, 2004.
5. Geyer, C., Daniilidis, K.: Catadioptric projective geometry. International Journal of Computer Vision **45** (2001) 223–243
6. Doran, C. Lasenby, A.: Geometric Algebra for Physicists. Cambridge University Press (2003)
7. Li, H., Hestenes, D., Rockwood, A.: Spherical conformal geometry with Geometric algebra. In Sommer, G. (Ed.): Geometric Computing with Clifford Algebras. Springer Verlag Berlin Heidelberg (2001) 61–76
8. McDonald, B.R: Geometric Algebra over Local Rings. Marcel Dekker, Inc. (1976)
9. Penrose, R., Rindler, W.: Spinors & Space-Time 1. Cambridge University Press (1984)
10. Perwass, C., Hildenbrand, D.: Aspects of Geometric Algebra in Euclidean, Projective and Conformal Space. Technical Report Nr.0308, University of Kiel (2002)
11. Rosenhahn, B., Sommer, G.: Pose estimation in conformal geometric algebra, Part II: Real-time pose estimation using extended feature concepts. Journal of Mathematical Imaging and Vision **22** (2005) 49–70
12. Rosenhahn, B., Perwass, C., Sommer, G. : Pose Estimation of free-form contours. Int. Journal of Computer Vision **62** (2005) 267–289

A New Methodology for Determination and Correction of Lens Distortion in 3D Measuring Systems Using Fringe Projection

Christian Bräuer-Burchardt

Fraunhofer IOF Jena,
Albert-Einstein-Str. 7, D-07745 Jena, Germany
braeuerc@iof.fhg.de

Abstract. A new methodology for the determination and correction of lens distortion in fringe projection systems for 3D object measurement is introduced. The calibration of the distortion is performed in the device ready for measurement based on the simultaneous determination of both projector and (remaining) camera distortion. The application of the algorithm allows a reduction of distortion errors up to 0.02 pixels in the projector chip and also in the camera chip.

1 Introduction

High precision measuring systems based on image data require high precision optical components. That means for the camera lenses that they should have a minimum of distortion effects. However, there are no really distortion free lenses, especially in the range of wide angle lenses.

Touchless 3D-measuring systems based on fringe projection use lenses in the range from weak to strong wide angles. That means that even if high quality lenses are used, a minimum of lens distortion can not be excluded. Depending on the requirements to the measuring uncertainty of the system the distortion effects must be corrected.

Depending on the measuring principle only the projection lens or both the projection and also camera lens(es) must be corrected. Recently the lens correction in such systems was usually ignored or dealt with some standard methods. Available systems are based on photogrammetric bundle adjustment. Tools for lens distortion correction are usually included [1]. However, these methods may be restricted concerning the used distortion models or the termination of the process of lens distortion determination is not achieved because of too strong correlation between the distortion parameters and the intrinsic camera parameters.

Conventionally, lens distortion is described by a distortion function including radial, decentering, and affine parameters [2,3,4]. Using wide angle lenses the main part of the distortion usually has the radial distortion. Therefore, in the majority of works no other distortion than the radial one is considered. This may be sufficient, if the required measuring accuracy is not very high or if the actual distortion is sufficiently described by the radial distortion. Some authors take into account de-

W. Kropatsch, R. Sablatnig, and A. Hanbury (Eds.): DAGM 2005, LNCS 3663, pp. 200–207, 2005.

centering distortion [3,4]. This may improve the correction. However, some other kind of distortion may still be present.

Kruck [5] suggests an approach including some 30 parameters describing the lens distortion. However, the use of so many parameters brings some disadvantages. First, a powerful calculation system for processing the data is necessary. Second, some of the parameters are not independent from each other. Third, the noise may influence the measurement and the reproducibility may be not sufficient.

Differing from standard methods Brakhage [6] introduces a method for fringe projection systems with telecentric projection lenses using Zernike-polynomials including the consideration of distance dependence. In the calibration strategy supposed by Chen [7] the distortion is described by polynomials calculated from residuals.

Here, the occurring distortion is described by a radial function added by a field of distortion vectors distributed over the whole detectable image plane [8]. Good experiences could be achieved using this kind of description. In the following the fringe projection devices are introduced, the distortion model and the new approach is described, the algorithms are given, and some results are presented.

2 Situation

The 3D measuring system "kolibri-flex" has been developed at the Fraunhofer IOF in Jena (see Fig.1). This system allows grasping the 3D surface geometry of arbitrarily formed objects of a size up to 400 x 400 x 200 mm. It is based on fringe projection. The measuring principle to obtain 3D object values is called phasogrammetry [9].

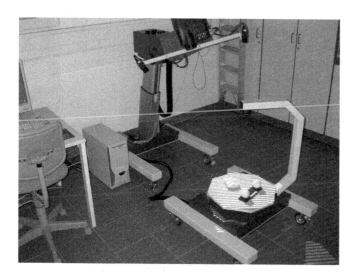

Fig. 1. 3D measuring system "kolibri-flex" using fringe projection

Phasogrammetry means the combination of photogrammetry and active fringe projection in closed mathematical form [9,10]. The basic principle of phasogrammetry includes the projection of at least two different positions, each one including two series of pattern sequences (e.g. Gray-Code-sequences in combination with phase-delayed grid lines) onto the object being measured whereas the second series is rotated 90° to the first one. The recording camera remains in same position according to the object. Therefore every point on the object is characterised by at least four phase values. The phase value $\xi^{(i)}$ and $\eta^{(i)}$ on the object point and its associated projection centres define spatial bundle of rays similar to those of the cameras in photogrammetry which can be used to calculate the coordinates.

Such a system can be extended to a flexibly measuring system by adding so called measuring cameras [9], which contribute to the measuring values. The "kolibri-flex" is such an extended system. In order to avoid distortion effects in the "kolibri" system the so called ADPA operator can be used which is implemented in the BINGO software [1] which is used in the system to perform the bundle adjustment.

Experiences with the "kolibri" system showed that satisfying results with the ADPA operator could be achieved using a high quality projector without measuring cameras. However, using a cheaper low quality projector or using the measuring cameras considerable deviations due to lens distortion occurred in the measurements of reference objects, and no correction with ADPA was possible.

Therefore our goal was to construct a robust method for determination and correction of all effects generated by lens distortion with maximum precision and minimum additional calibration effort. An additional demand was the use of the device in the state "ready for measurement" in order to avoid errors by the adjustment process.

3 Distortion Model

Lens distortion describes the deviation of the actual vision ray between the observed object point and the point in the image plane from the ideal one concerning the camera model used. Usually radial and eventually decentering distortion is modelled and determined, e.g. (see [3]) by

$$\Delta x = \Delta x_{rad} + \Delta x_{dec} = x'\left(a_2 r'^2 + a_4 r'^4 + ...\right) + b_1 \cdot (r'^2 + 2x'^2) + 2b_2 \cdot x' \cdot y'$$
$$\Delta y = \Delta y_{rad} + \Delta y_{dec} = y'\left(a_2 r'^2 + a_4 r'^4 + ...\right) + b_2 \cdot (r'^2 + 2y'^2) + 2b_1 \cdot x' \cdot y'$$
$$(1)$$

An influence of up to distortion 30 parameters may be analysed by the BINGO software [1]. However, our experiences with BINGO showed that even with 30 different distortion functions the actual distortion could not sufficiently modelled, and led to the decision to model the distortion as a matrix of distortion vectors in the image plane. This makes the description of any arbitrary distortion possible. The distortion function is represented by a reduced number of distortion vectors $\Delta v = (\Delta x, \Delta y)$ forming a matrix. Here, Δv includes all distortion shares. The amount of distortion between the distortion grid points is determined by bicubic spline interpolation.

If the radial share of the distortion is very high the distortion function can be separated into two parts: $\Delta v = \Delta v_{rad} + \Delta v_{rest}$, where Δv_{rad} describes the radial share and Δv_{rest} the remaining distortion. The radial share $\Delta v_{rad} = (\Delta x_{rad}, \Delta y_{rad})$ can be expressed by a function as

$$\Delta x_{rad} = (x - x_0)\left(\frac{r'}{r} - 1\right); \quad \Delta y_{rad} = (y - y_0)\left(\frac{r'}{r} - 1\right)$$

with

$$r = \frac{r'}{1 + d_0 + d_2 r'^2 + d_4 r'^4 + \dots}, \tag{2}$$

where r and r' are the undistorted and the distorted distance to the symmetry point $P=(x_0, y_0)$ of the distortion and $p=(x,y)$ the undistorted point coordinates. The remaining distortion $\Delta v_{rest} = (\Delta x_{rest}, \Delta y_{rest})$ can be described by a matrix of distortion vectors as shown in fig.2.

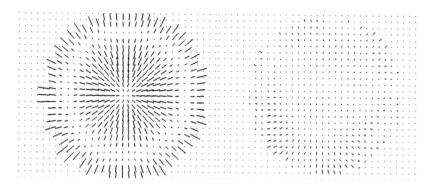

Fig. 2. Distortion matrix (restricted area) of a wide angle lens (f=12mm) with strong distortion (left), remaining part after removal of radial distortion (right). Distortion vectors are scaled by a factor of 40 stronger than image coordinate scaling.

4 Approach and Algorithms

The main problem to solve is generated by the fact, that the distortion of the projection lens can not be determined by analysis of an image of a well known calibration object. Because the projector produces and projects an image, the opposite way has to be gone. However, recording the projected image by another camera, distortion effects of this camera disturb the determination of the projector distortion.

The main idea of our method for projector distortion determination is to use a sufficiently corrected camera, or, alternatively, the simultaneous determination of the projector distortion and the camera distortion of the fringe projection system. This second approach has the big advantage to use the measuring device itself as the calibration tool. Subsequently, with the corrected projector lens a grid pattern can be produced which can be used to determine the lens distortion of the remaining cameras of the system.

Recently, in the "kolibri" systems lens distortion was estimated by a projection of stripes on a plane surface and a subjective comparison with calibrated grid patterns. This technique is only applicable having very strong distortion effects. It was not precise enough for the improved new "kolibri" system. Here, the amount of distortion is between 0.2 and 4µm in the projector chip, i.e. about 1/80 to ¼ of a projected pixel.

The idea to determine lens distortion of projector and cameras within the device was to use a plane surface as a calibration tool, project a pattern of phase values [9] onto this surface, and record this pattern by the camera. Between the distorted phase values and the undistorted camera coordinates a projective 2D-2D-mapping exists because of the planarity of the projected image points.

Considering such a "one projector – one camera" system the scheme of fig.3 illustrates the data flow and the influence of lens distortion. This leads to the algorithm *A1* for the determination of projector distortion assuming that the camera distortion is known or determined before. The criterion to evaluate the quality of the distortion determination is the averaged residual error (ARE, see also [2]) between the calculated $(x,y)_i$ and ideal $(x,y)^{id}_i$ coordinates before and after correction assuming that the estimation of the 2D-2D projective transform is true:

$$ARE = \frac{1}{n} \sum_{i=1}^{n} \sqrt{\left(x_i - x_i^{id}\right)^2 + \left(y_i - y_i^{id}\right)^2} \ . \tag{3}$$

The ideal coordinates $(x,y)^{id}_i$ are estimated by the best fit of the undistorted grid to the observed one.

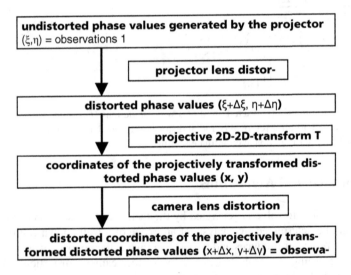

Fig. 3. Scheme of the data flow in the process of production of measuring values for lens distortion determination

Algorithm A1 (determination of projector lens distortion)

1. Produce corresponding point lists of phase values and corrected camera pixels
2. Estimate a 2D-2D projective transformation **T**
3. Apply $\mathbf{T}^{-1}$ to the corrected camera pixels
4. Calculate the difference between the transformed points and the original phase values
5. Eventually repeat nr. 2 to 4 with corrected phase values

The previous determination of the camera lens distortion can be either done using a calibration target or using an in relation to the projector distortion free camera. If the projector distortion is known or neglectable, algorithm *A2* can be used to determine camera distortion.

Algorithm A2 (determination of camera lens distortion)

1. Produce corresponding point lists of corrected phase values and camera pixels
2. Estimate a 2D-2D projective transformation **T**
3. Apply **T** to the phase values
4. Calculate the difference between the transformed phase values and the original camera point coordinates (pixels)
5. Eventually repeat nr. 2 to 4 with corrected camera pixels

A problem can occur when no distortion free camera is available, or the accuracy is not sufficient. In this case the solution may be an iterative distortion calculation determining alternately camera and projector distortion, which leads to algorithm *A3*. This algorithm requires a separation of the distortion effects of projector and camera. This can be achieved by repeating the image recording with changing positions between projector and camera (expressed by the rotation angle β) as it is performed in the normal measuring mode of the "kolibri-flex" device. The finishing criterion should be the minimal averaged error after correction.

Algorithm A3 (simultaneous camera and projector distortion determination)

1. Produce corresponding point lists of phase values and camera pixel coordinates in different arrangements between camera and projector (rotation of the projector, about six different rotation angles β)
   For each β
2. Estimate a 2D-2D projective transformation **T**
3. Apply **T** to the phase values
4. Calculate the difference between the transformed phase values and the camera pixel coordinates
5. Merge the difference matrices → reduction of distortion effects from projector
6. Estimate a 2D-2D projective transformation **T**$^{-1}$
7. Apply **T**$^{-1}$ to the camera pixel coordinates
8. Calculate the difference between the transformed camera pixel coordinates and the phase values
9. Merge the difference matrices → reduction of distortion effects from camera
10. Determine and analyse the quality measure

5 Experiments and Results

In order to evaluate the suggested methodology, a number of experiments has been performed. First, the determination of the distortion has been done using algorithm *A3*. Then, the determined distortion matrices were used to correct the distortion within the measuring process of the "kolibri-flex" system.

All in all three projectors and six camera lenses were included into the experiments. We used the projectors Davis CinemaTen (CT), InFokus LP120 (LP), and a self developed projector (KF). The six lenses Cinegon 1.4/8, Cinegon 1.4/12, Xeno-plan 17 (all by Schneider-Kreuznach), S5LPJ 2.8/12 (Sill), Lamegon 14, and Lametar 25 (both by Jenoptic) were used and analysed.

As the results the values for the ARE before and after correction are given, for the camera lenses also the percentage radial share psr (see formula 4) of the distortion and the determined distortion coefficient d_2 (see formula 2, $d_4=0$). The results for the projectors are given by table 1, the results for the camera lenses in table 2. The figures 4 and 5 show distortion matrices of the projectors CT and LP. The distortion vectors in the figs. 4 and 5 are scaled by a factor of 200 stronger than the image coordinates.

$$prs = 100 \cdot \sum_{i=1}^{n} \sqrt{(\Delta x_{rad})_i^2 + (\Delta y_{rad})_i^2} \bigg/ \sum_{i=1}^{n} \sqrt{(\Delta x)_i^2 + (\Delta y)_i^2} \qquad (4)$$

Table 1. Results distortion determination and correction of projector lenses

Projector	ARE before correction (pixel)	ARE after correction (pixel)
CT	0.030	0.012
LP	0.172	0.013
KF	0.100	0.026

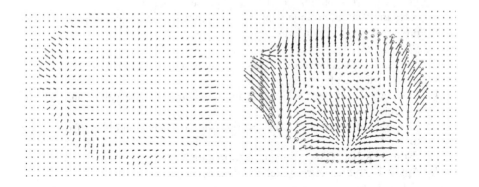

Fig. 4. Distortion matrix CT   **Fig. 5.** Distortion matrix LP

Table 2. Results of distortion determination and correction of camera lenses

Lens	Focal length (mm)	ARE before correction (pixel)	Radial share of dist. (%)	Radial coefficient $d_2 * 10^{-8}$ (pixel^{-2})	ARE after correction (pixel)
Cinegon8	8	0.28	99	-3.35	0.02
Cinegon12	12	0.18	99	-1.80	0.07
Sill	12.4	0.27	> 90	-1.64	0.04
Lamegon	14	< 0.10	n.s.	-	0.02
Xenoplan	17	0.37	85	-3.33	0.10
Lametar	25	< 0.06	n.s.	-	0.02

The influence of the application of distortion correction in a 3D measurement using LP was analysed. A stone slab with a size of 400 x 400 mm with a plane surface was measured before and after correction. The difference between the highest ant the lowest point (PV) of the measured plane decreased from 355 down to 32 µm.

The results show a reduction of the error by a factor between four and ten. It can be seen that the quality of the correction differs due to the lens quality. Furthermore, the restriction of the field of view may reduce the distortion effects and improve the result. Hence, an absolute statement about the lens quality can not be given.

6   Summary, Discussion, and Outlook

A new methodology to determine and correct lens distortion occurring in measuring systems using fringe projection was presented which considerably improves measurements of 3D object surfaces.

A remaining problem is the fact that no absolute separation of camera and projector distortion is possible using the algorithm for simultaneous determination of camera and projector distortion, when the image of the symmetry centre of distortion of the projector is close to the symmetry centre of the camera lens. This can be avoided by a weak change of the camera position. However, this means no restriction to the quality of the method, because a separation can always be achieved performing a usual lens distortion calibration procedure with more effort. Future work should be done in the analysis of lens distortion dependence on the object distance.

References

1. Kruck, E.: BINGO-F Benutzerhandbuch. Ges. f. Industriephotogramm. mbH, Aalen, 1995
2. Brown, D.C.: Close-range camera calibration. Photogram.Eng. 37(8) (1971) 855-66
3. Luhmann, Th.: *Nahbereichsphotogrammetrie*, Wichmann Verlag, 2003
4. Weng, J., Cohen, P., Herniou, M.: Camera calibration with distortion models and accuracy evaluation. PAMI(14), No 11 (1992) 965-80
5. Kruck, E.: Lösung großer Gleichungssysteme für photogrammetrische Blockausgleichungen mit erweitertem funktionalem Modell. Dissertation, Wiss. Arbeiten der Fachrichtung Vermessungswesen der Universität Hannover, Nr. 128, 1983
6. Brakhage, P., Notni, G., Kowarschik, R.: Image aberrations in optical three-dimensional measurement systems with fringe projection. Applied Optics, vol.43, nr.16 (2004) 3217-23
7. Chen, M. and Frankowski, G.: Kalibrierstrategie für optische 3D-Koordinatenmessgeräte, basierend auf streifenprojektionstechnischen und fotogrammetrischen Algorithmen. Technisches Messen 69, Oldenbourg (2002) 240-50
8. Bräuer-Burchardt, C.: A simple new method for precise lens distortion correction of low cost camera systems. In Pattern Recognition (Proc 26th DAGM), Springer LNCS (2004) 570-77
9. Notni, G., Kühmstedt, P., Heinze, M., Himmelreich, M.: Phasogrammetrische 3D-Messsysteme und deren Anwendung zur Rundumvermessung.. In Luhmann, Th. (ed.): In: Optische 3D-Messtechnik, Wichmann-Verlag (2003) 21-32
10. Schreiber, W., and Notni, G.: Theory and arrangements of self-calibrating whole-body three-dimensional measurement systems using fringe projection techniques. In: Opt. Eng. 39 (2000) 159-169

A Method for Fast Search of Variable Regions on Dynamic 3D Point Clouds

Eric Wahl[1] and Gerd Hirzinger[1]

Institute of Robotics and Mechatronics,
German Aerospace Center (DLR)
`eric.wahl@dlr.de`

Abstract. The paper addresses the region search problem in three-dimensional (3D) space. The data used is a dynamically growing point cloud as it is typically gathered with a 3D-sensing device like a laser range-scanner. An encoding of space in combination with a new region search algorithm is introduced. The algorithm allows for fast access to spherical subsets of variable size. An octree based and a balanced binary tree based implementation are discussed. Finally, experiments concerning processing time are shown.

1 Introduction

Many algorithms in 3D-vision use local information of a much larger scene [1,2]. Separating a subset is a necessary but nontrivial preliminary step, especially when using unorganized point clouds. It strongly depends on the 3D-data representations and therein the realization of spatial neighborhood relations.

A common procedure to organize the data, is applying a spatial subdivision tree. Tree representations differ in their strategies when partitioning space, but they agree on relying on a hierarchical structure. Each data point is mapped to a *unique index (key)* that determines the location in the tree. The indexed location is referred to as a *(tree-) node*. Accordingly, an index could be interpreted as the location on a one-dimensional space-filling curve in 3D. The dilemma is that such a curve does not preserve spatial proximity in all directions [3,4]. On the other hand, tree representations allow for organizing a sequential stream of orderless data dynamically, since an update with incoming data is possible, while access is still limited to complexity $O(log(N))$, where N is the number of nodes.

This work is related to the approach of Sagawa et. al. [5]. They introduced the *technique of the Bounds-Overlap-Threshold* for iterative closest point (ICP) search. The computational costs for registration tasks were reduced by limiting the search to a region within a selected threshold. Their approach accepts imprecision in return for faster computation. Furthermore, the algorithm only provides single points instead of a region. Since it is based on a *k-d tree*, an online balancing seems impractical.

Bodenmüller and Hirzinger use a tree representation capable for online surface-mesh generation [6]. The representation contains linked leaf-nodes, that facilitates access to the direct neighborhood. Adaption to searching a region of variable size would increase memory and processing costs for building the links and is thus infeasible.

W. Kropatsch, R. Sablatnig, and A. Hanbury (Eds.): DAGM 2005, LNCS 3663, pp. 208–215, 2005.

Advancing a closest point search, we introduce a novel search algorithm for regions of variable size. It is capable to separate local subsets of much larger point clouds. The approach can be implemented either on an octree or a balanced binary tree and is already embedded in a scene interpretation application [7], that uses the DLR multi-sensory device [8,9] for data acquisition.

The paper is organized as follows: Section 2 describes the index generation. Next, Section 3 introduces the region search algorithm. Section 4 includes experiments with respect to processing costs. Last, Section 5 closes the paper with a conclusion and prospects to future work.

2 Indexing

In this work, a hierarchical division of the space is applied, where space is a cube of edge size e_0. The first level of depth $d = 0$ consists of eight cubic cells of equal size. Every cell is divided in subcells, themselves. This is continued until a maximum depth d_{max} is reached. Cells of this level are referred to as *atomic cells*.

The *z-order*, also known as *morton code*, is used to address a cell. The function

$$m : \mathbf{p} \mapsto i \tag{1}$$

maps a point $\mathbf{p}$ to the index i, while

$$c : i \mapsto C \tag{2}$$

maps the index i to the cell C. The length l of an index is one octal digit per depth, where a digit defines one of the eight subcells. Accordingly, the prefix $\hat{i}_d(i)$ determines the d leading digits of the index i. It refers to the index of a higher located parent-cell $C_p = c(\hat{i}_d(i))$, that includes the cell $C = c(i)$.

The implementation of the space is realized as a tree. Thereby, a cell in space corresponds to a node in the tree. A node contains the mean point $\tilde{\mathbf{p}}$ of all points in the corresponding cell. This simultaneously allows for smoothing a point cloud and for restricting the point density to an upper bound.

In the following, two different types of (pointered) tree structures are applied.

2.1 The Octree

The octree uses the same structure as the hierarchical space division introduced above. Higher level cells are symbolized by nodes, while atomic cells refer to *leaf-nodes*. Only leaf-nodes contain information in terms of a 3D-point. Other nodes are exclusively used for traversing the tree. Therefore, an index can be interpreted as a path from the top to the bottom of the octree.

2.2 The Balanced Binary Tree

Adel'son-Vel'skiĭ and Landis [10] first introduced a balanced binary tree known as AVL-tree[1]. In this kind of tree, only atomic cells need to be realized as tree-nodes.

---

[1] The AVL-tree is used due to perfect balance and comparability to other trees, e.g. a red-black-tree.

The index of a cell still encodes the position of the node, but this position depends on the input order of data and does not exactly coincide with the spatial order. Memory costs for a balanced binary tree are lower than for an octree since binary trees need no additional nodes for higher level cells.

3   The Region Search Algorithm

The aim of every region search algorithm is to collect the points $\mathbf{p}$ that are within a radius r with respect to a region of interest (ROI)

$$\mathcal{F}(r, \mathbf{q}) = \{\mathbf{p} | \|\mathbf{p} - \mathbf{q}\| \leq r\} \tag{3}$$

around the center $\mathbf{q}$.

Step 1: Finding the Center of Search

The algorithm first needs to determine the starting point. For both tree variants the index $i_{\mathbf{q}} = m(\mathbf{q})$ is calculated. A cell has to be found, that is large enough to include the hole ROI, i.e. a cell of depth $d_{\mathcal{F}}$ is chosen if the edge size $e_{d_{\mathcal{F}}} = e_0/2^{d_{\mathcal{F}}}$ fulfills the condition

$$2r \leq e_{d_{\mathcal{F}}}. \tag{4}$$

By chance, the cell includes the complete ROI. Otherwise, if the center $\mathbf{q}$ is closer to the cell border than the size of the radius r, parts of the ROI penetrate neighboring cells. The sections of the ROI that are located in neighboring cells are further referred to as *outliers*. In 3D, each cell has a maximum number of 26 neighbors

$$\mathbf{P}_{[1...6]} = \mathbf{q} + \frac{\mathbf{u}_{[1...6]} - \mathbf{q}}{\|\mathbf{u}_{[1...6]} - \mathbf{q}\|} r, \tag{5}$$

$$\mathbf{P}_{[7...18]} = \mathbf{q} + \frac{\mathbf{v}_{[1...12]} - \mathbf{q}}{\|\mathbf{v}_{[1...12]} - \mathbf{q}\|} r, \tag{6}$$

$$\mathbf{P}_{[19...26]} = \mathbf{q} + \frac{\mathbf{w}_{[1...8]} - \mathbf{q}}{\|\mathbf{w}_{[1...8]} - \mathbf{q}\|} r, \tag{7}$$

where $u_{[1...6]}$ are the projections of $\mathbf{p}$ onto the six cell sides, $v_{[1...12]}$ are the projections of $\mathbf{p}$ onto the 12 cell edges, and $w_{[1...8]}$ are the eight cell corners. Condition 4 reduces the number of outliers to 7 neighbors. That leads to 8 starting points at most[2]. The following steps are individually applied for each starting point.

Step 2: Prefix Descent

All points $\mathbf{p}_s$ and $\mathbf{p}_t$ included in the space of a sub-cell $C = c(i)$ have the common prefix

$$\hat{i}_{d_{\mathcal{F}}}(m(\mathbf{p}_s)) \qquad \forall \{\mathbf{p}_s, \mathbf{p}_t | c(m(\mathbf{p}_s)) = c(m(\mathbf{p}_t))\}. \tag{8}$$

Therein, the algorithm descends the tree until a node with consistent prefix is found. If such a node $\mathbf{n}$ exists, the search continues therefrom, otherwise it terminates.

---

[2] That is the case, if the ROI is located in a corner of the cell.

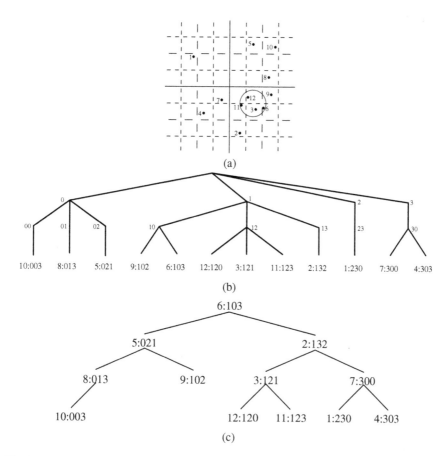

Fig. 1. (a) The example shows a space divided in hierarchical cells. A set of 12 input points $\mathbf{p}_i$ is used ($i \in [1, 12]$). The set $\Omega = \{230, 132, 121, 303, 021, 103, 300, 013, 102, 003, 123, 120\}$ contains the corresponding indices. The notation 1:230 refers to the point $\mathbf{p}_1$ with the index $i = 230$. The circle symbolizes the region of interest. All points inside of this region must be the result of the search. The size and position of the region leads to the prefix $\hat{i}_{d_{\mathcal{F}}=2}(i) = 12$. The cell is able but not presumed to include the focus. Therefore, the neighborhood has to be also examined. Two of the eight possible neighborhood positions point to cells with different prefixes and thus need exploration. (b) The two-dimensional version of an octree is the quadtree used here. The algorithm descends to the starting point in penultimate level, where the index and the prefix match. There, the points $\mathbf{p}_3$, $\mathbf{p}_{11}$ and $\mathbf{p}_{12}$ are received. Next, the prefixes $\hat{i}_{d_{\mathcal{F}}=2} = 10$ for the outliers are calculated and the points $\mathbf{p}_6$ and $\mathbf{p}_9$ are added to the result. (c) In the balanced binary tree the first match of the index with this prefix is searched. That leads to the point $\mathbf{p}_3$. The exploration of the subtree of point $\mathbf{p}_3$ adds the points $\mathbf{p}_{11}$ and $\mathbf{p}_{12}$. Then the outlier search starts for the prefix $\hat{i}_{d_{\mathcal{F}}=2} = 10$. It is successful in the root-node, where the point $\mathbf{p}_6$ is located. Calling the *explore*-operator on the left branch prunes the left side of the child and provides the point $\mathbf{p}_9$ on the right branch. Applying it on the right child prunes the right branch and leads to an already examined subtree, thereupon the search ends.

Step 3: Collecting Points

The collection of points depends on the tree organization. Hence, both trees have to be discussed separately.

Collecting Points in the Octree: Since the octree possesses a spatial organization, the search is straight-forward. All leaf-nodes in the subtree of node **n** are checked. If the distance of the mean point $\tilde{p}_n$ to the center **q** of the ROI is smaller than the radius, it is accepted. The complexity in the worst case is

$$O(8\log_8(d_{\mathcal{F}}) + 8^{1+d_{\max}-d_{\mathcal{F}}}\log_8(d_{\max} - d_{\mathcal{F}})). \tag{9}$$

That occurs, when the subtrees of all starting points contain the maximum number of entries and are of the same size.

Collecting Points in the Balanced Binary Tree: The position of a node in a balanced binary tree is less correlated with the spatial position than in the octree. Accordingly, additional operations are required in order to navigate. Comparing the prefix $\hat{i}_{d_{\mathcal{F}}}$ of node n to the prefix $\hat{i}'_{d_{\mathcal{F}}}$ of a child n′ of n by the operator

$$explore(\hat{i}_{d_{\mathcal{F}}}, \hat{i}'_{d_{\mathcal{F}}}) \begin{cases} \text{explore the right branch of } n', \text{ if } & \hat{i}'_{d_{\mathcal{F}}} < \hat{i}_{d_{\mathcal{F}}} \\ \text{explore both branches of } n', \text{ if } & \hat{i}'_{d_{\mathcal{F}}} = \hat{i}_{d_{\mathcal{F}}} \\ \text{explore the left branch of } n', \text{ if } & \hat{i}'_{d_{\mathcal{F}}} > \hat{i}_{d_{\mathcal{F}}} \end{cases} \tag{10}$$

allows for deciding, which branch needs further examination.

To avoid re-exploration of a subtree , the prefix $\hat{i}_{d_{\mathcal{F}}}$ of n is stored in an *explored-list* after examination of its complete subtree. The first element of the list is the prefix of the cell that contains the center of the ROI, followed by a maximum of 6 outlier prefixes. The index of each examined node is compared to all list elements. In case of a match, the search on the subtree terminates. Otherwise, the distance of the mean point of a node to the center **q** of the ROI is checked. If it passes, the point is collected.

In the worst case, all starting points are located in the top four levels of the tree, while the searched points are based in the leaf cells. Due to two instead of eight childs per node, the maximum tree depth is

$$3d_{\max} = \log_2 8^{d_{\max}}. \tag{11}$$

The limiting complexity is approximated by

$$O(32 + 2^{3d_{\max}-1}\log_2(3d_{\max} - 4)). \tag{12}$$

Fig. 1(a) illustrates the algorithm on a two-dimensional example. Fig. 1(b) shows the results on a quadtree (which is the 2D version of an octree), while Fig. 1(c) focuses on the balanced binary tree.

4   Experimental Evaluation

In this section, the processing speed for both the octree and the balanced binary tree is compared to the results of a naive approach. A comparison to ICP approaches is not appropriate since ICP approaches are limited to a search of single closest points.

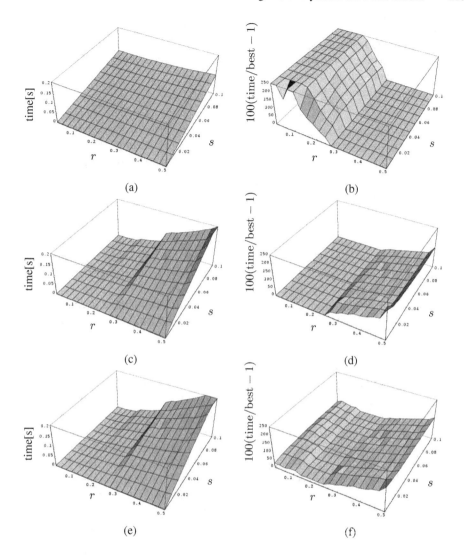

Fig. 2. The plots in the left column show absolute processing times, while the right column addresses the normalized processing times. Normalized times are divided by the measurement of the fastest algorithm regarding a pair of radius and saturation. The plots (a) and (b) are the result of the naive approach, (c) and (d) the result of the octree, while (e) and (f) are the result of the balanced binary tree.

The naive approach is implemented as a sequential pointered list. The use of an index is not necessary. Since no spatial organization exists, each list node is compared to the center of the ROI. Therefore, the complexity is N, as N is the number of nodes.

The input of every representation is an identical point cloud, i.e. a uniformly distributed set of points within a cube of unitary edge size. Note this is only a theoretical worst case example. Taking realistic data, such as a sampled surface consisting of several objects and background leads to much better but data-dependant results. Nevertheless, the mean processing times achieved with this method embedded in a 3D-scene interpretation approach are depicted in [7].

The term *saturation*

$$s = N/8^{d_{\max}} \tag{13}$$

describes the occupancy of the cube, where the divisor $8^{d_{\max}}$ is the maximum number of possible indices (that equals the maximum number of atomic cells). Accordingly, a saturation of $s = 1$ symbolizes the maximum number of 3D-points which can be encoded with an index of $d_{\max}$ digits. For the tests we used a subdivision space of depth $d_{\max} = 8$. It allows for a maximum number of about $16.8 \cdot 10^6$ entries.

For the experimental evaluation of the processing costs, the radius $r \in [0.01, 0.5]$ of the ROI $\mathcal{F}(r, \mathbf{q})$ was modified in 20 steps and the saturation $s \in [0.001, 0.1]$ of the representations in 10 steps. Each combination of r and s was repeated 500 times. That leads to a total of $20 \times 10 \times 500 = 10^5$ tests. The processing performance at an Intel Xeon 1.7GHz with 1GB RAM are depicted in Fig. 2.

Due to better visualization of the comparison results, we define a normalized notation of processing times. There, each pair (r, s) depicts the processing time of an approach with respect to the processing time of the fastest representation. The result is performed in percent and shifted to the origin, i.e. a value of 0 characterizes an approach as being faster than the others.

As mentioned above, the absolute processing times for the naive approach are a function of the saturation (see Fig. 2(a)), since it defines the length of the list. Furthermore, the processed operation is an expansive floating-point calculation of a distance in contrast to a simple integer comparison of an index.

For both tree representations the absolute processing costs arise either for the parameter r and s. This is caused by an increasing number of nodes which have to be examined in both cases. In the worst case, that is a ROI of similar size to the represented space all nodes have to be processed. Consecutively, additional costs for navigation and calculation of the index occur.

These contemplations are of minor importance, since the algorithm is designed for scene interpretation. There, focused objects are much smaller than the complete scene. A direct comparison of the normalized plots (Fig. 2(b), (d) and (f)) emphasizes the advantages of the search algorithm. It shows the dependency of the method to the radius r only. As desired small radii less than 30% of the edge size of the represented space, meet the expectations. The tree representations achieve significantly faster processing for this parameterization, while the naive approach exceeds the range of the plot.

Due to lower tree-depth and less operations during navigation, the octree outperforms the balanced binary tree with around 10% to 20% faster access. On the other hand, the octree needs $\sum_{i=0}^{d_{\max}-1} 8^i$ additional nodes for the top of the tree. It has to be considered, therefore, whether processing time or memory costs matter the most.

5   Conclusion

In this paper a novel combination of an encoding of 3D-points and a region search algorithm was introduced. The used input is a data stream as it is typical for sampling a scene with a 3D-sensing device.

It has been shown that the region search algorithm is feasible for an octree representation and a binary balanced tree representation. Both structures were selected to provide the necessary update ability. The search algorithm can be adapted to each tree representation and allows the access to arbitrary sized spherical subsets. The method shows the best performance for small and medium regions of interest. This is of special importance since the algorithm is embedded in a scene interpretation approach that needs to focus differently sized objects with respect to a large environment.

Comparing the octree to the balanced tree representation leads to the conclusion, that the octree is the best choice if memory costs are irrelevant. Keeping in mind that 3D sensing tends to produce very large data sets, the balanced binary tree is a very significant structure even though processing costs are higher.

References

1. Johnson, A.E., Hebert, M.: Using spin images for efficient object recognition in cluttered 3D scenes. IEEE Transactions on Pattern Analysis and Machine Intelligence **21** (1999) 433–449
2. Yamany, S.M., Farag, A.A.: Surface signatures: An orientation indepentent free-form surface representation scheme for the purpose of objects registration and matching. IEEE Transactions on Pattern Analysis and Machine Intelligence **24** (2002) 1105–1120
3. Samet, H.: Applications of Spatial Data Structures: computer graphics, image processing, and GIS. Addison-Wesley Publishing Company (1990)
4. Gaede, V., Günther, O.: Multidimensional access methods. ACM Computing Surveys **30** (1998) 170–231
5. Sagawa, R., Masuda, T., Ikeuchi, K.: Effective nearest neighbor search for aligning and merging range images. International Conference on 3-D Digital Imaging and Modelling (2003)
6. Bodenmüller, T., Hirzinger, G.: Online surface reconstruction from unorganized 3D-points for the DLR hand-guided scanner system. 2nd International Symposium on 3D Data Processing, Visualization, and Transmission 3DPVT'04 (2004)
7. Wahl, E., Hirzinger, G.: Local point cloud analysis for rapid scene interpretation. DAGM 2005 (27th Annual meeting of the German Association for Pattern Recognition) (2005)
8. Strobl, K.H., Sepp, W., Wahl, E., Bodenmüller, T., Suppa, M., Seara, J.F., Hirzinger, G.: The DLR multisensory hand-guided device: The laser stripe profiler. International Conference on Robotis & Automation (ICRA) (2004)
9. Suppa, M., Hirzinger, G.: A novel system approach to multisensory data acquisition. The 8th Conference on Intelligent Autonomous Systems IAS-8 (2004)
10. Adel'son-Vel'skiĭ, G.M., Landis, Y.M.: An algorithm for the organization of information. English translation: Soviet. Math. Dokl. 3 (1962) 1259–1263

6D-Vision: Fusion of Stereo and Motion for Robust Environment Perception

Uwe Franke, Clemens Rabe, Hernán Badino, and Stefan Gehrig

DaimlerChrysler AG, 70546 Stuttgart, Germany
{uwe.franke, clemens.rabe, hernan.badino,
stefan.gehrig}@daimlerchrysler.com

Abstract. Obstacle avoidance is one of the most important challenges for mobile robots as well as future vision based driver assistance systems. This task requires a precise extraction of depth and the robust and fast detection of moving objects. In order to reach these goals, this paper considers vision as a process in space and time. It presents a powerful fusion of depth and motion information for image sequences taken from a moving observer. 3D-position and 3D-motion for a large number of image points are estimated simultaneously by means of Kalman-Filters. There is no need of prior error-prone segmentation. Thus, one gets a rich 6D representation that allows the detection of moving obstacles even in the presence of partial occlusion of foreground or background.

1 Introduction

Moving objects are the most dangerous objects in many applications. The fast and reliable estimation of their motion is a major challenge for the environment perception of mobile systems and of driver assistance systems in particular. The three-dimensional information delivered by stereo vision is commonly accumulated in an evidence-grid-like structure [9]. Since stereo does not reveal any motion information, usually the depth map is segmented and detected objects are tracked over time in order to obtain their motion. The major disadvantage of this standard approach is that the performance of the detection highly depends on the correctness of the segmentation. Especially moving objects in front of stationary ones – eg. the bicycle in front of the parking vehicles shown in figure 1 – are often merged and therefore not detected. This can cause dangerous misinterpretations and requires more powerful solutions.

Our first attempt to overcome this problem was the so called flow-depth constraint [6]. Heinrich compared the measured optical flow with the expectation stemming from the known ego-motion and the 3D stereo information. Independently moving objects do not fulfil the constraint and can easily be detected. Unfortunately, this approach turned out to be very sensitive to small errors in the ego-motion estimation, since only two consecutive frames are considered.

Humans do not have the above mentioned problems since we simultaneously evaluate depth and motion in the retinal images and integrate the observations over time [10]. The approach presented in this paper follows this principle. The

W. Kropatsch, R. Sablatnig, and A. Hanbury (Eds.): DAGM 2005, LNCS 3663, pp. 216–223, 2005.

Fig. 1. Typical scene causing segmentation problems to standard stereo systems.

basic idea is to track points with depth known from stereo vision over two and more consecutive frames and to fuse the spatial and temporal information using Kalman Filters. The result is an improved accuracy of the 3D-position and an estimation of the 3D-motion of the considered point at the same time. Since we get a rich 6D-state vector for each point we like to refer to this method as 6D-Vision. Taking into account the motion information, the above mentioned segmentation problem can be solved much more easily and robust.

The fusion implies the knowledge of the ego-motion. Fortunately, practical tests reveal that for the detection of moving obstacles in front of a moving car the standard inertial sensors are sufficient. If neccessary, the ego-motion can be computed from image points found to be stationary (e.g. see [8] or [1]).

The mentioned accuracy improvement is already exploited by a satellite docking system described in [7]. After an application-specific initialization, predefined markers are tracked in the images of a pair of stereo cameras yielding a very precise estimation of the relative position. In [3] Dang combines stereo and motion to decide whether a group of points underlies the rigid motion.

In our real-time application we track about 2000 image points. So far, the best results are obtained using a version of the well-known Kanade-Lucas-Tomasi (KLT) tracker [11] that was optimized with respect to speed. The depth estimation is based on a hierarchical correlation based scheme [4]. However, any comparable optical flow estimation and any other stereo system can be used.

The paper is organized as follows: section 2 describes the system model and the measurement equation for the proposed Kalman Filter. Section 3 studies the rate of convergence of the considered system and presents a multi-filter system for improved convergence. Section 4 gives practical results including crossing objects and oncoming traffic.

2   System Description

In the following we use a right handed coordinate system with the origin on the road. The lateral x-axis points to the left, the height axis y points upwards and the z-axis represents the distance of a point straight ahead. This coordinate system is fixed to the car, so that all estimated positions are given in the coordinate system of the moving observer. The camera is at $(x, y, z)^T = (0, height, 0)^T$ looking in positive z-direction.

2.1   System Model

The movement of a vehicle with constant velocity v_c and yaw rate $\dot{\psi}$ over the time interval Δt can be described in this car coordinate system as

$$\Delta \underline{x}_c = \int_0^{\Delta t} \underline{v}_c (\tau) \, d\tau = \frac{v_c}{\dot{\psi}} \begin{pmatrix} 1 - \cos \dot{\psi} \Delta t \\ 0 \\ \sin \dot{\psi} \Delta t \end{pmatrix}.$$

The position of a world point $\underline{x} = (X, Y, Z)^T$ after the time Δt can be described in the car coordinate system at time step k as

$$\underline{x}_k = R_y (\psi) (\underline{x}_{k-1} + \underline{v}_{k-1} \Delta t - \Delta \underline{x}_c)$$

with its associated velocity vector $\underline{v}$ and the rotational matrix around the y-axis $R_y (\psi)$. Combining position and velocity in the 6D-state vector $\underline{\tilde{x}} = (X, Y, Z, \dot{X}, \dot{Y}, \dot{Z})^T$ leads to the discrete system model equation

$$\underline{\tilde{x}}_k = A_k \underline{\tilde{x}}_{k-1} + B_k v_c + \underline{w}_{k-1}$$

with the state transition matrix

$$A_k = \begin{pmatrix} R_y (\psi) & | & \Delta t R_y (\psi) \\ \overline{} & & \overline{} \\ 0 & | & R_y (\psi) \end{pmatrix}$$

and the control matrix

$$B_k = \frac{1}{\dot{\psi}} \begin{pmatrix} 1 - \cos \left(\dot{\psi} \Delta t \right) \\ 0 \\ -\sin \left(\dot{\psi} \Delta t \right) \\ 0 \\ 0 \\ 0 \end{pmatrix}.$$

The noise term $\underline{w}$ is assumed to be Gaussian white noise with covariance matrix Q.

2.2   Measurement Model

The measurement consists of two pieces of information: the image coordinates u and v of a tracked feature and the disparity d delivered by stereo vision working

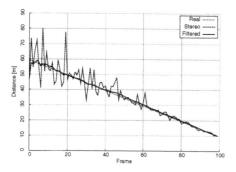
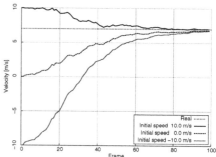

(a) Distance estimation of static world point.

(b) Velocity estimation of moving world point at a speed of $v_z = 7.0\,\frac{m}{s}$ using three different initializations.

Fig. 2. Estimation results of the presented Kalman Filter. The considered world point is at the initial position $(10.0\,\text{m}, 1.0\,\text{m}, 60.0\,\text{m})^T$. The observer moves at a constant speed of $v_z = 10\,\frac{m}{s}$ in positive z-direction (20 fps).

on rectified images. Assuming a pin-hole camera the non-linear measurement equation for a point given in the camera coordinate system is

$$\underline{z} = \begin{pmatrix} u \\ v \\ d \end{pmatrix} = \frac{1}{Z} \begin{pmatrix} X f_u \\ Y f_v \\ b f_u \end{pmatrix} + \underline{\nu}$$

with the focal lengths f_u and f_v and the baseline b of the stereo camera system. The noise term $\underline{\nu}$ is assumed to be Gaussian white noise with covariance matrix R.

2.3 Simulation Results

The benefit of filtering the three-dimensional measurement is illustrated by figure 2(a). It shows the estimated relative distance of a simulated static world point measured from an observer moving at a speed of $10\,\frac{m}{s}$. The initial position of the point is $(10.0\,\text{m}, 1.0\,\text{m}, 60.0\,\text{m})^T$. White gaussian noise was added to the image position and the disparity with a variance of $1.0\,\text{px}^2$. The dashed curve shows the unfiltered 3D position calculation which suffers from the additive noise. The continuous curve gives the excellent result of the filter.

In the above example the speed of the point was correctly initialized to zero. How does the filter perform if the point is in motion? Let us assume the point moves at a speed of $v_z = 7.0\,\frac{m}{s}$ in positive z-direction. Figure 2(b)shows the estimation results of three differently initialized filters. Although very large initial values of the P-Matrix are used, the speed of convergence is only fair. Better results can be obtained by a multi-filter approach described in the following.

3   Multiple Filters for Improved Rate of Convergence

As shown above in figure2(b), the closer the first guess is to the correct value, the less time it takes until the estimate is below a given error threshold. This strong dependency on the initial value can be overcome by running multiple Kalman Filters initialized at different speeds in parallel, estimating the world position and velocity using the same input data.

How can we decide which state is the best? One way is to calculate the distance between the real measurements and the predicted measurements using the Mahalanobis distance, also known as the normalized innovation squared (NIS) [2]:

$$D_M\left(\underline{z}, \underline{x}\right) = \left(\underline{z} - \underline{x}\right)\Sigma^{-1}\left(\underline{z} - \underline{x}\right)^{\top}$$

with the measurement $\underline{z}$, the predicted measurement $\underline{x}$ and the innovation co-variance matrix Σ.

Alternatively, the probability density function, also called likelihood, can be used as an indicator to decide whether a given measurement $\underline{z}$ matches a certain Kalman Filter model. This is used for example in the interacting multiple model estimator (IMM) [2]. However, the likelihood calculation tends to suffer from too small floating point data types.

In order to avoid these numerical problems, we base our decisions on the NIS criterion. Figure 3(a) shows the low pass filtered NIS values for the three differently initialized filters of figure 3(a). It is obvious that the initialization quality corresponds to the discrepancy in measurement space between the measured and predicted position.

Selecting one of the three (in general n) filter states as the correct one would ignore valuable information contained in the other filters. Assuming a limited initial state space, i.e. the tracked point has a limited absolute velocity, we initialize the filters on different velocities including the boundaries. Consequently, the real state must lie in between these boundaries and can be expressed as a weighted sum

$$\underline{\tilde{x}} = \frac{1}{\sum \beta_i} \sum_{i=0}^{n} \beta_i \underline{x}_i \qquad \text{with} \qquad \beta_i = \frac{1}{NIS_i}$$

where the weights β_i represent the matching quality of each Kalman Filter. It is beneficial not to base the decision or weighting on the current measurement quality only, since this would lead to undesired effects due to measurement noise. Therefore, we apply a low pass filtering to the weights thus accumulating the errors over a certain time.

Figure 3(b)shows the result obtained by the above approach, if the three filters are initialized at speeds -10.0, 0.0 and $10.0\ \frac{m}{s}$. For comparison, the same filter initialized at $-10.0\ \frac{m}{s}$ shown in figure 2(b) is considered. It can be seen that the multi-filter approach converges two times faster than the simple one. A comparison with figure (2b) reveals that the combined system shows a better performance than each of the three single filters.

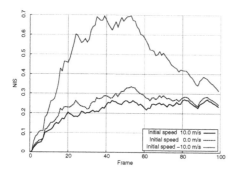
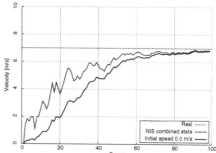

(a) Low pass filtered normalized innovation squared of the filters from figure 2(b).

(b) Improved convergence obtained by the Multi Kalman Filter system.

Fig. 3. Multi Kalman Filter estimation result (20 fps)

Fig. 4. Velocity estimation results for cyclist moving in front of parking cars. The arrows show the predicted position of the world point in 0.5 s. The right image was taken 0.5 s later allowing a comparison of the estimation from the left image. Blue encodes stationary points.

4   Real World Results

The five most probable practical situations are: stationary objects, vehicles driving in the same direction as our own vehicle with small relative speed, oncoming traffic, traffic from left, and traffic from right. The sketched multi-filter approach offers the chance to run independent filters tuned to any of these five situations in order to reach the desired fast convergence.

Let us first concentrate on the crossing situation already shown in figure 1. The result of the velocity estimation is given in figure 4. The cyclist drives in front of parking vehicles while the observer moves towards him at a nearly constant speed of $4\frac{m}{s}$. The arrows show the predicted position of the corresponding world point in 0.5 s projected into the image. The colors encode the estimated lateral speed; the warmer the colour the higher the velocity. In order to prove the results,

Fig. 5. Velocity estimation results for oncoming car. The observer moves at a constant speed of 50 $\frac{km}{h}$.

the right image in figure 4 shows the same situation 0.5 s later. As can be seen, the prediction shown in the left image was very accurate.

Figure 5 shows the estimation results for a typical oncoming traffic situation in which the observer moves at a constant speed of 50 $\frac{km}{h}$. Here the color encodes the Euclidean velocity of the tracked points. The prediction matches the real position shown in the right image.

Practical tests at intersections and on highways reveal that the algorithm is highly robust with respect to measurement noise, induced by pitch and yaw of the vehicle. Simply spoken, it doesn't matter how a point in the world precisely moves from A to B, because those details are filtered out by the Kalman Filter. On the other hand, it turns out that measurement outliers sometimes cause serious misinterpretations. This problem is overcome by using a standard 3σ-test to detect and reject those outliers.

5   Summary

The proposed fusion of stereo and optical flow simultaneously improves the depth accuracy and allows estimating position and motion of each considered point. Segmentation based on this 6D-information is much more reliable and a fast recognition of moving objects becomes possible. In particular, objects with certain direction and speed of motion can directly be detected on the image level without further non-linear processing or classification steps that may fail if unpredicted objects occur.

Since the fusion is based on Kalman Filters, the information contained in a number of frames is integrated. This leads to much more robust estimations than differential approaches like pure evaluation of the optical flow. The proposed multi-filter approach adopted from our depth-from-motion work [5] speeds up the rate of convergence of the estimation, which is important for fast reactions. For example, practical tests confirm that a crossing cyclist at an intersection is detected within 4-5 frames. The implementation on a 3.2 GHz Pentium 4 proves that the described approach runs in real-time. Currently, we select and track about 2000 image points at 12-16 Hz, depending on the used optical flow algorithm (the images have VGA resolution).

The ego-motion is assumed to be known throughout the paper. For many in-door robotic applications on flat surfaces the usage of inertial sensors will be sufficient. At the moment, the ego-motion of our demonstrator vehicle (UTA, a Mercedes Benz E-Class vehicle) is determined based on the inertial sensors only. Thanks to the Kalman Filter, the results are sufficient for obstacle avoidance. The most dominant pitching motion results in an apparent vertical motion that is ignored for this application. Nevertheless, in order to reach maximum accuracy, the next step will be to estimate the six degree of freedom ego-motion precisely using those image points that have been classified as static.

References

1. Badino, H.: A Robust Approach for Ego-Motion Estimation Using a Mobile Stereo Platform. 1st International Workshop on Complex Motion (IWCM04), Günzburg, Germany, October 2004
2. Bar-Shalom, Y., Kirubarajan, T., Li, X.: Estimation with Applications to Tracking and Navigation. John Wiley & Sons, Inc., 2002
3. Dang, T., Hoffmann, C., Stiller, C.: Fusing Optical Flow and Stereo Disparity for Object Tracking. Proc. of the IEEE V. International Conference on Intelligent Transportation Systems, Singapore, 3-6 September, pp. 112–117, 2002.
4. Franke, U.: Real-time Stereo Vision for Urban Traffic Scene Understanding. IEEE Conference on Intelligent Vehicles 2000, October 2000, Dearborn
5. Franke, U., Rabe, C.: Kalman Filter based Depth from Motion Estimation with Fast Convergence. to appear in IEEE Conference on Intelligent Vehicles 2005, June 2005, Las Vegas
6. Heinrich, S.: Real Time Fusion of Motion and Stereo using Flow/Depth constraint for Fast Obstacle Detection. DAGM 2002, September 2002
7. Lin, C.-F.: Three-dimensional relative positioning and tracking using LDRI. US patent no 6,677,941, Jan. 13, 2004
8. Mallet, A., Lacroix, S., Gallo, L.: Position estimation in outdoor environments using pixel tracking and stereovision. Proc. of the 2000 IEEE International Conference on Robotics and Automation ICRA 2000, pp. 3519–3524, San Francisco, April 2000
9. Martin, M., Moravec, H.: Robot Evidence Grids. The Robotics Institute, Carnegie Mellon University, Pittsburgh, PA, March 1996 (CMU-RI-TR-96-06)
10. Sekuler, R.,Watamaniuk, S.,Blake R.: Perception of Visual Motion. In Stevens' Handbook of Experimental Psychology, Volume 1, Sensation and Perception, Jan. 2004
11. Tomasi, C., Kanade, T.: Detection and Tracking of Point Features. School of Computer Science, Carnegie Mellon University, Pittsburgh, PA, April 1991 (CMU-CS-91-132)

A Method for Determining Geometrical Distortion of Off-The-Shelf Wide-Angle Cameras

Helmut Zollner and Robert Sablatnig

Pattern and Image Processing Group (PRIP),
Techn. Univ. Wien, 1040 Vienna, Austria
{zollnerh, sab}@prip.tuwien.ac.at

Abstract. In this work we present a method for calibrating and removing nonlinear geometric distortion of an imaging device. The topic is of importance since most reasoning in projective geometry requires the projection to be strictly line preserving. The model of radial-symmetric pincushion or barrel distortions, is generally not sufficient to compensate for all non-linearities of the projection, this is true especially for wide-angle cameras. Therefore we applied a more complex parametric model to compensate for the non-central distortion effects. The only a-priori knowledge that is used is the straightness of some edges in the recorded image. In our experiments we could show that the method is applicable especially for off-the-self cameras with medium quality optics.

1 Introduction

In the field of camera calibration, distortion is widely considered as a correction of inaccurate camera features and is part of the generic camera model [8]. This approach is not feasible for auto-calibration without a predefined calibration target, since linear projection is preconditioned. Hence, an accurate method and robust solution for the distortion problem is needed without using predefined calibration targets. In [4] no a-priori knowledge is needed for distortion estimation at all which is allowed by the simplicity of the distortion model. In return only radial-symmetric distortion can modeled. For omni-directional cameras the pinhole projection cannot be used at all. Camera and distortion models for this type of optics are studied in [6]. Especially the distortion model can be also used for wide-angle lenses. Numerous other parametric models were also presented in [3] and more recently in [5]. A non-parametric distortion model was studied in [7].

Actual photographic devices never comply with a strictly affine or projective camera model, which is basic for further geometric reasoning. Physically this is due to numerous non-zero tolerances of dimensions of lenses and imperfections of the camera components. In optical engineering some so-called aberrations featuring special deviations to ideal optical instruments are distinguished. As we assume the camera system to be achromatic [1], this work is restricted to pure geometric aberrations.

---

[1] The refraction angle of ray passing throw the optics is independent of it corresponding wavelength

W. Kropatsch, R. Sablatnig, and A. Hanbury (Eds.): DAGM 2005, LNCS 3663, pp. 224–229, 2005.

As the magnitude of these aberrations also depends on the field of view of the imaging device, we investigated our method using wide-angle cameras with a field of view more than 120°, since using other optics makes some of these deviations too small to measure and at least very sensitive to noise.

This paper is structured in three parts. Starting with the formal description of distortion model and explanation of the parameters we will then introduce our approach for the parameter estimation. The next section comprises a summary of our experiments and results. Finally we will present our conclusions and give a short outlook of our future plans.

2   Geometric Camera Distortion Model

The most significant distortion effect is present in the radial component. Especially for narrow angle optics this might be the only considerable non-linear projection feature that has to be considered. Hence the notion of ignoring other distortion components is widely accepted in practice, since the terms describing these models are easily invertible. In contrast, using off-the-shelf wide-angle optics, that are in general not very central, a simple radial distortion model is not sufficient as it turned out in our experiments. Several solutions like using a non-parametric distortion model or some non-polynomial models have been proposed in recent years. In our work, we go back to a strictly polynomial model, that was first introduced in [9]. In this distortion model, we can distinguish three types of distortion:

- radial-symmetric distortion: this is the well-known distortion which is symmetric around a defined distortion center, which is also the minimum of the function. Geometrically this a projection from a spherical to a flat surface.
- radial-tangential distortion: if distortion is not perfectly symmetrical around a single point, the distortion is itself non-central and consists of two strictly distinguished components.
- prism-distortion: is caused by errors in orthogonality of the optical axis of the lens and the image sensor and can occur for central and non-central cameras.

Let the recorded image points of the camera be $P = [u', v']$. Then the full distortion model is now given by:

$$P_{undist} = \begin{bmatrix} u' - c_x \\ v' - c_y \end{bmatrix} = \begin{bmatrix} u \\ v \end{bmatrix} + \delta(u, v),$$

$$\delta(u, v) = \delta_{prism}(u, v) + \delta_{tang}(u, v) + \delta_{radial}(u, v),$$

(1)

where

$$\delta_{prism}(u, v) = \begin{bmatrix} s_1(u^2 + v^2) \\ s_2(u^2 + v^2) \end{bmatrix}, \quad \delta_{tang}(u, v) = \begin{bmatrix} p_1(3u^2 + v^2) + 2p_2 uv \\ p_2(u^2 + 3v^2) + 2p_1 uv \end{bmatrix},$$

$$\delta_{radial}(u, v) = \begin{bmatrix} k_1 u(u^2 + v^2) \\ k_1 v(u^2 + v^2) \end{bmatrix}$$

(2)

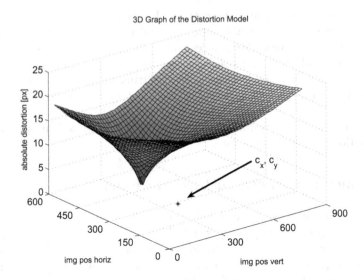

Fig. 1. Visualization of the euclidean distance $|\delta|$ between distorted (original) and corrected image coords across the original image area. Notice: the minimum is not at the center of the radial distortion component $[c_x, c_y]$.

The distortion functions are all derived from Taylor series. Only the 2nd degree terms are used, since it is well-known that higher order terms do not produce any substantially better results in practice and secondly they would also increase complexity and noise sensitivity . Accordingly the model has 7 free parameters. It is important to note that $[c_x, c_y]$ does neither designate the position of principal point nor the exact coordinates of the point of minimal distortion as is illustrated in Figure 1. Hence there is no distortion center at all, since we introduced the radial-tangential factor, which generally implies non-central distortion. Alternatively the model can be simplified by keeping c_x and c_y constant. Obviously these values should be around the coordinates of the image center, but principally we can choose any position — even at the image border. That of course will heavily disrupt the shape of the corrected image area by enlarging the prism distortion effect quite strongly.

3   Parameter Estimation

In previous work several methods for robust distortion estimation were introduced. In [6] point correspondences together with a special modification of the non-polynomial division model are used in order to solve for quadratic eigenvalue problem. Using a very simple radial distortion model, even blind estimation of its parameters is possible, which has been demonstrated by Farid and Popescu in [4]. In our case we use defined flat pattern of concentric compound regions with piecewise linear circumference, e.g. some squares, hexagons, octagons. As we now know all edgels within a picture of the pattern sit on straight lines. Hence straightness constraints can be applied to the estimation problem in order to produce a line-preserving image. The argumentation for using only line-features is the same as already formulated in [5]. The resulting projection is strictly linear and can be further calibrated according to a pinhole model. We do not enforce any kind of angle-constraint, since, even if we do not get the right angles, this can be corrected, because shear operations in the image space are always line-preserving.

For edge extraction we use a Canny edge detector and rearrange the resulting edgels together with the covariances (uncertainties) as a sorted list representing the polygon and its uncertainty. In order to identify the corners we use a curvature analysis algorithm introduced in [1].

The resulting sample polygons are subject to a linear least square fit which uses the following error function χ^2:

Let $\mathbf{P} = \{P_1, ...P_n\}$ where $P_i = (u_i, v_i)$ is an ordered set of extracted edgels.

$$\chi^2 = \frac{1}{n^2} \cdot (a \sin^2 \phi - 2 |b| |\sin \phi| \cos \phi + c \cos^2 \phi), \tag{3}$$

where

$$a = \sum_{j=1}^{n} u_j^2 - \frac{1}{n} \left(\sum_{j=1}^{n} u_j \right)^2 \qquad b = \sum_{j=1}^{n} u_j v_j - \frac{1}{n} \sum_{j=1}^{n} u_j \sum_{j=1}^{n} v_j \tag{4}$$

$$c = \sum_{j=1}^{n} v_j^2 - \frac{1}{n} \left(\sum_{j=1}^{n} v_j \right)^2 \tag{5}$$

$$\alpha = a - c \qquad \beta = \frac{\alpha}{2\sqrt{\alpha^2 + 4b}} \tag{6}$$

$$|\sin \phi| = \sqrt{\frac{1}{2} - \beta}, \qquad \cos \phi = \sqrt{\frac{1}{2} + \beta} \tag{7}$$

The angle ϕ in Equation 4 corresponds directly to the angle of the fitted line with u-axis. The error function is very similar to the one introduced in [2]. We introduced the additional term $\frac{1}{n^2}$ in Equation 4, since it improved the convergence behavior in our experiments by a factor of ten yielding results differing from the ones computed with the original model in [2] at the 7th to 9th decimal place for the parameters.

The initial setup for the distortion model is a zero vector. After the first run with resulting residual Outlier-points are eliminated and the corner detection is applied a second time. If the relative difference between the previous residual [2] and the current one is less than a threshold the estimation is finished. In the other case we iterate the procedure until the stop condition is fulfilled. The result of the operation is a full distortion model and a list of Outlier points. These outliers can be also used to determine asymmetric lens defects.

---

[2] Now computed without the Outlier-points.

4   Experiments

We used the intensity images of a 1/3 inch standard CCD-camera. Mounted with 3.8mm wide-angle lens the images cover the scene with an effective angle of view of about 135°. The size of the images was 768x576 pixel. A flat print-out of concentric rectangles of unknown proportions and size serves as a calibration pattern. We used one light source directed roughly perpendicular to this surfaces, producing roughly uniform illumination for recording. We were able to detect the edges with a standard deviation of less than 0.3 [px] using a Canny edge detector (see Figure 2). Out of about 10,000 edgels we selected the corners with the algorithm suggested in [1]. By the decrease of the amount of sample points the corner detector gets more sensitive resulting in some additional redundant corners. Since this effect is due to the distortion, which is expected to be smaller in central areas, we may exclude the innermost edgels from the estimation, where the polygon is most likely broken into smaller unwanted parts.

In order to evaluate the accuracy of our results we used an error metric which directly relates to the straightness of the resulting projection. We fitted

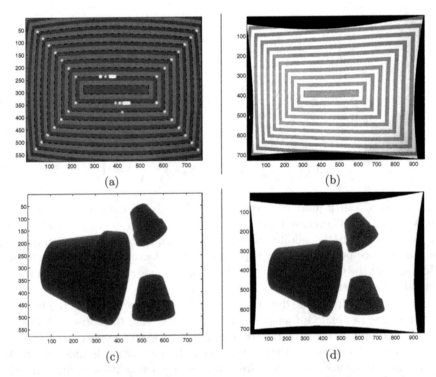

Fig. 2. (a) The original image of the calibration pattern with detected edges and corners. (b) Correction according to estimation after 3 iterations (c) Image of several pots recorded with same camera (d) Corrected image of the pots.

a line in between the remaining test points for each section of all polygons in a least-square sense and measured their perpendicular distance to this reference. The standard deviation of this distances was in the range of 0.5-0.7 pixels. If we only take into account the outermost section we can roughly bound the accuracy to 0.7 pixels. Indeed in this case it might not be quite correct to speak of an accuracy measurement rather than a quantitative indication of how close to perfectly line-preserving the resulting projection is.

5   Conclusion and Outlook

We were able to demonstrate the applicability of a complex polynomial distortion model using wide-angle off-the-self lenses. The resulting parametric models can be used to stratify images and their features. We introduced a distortion model with some minor changes to the one proposed in [9]. Due to the optimization strategy which is similar to the widely applied RANSAC algorithm, the method is robust against local deviations and can also be apply for detecting them. A major objection for using polynomial models is that they are not directly invertible. In the future work we will investigate that problem closely. Finally we plan to integrate the distortion estimator in a framework for auto-calibration where is used to correct all image features in order to produce a virtually line-preserving projection.

References

1. Dmitry Chetverikov and Zs. Szab. A Simple and Efficient Algorithm for Detection of High Curvature Points in Planar Curves. Technical report, 1999.
2. R. Deriche, R. Vailant and O. Faugeras. From Noisy Edge Points to 3d Reconstruction of a scene: A Robust Approach and its Uncertainty Analysis. In *Proc. of the 7th Scandinavian Conf. on Image Analysis*, pages 225–232, Alborg, Denmark, Aug 1991.
3. Frederic Devernay and Olivier D. Faugeras. Straight lines have to be straight. *Machine Vision and Applications*, 13(1):14–24, 2001.
4. H. Farid and A.C. Popescu. Blind Removal of Lens Distortions. *Journal of the Optical Society of America*, 18(9):2072–2078, 2001.
5. A. Habib and M. Morgan. Automatic Calibration of Low Cost digital cameras. *SPIE Journal of Optical Engeneering*, 42(4):948–955, 2003.
6. B. Micusik and T. Pajdla. Using RANSAC for Omnidirectional Camera Model Fitting. In Ondrej Drbohlav, editor, *Computer Vision - CVWW*, Vatice, Czech Republic, Feb 2003. Czech Pattern Recognition Society.
7. J. Pers and S. Kovacic. Nonparametric, Model-Based Radial Lens Distortion Correcting Using Tilted Camera Assumption. In H. Kropatsch, W. Wildenauer, editor, *Computer Vision - CVWW*, pages 286–295, Bad Ausee, Austria, February 2002.
8. R. Y. Tsai. A Versatile Camera Calibration Technique for High Accuracy 3D Machine Vision Metrology using Off-the-Shelf TV Cameras and Lenses. Technical Report RC 51342, IBM, oct 1985.
9. Juyang Weng, Paul Cohen, and Marc Herniou. Camera Calibration with Distortion Models and Accuracy Evaluation. *IEEE Trans. Pattern Anal. Mach. Intell.*, 14(10):965–980, 1992.

A System for Marker-Less Human Motion Estimation

B. Rosenhahn[1,4], U. G. Kersting[2], A. W. Smith[2], J. K. Gurney[2], T. Brox [3],
and R. Klette[1]

[1]Computer Science Department, [2]Department of Sport and Exercise Science,
The University of Auckland, New Zealand
bros028@cs.auckland.ac.nz
[3]Math. Image Analysis Group, Saarland University, Germany
[4] From November 2005: Max Planck Center Saarbrücken,
rosenhahn@mpi-sb.mpg.de

Abstract. In this contribution we present a silhouette based human motion estimation system. The system components contain silhouette extraction based on
level sets, a correspondence module, which relates image data to model data and
a pose estimation module. Experiments are done in a four camera setup and we
estimate the model components with 21 degrees of freedom in two frames per
second. Finally, we perform a comparison of the motion estimation system with a
marker based tracking system to perform a quantitative error analysis. The results
show the applicability of the system for marker-less sports movement analysis.

1 Introduction

Human motion estimation from image sequences means to determine the rigid body
motion [11] and joint angles of a 3D human model from 2D image data. Due to redun-
dancies multi-view approaches are necessary. Often simplified models are used, e.g. by
using stick, ellipsoidal, cylindrical or skeleton models [1,9,7]. We recently introduced
an approach for silhouette based human motion estimation [14] which uses free-form-
surface patches to estimate the pose and joint angles of the upper torso. In [15] we
further applied local and global morphing techniques to get realistic motions of the upper torso model. These basic modules are now extended to a complete human motion
estimation system. The system consists of an advanced image segmentation method,
dynamic occlusion handling and kinematic chains of higher complexity (21 degrees of
freedom). Finally we perform a comparison of the system with a commercial marker
based tracking system [10] used to analyze sports movements[1]. We perform and analyze exercises, such as push ups or sit ups. The algorithm proves as stable, robust and
fairly accurate.

The contribution is organized as follows: We will start with the basic setup of the
motion capture system. Then we will continue with the system modules. Here we will
briefly describe image segmentation based on level sets, pose estimation and the dynamic occlusion handling to deal with partial occlusion in certain frames. The next

---

[1] Motion Analysis Corporation is one of the leading provider of optical motion capture systems in entertainment, video-games, film, broadcasting, virtual reality, medicine, sports, and
research.

W. Kropatsch, R. Sablatnig, and A. Hanbury (Eds.): DAGM 2005, LNCS 3663, pp. 230–237, 2005.

section presents the experimental results and the quantitative error analysis followed by a brief discussion.

2 The Human Motion Tracking System

A 3D object model builds the a priori knowledge of the system, which is in this case given as two free-form surface patches with two kinematic chains. Each kinematic chain

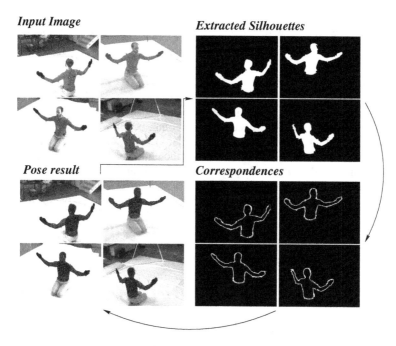

Fig. 1. The capture system consists of iterating the following steps: Segmentation, correspondence estimation, pose estimation

consists of seven joints (three for the shoulder, two for the elbow and two for the wrist). Furthermore we added one back segment joint to the torso surface patch. The estimation procedure is dealing with 21 unknowns, six for the pose parameters (three for rotation and three for translation), 7 for each arm and one backbone joint. During correspondence estimation (along four frames) we collect around 5000 point correspondences (slightly varying dependent on the visible information) and still track in two frames per second for the four camera sequence. Using the 3D model and four images from a (triggered) calibrated camera sequence, the motion tracking system consists of three main components, namely silhouette extraction, matching and pose estimation. All components are iterated to stabilize segmentation on the one hand and pose estimation on the other hand.

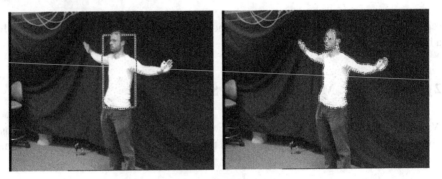

Fig. 2. Silhouette extraction based on level set functions. Left: Initial segmentation. Right: Segmentation result

2.1 Image Segmentation

Image segmentation usually means to estimate boundaries of objects in an image. This task can become very difficult, since noise, shading, occlusion or texture information between the object and the background may distort the segmentation or even make it impossible. Our approach is based on image segmentation based on level sets [12,4,5,2]. A level set function $\Phi \in \Omega \mapsto \mathbf{R}$ splits the image domain Ω into two regions Ω_1 and Ω_2 with $\Phi(x) > 0$ if $x \in \Omega_1$ and $\Phi(x) < 0$ if $x \in \Omega_2$. The zero-level line thus marks the boundary between both regions. The segmentation should maximize the total a-posteriori probability given the probability densities p_1 and p_2 of Ω_1 and Ω_2, i.e., pixels are assigned to the most probable region according to the Bayes rule. Ideally, the boundary between both regions should be as small as possible. This can be expressed by the following energy functional that is sought to be minimized:

$$E(\Phi, p_1, p_2) = - \int_{\Omega} \left(H(\Phi) \log p_1 + (1 - H(\Phi)) \log p_2 + \nu |\nabla H(\Phi)| \right) dx \qquad (1)$$

where $\nu > 0$ is a weighting parameter and $H(s)$ is a regularized version of the Heaviside function, e.g. the error function. Minimization with respect to the region boundary represented by Φ can be performed according to the gradient descent equation

$$\partial_t \Phi = H'(\Phi) \left(\log \frac{p_1}{p_2} + \nu \operatorname{div} \left(\frac{\nabla \Phi}{|\nabla \Phi|} \right) \right) \qquad (2)$$

where $H'(s)$ is the derivative of $H(s)$ with respect to its argument. The probability densities p_i are estimated according to the *expectation-maximization principle*. Having the level set function initialized with some contour, the probability densities within the two regions are estimated by the gray value histograms smoothed with a Gaussian kernel K_σ and its standard deviation σ.

This rather simple and fast approach is sufficient for our laboratory set-up, though it is also conceivable to apply more elaborated region models including texture features. Figure 2 shows an example image and the contour evolution over time. As can be seen, the body silhouette is well extracted, but there are some deviations in the head region, due to the dark hair. Such inaccuracies can be compensated from the pose estimation procedure. For our algorithm we can make a tracking assumption. Therefore, we initialize the silhouette with the pose of the last frame which greatly reduces the number of iterations needed. The implementation is fast; the algorithm needs 50 ms per frame and 200 ms image processing time for a four-camera setup.

2.2 Pose Estimation

For pose estimation we assume a set of point correspondences (X_i, x_i), with 4D (homogeneous) model points X_i and 3D (homogeneous) image points x_i. Each image point is reconstructed to a Plücker line $L_i = (n_i, m_i)$, with a (unit) direction n_i and moment m_i [11].

Every 3D rigid motion can be represented in an exponential form

$$M = \exp(\theta\hat{\xi}) = \exp\begin{pmatrix} \hat{\omega} & v \\ 0_{3\times1} & 0 \end{pmatrix}$$

where $\theta\hat{\xi}$ is the matrix representation of a twist $\xi = (\omega_1, \omega_2, \omega_3, v_1, v_2, v_3) \in se(3) = \{(v, \omega)|v \in \mathbf{R}^3, \omega \in so(3)\}$, with $so(3) = \{A \in \mathbf{R}^{3\times3}|A = -A^T\}$.

In fact, M is an element of the one-parametric Lie group $SE(3)$, known as the group of direct affine isometries. A main result of Lie theory is, that to each Lie group there exists a Lie algebra which can be found in its tangential space, by derivation and evaluation at its origin; see [11] for more details. The corresponding Lie algebra to $SE(3)$ is denoted as $se(3)$. A twist contains six parameters and can be scaled to $\theta\xi$ with a unit vector ω. The parameter $\theta \in \mathbf{R}$ corresponds to the motion velocity (i.e., the rotation velocity and pitch). For varying θ, the motion can be identified as screw motion around an axis in space. To reconstruct a group action $M \in SE(3)$ from a given twist, the exponential function $\exp(\theta\hat{\xi}) = M \in SE(3)$ must be computed. This can be done efficiently by using the Rodriguez formula [11],

$$\exp(\hat{\xi}\theta) = \begin{pmatrix} \exp(\theta\hat{\omega}) & (I - \exp(\hat{\omega}\theta))(\omega \times v) + \omega\omega^T v\theta \\ 0_{1\times3} & 1 \end{pmatrix}, \text{ for } \omega \neq 0$$

with $\exp(\theta\hat{\omega})$ computed by calculating

$$\exp(\theta\hat{\omega}) = I + \hat{\omega}\sin(\theta) + \hat{\omega}^2(1 - \cos(\theta)).$$

Note that only sine and cosine functions of real numbers need to be computed.

For pose estimation we combine the reconstructed Plücker lines with the screw representation for rigid motions and apply a gradient descent method: Incidence of the transformed 3D point X_i with the 3D ray L_i can be expressed as

$$(\exp(\theta\hat{\xi})X_i)_{3\times1} \times n_i - m_i = 0.$$

Indeed, X_i is a homogeneous 4D vector, and after multiplication with the 4×4 matrix $\exp(\theta\hat{\xi})$ we neglect the homogeneous component (which is 1) to evaluate the cross product with n_i. We now linearize the equation by using $\exp(\theta\hat{\xi}) = \sum_{k=0}^{\infty} \frac{(\theta\hat{\xi})^k}{k!} \approx I + \theta\hat{\xi}$, with I as identity matrix. This results in

$$((I + \theta\hat{\xi})X_i)_{3\times1} \times n_i - m_i = 0$$

and can be reordered into an equation of the form $A\xi = b$. Collecting a set of such equations (each is of rank two) leads to an overdetermined system of equations, which can be solved using, for example, the Householder algorithm. The Rodriguez formula can be applied to reconstruct the group action M from the estimated twist ξ. Then the 3D points can be transformed and the process is iterated until the gradient descent approach converges.

Joints are expressed as special screws with no pitch of the form $\theta_j \hat{\xi}_j$ with known $\hat{\xi}_j$ (the location of the rotation axes as part of the model representation) and unknown joint angle θ_j. The constraint equation of a jth joint has the form

$$(\exp(\theta_j \hat{\xi}_j) \ldots \exp(\theta_1 \hat{\xi}_1) \exp(\theta \hat{\xi}) X_i)_{3 \times 1} \times n_i - m_i = 0$$

which is linearized in the same way as the rigid body motion itself. It leads to three linear equations with the six unknown pose parameters and j unknown joint angles. Collecting a sufficient number of equations leads to an overdetermined system of equations.

Note, that since we work with reconstructed 3D lines, we can gain equations from different cameras (calibrated with respect to the same world coordinate system) and put them together in one system of equations and solve them simultaneously. This is the key idea to deal with partial occlusions: A joint which is not visible in one camera must be visible in another one to get a solvable system of equations. A set of four cameras around the subject covers a large range and allows to analyze quite complex motion patterns.

2.3   Correspondence Estimation

After image segmentation correspondences between the object model and the extracted silhouettes are established. Therefore, we follow a modified version of an ICP algorithm [14] and use a voting method to decide, whether a point belongs to the torso or one of the arms. These correspondences are applied on the pose estimation module resulting in a slightly transformed object. This is used to establish new correspondences until the overall pose converges.

3   Experiments

A lack of many studies is that only a visual feedback about the pose result is given, by overlaying the pose result with the image data, e.g. [14]. To enable a quantitative error analysis, we use a commercial marker based tracking system for a comparison. Here, we use the Motion Analysis software [10], with an 8-Falcon-camera system. For data capture we use the Eva 3.2.1 software and the Motion Analysis Solver Interface 2.0 for inverse kinematics computing [10]. In this system a human has to wear a body suit and retroflective markers are attached to it. Around each camera is a strobe light led ring and a red-filter is in front of each lens. This gives very strong image signals of the markers in each camera. These are treated as point markers which are reconstructed in the eight-camera system. The system is calibrated by using a wand-calibration method. Due to the filter in front of the images we had to use a second camera set-up which

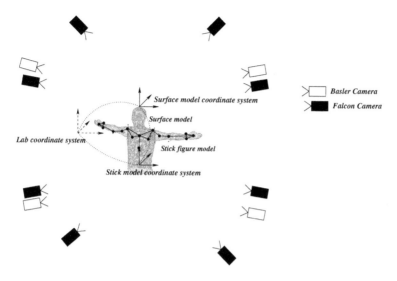

Fig. 3. The coordinate systems in the lab setup

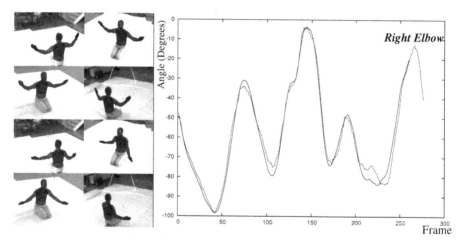

Fig. 4. Tracked arms: The angle diagrams show the elbow values of the Motion analysis system (dotted) and the silhouette system (solid)

provides *real* image data. This camera system is calibrated by using a calibration cube. After calibration, both camera systems are calibrated with respect to each other. Then we generate a stick-model from the point markers including joint centers and orientations. This results in a complete calibrated set-up we use for a system comparison. It is visualized in figure 3.

The images in the upper left of figure 1 show the body-suit with the attached markers. These lead to minor errors during silhouette extraction, which are omitted here. Figure 4 shows the first test sequence, where the subject is just moving the arms forwards and backwards. The diagram on the right side shows the estimated angles of the right elbow. The marker results are given as dotted lines and the silhouette results in solid lines. The overall error between both angles diagrams is 2.3 degrees, including the tracking failure between frames 200 till 250.

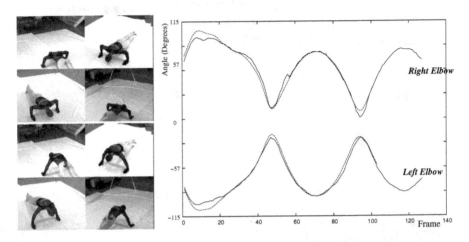

Fig. 5. Tracked Push-ups: The angle diagrams show the elbow values of the Motion analysis system (dotted) and the silhouette system (solid)

Figure 5 shows the second test sequence, where the subject is performing a series of push-ups. Here the elbow angles are much more characteristic and also well comparable. The overall error is 1.7 degrees. Both sequences contain partial occlusions in certain frames. But this can be handled from the algorithm.

4   Discussion

The contribution presents a human motion estimation system. The system extracts silhouettes by using level-set functions and uses a model with 21 degrees of freedom in a four-camera set-up. Finally we perform a comparison of the marker-free approach with a commercial marker based tracking system. In [13] eight bio-mechanical measurement systems are compared (including the Motion Analysis system). There is also performed a rotation experiment which shows, that the RMS² errors are typically within three degrees. Our error measures fit in this range quite well.

Marker-less human motion tracking is highly challenging for sports, exercise and clinical analysis and the system evaluation shows, that our approach is leading in the right direction for a marker-less stable and accurate human motion estimation system. Future works will continue with silhouette extraction in more complex environments, so that we can also analyze sports movements in non-lab environments.

---

² root mean square.

Acknowledgments

This work has been supported by the DFG grants RO 2497/1-1 and RO 2497/1-2.

References

1. Bregler C. and Malik J. Tracking people with twists and exponential maps. *IEEE Computer Society Conference on Computer Vision and Pattern Recognition*, Santa Barbara, California, pp. 8-15, 1998.
2. Brox T., Rousson M., Deriche R., Weickert J. Unsupervised segmentation incorporating colour, texture, and motion In *Computer Analysis of Images and Patterns*, Springer LNCS 2756, N.Petkov, M.A.Westenberg (Eds.), pp. 353-360, Proc. CAIP 2003 Conference, Groningen, The Netherlands, 2003.
3. Campbell R.J. and Flynn P.J. A survey of free-form object representation and recognition techniques. *Computer Vision and Image Understanding (CVIU)*, Vol. 81, pp. 166-210, 2001.
4. Caselles V., Catté F., Coll T. and Dibos F. A geometric model for active contours in image processing. *Numerische Mathematik*, 66:1–31, 1993.
5. Chan T. and Vese L. An active contour model without edges. In M. Nielsen, P. Johansen, O. F. Olsen, and J. Weickert, editors, *Scale-Space Theories in Computer Vision*, volume 1682 of *Lecture Notes in Computer Science*, pages 141–151. Springer, 1999.
6. Cremers D., Kohlberger T., and Schnörr Ch. Shape statistics in kernel space for variational image segmentation. *Pattern Recognition*, No. 36, Vol. 9, pp. 1929-1943, 2003.
7. Fua P., Plänkers R., and Thalmann D. Tracking and modeling people in video sequences. *Computer Vision and Image Understanding*, Vol. 81, No. 3, pp.285-302, March 2001.
8. Gavrilla D.M. The visual analysis of human movement: A survey *Computer Vision and Image Understanding*, Vol. 73 No. 1, pp. 82-92, 1999.
9. Mikic I., Trivedi M, Hunter E, and Cosman P. Human body model acquisition and tracking using voxel data *International Journal of Computer Vision (IJCV)*, Vol. 53, Nr. 3, pp. 199–223, 2003.
10. Motion Analysis Corporation www.motionanalysis.com last accessed February 2005.
11. Murray R.M., Li Z. and Sastry S.S. A Mathematical Introduction to Robotic Manipulation. *CRC Press*, 1994.
12. Osher S. and Sethian J. Fronts propagating with curvature-dependent speed: Algorithms based on Hamilton–Jacobi formulations. *Journal of Computational Physics*, Vol.79, pp. 12-49, 1988.
13. Richards J. The measurement of human motion: A comparison of commercially available systems *Human Movement Science*, Vol. 18, pp. 589-602, 1999.
14. Rosenhahn B., Klette R. and Sommer G. Silhouette based human motion estimation. *Pattern Recognition 2004, 26th DAGM-symposium,* Tübingen, Germany, C.E. Rasmussen, H.H. Bülthoff, M.A. Giese, B. Schölkopf (Eds), LNCS 3175, pp 294-301, 2004, Springer-Verlag Berlin Heidelberg.
15. Rosenhahn B. and Klette R. Geometric algebra for pose estimation and surface morphing in human motion estimation *Tenth International Workshop on Combinatorial Image Analysis (IWCIA)*, R. Klette and J. Zunic (Eds.), LNCS 3322, pp. 583-596, 2004, Springer-Verlag Berlin Heidelberg. Auckland, New Zealand.
16. Zang Z. Iterative point matching for registration of free-form curves and surfaces. *International Journal of Computer Vision*, Vol. 13, No. 2, pp. 119-152, 1999.

A Fast Algorithm for Statistically Optimized Orientation Estimation

Matthias Mühlich[1,2] and Rudolf Mester[1]

[1] J.W. Goethe University,
Robert-Mayer-Str. 2-4, 60054 Frankfurt, Germany
[2] RWTH Aachen University, Sommerfeldstr. 24, 52074 Aachen, Germany
{muehlich, mester}@iap.uni-frankfurt.de

Abstract. Filtering a signal with a finite impulse response (FIR) filter introduces dependencies between the errors in the filtered image due to overlapping filter masks. If the filtering only serves as a first step in a more complex estimation problem (e.g. orientation estimation), then these correlations can turn out to impair estimation quality.

The aim of this paper is twofold. First, we show that orientation estimation (with estimation of optical flow being an important special case for space-time volumes) is a Total Least Squares (TLS) problem: $\mathbf{Tp} \approx \mathbf{0}$ with sought parameter vector $\mathbf{p}$ and given TLS data matrix $\mathbf{T}$ whose statistical properties can be described with a *covariance tensor*. In the second part, we will show how to improve TLS estimates given this statistical information.

1 Introduction

1.1 Gradient-Based Orientation Estimation

The detection of edges (grey value discontinuities) is an important problem in image processing, especially if we consider $N+1$ dimensional *space-time volumes* that are spanned by N space dimensions and one dimension representing time. Orientations in these volumes can be interpreted as *motion equation*.

Edges are determined by grey value discontinuity in all orthogonal directions. Therefore, one can find orientations in N-dimensional data by computing gradients in a certain image window. Ideally, there is no discontinuity along the edge and all gradients are orthogonal to the sought direction. If the gradients are written as row vectors of a matrix $\mathbf{T}$, then the orientation estimation problem can be written as TLS problem $\mathbf{Tp} \approx \mathbf{0}$.

For computing the derivative along some coordinate axis, one needs a 1D-derivative filter, e.g. $\mathbf{D}_3 = \begin{bmatrix} 1 & 0 & \text{-1} \end{bmatrix}$. The subscript 3 denotes a 3-element filter (following the notation of Jähne, e.g. in [1]). A well known problem for differential filters is that the transfer function is high for large frequencies [2,1]. In other words: they are extremely sensitive to noise. But there is an easy solution: we only have to differentiate in one direction; there are $N-1$ dimensions left which can be used for averaging, thus reducing the influence of noise on the estimate. This general concept is known as *regularized edge detection* [2].

W. Kropatsch, R. Sablatnig, and A. Hanbury (Eds.): DAGM 2005, LNCS 3663, pp. 238–245, 2005.
© Springer-Verlag Berlin Heidelberg 2005

For computational efficiency, we should take care to construct separable filters only. Consequently, we only need one 1D averaging filter that is applied to all remaining dimensions in sequence, e.g. $\mathbf{A}_{box3} = \begin{bmatrix} 1 & 1 & 1 \end{bmatrix}$ (3-element box filter) or $\mathbf{A}_{bin3} = \begin{bmatrix} 1 & 2 & 1 \end{bmatrix}$ (3-element binomial filter).[1] For instance, the *Sobel operator* combines binomial averaging and first derivative.

1.2   TLS Error Modelling

Let $\mathcal{S}$ denote some image window which will be analyzed to estimate the orientation at its center pixel. By vectorizing (i.e. stacking columns on top of each other), we can construct a vector $\mathbf{s} \in \mathbb{R}^{N_s}$ representing the input signal. Analogously, we represent the filter output as image $\mathcal{Z}$ or, in vectorized form, as $\mathbf{z} \in \mathbb{R}^{N_z}$. We assume $N_z < N_s$ to avoid border effects (i.e. cut off border in filtered image). The purpose of vectorization is reformulating filtering of an image (or general N-D signal) with filter operator $\mathbf{F}$ (i.e. $\mathcal{Z} = \mathbf{F}\mathcal{S}$) as matrix multiplication

$$\mathbf{z} = \mathbf{F}\,\mathbf{s} \tag{1}$$

with matrix $\mathbf{F} \in \mathbb{R}^{N_z \times N_s}$. Now let $\mathbf{z}_k = \mathbf{F}_k\mathbf{s}$ be the output vector produced with some filter matrix $\mathbf{F}_k$; in general, we have $k = 1, \ldots, N$ (with $N = 2$ for orientation estimation in image). The constraint that gradients are orthogonal to the sought orientation then leads to

$$\underbrace{\begin{pmatrix} | & & | \\ \mathbf{z}_1 & \cdots & \mathbf{z}_N \\ | & & | \end{pmatrix}}_{\mathbf{T}} \mathbf{p} = \mathbf{T}\mathbf{p} = \mathbf{0} \; . \tag{2}$$

Problems of this type are known as TLS problems and commonly solved by taking the singular vector corresponding to the smallest singular vector of $\mathbf{T}$ (which is identical to the eigenvector of $\mathbf{T}^T\mathbf{T}$ ["structure tensor"] corresponding to its smallest eigenvalue). We will denote this approach as *plain TLS* or *PTLS*.

The sought orientation $\mathbf{p}$ (a unit vector) is orthogonal to all gradients – at least if there are no errors in the gradients. But errors in the input data will inevitably lead to errors in the filtered images and hence in the TLS data matrix $\mathbf{T}$ as well. PTLS is statistically optimal if and only if all errors in the random matrix $\mathbf{T}$ are independent and identically distributed (iid) [3] – which is clearly *not* the case here as overlapping filters will produce highly correlated errors.

In order to improve orientation estimation, we should therefore describe the errors in the TLS data matrix in terms of their statistical moments. We start by decomposing $\mathbf{T}$ into its true but unknown part $\bar{\mathbf{T}}$ (for which $\bar{\mathbf{T}}\mathbf{p} = 0$ holds

---

[1] The mean grey value does not change if and only if the sum of the coefficients in an averaging filter is normalized to one. Therefore, the 3-element filters defined above are commonly defined with an additional factor $\frac{1}{3}$ resp. $\frac{1}{4}$. But for orientation estimation, this scaling is irrelevant (we estimate a *homogeneous* vector), and therefore, we omit normalization factors and use integers here.

exactly) and the error part $\check{\mathbf{T}}$ which can be assumed as zero-mean random matrix without loss of generality (otherwise, subtract mean from measurement first):

$$\mathbf{T} = \bar{\mathbf{T}} + \check{\mathbf{T}} . \tag{3}$$

In the same way as a covariance matrix characterizes a random vector, the second order statistical moments of a random matrix are characterized by a tensor of tensor rank 4 which is known as *covariance tensor*.

For two-dimensional orientation estimation, Ng et al gave a solution in [4] which assumes simple iid errors in the images but handles the resulting (much more complicated!) noise model for the gradients better than PTLS. However, a complicated and time-consuming iterative scheme was necessary. We will show that the model (3) allows to replace PTLS with a better *closed-form* solution.

1.3   Equilibration and Unbiased Orientation Estimation

PTLS (and the eigensystem analysis it is built on) implicitly approximates $\mathbf{T}$ with a rank-deficient matrix $\hat{\mathbf{T}}$ (an estimate for the true data matrix) such that the Frobenius norm $\|\mathbf{T} - \hat{\mathbf{T}}\|_F$ is minimized. Alternatively, we can perform rank reduction in an reweighted space

$$\|\mathbf{W}_L(\mathbf{T} - \hat{\mathbf{T}})\mathbf{W}_R\|_F \quad \rightarrow \quad \min \tag{4}$$

with suitably chosen non-singular weight matrices $\mathbf{W}_L$ and $\mathbf{W}_R$; this technique is known as equilibration [5]. A subset of possible right equilibrations (i.e. choices for $\mathbf{W}_R$) are the data normalization transformation [6] which are known to improve estimation quality in apparently similar TLS problems like fundamental matrix estimation or ellipse fitting.

But for orientation estimation, the TLS data matrix does not contain products of homogenized measurements (in contrast to the two problems mentioned above); it is linear in the input data. Therefore, all errors are already within the same order of magnitude and a data normalization does not help. The key to an improved orientation estimate is *left* equilibration and this is related to the fact that we have to de-correlate the individual gradients, i.e. rows of the TLS data matrix $\mathbf{T}$. At the same time, this also explains why other general parameter estimation schemes (HEIV, Renormalization, FNS, IETLS [7]) are not applicable for orientation estimation: they all assume *uncorrelated* measurements.

2   Derivation of the Covariance Tensor

2.1   Setup for the General N-Dimensional Problem

We will derive the covariance tensor of the TLS data matrix $\mathbf{T}$ for regularized orientation estimation in N-dimensional signals; this means that we apply N separable filters $\mathbf{F}_1$ to $\mathbf{F}_N$ where $\mathbf{F}_k$ stands for differentiating along the k-th coordinate axis and averaging in all other dimensions. Differential and averaging filter coefficients are modelled as $[d_{-b} \ldots d_b]$ and $[a_{-b} \ldots a_b]$, respectively.

The filter width is therefore assumed to be $2b + 1$. Also notice that the coefficient subscripts are counted form $-b$ to b, i.e. we cannot simple write them in vector form (where counting always starts with 1). So let us define the following convention: vectors with an underline (e.g. $\underline{\mathbf{a}}$) indicate such odd-sized filter coefficient vectors where index 0 always refers to the central value. Additionally, we define that a vector written with square brackets (e.g. $\underline{\mathbf{a}} = [1, 2, 1]$) represents such a special filter vector (here: $(\underline{\mathbf{a}})_{-1} = 1$, $(\underline{\mathbf{a}})_0 = 2$ and $(\underline{\mathbf{a}})_1 = 1$).

Let $n \times \cdots \times n$ be the size of the filter output signals; the vectorized filter output signals then are $N_z = n^N$ dimensional. In order to avoid border effects, we then need input signals of size $N_s = m^N$ with $m = n + 2b$ (i.e. b overlap on each side). For regularized orientation estimation, a differential filter $\underline{\mathbf{d}}$ (e.g. $[1, 0, -1]$) and an averaging filter $\underline{\mathbf{a}}$ (e.g. $[1, 3, 1]$) are given and the complete k-th filter mask is defined by differentiation with respect to the k-th direction and averaging in the other $N - 1$ directions.

Vectorization of input and output images together with separable filters allows to express the filter matrices $\mathbf{F}_1$ to $\mathbf{F}_N$ as Kronecker matrix products (see [8] for a definition of this special tensor product)

$$\mathbf{F}_k = \mathbf{F}_k^{(N)} \otimes \cdots \otimes \mathbf{F}_k^{(1)} \quad \text{with} \quad \mathbf{F}_k^{(j)} = \text{spdiag}\left[\underline{\mathbf{f}}_k^{(j)}, n, m\right] \tag{5}$$

where $\underline{\mathbf{f}}_k^{(j)}$ is the 1D filter of filter mask k used to filter the j-th dimension. For regularized orientation estimation, this 1D filter is either the differential filter ($\underline{\mathbf{f}}_k^{(j)} = \underline{\mathbf{d}}$ for $j = k$) or the averaging filter ($\underline{\mathbf{f}}_k^{(j)} = \underline{\mathbf{a}}$ for $j \neq k$). The function $\text{spdiag}[\cdot, \cdot, \cdot]$ is given by:

Definition 1. *With $\mathbf{F} = \text{spdiag}[\underline{\mathbf{v}}, n, m]$ we mean a multi-diagonal $n \times m$-matrix (with $|m - n|$ being an even number) which is defined by*

$$(\mathbf{F})_{ij} = (\underline{\mathbf{v}})_{(j-i)+(n-m)/2} \tag{6}$$

Example: $\text{spdiag}[[1, 2, 3], 3, 5]$ *is the 3×5-matrix* $\begin{pmatrix} 1\,2\,3\,0\,0 \\ 0\,1\,2\,3\,0 \\ 0\,0\,1\,2\,3 \end{pmatrix}$.

It follows that only two different factors appear in the Kronecker product (5) in case of regularized orientation estimation: either $\mathbf{F}_A := \text{spdiag}[\underline{\mathbf{a}}, n, m]$ or $\mathbf{F}_D := \text{spdiag}[\underline{\mathbf{d}}, n, m]$.

2.2 Covariance Tensor of TLS Error Matrix

For the general N-dimensional problem, we define the matrices $\mathbf{C}_{pq}$ (cross-covariance between p-th and q-th filter output; auto-covariance for $p = q$), which can be viewed as slices of the covariance tensor of the TLS data matrix: $(\mathbf{C}_{pq})_{ij} = \text{Cov}[(\mathbf{T})_{ip}, (\mathbf{T})_{jq}]$. Using (1), we obtain

$$\mathbf{C}_{pq} = \text{Cov}[\mathbf{z}_p, \mathbf{z}_q] = \mathbf{F}_p \,\text{Cov}[\mathbf{s}]\, \mathbf{F}_q^T . \tag{7}$$

Assuming white noise in the original signal (extension is straightforward), we get $\mathbf{C}_{pq} = \mathbf{F}_p \mathbf{F}_q^T$ for the cross-covariance matrices. Recalling that the filter matrices $\mathbf{F}_p$ and $\mathbf{F}_q$ are Kronecker matrix products (see (5)), we can use the identity

$$(\mathbf{A} \otimes \mathbf{B})(\mathbf{C} \otimes \mathbf{D})^T = (\mathbf{A}\mathbf{C}^T) \otimes (\mathbf{B}\mathbf{D}^T) \tag{8}$$

and the formula

$$\text{spdiag}\,[\underline{a}, p, q]\,(\text{spdiag}\,[\underline{b}, p, q])^T = \text{spdiag}\,[\text{xcorr}\,[\mathbf{a}, \mathbf{b}]\,, p, p] \tag{9}$$

(for $q - p + 1 \geq \text{length}(\underline{a})$) to find

$$\mathbf{C}_{pq} = \mathbf{C}_{pq}^{(N)} \otimes \cdots \otimes \mathbf{C}_{pq}^{(1)} \tag{10}$$

with

$$\mathbf{C}_{pq}^{(j)} = \text{spdiag}\left[\text{xcorr}\left[\underline{\mathbf{f}}_p^{(j)}, \underline{\mathbf{f}}_q^{(j)}\right], n, n\right] \tag{11}$$

where xcorr $[\underline{a}, \underline{b}]$ defines the (auto-)cross-correlation of the vectors $\underline{a}$ and $\underline{b}$:

Definition 2 (Cross-correlation). *Let $\underline{a}$ and $\underline{b}$ denote two filter vectors. Then xcorr $[\underline{a}, \underline{b}]$ defines the cross-correlation between $\underline{a}$ and $\underline{b}$. Formally, it is defined by*

$$(\text{xcorr}\,[\underline{a}, \underline{b}])_i = \sum_{\nu=-\infty}^{\infty} (\underline{a})_\nu (\underline{b})_{i+\nu} \,. \tag{12}$$

With (10), we have now derived a general method for computing the covariance tensors for filter problems and we will now apply these results to regularized differential filters. Looking at equation (11), we see that only three possible cross-covariance matrices for individual directions can appear. We therefore define

$$\mathbf{A} = \text{spdiag}\,[\text{xcorr}\,[\underline{a}, \underline{a}]\,, n, n] \tag{13}$$
$$\mathbf{D} = \text{spdiag}\,[\text{xcorr}\,[\underline{d}, \underline{d}]\,, n, n] \tag{14}$$
$$\mathbf{C} = \text{spdiag}\,[\text{xcorr}\,[\underline{a}, \underline{d}]\,, n, n] \tag{15}$$

and obtain

$$\mathbf{C}_{pq}^{(j)} = \begin{cases} \mathbf{D} & \text{for } p = q = j \\ \mathbf{A} & \text{for } p \neq j \text{ and } q \neq j \\ \mathbf{C} & \text{else (i.e. either } p = j \text{ or } q = j, \text{ but not both)} \end{cases} \tag{16}$$

With (10), we see that for identical indices (i.e. $p = q$) we get $\mathbf{D}$ at position p and $\mathbf{A}$ for all other factors in the Kronecker product. For different indices, we get $\mathbf{C}$ at positions p and q and $\mathbf{A}$ for the remaining factors. By deriving all tensor slices $\mathbf{C}_{pq}$, we succeeded in our task to determine the covariance tensor for general N-dimensional FIR filters.

Example 1 (3D orientation estimation). We obtain

$$\mathbf{C}_{11} = \mathbf{D} \otimes \mathbf{A} \otimes \mathbf{A} \qquad\qquad \mathbf{C}_{12} = \mathbf{C}_{21} = \mathbf{C} \otimes \mathbf{C} \otimes \mathbf{A}$$
$$\mathbf{C}_{22} = \mathbf{A} \otimes \mathbf{D} \otimes \mathbf{A} \qquad\qquad \mathbf{C}_{13} = \mathbf{C}_{31} = \mathbf{C} \otimes \mathbf{A} \otimes \mathbf{C}$$
$$\mathbf{C}_{33} = \mathbf{A} \otimes \mathbf{A} \otimes \mathbf{D} \qquad\qquad \mathbf{C}_{23} = \mathbf{C}_{32} = \mathbf{A} \otimes \mathbf{C} \otimes \mathbf{C}$$

(left column for the tensor slices with identical second and fourth index and right column for the other slices).

In the introduction, we asked: given a set of linear finite impulse response filters, how can one compute the covariance tensor for the TLS model $\mathbf{Tp} \approx \mathbf{0}$? The general answer was given in equations (10) and (11). For regularized orientation estimation, the answer can be simplified further because only three different matrices can appear in the Kronecker products.

2.3 The NETLS Algorithm

In section 1.3, we showed that the equilibration technique uses weight matrices $\mathbf{W}_L$ and $\mathbf{W}_R$ to improve the statistical properties of the TLS data matrix $\mathbf{T}$. The choice of these weight matrices clearly depends on the covariance tensor of $\mathbf{T}$; however, the full derivation is a tedious task and we will only summarize the final formulas as MATLAB code. Listing L-1 shows how to computes an equilibrated TLS estimate from a given rank-4 covariance tensor of $\mathbf{T}$.

The mathematical core of this algorithm is the computation of two matrices $\mathbf{Z}_L$ and $\mathbf{Z}_R$ as sums over all tensor slices with identical row resp. column indices (however, we realized this summation using a special tensor decomposition for increased computational efficiency). The sought equilibration matrices $\mathbf{W}_L$ and $\mathbf{W}_R$ are then found as inverted Cholesky factors of these sums. These equilibration matrices effectively de-correlate the entries of the TLS data matrix and thus lead to improved estimates.

Due to space limitations, we have to omit the whole theoretical background here. We will sketch the basic idea, hoping that the NETLS procedure appears at least plausible to the reader then: for computing covariance information, one has to consider matrix-valued weights *twice* (from left and right) and therefore chosing the weights as inverted matrix roots of the row vector resp. column vector covariance matrices is the appropriate method to decorrelate the individual errors in the matrix elements (because the covariance matrices become the identity matrix after reweighting). Mathematical details and the derivation of the NETLS algorithm can be found in [9].

3   Experiments

Orientation estimation is an estimation problem where extremely high noise levels appear frequently; additionally, we can have the aperture problem if the local signal is rank-deficient. For instance, a moving 2D *edge* defines a planar subspace in the space-time volume, not a linear subspace (which is only defined by image *points*). These two problems make all iterative estimation schemes relying on previous estimates risky for bad signal-to-noise ratios.

In [9], we tested various non-iterative and iterative approaches for orientation estimation and used the mean squared axial error (MSAE)

$$\text{MSAE} = \frac{4}{m} \left(1 - \sum_{i=1}^{m} \frac{(\mathbf{a}_i^T \bar{\mathbf{a}})^2}{(\mathbf{a}_i^T \mathbf{a}_i)(\bar{\mathbf{a}}^T \bar{\mathbf{a}})} \right) . \tag{17}$$

```
1  function p = EstimateNETLSCorr(T,C)
2  % compute NETLS solution for correlated data
3  % INPUT: T MxN TLS data matrix
4  % INPUT: C MxNxMxN covariance tensor: C(i,p,j,k) = Cov[(T)_{ip},(T)_{jq}]
5
6  [M,N,d3,d4] = size(C);
7
8  % make single-symmetric, re-arrange weight tensor and decompose it
9  C = (C + permute(C,[1 4 3 2])) / 2;
10 CRight = permute(C,[1 3 2 4]);
11 MMat = reshape(CRight,[M*M,N*N]);
12 [U,S,V] = svd(MMat,0);
13 alpha = diag(S);
14 num = N*(N+1)/2;
15
16 % compute equilibration weights
17 ZL = zeros(M,M);
18 ZR = zeros(N,N);
19 for k = 1:num
20    XTemp = reshape(U(:,k),[M,M]);
21    YTemp = reshape(V(:,k),[N,N]);
22    ZL = ZL + alpha(k) * XTemp * trace(YTemp);
23 end
24 WL = inv(chol(ZL))';
25 for k = 1:num
26    XTemp = WL*reshape(U(:,k),[M,M])*WL';
27    YTemp = reshape(V(:,k),[N,N]);
28    ZR = ZR + alpha(k) * YTemp * trace(XTemp);
29 end
30 WR = inv(chol(ZR))';
31
32 % estimate
33 TTrans = WL*A*WR';
34 [U,S,V] = svd(TTrans);
35 p = WR'*V(:,N);
36 p = p/norm(p);
```

Listing L-1. NETLS algorithm for correlated data.

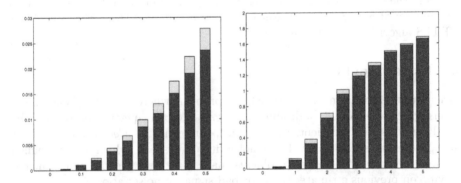

Fig. 1. Orientation estimation with NETLS for different noise levels; left image: low noise level; right image: higher noise levels. The full bar indicates PTLS mean squared axial error (MSAE) while the dark part is the MSAE for NETLS.

between a set of estimates $\mathbf{a}_i$ and the true solution $\bar{\mathbf{a}}$ as quality criterion. As a result, we propose to use the NETLS algorithm presented in subsection 2.3.

Fig. 1 shows experimental results for regularized edge detection in two dimensions with averaging filter $[.2, .6, .2]$. The MSAE for 10,000 simulations is plotted for different noise levels (left graphics for lower noise levels, right graphics for higher noise levels). The MSAE is bounded (for pure noise, no estimation scheme can estimate anything useful); the maximum value is reached if the distribution of estimates has no mean axis anymore (both eigenvalues of the expected scatter matrix become equal, e.g. for the uniform distribution). For low and medium noise levels, NETLS is roughly 15 % better than PTLS; the difference is reduced for higher noise. This is a considerable improvement, especially if we consider that NETLS computes a non-iterative closed-form solution.

The example presented here is a rather simple one: 3-element filters in two dimensions. But we stress that we provided the whole theory for statistically optimized orientation estimation from *arbitrary sets of filters* and in *general N-dimensional space* (even the orientation estimation problem is not limited to *first* order derivatives, see e.g. [10]). Standard eigensystem analysis suffers from the fact that overlapping filters produce correlated data. With the methods presented in this paper, we finally have some tool to overcome this deficiency.

References

1. Scharr, H., Körkel, S., Jähne, B.: Numerische Isotropieoptimierung von FIR-Filtern mittels Querglättung. In: Proc. DAGM 97. (1997) 367–374
2. Jähne, B.: Digitale Bildverarbeitung. 4 edn. Springer (1997)
3. van Huffel, S., Vandewalle, J.: The Total Least Squares problem: Computational aspects and analysis. SIAM (Society for Industrial and Applied Mathematics), Philadelphia (1991)
4. Ng, L., Solo, V.: Errors-in-variables modeling in optical flow estimation. IEEE Transactions on Image Processing **10** (2001) 1528–1540
5. Mühlich, M., Mester, R.: Subspace methods and equilibration in computer vision. Technical Report XP-TR-C-21, J.W.G.University Frankfurt (1999)
6. Hartley, R.I.: In defence of the eight-point algorithm. IEEE Transaction on Pattern Analysis and Machine Intelligence **6** (1997) 580–593
7. Mühlich, M., Mester, R.: Optimal homogeneous vector estimation. In: Scandinavian Conference on Image Analysis, Jönssu, Finland. (2005) *accepted*.
8. Horn, R., Johnson, C.: Topics in Matrix Analysis. Cambridge University Press (1991)
9. Mühlich, M.: Estimation of Homogeneous Vectors and Applications in Computer Vision – Extended Version. PhD thesis, J. W. Goethe-Universität Frankfurt (2004)
10. Mester, R.: A system-theoretical view on local motion estimation. In: Proc. IEEE SouthWest Symposium on Image Analysis and Interpretation, Santa Fé (NM), IEEE Computer Society (2002) 201–205

A Direct Method for Real-Time Tracking in 3-D Under Variable Illumination

Wolfgang Sepp

Institute of Robotics and Mechatronics,
German Aerospace Center (DLR),
82234 Wessling, Germany
wolfgang.sepp@dlr.de

Abstract. 3-D tracking of free-moving objects has to deal with brightness variations pronounced by the shape of the tracked surface. Pixel-based tracking techniques, though versatile, are particularly affected by such variations. Here, we evaluate two illumination-adaptive methods for a novel efficient pixel-based 3-D tracking approach. Brightness adaption by means of an illumination basis is compared to with a template update strategy with respect to both robustness and accuracy on tracking in 6 degrees-of-freedom.

1 Introduction

Numerous applications in the fields of robotics, augmented reality, and human-machine interfaces demand solutions for object related pose tracking. Vision-based tracking systems are particularly interesting owing to their low cost and high accuracy. The most popular systems are based on infrared reflecting markers, which can be tracked very robustly. However, these systems require some kind of augmentation of the target object and require dedicated infrared cameras.

On the other side, passive visual tracking methods offer a natural way of tracking objects. Feature-based tracking techniques based on 3-D edges and corners are prevalently stable under changes of illumination but cannot be applied to free-form surfaces. These techniques are outperformed by pixel-based tracking based on template matching, and therefore are not limited to certain shapes. However, latter techniques are affected by illumination changes between the templates.

This paper compares two adaptive methods for direct (pixel-based) tracking of free-moving objects in 6 Degrees-of-Freedom (DoF) with illumination changes. Here, an exact registration and not simply a rough match between target and object template is desired. Thus, accurate models of illumination are required. The first method considered extends tracking to more parameters including the coefficients of an illumination base. The second method updates the tracked 3-D texture template over time. These methods are evaluated with regard to object velocity and accuracy of the tracked pose.

W. Kropatsch, R. Sablatnig, and A. Hanbury (Eds.): DAGM 2005, LNCS 3663, pp. 246–253, 2005.
© Springer-Verlag Berlin Heidelberg 2005

1.1   Previous Work

Sum-of-squared differences (SSD) alignment reaches back to the work of Lucas and Kanade [9] upon which many 2-D tracking algorithms are based. The work did also consider contrast and brightness adjustment within the SSD description of the problem. Extending this tracking method to 3-D requires an efficient formulation of the problem which proves to be increasingly demanding toward full 6-DoF motion.

Diehl et al. [7] developed a fast method for tracking 4-DoF motion of planar objects where illumination effects are neglected. If a reference texture is registered to the model, then planar tracking can be extended to more DoF. Baker et al. [1] solve the 8-D homography while Buenaposada et al. [4] compute the 6-DoF motion explicitly without taking changes in illumination into account.

La Cascia et al. [5] use numerical difference decomposition to minimize the residual error of the projected surface texture from the current view to the reference view. Variations in illumination are compensated by using illumination templates along the lines of Hager and Belhumeur [8].

Some efforts have been undertaken to upgrade tracking of primitive planar surfaces to more general surfaces. Cernuschi-Frias et al. [6] presented an estimation model for simple parameterized surfaces by matching two views on the surface. The approach is based on an orthographic imaging model and has been evaluated for up to 4-DoF geometric surfaces and without handling of illumination changes. The approach of Sepp et al. [12] iteratively estimates the pose of 3-D free-form surface patches in stereo images. A small stereo baseline ensures that illumination changes on the surface, including shadows, need not be modeled explicitly. The computational expense of the method however does not fit the requirements for tracking at frame rate. Recently, Ramey et al. [11] were able to track the coefficients of a b-spline 2 1/2-D surface in stereo images. They used the zero-mean SSD as comparison measure to gain robustness against brightness variations. Promising results have been achieved by Belhumeur et al. [2] whose approach establishes the basis vectors for an optical-flow (pose) subspace and an illumination subspace. The coefficients of these vectors are mapped to 6-DoF object motion under the orthographic projection model. The method, however, has the drawback of a long training session.

Recently Sepp et al. [13] presented an approach capable of tracking arbitrary 3-D surfaces in 6-DoF under full perspective projection in real-time. Yet, this approach has not been evaluated under illumination changes. In this paper we empirically evaluate two illumination-adaptive methods for a similar approach.

2   Direct Method for Tracking in 3-D

The 3-D surface patch to be tracked is modeled as an arbitrary set of points $X = \{\mathbf{x}_0, \mathbf{x}_1, .., \mathbf{x}_N\} \subset \mathbb{R}^3$. No assumption is made about the topology of the points such as for instance a 2-D grid. Therefore, no constraints other than visibility are imposed on the surface. The rigid body transformation of a point $\mathbf{x} \in X$ is described by

$$m(\mathbf{x}, \mu) = R(\mu)\,\mathbf{x} + t(\mu) \tag{1}$$

for a pose $\mu \in \mathbb{R}^6$ and the associated 3-D rotation $R(\mu)$ and translation $t(\mu)$. A point in camera frame is mapped to the image under the full perspective projection

$$p(\mathbf{x}) = \left(\frac{\mathbf{k}_1^T \cdot \mathbf{x}}{\mathbf{k}_3^T \cdot \mathbf{x}}, \frac{\mathbf{k}_2^T \cdot \mathbf{x}}{\mathbf{k}_3^T \cdot \mathbf{x}}\right)^T \quad , \quad K = \begin{pmatrix} \mathbf{k}_1^T \\ \mathbf{k}_2^T \\ \mathbf{k}_3^T \end{pmatrix} \tag{2}$$

where $K \in \mathbb{R}^{3\times 3}$ is the matrix of intrinsic camera parameters. Let $I(\mathbf{u})$ be a brightness value of the *current* image of a live stream at position $\mathbf{u} \in \mathbb{R}^2$ and let $T(\mathbf{u})$ be the brightness value for the *reference* image. In the following ${}^{P}I(\mathbf{x}) \equiv I(p(\mathbf{x}))$ and ${}^{Po}T(\mathbf{x}) \equiv T(p(m(\mathbf{x}, \mu^0)))$.

With these definitions, tracking is formulated as minimization problem $\hat{\delta\mu}^* = \arg\min_{\delta\mu} O(\delta\mu)$ of a least-squares, *compositional* objective function

$$O(\delta\mu) = \sum_{\mathbf{x} \in X} \left[{}^{P}I(m(m(\mathbf{x}, \delta\mu), \hat{\mu})) - {}^{Po}T(\mathbf{x})\right]^2 . \tag{3}$$

This error function measures the dissimilarity between the surface texture in the current view under the chained poses $\delta\mu, \hat{\mu}$ and the texture in the reference view under the initially registered pose μ^0. The pose variation $\hat{\delta\mu}^*$ that minimizes (3) gives the pose estimation for the current image I, that is

$$\hat{\mu}^* = \hat{\mu} \circ \hat{\delta\mu}^* \quad \text{according to} \quad m(\mathbf{x}, \hat{\mu}^*) = m\left(m\left(\mathbf{x}, \hat{\delta\mu}^*\right), \hat{\mu}\right) \quad . \tag{4}$$

The above objective function is minimized with a Gauss-Newton approximation to the Hessian by repeatedly solving the linear equation system

$$\sum_{\mathbf{x} \in X} [\partial_{\delta\mu}{}^{P}I]^T [\partial_{\delta\mu}{}^{P}I]\Big|_{\delta\mu=0,\hat{\mu}} \hat{\delta\mu} = \tag{5}$$

$$- \sum_{\mathbf{x} \in X} [\partial_{\delta\mu}{}^{P}I]^T\Big|_{\delta\mu=0,\hat{\mu}} \left[{}^{P}I\big|_{\delta\mu=0,\hat{\mu}} - {}^{Po}T\right]$$

for the pose variation $\hat{\delta\mu}$. In practice (5) is not efficient since the image Jacobian has to be recomputed for every frame in the live-stream. Here, the computational expense can be lowered by taking advantage of an approximative image constancy assumption[1] in 3-D at the optimal pose $\hat{\mu} \circ \hat{\delta\mu}^*$, that is

$$ {}^{P}I\left(m\left(m\left(\mathbf{x}, \hat{\delta\mu}^*\right), \hat{\mu}\right)\right) = {}^{Po}T(\mathbf{x}) \quad . \tag{6}$$

The spatial gradient remains constant under this approximation, that is

$$\partial_1{}^{P}I\Big|_{\hat{\delta\mu}^*,\hat{\mu}} \cdot \partial_1 m\Big|_{\hat{\delta\mu}^*,\hat{\mu}} \cdot \partial_1 m\Big|_{\hat{\delta\mu}^*} = \partial_1{}^{Po}T , \tag{7}$$

---

[1] The extended image constancy assumption holds if the surface normal is *parallel* to the camera ray under the current and the initial rigid body transformation.

where operator ∂_i denotes the derivative of the following function with respect to their i-th argument. Thus, the image Jacobian of (5) simplifies to

$$\partial_{\delta\mu}{}^{P}I\Big|_{\hat{\delta\mu}^*,\hat{\mu}} = \partial_1{}^{P}I\Big|_{\hat{\delta\mu}^*,\hat{\mu}} \cdot \partial_1 m\Big|_{\hat{\delta\mu}^*,\hat{\mu}} \cdot \partial_2 m\Big|_{\hat{\delta\mu}^*} \tag{8}$$

$$= \partial_1{}^{Po}T \cdot \partial_1 m^{-1}\Big|_{\hat{\delta\mu}^*} \cdot \partial_2 m\Big|_{\hat{\delta\mu}^*} .$$

Since the Jacobian is evaluated at $\delta\mu = 0$, it can be further simplified to

$$\partial_{\delta\mu}{}^{P}I(m(m(\mathbf{x},\delta\mu),\hat{\mu})) = \partial_1{}^{Po}T(\mathbf{x}) \cdot \partial_2 m(\mathbf{x},0) \tag{9}$$

under the assumption that $m(\mathbf{x},0)$ equals the identity transformation. Hence, the image Jacobian and Hessian are constant in the compositional framework for every live-stream image.

While the image constancy assumption holds in 2-D leading to the inverse compositional method of Baker and Matthews [1] this equality is only approximatively satisfied for general surfaces in 3-D.

3   Illumination Adaptive Methods

The objective function (3) does not consider illumination changes of the surface texture due to a moving object or moving light source. In the following, two methods are considered to cope with these effects.

3.1   Illumination Subspace

Belhumeur and Kriegman [3] proved that illumination variation form a convex polyhedral cone in $\mathbb{R}^N$. That is, an image and its illumination changes can be reconstructed by a linear combination of orthogonal image vectors $\mathbf{B}_1, \mathbf{B}_2, \ldots, \mathbf{B}_M$. So, illumination compensation is added to the objective function (3) in the form

$$O(\delta\mu) = \sum_{\mathbf{x}\in X} [{}^{P}I(m(m(\mathbf{x},\delta\mu),\hat{\mu})) + {}_{\mathbf{x}}B\lambda - {}^{Po}T(\mathbf{x})]^2 , \tag{10}$$

where ${}_{\mathbf{x}}B = ({}_{\mathbf{x}}B_1, {}_{\mathbf{x}}B_2, \ldots, {}_{\mathbf{x}}B_M)$ is a row vector of brightness values of the illumination base for model point $\mathbf{x}$ and λ is the parameter column vector of coefficients to this illumination base. The overall parameters are determined in accordance with [8] by the solution of the linear equation system

$$\sum_{\mathbf{x}\in X} \big[\partial_{\delta\mu}{}^{P}I , {}_{\mathbf{x}}B\big]^{\mathrm{T}} \big[\partial_{\delta\mu}{}^{P}I , {}_{\mathbf{x}}B\big]\Big|_{\delta\mu=0,\hat{\mu}} \begin{pmatrix} \hat{\delta\mu} \\ \hat{\lambda} \end{pmatrix} = \tag{11}$$

$$- \sum_{\mathbf{x}\in X} \big[\partial_{\delta\mu}{}^{P}I , {}_{\mathbf{x}}B\big]^{\mathrm{T}}\Big|_{\delta\mu=0,\hat{\mu}} \big[{}^{P}I|_{\delta\mu=0,\hat{\mu}} - {}^{Po}T\big] ,$$

for pose variation $\hat{\delta\mu}$ and illumination coefficients $\hat{\lambda}$. Note, that omitting illumination compensation in the image constancy assumption allows for the efficient minimization techniques of Sect. 2.

3.2   Template Update Method

Matthews et al. [10] developed a strategy for updating a tracked template without drifts between the updated template and the original one. At the i-th image of the live-stream, minimization starts at the previous pose estimation $\hat{\mu}_{i-1}^{\star}$ with an updated template $^{\text{Po}}T_i$ which reads for compositional tracking

$$\hat{\delta\mu}_i = \arg\min_{\delta\mu} \sum_{\mathbf{x}\in X} \left[^{\text{P}}I_i\big(m\big(m(\mathbf{x}, \delta\mu), \hat{\mu}_{i-1}^{\star}\big)\big) - ^{\text{Po}}T_i(\mathbf{x}) \right]^2 \quad . \tag{12}$$

Subsequently, minimization is continued with the reference template $^{\text{Po}}T_0$

$$\hat{\delta\mu}_i^{\star} = \arg\min_{\delta\mu} \sum_{\mathbf{x}\in X} \left[^{\text{P}}I_i\Big(m\Big(m(\mathbf{x}, \delta\mu), \hat{\mu}_{i-1}^{\star} \circ \hat{\delta\mu}_i\Big)\Big) - ^{\text{Po}}T_0(\mathbf{x}) \right]^2 \quad . \tag{13}$$

The final pose estimation reads $\hat{\mu}_i^{\star} = \hat{\mu}_{i-1}^{\star} \circ \hat{\delta\mu}_i \circ \hat{\delta\mu}_i^{\star}$ and the template is updated following the rule

$$^{\text{Po}}T_{i+1}(\mathbf{x}) = \begin{cases} ^{\text{P}}I_i(m(\mathbf{x}, \hat{\mu}_i^{\star})) & : \quad \|\hat{\delta\mu}_i^{\star}\| < \epsilon \\ ^{\text{Po}}T_i(\mathbf{x}) & : \quad \text{else} \end{cases} \tag{14}$$

Thus, the template is updated only when subsequent minimization with the reference template leads to the same minimum. Here, this strategy is used to update the brightness appearance of the tracked surface in order to account for changing illumination conditions.

4   Evaluation

In the following, experiments are performed on a standard Pentium Xeon 1.7GHz. Video images are gathered with a interlaced camera at PAL resolution and $56° \times 48°$ horizontal and vertical apertures. The internal parameters of the camera together with the distortion coefficients for a 3rd degree polynomial distortion model are determined offline.

The test set consists of two objects. The first surface patch is part of the label of an ordinary 1.5l soda bottle. The patch is modeled as a $83.17°$ segment of a cylindrical body of radius 4.6cm. Sampling at intervals of 1mm produces

Fig. 1. Texture-registered 3-D point cloud of the objects *bottle* and *sculpture*

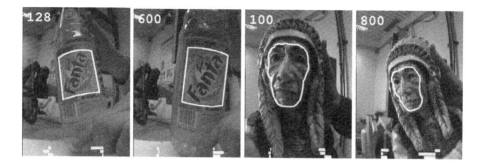

Fig. 2. Screenshots of the tracked sequences *bottle* and *sculpture*. The region of the tracked 3-D model points is manually outlined for better visualization.

4624 surface points. The second surface is the face of a sculpture. By using a 3-D digitizing system, 3668 3-D points of this object are acquired.

The reference textures of the objects are acquired prior tracking. For the first object, the reference image is manually registered to the corresponding 3-D model (see Fig. 1). The point cloud of the sculpture is automatically registered with the image using the same 3-D digitizing system as mentioned above. A video stream of the objects is recorded at 25Hz starting from the vicinity of the reference pose (see Fig. 2). Four different object velocities are simulated by sub-sampling the sequence with different step sizes. In order to cope with real-world (computing) constraints the number of total minimization steps is limited to 22. In the case of the update strategy, the first 14 steps are performed with the updated template. The dimensionality of the illumination subspace is set to 2 for sequence *bottle* and to 3 for the sequence *sculpture*.

4.1   Robustness

The first experiment evaluates the gain in robustness of the two methods for brightness adaption. Increasing the target velocity implicitly accelerates the brightness variation on the surface. Thus, improved robustness would result in a persistent sequence of the tracked target. Table 1 reports the number of frames successfully tracked until the object was lost. The use of the illumination sub-

Table 1. Robustness under different velocities of sequences *bottle* and *sculpture*. The tables shows the number of successfully tracked frames.

bottle	vel 1	vel 2	vel 3	vel 4
compositional	719	319	137	1
+ill. subspace	528	258	137	1
+template update	719	350	137	102
# of frames	719	359	239	228

sculpture	vel 1	vel 2	vel 3	vel 4
compositional	903	451	287	205
+ill. subspace	903	431	284	100
+template update	903	451	286	215
# of frames	903	451	301	225

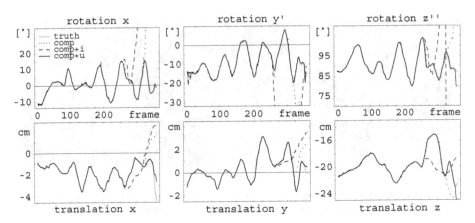

Fig. 3. Cartesian 6-DoF trajectories of sequence *bottle* at velocity 2 for tracking with the illumination subspace method or the template update strategy. The trajectories match the ground truth until the target was lost.

Table 2. Accuracy over the first 250 frames in sequence *bottle* with velocity 2

bottle	$\sigma_{rx}[°]$	$\sigma_{ry}[°]$	$\sigma_{rz}[°]$	$\sigma_{tx}[mm]$	$\sigma_{ty}[mm]$	$\sigma_{tz}[mm]$
compositional	0.29	0.58	0.12	0.17	0.32	0.38
+ill. subspace	0.35	0.75	0.16	0.19	0.32	0.48
+template update	0.22	0.25	0.10	0.15	0.32	0.28

space degrades the compositional approach for sequences with fair illlumination changes while the template update strategy clearly improves overall robustness.

4.2   Accuracy

The second experiment compares both methods for brightness adaption regarding their accuracy. Retro-reflecting markers are attached to the *bottle* object and tracked with a commercially available system. The missing coordinate transformation of marker frame to object frame and world frame to camera frame are estimated offline by means of least-squares fitting over a tracked sequence.

Figure 3 shows the trajectories of the tracked sequence at velocity 2 while Table 2 reports the standard deviations to the ground-truth trajectories. The standard deviations and the displayed trajectories show the superiority of the template update strategy for illumination adaption.

5   Summary and Conclusions

Tracking in the 2-D image plane has been recently extended to 3-D with 6 degrees-of-freedom. Here, we proposed a novel method for efficient 3-D tracking and evaluated two adaptation methods for brightness variations.

The experiments qualitatively and quantitatively showed that extending tracking to more parameters, e.g. for an illumination subspace, degrades the tracked

6-DoF poses. On the other hand, the template update strategy of Matthews et al. [10] increases both, robustness in tracking and accuracy in the trajectories and is therefore the method of choice for tracking objects in 6-DoF with the proposed compositional approach.

Acknowledgment

The author would like to thank Bernhard Thaler for his support on the evaluation. The work was partly supported by the FP-6 IP *SMErobot* no. 011838-2.

References

1. Simon Baker and Iain Matthews. Lucas-kanade 20 years on: A unifying framework. *International Journal of Computer Vision*, 56(3):221 – 255, March 2004.
2. Peter N. Belhumeur and Gregory D. Hager. Tracking in 3d: Image variability decomposition for recovering object pose and illumination. *Pattern Analysis & Applications*, 2:82–91, 1999.
3. Peter N. Belhumeur and David J. Kriegman. What is the set of images of an object under all possible illumination conditions. *International Journal of Computer Vision*, 28(3):245–260, July 1998.
4. José M. Buenaposada and Luis Baumela. Real-time tracking and estimation of plane pose. In *Proc. ICPR*, volume II, pages 697–700, August 2002. Quebec, Canada.
5. Marco La Cascia, Stan Sclaroff, and Vassilis Athitsos. Fast, reliable head tracking under varying illumination: an approach based on registration of texture-mapped 3d models. *IEEE Trans. on PAMI*, 22(4):322–336, 2000.
6. Bruno Cernuschi-Frias, David B. Cooper, Yi-Ping Hung, and Peter N. Belhumer. Toward a model-based bayesian theory for estimating and recognizing parameterized 3-d objects using two or more images taken from different positions. *IEEE Trans. on PAMI*, 11(10):1028–1052, 1989.
7. Norbert Diehl and Hans Burkhardt. Planar motion estimation with a fast converging algorithm. In *Proc. 8th ICPR*, pages 1099–1102, 1986.
8. Gregory D. Hager and Peter N. Belhumeur. Efficient region tracking with parametric models of geometry and illumination. *IEEE Trans. on PAMI*, 20(10):1025–1039, October 1998.
9. Bruce D. Lucas and Takeo Kanade. An iterative image registration technique with an application to stereo vision (darpa). In *Proceedings of the International Joint Conference on Artificial Intelligence*, pages 674–679, 1981.
10. Iain Matthews, Takahiro Ishikawa, and Simon Baker. The template update problem. In *Proc. of the British Machine Vision Conference*, September 2003.
11. Nicholas A. Ramey, Jason J. Corso, William W. Lau, Darius Burschka, and Gregory D. Hager. Real time 3d surface tracking and its applications. In *Proc. of Workshop on Real-time 3D Sensors and Their Use (at CVPR 2004)*, 2004.
12. Wolfgang Sepp and Gerd Hirzinger. Featureless 6dof pose refinement from stereo images. In *Proc. ICPR*, volume IV, pages 17–20, August 2002. Quebec, Canada.
13. Wolfgang Sepp and Gerd Hirzinger. Real-time texture-based 3-d tracking. In *Proc. 25th Pattern Recognition Symp., DAGM'03*, Sept. 2003. Magdeburg, Germany.

Efficient Combination of Histograms for Real-Time Tracking Using Mean-Shift and Trust-Region Optimization

F. Bajramovic[1], Ch. Gräßl[2,*], and J. Denzler[1]

[1] Chair for Computer Vision, Friedrich-Schiller-University Jena
{bajramov, denzler}@informatik.uni-jena.de
http://www4.informatik.uni-jena.de
[2] Chair for Pattern Recognition, University of Erlangen-Nuremberg
graessl@informatik.uni-erlangen.de
http://www5.informatik.uni-erlangen.de

Abstract. Histogram based real-time object tracking methods, like the Mean-Shift tracker of Comaniciu/Meer or the Trust-Region tracker of Liu/Chen, have been presented recently. The main advantage is that a suited histogram allows for very fast and accurate tracking of a moving object even in the case of partial occlusions and for a moving camera. The problem is which histogram shall be used in which situation. In this paper we extend the framework of histogram based tracking. As a consequence we are able to formulate a tracker that uses a weighted combination of histograms of different features. We compare our approach with two already proposed histogram based trackers for different historgrams on large test sequences availabe to the public. The algorithms run in real-time on standard PC hardware.

1 Introduction

Data driven, real-time object tracking is still an important and in general unsolved problem with respect to robustness in natural scenes. Obviously, for many different, high-level tasks in computer vision, there is the need for tracking a moving object in real-time without having specific knowledge about its 2D or 3D structure. In general, it is necessary in surveillance tasks, action recognition, navigation of autonomous robots, etc. Usually, tracking is initialized based on change detection in the scene. From this moment on, the position of the moving target is identified in each consecutive frame.

Several approaches for 2D data driven tracking have been presented in the past, for example feature based [1], template based [2,3], and, most recently, histogram based methods [4,5]. In all cases, tracking, i.e. correspondence between successive frames, is solved by defining and solving an optimization problem. The main difference between the approaches consists in the representation of the object and the way the optimization problem is solved.

---

* This work was partially funded by the European Commission 5th IST Programme - Project VAMPIRE. Only the authors are responsible for the content.

W. Kropatsch, R. Sablatnig, and A. Hanbury (Eds.): DAGM 2005, LNCS 3663, pp. 254–261, 2005.

In this paper, we focus on histogram based methods, where the object to be tracked is identified by a histogram of a priori defined features. One prominent example for a feature is color resulting in a color histogram used to identify the object. We present an extension of histogram based tracking where instead of a single histogram a weighted combination of several different histograms can be used. We refer to this tracker in the following as *combined histogram tracker* (CHT). For tracking, we formulate the optimization problem in a general way, such that the Mean-Shift [6] as well as the Trust-Region [7] optimization can be applied. This allows for a maximum of flexibility for the parameters that are estimated during tracking, for example, translation, rotation, and scaling. We compare the CHT with already presented histogram trackers using only one specific histogram. The results show a significantly better performance of the CHT with respect to accuracy during tracking, and at the same time without loosing its real-time capability.

The paper is structured as follows. In section 2 we introduce histogram based tracking methods together with two already presented local optimization methods, the Mean-Shift and the Trust-Region algorithm. In section 3 we present a rigorous mathematical description for the CHT. We show how the optimization problem can be solved again using the Mean-Shift and the Trust-Region algorithm. Section 4 deals with the experiments. We show results on a large set of labeled image sequences available to the public, which allows quantitative evaluation and comparison. The paper concludes with a discussion and an outlook to future work.

2   Region Based Object Tracking Using Histograms

2.1   Representation and Tracking

In general, the target is identified by an image region $R(\boldsymbol{x}(t))$, where $\boldsymbol{x}(t)$ contains the time variant parameters of the region, also referred to as the state of the region. One simple example for a region $R(\boldsymbol{x}(t))$ is a rectangle of fixed dimensions. The state of the region $\boldsymbol{x}(t) = (m_x(t), m_y(t))^T$ is the center of gravity of that rectangle in pixel coordinates $m_x(t)$ and $m_y(t)$ for each time step t. With this simple model translation of a target region can be easily described by estimating $\boldsymbol{x}(t)$, i.e. center of gravity of the rectangle, over time. If the size of the region is also included in the state, estimation of scale is possible.

The information contained within the region is used to model the moving object. The information may consists of the color, the gray value, or certain other features, like the gradient. At each time step t and for each state $\boldsymbol{x}(t)$ the representation of the moving object consists of a probability density function $p(\boldsymbol{x}(t))$ of the chosen features within the region $R(\boldsymbol{x}(t))$. In practice, this density function has to be estimated from image data. For performance reasons, a weighted histogram $\boldsymbol{q}(\boldsymbol{x}(t)) = (q_1(\boldsymbol{x}(t)), q_2(\boldsymbol{x}(t)), \ldots, q_N(\boldsymbol{x}(t)))^T$ of N bins $q_i(\boldsymbol{x}(t))$ is used as a non-parametric estimation of the true density, although it is well known that this is not the best choice from a theoretical point of view [8]. Each individual bin $q_i(\boldsymbol{x}(t))$ is computed by

$$q_i(\boldsymbol{x}(t)) = C_{\boldsymbol{x}(t)} \sum_{\boldsymbol{u} \in R(\boldsymbol{x}(t))} L_{\boldsymbol{x}(t)}(\boldsymbol{u}) \delta(b_t(\boldsymbol{u}) - i), i = 1, \ldots, N \qquad (1)$$

with $L_{x(t)}(u)$ being a suited weighting function introduced below, $b_t(u)$ the function that maps the pixel u to the number j of the bin which the feature at position u falls into ($j \in \{1, \ldots, N\}$), and δ being the Kronecker-Delta function. The value $C_{x(t)} = 1/\sum_{u \in R(x(t))} L_{x(t)}(u)$ is a normalizing constant. In other words, (1) counts all occurrences of pixels that fall into bin i, where the increment within the sum is given by the weighting function $L_{x(t)}(u)$.

Object tracking can now be defined as an optimization problem. Starting with an initial target region — for example, manually or automatically defined in the first image at $t = 0$ — an initial histogram $q(x(0))$ can be computed. For $t > 0$ the corresponding region is defined by

$$x(t) = \underset{x}{\operatorname{argmin}} \, D(q(x(0)), q(x)) \tag{2}$$

with $D(\cdot, \cdot)$ being a suited distance function defined on histograms. In our work we use two local optimization techniques, the Mean-Shift algorithm [4] and the Trust-Region algorithm [5]. In the context of histogram based tracking, also a global optimization using a particle filter can be applied [9].

2.2 Kernel and Distance Functions

There are two open aspects left: the choice of the weighting function $L_{x(t)}(u)$ in equation (1) and the distance function $D(\cdot, \cdot)$. The weighting function is typically chosen as a kernel, whose support is exactly the region $R(x(t))$. Different kernel profiles can be used, like the Epanechnikov, the biweight, or the truncated Gauss profile [10].

For the optimization problem in (2) several distance functions on histograms have been proposed, like the Bhattacharya distance, the Kulback-Leibler distance, the Euclidean distance or the scalar product distance. It is worth noting that for the following optimization no metric is necessary. The main restriction on the given distance functions in our work is the following special form

$$D(q(x(0)), q(x(t))) = \hat{D}\left(\sum_{n=0}^{N} d(q_n(x(0)), q_n(x(t)))\right) \tag{3}$$

with a monotone, bijective function $\hat{D}$, and a function $d(a, b)$, which is twice differentiable for b. Now, substituting (3) into (2) we get

$$x(t) = \underset{x}{\operatorname{argmax}}\left(-sgn(\hat{D})\sum_{n=0}^{N} d(q(x(0)), q(x))\right) \tag{4}$$

where $sgn(\hat{D}) = 1$ or $sgn(\hat{D}) = -1$ if $\hat{D}$ is monotonly increasing or decreasing, respectively. More details can be found in [10].

2.3 Optimization

This section deals with the optimization of (4) using the Mean Shift algorithm. Hints are given in the end how the optimization can be solved by Trust Region optimization.

The main idea is to do a Taylor series expansion of the right hand side of (4). After a couple of computations and simplifications (for details, see [10]) we get

$$x(t) \approx \underset{x}{\mathrm{argmax}} \left(C_0 \sum_{u \in R(x)} L_x(u) \underbrace{\sum_{n=1}^{N} \delta(b_t(u) - n) \tilde{w}_t(n)}_{\tilde{w}_t(b_t(u))} \right) \tag{5}$$

with the weights

$$\tilde{w}_t(b_t(u)) = -sgn(\hat{D}) \frac{\partial d(a,b)}{\partial b} \Bigg|_{(a,b)=\left(q_{b_t(u)}(x(0)), q_{b_t(u)}(x)\right)} \tag{6}$$

This special reformulation allows us to interpret the weights $\tilde{w}_t(b_t(u))$ as weights on the pixel coordinates u. For a certain distance function $D(\cdot, \cdot)$ we need to calculate the corresponding pixel weights. Finally, we can apply the Mean-Shift algorithm for the optimization of (5), since (5) is a weighted kernel density estimation. Due to lack of space, for details, on how the Mean-Shift algorithm is applied, the reader is referred to [11,10]. Alternatively, the Trust-Region optimization algorithm can be applied. In this case, we need the gradient and Hessian matrix of the right hand side of (4). Both quantities can be derived in closed form [10]. The advantage of the Trust Region method is, that — besides estimation of translation of the target region — also rotation and scale can be integrated in the optimization problem [10].

2.4 Example

Now we give an example for the equations and quantities presented above. Using the Bhattacharyya distance between histograms (as in [4]), defined as

$$D(q(x(0)), q(x(t))) = \sqrt{1 - B(q(x(0)), q(x(t)))} \tag{7}$$

with

$$B(q(x(0)), q(x(t))) = \sum_{n=1}^{N} \sqrt{q_n(x(0)) \cdot q_n(x(t))} \tag{8}$$

we have $\hat{D}(a) = \sqrt{1 - a}$, $d(a,b) = \sqrt{a \cdot b}$ and

$$\tilde{w}_t(n) = \frac{1}{2} \sqrt{\frac{q_n(x(0))}{q_n(x(t)}} \tag{9}$$

3 Combination of Histograms

Up to now, the formulation of histogram based tracking relies on a certain histogram of n-dimensional features, defined a priori for the tracking task at hand. Some examples are gray value histograms ($n = 1$), edge histograms ($n = 1$) or RGB color histograms

($n = 3$). Certainly, using several different features for representing the object to be tracked will result in better tracking performance, especially, if the different features are weighted dynamically according to the situation in the scene. For example, color might be a problem, if illumination changes. In this case, information on the edges might be more useful. On the other side, a unique color of the moving object in a highly textured environment will favour for color and against edges. One idea would now be, to combine several features into one histogram of larger dimension. The problem with that idea is the curse of dimensionality: higher dimensional features result in very sparse histograms so that the estimation of the true, underlying density becomes very inaccurate. This problem prevents us from just combining different features to a bigger feature vector with larger dimension.

We propose now a different solution for combining histograms of different feature for object tracking. The key idea is to use a weighted combination of several histograms with low dimensions instead of one weighted histogram with high dimension. Let $\mathcal{H} = \{1, \dots, H\}$ be the set of features used for representing the object. For each feature $h \in \mathcal{H}$ we define a separate function $b_t^{(h)}(\boldsymbol{u})$. The number of bins in histogram h is N_h and might differ between the histograms. Also, for each histogram a different weighting function $L_{\boldsymbol{x}(t)}^{(h)}(\boldsymbol{u})$ can be applied, i.e. different kernels for each individual histogram are possible if necessary. This results in H different weighted histograms $\boldsymbol{q}^{(h)}(\boldsymbol{x}(t))$ with the bins

$$q_i^{(h)}(\boldsymbol{x}(t)) = C_{\boldsymbol{x}(t)}^{(h)} \sum_{\boldsymbol{u} \in R(\boldsymbol{x}(t))} L_{\boldsymbol{x}(t)}^{(h)}(\boldsymbol{u}) \delta(b_t^{(h)}(\boldsymbol{u}) - i), h \in \mathcal{H}, i = 1, \dots, N_h \quad (10)$$

We now define a combined representation of the object by $\phi(\boldsymbol{x}(t)) = \left(\boldsymbol{q}^{(h)}(\boldsymbol{x}(t))\right)_{h \in \mathcal{H}}$ and a new distance function (compare (2)), based on the weighted sum of the distances for the individual histograms

$$D^* = \sum_{h \in \mathcal{H}} \beta_h D_h(\boldsymbol{q}^{(h)}(\boldsymbol{x}(0)), \boldsymbol{q}^{(h)}(\boldsymbol{x}(t))) \quad (11)$$

where $\beta_h \geq 0$ being the contribution of the individual histogram h to the object respresentation. The quantities β_h can be adjusted to best model the object in the current context of tracking. Currently, we set these parameters empirically. In future work we plan to find the optimal values automatically and to dynamically adjust them during tracking.

As before, for the Mean-Shift as well as for the Trust-Region method we can formulate a corresponding optimization problem. If we use the same weighting function $L_{\boldsymbol{x}(t)}(\boldsymbol{u})$ for all histograms and as state $\boldsymbol{x} = (m_x, m_y)^T$ the position of the moving object in the image plane, we get

$$\boldsymbol{x}(t) \approx \underset{\boldsymbol{x}}{\operatorname{argmax}} \, C_0 \sum_{\boldsymbol{u} \in R(\boldsymbol{x})} L_{\boldsymbol{x}}(\boldsymbol{u}) \underbrace{\sum_{h \in \mathcal{H}} \tilde{w}_{h,t}(b_t^{(h)}(\boldsymbol{u}))}_{w_{h,t}(\boldsymbol{u})} \quad (12)$$

which is again a weighted kernel density estimation. The constant C_0 can be shown to be independent of x. The corresponding pixel weights are

$$w_{h,t}(u) = \sum_{h \in \mathcal{H}} \tilde{w}_{h,t}(b_t^{(h)}(u)) \tag{13}$$

$$= \sum_{h \in \mathcal{H}} -\beta_h sgn(D_h) \frac{\partial d_h(a,b)}{\partial b} \Bigg|_{(a,b)=(q^{(h)}(x(0)), q^{(h)}(x))} \tag{14}$$

where $d_h(a,b)$ is defined as in (3) for each individual feature h. For the Trust-Region optimization again gradient and Hessian matrix have to be derived. Details can be found in [10].

4 Experiments

We will now show that a weighted combination of different histograms is suited to improve tracking performance. In the experiments we use the test videos of the CAVIAR project [12], originally recorded for action and behaviour recognition experiments. Although, we do not have this kind of application in mind, the videos are prefectly suited, since they are recorded in natural environment, with change in illumination and scale of the moving persons as well as partial occlusions. Most important, the moving persons are hand-labelled, i.e. for each frame a reference rectangle is stored.

To evaluate the results of the original Mean-Shift and Trust-Region tracker as well as our proposed CHT we used an area based criterion. We measure the difference e of the returned region A and the ground-truth region B by

$$e(A, B) = 1 - \frac{|A \cap B|}{\frac{1}{2}(|A| + |B|)} \tag{15}$$

This error metric is zero, if the two regions are identical, and one if they do not overlap. If the two regions have the same size, the error increases with increasing distance between the center of both regions. Also, equal center but different size if taken care of.

In the experiments we combined three different histograms. The first is the standard color histogram consisting of the RGB channels, abbreviated in the figures as *rgb*. The second histogram is computed from a sobel edge strength image (*gradn*), with the edge strength normalized to fit the gray value range from 0 to 255. The third histogram is computed from a corner interest map (*minev*). This interest map is based on the interest operator returning the smallest eigenvalue of the structure matrix from a 5×5 window around the respective pixel [13]. Thus, high values in the interest map correspond to corners in the image. For simplicity reasons, we call this histogram a corner histogram.

In Figure 1 for the Mean-Shift the accuracy of tracking is documented using the error percentile. For a certain percentile pz (x–axis) we measure the largest error $e(A, B)$ (y–axis, compare (15) taking into account the $pz\%$ best images only. In the left figure, we only evaluated images until object lost, in the right figure all images are considered. The reader can verify, that a combination of RGB with a gradient histogram leads to a significant improvement of tracking stability compared to a pure RGB histogram

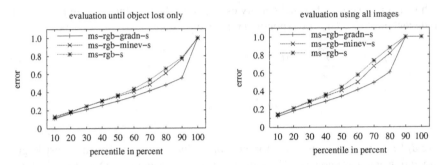

Fig. 1. Error percentile using CHT of RGB and gradient (rgb-gradn) and RGB and corner histogram (rgb-minev) as well as pure RGB histogram tracker (rgb). Results are give for the Mean-Shift-Tracker with scale estimation, Biweight-Kernel, Kullback-Leibler distance for all individual histograms.

Fig. 2. Tracking result for one of the images sequences from the CAVIAR test bed (first and last image of the sucessfully tracked person). Ground truth and computed region of the moving person (ellipses) are almost the same, even in the case of change in scale.

tracker as well as a tracker with a combination of RGB and corner histogram. We got similar results for the corresponding Trust-Region tracker and our extension to combined histograms. The weights β_h for combining RGB with corner and edge histogram (compare (11)) has been empirically set to 0.8 and 0.2, respectively. To automatically find these weights for a certain object and to adjust them dynamically during tracking is one of the focus of our future work.

The computation time for one images is on average less than 2 msec on a PIV, 3.2 GHz compared to approximately 1 msec for a tracker using one histogram only. One example of a successful tracking including correct scale estimation is shown in Figure 2.

5　Conclusion

In our paper we have presented a mathematically consistent extension of histogram based tracking, which we call combined histogram tracker. We could show that the corresponding optimization problems can still be solved using the Mean-Shift as well as the Trust-Region algorithm without loosing real-time capability. The formulation allows the combination of an arbitrary number of histograms with varying dimensions as wells as individual distance functions between two histograms. This allows for a maximum of flexibility in the application of the method. In the experiments we have shown for three different feature histograms that a combination of two of them can improve tracking accuracy and stability. The improvement of course depends on the chosen histogram and on the object to be tracked itself. One important result is, that tracking can still be performed in real-time on standard PC hardware. In the end we like to stress again, that similar results are achieved using the Trust-Region algorithm, although the presentation in this paper was focused on the Mean-Shift algorithm. For more details, the reader is referred to [10].

In our future work we will investigate the adaptive combination of histograms during tracking such that the weights of the histograms are dynamically adjusted depending on the context of tracking, the objects, and background. Also, we are going to compare systematically the CHT with state of the art 2-d tracker, like the tracker of Perez [9].

References

1. Denzler, J., Niemann, H.: Active rays: Polar–transformed active contours for real–time contour tracking. Journal on Real–Time Imaging **5** (1999) 203–213
2. Hager, G.D., Belhumeur, P.N.: Efficient Region Tracking With Parametric Models of Geometry and Illumination. IEEE Transactions on Pattern Analysis and Machine Intelligence **20** (1998) 1025–1039
3. Jurie, F., Dhome, M.: Hyperplane Approximation for Template Matching. IEEE Transactions on Pattern Analysis and Machine Intelligence **24** (2002) 996–1000
4. Comaniciu, D.: Bayesian Kernel Tracking. In: Annual Conference of the German Society for Pattern Recognition. (2002) 438–445
5. Liu, T.L., Chen, H.T.: Real-Time Tracking Using Trust-Region Methods. IEEE Transactions on Pattern Analysis and Machine Intelligence **26** (2004) 397–402
6. Cheng, Y.: Mean Shift, Mode Seeking, and Clustering. IEEE Transactions on Pattern Analysis and Machine Intelligence **17** (1995) 790–799
7. Conn, A.R., Gould, N.I.M., Toint, P.L.: Trust-Region Methods. SIAM (2000)
8. Wand, M.P., Jones, M.C.: Kernel Smoothing. Chapman and Hall (1995)
9. Perez, P., Hue, C., Vermaak, J., Gangnet, M.: Color-Based Probabilistic Tracking. In: 7th European Conference on Computer Vision. Volume 1. (2002) 661–675
10. Bajramovic, F.: Kernel-basierte Objektverfolgung. Technical Report Masters thesis at Computer Vision Group, Department of Mathematics and Computer Science, University of Passau (2004)
11. Comaniciu, D., Meer, P.: Mean Shift: A Robust Approach Toward Feature Space Analysis. IEEE Transactions on Pattern Analysis and Machine Intelligence **24** (2002) 603–619
12. CAVIAR: Ec funded caviar project, ist 2001 37540, url: http://homepages.inf.ed.ac.uk/rbf/caviar/ (2004)
13. Trucco, E., Verri, E.: Introductory Techniques for 3-D Computer Vision. Prentice Hall (1998)

Spiders as Robust Point Descriptors

Adam Stanski and Olaf Hellwich

Computer Vision & Remote Sensing Group, Technical University of Berlin,
FR 3-1, Franklinstr. 28/29, 10587 Berlin, Germany
{astanski, hellwich}@cs.tu-berlin.de

Abstract. This paper introduces a new operator to characterize a point in an image in a distinctive and invariant way. The robust recognition of points is a key technique in computer vision: algorithms for stereo correspondence, motion tracking and object recognition rely heavily on this type of operator. The goal in this paper is to describe the salient point to be characterized by a constellation of surrounding anchor points. Salient points are the most reliably localized points extracted by an interest point operator. The anchor points are multiple interest points in a visually homogenous segment surrounding the salient point. Because of its appearance, this constellation is called a spider. With a prototype of the spider operator, results in this paper demonstrate how a point can be recognized in spite of significant image noise, inhomogeneous change in illumination and altered perspective. For an example that requires a high performance close to object / background boundaries, the prototype yields better results than David Lowe's SIFT operator.

1 Introduction

Numerous algorithms in computer vision require the recognition of the same point in images that differ in perspective, illumination, position of objects, image noise, etc. Homologous points are needed for depth reconstruction of two stereo images, for motion tracking and in most object recognition methods (e.g. [1]). Regardless of the application, the problem always remains the same: How can the position of a point be described in a distinctive and invariant way? Distinctive in the sense that the description is strongly differing from that of other points. Invariant in a way that a change in the surrounding area of a point caused by rotation, scaling, variation of illumination, etc. does not alter its description beyond recognition.

In this paper the problem is solved with spiders. A spider characterizes a salient point with a constellation of anchor points, whose positions are stored relative to the salient point. The following three steps summarize the approach:

1. *Interest Point Localization:* An interest point operator is utilized to localize points and associates each one with a reliability to be repeatedly found in an altered image. Some points with high reliability are chosen as the salient point of spiders.
2. *Extraction of Image Segment:* For each salient point, a segment of the image is determined that is visually homogenous. All points extracted by the interest point operator, which are also part of this segment, are the anchor points belonging to this salient point. A salient point with multiple surrounding anchor points forms a spider.

W. Kropatsch, R. Sablatnig, and A. Hanbury (Eds.): DAGM 2005, LNCS 3663, pp. 262–268, 2005.
© Springer-Verlag Berlin Heidelberg 2005

3. *Comparison of Spiders*: To determine the similarity of two salient points, the constellation of their anchor points has to be compared. However, when observed from a different perspective, the geometric constellation of the anchor points is distorted. Therefore, an affine transformation to compensate for this distortion is estimated before comparing two spiders.

Figure 1 gives an example of a typical spider in an image, determined by the prototype of the spider operator:

Fig. 1. An example of the determination of a spider. From left to right: 1) The original image (a part of the Lena image). 2) Interest points extracted with Lowe's scale space extrema operator are highlighted. A reliable point is marked, which is used as a salient point for the spider in the following. 3) A segment of pixels with a locally averaged brightness similar to the salient point is highlighted. Interest points in this area are used as the anchor points of the spider. 4) The final spider with 14 anchor points.

2 Related Research

The concept that is most often used to describe a point is the simplest one, too: the area surrounding a point is compared pixel by pixel. Usually this area is square or circular in shape, with the salient point at its center. Two points are compared by aggregating the differences of every corresponding pair of pixels. There are several ways to do this. For example, the difference between two pixels can be described by the difference of their intensities (absolute intensity differences) or their squared intensity (squared intensity differences). The aggregation may be based on simple addition (e.g. sum-of-squared-differences) or on additional normalization (e.g. normalized-grayscale-correlation). This class of methods is successfully used in, for example small baseline stereo matching (e.g. Scharstein [6]) and object recognition (e.g. Leibe [2]). The algorithms are fast, simple, robust with respect to image noise and partly invariant in relation to homogenous changes of illumination or contrast. However, other changes of the image, such as changes in perspective or rotation, change the description of a point so much that it can no longer be identified by these methods.

Another concept for the description of a point is based on calculations on a group of pixels. The calculation aims at generating features that identify a point more distinctively and with increased invariance than possible by direct comparison of pixels. Two examples of current methods that calculate features from scaled round or affine transformed squared regions are proposed by Mikolaiczyk and Schmid [4] and Lowe [3]. The method in the first paper begins with determining interest points with an affine-invariant Harris operator. In a second step their scale is calculated by searching for local scale space extremas. Finally, the affine shape of the surrounding area of a point is estimated by a second moment matrix.

Lowe's method can also be divided into multiple steps. First, the scale of a point is determined by detecting local scale space extremas. In a second step, a quadratic function is fitted to the results, so that the position and scale of the points can be calculated more precisely. In a third step the orientation of points is determined by local image gradients. Finally, the surrounding area is normalized relative to scale and orientation in order to describe the point with the SIFT descriptor – a feature based on several local gradients in the surrounding area.

Lowe's method provides a higher density of distinctive points than the approach of Mikolaiczyk and Schmid. However, the interest points calculated by Lowe in the first step are only scale-invariant, which diminishes the tolerance of his method compared to a full affine transformation. Both approaches cannot maintain their generally good performance when it comes to object / background boundaries. This is impossible for a point on the silhouette of an object as there are too many pixels in the surrounding area that belong to the background, which falsifies the calculation. For example, points in images containing trees, animals or people cannot be detected in a reliable way, if the parts of the objects (here branches and limbs) are only a few pixels wide.

Two approaches that solve this problem are proposed by Mikolajczyk, Zisserman und Schmid [5] and by Tuytelaars und Van Gool [8]. The first paper uses a description related to Lowe's SIFT Descriptor. However, the initial points are determined on edges and their scale is calculated relative to the opposite edge. Every point is now described by two independent descriptors: each describing the pixel on one side of the edge on which the point is situated. In case a point is indeed close to the silhouette of an object, one descriptor will refer only to the object and the other one only to the background. In the second paper from Tuytelaars and Van Gool, edges are also utilized to determine the area on which the description of a point is based. A parallelogram is fit to every two edges that form a corner. The description of a point is now calculated based on the pixels inside this parallelogram. As the edges the parallelogram was fit to usually do not extend beyond object boundaries, it rarely crosses an object border. Both approaches work with Canny edge detection, which utilizes two thresholds. Slight changes in an image can therefore cause an interruption of edges; they may not be detected at all or connected differently. This lack of stability has a negative effect on the performance of both methods.

3 Interest Point Localization

The first step of the proposed spider operator is to detect stable points. The most important property of these points is that they can be localized in spite of changed light conditions, viewpoint on a scene, etc. Multiple candidates with this characteristic were examined, such as points detected with the Harris operator or the ends of edges. The prototype examined in this paper utilizes scale space extremas, as described by Lowe in [3]. The interest points detected by Lowe's operator are the centers of round areas of different size that are lighter or darker than their environment. Basically, they are light or dark blobs in the image. Utilizing multiple interest point operators is another possibility, as long as all of them yield stable points.

The implemented version of the scale space extrema operator yields more stable points than the Harris operator and a newly developed approach looking for the ends of edges in an image. However, it does not achieve quite the same good results as given by Lowe for unknown reasons. While trying to obtain a higher performance, a new way to determine the reliability of the points was identified that enhances their stability. Instead of using the absolute value of a scale space extrema as a criterion for its stability, its relative value is used in the prototype: The reliability of a maximum depends on its value minus the highest value of the 98 pixels, which have a chessboard distance of 2 to this maximum of the 3d scale space. The reliability of a minimum found in scale space depends on the lowest of these values minus the value of this minimum.

4   Extraction of Image Segment

After a salient point is located, the segment which belongs to this point must be determined. A segment is a connected area of the image, in which each pixel has a high reliability of being on the same plain as the salient point. A segment is approximated by extracting an area, which is visually similar to the salient point. Multiple techniques known from image segmentation based on color gradients, textures or boundary smoothness could be applied here.

The prototype of the spider operator simply aggregates adjacent pixels starting from the salient point, as long as the difference of the brightness between the pixel and the salient point is below a threshold. This aggregation is performed on a Gaussian blurred image to reduce the influence of single pixels.

All points that are extracted by the interest point operator and are also part of the segment of a salient point form its anchor points. Usually, a salient point can be recognized even if its segment is extracted differently in an altered image, as long as the majority of its anchor points is detected in both images.

5   Comparison of Spiders

If two images show the same point from an altered perspective, the spiders calculated on the two views of the point will be different also. An example of this can be seen in the two leftmost images of figure 2, of which one is a rotated and scaled version of the other. To identify the two points as the same, the perspective distortion of one spider has to be eliminated by a transformation, thereby changing the shape of the spider, so that its appearance becomes similar to the other. The method for matching two spiders is illustrated in figure 2 and described in the remainder of this section.

To calculate this transformation in practice the following three assumptions are made: 1) The salient point and all anchor points are assumed to be coplanar. This should be the case in the segment of a salient point and reduces the necessary calculations as well as the number of anchor points required. 2) The perspective distortion is estimated with an affine transformation, which also reduces the computational effort. 3) As it is assumed that the salient point of both spiders is identical and that the coordinates of the anchor points are given relative to the salient point, translations need not to be considered. This leaves us with a matrix containing only four unknowns, which transforms an anchor point (x_1, y_1) of a spider S_1 into a point (x_2, y_2) of a spider S_2:

$$\begin{bmatrix} x_2 \\ y_2 \end{bmatrix} = \begin{bmatrix} m_1 & m_2 \\ m_3 & m_4 \end{bmatrix} \begin{bmatrix} x_1 \\ y_1 \end{bmatrix} \qquad (1)$$

The determination of anchor points is error-prone. Thus, to match two spiders with this transformation, the error of the position of its anchor points has to be estimated. As they should be well localized, the probability of detecting an anchor point decreases with an increased distance to its correct position. Therefore, a least-squares optimal solution is chosen. However, this is a very poor estimate for some cases, e.g. if the search for an anchor point reveals that multiple positions in a large area are likely to be its correct position. Hence, an additional reliability is determined for each anchor point, which can be interpreted as the probability that its detected position is close to its correct location. The lower the reliability of a point, the weaker the influence of its detected location on the matching of spiders should be. As an anchor point is matched with a corresponding one, both of their reliabilities determine their influence on the whole matching. This is achieved by scaling a pair of corresponding anchor points P_1 and P_2 with their combined reliabilities r_1 and r_2:

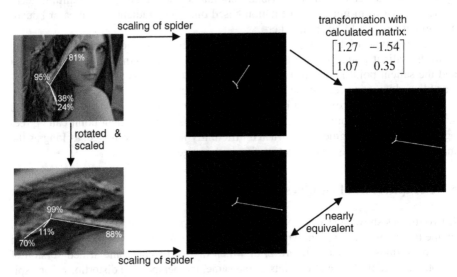

Fig. 2. Simplified example for the comparison of two spiders. Upper left: the original image with a spider and the reliabilities of all four anchor points. Lower left: a version of the original image scaled by factor 1.3 horizontally and 2.0 vertically, than rotated clockwise by 68.4°. The spider in this image is distorted, because of the transformation of the image. Middle column: the spiders from the two left images, whose anchor points are scaled with equation 2 according to their reliability. The two most unreliable anchor points (with 38% and 24% in the upper and 11% and 70% in the lower image) are shortened strongly, so that one of them is barely visible. Right image: By transformation with the given matrix, which was determined with equation 5, the upper spider becomes nearly equivalent with the lower spider. This makes it possible to determine reliably that both salient points are actually the same.

$$\begin{bmatrix} x_1' \\ y_1' \end{bmatrix} = \begin{bmatrix} r_1 & r_2 \end{bmatrix} \begin{bmatrix} x_1 \\ y_1 \end{bmatrix} \quad \text{and} \quad \begin{bmatrix} x_2' \\ y_2' \end{bmatrix} = \begin{bmatrix} r_1 & r_2 \end{bmatrix} \begin{bmatrix} x_2 \\ y_2 \end{bmatrix} \tag{2}$$

It is possible to determine an optimal solution for the stated problem (see e.g. Strang [7]). First, equations 1 and 2 are converted into a linear equation. Each anchor point contributes to two more rows in the matrix and the last vector (at least two points are required):

$$\begin{bmatrix} r_1 r_2 x_1 & r_1 r_2 y_1 & 0 & 0 \\ 0 & 0 & r_1 r_2 x_1 & r_1 r_2 y_1 \\ \vdots & \vdots & \vdots & \vdots \end{bmatrix} \begin{bmatrix} m_1 \\ m_2 \\ m_3 \\ m_4 \end{bmatrix} = \begin{bmatrix} r_1 r_2 x_2 \\ r_1 r_2 y_2 \\ \vdots \end{bmatrix} \tag{3}$$

This inhomogeneous linear equation can be written as:

$$Ax = b \tag{4}$$

By rewriting this formula and calculating the pseudo inverse with a singular value decomposition the parameters x of an affine transformation that converts spider S_1 into spider S_2 are determined (Moore-Penrose inverse):

$$x = \left[A^T A \right]^+ A^T b \tag{5}$$

6 Comparison of Results

In the following, the spider prototype is compared with the SIFT operator using an example where object / background segmentation is of the essence. Figure 3 shows

Fig. 3. Comparison of the SIFT and the spider operator. From left to right: 1) The SIFT operator matches 6 points on the object, of which 3 are correct. 2) The spider operator matches 8 points, of which 7 are correct. 3) An example of two of the spiders that are matched correctly. The upper has 28 anchor points; the lower is formed by 22 points.

two images with a fork moved in front of a fixed background. The first column displays lines connecting each pair of points matched by the SIFT operator. The original version of the SIFT operator as provided by David Lowe on his website is used (Version 3, August 2004). Matching points on the background were discarded for simplicity. 3 of the 6 point pairs are correct. The false correspondences are due to the low information content in the area between the spikes of the fork.

The second column displays the results of the spider operator. 7 of the 8 pairs are correct matches. As the spider operator uses information from a visually similar segment to describe a point, it can utilize the structure of the fork instead of being limited to local information. This is exemplified in the last column, which displays one of the correctly matched spiders.

7 Conclusions

In this paper, a new operator for recognizing a point under varying perspective and lighting conditions was introduced. It provides a basis for various applications, like wide-baseline stereo, motion tracking or object recognition. The operator characterizes a salient point with a constellation of surrounding anchor points, which are interest points detected in a visually homogenous neighborhood of the salient point. An algorithm for matching spiders determined from altered perspectives on a scene was developed. In an example, the prototype of the spider operator yields a better result than the SIFT operator when applied to a jagged object. As this is only a single example, additional experiments have to be performed to make a statement about the general quality of the spider operator.

References

1. Forsyth, D. A. and Ponce, J.: Computer Vision – A Modern Approach (2003)
2. Leibe, B. and Schiele, B.: Scale Invariant Object Categorization Using a Scale-Adaptive Mean-Shift Search. DAGM'04 Annual Pattern Recognition Symposium. Springer LNCS, Volume 3175 (2004)
3. Lowe, D.: Distinctive Image Features from Scale-Invariant Keypoints. International Journal of Computer Vision, Volume 60 (2004)
4. Mikolajczyk, K. and Schmid, C.: Scale & Affine Invariant Interest Point Detectors. International Journal of Computer Vision, Volume 60 (2004)
5. Mikolajczyk, K., Zisserman, A., and Schmid, C.: Shape recognition with edge-based features. Proceedings of the British Machine Vision Conference, Norwich, U.K. (2003)
6. Scharstein, D. and Szeliski, R.: A Taxonomy and Evaluation of Dense Two-Frame Stereo Correspondence Algorithms. International Journal of Computer Vision, Volume 47 (2002)
7. Strang, G.: Introduction to Linear Algebra, Third Edition (2003)
8. Tuytelaars, T. and Gool, L.V.: Matching Widely Separated Views Based on Affine Invariant Regions. International Journal of Computer Vision, Volume 59 (2004)

A Comparative Evaluation of Template and Histogram Based 2D Tracking Algorithms

B. Deutsch[1,*], Ch. Gräßl[1,**], F. Bajramovic[2], and J. Denzler[2]

[1] Chair for Pattern Recognition, University of Erlangen-Nuremberg
{deutsch, graessl}@informatik.uni-erlangen.de
http://www5.informatik.uni-erlangen.de
[2] Chair for Computer Vision, Friedrich-Schiller-University Jena
{bajramov, denzler}@informatik.uni-jena.de
http://www4.informatik.uni-jena.de

Abstract. In this paper, we compare and evaluate five contemporary, data-driven, real-time 2D object tracking methods: the region tracker by Hager et al., the Hyperplane tracker, the CONDENSATION tracker, and the Mean Shift and Trust Region trackers. The first two are classical template based methods, while the latter three are from the more recently proposed class of histogram based trackers. All trackers are evaluated for the task of pure translation tracking, as well as tracking translation plus scaling. For the evaluation, we use a publically available, labeled data set consisiting of surveillance videos of humans in public spaces. This data set demonstrates occlusions, changes in object appearance, and scaling.

1 Introduction

Data driven real-time 2D object tracking is a preliminary for many different computer vision tasks, like face and gesture recognition, surveillance tasks, or action recognition. Recently, two promising classes of 2D data driven tracking methods have been proposed: template, or region based, tracking methods and histogram based methods. The idea of template based tracking is to track a moving object by defining a region of pixels belonging to that object and, using local optimization methods, to estimate the transformation parameters of that region between two consecutive images. In histogram based methods, the idea is to represent an object by a distinctive histogram, for example a color histogram. Tracking is then performed by searching for a similar region in the image whose histogram best matches the object histogram from the first image. In this paper, we present a comparative evaluation of five different object trackers, two region based [1,2] and three histogram based approaches [3,4,5]. We test the performance of each tracker both for pure translation and for translation with scaling. Due to the rotational invariance of the histogram based methods, further motion models, such

---

* This work was partially funded by the German Science Foundation (DFG) under grant SFB 603/TP B2. Only the authors are responsible for the content.
** This work was partially funded by the European Commission 5th IST Programme - Project VAMPIRE. Only the authors are responsible for the content.

W. Kropatsch, R. Sablatnig, and A. Hanbury (Eds.): DAGM 2005, LNCS 3663, pp. 269–276, 2005.
© Springer-Verlag Berlin Heidelberg 2005

Fig. 1. Example of template matching: The left image is the reference image from which the reference template was extracted. The region points are marked by crosses. In the other two images, the reference region has been transformed (center: translation, right: translation and scaling) to match with the reference template. The reference region is marked by the dashed rectangle.

as rotation or general affine motion, are not considered. In the evaluation, we focus especially on natural scenes with changing illuminations and partial occlusions based on a publicly available data set [6].

The paper is structured as follows: in Section 2, we give a short introduction to the mathematics of both tracking principles. Section 3 deals with the test set and evaluation criteria that we use for our comparative study. The main contribution consists of the evaluation of the different tracking algorithms in Section 4. The paper ends with a short conclusion and discussion of the results.

2   Data Driven 2D Object Tracking

In the following two sections, we summarize two different classes of data driven object tracking in the image plane: template matching methods and histogram matching methods.

2.1   Template Matching

One type of algorithm for data driven object tracking is based on template-matching. During an initialization step, the intensity values are extracted from image points belonging to the object. These points form the *reference region* $r = (x_1, x_2, \ldots, x_N)^T$, where $x_i = (x_i, y_i)^T$ is a 2D point. The gray-level intensity of a point x at time t is given by $f(x, t)$. Consequently, the vector $f(r, t)$ contains the intensities of the entire region r at time t and is called a *template*. The template at the starting time t_0 is denoted as the *reference template*. Template matching can now be described as computing the motion parameters $\mu(t)$ that minimize the least-square intensity difference between the reference template and the current template:

$$\mu(t) = \operatorname*{argmin}_{\mu} \| f(r, t_0) - f(g(r, \mu), t) \|_2 \, . \tag{1}$$

The function $g(r, \mu)$ performs a geometrical transformation of the the region, parameterized by vector μ. Several such transformations can be considered, e.g., [2] use a parameterization which not only deals with translation, rotation, and scaling, but also with affine and projective transformations. In this paper, we restrict ourselves to translation and scale estimation, as illustrated in Fig. 1.

The minimization in Eq. 1 is computationally expensive if done by a brute-force search. It is more efficient to approximate μ through a linear system

$$\hat{\mu}(t+1) = \hat{\mu}(t) + A(t+1)\left(f\left(r, t_0\right) - f\left(g\left(r, \mu(t)\right), t+1\right)\right). \tag{2}$$

We compare two approaches for computing matrix $A(t)$ from Eq. 2. Jurie and Dhome [2] perform a short training step, where random transformations are simulated in the reference image. Typically, on the order of 1000 transformations are executed and their motion parameters $\tilde{\mu}_i$ and difference vectors $f\left(r, t_0\right) - f\left(g\left(r, \tilde{\mu}_i\right), t_0\right)$ collected. Afterwards, matrix A is derived through a least squares approach. Note that A can be made independent from t in this approach. For details, we refer to the original paper. A more analytical way is proposed by Hager et al. [1], who use a first order Taylor approximation. During initialization, the gradients of the region points are used to build a Jacobian matrix. Although A cannot be made independent from t, the transformation can be performed very efficiently and the approach has real-time capability.

2.2 Histogram Matching

In histogram based tracking methods, the target is again identified by an image region $r(\mu(t))$, where $\mu(t)$ contains the time variant parameter of the region, also referred to as the state of the region. One simple example for a region $r(\mu(t))$ is a rectangle of fixed dimensions. The state of the region $\mu(t) = (m_x(t), m_y(t))^T$ is the center of that rectangle in pixel coordinates, $m_x(t)$ and $m_y(t)$, for each time step t. With this simple model, translation of a target region can be easily described by estimating $\mu(t)$, i.e. center of gravity of the rectangle, over time. If the size of the region is also included in the state, estimation of the scale is possible.

The information contained within the region is used to model the moving object, but instead of focusing on individual pixels and their values, the distribution of features defined at each pixel is used. The information may consist of the color, the intensity, or certain other features like the gradient. At each time step t and for each state $\mu(t)$, the representation of the moving object consists of a probability density function $p(\mu(t))$ of the chosen features within the region $r(\mu(t))$. In practice, this density function has to be estimated from image data. For performance reasons, a weighted histogram $q(\mu(t)) = (q_1(\mu(t)), q_2(\mu(t)), \ldots, q_N(\mu(t)))^T$ of N bins is used as a non-parametric estimation of the true density. Each individial bin $q_i(\mu(t))$ of the histogram is computed by

$$q_i(\mu(t)) = C_{\mu(t)} \sum_{u \in r(\mu(t))} L_{\mu(t)}(u)\delta(b_t(u) - i), i = 1, \ldots, N \tag{3}$$

with $L_{\mu(t)}(u)$ being a suitable weighting function, $b_t(u)$ the function that maps the pixel u to the number j of the bin which the feature at position u falls into ($j \in \{1, \ldots, N\}$), and δ being the Kronecker-Delta function. The value

$$C_{\mu(t)} = \frac{1}{\sum_{u \in r(\mu(t))} L_{\mu(t)}(u)} \tag{4}$$

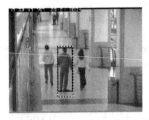

Fig. 2. Stills from three of the videos used. The solid box marks the hand-labled ground truth. The dashed box is the tracker's current estimate. In the right-most image, the tracker has been distracted by a temporary occlusion from another person, and subsequently lost the real target.

is a normalizing constant. In other words, (3) counts all occurances of pixels that fall into bin i, where the increment within the sum is weighted by $L_{\mu(t)}(u)$.

Object tracking can now be defined as an optimization problem. Starting with an initial target region—for example, manually or automatically defined in the first image at $t = t_0$—an initial histogram $q(\mu(t_0))$ can be computed. For $t > t_0$, the corresponding region is defined by

$$\mu(t) = \underset{\mu}{\operatorname{argmin}} \, D(q(\mu(t_0)), q(\mu(t))) \tag{5}$$

with $D(\cdot, \cdot)$ being a suitable distance function defined on histograms. In our work we compare two local optimization techniques, the Mean Shift algorithm [7,8] and the Trust Region algorithm [4,9], as well as a global optimization technique using particle filters [5,10].

3   Test Set and Evaluation Criteria

The experiments were performed on publically available videos from the CAVIAR [6] project. These are surveillance-type videos from a fixed camera, showing human beings performing a variety of actions. The videos come with hand-labeled ground truth information, which allows an independent evaluation of our trackers. The ground truth information describes rectangles surrounding the individual humans in each scene.

Figure 2 shows sample images from three of the videos used. The change in the tracked person's appearance, as well as the heterogeneous background, makes this a relatively difficult problem.

In each experiment, a specific person was to be tracked. The tracking system was given the frame number of the first unoccluded appearence of the person, the ground truth rectangle around the person, and the frame of the person's dissappearance. Each tracker was initialized with this enclosing rectangle. Aside from this initialization, the trackers had no access to the ground truth information.

For each frame, two measurements between the tracked region and the ground truth region were recorded. The first is defined as the fraction of non-overlapping area by the total area of both regions:

$$e_r(A, B) := \frac{|A \setminus B| + |B \setminus A|}{|A| + |B|} \tag{6}$$

Table 1. Timing results from the first sequence, in milliseconds. For each tracker, the time taken for initialization, and the average time per frame, are shown for scaling and non-scaling versions.

	Without scaling		With scaling	
	initial	per frame	initial	per frame
Hager & Belhumeur	5	2.33	5	2.87
Hyperplane	528	2.16	536	2.19
Mean Shift	2	1.03	2	2.74
Trust Region	9	4.01	18	8.63
CONDENSATION	11	79.71	11	109.95

where A and B are image regions, represented as sets of image points, and $| \cdot |$ is the cardinal number of a set. Identical regions have a region error of $e_r(A, A) = 0$, while non-overlapping rectangles have a region error of 1. The second measurement, denoted e_c, is the Euclidean distance between both rectangles' centers, measured in pixels.

Twelve experiments were performed on seven videos (some videos were reused, tracking a different person each time).

4 Experimental Results

The following five trackers were compared: The region tracking algorithm of Hager et al.[1], working on a three-level Gaussian image pyramid hierarchy to enlarge the basin of convergence. The Hyperplane tracker, using a 150 point region and initialized with 1000 training perturbation steps. The Mean Shift and Trust Region algorithms, using an Epanechnikov weighting kernel, the Bhattacharyya distance measure and the HSV color histogram feature from [5] for maximum comparability. Finally, the CONDENSATION based color histogram approach from Pérez et al.[5], with 400 particles diffused by a zero-mean Gaussian distribution with a variance of 5 pixels in each dimension. All trackers were tested with pure translation, and with translation and scaling.

All tests were timed on a 2.8 GHz Intel Xeon processor. The methods differ greatly in the times taken for initialization (once per sequence) and tracking (once per frame). Table 1 shows the timing results from the first sequence. Notable points are the long initialization phase of the Hyperplane tracker due to training, and the long per-frame time of the CONDENSATION tracker due to the large number of particles.

The trackers' output was compared to the ground truth with the two evaluation criteria introduced in section 3 (distance between centers e_c, and fraction of region overlap e_r). For each tracker, the errors from all sequences were concatenated and sorted.

Figure 3 shows the measured distance error e_c and the region error e_r for all trackers, both with and without scaling.

Performance varies widely between all tested trackers, showing strengths and weaknesses for each individual method. There appears to be no method which is universally "better" than others.

The structure-based region trackers, Hager and Hyperplane, are potentially very accurate, as can be seen at the left-hand side of each graph, where they display a larger number of frames with low errors. However, both are prone to losing the target quicker,

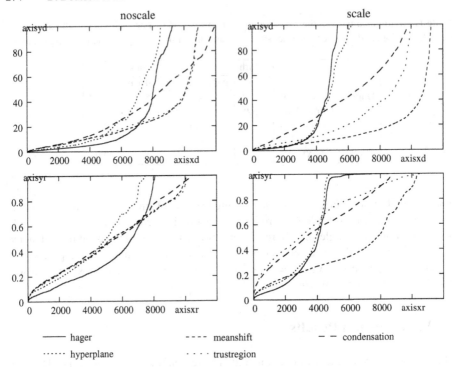

Fig. 3. The result graphs. The top row shows the distance error e_c, the bottom row shows the region error e_r. The left-hand column contains the results for trackers without scaling, the right-hand column those with scaling. The horizontal axis does not correspont to time, but to sorted aggregation. The vertical axis for e_c has been truncated to 100 pixels to emphasize the relevant details.

causing their errors to climb faster than the other three methods. Particularly when scaling is also estimated, the additional degree of freedom typically provides additional accuracy, but causes the estimation to diverge sooner. This is a consequence of the strong changes of appearance of the tracked regions in these image sequences.

The CONDENSATION method, for the most part, is not as accurate as the two local optimization methods, Mean Shift and Trust Region. We believe this is partly due to the fact that basic CONDENSATION does not provide intra-frame refinement, and that time constraints necessitate the use of a quickly computable particle evaluation function. However, the strength of the CONDENSATION approach lies in its robustness against local optima: it is capable of reacquiring a lost (or nearly lost) target, which shows in the flatness of the error curves towards the high end.

Figure 4 shows a direct comparison between a locally optimizing structural tracker (Hager) and the globally optimizing histogram based CONDENSATION tracker. It is clearly visible that the Hager tracker provides more accurate results, but cannot reacquire a lost target. The CONDENSATION tracker, on the other hand, can continue to track the person after it reappears.

The Mean Shift and Trust Region trackers perform equally well and provide the overall best tracking when scaling is not estimated. When scaling is introduced, how-

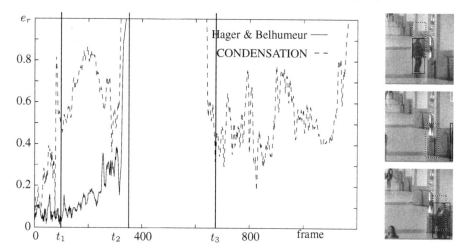

Fig. 4. Comparison of the Hager and CONDENSATION trackers using the e_r error measure (cf. Sec. 3). The black rectangle shows the ground truth. The white rectangle is from the Hager tracker, the dashed rectangle from the CONDENSATION tracker. The top, middle and bottom images are from frames t_1, t_2, and t_3 respectively. The tracked person (almost) leaves the camera's field of view in the middle image, and returns near the left image. The Hager tracker is more accurate, but loses the person irretrievably, while the CONDENSATION tracker is able to reacquire the person.

ever, the Mean Shift algorithm performs noticably better than the Trust Region approach. This is especially visible when comparing the region error e_r (figure 3, bottom right), where the error in the scaling component plays an important role.

Another very interesting thing to note is that tracking translation and scaling, as opposed to tracking translation only, generally did *not* improve the results on these sequences. In fact, the performance of all trackers deteriorated, even when measuring the fraction of region non-overlap (where any changes in target scale will automatically penalize trackers which do not estimate scaling).

For the structure-based trackers, Hager and Hyperplane, the changing appearance of the tracked persons is a strong handicap. The extra degree of freedom opens up more chances to diverge towards local optima, which causes the target to be lost sooner.

The trackers using histogram features, on the other hand, suffer from the fact that the features themselves are typically rather invariant under scaling. Once the scale, and therefore the size of the region, is wrong, small translations of the target can go completely unnoticed.

5   Conclusion

In this paper, we presented a comparative evaluation of five state of the art algorithms for data-driven object tracking, namely Hager's region tracking technique [1], Jurie's Hyperplane approach [2], the probabilistic color histogram tracker by Perez [5], Comaniciu's Mean Shift tracking approach [3], and the Trust Region method introduced by Chen [11]. All of those trackers have the ability to estimate the position and scale of an object in the image in real-time. For the comparison, the CAVIAR video database, which includes ground-truth data, has been employed. The results of our experiments shows that, in cases of strong appearance change, the region based methods of [2,1] tend to lose the object more often than the histogram based methods. On the other side, if the appearance change is weak, the region based methods surpass the other approaches in tracking accuracy. Comparing the histogram based methods among each other, the Mean Shift approach [3] leads to the best results. The experiments also show that the probabilistic color histogram tracker [5] is not quite as accurate as the other techniques, but is more robust in case of occlusions and appearance changes.

References

1. Hager, G., Belhumeur, P.: Efficient region tracking with parametric models of geometry and illumination. IEEE Transactions on Pattern Analysis and Machine Intelligence **20** (1998) 1025–1039
2. Jurie, F., Dhome, M.: Hyperplane approach for template matching. IEEE Transactions on Pattern Analysis and Machine Intelligence **24** (2002) 996–1000
3. Comaniciu, D., Meer, P., Ramesh, V.: Kernel-Based Object Tracking. IEEE Transactions on Pattern Analysis and Machine Intelligence **25** (2004) 564–575
4. Liu, T.L., Chen, H.T.: Real-Time Tracking Using Trust-Region Methods. IEEE Transactions on Pattern Analysis and Machine Intelligence **26** (2004) 397–402
5. Perez, P., Hue, C., Vermaak, J., Gangnet, M.: Color-Based Probabilistic Tracking. In: 7th European Conference on Computer Vision. Volume 1. (2002) 661–675
6. CAVIAR: EU funded project, IST 2001 37540,
   URL: http://homepages.inf.ed.ac.uk/rbf/CAVIAR/ (2004)
7. Comaniciu, D.: Bayesian Kernel Tracking. In: Annual Conference of the German Society for Pattern Recognition. (2002) 438–445
8. Cheng, Y.: Mean Shift, Mode Seeking, and Clustering. IEEE Transactions on Pattern Analysis and Machine Intelligence **17** (1995) 790–799
9. Conn, A.R., Gould, N.I.M., Toint, P.L.: Trust-Region Methods. SIAM (2000)
10. Isard, M., Blake, A.: Condensation – Conditional Density Propagation for Visual Tracking. International Journal of Computer Vision **29** (1998) 5–28
11. Chen, H.T., Liu, T.L.: Trust-Region Methods for Real-Time Tracking. In: 8th IEEE International Conference on Computer Vision. Volume 2. (2001) 717–722

Bayesian Method for Motion Segmentation and Tracking in Compressed Videos

Siripong Treetasanatavorn[1], Uwe Rauschenbach[2], Jörg Heuer[2], and André Kaup[1]

[1] University of Erlangen-Nuremberg, Chair of Multimedia Communications and
Signal Processing, Cauerstraße 7, D-91058 Erlangen, Germany
`siripongtr@ieee.org, kaup@LNT.de;`
[2] Siemens AG, CT IC 2, Otto-Hahn-Ring 6, D-81739 Munich, Germany
`{uwe.rauschenbach, joerg.heuer}@siemens.com`

Abstract. This contribution presents a statistical method for segmentation and tracking of moving regions from the compressed videos. This technique is particularly efficient to analyse and track motion segments from the compression-oriented motion fields by using the Bayesian estimation framework. For each motion field, the algorithm initialises a partition that is subject to comparisons and associations with its tracking counterpart. Due to potential hypothesis incompatibility, the algorithm applies a conflict resolution technique to ensure that the partition inherits relevant characteristics from both hypotheses as far as possible. Each tracked region is further classified as a background or a foreground object based on an approximation of the logical mass, momentum, and impulse. The experiment has demonstrated promising results based on standard test sequences.

1 Introduction

Video analysis for meaningful moving clusters or regions is an important process in numerous scenarios addressing visual motion content. The significance of such cues was indicated by recent investigations [1,2] that humans tend to perceive visual motion in terms of syntactic and semantic objects. Based on this motivation, this paper proposes a statistical method to analyse and track motion segments that correspond to the background or the foreground objects. The target application is in a heterogeneous communication scenario, e.g. video messaging [3], where the future provider requires intelligent video adaptation to scale with an increasing number of terminal classes, configurations, and usage contexts given a limited resource. The success of this process, however, depends on the comprehensibility of the adapted presentations. This requirement can be fulfilled by pre-processing the adaptation with a video content analysis.

In this context, the paper addresses the problem in segmentation and tracking of moving regions. The novelties of this contribution lie in a statistical modelling and an algorithm for motion segmentation and tracking from the pre-encoded motion fields of the compressed videos. The prime challenge lies in difficulty to analyse meaningful motion semantics and the corresponding spatiotemporal video structure from the coded visual information only. This technique applies the Gibbs-Markov random field theory [4] and the Bayesian estimation framework [5] by extending the *stochastic motion*

W. Kropatsch, R. Sablatnig, and A. Hanbury (Eds.): DAGM 2005, LNCS 3663, pp. 277–284, 2005.

coherency model [6]. The paper focusses on the case that there exist two initial partition hypotheses, i.e., an initial local partition versus a projection-based tracking predictor. As such, the final result shall inherit relevant characteristics from both hypotheses through the guide of the proposed model. For each observed motion field, the algorithm estimates a reliability measure array using an initial assessment of the local motion coherency [7]. The two competing partition hypotheses are approximated through the use of the individual field optimisation [6] and the prediction using results from the preceding fields [7]. The algorithm detects potential conflicts from the two configuration sets and resolves them by applying a model-based reconciliation technique. In this process, the algorithm evaluates the Bayesian analysis model to ensure that the partition is characterised by the designed likelihood, the local/region coherency [6], and the contour smoothness [8]. Upon this result, the method classifies the detected spatiotemporal regions in terms of the background or the foreground objects.

Related techniques were present in the literature. A compressed-video segmentation typically requires a pre-processing step to analyse the confidence indicators [9], where a number of techniques applies a statistical analysis, e.g. Bayes estimation [8,10], to address uncertainty of the acquired video data. On the tracking part, most techniques apply contour [11] or edge [12] features to correspond visual information between frames. A hybrid approach applying the human computer interaction method has been demonstrated as a promising technique to leverage high-level semantic information [13].

The paper is organised as follows. Sect. 2 discusses the Bayesian analysis model that is characterised by the likelihood, the regularisation density, and the *a priori* region border density. Sect. 3 presents the algorithm for moving-region segmentation, tracking, and classification. Sect. 4 reports the experimental results. Sect. 5 concludes the paper.

2   Bayesian Analysis Model

The segmentation and tracking are considered in this paper as an estimation problem. It employs the *maximum a posteriori* probability (MAP) estimation technique and the Gibbs-Markov random field theory [4]. For an observed (known) motion field $\mathcal{V}$, the analysis model characterises the solicited partition $\mathcal{Q}$ in terms of a probability density $\Pr(\mathcal{Q}, \mathcal{Q}', \mathcal{V})$, provided an initial partition $\mathcal{Q}$ and its predictor $\mathcal{Q}'$ that is derived from a partition projection scheme [7]. Using the Bayes rule $\Pr(\mathcal{Q}, \mathcal{Q}', \mathcal{V})$ can be written as:

$$\Pr(\mathcal{Q}, \mathcal{Q}', \mathcal{V}) \propto \Pr(\mathcal{Q}'|\mathcal{V}, \mathcal{Q}) \cdot \Pr(\mathcal{V}|\mathcal{Q}) \cdot \Pr(\mathcal{Q}), \qquad (1)$$

which specifies the constituents of this model. The first multiplicand denotes the likelihood of the predicted partition $\mathcal{Q}'$ given the motion field $\mathcal{V}$ and the initial configuration of partition $\mathcal{Q}$ (cf. Sect. 2.1). The second multiplicand regularises the likelihood using the stochastic motion coherency analysis (cf. Sect. 2.2). The last term evaluates the *a priori* probability density of the partition (cf. Sect. 2.3).

2.1   The Congruity-Based Momentum Likelihood

Given a motion field $\mathcal{V}$, the likelihood $\Pr(\mathcal{Q}'|\mathcal{V}, \mathcal{Q})$ is characterised by the momentum magnitude of the congruity analysis from a local partition $\mathcal{Q}$ [6] against an initial tracking result or a predictor $\mathcal{Q}'$. Let partition $\mathcal{Q}$ consist of μ regions Θ_r, $r = 1, \ldots, \mu$ that is defined in the universe U of the 2-D motion vector coordinates, $\mathbf{x} = [x \quad y]^T \in U$. Since not every coded motion block can be analysed, the universe U contains only co-ordinates of valid motion vectors (excluding intracoded blocks). Likewise, the predictor Q' is represented by Θ'_s, $s = 1, \ldots, \mu'$. The congruity analysis requires a correspondence set between the two partitions. A region on the partition Q is associated with at most only one region on the partition Q', and vice versa. The r-th region on the partition Q is corresponded to a region counterpart $\Gamma(r)$ on the predictor Q' using

$$\Gamma(r) = \arg\max_s \left[\sum_{\mathbf{x} \in \Omega(r,s)} |w(\mathbf{x}) \cdot \mathbf{v}(\mathbf{x})| \right], \tag{2}$$

with $\Omega(r, s)$ being an intersection test set $\Omega(r, s) = \Theta_r \cap \Theta'_s$, $w(\mathbf{x})$ a reliability measure denoting a logical *mass*, and $\mathbf{v}(\mathbf{x})$ an encoded motion vector representing a logical *velocity*. The function $w(\mathbf{x})$ is estimated by the local motion coherency [7], $w(\mathbf{x}) = \exp[-G_\mu \cdot \Delta_\alpha(\mathbf{x}, \mu)] / Z_\alpha$. For the local statistical justification, an observed local incoherence function $\Delta_\alpha(\mathbf{x}, \mu)$ (cf. [6]) is scaled by G_μ, the reciprocal of the normalised standard deviation [7]. The parameter Z_α is a constant ensuring that each estimate lies between 0 and 1. Upon this definition, an *associated* membership set Π_r between the r-th region on Q and the $\Gamma(r)$-th region on Q' can be derived by using (2); as a consequence, we also obtain the incongruity set Υ:

$$\Pi_r = \Theta_r \cap \Theta'_{\Gamma(r)}; \quad \Upsilon = U - \bigcup_{r=1}^{\mu} \Pi_r. \tag{3}$$

For each region r on the partition Q, set Π_r is defined by an intersection of Θ_r and Θ'_s, with $s = \Gamma(r)$. The set Υ is computed based on the constellation of Π_r. As such, the congruity-based momentum likelihood can be evaluated in the detected set Υ by:

$$\Pr(Q'|V, Q) = \frac{1}{Z_\Upsilon} \exp\left[-\mathcal{E} \cdot \sum_{\mathbf{x} \in \Upsilon} |w(\mathbf{x}) \cdot \mathbf{v}(\mathbf{x})|\right], \tag{4}$$

with $\mathcal{E}$ being a configurable parameter and Z_Υ a normalisation constant. In order to justify the magnitude of the logical *momentum* (see more in Sect. 3), $\mathcal{E}$ is chosen at the reciprocal of the entire momentum in the universe U, i.e., $(\sum_{\mathbf{x} \in U} |w(\mathbf{x}) \cdot \mathbf{v}(\mathbf{x})|)^{-1}$.

Fig. 1 demonstrates this analysis using frame 15 of the sequence *Foreman*. A unique color was painted at each region. The algorithm generated a predictor hypothesis (Q', Fig. 1(b)) based on the segmentation result from frame 12 (Fig. 1(a)). Applying the reliability array ($w(\mathbf{x})$, Fig. 1(c)), the second hypothesis (Q, Fig. 1(d)) can be optimised from the current motion field in frame 15. Upon the hypothesis association by (2) and (3), the incongruity set Υ was detected around the face borders as marked in Fig. 1(e) (this subfigure was enlarged) with the red color. This is the basis for the likelihood of this model. Further experimental results can be found in Sect. 4.

2.2 The Likelihood Regularisation: Stochastic Motion Coherency

The likelihood is regularised by the *a posteriori* probability $\Pr(V|Q)$ of the partition Q. The method chooses the stochastic motion coherency analysis [6] to model this

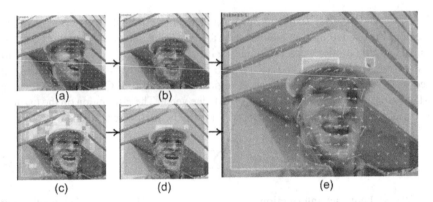

(a)   (b)   (c)   (d)   (e)

Fig. 1. Illustrating an experimental result from sequence *Foreman* at frame 15

observation. Let us assume that partition $\mathcal{Q}$ consists of λ regions Ψ_t, $t = 1, \ldots, \lambda$. The probability $\Pr(\mathcal{V}|\mathcal{Q})$ is proportional to the multiplication of the local/region coherency:

$$
\Pr(\mathcal{V}|\mathcal{Q}) \propto \underbrace{\exp\left[-\sum_{t=1}^{\lambda}\left\{G_t \cdot \sum_{\mathbf{x}\in\Psi_t} \Delta_\alpha(\mathbf{x}, t)\right\}\right]}_{Local\ Motion\ Coherency} \cdot \underbrace{\exp\left[-\sum_{t=1}^{\lambda}\left\{H_t \cdot \sum_{\mathbf{x}\in\Psi_t} \Delta_\beta(\mathbf{x}, t)\right\}\right]}_{Region\ Motion\ Coherency} \quad (5)
$$

This function evaluates the two-level Gibbs distribution-based motion coherency at each vector coordinate $\mathbf{x}$ in the assigned t-th region. At the neighbourhood level, the local motion smoothness is examined through the observation of the local incoherence $\Delta_\alpha(\mathbf{x}, t)$ at the eight nearest neighbours. At the region level, the region model fit is investigated by the region incoherence $\Delta_\beta(\mathbf{x}, t)$ using the t-th region motion model estimate. This latter criterion ensures that each motion vector in the assigned region is well described by the region model. This is an important measure to allow clustering of distant motion vectors, especially when the object motion is undergone by zoom and rotation significantly. Further details can be found in Ref. 6,7.

2.3   The A-Priori Density of Region Boundary

The last term in (1) is the *a priori* density of the region shapes on the partition $\mathcal{Q}$. The model chooses the density that favours smooth boundaries akin to the property of most physical regions [4,8]. The *a priori* density is modelled by:

$$
\Pr(\mathcal{Q}) = \frac{1}{Z_\chi} \exp\left[-\mathcal{H}(\mathcal{Q})\right] = \frac{1}{Z_\chi} \exp\left[-\mathcal{N}_B B - \mathcal{N}_C C\right], \quad (6)
$$

with $\mathcal{H}(\mathcal{Q})$ being the energy of the partition state. This energy function linearly scales with two counts of the motion vector pairs at region borders (i.e., of different region labels). The model specifies independent weights B and C to the counts $\mathcal{N}_B$ and $\mathcal{N}_C$ for the horizontal or vertical border pairs and for the diagonal ones, respectively.

3   Algorithm for Segmentation, Tracking, and Classification

The method assesses the reliability extent of each motion vector (cf. Sect. 2.1) and ensures that only reliable members are utilised in the process. For each observed motion field, the algorithm initialises two competing partition hypotheses referred to as an initial partition Q and its predictor Q' in Sect. 2.1. The segment optimisation of the first frame is based on the individual field only [6]. For the subsequent frames, the algorithm additionally initialises the second hypothesis using the partition projection and relaxation [7]. This technique predicts the partition Q' based on the partition results from the preceding frames. These two hypotheses are associated using (2) and (3).

As incongruities or conflicts may arise from the hypothesis association, the optimisation process requires a conflict detection and resolution technique. To minimise affects of the non-representative members in the region model estimation, the algorithm assigns a new region to every non-empty incongruity fraction $\Upsilon_{r,s}$. It identifies $\Upsilon_{r,s}$ by intersecting the *non-associated* set $\Theta_r - \Pi_r$, $r = 1, \ldots, \mu$ with the *non-used* predicted set Θ'_s, $s = 1, \ldots, \mu', s \neq \Gamma(r)$, i.e. $\Upsilon_{r,s} = (\Theta_r - \Pi_r) \cap \Theta'_s$. Using this technique, the partition shall consist of λ non-overlapped regions Ψ_t, $t = 1, \ldots, \lambda$. This set is an aggregation of the associated membership set Π_r, $r = 1, \ldots, \mu$ and the $\lambda - \mu$ newly-defined fractions $\Upsilon_{r,s}$, corresponding to the result of the initial reconciliation.

Now, the algorithm must ensure that the associated partition has the most optimal configuration specified by the Bayesian analysis model. For this reason, the probability $\Pr(Q, Q', V)$ is evaluated and improved by adjusting the configuration of Q. The evaluation is quantified by taking the negative logarithm to (1). Through the use of (4), (5), and (6), this operation leads to the MAP cost estimate:

$$f(Q, Q', V) = \mathcal{E} \cdot \underbrace{\sum_{\mathbf{x} \in \Upsilon} |w(\mathbf{x}) \cdot \mathbf{v}(\mathbf{x})|}_{Hypothesis\ Incongruity} + \sum_{t=1}^{\lambda} \Bigg[G_t \cdot \underbrace{\sum_{\mathbf{x} \in \Psi_t} \Delta_\alpha(\mathbf{x}, t)}_{Local\ Heterogeneity}$$

$$+ \ H_t \cdot \underbrace{\sum_{\mathbf{x} \in \Psi_t} \Delta_\beta(\mathbf{x}, t)}_{Region\ Heterogeneity} \Bigg] + \underbrace{\mathcal{N}_B B + \mathcal{N}_C C}_{Contour\ Roughness} + L. \tag{7}$$

The desired partition Q that maximises $\Pr(Q, Q', V)$ shall minimise this cost function. L corresponds to the logarithm of the normalisation constants specified in the model. The algorithm attempts to relax region borders using a label substitution technique. For every block at the region borders (i.e., at least one neighbour has a different label) it finds a set of potential substitutions that reduce the MAP cost based on labels of the eight nearest neighbours. Only the configuration that leads to the highest cost reduction shall take place. This scheme proceeds in multiple raster-scan iterations until no cost improvement is found. In the second step, the algorithm attempts to merge regions in a pairwise manner through the guide of the MAP cost change. In each iteration, only the merge configuration that reduces MAP cost function the most shall take place. This process repeats until the best merge configuration no longer decreases the MAP cost.

Table 1. Results of the tracked region classification from sequences *Foreman* and *Table Tennis* in the first 15 frames (Lifespan is in frame, Mass in frame·MB, and Impulse Magnitude in pel·MB)

Sequence	Region	Lifespan	Logical Mass	Logical Impulse Magnitude	Classification
Foreman	0	15	**2519.40**	1457.94	Background
	1	15	392.39	**1277.77**	Significant Object
Table Tennis	0	15	**3365.45**	109.14	Background
	1	15	396.27	**590.27**	Significant Object

A series of tracked partitions forms a set of spatiotemporal regions. The algorithm classifies them into background or foregrounds. Given that the reliability measure represents the logical *mass* at the corresponding grid of the field lattice, a total spatiotemporal mass $\mathcal{M}_t$ of the t-th tracked region is calculated by accumulating the reliability measures in the set $\Psi(t)$ of the t-th region throughout its lifespan $[\tau_0(t), \tau_\infty(t)]$:

$$
\mathcal{M}_t = \int_{\tau_0(t)}^{\tau_\infty(t)} \sum_{\mathbf{x} \in \Psi(t)} w(\mathbf{x}) \, d\tau.
\tag{8}
$$

The tracked region having the largest mass $\mathcal{M}_t$ shall be classified as the background. This rule indicates that the background is the *largest reliable region* of the entire sequence. At each t-th tracked region, we derive the momentum magnitude by summing up the mass-motion amount, i.e., $\mathcal{P}_t = \sum_{\mathbf{x} \in \Psi(t)} |w(\mathbf{x}) \cdot \mathbf{v}(\mathbf{x})|$, and the force magnitude by averaging the momentum magnitude in the time gap towards the reference frame, i.e., $\mathcal{F}_t = \mathcal{P}_t / \Delta\tau$. An integration of this force magnitude throughout a region lifespan results in the *logical impulse magnitude* exerted by the movement of this region:

$$
\mathcal{I}_t = \int_{\tau_0(t)}^{\tau_\infty(t)} \mathcal{F}_t \, d\tau = \int_{\tau_0(t)}^{\tau_\infty(t)} \frac{\sum_{\mathbf{x} \in \Psi(t)} |w(\mathbf{x}) \cdot \mathbf{v}(\mathbf{x})|}{\Delta\tau} \, d\tau.
\tag{9}
$$

The significance from each foreground region is sorted based on the impulse magnitude estimation. The tracked region that produces the highest impulse magnitude shall be classified as the significant foreground object. In the simulation, the algorithm chooses the Simpson's numerical integration [14], as this estimation bounds the integration error up to the fourth derivative, while requiring a relatively low computational effort.

4   Results

Sequences *Foreman* and *Table Tennis* in CIF format were experimented. The motion fields were estimated using the 16-pixel search range and the 512-kbps rate control (TM5 algorithm) based on an MPEG-4 encoder [15]. Fig. 2 and 3 depict the results from both sequences at frames 6, 9, 12, and 15 (cf. Fig. 2,3(a), left to right). The algorithm segmented and tracked motion-semantic regions as depicted in Fig. 2,3(b). The foreman face in Fig. 2(c) as well as the arm and the hand in Fig. 3(b) were well extracted. The emphasis is on the color preservation on these tracked regions at a sequence level.

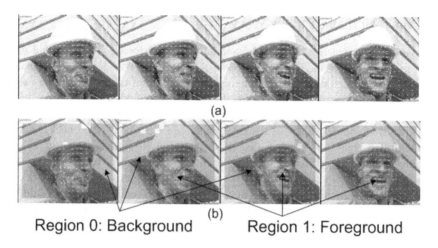

Fig. 2. Results from sequence *Foreman*

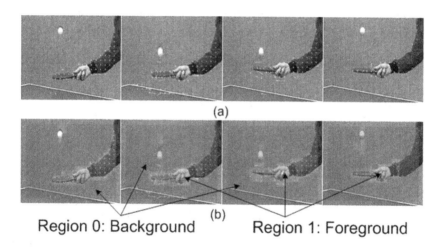

Fig. 3. Results from sequence *Table Tennis*

In the next step, these tracked regions were classified to either background or foregrounds based on the logical mass and impulse magnitude estimates. Table 1 and Fig. 2, 3(b) show that in each sequence region with the largest mass (region 0 in both cases) was attributed to the background. Based on an order of the impulse magnitude estimates, the significant object was chosen at region 1 in the sequence *Foreman*. This region represents most parts of the foreman face (cf. Fig. 2(b)). Since region 0 has already been classified as the background, it was not considered in the foreground classification. For the second example in Fig. 3(b), the arm and the hand were altogether identified as a representative foreground object as anticipated. On a 500-MHz machine this non-optimised simulation required 10.47 and 9.02 second-per-frame to analyse the sequences *Foreman* and *Table Tennis*, respectively.

5   Conclusion and Future Work

This paper presents a Bayesian model and an algorithm for segmentation and tracking of motion fields in the compressed video sequences. It was demonstrated that the motion-semantic regions can be efficiently partitioned and tracked from the motion field sequences by using the proposed technique. The method novelties lie in the hypothesis association and the conflict resolution based on the tracking predictor and the local analysis hypotheses. These tracking results are classified as the background or the foreground objects by bearing analogy of the reliability measure and the velocity magnitude to the logical mass and momentum concepts, respectively. Upon standard test sequences, the experiment has demonstrated promising results. Future work shall improve shapes, structures, and precision of the detected region contours. Additional features such as inter- and intra-coded transform coefficients should be considered.

Acknowledgments

The first author gratefully acknowledges Siemens *Youth and Knowledge* Fellowship Grant. He also wishes to thank Klaus Illgner for many fruitful discussions, as well as Jens Bialkowski and Marcus Barkowsky for assistance in result visualisation.

References

1. Wesenick, M.B.: Limitations of Human Visual Working Memory. PhD thesis, Ludwig-Maximilians-Universität München (2004)
2. Jaimes, A.: Conceptual Structures and Computational Methods for Indexing and Organization of Visual Information. PhD thesis, Columbia University (2003)
3. Kaup, A., Treetasanatavorn, S., Rauschenbach, U., Heuer, J.: Video analysis for universal multimedia messaging. In: Proc. IEEE SSIAI. (Apr. 2002) 211–215
4. Li, S.: Markov Random Field Modeling in Image Analysis. Springer-Verlag, Tokyo (2001)
5. Mayntz, C., Aach, T.: Nichtlineare Bayes-Restauration mittels eines verallgemeinerten Gauß-Markov-Modells. In: Proc. DAGM Mustererkennung. (Sept. 1999) 111–119
6. Treetasanatavorn, S., et al.: Stochastic motion coherency analysis for motion vector field segmentation on compressed video sequences. In: Proc. WIAMIS. (Apr. 2005)
7. Treetasanatavorn, S., et al.: Model based segmentation of motion fields in compressed video sequences using partition projection and relaxation. In: Proc. VCIP. (Jul. 2005) to appear.
8. Aach, T., Kaup, A.: Bayesian algorithms for adaptive change detection in image sequences using Markov random fields. Sig. Proc.: Image Communication 7 (Aug. 1995) 148–160
9. Wang, R., Zhang, H.J., Zhang, Y.Q.: A confidence measure based moving object extraction system built for compressed domain. In: Proc. IEEE ISCAS. Volume V. (May 2000) 21–24
10. Chang, M.M., Tekalp, A.M., Sezan, M.I.: Simultaneous motion estimation and segmentation. IEEE Transactions on Image Processing 6 (Sept. 1997) 1326–1333
11. Kass, M., Witkin, A., Terzopoulos, D.: Snakes: Active contour models. International Journal of Computer Vision 1 (Jan. 1988) 321–331
12. Drummond, T., Cipolla, R.: Real-time visual tracking of complex structures. IEEE Transactions on Pattern Analysis and Machine Intelligence 24 (July 2002) 932–946
13. Gu, C., Lee, M.C.: Semiautomatic segmentation and tracking of semantic video objects. IEEE Transactions on Circuits and Systems for Video Technology 8 (Sept. 1998) 572–584
14. Kreyszig, E.: Advanced Engineering Mathematics. 6 edn. John Wiley & Sons (1988)
15. Microsoft: (ISO/IEC 14496 Video Reference Software) Microsoft-FDAM1-2.3-001213.

Nonlinear Body Pose Estimation
from Depth Images

Daniel Grest, Jan Woetzel, and Reinhard Koch

Christian-Albrechts-University Kiel,
Multimedia Information Processing, Germany
{grest, jw, rk}@mip.informatik.uni-kiel.de

Abstract. This paper focuses on real-time markerless motion capture. The body pose of a person is estimated from depth images using an Iterative Closest Point algorithm. We present a very efficient approach, that estimates up to 28 degrees of freedom from 1000 data points with 4Hz. This is achieved by nonlinear optimization techniques using an analytically derived Jacobian and highly optimized correspondence search.

1 Introduction

Motion capture and body pose estimation are very important tasks in many applications. Motion capture products used in the film industry or for computer games are usually marker based to achieve high quality and fast processing.

A lot of research is devoted to make markerless motion capture applicable. There are very different approaches using very different kind of information, e.g. tracking features, contour information, color tracking, or depth data. An overview of markerless motion capture systems and algorithms is given in [7].

In some applications highly accurate motion data is not needed every frame. In Human-Computer-Interaction applications the focus is usually more on real-time evaluation and robustness with respect to lighting, background etc. Therefore this paper focuses on markerless motion capture that estimates body pose in at least near to real-time.

We estimate human motion from depth data calculated from stereo images. The proposed approach uses an estimation method similar to Rosenhahn [9] and Malik & Bregler [2]. Our approach however uses standard non-linear optimization methods that involves an analytically derived Jacobian of the optimization function. Therefore it can be applied to methods like gradient descent, Quasi-Newton, *Levenberg-Marquardt (LM)* etc. Authors of recent work, which is very similar to our, seem not to be aware of this possibility. Their work might benefit from the derivations and results presented here.

Recent work most similar to this one are, as far as we know, that of D. Demirdjian [4] and M. Bray [1]. Both estimate the body pose from depth data and have an Iterative Closest Point (ICP) approach to find necessary correspondences. Other similar work on body pose estimation using depth data can also be found in [8,6], which is however not fast enough for real-time purposes.

The approach of Demirdjian is fast enough to fulfill real-time requirements as poses are estimated with 10Hz. An ICP estimation is done for each body segment

W. Kropatsch, R. Sablatnig, and A. Hanbury (Eds.): DAGM 2005, LNCS 3663, pp. 285–292, 2005.

separately. Later, the underlying movement constraints (segments are connected by joints) are applied by projecting the evaluated transformations onto the set of possible articulated transformations. As the authors state themselves in [4] '*constraint projection methods may give an sub-optimal solution, but are easier to implement than direct approaches*'. The direct approach was implemented in our work and showed to be fast enough for real-time requirements in spite of its complexity.

In [1] the pose of a human hand is estimated from depth data obtained by a structured light sensor. Movement of points is described as a concatenation of rigid body motions. However the derivative is calculated by numerical methods, which takes a significant amount of time. Different nonlinear optimization methods are applied to the pose estimation problem and a extended gradient descent method, the stochastic meta descent, is proposed to give the best results. Estimation takes 4 seconds per frame from 45 data points.

Our approach uses an analytically derived Jacobian for the optimization, which decreases the computation time significantly. Further optimizations for efficient correspondence calculations enable us to estimate body pose from 1000 data points in 250ms on a Pentium4 3Ghz.

2   Body Model

Depending on the kind of work different body models are used for the estimation process. The models range from simple stick figures [2] over models consisting of scalable spheres (meta-balls) [8] to linear blend skinned models [1]. We use models consisting of rigid, fixed meshes in each body segment, that try to make a balance between fast computation, which requires low resolution models with few points, and accurate modeling of the person. The movement capabilities are the same as defined in the MPEG4 standard. An example for the movement capabilities of the arm are shown in figure (1).

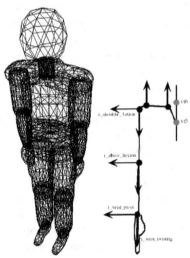

The body model is fitted to the current observed person offline by scaling each segment separately in size. To fit the template model a contour based monocular algorithm

Fig. 1. The body model (left) and the joints of the arm (right)

is used. The person is captured in specific predefined poses in front of a known static background and the scale values for each body segment are evaluated by hierarchical nonlinear optimization.

3   Body Pose Estimation

We will show in this section how nonlinear optimization methods can be applied to the problem of body pose estimation. This approach is used within a variety of applications, e.g. [1,8], but usually relies on numerical derivatives, which are inaccurate and time consuming to compute.

3.1 Rigid Body Motion as Rotation Around Arbitrary Axis

A rigid body motion (RBM) in $\mathbb{R}^3$ may be expressed as a rotation around an arbitrary axis plus a translation along that axis. There are different formulations for rigid body motions, e.g. twists [2], which use a exponential term e^{ψ} or rotors [9], which may be seen as an extension of quaternions. Important here is not a complete RBM, but a rotation around an arbirtrary axis, which is given in standard vector notation of the Euclidean space as follows.

Consider the normal vector $\boldsymbol{w}$, which describes the direction of the axis, and the point $\boldsymbol{q}$ on the axis, which has the shortest distance to the origin, i.e. $\boldsymbol{q}$ lies on the axis and $\boldsymbol{q}^T\boldsymbol{w} = 0$, refer to figure (2). The rotation of a point $\boldsymbol{x}$ around that axis may then be written as

$$
\begin{aligned}
\boldsymbol{y} &= \boldsymbol{x} + \sin\theta(\boldsymbol{w} \times (\boldsymbol{x} - \boldsymbol{q})) + (1 - \cos\theta)(\boldsymbol{q} - \boldsymbol{x}^p) \\
&= \boldsymbol{x} + \sin\theta(\boldsymbol{w} \times (\boldsymbol{x} - \boldsymbol{q})) + (\boldsymbol{q} - \boldsymbol{x}^p) - \cos\theta(\boldsymbol{q} - \boldsymbol{x}^p) \qquad (1) \\
&\equiv R_{\boldsymbol{w},\boldsymbol{q}}(\theta) \circ \boldsymbol{x}
\end{aligned}
$$

where $\boldsymbol{x}^p = \boldsymbol{x} - (\boldsymbol{x}^T\boldsymbol{w})\boldsymbol{w}$ is the projection of $\boldsymbol{x}$ onto the plane through the origin with normal $\boldsymbol{w}$. Note that $\boldsymbol{q}$ is also on that plane. This expression is very useful as the derivative $R'_{\boldsymbol{w},\boldsymbol{q}}(\theta) = \frac{\partial R_{\boldsymbol{w},\boldsymbol{q}}(\theta)}{\partial\theta}$ is easy to calculate:

$$
R'_{\boldsymbol{w},\boldsymbol{q}}(\theta) = \cos\theta(\boldsymbol{w} \times (\boldsymbol{x} - \boldsymbol{q})) + \sin\theta(\boldsymbol{q} - \boldsymbol{x}^p) \qquad (2)
$$

3.2 Concatenation of Rotations

The MPEG4 body model is a mixture of articulated objects. The movement of a point, e.g. on the hand, may therefore be expressed as a concatenation of rotations. As the rotation axis are known, e.g. the flexion of the elbow, the rotation has only one DOF, the angle around that axis. In addition to the joint angles there are 6 DOF for the position and orientation of the object within the global world coordinate frame. For an articulated object with $p - 6$ joints the transformation may be written as:

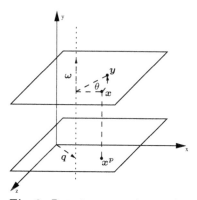

Fig. 2. Rotation around an arbitrary axis in space

$$
f(\boldsymbol{\theta}, \boldsymbol{x}) = (\theta_1, \theta_2, \theta_3)^T + R_x(\theta_4) \circ R_y(\theta_5) \circ R_z(\theta_6) \circ R_{\boldsymbol{w},\boldsymbol{q}}(\theta_7) \circ \cdots \circ R_{\boldsymbol{w},\boldsymbol{q}}(\theta_p) \circ \boldsymbol{x}
$$
$$(3)$$

where $(\theta_1, \theta_2, \theta_3)^T$ is the global translation, R_x is the rotation around the global x-axis etc. and $R_{\boldsymbol{w},\boldsymbol{q}}(\theta_i), i \in 7..p$ denotes the rotation around the known axis $(\boldsymbol{w}_i, \boldsymbol{q}_i)$ with angle θ_i.

Note that 'o' does here not denote multiplication but concatenation of rotations around arbitrary axis' in space, which must evaluated by recursive insertion, as we use the description of equations (1) and (2). Equation (3) gives the position of a point x on a specific segment of the body (e.g. the foot), with respect to joint angles θ and an initial body pose.

The first derivatives of $f(\theta, x)$ with respect to θ give the Jacobian matrix, which is $J_{ki} = \frac{\partial f_k}{\partial \theta_i}$. Of special interest is here the derivative at some specific position θ^t, which reads $J_{ki}^t = \frac{\partial f_k}{\partial \theta_i}\big|_{\theta^t}$.

The Jacobi matrix for the movement of the point x in a kinematic chain is

$$J^t = \begin{bmatrix} 1 & 0 & 0 & & & & & & \\ 0 & 1 & 0 & \frac{\partial f}{\partial \theta_4} & \frac{\partial f}{\partial \theta_5} & \frac{\partial f}{\partial \theta_6} & \frac{\partial f}{\partial \theta_7} & \cdots & \frac{\partial f}{\partial \theta_p} \\ 0 & 0 & 1 & & & & & & \end{bmatrix} \tag{4}$$

with

$$\frac{\partial f}{\partial \theta_6} = R_x(\theta_4^t) \circ R_y(\theta_5^t) \circ R_z'(\theta_6^t) \circ (R_{\omega,q}(\theta_7^t) \circ \cdots \circ R_{\omega,q}(\theta_p^t) x)$$

$$\frac{\partial f}{\partial \theta_i} = R_x(\theta_4^t) \circ \cdots \circ (R_{\omega,q}(\theta_{i-1}^t) \circ R_{\omega_i,q}'(\theta_i^t) \circ R_{\omega,q}(\theta_{i+1}^t) \circ \cdots \circ R_{\omega,q}(\theta_p^t) x \tag{5}$$

where x corresponds to the initial pose with $\theta = 0$ and $\frac{\partial f}{\partial \theta_{4,5}}$ are similar to $\frac{\partial f}{\partial \theta_6}$.

The partial derivative $\frac{\partial f_k}{\partial \theta_i}$ gives the direction in which the point x will move, if θ_i is changed, which is the tangent vector on the circle, on which x moves around (ω_i, q_i).

3.3   Simplifying the Jacobian

There is a special case to be considered, if θ^t is zero. The partial derivative $\frac{\partial f}{\partial \theta_i}$ then simplifies to:

$$\frac{\partial f}{\partial \theta_i}\bigg|_0 = \frac{\partial R_{\omega,q}(\theta_i)}{\partial \theta_i}\bigg|_0 = \omega_i \times (x - q_i), \tag{6}$$

With this simplification the partial derivatives $\frac{\partial f}{\partial \theta_{4,5,6}}$ for the global rotation are exactly the same as a linearized rotation matrix. When used within Newton Iteration the above equation leads also to a similar, if not equal, linear equation system as for 3D-3D correspondences in Rosenhahn [9].

4   Nonlinear Optimization by Newton Iteration

Assume the intially known model points $X^0 = (x^0{}_1, x^0{}_2, ..., x^0{}_n)$ are observed at $Y = (y_1', y_2', ..., y_n')$. The task of pose estimation is to find the parameters θ that map X to Y, where each point is transformed by $f^\theta \equiv f(\theta, x)$. If the observed points Y are disturbed by noise, a best fit has to be found.

As this minimization problem for pose estimation involves concatenations of sin and cos, it is analytically hard to calculate. However an assumption can be made that simplifies the problem and makes it possible to evaluate θ by an iterative method. The assumption made for Newton Iteration is that the function f^θ is locally linear at some point θ^t.

The minimization problem now reads $min_\theta \ |Y - F(\theta)|_2$ with $F : \mathbb{R}^p \to \mathbb{R}^{3n}$ and $F(\theta) = \left(f^\theta(x_1^0), f^\theta(x_2^0), .., f^\theta(x_n^0) \right)^T$.

The locally linear assumption leads to:

$$F(\theta^t + \Delta\theta) \approx F(\theta^t) + \left. \frac{\partial F}{\partial \theta} \right|_{\theta^t} \cdot \Delta\theta \qquad (7)$$

The derivative $\left. \frac{\partial F}{\partial \theta} \right|_{\theta^t}$ of F at position θ^t is the Jacobi matrix from above, now for all points from the set X.

Let $\epsilon^t = Y - F(\theta^t)$ be the error at iteration step t. In each iteration $\Delta\theta$ is estimated by solving a linear minimization problem:

$$min_{\Delta\theta} \ |\epsilon^t - J\Delta\theta|_2 \qquad (8)$$

The solution is given by $\Delta\theta = J^+ \epsilon^t$, where $J^+ = (J^T \ J)^{-1} J^T$ is the Pseudo-inverse of J. This may also be solved efficiently by Gauss-Elimination using the linear equation system $(J^T \ J)\Delta\theta = J^T \epsilon^t$, which may be faster than building the inverse of $(J^T \ J)$.

As stated above the derivatives becomes much simpler if θ^t is zero. This can be achieved by estimating only the relative transforms in each iteration step of the Newton Iteration, which requires recalculation of the known parameters of $F(\theta)$. These are the known axes $\omega_1, .., \omega_p$ and their corresponding points $q_1, .., q_p$ in world coordinates. Additionally the new point set X^{t+1} must be evaluated from X^t with respect to the estimated values $\Delta\theta$.

5 ICP Approach

The optimization above assumes that correspondences between the observed points and the model points are known. As the observed points are calculated from depth maps, these correspondences are not known. Equal to [9,1,2,4] we take an Iterative Closest Point (ICP) approach. For each observed point the nearest point on the model is assumed to be the corresponding one. With these correspondences the body pose of the model is calculated. Those two steps are then repeated i times or until the change in the pose parameters is below a certain threshold. Similar to other works, we assume that the model of the observed person is given and that the initial position and initial pose in the first frame are approximately known. Also we assume that there is an upper bound on the displacement of each point on the known model from frame to frame. To fit the body model to the observed point set, a segmentation of the person from the background is necessary. In [1] this is done by using skin color. We assume here only that there are no scene objects (or only negligible parts) within a certain distance to the person by using reweighted least-squares for equation (8).

The calculation of correspondences involves several steps, which are optimized in the following ways.

1. The depth image is randomly subsampled and the 3D-points are calculated from the known focal length and principal point of the camera. To do this efficiently the camera coordinate system is assumed to be equal with the world coordinate system and the body model is positioned initially, such that it is close to the observed point set.

2. The visible points of the model are calculated by rendering each triangle of the body model in a different unique color. The RGB-color of each triangle is then used as an index to get the 3D-points of the triangle by a simple array subscript similar to [3]. The segment to which the model point belongs is also found by an array subscript. For efficient nearest neighbor search, the visible points are ordered into an associative array that uses a binary search tree, where the main order value is that coordinate of the model that has the largest extent, usually the height of the person.

3. Nearest neighbor search. For each observed point the associative array is searched for the point with the next height-value. As the height distance is a lower bound for the Euclidean distance, the search can be stopped, if the height distance is larger than the Euclidean distance to the next point.

6   Depth Estimation

Our motion estimation is based on dense depth information which could be estimated directly from correspondences between images. Traditionally, pair-wise rectified stereo images were analyzed exploiting geometrical constraints along the epipolar lines. More recently, generalized approaches were introduced that can handle multiple images and higher order constraints. See [10] for an overview. Achieving realtime performance on standard hardware has become reality with the availability of free programmable graphics hardware (GPU) and the additional benefit of keeping the CPU free for other tasks like our pose estimation [11]. The results presented here are calculated from depth images generated by a dynamic programming based disparity estimator with a pyramidal scheme for dense correspondence matching along the epipolar lines [5].

7   Results

We tested our implementation with depth images from a real sequence, where a person moved his arms at first in a waving manner, and later crossing his arms in front of his chest. The arms close to the body is a very difficult pose. All contour based approaches will fail here. In figure (3) three images from the sequence are shown. The top row shows the depth images with lighter values indicating closer points. The middle row shows the original images overlayed with the estimated model pose in grey. The bottom row shows the same model pose as seen from another position. The model's position is estimated below the real person throughout the sequence, because the model was fitted offline beforehand to the person showing a bare upper body. This shows the robustness of the estimation with respect to inaccurate model geometry. For this sequence 14 DOF were estimated: The global transform, the three shoulder angles and the elbow flexion. Important for the accuracy and speed are the number of iterations and the number of data points (the subsampling rate). The fastest result were achieved by taking approx. 800 data points and ca. 10 iterations per frame. Taking less iterations or data points can lead to invalid tracking for large motions between frames. The processing of one frame took 200ms on a

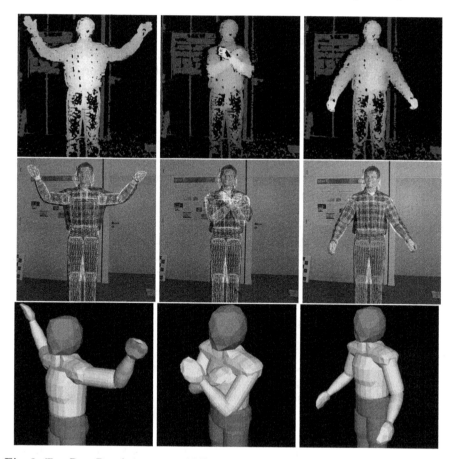

Fig. 3. Top Row:Depth images, middle row: original image overlayed with esimtated model pose, bottom row: model view from the side

Table 1. Comparison with related work

	Demirdjan	Bray	Our
DOF	ca. 18	30	28
correspondences	unknown	45	1000
model complexity	6 simple	complex hand model	18 seperately
	cylinders	linear blend skinned	fitted body parts
speed	6-10fps	0.22 fps	4 fps
	Pentium4 2Ghz	fps Sunfire 1.2Ghz	Pentium4 3 Ghz

3Ghz Pentium 4 on the average. For a bowing sequence with synthetic data, that involved movement of the arms, legs and head, 26 DOF were estimated. The estimation time increased only slightly to 250ms per frame with about 10 iterations and 1000 data points.

Table (1) shows the effectiveness of our approach. We are able to use far more correspondences for the estimation than Bray. This is probably due to the analytically derived Jacobian. Processing more data points stabilizes the estimation significantly if noisy depth data has to be used. The approach of Demirdjan is faster than our, however the estimation method is inferior [4] to our direct approach and uses a simpler model and probably less correspondences.

8   Conclusions and Outlook

We showed how body pose estimation by nonlinear optimization methods can be improved using the correct derivatives and described an optimized ICP approach that calculates body pose from depth images in near to real-time. We are optimistic to accelerate our algorithm to more than 10fps by the use of a simpler model and a smarter way of subsampling the depth image, such that less correspondences are sufficient. The stereo algorithm [11] can provide depth images with up to 20fps and is therefore well suited for real-time body pose estimation within HCI applications. Further constraints like self collision and limiting the joint movement to realistic angles will further increase the performance. To integrate constrained motion into Newton Iteration barrier functions can be used. First experiments with barrier functions for the elbow flexion showed promising results. Additional cameras from other views can be easily integrated in the estimation, as they simply provide additional correspondences.

References

1. M. Bray, E. Koller-Meier, P. Mueller, L. Van Gool, and N. N. Schraudolph. 3d hand tracking by rapid stochastic gradient descent using a skinning model. In *CVMP*. IEE, March 2004.
2. C. Bregler and J. Malik. Tracking people with twists and exponential maps. In *Proceeding IEEE CVPR*, pages 8–15, 1998.
3. Roman Calow, Bernd Michaelis, and Ayoub Al-Hamadi. Solutions for model-based analysis of human gait. In B. Michaelis, editor, *Proc. of DAGM-Symposium*, pages 540–547, Magdeburg, 2003.
4. D. Demirdjian, T. Ko, and T. Darrell. Constraining human body tracking. In *Proceedings of ICCV*, Nice, France, October 2003.
5. L. Falkenhagen. Hierarchical block-based disparity estimation considering neighbourhood constraints, 1997.
6. David G. Lowe. Fitting parameterized three-dimensional models to images. In *Trans. on Pattern Analysis and Machine Intelligence*, pages 13(5):441–450, 1991.
7. T. B. Moeslund and E. Granum. A survey of computer vision-based human motion capture. *Computer Vision and Image Understanding: CVIU*, 81(3):231–268, 2001.
8. Ralf Plaenkers and Pascal Fua. Model-based silhouette extraction for accurate people tracking. In *Proc. of ECCV*, pages 325–339. Springer-Verlag, 2002.
9. B. Rosenhahn and G. Sommer. Adaptive pose estimation for different corresponding entities. In *Proc. of DAGM*, pages 265–273. Springer-Verlag, 2002.
10. D. Scharstein, R. Szeliski, and R. Zabih. A taxonomy and evaluation of dense two-frame stereo correspondence algorithms. In *Proceedings of IEEE Workshop on Stereo and Multi-Baseline Vision*, Kauai, HI, December 2001.
11. J. Woetzel and R. Koch. Real-time multi-stereo depth estimation on GPU with approximative discontinuity handling. In *CVMP 2004, London, UK*, March 2004.

Conservative Visual Learning for Object Detection with Minimal Hand Labeling Effort *

Peter Roth[1], Helmut Grabner[1], Danijel Skočaj[2], Horst Bischof[1], and Aleš Leonardis[2]

[1] Inst. for Computer Graphics and Vision,
Graz University of Technology, Austria
{pmroth, hgrabner, bischof}@icg.tu-graz.ac.at
[2] Faculty of Computer and Information Science,
University of Ljubljana, Slovenia
{danijels, alesl}@fri.uni-lj.si

Abstract. We present a novel framework for unsupervised training of an object detection system. The basic idea is to (1) exploit a huge amount of unlabeled video data by being very conservative in selecting training examples; and (2) to start with a very simple object detection system and using generative and discriminative classifiers in an iterative co-training fashion to arrive at increasingly better object detectors. We demonstrate the framework on a surveillance task where we learn a person detector. We start with a simple moving object classifier and proceed with robust PCA (on shape and appearance) as a generative classifier which in turn generates a training set for a discriminative AdaBoost classifier. The results obtained by AdaBoost are again filtered by PCA which produces an even better training set. We demonstrate that by using this approach we avoid hand labeling training data and still achieve a state of the art detection rate.

1 Introduction

Starting with face detection [14,19] there has been a considerable interest in visual object detection in recent years, e.g., pedestrians [20], cars [1], bikes [12], etc. This is sometimes also referred to as visual categorization as opposed to object recognition [4,12]. At the core of most object detection algorithms is usually a classifier, e.g., AdaBoost [5], Winnow [9], neural network [14] or support vector machine [18]. The proposed approaches have achieved considerable success in the above mentioned applications.

* This work has been supported by the Austrian Joint Research Project Cognitive Vision under projects S9103-N04 and S9104-N04, by the Federal Ministry for Education, Science and Culture of Austria under the CONEX program, by the SI-A project, by the Federal Ministry of Transport, Innovation and Technology under P-Nr. I2-2-26p Vitus2, by the Research program Computer Vision P2-0214 (RS), by EU FP6-004250-IP project CoSy and by EU FP6-511051-2 project MOBVIS.

W. Kropatsch, R. Sablatnig, and A. Hanbury (Eds.): DAGM 2005, LNCS 3663, pp. 293–300, 2005.

However, a requirement of all these methods is a training set which in some cases needs to be quite large. The problem of obtaining enough training data increases even further because the methods are view based, i.e., if the view-point of the camera changes the classifier needs to encompass this variability (e.g., car from the side and car from the back). Training data is usually obtained by hand labeling a large number of images which is a time consuming and tedious task. Clearly this is not practicable for applications requiring a large number of different view-points (e.g., video surveillance by large camera networks). Therefore, it is essential that a representative set of labeled object data is obtained. Negative examples (i.e., examples of images not containing the object) are usually obtained by a bootstrap approach [17]. One starts with a few negative examples and trains the classifier. The obtained classifier is applied to images not containing the object. Those sub-images where a (wrong) detection occurs are added to the set of negative examples and the classifier is retrained. This process can be repeated several times. Obtaining reliable positive examples is, however, a more difficult problem, since discriminant classifiers are very sensitive to false training data.

The main contribution of this paper is to propose a novel framework (depicted in Fig. 1) avoiding hand labeling of training data for object detection tasks. The basic idea is to use the huge amount of unlabeled data that is readily available for most detection task (i.e., just mount a video camera and observe the scene).

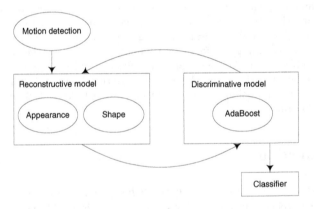

Fig. 1. The proposed conservative learning framework

We use two types of models, a reconstructive one which assures robustness and serves for verification, and discriminative one, which actually performs the detection. To get the whole process started we use a simple motion detector to detect potential objects of interest. In fact, we miss a considerable amount of objects (which can be compensated by just using longer sequences) and we will get also a lot of miss-detections (which will be reduced in the subsequent steps). The output from the motion detector can be used to robustly build a first initial reconstructive representation (to further increase the robustness we are using one representation on shape and the other on appearance). In particular, we use robust PCA [15] at this stage so that most of the miss-detections (background, false detections, over-segmentations, etc.) are not incorporated in the reconstructive model. This is very crucial as the discriminative classifier needs to be trained with "clean" images to produce good classification results. The discriminative model is then used to detect new objects in new images. The output of the discriminative classifier is then verified by the reconstructive model, and detected false positives can be fed back into the discriminative classifier as negative examples (and true positives as positive examples) to further improve the discriminative model. In fact, it has been shown in the active learning community [13], that it is more effective to sample the current estimate of the decision boundary than the unknown true boundary. This is exactly achieved by our combination of reconstructive and discriminative classifiers. Exploiting the huge amount of video data, this process can be iterated to produce a stable and robust classifier.

The outlined approach is similar to the recent work of Nair and Clark [11] and Levin et al. [8]. Nair and Clark propose to use motion detection for obtaining the initial training set and then Winnow as a final classifier. Their approach does not include generative classifiers, nor does it iterate the process to obtain more accurate results. In that sense our framework is more general. Levin et al. use the so called co-training framework to start with a small training set and to increase it by using a co-training of two classifiers operating on different features. We show that using a combination of generative and discriminative classifiers helps to increase the performance of the discriminative one.

The rest of the paper is organized as follows. In Section 2 we detail our approach. In order to make the discussion concrete we will use person detection from videos. The experimental results in Section 3 demonstrate the approach on some challenging video sequences with groups of people and occlusions. Finally, we present some conclusions and work in progress.

2   Our Approach

In this section we will explain the modules used in our implementation of the framework depicted in Fig. 1. We used a motion detection procedure based on a simple approximated median background model, a robust PCA as a reconstructive model, and AdaBoost as a discriminative classifier. But note that the particular methods are not crucial and other types of classifiers might be used as well.

2.1   Motion Detection

Having a stationary camera a common approach to detect moving objects is to threshold the difference image between the current frame and a background model. A widely used and simple method for generating a background model is a pixel-wise temporal median filter. To reduce computational costs and memory requirement McFarlane and Schofield [10] developed the approximated median a computationally more efficient method.

The obtained motion blobs can be labeled as persons if the aspect ratio of their bounding box is within the prespecified limits. We are very conservative in this step, i.e., we will miss many potential persons, but we nevertheless will obtain a few false negatives.

2.2 Reconstructive Model

We use a PCA-based subspace representation as a reconstructive model. This low-dimensional representation captures the essential reconstructive characteristics by exploiting the redundancy in the visual data. As such, it enables "hallucinations" and comparison of the visual input with the stored model. In this way the inconsistent data can be rejected and the discriminative model can be trained from clear data only.

To be more specific, once the subspace representation has been built from the training images, we can verify if an input image can be modeled with this model simply by checking its reconstruction error. We can thus project the image into the eigenspace (using the standard projection or a robust procedure [6]), reconstruct the obtained coefficients and determine the reconstruction error, which is a good verification measure. Having a consistent model of training images, we can successfully evaluate new images by considering this measure.

It turns out that a similar approach can be used also in the learning stage, thus during the estimation of the principal subspace. By considering the reconstruction error, the robust learning procedure can discard inconsistencies in the input data and train the model from consistent data only [3,15,16]. We use a similar but simplified approach and by checking the consistency of the input images (patches) we accept or reject potential patches as positive or negative training examples for the discriminative learner.

To further increase the robustness of the reconstructive model, we build two subspace representations in parallel: appearance-based and shape-based representation. The former is created from the cropped and resized appearance patches, which are detected by the motion detector. Since the output of this detector is also a binary segmentation mask, this mask is used to calculate the shape images based on the Euclidean distance transform [2]. The mean and the first five eigenvectors of the appearance-based and shape-based model are shown in Figs. 2(a,b).

Having these models, each image can be checked whether is consistent with them or not. Figs. 2(c,d) depict an image and its appearance and shape reconstructions in the case of a correct and a false detection. In the latter case, the

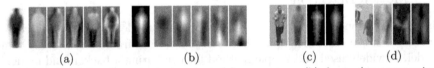

(a)   (b)   (c)   (d)

Fig. 2. Mean and first five principal vectors: (a) appearance, (b) shape. Appearance image, its reconstruction, shape image, its reconstruction: (c) in case of correct detection, (d) in case of false detection.

reconstruction error is significantly larger (i.e., the original image and its reconstruction differ significantly), thus the patch, which encompasses parts of two
pedestrians instead of a single one, gets discarded. Since the main idea of conservative learning is to consider only the images (patches), which are sufficiently consistent with the current model (and would not change it significantly), we accept
only the images, which are close enough to both, the appearance and the shape
model. We thus assure that the discriminative learner gets only the clean data.

2.3   Discriminative Model

In principle our proposed concept can be used with any discriminative classifier,
but due to its popularity we have used the classical AdaBoost classifier from
Viola and Jones [19]. It allows a very fast processing while achieving a high
detection rate. The main assumption from Viola and Jones is that a small set
of important features can separate the object classes from the background. This
feature selection is done by boosting.

To improve the performance we use in addition to the Haar Wavelets local
edge oriented histograms, similar to Levi and Weiss [7]. To detect an object the
classifier is evaluated at many possible positions and scales on the image. Since
both feature types can be calculated with integral images, this can be done very
efficiently for each sub-window.

3   Experimental Results

We have created challenging indoor surveillance video sequences showing a corridor in a public building. We have recorded images over several days. A simple
motion detector triggers the camera and then each second one image is recorded.
In total we have recorded over 35000 images.

For training the classifiers a sequence containing approximately 4500 frames
has been used. In order to have a challenging test situation we created an independent test set containing groups of persons, persons partially occluding each
other and persons walking in different directions. The test set consists of 300
frames (235 persons) and was manually annotated.

3.1   Description of Experiments

We applied the conservative learning framework as outlined above. To demonstrate the success of the individual steps, we trained an AdaBoost classifier after
each step, and applied it to the test set. The AdaBoost classifiers have all the
same VC-dimension (i.e., we used 60 weak classifiers). For evaluation we used
non-local maximum suppression of the detections.

AdaBoost1: On the training sequence the motion detection produced 412 detections that where considered as persons (approximately 10% false positives), in addition 1000 negative examples are created by randomly sampling
image regions where no motion was detected.

AdaBoost2: A robust reconstructive representation obtained by PCA is computed from the output of the motion detector. This representation is used to verify the output of motion detection to create the set of positive examples. From the 412 detections only 140 positive examples are extracted. The set of negative examples is the same as for AdaBoost1.

AdaBoost3: The detections of AdaBoost2 are verified by the reconstructive model (subdivided into 3 groups: true positives, false positives, any others). Detected false positives are fed back into the AdaBoost as negative examples and true positives as positive examples (76 patches were added to positive examples, 209 to negative examples). Note that these are extremely valuable examples because they sample the current decision boundary.

3.2   Results

As an evaluation criterion we used similar to [1], precision, recall and the F-measure that can be considered as tradeoff between recall and precision. The results of the experiments on the test set are summarized in Table 1:

Table 1. Experimental results on the test set.

method	true-pos.	false-pos.	recall	precision	F-measure
AdaBoost1	229	605	97.4 %	27.5 %	42.9 %
AdaBoost2	216	160	91.9 %	57.4 %	70.7 %
AdaBoost3	220	12	93.6 %	94.8 %	94.2 %

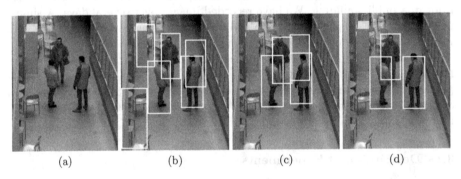

| (a) | (b) | (c) | (d) |

Fig. 3. Detected persons: (a) Motion, (b) AdaBoost1, (c) AdaBoost2, (d) AdaBoost3.

From the experimental results one can clearly see that the number of false positives is considerably reduced by the different stages of the classifier (this is exactly what is to be expected from conservative learning). The F-measure improves from initially 42% to more than 90%. To show the benefit of our approach an AdaBoost classifier was trained with hand labeled positive examples. Using this classifier we detected 224 persons and got 126 false positives (F-measure: 77%). Thus, the result is comparable to AdaBoost2.

Fig. 3 shows some example detections obtained by the different classifiers. Since the persons are not moving there is no motion detected (a). The AdaBoost classifier trained with the noisy data (b) yields a lot of false positives. The classifiers trained with the clean data (c) and with the verified false positives (d) provide much better results.

(a)   (b)   (c)   (d)

Fig. 4. Examples of detected persons applying the final classifier.

Fig. 4 shows examples of correctly detected persons applying the final classifier. The bright clothed women (a) is as well detected (while the cleaning cart is not detected), so is the dark man (b), the man with the knapsack (c) and the persons close together (d).

4   Conclusion

We have presented a novel framework for unsupervised training of an object detection system. The basic idea is to start with a very simple object detection system and then using reconstructive and discriminative classifiers in an iterative fashion (by being very conservative in accepting when a training sample should be added to the training set) to generate better object detectors. We have demonstrated the framework on a surveillance task where we have learned a pedestrian detector. We have started with a simple moving object classifier and then used PCA (on shape and appearance) as a reconstructive classifier which in turn was used to generate a training set for an discriminative AdaBoost classifier. The results obtained by AdaBoost are again filtered by PCA which produces an even better training set. In fact, using this strategy we produce a training set for the AdaBoost classifier which is optimal in the sense that we always sample at the current estimate of the decision surface [13] and not at the unknown theoretic decision boundary.

The framework we have presented is quite general and can be extended in several directions. Our next step is to use online classifiers. In fact, for PCA we have already on-line algorithms, using also on-line AdaBoost will avoid collecting training data in batches and training the system off-line in different phases. In addition, we plan to increase the diversity of different classifiers and to include also voting in the process.

References

1. S. Agarwal, A. Awan, and D. Roth. Learning to detect objects in images via a sparse, part-based representation. *IEEE Trans. PAMI*, 26(11):1475–1490, 2004.
2. H. Breu, J. Gil, D. Kirkpatrick, and M. Werman. Linear time euclidean distance transform algorithms. *IEEE Trans. PAMI*, 17(5):529–533, 1995.
3. F. De la Torre and M. J. Black. A framework for robust subspace learning. *IJCV*, 54(1):117–142, 2003.
4. R. Fergus, P. Perona, and A. Zisserman. Object class recognition by unsupervised scale-invariant learning. In *Proc. CVPR 2003*, pages 264–271, 2003.
5. Y. Freund and R. Shapire. A decision-theoretic generalization of online learning and an application to boosting. *J. of Computer and System Sciences*, 55:119–139, 1997.
6. A. Leonardis and H. Bischof. Robust recognition using eigenimages. *Computer Vision and Image Understanding*, 78:99–118, 2000.
7. K. Levi and Y. Weiss. Learning Object Detection from a Small Number of Examples: The Importance of Good Features. In *Proc. CVPR 2004*, 2004.
8. A. Levin, P. Viola, and Y. Freund. Unsupervised improvement of visual detectors using co-training. In *Proc. ICCV*, pages 626–633, 2003.
9. N. Littlestone. Learning quickly when irrelevant attributes abound. *Machine Learning*, 2:285–318, 1987.
10. N.J.B. McFarlane and C.P. Schofield. Segmentation and tracking of piglets. *Machine Vision and Applications*, 8(3):187–193, 1995.
11. V. Nair and J.J. Clark. An unsupervised, online learning framework for moving object detection. In *Proc. CVPR 2004*, pages 317–324, 2004.
12. A. Opelt, M. Fussenegger, Axel Pinz, and Peter Auer. Weak hypotheses and boosting for generic object detection and recognition. In *Proc. ECCV 2004*, volume II, pages 71–84, 2004.
13. Jin-Hyun Park and Young-Kiu Choi. On-line learning for active pattern recognition. *IEEE Signal Processing Letters*, 3(11):301–303, 1996.
14. H. Rowley, S. Baluja, and T. Kanade. Neural network-based face detection. *IEEE Trans. PAMI*, 20(1):23–38, 1998.
15. D. Skočaj, H. Bischof, and A. Leonardis. A robust PCA algorithm for building representations from panoramic images. In *Proc. ECCV 2002*, volume IV, pages 761–775, 2002.
16. D. Skočaj and A. Leonardis. Weighted and robust incremental method for subspace learning. In *Proc. ICCV 2003*, volume II, pages 1494–1501, 2003.
17. K. Sung and T. Poggio. Example-based learning for view-based face detection. *IEEE Trans. PAMI*, 20:39–51, 1998.
18. V.N. Vapnik. *The Nature of Statistical Learning Theory*. Springer, 1995.
19. P. Viola and M. Jones. Rapid object detection using a boosted cascade of simple features. In *Proc. CVPR 2001*, pages 511–518, 2001.
20. P. Viola, M.J. Jones, and D. Snow. Detecting pedestrians using patterns of motion and appearance. In *Proc. ICCV 2003*, volume 2, pages 734–741, 2003.

Rapid Online Learning of Objects in a Biologically Motivated Recognition Architecture

Stephan Kirstein, Heiko Wersing, and Edgar Körner

Honda Research Institute Europe GmbH,
Carl Legien Str. 30, 63073 Offenbach am Main, Germany
{stephan.kirstein, heiko.wersing, edgar.koerner}@honda-ri.de

Abstract. We present an approach for the supervised online learning of object representations based on a biologically motivated architecture of visual processing. We use the output of a recently developed topographical feature hierarchy to provide a view-based representation of three-dimensional objects using a dynamical vector quantization approach. For a simple short-term object memory model we demonstrate real-time online learning of 50 complex-shaped objects within three hours. Additionally we propose some modifications of learning vector quantization algorithms that are especially adapted to the task of online learning and capable of effectively reducing the representational effort in a transfer from short-term to long-term memory.

1 Introduction

Most research on trainable object recognition algorithms has so far focused on learning based on collecting large data sets and then performing offline training of the corresponding classifiers. Since in these approaches learning speed is not a primary optimization goal, typical offline training times last many hours. Another problem is that most classifier architectures like e.g. multi layer perceptrons or support vector machines do not allow online training with the same performance as for offline batch training. Due to these drawbacks, research in man-machine interaction for robotics dealing with online learning of objects has used histogram-based feature representations [8] or hashing techniques [1] that offer fast processing, but only limited representational and discriminatory capacity. An interesting approach to supervised online learning for object recognition was proposed by Bekel et al. [2]. Their VPL classifier consists of feature extraction based on vector quantization and PCA and supervised classification using a local linear map architecture.

We suggest to use a biologically motivated strategy similar to the hierarchical processing in the ventral pathway of the human visual system to speed up object learning considerably. The main idea is to use a sufficiently general feature representation that remains unchanged, while object-specific learning is accomplished only in the highest levels of the hierarchy. We perform supervised online learning of objects using a short-term memory with a similarity-based adaptive collection of view templates using the intermediate level feature representation of

W. Kropatsch, R. Sablatnig, and A. Hanbury (Eds.): DAGM 2005, LNCS 3663, pp. 301–308, 2005.

the proposed visual hierarchy from [9]. Additionally we propose an incremental learning vector quantization model to achieve a reduction of the representational effort that is related to the transfer from short-term to long-term memory.

After a short introduction to the hierarchical feature processing model we introduce our short-term and refined long-term memory model, based on an incremental learning vector quantization approach in Sect. 2. We demonstrate its effectiveness for an implementation of real-time online object learning of 50 objects in Sect. 3, and give our conclusions in Sect.4.

2   Hierarchical Online Learning Model

Our online learning model consists of three major processing stages: First the input image is processed using a topographically organized feature hierarchy. Object views are then stored using the feature map representation in a template-based short-term memory, that allows immediate online learning and recognition. Finally the short-term memory representatives are accumulated into a condensed long-term memory. We now describe these three stages in more detail:

Initial Processing Architecture. Our hierarchy is based on a feed-forward architecture with weight-sharing [4] and a succession of feature-sensitive and pooling stages (see Fig.1 and [9] for details). The output of the feature representation of the complex feature layer (C2) can be used for robust object recognition that is competitive with other state-of-the-art models [9]. We augment the shape representation from [9] with downsampled color maps in the three RGB channels of the input image with the same resolution as the C2 shape features. We denote the output of the hierarchy for a given input image $\mathbf{I}_i$ as $\mathbf{x}^i(\mathbf{I}_i)$.

Online Vector Quantization as Short-Term Memory. Object views are stored in a set of M representatives $\mathbf{r}^l$, $l = 1,\ldots,M$, that are incrementally collected, and labelled with class Q^l. We define R_q as the set of representatives $\mathbf{r}^l$ that belong to object q. The acquisition of templates is based on a similarity threshold S_T. New object views are only collected into the short-term memory (STM) if their similarity to the previously stored views is less than S_T. The parameter S_T is critical, characterizing the compromise between representation resolution and computation time. We denote the similarity of view $\mathbf{x}^i$ and representative $\mathbf{r}^l$ by A_{il} and compute it based on C2 feature space distance by $A_{il} = \exp(-||\mathbf{x}^i - \mathbf{r}^l||^2/\sigma)$. Here, σ is chosen for convenience such that the average similarity in a generic recognition setup is approximately equal to 0.5.

For one learning step the similarity A_{il} between the current training vector $\mathbf{x}^i$, labelled as object q and all representatives $\mathbf{r}^l \in R_q$ of the same object q is calculated and the maximum value is computed as $A_i^{max} = \max_{l \in R_q} A_{il}$. The training vector $\mathbf{x}^i$ with its class label is added to the object representation, if $A_i^{max} < S_T$. If M representatives were present before, then choose $\mathbf{r}^{M+1} = \mathbf{x}^i$ and $Q^{M+1} = q$. Otherwise we assume that the vector $\mathbf{x}^i$ is already sufficiently well represented by one $\mathbf{r}^l$, and do not add it to the representation. We call this template-based representation online vector quantization (oVQ). The non-

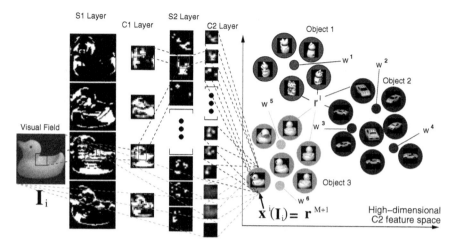

Fig. 1. The visual hierarchical network structure. Based on a color image input $\mathbf{I}_i$ (64×64), shape and color processing is separated in the feature hierarchy and fused in the view-based object representation. In the shape pathway the S1 feature-matching layer computes an initial linear sign-insensitive receptive field summation, a Winner-Take-Most mechanism between features at the same position and a final threshold function. We use Gabor filter receptive fields, to perform a local orientation estimation in this layer. The C1 layer subsamples the S1 features by pooling down to 16×16 resolution using a Gaussian receptive field and a sigmoidal nonlinearity. The 50 features in the intermediate layer S2 are trained by sparse coding and are sensitive to local combinations of the features in the planes of the C1 layer. The layer C2 again performs spatial integration and reduces the resolution to 8×8. When the color pathway is used, three downsampled 8×8 maps of the individual RGB channels are added to the C2 feature maps. The short-term memory consists of template vectors $\mathbf{r}^l$ that are computed as the output $\mathbf{x}^i(\mathbf{I}_i)$ of the hierarchy and added based on sufficient Euclidean distance in the C2 feature space to previously stored representatives of the same object. The refined long-term memory representatives $\mathbf{w}^k$ are learned from the labelled short-term memory nodes $\mathbf{r}^l$ using an incremental vector quantization approach.

destructive incremental learning process allows online learning and recognition at the same time, without a separation into training and testing phases. To model a limited STM capacity we set in some simulations an upper limit of 10 objects that can be represented and if the 11th object is presented, representatives of the oldest learned object are removed from the STM.

Recognition of a unclassified test view $\mathbf{I}_j$ can be done with a nearest neighbour search of the hierarchy output $\mathbf{x}^j(\mathbf{I}_j)$ to the set of STM representatives. The winning node $l_{\max}$ satisfies $l_{\max} = \arg\max_l(A_{jl})$ and then the class label $Q^{l_{\max}}$ of the winning representative $\mathbf{r}^{l_{\max}}$ is assigned to the current test view $\mathbf{x}^j$.

Incremental LVQ as Long-Term Memory. The labelled STM representatives $\mathbf{r}^l$ in the C2 feature space provide the input ensemble for our proposed long-term memory (LTM) representation, which is optimized and built up incrementally based on the set of STM nodes $\mathbf{r}^l$, where we assume a limited STM capacity with only the most recently shown objects being represented. In contrast to the typical usage of learning vector quantization networks [7], where every class is trained with a fixed number of LVQ nodes, we use an incremental approach, related to other models like e.g. the growing neural gas [3]. Another related work not dealing with incremental learning, but with clustering of nonstationary or changing datasets was proposed by [5].

For training our incremental LVQ (iLVQ) model, a stream of randomly selected input STM training vectors $\mathbf{r}^l$ is presented, and classified using labelled iLVQ representatives in a Euclidean metrics. The training classification errors are collected, and each time a given sufficient number of classification errors has occurred a set of new iLVQ nodes is inserted. The addition rule is designed to promote insertion of nodes at the class boundaries. During training, iLVQ nodes are adapted with standard LVQ weight learning that moves nodes into the direction of the correct class and away from wrong classes. An important change to the standard LVQ is an adaptive modification of the individual node learning rates to deal with the stability-plasticity dilemma of online learning. The learning rate of winning nodes is more and more reduced to avoid too strong interference of newly learned representatives with older parts of the object LTM.

We denote the set of iLVQ representative vectors at time step t by $\mathbf{w}^k(t)$, $k = 1, \ldots, K$, where K is the current number of nodes. C^k denotes the corresponding class label of the iLVQ center $\mathbf{w}^k$. The training of the iLVQ nodes is based on the current set of STM nodes $\mathbf{r}^l$ with class Q^l that serve as input vectors for the LTM. Each iLVQ node $\mathbf{w}^k$ obtains an individual learning rate $\Theta_k(t) = \Theta(0) \exp(-a_k(t)/d)$ at step t, where $\Theta(0)$ is an initial value, d is a scaling factor, and $a_k(t)$ is an iteration-dependent age factor. The age factor a_k is incremented when the corresponding $\mathbf{w}_k$ becomes the winning node.

New iLVQ nodes are always inserted, if a given number $G_{\max}$ of training vectors was misclassified during iterative presentation of the $\mathbf{r}^l$. The value of $G_{\max} = 30$ is a compromise between convergence speed and representation resolution. Within this error history, misclassifications are memorized with corresponding input $\mathbf{r}^l$ and winning iLVQ node $\mathbf{w}^{k_{\max}}(\mathbf{r}^l)$. We denote S_p as the set of previously misclassified $\mathbf{r}^l$ within this error history that were of original class $p = Q^l$. For each nonempty S_p a new node $\mathbf{w}^m$ is added to the representation. It is initialized to the element of $\mathbf{r}^l \in S_p$ that has the minimal distance to its corresponding winning iLVQ node $\mathbf{w}^{k_{\max}}(\mathbf{r}^l)$ and the class of the iLVQ node is given as $C^m = Q^l$. This insertion rule adds new nodes primarily near to class borders. The formal definition of the iLVQ learning algorithm is then:

1. Choose randomly $\mathbf{r}^l$ from the set of STM nodes. Find winning iLVQ node $k_{\max} = \arg\max_k(-\|\mathbf{r}^l - \mathbf{w}^k\|)$ and update $\mathbf{w}^{k_{\max}}(t+1) = \mathbf{w}^{k_{\max}}(t) + \kappa\Theta_{k_{\max}}(t)(\mathbf{r}^l - \mathbf{w}^{k_{\max}}(t))$, where $\kappa = 1$ if $C^{k_{\max}} = Q^l$ and $\kappa = -1$ otherwise. The learning rate is given as $\Theta_{k_{\max}}(t) = \Theta(0) \exp(-a_{k_{\max}}(t)/d)$.
2. Increment $a_{k_{\max}}(t+1) = a_{k_{\max}}(t) + 1$.
3. If $C^{k_{\max}} \neq Q^l$ increase $G(t+1) = G(t) + 1$. Add $\mathbf{r}^l$ to the current set of misclassified views S_{Q^l} of object Q^l.
4. If $G = G_{\max}$, then do for each $S_p \neq \emptyset$: Find the object index C^m of the iLVQ representative $\mathbf{w}^m$ with minimal distance to the wrongly classified elements

in S_p according to $||\mathbf{r}^l - \mathbf{w}^m|| = \min_{l|\mathbf{r}^l \in S_p} ||\mathbf{r}^l - \mathbf{w}(\mathbf{r}^l)||$, where $\mathbf{w}(\mathbf{r}^l)$ is the winning iLVQ node for view $\mathbf{r}^l$. Insert a new iLVQ node with $\mathbf{w} = \mathbf{r}^l$. Reset $G = 0$ and $S_p = \emptyset$ for all p. Goto step 1 until sufficient convergence.

Classification of a test view $\mathbf{x}^j(\mathbf{I}_j)$ is done by determining the winning iLVQ node $\mathbf{w}^{k_{\max}}$ with smallest distance to $\mathbf{x}^j$ and assigning the class label $C^{k_{\max}}$.

The C2 feature vectors are sparsely activated with only about one third of nonzero entries. During our investigation of the iLVQ approach we noted that convergence can be improved by applying the weight update of $\mathbf{w}(\mathbf{r}^l)$ nodes only on the nonzero entries of the input vectors $\mathbf{r}^l$. The weight update is then defined componentwise as $w_i^{k_{\max}}(t+1) = w_i^{k_{\max}}(t) + H(r_i^l)\kappa\Theta_{k_{\max}}(t)(r_i^l - w_i^{k_{\max}}(t))$, where H is the Heaviside function. We call this modification *sparse* iLVQ.

3   Experimental Results

Setup. For our experiments we use a setup, where we show objects, held in hand with a black glove before a black background. Color images are taken with a camera, segmented using local entropy-thresholding [6], and normalized in size (64x64 pixels). We show each object by rotating it freely by hand for

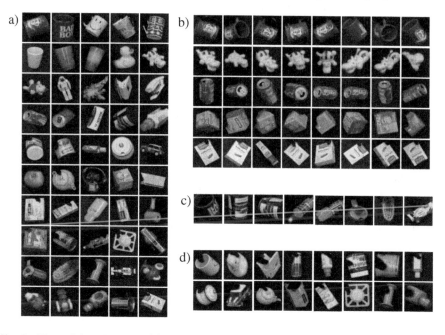

Fig. 2. Test object images. (a) 50 freely rotated objects, taken in front of a dark background and using a black glove for holding. (b) Some rotation examples. (c) A few examples for incomplete segmentation. (d) Examples for minor occlusion effects. The main difficulties of this training ensemble are the high appearance variation of objects during rotation around three axes, and shape similarity among cans, cups and boxes, combined with segmentation errors (c), and slight occlusions (d).

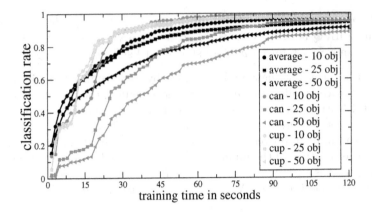

Fig. 3. Classification rate of two selected objects dependent on the training time for learning the 10th, 25th, and 50th object, and same learning curves averaged over 20 object selections. While training proceeds, at each point classification rate is measured on all 750 available test views of the current object. Good recognition performance can be achieved within two minutes, also for the 50th object.

some minutes, such that 750 input images $\mathbf{I}_i$ for each object are collected (see Fig.2). Another set of 750 images for each object is recorded for testing.

Online Learning using Short-Term Memory. In the first experiment we investigate the time necessary for training the template-based oVQ short-term memory with up to 50 objects. The training speed is limited by the frame rate of the used camera (12.5 Hz), the computation time needed for the entropy segmentation, the extraction of the corresponding sparse C2 feature vector $\mathbf{x}^i$ with 3200 shape dimensions and 192 color dimensions and the calculation of similarities A_{il} (see Sect.2). The similarity threshold was set to $S_T = 0.85$ for this experiment, and there was no limit imposed on the number of STM representatives. Altogether we achieve an average frame rate of 7 Hz on a 3GHz Xeon processor. For the shown curves of a cup and a can from our database we trained 9, 24 or 49 objects and incrementally added the cup or can as an additional object. Figure 3 shows how long it takes until the newly added object can be robustly separated from all other objects. At the given points the correct classification rate of the current object is computed using the 750 views from the disjoint test ensemble. Additionally we show the learning curves, averaged over 20 randomly chosen object selections. On average, training of one object can be done in less than 2 minutes, with rapid convergence. For all other experiments we used all available views (750 views per object) for training and testing our models.

To evaluate the quality of the feature representation obtained from the visual hierarchy, we compared the use of 8x8x50 C2 shape feature maps, 8x8x(50+3) C2 features with coarse RGB color maps, and plain 64x64x3 pixel RGB images as input $\mathbf{x}_i$ for the STM. The last setting captures the baseline similarity of the plain images in the ensemble, and serves as a reference point, since there are currently no other established standard methods for online learning available.

Table 1. Classification rates and number of representatives #R of the online learning oVQ model for different similarity thresholds S_T and different inputs

S_T	input data	#R	error rate
0.55		140	86.9%
0.65	plain	474	76.8%
0.75	color	1956	55.4%
0.85		8832	27.7%
0.90		17906	15.2%
0.55		701	57.8%
0.65		2335	35.1%
0.75	shape	7138	17.2%
0.85		19283	9.4%
0.90		28921	8.3%
0.55		2740	24.5%
0.65	shape	6451	12.5%
0.75	+coarse	14223	6.9%
0.85	color	27104	5.8%
0.90		33831	5.7%

Table 2. Comparison of classification rates of oVQ, incremental LVQ, sparse LVQ, incremental LVQ* with limited short term memory and sparse LVQ* with memory. For all tests we used a similarity threshold of $S_T = 0.85$. The number of selected representatives #R is shown.

method	input data	#R	error rate
oVQ	color+shape	27104	5.8%
iLVQ	color+shape	7304	11.4%
sp. iLVQ	color+shape	3665	9.0%
iLVQ*	color+shape	4574	12.2%
sp. iLVQ*	color+shape	3167	9.9%
oVQ	shape	19283	9.4%
iLVQ*	shape	8320	20.9%
sp. iLVQ*	shape	3780	14.6%

Additionally we varied the similarity threshold S_T to investigate the tradeoff between representation accuracy and classification errors. The results are shown in Tab.1. For a fair comparison, error rates for roughly equal numbers of chosen representatives should be compared. The hierarchical shape features reducing the error rates considerably, compared to the plain color images, especially for a small number of representatives #R. The addition of the three RGB feature maps reduces error rates by about one third. For training of all 50 objects that can be done within about three hours, the remaining classification error is about 6% using color and shape and 8% using only shape.

Long-Term Memory and iLVQ. In Tab.2 we show the performance of the iLVQ long-term memory model. We compare the effect of using only a limited memory history for the STM (denoted iLVQ*), in relation to using all data, and the results for the sparse learning rule adaptation described in Sect.2 (denoted sp.iLVQ). The necessary number of representatives #R can be strongly reduced by a factor of 6 and more with the iLVQ network, however, at the price of a slightly reduced classification performance. The differences between the incremental LVQ and the sparse LVQ are that the sparse LVQ reaches slightly better results with fewer number of representatives #R. More important, the sparse iLVQ converges about ten times faster than iLVQ with the standard learning rule, resulting in a training time of only about 3-4 hours. For the experiments using only a limited STM of 10 objects, it can be seen that iLVQ can handle this with almost no performance loss and uses even less resources for representation. We also performed a test using stochastic gradient-based training of linear discriminators (based on the $\mathbf{r}^l$) for each object, where, however the same limited memory history of views from the past 10 objects was applied. Although performance on the current training window of 10 objects normally is below 5% error, the network quickly fails to distinguish objects from the earlier training phases and achieves only a complete final error rate of 73% on all 50 objects.

4   Conclusion

We have shown that the hierarchical feature representation is well suited for online learning using an incremental vector quantization model approach. Of particular relevance is the technical realization of the appearance-based online learning of complex shapes for the context of man-machine interaction and humanoid robotics. This capability introduces many new possibilities for interaction and learning scenarios for incrementally increasing the visual knowledge of a robot. Also for the realistic setting of a limited short-term memory length of 10 objects, we can achieve real-time learning of 50 objects with less than 10% classification error. Although we assume segmentation of the objects in this study, it has been shown previously that the visual hierarchy can also be applied with good results both to learning and recognition of unsegmented objects in clutter [9]. The application to the unsegmented case will therefore be the next step in extending the online object learning approach presented here.

Acknowledgments: We thank C. Goerick, M. Dunn, J. Eggert and A. Ceravola for providing the image acquisition and processing system infrastructure.

References

1. Arsenio, A.: Developmental learning on a humanoid robot. Proc. Int. Joint Conf. Neur. Netw. (2004), Budapest 3167–3172
2. Bekel, H., Bax I., Heidemann G., Ritter H.: Adaptive Computer Vision: Online Learning for Object Recognition. Proc. DAGM, (2004) 447–454
3. Fritzke, B.: A growing neural gas network learns topologies. In G. Tesauro et. al., eds., Adv. Neur. Inf. Proc. Systems. 7. MIT Press, Cambridge MA (1995) 625–632
4. Fukushima, K.: Neocognitron: A self-organizing neural network model for a mechanism of pattern recognition unaffected by shift in position. Biological Cybernetics **36 (4)** (1980) 193–202
5. Guedalia, I. D., London, M., Werman, M. An on-line agglomerative clustering method for non-stationary data. Neural Computation, **11(2)** (1999) 521–540
6. Kalinke T., von Seelen, W.: Entropie als Mass des lokalen Informationsgehalts in Bildern zur Realisierung einer Aufmerksamkeitssteuerung. Mustererkennung (1996), Jähne et al., 627–634
7. Kohonen, T.: Self-Organizing and Associative Memory. Springer Series in Information Sciences, Springer-Verlag, third edition (1989)
8. Steels, L., Kaplan, F.: AIBO's first words: The social learning of language and meaning. Evolution of Communication, **vol. 4, no. 1** (2001) 3–32
9. Wersing, H., Körner, E.: Learning Optimized Features for Hierarchical Models of Invariant Object Recognition. Neural Computation **15 (7)** (2003) 1559–1588

Semidefinite Clustering for Image Segmentation with A-priori Knowledge

Matthias Heiler[1], Jens Keuchel[2], and Christoph Schnörr[1]

[1] Computer Vision, Graphics, and Pattern Recognition Group,
Department of Mathematics and Computer Science,
University of Mannheim, 68131 Mannheim, Germany
{heiler, schnoerr}@uni-mannheim.de
[2] ETH Zurich, Institute of Computational Science,
Hirschengraben 84, CH-8092 Zurich
Jens.Keuchel@inf.ethz.ch

Abstract. Graph-based clustering methods are successfully applied to computer vision and machine learning problems. In this paper we demonstrate how to introduce a-priori knowledge on class membership in a systematic and principled way: starting from a convex relaxation of the graph-based clustering problem we integrate information about class membership by adding linear constraints to the resulting semidefinite program. With our method, there is no need to modify the original optimization criterion, ensuring that the algorithm will always converge to a high quality clustering or image segmentation.

1 Introduction

When working on clustering problems we often have some a-priori knowledge available: certain samples are known to belong to the same class of objects, or we can make assumptions on the size of the clusters. Occasionally, multiple different clusterings are meaningful and we want to target an algorithm toward one particularly interesting solution. In the extreme case we have a small set of labeled objects and want to generalize their labels to a larger set of new, unseen objects. Instead of training a classifier on the labeled objects only we can employ semi-supervised clustering for this task. This application is usually referred to as *transductive inference*.

Fig. 1 visualizes the idea: given a dataset with a number of "sensible looking" clusterings, find the best (here: binary) clustering consistent with some a-priori information on common class membership. This information is provided in the form of *equivalence constraints* on the class labels of some points. For instance, in Fig. 1(b) a point from the left-most cluster is linked to a point in the middle cluster by a constraint which forces these points to have equal class labels. Interestingly, our results show that such a constraint does not influence these two points only, but the information is propagated through their corresponding clusters.

Our work relates to *graph-based clustering* methods used in machine learning and computer vision [1,2]. Since the corresponding *combinatorial optimization*

W. Kropatsch, R. Sablatnig, and A. Hanbury (Eds.): DAGM 2005, LNCS 3663, pp. 309–317, 2005.

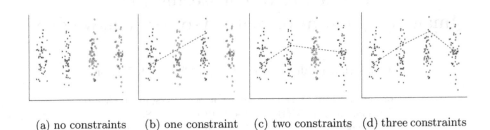

(a) no constraints   (b) one constraint   (c) two constraints   (d) three constraints

Fig. 1. Effects of a-priori information: adding constraints (dashed lines) between few points leads to completely different clusterings

problems are NP-hard, a common approach is to compute approximative solutions using eigenvectors or min-flow calculations [1,3]. In this paper, we use an alternative technique that is based on a *semidefinite programming (SDP) relaxation*. Besides its conceptual advantages over spectral relaxation, this method has recently been applied successfully in the context of machine learning [4] and image partitioning [5].

Concerning a-priori information, most spectral and min-flow methods currently require to modify the cost function of the original clustering problem [1,6]. In contrast, the semidefinite relaxation method puts additional constraints on the set of admissible solutions and finds a high quality solution according to the *original* clustering criterion within this restricted set. For the special problem of semi-supervised image segmentation, besides graph-based optimization techniques [7,6] various other approaches were also presented recently [8,9].

We introduce the graph-based clustering framework used in Section 2 and explain how to integrate a-priori knowledge on cluster size and membership. Section 3 presents our semidefinite relaxation approach along with a geometric interpretation. Some experiments in Section 4 show that adding very few constraints already yields appealing results. Section 5 concludes the paper.

2   Graph-Based Clustering

In order to cluster n objects we need to compute a suitable similarity matrix $W \in \mathbb{R}^{n \times n}$ with W_{ij} being large when the objects i and j are similar. Interpreting the objects as vertices of a fully connected graph $G(V, E)$ with edge weights W_{ij}, a classical *binary* partitioning approach from spectral graph theory (see, e.g., [10,11]) is based on the following problem formulation:

$$\max_{x \in \{-1,+1\}^n} x^\top W x \quad \Longleftrightarrow \quad \min_{x \in \{-1,+1\}^n} x^\top L x \qquad (1)$$

where $L = \mathrm{diag}(We) - W$ denotes the Laplacian matrix of the graph (with $e = (1, \ldots, 1)^\top \in \mathbb{R}^n$). Problem (1) has a clear interpretation: find a binary partitioning with maximum similarity of the objects within each cluster, or, equivalently, determine a cut through G with minimal weight.

Unfortunately, problem (1) can result in very imbalanced partitions, especially when the similarity matrix W contains positive entries only: putting every object into one cluster produces the optimal cut of weight 0. As a remedy, different approaches have been proposed in the literature. Several authors (e.g. [3,12]) suggest to scale the objective function in (1) appropriately in order to favor balanced cuts. Another approach uses an additional *balancing constraint*,

$$c^\top x = a, \tag{2}$$

where $a \geq 0$ specifies the difference between the weighted number of objects in each cluster. For example, setting $c = e, a = 0$ requires that G is partitioned into clusters of identical size (equipartition problem [10]).

As the resulting problems are NP-hard they are often solved approximately using spectral techniques: dropping the integer constraint, extremal eigenvectors of W or L (or of normalized versions of these matrices) are computed and thresholded according to some suitable criterion. In Section 3, we propose a different method to relax and solve constrained problems of type (1), which not only takes the integer constraint on x into account more accurately than spectral techniques [5], but also permits to include linear and quadratic constraints on x *without* changing the original objective function.

Incorporating a-priori knowledge: Aside from similarities of the objects given by W, we may often know that some objects belong to the same class. For two objects i and j, this is modeled in our framework by the constraint

$$x_i x_j = 1. \tag{3}$$

Conversely, if i and j belong to *different* classes, we can use the constraint

$$x_i x_j = -1. \tag{4}$$

In contrast to other approaches [13], adding such *non-equivalent* constraints with our method is not more difficult than adding *is-equivalent* constraints (3): both lead to *quadratic equalities*.

Another example of a-priori information was given above: if the *size* of a cluster is known in advance we can use the linear constraint (2) with an appropriate value for a to demand a corresponding partitioning of G.

Note that in contrast to established methods [1], integrating a-priori knowledge into our framework leads to very clear and concise models: entries of the similarity matrix and the corresponding graph remain unchanged. We do not alter the original problem more than absolutely necessary to account for the additional information.

3   Semidefinite Programming (SDP) Relaxation

In [5], an approach to approximately solve the combinatorial problem (1) with an additional balancing constraint (2) is presented. This method basically consists of three steps: first, the decision variables are lifted into a higher-dimensional space where the corresponding problem is relaxed to a *convex* optimization problem [14]. Then, the global optimum of this relaxation is found using interior point techniques. Finally, the decision variables are recovered from the solution using a small number of random hyperplanes [15]. Next, we extend this idea to take a-priori knowledge into account by adding constraints of the form (3) and (4).

The basic lifting step of the SDP relaxation is based on the observation that the objective function in (1) can be rewritten in the form of a standard matrix inner product as $x^{\top} W x = \mathrm{tr}(W x x^{\top}) =: W \bullet x x^{\top}$. Interpreting this as an optimization problem in a higher dimensional matrix space, the relaxation consists of replacing the positive semidefinite *rank one* matrix $x x^{\top} \in \mathbb{R}^{n \times n}$ by a positive semidefinite matrix $X \succeq 0$ of *arbitrary rank*. Since the combinatorial constraints on the entries of x in (1) can be lifted easily into this matrix space by requiring $X_{ii} = 1$, we obtain the following basic relaxation of (1):

$$\max_{X \succeq 0} \quad W \bullet X \tag{5}$$
$$\text{subject to} \quad X_{ii} = 1 \quad \forall i = 1, \ldots, n$$

While solving this relaxation is trivial in case of a positive matrix W (cf. Section 2), it is also applicable if W contains negative entries. Moreover, note that the integer constraint on x is still accounted for in (5), which contrasts spectral relaxation techniques which usually drop it completely [3].

Problem (5) belongs to the class of *semidefinite programs*, for which the global optimum can be computed to arbitrary precision in polynomial time (see, e.g., [16]). For this problem class, the additional constraints on x which describe the a-priori knowledge can easily be incorporated by lifting them into the matrix space: the balancing constraint (2) is squared to become $c^{\top} x x^{\top} c = a^2$, which results in the linear constraint $c c^{\top} \bullet X = a^2$ after relaxation. Each equivalence constraint of the form (3) can be transformed directly to $X_{ij} = X_{ji} = 1$. To represent this as a linear constraint based on a symmetric matrix, we use the alternative formulation $X_{ij} + X_{ji} = 2$. Due to the constraints $X_{ii} = 1$ and the fact that X is positive semidefinite, this imposes no additional relaxation as no entry of X can become larger than 1. Equivalently, the non-equivalence constraints (4) are represented by $X_{ij} + X_{ji} = -2$.

Let P_1 (P_2) denote the set containing the pairs (i, j) of objects that are known to belong to the same class (different classes). Representing all constraints in linear form, we finally obtain the following semidefinite program:

$$\max_{X \succeq 0} \quad W \bullet X$$
$$\text{subject to} \quad e_i e_i^{\top} \bullet X = 1 \quad \forall i = 1, \ldots, n \tag{6a}$$
$$(e_i e_j^{\top} + e_j e_i^{\top}) \bullet X = 2 \quad \forall (i, j) \in P_1 \tag{6b}$$
$$(e_i e_j^{\top} + e_j e_i^{\top}) \bullet X = -2 \quad \forall (i, j) \in P_2 \tag{6c}$$
$$c c^{\top} \bullet X = a^2 \tag{6d}$$

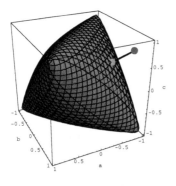 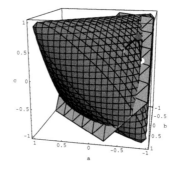

Fig. 2. SDP clustering as matrix approximation. Depicted is the set $M_{\succeq 0}$ of all positive semidefinite symmetric matrices of dimension 3×3 with diagonal fixed to unity (blue object). For a matrix W with negative eigenvalues (red point) the solution X of problem (5) (green point) is given by the projection of W onto $M_{\succeq 0}$ (left). Incorporating a-priori information about relative cluster sizes (2) leads to an additional linear constraint (right, green plane). The SDP relaxation finds a solution X (white point) satisfying this linear constraint and approximating W (red point) optimally.

where $e_i \in \mathbb{R}^n$ denotes the ith standard unit vector. Note that the (non-)equivalence constraints (3),(4) can also be combined into a single constraint: adding the matrices from (6b),(6c) as $E_{P_k} = \sum_{(i,j) \in P_k} (e_i e_j^\top + e_j e_i^\top)$ gives the equivalent constraints $E_{P_1} \bullet X = 2|P_1|$ and $E_{P_2} \bullet X = -2|P_2|$, respectively. As already mentioned above, this results in no further relaxation.

After a solution X of (6) is found we apply the *randomized hyperplane technique* [15] to recover a binary solution x. In this step, no adaption is necessary to enforce the additional (non-)equivalence constraints (3),(4) as the corresponding constraints (6b),(6c) already do this efficiently. Depending on the application we also may not enforce the balancing constraint (2): since the a-priori knowledge on the size of the clusters usually is given only approximately, it merely serves as a bias to guide the search for convenient clusters than as a strict requirement. For more details on the SDP relaxation approach, we refer to [5].

Fig. 2 visualizes the geometry of our method: solving (6) corresponds to projecting the problem matrix W (which is not necessarily positive semidefinite) onto the set $M_{\succeq 0}$ of all positive semidefinite matrices with diagonal fixed to unity, which is equivalent to finding the closest approximation of W within $M_{\succeq 0}$.

The resulting solution matrix $X \in M_{\succeq 0}$ is, by construction, positive semidefinite and therefore can be interpreted as a matrix whose entries are inner products of points located on the unit sphere in some Euclidean space. The randomized hyperplane algorithm then places a cut through this sphere and retrieves a binary clustering which maximizes the original objective function in (1). Geometrically, this is a projection of X onto the closest vertex of the set $M_{\succeq 0}$ (Fig. 2, left).

The linear constraints (6b)–(6d) further limit the set of admissible solutions: whereas constraint (6d) represents a plane cutting through $M_{\succeq 0}$ (Fig. 2, right), the constraints (6b),(6c) correspond to tangential planes. Together, they move the solution X toward vertices obeying the a-priori knowledge *and* representing a good clustering measured in terms of the original objective function $x^\top W x$.

4   Experiments

As a proof-of-concept we created a very simple dataset consisting of four clearly separated clusters of 50 points each distributed according to a Gaussian distribution (Fig. 1(a)). Using a centered Gaussian kernel as similarity measure we compute multiple clusterings by subsequently adding constraints on the class labels. Fig. 1 shows that the constraints were met in each case and led to completely different clusterings. Although we did not provide a-priori information about the size of the clusters the centered kernel favored balanced solutions and flipped the unconstrained clusters accordingly.

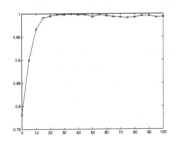

Fig. 3. The soybean experiment

Following [17] we tested our approach on the soybean dataset which comprises 35 attributes for 47 objects from four classes. To apply our method to this *multiclass problem* we assigned each class a *two bit binary code* and clustered on the corresponding binary digits using a centered exponential kernel as similarity measure. As in [17] consistency w.r.t. the known correct clustering was determined using the *Rand index* [18] and 10-fold crossvalidation. With the class labels as ground truth we generated random constraints on the training sets, clustered, and measured accuracies on the corresponding test sets. The mean performance over 10 repeated experiments is visualized in Fig. 3: without any constraints 78% of the instances are correctly clustered. This is worse than the 87% reported for kmeans [17]. However, with only 5 constraints this improves to 90% correctly clustered points ($\approx$ 88% for kmeans), and we need only 15 constraints to achieve an accuracy of 99% (kmeans needs 100 constraints). Thus, for this dataset adding a-priori constraints is highly effective, leading to dramatic improvements in accuracy.

In Fig. 4 we show segmentations obtained for images from the Berkeley segmentation dataset [19] using a similarity measure based on color and spatial proximity (cf. [21]). In order to reduce the problem size appropriately, the images were over-segmented in a preprocessing step by applying the mean shift algorithm [20], which results in less than 1000 image patches [21]. These are clustered by our SDP relaxation with and without additional equivalence constraints. It is clearly visible that adding very few constraints can lead to dramatically different and visually more appealing segmentations.

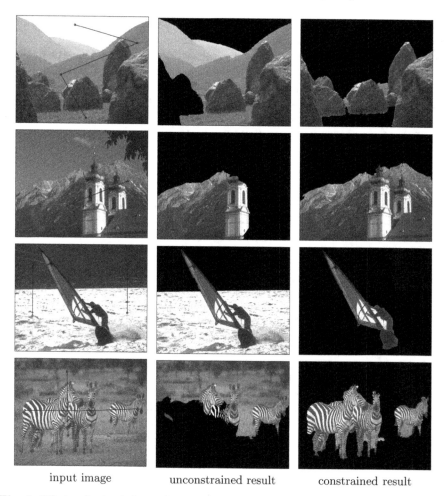

input image   unconstrained result   constrained result

Fig. 4. Effects of prior information on image segmentation. An unsupervised segmentation based on color and spatial proximity may not partition the image in a visually meaningful way (2nd column). Adding only 1–3 equivalence constraints (blue lines in 1st column) can dramatically improve the segmentation (3rd column).

5   Conclusion

We presented a method for clustering and segmentation based on a semidefinite relaxation of the well-known minimal cut problem on graphs. The advantage over alternative approaches is that it allows incorporating a-priori knowledge in the clustering process without changing the target function. Instead, available equivalence information is modeled by additional constraints on the optimization problem. This simplifies interpretation of the results and ensures that different constraints can be combined arbitrarily.

We gave two examples for a-priori information which lead to linear constraints on the set of admissible solutions of the semidefinite relaxation and explained their geometric meaning. In an experimental section we showed that the method works in practice and can lead to improved image segmentation results.

In the future, we will investigate how to integrate further types of a-priori information and evaluate the method for constrained multiclass-clustering. Besides using binary codes, binary clustering can be applied hierarchically [21] or the SDP relaxation can be extended to multiclass settings.

References

1. A. Blum and S. Chawla, "Learning from labeled and unlabeled data using graph mincuts," in *ICML*, pp. 19–26, 2001.
2. Y. Weiss, "Segmentation using eigenvectors: A unifying view," in *ICCV*, pp. 975–982, 1999.
3. J. Shi and J. Malik, "Normalized cuts and image segmentation," *IEEE PAMI*, vol. 22, no. 8, pp. 888–905, 2000.
4. G. Lanckriet, N. Cristianini, P. Bartlett, L. E. Ghaoui, and M. Jordan, "Learning the kernel matrix with semi-definite programming," in *ICML*, pp. 323–330, 2002.
5. J. Keuchel, C. Schnörr, C. Schellewald, and D. Cremers, "Binary partitioning, perceptual grouping, and restoration with semidefinite programming," *IEEE PAMI*, vol. 25, no. 11, pp. 1364–1379, 2003.
6. S. X. Yu and J. Shi, "Segmentation given partial grouping constraints," *IEEE PAMI*, vol. 26, no. 2, pp. 173–183, 2004.
7. Y. Boykov and M.-P. Jolly, "Interactive graph cuts for optimal boundary & region segmentation of objects in n-d images," in *ICCV*, vol. 1, pp. 105–112, 2001.
8. L. Hermes and J. M. Buhmann, "Semi-supervised image segmentation by parametric distributional clustering," in *Energy Min. Meth. in Comp. Vis. a. Patt. Recog. (EMMCVPR)*, no. 2683 in LNCS, pp. 229–245, Springer, 2003.
9. R. Nock and F. Nielsen, "Grouping with bias revisited," in *CVPR*, 2004.
10. B. Mohar and S. Poljak, "Eigenvalues in combinatorial optimization," in *Combinatorial and Graph-Theoretical Problems in Linear Algebra* (R. Brualdi, S. Friedland, and V. Klee, eds.), vol. 50 of *IMA Vol. Math. Appl.*, pp. 107–151, Springer, 1993.
11. P. Perona and W. Freeman, "A factorization approach to grouping," in *ECCV'98* (H. Burkhardt and B. Neumann, eds.), LNCS, pp. 655–670, Springer, 1998.
12. S. Sarkar and P. Soundararajan, "Supervised learning of large perceptual organization: Graph spectral partitioning and learning automata," *IEEE PAMI*, vol. 22, no. 5, pp. 504–525, 2000.
13. T. Hertz, N. Shental, A. Bar-Hillel, and D. Weinshall, "Enhancing image and video retrieval: Learning via equivalence constraints," in *CVPR*, 2003.
14. L. Lovász and A. Schrijver, "Cones of matrices and set-functions and 0-1 optimization," *SIAM J. Optimization*, vol. 1, no. 2, pp. 166–190, 1991.
15. M. Goemans and D. Williamson, "Improved approximation algorithms for maximum cut and satisfiability problems using semidefinite programming," *J. of the ACM*, vol. 42, no. 6, pp. 1115–1145, 1995.
16. Y. Nesterov and A. Nemirovskii, *Interior Point Polynomial Methods in Convex Programming.* SIAM, 1994.
17. K. Wagstaff, C. Cardie, S. Rogers, and S. Schroedl, "Constrained k-means clustering with background knowledge," in *ICML*, pp. 577–584, 2001.

18. W. M. Rand, "Objective criteria for the evaluation of clustering methods," *J. of the Am. Stat. Assoc.*, vol. 66, no. 336, pp. 846–850, 1971.
19. D. Martin, C. Fowlkes, D. Tal, and J. Malik, "A database of human segmented natural images and its application to evaluating segmentation algorithms and measuring ecological statistics," in *ICCV*, pp. 416–423, 2001.
20. D. Comaniciu and P. Meer, "Mean shift: A robust approach toward feature space analysis," *IEEE PAMI*, vol. 24, no. 5, pp. 603–619, 2002.
21. J. Keuchel, C. Schnörr, and M. Heiler, "Hierarchical image segmentation based on semidefinite programming," in *Proc. DAGM*, 2004.

Separable Linear Discriminant Classification

Christian Bauckhage and John K. Tsotsos

Centre for Vision Research, York University, Toronto, ON, M3J 1P3
http://cs.yorku.ca/LAAV

Abstract. Linear discriminant analysis is a popular technique in computer vision, machine learning and data mining. It has been successfully applied to various problems, and there are numerous variations of the original approach. This paper introduces the idea of *separable* LDA. Towards the problem of binary classification for visual object recognition, we derive an algorithm for training separable discriminant classifiers. Our approach provides rapid training and runtime behavior and also tackles the small sample size problem. Experimental results show that the method performs robust and allows for online learning.

1 Introduction

Linear discriminant analysis (LDA) is a powerful tool for dimensionality reduction and classification [1,2]. Its applications and extensions are far too numerous to allow for an exhaustive review here. Instead, in this paper, we will restrict our discussion to the linear discriminant analysis of two classes. We shall call the two classes ω_p and ω_n where the subscripts p and n stand for *positive* and *negative*, respectively. Given a set of feature vectors $\{x_1, x_2, \ldots, x_L\}$ containing positive and negative examples, binary LDA seeks a projection $w^T x_i$ of the samples that maximizes the inter-class distance of the resulting scalars.

The most widely applied technique for finding the direction w of the optimal projection dates back to seminal work by Fisher [3]. He proposed to determine w by maximizing the Rayleigh quotient $w^T S_b w / w^T S_w w$ where S_b and S_w are matrices that denote the between-class and within-class scatter of the data. Following this proposal, w results from solving the generalized eigenvalue problem $S_b w = \alpha S_w w$. Once w has been found, binary classification simply requires selecting a suitable threshold.

A well known but underexploited fact that Fisher himself pointed out [3] is that binary LDA is equivalent to the least mean squares (LMS) fitting of a hyperplane that separates ω_p and ω_n. The projection direction corresponds to the normal vector of the plane. This paper makes use of this equivalence. Aiming at image data and visual object detection, we introduce an iterative LMS approach to *separable* LDA. The resulting binary classifiers are especially suited for appearance based object recognition, because classifying image content is reducible to a convolution operation. Our practical experience has revealed several favorable characteristics of this approach. First, it is as fast as the popular cascaded weak classifiers [4]. Second, on standard databases of images of objects in complex natural scenes, it performs as reliably as recent, more sophisticated non-linear approaches [5,6,7]. Third, in contrast to the cited methods, the training time of our approach is sufficiently short to enable online learning.

W. Kropatsch, R. Sablatnig, and A. Hanbury (Eds.): DAGM 2005, LNCS 3663, pp. 318–325, 2005.
© Springer-Verlag Berlin Heidelberg 2005

Next, we derive our algorithm and discuss its characteristics. Section 3 presents experiments on using separable LDA to detect and track objects in natural environments. A summary and an outlook will end this contribution.

2 Separable LDA for Classifying Image Data

Faced with the problem of fast and adaptive classification of image data, the idea of separable LDA arose from the following two observations.

Most approaches to appearance based object recognition transform image patches X of size $m \times n$ into vectors $x \in \mathbb{R}^{mn}$. The first step towards fast linear discriminant analysis for visual processing is to keep the matrix representation and to consider the Frobenius inner product of matrices $W \cdot X = \sum_{i,j} W_{ij} X_{ij}$ instead of the inner product of high dimensional vectors.[1]

As a consequence, LDA classification of image content becomes a problem of linear filtering. If W denotes a $m \times n$ filter matrix, its convolution with a digital image I will result in a filter response map Y, where an entry Y_{ij} corresponds to the LDA projection of the image patch X_{ij} centered at image coordinate (i, j), i.e. $Y_{ij} = W \cdot X_{ij}$.

The second step towards fast linear discriminant classification considers well known facts about linear filtering. Convolving an image with an $m \times n$ matrix requires $O(mn)$ operations per pixel. Even on modern computers, this may be prohibitive if m and n are rather large. Assume, however, W was given as a basis function expansion

$$W = \sum_{i=1}^{k} u_i v_i^T \tag{1}$$

where $u_i \in \mathbb{R}^m$ and $v_i \in \mathbb{R}^n$ such that the basis functions are separable matrices of rank 1. Then, the two-dimensional convolution can be computed as a sequence of one-dimensional convolutions $\sum_i (I * u_i) * v_i^T$. If the matrix W was rank deficient, i.e. $k < \min\{m, n\}$, this would reduce the effort to $O(k(m + n))$ and therefore would provide a fast linear approach to object detection. The following subsection discusses how to derive such separable *filter* or *projection matrices* from training data.

2.1 Learning Separable k-Term Projection Matrices

For convenience, we shall first consider the derivation of a $k = 1$ term separable LDA projection, i.e. we will examine the case $W = uv^T$.

Assume a sample $\{X_\alpha, y_\alpha\}_{\alpha=1,\dots,N}$ of image patches X_α with corresponding class labels y_α. Due to the general equivalence

$$uv^T \cdot X = \sum_{k,l} (uv^T)_{kl} X_{kl} = \sum_{k,l} u_k v_l X_{kl} = u^T X v \tag{2}$$

a one term separable LDA projection can be found from minimizing the LMS error $E(u, v) = \frac{1}{2} \sum_\alpha (y_\alpha - u^T X_\alpha v)^2$ using the following iterative procedure:

---

[1] Of course, the difference between both views is a mere conceptual one; with the common substitution $k = i \cdot n + j$ we have the equivalence $\sum_k w_k x_k = \sum_{i,j} W_{ij} X_{ij}$.

1. Randomly initialize $u \in \mathbb{R}^m$.
2. Given u, solve $E(u, v) = $ min for v. A solution can be found by requiring $\nabla_v E(u, v) = 0$. If the $n \times n$ correlation matrix $C_u = \sum_\alpha X_\alpha^T u u^T X_\alpha$ is non singular, the optimal v^* amounts to

$$v^* = C_u^{-1} D_u u \tag{3}$$

where $D_u = \sum_\alpha y_\alpha X_\alpha$.
3. Given v^*, solve $E(u, v^*) = $ min for u in a similar way.

As the procedure starts with an arbitrary u, steps 2. and 3. have to be iterated until a convergence criterion is met. Inserting (3) into the LMS error function reveals that the length of u 'cancels out'. The vector u can therefore be constrained to be of unit length $\|u\| = 1$. Although this requires normalizing u after each iteration, it guarantees that the procedure will converge because $E(u, v^*)$ becomes a convex function over the unit ball in $\mathbb{R}^m$. Moreover, the unit length constraint provides a convenient convergence criterion. Our implementation uses $\|u_t - u_{t-1}\| \le \epsilon$ which converges quickly.

As the resulting projection matrix uv^T has only $m + n$ independent parameters whereas a non-separable one would provide $m \cdot n$ parameters, the one-term separable projection will be less flexible than the usual solution. This suggests we consider k-term basis expansions where $k > 1$. Note that uv^T is of rank 1. If one demands $W = \sum_{i=1}^k u_i v_i^T$ to provide more independent parameters than uv^T, it has to be of higher rank. A simple way to guarantee a higher rank of W, say k, that simultaneously ensures separability of the individual terms in the basis function expansion is to require the u_i and v_i to be pairwise orthogonal, i.e $u_i^T u_j = 0$ and $v_i^T v_j = 0$ for $i \ne j$.

Forward additive stage-wise modeling [2] provides a straightforward approach to determining such sets of orthogonal parameter vectors. If $W = \sum_{i=1}^k u_i v_i^T$ is a k term solution for the LDA projection matrix, a $k + 1$ term representation can be found by minimizing $E(u_{k+1}, v_{k+1})$. To assure orthogonality, our iterative minimization procedure has to be extended such that, after *each* iteration, the vectors v_{k+1} and u_{k+1} are orthogonalized with respect to the $\{v_i\}_{i=1,\ldots,k}$ and $\{u_i\}_{i=1,\ldots,k}$ determined so far. Orthogonalization can be done applying the Gram-Schmidt procedure.

Before presenting our results obtained with this approach, we first emphasize some of its favorable properties.

2.2 Properties and Benefits of Separable LDA

Separable LDA should not be confused with orthogonal LDA. Our approach does not seek a set of orthogonal discriminant directions as in the case of O-LDA [1]. Rather, we determine a discriminant direction under the constraint that the projection matrix is given as a sum of k pairwise orthogonal matrices of rank 1.

Separable LDA differs from the singular value decomposition of an unconstrained projection matrix. LMS optimization can learn an unconstrained $m \times n$ matrix W. Using SVD, it can be decomposed into a sum of r separable rank 1 matrices, where r is the rank of W. Since W is usually of full rank, $r = \min\{m, n\}$. If, w.l.o.g., we assume $r = m$, a separated convolution will require $m(m + n) > mn$ operations per pixel and will thus be even more expensive than the usual variant. A rank deficient SVD expansion of $k < r$ terms is less expensive, but practical experience shows that it not useful. In contrast to the SVD-based method, our approach derives the projection matrix directly from data rather than from an unconstrained W. Hence, even for $k \ll r$, it yields reasonable results and also runs quickly.

Separable LDA differs from 2D LDA, as introduced by Ye et al. [8], who present an iterative SVD algorithm that projects $m \times n$ matrices onto $l_1 \times l_2$ matrices where $l_1 < m$ and $l_2 < n$. For projections onto a one-dimensional subspace ($l_1, l_2 = 1$), their approach is equivalent to our solution for 1-term separable LDA. However, as it does not allow for $k > 1$ term representations, their algorithm provides fever independent parameters than our approach to binary LDA.

Separable LDA differs from image coding using the tensor rank principle proposed by Shashua and Levin [9]. Although it resembles our approach, their algorithm has a fundamentally different purpose and considers a different optimization criterion. While separable LDA seeks a k-term projection matrix of low rank, Shashua and Levin estimate a minimal set of second order tensors of rank 1 having a linear span that includes the given set of training images.

Separable LDA projection matrices are learned quickly. LDA based on unconstrained LMS optimization or on solving the generalized eigenvalue problem $S_b w = \alpha S_w w$ requires the computation and inversion of covariance matrices of sizes $mn \times mn$. For larger values of m and n and many training examples, training becomes tedious, even on modern computers. However, the covariance matrices C_u and C_v that appear in the learning stage of separable LDA are of considerably reduced sizes $n \times n$ and $m \times m$, respectively. Therefore, in addition to its fast runtime, our technique significantly shortens training time.

Separable LDA tackles the small sample size problem. This property is closely related to the previous one. The term *small sample size problem* refers to the effect that the within-class scatter matrix S_w is often singular because the number of training samples is much smaller than the dimension of the embedding space [1]. Again, as the covariance matrices C_u and C_v are of considerably small dimensionality, small sample sizes will not hamper separable LDA.

Separable LDA can be expected to perform well in visual object detection and recognition. Fast training and operation times allow the use of fairly large values for m and n so that the resulting linear classifiers will process data from very high dimensional feature spaces. However, according to Cover's theorem [10], the probability of finding a suitable hyperplane that separates two arbitrary classes increases with the dimension of the embedding space.

3   Experiments

This section presents two application examples for the algorithm derived above. First, we regard the problem of robust offline object detection in real world environments. Afterwards, we consider online learning for tracking of articulated objects.

Note that in all experiments the input was normalized to zero mean $\tilde{X} = X - \mu$, where μ denotes the mean of all training examples. In the classification stage, this

Fig. 1. Exemplary detection results ($k = 9$, $\theta = 3.6$) obtained on the UIUC database of cars [5]

accounts only for a single operation per pixel, since $(X - \mu) \cdot W = X \cdot W - \mu \cdot W$, where the constant $\mu \cdot W$ can be computed beforehand.

With respect to the classification threshold θ applied in our experiments, we must point out that determining the theoretically optimal threshold for LDA-based classification requires knowledge of the class covariance matrices. However, in the previous section, we saw that separable LDA avoids the estimation of class covariance matrices, and we stressed the advantages this entails. In order not to lose these advantages, we adopted a heuristic to automatically determine a suitable θ. We computed the mean μ_p and variance σ_p from the projections of the positive training samples onto the discriminant direction, and θ was set to $\mu_p - \sigma_p$. Figure 2(b) indicates that this is good practice in many cases.

3.1 Object Detection in Real World Environments

Experiments in offline object detection were carried out using the UIUC database of cars [5,11]. It contains side views of cars of arbitrary shape and color in natural environments; typical examples are shown in Figure 1. In our experiments, the set ω_p of positive training examples (label +1) consisted of 124 images of cars of size 80×30. The set ω_n of negative examples (label -1) consisted of 1776 patches randomly cut from the background of half of the images in the database; testing was done on the other half.

In order to reduce effects of varying illumination and color, the classifiers considered in our experiments were trained and applied to gradient magnitude images. These were obtained using recursive Gaussian filtering according to Deriche [12]. After training, the test images were convolved with the resulting matrices. A car was said to be detected where the classifier response exceeded the threshold θ. The response maps were subjected to a non-maximum suppression to reduce the number of false positives.

As the UIUC database includes manually annotated ground truth, detection results can be colored correspondingly (see Figure 1). Figure 2(a) plots the precision recall curve we obtained for classifiers of different rank k. The $k = 9$ classifier yielded the best ratio of recall and precision. Figure 2(b) shows how it discriminates the training images. For the classifiers $k = 9$, $k = 6$ (lowest recall) and $k = 17$ (highest recall) we varied the classification thresholds in the intervals $[\theta(k) - 1, \theta(k) + 1]$ to examine how it would influence the performance. The resulting precision recall curves are shown in Figure 2(c). It turned out that improvements were possible. In terms of equal error rate (EER), i.e. the point of equal recall and precision, the classifier with $k = 9$ and $\theta = 3.6$ performed best; it yielded an EER of 86%.

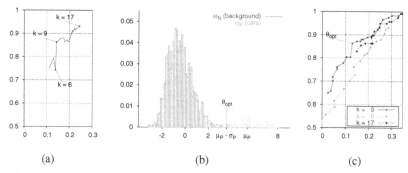

(a)   (b)   (c)

Fig. 2. Quantitative results obtained on the UIUC database of cars. 2(a) $1-$precision vs. recall for different k; the classification threshold θ was set to $\mu_p(k) - \sigma_p(k)$. 2(b) histogram resulting from projecting the training data using $k = 9$. 2(c) $1-$precision vs. recall curves obtained from varying θ for $k \in \{6, 9, 17\}$; the classifier with $k = 9$ and $\theta_{opt} = 3.6$ provides an EER of 86%.

Table 1. Comparison of results reported in contributions dealing with the UIUC database of cars

method	Agarwal et al.[5]	separable LDA	Fergus et al. [6]	Garg et al. [7]	Leibe et al. [13]
EER	77%	86%	88%	88%	97%

Fig. 3. Exemplary results ($k = 7$, $\lambda = 10$, $\theta = \mu_p - \sigma_p$) obtained on frames 41, 89, 304 and 310 of the rotating can sequence recorded by Black and Jepson [14].

It is interesting to note that our linear and holistic approach performs comparably to sophisticated methods found in recent literature. Table 1 lists equal error rates other researchers reported for the UIUC database. Except for our method, all figures result from part-based approaches that learn lexica of salient object parts and statistical models of part relations. Runtimes or training times of these approaches have not been reported but, due to the need for building lexica, at least the training times can be expected to exceed real time. Given a naïve C implementation, our method performed as follows: on a 3GHz Xeon PC, training with 1900 examples took 13 seconds. File I/O and processing of 99 test images of an average size of 120×116 pixels was done at a rate of 3.2Hz.

3.2 Online Learning for Tracking of Articulated Objects

Encouraged by the runtime behavior of our approach, we explored its potential in online learning from image sequences and experimented with material provided by Black and Jepson [14]. Next, we discuss a typical example.

The *rotating can* sequence shows a tin can that is being moved and rotated in front of a static camera (see Figure 3). For our experiments, we applied 141×81 image patches to train classifiers of various ranks k. After manually specifying the center of the can in the first frame of the sequence, 30 image patches are randomly selected from its neighborhood to serve as positive training examples (class ω_p, label +1); 240 patches randomly selected from outside the neighborhood were used as counter examples (class ω_n, label -1). Training and classification both considered simple pixel intensity information.

The classifier matrix resulting from training on the first frame was convolved with the subsequent frames of the sequence. This was done in a brute force manner: the entire image was processed, without considering regions of interest. The can was assumed to be recognized where the classifier response exceeded the threshold θ. Again, non-maximum suppression was applied to reduce the number of false positives. Due to its rotation, the can's appearance changes throughout the sequence. Thus, after λ frames, each classifier was retrained. We experimented with $\lambda \in \{3, 6, 9, \ldots, 30\}$.

The graphs in Figure 4 show 1-precision and recall curves for classifiers of rank $k \in \{4, 7, 10\}$. They are plotted as functions of the operation frequency, which, in turn, is a function of λ. As one would expect, the 4 term classifiers perform fastest. Owing to the needs of video processing, we improved the memory management of our implementation. Consequently, on a 3GHz Xeon PC, the 400 frames of size 320×240 were processed at an operation frequency of up to 9Hz, including file I/O *and* retraining. A practically suitable ratio of speed and reliability was obtained for a $k = 7$ classifier retrained every 9 frames. At a frequency of 4.3Hz, it produces a recall of 94% and a 1-precision value of 3%.

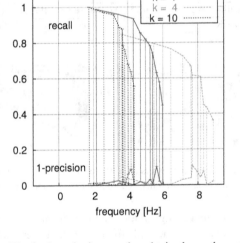

Fig. 4. Quantitative results obtained on the rotating can sequence. The graphs show recall and 1−precision for classifiers of different k plotted as functions of the operation frequencies of various update rates λ. The $k = 7$ classifier updated every 9 frames operates at 4.3 Hz and produces a recall of 94% and 1−precision of 3%.

4   Summary and Outlook

This paper presented an approach to separable linear discriminant classification for image analysis. Based on the idea of understanding LDA projection as a convolution operation, we express the projection matrix as a basis function expansion of separable rank 1 matrices, in order to ensure rapid runtime behavior. We introduced an iterative two step least mean squares procedure to learn corresponding basis functions from training data. Due to the separability of the projection operator, both application and training are very fast. Furthermore, small sample sizes do not corrupt the training process. Experimental results obtained on a standard testbed for object detection revealed that separable LDA performs as fast and as reliably as more elaborate state-of-the-art techniques. In addition, however, it also provides an avenue to online learning in image sequence processing.

Currently, we are working on a thorough experimental and theoretical analysis of separable LDA. Our focus is on questions to which this paper only alludes: Is there a significant difference in performance between usual binary LDA and k-term separable LDA? How can a suitable number k of terms be determined automatically How can our approach be extended to multiple classes? Is there a framework that could unify our approach to computing k-term separable matrices with the approaches proposed in [8] and [9] that consider 1-term higher order tensors of rank 1?

Acknowledgments

We would like to thank Andrei Rotenstein for fruitful discussions and valuable suggestions. We also want to thank our anonymous reviewers. Their precise comments and pointers to recent related literature helped to improve this contribution.

References

1. Fukunaga, K.: Introduction to Statistical Pattern Recognition. Academic Press (1990)
2. Hastie, T., Tibshirani, R., Friedman, J.: The Elements of Statistical Learning. Springer (2001)
3. Fisher, R.: The Use of Multiple Measurements in Taxonomic Problems. Ann. Eugenics **7** (1936) 179–188
4. Viola, P., Jones, M.: Rapid Object Detection using a Boosted Cascade of Simple Features. In: Proc. CVPR. Volume I. (2001) 511–518
5. Agarwal, S., Awan, A., Roth, D.: Learning to Detect Objects in Images via a Sparse, Part-based Representation. IEEE T. Pattern Anal. Machine Intell. **26** (2004) 1475–1490
6. Fergus, R., Perona, P., Zisserman, A.: Object Class Recognition by Unsupervised Scale-Invariant Learning. In: Proc. CVPR. Volume II. (2003) 264–272
7. Garg, A., .Agarwal, S., Huang, T.: Fusion of Global and Local Information for Object Detection. In: Proc. ICPR. Volume III. (2002) 723–727
8. Ye, J., Janardan, R., Li, Q.: Two-Dimensional Linear Discriminant Analysis. In Saul, L., Weiss, Y., Bottou, L., eds.: Advances in Neural Information Processing Systems 17. MIT Press, Cambridge, MA (2005) 1569–1576
9. Shashua, A., Levin, A.: Linear Image Cosing for Regression and Classification using the Tensor-rank Principle. In: Proc. CVPR. Volume I. (2001) 42–40
10. Cover, T.: Geometrical and Statistical Properties of Systems of Linear Inequalities with Applications to Pattern Recognition. IEEE T. on Electronic Computers **14** (1965) 326–334
11. http://l2r.cs.uiuc.edu/~cogcomp/Data/Car/ (retrieved spring 2005)
12. Deriche, R.: Recursively Implementing the Gaussian and Its Derivatives. In: Proc. ICIP. (1992) 263–267
13. Leibe, B., Schiele, B.: Scale-Invariant Object Categorization using a Scale-Adaptive Mean-Shift Search. In: Proc. DAGM. Volume 3175 of LNCS., Springer (2004) 145–153
14. Black, M., Jepson, A.: EigenTracking: Robust matching and tracking of articulated objects using a view-based reprenstation. Int. J. Comput. Vis. **26** (1998) 63–84

Improving a Discriminative Approach to Object Recognition Using Image Patches

Thomas Deselaers, Daniel Keysers, and Hermann Ney

Lehrstuhl für Informatik VI – Computer Science Department,
RWTH Aachen University – D-52056 Aachen, Germany
{deselaers, keysers, ney}@informatik.rwth-aachen.de

Abstract. In this paper we extend a method that uses image patch histograms and discriminative training to recognize objects in cluttered scenes. The method generalizes and performs well for different tasks, e.g. for radiograph recognition and recognition of objects in cluttered scenes. Here, we further investigate this approach and propose several extensions. Most importantly, the method is substantially improved by adding multi-scale features so that it better accounts for objects of different sizes. Other extensions tested include the use of Sobel features, the generalization of histograms, a method to account for varying image brightness in the PCA domain, and SVMs for classification. The results are improved significantly, i.e. on average we have a 59% relative reduction of the error rate and we are able to obtain a new best error rate of 1.1% on the Caltech motorbikes task.

1 Introduction

The learning of representations that allow for recognition and classification of objects in cluttered scenes is a significant open problem in computer vision. A very promising approach to this problem assumes that the objects to be learned and recognized consist of a collection of parts, and that different objects can share some of the parts. Additionally, changes in the geometrical relation between image parts can be modeled to be flexible to tolerate some deformations. This approach can handle occlusions well, because if some parts of an object are occluded, the other parts can still be detected and recognized perfectly.

Related work includes Mohan and colleagues [13] who use pre-determined parts of human bodies to detect humans in cluttered scenes. Dorko and Schmid [4] use image patches to classify cars, but the extracted patches from the training set are labelled by whether they are part of a car or not. Leibe and Schiele [10] use scale-invariant interest points and manually segmented training data for classification. In contrast to these approaches, we need only weak supervision in training, i.e. only information about the presence of an object in the image. Fergus and colleagues [5] and Weber and colleagues [14] statistically model position, occurrence, and appearance of object parts.

W. Kropatsch, R. Sablatnig, and A. Hanbury (Eds.): DAGM 2005, LNCS 3663, pp. 326–333, 2005.
© Springer-Verlag Berlin Heidelberg 2005

In [3] we present and compare several approaches to use histograms of image patches for the recognition of objects in cluttered scenes. It was shown that an approach using histograms of vector quantized image patches and discriminative training performed best among the tested approaches (global patch search & direct voting, nearest neighbor, naive Bayes, generative Gaussians, and discriminative training). In this work, we further investigate this approach and propose several extensions: 1. As proposed in [9], we use image patches in various scales, enabling us to account for objects at different scales. 2. We use Sobel filtered images in addition to the gray values to account for edge structures in the images. 3. As the histograms created are very sparse (e.g. there are approx. 1000 data points in a 4096 bin histogram), we generalize the histograms to use non-binary bin assignments. 4. To account for different lighting conditions, we incorporate a method for brightness normalization.

2   Baseline Approach

The method for discriminative training of image patch histograms, which has been proposed in [3], consists of two steps: 1. feature extraction and 2. training and classification. These steps are briefly summarized in the following sections.

2.1   Feature Extraction

Given an image, we use up to 500 square image patches as features. These patches are extracted around interest points obtained using the method proposed by Loupias and colleagues [11]. Additionally, we use 300 patches from a uniform grid of 15×20 cells that is projected into the image. In contrast to the interest points from the detector, these points can also fall onto very homogeneous areas of the image. This property is important for capturing homogeneity in objects in addition to points that are detected by interest point detectors, which are usually of high variance. Figure 1 shows the points of interest detected in a typical image. The patches are allowed to extend beyond the image border, in which case the part of the patch falling outside the image is padded with zeroes. After the patches are extracted, a PCA dimensionality reduction is applied to reduce the large dimensionality of the data, keeping 40 coefficients. These data are then clustered with a Linde-Buzo-Gray algorithm using the Euclidean distance. Then we discard all information for each patch except its closest corresponding cluster center identifier. For the test data, this identifier is determined by evaluating the Euclidean distance to all cluster centers for each patch. Thus, the clustering assigns a cluster $c(x) \in \{1, \ldots C\}$ to each image patch x and allows us to create histograms of cluster frequencies by counting how many of the extracted patches belong to each of the clusters. The histogram representation $h(X)$ with C bins is then determined by counting and normalization such that $h_c(X) = \frac{1}{L_X} \sum_{l=1}^{L_X} \delta(c, c(x_l))$, where δ denotes the Kronecker delta function, $c(x_l)$ is the closest cluster center to x_l, and x_l is the l-th image patch extracted from image X.

Fig. 1. Patch extraction: salient points and uniform grid

2.2   Decision Rule

Having obtained this representation by histograms of image patches, we define a
decision rule for the classification of images. In [3] we observed that the method
using discriminative training of log-linear models outperforms other methods.

The approach based on maximum likelihood of the class-conditional distributions does not take into account the information of competing classes during
training. We can use this information by maximizing the class posterior prob-
ability $\prod_{k=1}^{K} \prod_{n=1}^{N_k} p(k|X_{kn})$ instead. Assuming a Gaussian density with pooled
covariances for the class-conditional distribution, this maximization is equivalent
to maximizing the parameters of a log-linear or maximum entropy model

$$p(k|h) = \frac{1}{Z(h)} \exp\left(\alpha_k + \sum_{c=1}^{C} \lambda_{kc} h_c \right),$$

where $Z(h) = \sum_{k=1}^{K} \exp\left(\alpha_k + \sum_{c=1}^{C} \lambda_{kc} h_c \right)$ is the renormalization factor. (Note
that also the generative Gaussian model can be rewritten in this form. Further-
more, we can always find a generative model that results in the same posterior
distribution [7].) The maximizing distribution is unique and the resulting model
is also the model of highest entropy with fixed marginal distributions of the features [7]. Efficient algorithms to determine the parameters $\{\alpha_k, \lambda_{kc}\}$ exist. We
use a modified version of generalized iterative scaling [1]. Bayes' decision rule is
used for classification.

3   Extensions to the Method

In [3], we thoroughly investigated several decision rules and classification methods. In this work, we further investigate the feature extraction method and test
several extensions.

Multi-scale features. In the original approach, all patches extracted were of
the same size and we have experimentally evaluated which image patch size
performed best on the given tasks. This can lead to problems if the objects to be
recognized are of different scales. Here we propose to extract patches of different
sizes. That is, at each feature extraction point, we extract square patches of 7, 11,
21, and 31 pixels width. To be able to use these patches in the proposed training

and classification framework, all extracted patches are scaled to a common size of 15×15 pixels using the Bresenham scaling algorithm.

Derivatives. In many applications of pattern recognition, derivatives can improve classification performance significantly, e.g. in automatic speech recognition, derivatives are normally used. Also in the recognition of handwritten characters, derivatives can strongly improve the results [8], as the local derivatives allow mapping of edges to edges. To take advantage of these effects, we enrich the patches by their horizontally and vertically Sobel filtered versions. That is, the data is tripled by adding horizontally and vertically Sobel-filtered patches. Then, the PCA transformation is applied to all three versions (gray values, horizontal Sobel, vertical Sobel) at once and the dimensionality is reduced from $3 \cdot 15^2 = 675$ to 40 in total to allow for efficient processing in the remaining steps (clustering and histogramization).

Histogram smoothing. A weakness of the original approach might be that the histograms are high dimensional and very sparse, e.g. the histograms have 4096 bins but only 800 patches (2400 for multi-scale features) are extracted per image. Thus, most of the bins are empty and cannot contribute to the result. To have smoother histograms, we generalize the histograms to use non-binary bin assignments, i.e. patches do not only contribute to their closest cluster center but to all cluster centers that are sufficiently similar. That is, given an image patch and the Euclidean distance $d_i := d(x, c_i)$ to cluster center c_i, the corresponding histogram count h_i is updated as

$$h_i \leftarrow h_i + \frac{\exp(-\frac{d_i}{\alpha})}{\sum_{i'} \exp(-\frac{d_{i'}}{\alpha})}.$$

By changing α, the strength of smoothing can be changed.

Brightness normalization. Another issue which is a well-known problem in computer vision is that different images are often taken under different lighting conditions, and thus the brightness of otherwise very similar images can vary significantly. Evidently, the brightness of an image should usually not change class membership, but e.g. the Euclidean distance between two images that are identical except for their brightness can be very high. A practical approach for brightness normalization in this context is given in the PCA transformation: The first PCA vector for a collection of image patches usually captures the change in brightness and thus contributes most to the overall brightness of the image patches. Thus we propose to discard the first component of the PCA transformed vectors in order to discard information about global brightness of image patches [12]. Figure 2 illustrates this effect: For each of the three tasks (airplanes, faces, motorbikes), it shows the first component of the PCA matrix (clearly capturing global patch brightness) and an example of a bright and a dark patch reconstructed from the PCA transformed and dimensionality reduced representations, one with and one without the first PCA component. It can be observed that the differences in brightness are reduced for the patches which have been reconstructed without the first PCA component.

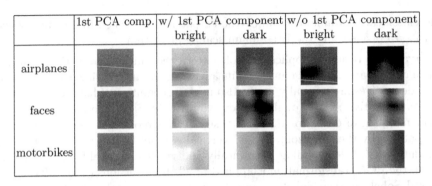

Fig. 2. For each of the three tasks: First PCA component, a bright image patch and a dark image patch reconstructed from the PCA vectors using all 40 PCA components, and the same patches reconstructed from the PCA vectors discarding the first PCA component.

Support-Vector-Classifier. As support-vector-machines (SVM) are a known to be a good classification method, the maximum likelihood approach was exchanged in favor of a support-vector classified from libsvm[1]. We tried radial basis functions and linear functions as kernels and optimized the parameters using the training data.

4   Databases

Fergus and colleagues [5] use different datasets for unsupervised object training and recognition of objects. The task is to determine whether an object is present in an image or not. For this purpose, several sets of images containing certain objects (airplanes, faces, and motorbikes) and a set of background images not containing any of these objects are available[2], which we use in the experiments. The images are of various sizes, and for the experiments they were converted to gray images. The airplanes and the motorbikes task consists of 800 training and 800 test images each. The faces task consists of 436 training and 434 test images. For each of these tasks, half of the images contain the object of interest and the other half does not. An example image of each set is shown in Figure 3. For our experiments we scaled all images to a common height of 225 pixels as our approach implicitly learns the importance of the image size for classification otherwise [3].

5   Experimental Results

In Table 1 we give the results for the baseline method from [3] and the results obtained with the proposed extensions in comparison to results from the literature. All experiments were carried out using 4096 dimensional histograms.

---

[1] http://www.csie.ntu.edu.tw/~cjlin/libsvm/
[2] http://www.robots.ox.ac.uk/~vgg/data

Fig. 3. Examples from the Caltech database (airplanes, faces, motorbikes, background)

Table 1. Summary of results and comparison to results from other publications

Method		airplanes	faces	motorbikes
Discriminative Model	[3]	2.6	5.8	1.5
+ multi-scale features		**1.1**	5.0	1.9
+ multi-scale & Sobel features		4.5	13.6	2.6
+ multi-scale feat. & fuzzy hist.		2.6	8.1	1.4
+ multi-scale & brightness norm.		1.4	**3.7**	**1.1**
lin. SVM + multi-scale & brightness norm.		2.4	7.8	2.1
rbf. SVM + multi-scale & brightness norm.		2.1	9.4	2.1
Statistical Model	[5]	9.8	3.6	7.5
Texture features	[2]	**0.8**	1.6	7.4
Segmentation	[6]	2.2	**0.1**	10.4

Comparing the results using multi-scale features to the results from the baseline method where only patches of one size were extracted, a clear improvement can be seen in two of the three tasks. The result for the motorbikes task was not improved. These results can be explained by the fact that the scale of the motorbikes is very homogeneous and thus, multi-scale features cannot improve the results. Due to the positive results, all experiments in the following were performed using multi scale features.

The results where Sobel features were used are worse than those from the baseline method. This unexpected result may be due to the combined PCA transformation of brightness and contrast information. We will further investigate the reasons for these effects.

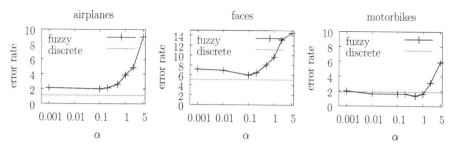

Fig. 4. Error rates for the Caltech tasks depending on the smoothing factor α in fuzzy histograms

In a next step, we evaluated the possible advantages of fuzzy histograms. Figure 4 shows the effect of choosing different parameters α to smooth the image patch histograms. In these experiments we used 4096 clusters and multi

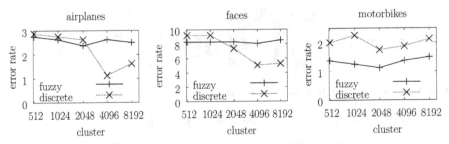

Fig. 5. Error rates for the Caltech tasks depending on the number of clusters using fuzzy histograms and discrete histograms

scale features. The figures show that the fuzzy histograms do not improve the results in this setting. In Figure 5 we compare fuzzy histograms with discrete histograms using different numbers of histogram bins. It can be seen that fuzzy histograms outperform discrete histograms in the case of only few clusters. As the clustering process is computationally very expensive, but the creation of fuzzy histograms is not more expensive than the creation of discrete histograms given a cluster model, fuzzy histograms can be used to obtain reasonable results when computing power for the training is limited. It can also be clearly seen that the number of clusters has less impact on the classification performance when fuzzy histograms are used. The results in Table 1 show that the use of fuzzy histograms does not yield a significant improvement over the baseline method.

The results from evaluating the proposed method for brightness normalization can be seen in Table 1. It can be seen that strong improvements are possible here. A significant improvement is observed in the faces task because some of the images were taken indoors and some images where taken outdoors.

Finally, SVMs were tested and the results cannot be improved. Thus, apart from losing the possibility to visually see which patches are discriminative for which class we loose classification performance using SVMs.

The result presented in [6] is much better for the faces task, because a specialized method for face detection was applied to the data.

6   Conclusion and Outlook

In this paper we extended a method for object classification in cluttered scenes into different directions. We proposed to use multi-scale feature, Sobel features, generalized histograms, and brightness normalization. We could show experimentally that multi-scale features and brightness normalization strongly improve the results, and that generalized histograms can be used to reduce computation time in training with only slight degradation in classification performance. Using Sobel features did not improve the results. It might be an interesting option to apply PCA transformation to the gray values and Sobel features separately. Furthermore, we plan to explicitly model local variability in images. Another point where improvements are probably possible is to consider spatial information along with the extracted patches. All spatial information is currently discarded.

The results of the recent evaluation within the PASCAL Visual Object Classes Challenge[3] underline the quality of the approach.

Acknowledgments

We would like to thank Etienne Loupias for providing the source code for his salient point detector. This work was partially funded by the DFG (Deutsche Forschungsgemeinschaft) under contract NE-572/6.

References

1. J. N. Darroch and D. Ratcliff. Generalized Iterative Scaling for Log-Linear Models. *Annals of Mathematical Statistics*, 43(5):1470–1480, 1972.
2. T. Deselaers, D. Keysers, and H. Ney. Features for Image Retrieval – A Quantitative Comparison. In *DAGM Symposium, Pattern Recognition*, Tübingen, Germany, pages 228–236, Sep. 2004.
3. T. Deselaers, D. Keysers, and H. Ney. Discriminative Training for Object Recognition using Image Patches. In *CVPR*, San Diego, CA, in press, June 2005.
4. G. Dorko and C. Schmid. Selection of Scale-Invariant Parts for Object Class Recognition. In *ICCV*, volume 1, Nice, France, pages 634–640, Oct. 2003.
5. R. Fergus, P. Perona, and A. Zissermann. Object Class Recognition by Unsupervised Scale-Invariant Learning. In *CVPR*, Blacksburg, VG, pp. 264–271, June 2003.
6. M. Fussenegger, A. Opelt, A. Pinz, and P. Auer. Object Recognition Using Segmentation for Feature Detection. In *ICPR*, vol. 3, Cambridge, UK, pp. 41–48, Aug. 2004.
7. D. Keysers, F.-J. Och, and H. Ney. Maximum Entropy and Gaussian Models for Image Object Recognition. In *DAGM Symposium, Pattern Recognition*, Zürich, Switzerland, pages 498–506, Sep. 2002.
8. D. Keysers, C. Gollan, and H. Ney. Local Context in Non-linear Deformation Models for Handwritten Character Recognition. In *ICPR*, vol. 4, Cambridge, UK, pages 511–514, Aug. 2004.
9. T. Kölsch, D. Keysers, H. Ney, and R. Paredes. Enhancements for Local Feature Based Image Classification. In *ICPR*, vol. 1, pp. 248–251, Aug. 2004.
10. B. Leibe and B. Schiele. Scale Invariant Object Categorization Using a Scale-Adaptive Mean-Shift Search. In *DAGM Symposium, Pattern Recognition*, pp. 145–153, Aug. 2004.
11. E. Loupias, N. Sebe, S. Bres, and J. Jolion. Wavelet-based Salient Points for Image Retrieval. In *ICIP*, vol. 2, Vancouver, Canada, pages 518–521, Sep. 2000.
12. A. Martinez and A. Kak. PCA versus LDA. *IEEE TPAMI* 23(2):228–233, Feb. 2001.
13. A. Mohan, C. Papageorgiou, and T. Poggio. Example-based Object Detection in Images by Components. *IEEE TPAMI*, 23(4):349–361, Apr. 2001.
14. M. Weber, M. Welling, and P. Perona. Unsupervised Learning of Models for Recognition. In *ECCV*, vol. 1, Dublin, Ireland, pp. 18–32, June 2000.

---

[3] http://www.pascal-network.org/challenges/VOC/

Comparison of Multiclass SVM Decomposition Schemes for Visual Object Recognition

Laine Kahsay, Friedhelm Schwenker, and Günther Palm

University of Ulm, Department of Neural Information Processing,
Albert-Einstein-Allee 11, D-89069 Ulm
Phone: +49 731 5024151, Fax: +49 731 5024156
{kahsay, fschwenker, Palm}@neuro.informatik.uni-ulm.de

Abstract. We consider the problem of multiclass decomposition schemes for Support Vector Machines with Linear, Polynomial and RBF kernels. Our aim is to compare and discuss popular multiclass decomposing approaches such as the One versus the Rest, One versus One, Decision Directed Acyclic Graphs, Tree Structured, Error Correcting Output Codes. We conducted our experiments on benchmark datastes consisting of camera images of 3D objects. In our experiments we found that all the multiclass decomposing schemes for SVMs performed comparably very well with no significant statistical differences in cases of nonlinear kernels. In case of linear kernels the multiclass schemes OvR, OvO and DDAG outperform Tree Structured and ECOC.

1 Introduction

The task of learning from examples for pattern recognition applications is to find an approximating classifier mapping f for an unknown function F given a finite set of training examplars $(x_i, F(x_i))$. Provided, F is a binary function, many algorithms are available, e.g. Classification Trees (CT), Linear Discriminate Analysis (LDA), K-Nearest-Neigbors (KNN), Learning Vector Quantization (LVQ), and Artificial Neural Networks (ANN) such as perceptrons, Multi-Layer-Perceptrons (MLP) or Radial Basis Function (RBF) Networks [4,9]. These learning schemes are well defined to learn binary-valued classifier mappings, but in real-world applications the classifier has to take values from a discrete set of $K > 2$ classes, for instance in medical diagnosis, optical character recognition, phoneme classification, and 3D visual object recognition [4]. Some of these learning schemes can be easily extended to the multiclass problem, e.g. KNN, LVQ and DT, but many ANNs are more difficult to generalize to the multiclass setting. The typical ANN approach to the multiclass problem is to train K individual binary classifiers $f_1, \ldots, f_K$ one for each class, and then to apply an unseen input x to each classifier f_i and assign the class j to x for the classifier f_j with the highest output value $f_j(x)$.

Support Vector Machines (SVMs) are an important alternative to MLPs or RBF networks [20,2]. The advantage of SVMs is that the learning task is a convex optimization problem instead of a general nonlinear optimization problem

W. Kropatsch, R. Sablatnig, and A. Hanbury (Eds.): DAGM 2005, LNCS 3663, pp. 334–341, 2005.

in case of multilayered neural nets, such as MLPs or RBFs. The simplest model of SVMs constructs a maximal margin hyperplane separating a set of positive samples from a set of negative samples. Linearly non separable problems can be tackled by utilizing the kernel function method [18] (section 2). In section 3 multiclass decomposition schemes for SVMs are described. Here in this study we conducted our experimental evaluation on real world benchmark datasets for object recognition problems consisting up to 100 classes. A description of the experiments, datasets and results is given in section 4. In [1,17] multiclass decomposing for SVMs is discussed and evaluated by using benchmark datasets from the UCI repository with number of classes ranging up to only 26. Further more we have included additionally the Tree Structured SVMs [19] in our study. Finally in section 5 we discuss results.

2   Support Vector Machines (SVMs)

Given ℓ training samples (x_i, y_i) where each sample is a d-dimension vector $(x_i \in R^d)$ and is labeled as $y_i \in \{1, -1\}$. A separating hyperplane $H(w, b)$ in R^d can then be written as:

$$H(w, b) = \{x \in R^d \mid w \cdot x + b = 0\} \tag{1}$$

where $b \in R$, and $w \in R^d$ is a vector orthogonal to the hyperplane; and the decision function would be $f(x) = sign(wx + b)$. Since the hyperplane $H(w, b)$ given by Eq. (1) can be equally expressed by all pairs $(\lambda w, \lambda b)$ for all $\lambda \in R^+$, it is appropriate to consider a hyperplane in canonical form with respect to x_i [20], where the scaling λ is implicitly set, such that, $\min \{x_i : \mid w \cdot x_i + b \mid\} = 1$. This is also equivalent to saying that the sample point closest to the hyperplane has a distance of $1/\|w\|$ leading to an over all margin distance of $2/\|w\|$. To maximize the margin the task would therefore be the minimization of $T(w) := \frac{1}{2}\|w\|^2$, subject to $y_i(w \cdot x_i + b) \geq 1$, $i = 1, \cdots, \ell$. Further more, the learning task is reduced to the maximization of the primal Lagrangian:

$$\max_{w,b} L(w, b, \alpha) := \frac{1}{2}\|w\|^2 - \sum_{i=1}^{\ell} \alpha_i(y_i(w \cdot x_i + b) - 1) \tag{2}$$

where $\alpha_i \geq 0$ are Lagrangian multipliers. By taking the derivative of the primal with respect to w and b and making appropriate re-substitution, the dual form of the primal is formulated as it is more convenient to deal with.

$$\max_{w} W(\alpha) := \frac{1}{2}\|w\|^2 - \sum_{i=1}^{\ell}\sum_{j=1}^{\ell} \alpha_i\alpha_j y_i y_j (x_i \cdot x_j), \tag{3}$$

subject to $\alpha_i \geq 0, i = 1, \cdots, \ell$ and $\sum_{i=1}^{\ell} \alpha_i y_i = 0$. Sample points corresponding to the multipliers $\alpha_i > 0$ are termed as the *Support Vectors* (SVs) [18,2].

To deal with linearly non-separable problems, more general decision surfaces need to be considered. This can be accomplished by using a nonlinear mapping $\Phi(x)$ that transforms the input data into a high dimension *feature space*, where it would be possible to construct an optimal separating hyperplane. This procedure is justified by Cover's Theorem [18]. The formulation of the new optimization problem is simply done by replacing all occurrences of x with $\Phi(x)$ in Eq. (3).

$$\max_{w} W(\alpha) := \frac{1}{2}\|w\|^2 - \sum_{i=1}^{\ell}\sum_{j=1}^{\ell}\alpha_i\alpha_j y_i y_j(\Phi(x_i)\cdot\Phi(x_j)) \qquad (4)$$

subject to $\alpha_i \geq 0, i = 1,\cdots,\ell$ and $\sum_{i=1}^{\ell}\alpha_i y_i = 0$. Note that, there is no need to explicitly map the data into the high-dimensional feature space and compute the dot products $\Phi(x_i)\cdot\Phi(x_j)$, as it is possible to find a *kernel function* [18] $K(x_i, x_j) = \Phi(x_i)\cdot\Phi(x_j)$. After computing the optimal values α_i^*, the decision function would be $f(x) = sign(\sum_{i=1}^{\ell}\alpha_i^* y_i K(x, x_i) + b)$.

3   Multiclass Decomposition Schemes

In our experiments we have studied different decomposition schemes for multiclass classification problem using SVMs. In the following sub-sections each of the multiclass approaches listed below are discussed.

- One versus the Rest (O-vs-R)
- One versus One (O-vs-O)
- Decision Directed Acyclic Graphs (DAG)
- Tree Structured (TS)
- Error Correcting Output Codes (ECOC)

3.1   One Versus the Rest (OvR)

This scheme is the most intuitive method of decomposition, where the task of solving a K-class problem is done by constructing a set of binary classifiers $f_1 \cdots f_K$. Each of the f_k classifiers is trained to separate the kth class from the rest of the classes, and hence the name One-versus-the-Rest (OvR). The classification of an unknown sample x is performed according to maximal output value of functions $f_k(x)$ without applying the signum function, i.e. *winner-takes-all*.

$$\operatorname*{argmax}_{k} f_k(x) = \sum y_i \alpha_i^k K(x, x_i) + b^k \qquad (5)$$

The values of $f_k(x)$ can also be used as a measure of reject decision. This is done by taking the difference between the two largest $f_k(x)$ as a measure of confidence in the classification of unknown sample x. If this difference falls below a certain threshold value, then the sample may be rejected.

3.2   One Versus One (OvO)

This method has a simple conceptual approach in which a binary classifier is trained for each pair of classes resulting in $\binom{K}{2}$ classifiers. Compared to OvR, it has large number of classifiers which might suggest large training time. But, since the size of individual problems is significantly smaller than the whole, it is actually possible to save time during training, and is faster during evaluation as the number of SVs for each binary problem is usually much smaller [10,8,7]. The separating boundaries are constructed by defining a decision function f_{pq} for each pair of classes (p, q), $p \neq q$, as follows,

$$x \overset{f_{pq}}{\mapsto} \begin{cases} +1, & x \text{ in class } p \\ -1, & x \text{ in class } q \end{cases} \tag{6}$$

The class prediction of an unknown sample x is made by taking the maximum value of the sums of the output of signum function ($\max_p f_p := \sum_q f_{pq}$, for $p \neq q$). The winner class gets exactly $(K-1)$ positive votes for cases where there are no tie situations. In tie situation, where more than one classes get equal positive vote, one has to take into consideration the confidence by measuring the real values of the decision function instead of the output of a signum function.

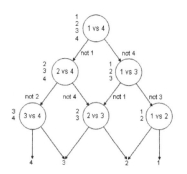

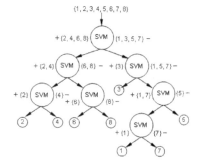

Fig. 1. DDAG for a 4-class problem

Fig. 2. Tree Structure for an 8-class problem

3.3   Decision Directed Acyclic Graphs (DDAG)

The OvO scheme has some inefficiency with respect to evaluation time, especially when the number of classes is very large it grows super linearly with the number of classes. One remedy to this problem is to use Decision Directed Acyclic Graphs (DDAG) introduced in [16]. In a K-class problem, the DDAG tree includes $\binom{K}{2}$ nodes which embed binary classifiers between the pth and q^{th} pair of classes; see Fig. (1). The K leaves of the tree represent predicted class labels of unknown sample. The total depth of the DDAG is $K - 1$. During training the DAG scheme is necessarily the same as the OvO scheme producing $\binom{K}{2}$ binary classifiers. However, during evaluation, only $K - 1$ decision nodes are traversed. This systematic approach of evaluation in DDAG outperforms the evaluation in OvO scheme by a factor of $K/2$ times in speed.

3.4   Tree Structured (TS)

The strategy here is to decompose a K-class problem into two disjoint subsets recursively until every subset contains one class only [19]; see Fig. (2). The nodes of the tree embed binary classifies while the leaves yield the label of a class prediction. For a K-class problem $(K-1)$ SVMs must be trained, however, approximately $\log_2(K)$ decision functions are evaluated. In the design of a Tree Structure, there is no definite way to construct two disjoint subsets of classes at each node. For all practical purposes it is recommended to do the splitting according to some similarity measures such as using a clustering algorithm or other measures of similarities [19].

3.5   Error-Correcting Output Codes (ECOC)

Introduced by Dietterich and Bakiri [3,1], the strategy here is to decompose a K-class problem into binary problems based on a distributed output codes in which each class is assigned a unique N-bit codeword. The K codewords are combined together to form a code matrix M. During training N binary classifiers are trained, where each classifier belongs to one bit position in the codewords. Class prediction is done using Hamming decoding that compares the Hamming distance between the computed code of unknown sample and the codewords of the classes. Hamming decoding ignores the 'confidence' $|f_j(x)|$ of predictions. Another approach of decoding that takes into consideration the confidence is the Loss based decoding. To classify an unknown sample x, first the output of each decision function is computed, i.e. $f_1(x), f_2(x), \cdots, f_N(x)$. Then for each class i the total loss $\sum_{j=1}^{N} L(M(i,j)f_j(x))$ is computed, where each $M(i,j)$ are the entries of the code matrix and $L(z)$ is the loss function. Finaly the class label of the unknown is chosen to be the ith class that minimizes the total loss. The encoding and decoding technique of the ECOC constitutes some error-correcting capabilities measured by the minimum Hamming distance d between any pair of codewords. In general a good error-correcting output code-matrix should have well separated rows and columns [3].

4   Experiments and Results

All our experiments were carried on the following datasets containing camera images of 3-D objects.

- *Obst dataset* - 7 types of fruits, 840 images with 120 instance from each [5].
- *Faces dataset* - 40 subjects, 400 images with 10 instance from each[11].
- *Coil-20 dataset* - 20 objects, 1440 images with 72 instances from each[13].
- *Coil-100 dataset* - 100 objects, 7200 images with 72 instances from each [13].

Each image in the datasets was pre-processed using Orientation Histograms [6] to extract *feature vectors*. Orientation Histogram were computed for each gray image by sub-dividing it into 3×3 rectangular regions with an overlap of about

20% between adjacent regions. For each of the nine sub-regions in the image, the Orientation Histograms were computed in 8-bins and then concatenated together to give a 72-dimensional feature vector for each entry[5]. All the experiments were conducted on OvR, OvO, DDAG, TS and ECOC decomposing schemes for SVMs using Linear, Polynomials *(degrees 2 and 3)*, and RBF $(exp\{-\frac{\|x_i - x_j\|}{2\sigma^2}\}, \sigma = 1$ *and* $\sigma = 2)$ kernel functions. Training of the SVMs was done using the Sequential Minimal Optimization (SMO) algorithm [15]. The value of the meta-parameter C for the SVM was set to 10 which offered good solutions.

Table 1. Obst dataset:

	Linear	Poly $d=2$	Poly $d=3$	RBF $\sigma=1$	RBF $\sigma=2$
OvR	86.9	92.9	93.9	95.8	96.0
OvO	89.1	94.2	94.8	92.7	96.6
DAG	89.5	94.1	94.9	92.7	96.6
Tree	86.1	93.2	95.0	86.9	95.9
ECOC	84.4	94.7	94.4	95.8	96.2

Table 2. Coil-20 dataset

	Linear	Poly $d=2$	Poly $d=3$	RBF $\sigma=1$	RBF $\sigma=2$
OvR	99.6	99.8	68.3	100.0	100.0
OvO	100.0	100.0	43.2	99.8	100.0
DAG	100.0	100.0	34.8	99.8	100.0
Tree	100.0	100.0	100.0	99.9	100.0
ECOC	89.0	99.9	91.9	100.0	100.0

Table 3. Faces dataset

	Linear	Poly $d=2$	Poly $d=3$	RBF $\sigma=1$	RBF $\sigma=2$
OvR	99.7	100.0	100.0	98.5	100.0
OvO	99.5	99.5	99.2	88.2	99.5
DAG	99.7	99.5	99.2	88.2	99.5
Tree	94.1	98.5	97.8	78.8	98.2
ECOC	69.1	99.2	99.8	93.5	99.5

Table 4. Coil100 dataset

	Linear	Poly $d=2$	Poly $d=3$	RBF $\sigma=1$	RBF $\sigma=2$
OvR	91.2	99.4	96.2	99.8	99.7
OvO	99.4	99.7	96.8	99.7	99.7
DAG	99.3	99.6	96.9	99.7	99.7
Tree	86.5	98.7	94.1	99.6	99.1

To estimate the percentage of accuracy we performed *10-times-10-Fold cross-validation* for all the datasets with the exception of the Coil-100 dataset, in which case only a single run of *10-Fold cross-validation* was made. Our results are summarized in Tables 1-4. All numeric data in the results represent the median value of the percentage of accuracy from all the averages of the *10-times-10-fold cross-validation*. The standard deviation during evaluation was less than 0.6% in almost all cases with some exception for the COIL-20 dataset in using polynomial kernel of degree 3 where the deviation is 0.04% for the Tree-SVM, 2.1% for the ECOC and 4.9% for the OvsR.

5   Conclusion

We have observed that SVMs perform very well as learning systems with good ability to generalize even across objects of similar appearance as this is evident from the results obtained for the Obst dataset, which contains seven similar fruits. The use of Polynomial $(d = 2)$ and the RBF $(\sigma = 2)$ kernels showed relatively better performance in almost all cases as can be seen in Tables (1-4). This implies that careful choice of kernel functions improves the performance of multiclass classification. Another important observation is that all the multiclass decomposing schemes show comparably similar performance. A slight exception being the use of linear kernel in some datasets. This lower performance in linear kernel is mostly noticeable in the ECOC scheme, which could be due to the resulting binary problems being more complex and harder as to be solved linearly.

The Tree-Structure SVMs may still achieve better results if one could improve the way the samples are split at each node. One possible way of improvement would be to consider nodes with overlapped decision regions, which may require slightly more SVMs to be trained. This is to say some classes may be allowed to appear on both positive and negative sides at a node if their samples are in good proportion on both subsets during the clustering or splitting. Furthermore, tree-sturctured SVMs offer the opportunity to utilize different types of features in the decision nodes. Integeration of multiple features (shape, color, etc...) in the recognition of 3D objects is particularly important in the multiclass object recognition applications where it is difficult to discriminate objects based on a single feature; see [5,12,14]. The OvR approach besides being the most intituitive, it scored at least as comparable results as others. The advantage of the OvO and DAGs over the other schemes is that they have minimal training time due to the reduced number of samples considered in each sub-problem. A rather unexpected result in Table (2) is observed on the results of COIL-20 in using polynomial kernel of degree 3. Here, the schemes DDAG, O-vs-O and O-vs-R have shown lower performance (<70%), on the other hand the tree-structured SVMs have scored exceptionally highest accuracy (100%) followed by ECOC (91%). Since, the problem is not appearing in other cases and datasets, it could be due to some special 'properties' specific to the COIL-20 dataset.

It is important mentioning here the Orientation Histograms (see section 4) that were applied to extract feature vectors have yielded good results proving that they are very good techniques among others to extract features for object recognition from camera images.

References

1. E. L. Allwein, R. E. Schapire, and Y. Singer. Reducing Multiclass to Binary: Unifying Approach for Margin Classifiers. In *Proc. 17th Int'l Conf. on Machine Learning*, pages 9–16, 2000.
2. C. Cortes and V. Vapnik. Support Vector Networks. *Machine Learning*, 20:273–297, 1995.
3. T. G. Dietterich and G. Bakiri. Solving multiclass learning problems via error-correcting output codes. *Jour. of Artificial Intelligence Research*, 2:263–286, 1995.
4. R. Duda, P. Hart, and D. Stork. *Pattern Classification*. John Wiley & Sons, New York, 2001.
5. R. Fay, U. Kaufmann, F. Schwenker, and G. Palm. Learning Object Recognition in a NeuroBotic System. In Horst-Michael Groß, Klaus Debes, and Hans-Joachim Böhme, editors, *3rd Workshop on SelfOrganization of AdaptiVE Behavior SOAVE 2004*, pages 198–209. VDI, Dsseldorf, 2004.
6. W. T. Freeman and M. Roth. Orientation histogram for hand gesture recognition. In *IEEE Int'l Workshop on Automatic Face and Gesture Recognition, Zurich*, pages 296–301, 1995.

7. J.H. Friedman. Another approach to polychotomous classification. Technical report, Stanford University, Department of Statistics, 1996.
8. T. Hastie and R. Tibshirani. Classification by pairwise coupling. *The Annals of Statistics*, 2:451–471, 1998.
9. Trevor Hastie, Robert Tibshirani, and J. H. Friedman. *The elements of statistical learning: data mining, inference, and prediction*. New York: Springer-Verlag, 2001.
10. U. Kreßel. Pairwise classification and support vector machines. In B. Schölkopf, C. Burges, and A. Smola, editors, *Advances in Kernel Methods*, chapter 15, pages 255–268. The MIT Press, 1999.
11. S. Lawrence, L. Giles, A. C. Tsoi, and A. D. Back. Face recognition: A convolutional neural network approach. *IEEE TNN*, 8(1):98–113, 1997.
12. B. W. Mel. SEEMORE: Combining color, shape and texture histogramming in a neurally-inspired approach to visual object recognition. *Neural Computation*, 9(4):777–804, 1997.
13. S. Nene, S. Nayar, and H. Murase. Columbia Object Image Library. Technical Report CUCS-005-96 and CUCS-006-96, Columbia University, 1996.
14. M. E. Nilsback and B. Caputo. Cue integration through discriminative accumulation. In *CVPR (2)*, pages 578–585, 2004.
15. J. C. Platt. Sequential Minimal Optimization: A Fast Algorithm for Training SVMs. Technical Report MSR-TR-98-14, Microsoft Research, 1998.
16. J. C. Platt, N. Cristianini, and J. Shawe-Taylor. Large Margin DAGS for Multiclass Classification. In S.A. Solla, T.K. Leen, and K.-R. Mueller, editors, *Advances in Neural Information Processing Systems 12*, pages 547–553, 2000.
17. R. Rifkin and A. Klautau. In defense of one-vs-all classification. *Journal of Machine Learning Research*, 5:101–141, 2004.
18. B. Schölkopf and A. J. Smola. *Learning with Kernels: Support Vector Machines, Regularization, Optimization and Beyond*. MIT Press, Cambridge, MA, 2002.
19. F. Schwenker. Solving Multi-Class Pattern Recognition Problems with Tree Structured Support Vector Machines. In B. Radig and S. Florczyk, editors, *Mustererkennung 2001*, pages 283–290. Springer, 2001.
20. V. Vapnik. *The Nature of Statistical Learning Theory*. Springer, N.Y., 1995.

Shape Priors and Online Appearance Learning for Variational Segmentation and Object Recognition in Static Scenes

Martin Bergtholdt and Christoph Schnörr

Computer Vision, Graphics, and Pattern Recognition Group,
Department of Mathematics and Computer Science,
University of Mannheim, 68131 Mannheim, Germany
{bergtholdt, schnoerr}@uni-mannheim.de

Abstract. We present an integrated two-level approach to computationally analyzing image sequences of static scenes by variational segmentation. At the top level, estimated models of object appearance and background are probabilistically fused to obtain an a-posteriori probability for the occupancy of each pixel. The data-association strategy handles object occlusions explicitly.

At the lower level, object models are inferred by variational segmentation based on image data and statistical shape priors. The use of shape priors allows to distinguish between recognition of known objects and segmentation of unknown objects. The object models are sufficiently flexible to enable the integration of general cues like advanced shape distances. At the same time, they are highly constrained from the optimization viewpoint: the globally optimal parameters can be computed at each time instant by dynamic programming.

The novelty of our approach is the integration of state-of-the-art variational segmentation into a probabilistic framework for static scene analysis that combines both on-line learning and prior knowledge of various aspects of object appearance.

1 Introduction

Since the seminal work of Mumford and Shah on variational image segmentation [13], research has focused on generalizations of the Mumford-Shah functional along several directions.

A first direction concerns algorithmic schemes and contour representation by level sets for efficiently computing a good local minimum [3,18,19]. A second line of research investigates probabilistic models of image classes for variational segmentation that are richer than the piecewise-smooth image model underlying the original Mumford-Shah functional [22,14,12,11]. Thirdly, statistical shape priors have been considered recently to complement data-driven variational approaches with a model-driven component [8,7,16,5,4,15,21].

This work contributes to the latter two directions in a twofold novel way. Firstly, probabilistic representations for *spatially structured* intensity distributions – as opposed to homogeneous textures - like the appearance of clothes,

W. Kropatsch, R. Sablatnig, and A. Hanbury (Eds.): DAGM 2005, LNCS 3663, pp. 342–350, 2005.

are learnt on-line. Secondly, statistical shape priors based on a *psychophysically relevant* shape distance and prototypical views are learnt off-line from examples through structure-preserving Euclidean embedding and clustering. Both shape distance and embedding, as well as the incorporation of this knowledge into the overall variational approach as a statistical prior, distinguish our work from related hierarchical shape representations introduced by Gavrila for pedestrian detection in traffic scenes through template matching ([9,10]).

Organization. In section 2, we describe the overall probabilistic model for image intensity, conditioned on estimated models of object appearance. The components of this model and the parameters that constitute object appearance in terms of intensity and shape, are explained in section 3. Section 4 describes the computation of optimal contours and data association through variational segmentation. We conclude with a discussion of experimental results and pointing out further work.

2   Probabilistic Image Model

At every time instant t, image intensity $I(\mathbf{x}, t)$ depends at each location $\mathbf{x} \in \Omega$ on the presence of N objects $\mathcal{O} = \{O_0; O_1, \ldots, O_N\}$, where O_0 denotes the background. Each object $O_k, k = 1, \ldots, N$, is specified by parameters, $O_k = \{\Theta_k, \mathbf{c}_k(s)\} \in \mathcal{O}$ which have the following meaning:

- Θ_k parametrizes a distribution p_{Θ_k} which models object appearance in terms of intensity. These distributions form the components of the overall image intensity distribution in eqn. (1). They are described in section 3.2.
- $\mathbf{c}_k(s)$ denotes the boundary contour of image region Ω_k occupied by object O_k, $\mathbf{c}_k(s) := \partial \Omega_k$ (Ω_k image region of object O_k)

With each object region Ω_k, we associate its characteristic function: $\chi_k(\mathbf{x}) = 1$ if $\mathbf{x} \in \Omega_k$ and 0 otherwise.

Given the parameters of all objects $\mathcal{O}$, the probabilistic image model reads:

$$p\big(I(\mathbf{x}) \,|\, \mathcal{O}\big) = \sum_{k=0}^{N} \pi_k(\mathbf{x}) \, p_{\Theta_k}\big(I(\mathbf{x}) \,|\, \mathbf{c}_k\big) \,, \quad \pi_k(\mathbf{x}) = \frac{\chi_k(\mathbf{x})}{\sum_{j=0}^{N} \chi_j(\mathbf{x})} \,, \quad \forall \mathbf{x} \in \Omega \ (1)$$

Parameters π_k are deterministically obtained from the object regions, the factors $p_{\Theta_k}\big(I(\mathbf{x}) \,|\, \mathbf{c}_k\big)$ are detailed in section 3.2. This "mixture of objects" model is less restrictive than partitioning models that divide an image into mutually exclusive regions, since in our case several objects are allowed to occupy the same image location (occlusions).

Basically, eqn. (1) models object appearance in terms of both *intensity and shape*. For each object O_k (including background), a parameterized intensity model is learnt and updated from frame to frame. This intensity information is combined with statistical prior information about possible object shapes, which has been learnt off-line. Through optimizing the contours $\mathbf{c}_k$ (see section 4), object regions Ω_k compete with each other in order to provide the "best explanation" of given image data.

3   Object Appearance

3.1   Statistical Shape Priors

We assume that, for each object class, a database is given containing shapes of different object views. These data are represented by a small subset of representative, prototypical views, obtained by pairwise dissimilarity clustering.

In order to cope with non-rigid objects like human shapes, we adopted from [1] the shape distance:

$$d_E(\mathbf{c}_1, \mathbf{c}_2) = \min_g E(g; \mathbf{c}_1, \mathbf{c}_2) \,, \qquad (2)$$

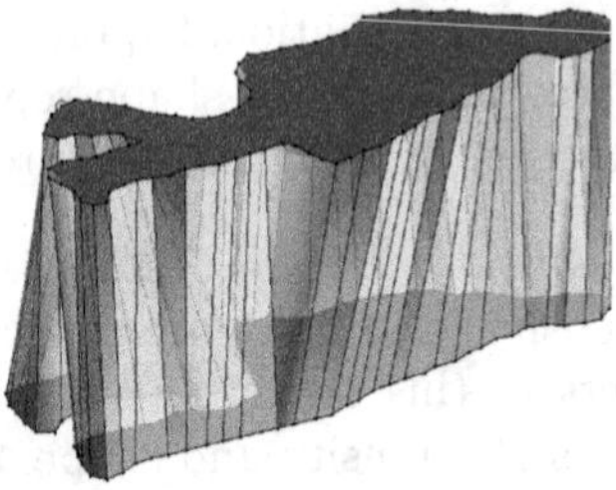

which is computed by minimizing the matching functional:

Fig. 1. Matching by minimizing (3) leads to an accurate correspondence of *parts* of non-rigid objects

$$E(g; \mathbf{c}_1, \mathbf{c}_2) = \oint_0^1 \left\{ \frac{[\kappa_2(s) - \kappa_1(g(s))g'(s)]^2}{|\kappa_2(s)| + |\kappa_1(g(s))g'(s)|} + \lambda \frac{|g'(s) - 1|^2}{|g'(s)| + 1} \right\} ds \qquad (3)$$

over all smooth reparametrizations $g : [0,1] \longrightarrow [0,1]$. Here, κ_1, κ_2 denote the curvature functions of the contours $\mathbf{c}_1, \mathbf{c}_2$. Functional (3) involves bending (change of curvature) and stretching $g'(s)$ of contours, which allows to group contours that are *perceptually close* to each other, despite transformed parts (cf. [1]). The minimization in (2) is carried out by dynamic programming over all piecewise-linear and strictly monotonously increasing functions g. Figure 1 illustrates the result for two human shapes.

To determine representative shapes by clustering, we compute an Euclidean embedding $\{\mathbf{p}_k\}_{k=1,2,\ldots}$ of the given shape examples such that $\|\mathbf{p}_i - \mathbf{p}_j\| \approx$

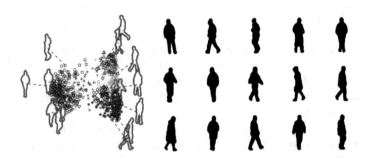

Fig. 2. Left, clustering of the views of human shapes, projected to the first two principal components. The clusters are indicated by prototypical shapes (cluster centers) dominating a range of corresponding views. Right, the templates corresponding to the cluster centers used in our experiments.

$d_E(\mathbf{c}_i, \mathbf{c}_j)$, $\forall i, j$ [6], followed by k-means clustering [2]. As a result of this procedure, we obtain for each object class a small set of representative shapes, henceforth called *templates* $\mathcal{T} = \{\mathbf{c}_1^t, \ldots, \mathbf{c}_T^t\}$, see figure 2. We assume equal prior probabilities for the templates.

3.2 Object Intensity

We model the background O_0 by Gaussian mixture distributions for each pixel with - in our implementation - three components [17]. This simple approach proved to be effective and runs in real-time on current PCs.

For each foreground object $O_1, \ldots, O_N$, we combine this approach with the statistical shape information described in the previous section as follows.

Each template $\mathbf{c}_j^t$ in $\mathcal{T}$ is represented in *normalized* coordinates $\mathbf{x}'$. For the current contour $\mathbf{c}_k$ of object O_k in the *image*, we compute in parallel the optimal matchings to all templates $\mathbf{c}_j^t$ in $\mathcal{T}$ through (2), and corresponding registrations of the enclosed regions by thin-plate splines [20] using the correspondences on the boundary. This establishes a one-to-one correspondence between image and template coordinates $\mathbf{x}, \mathbf{x}'$, see figure 3.

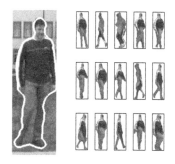

Fig. 3. A human shape and images in normalized coordinates. Note the plausible distortions of intensity. Also note that some matchings for perceptually dissimilar templates are wrong, but these integrate out over time.

The distribution $p_{\Theta_k}(I(\mathbf{x}) \mid \mathbf{c}_k)$ in (1) modeling the intensity of object O_k is then given by marginalizing out the shape templates:

$$p_{\Theta_k}(I(\mathbf{x}) \mid \mathbf{c}_k) = \sum_{j=1}^{T} p(I(\mathbf{x}) \mid \mathbf{c}_j^t) \, p(\mathbf{c}_j^t \mid \mathbf{c}_k) \, ,$$

where $p(I(\mathbf{x}) \mid \mathbf{c}_j^t)$ records – analogously to the background – for each template $\mathbf{c}_j^t$ a pixel-wise Gaussian mixture model in normalized coordinates $\mathbf{x}'$:

$$p(I(\mathbf{x}) \mid \mathbf{c}_j^t) = \sum_{i=1}^{3} \pi_i^j(\mathbf{x}') \mathcal{N}(I(\mathbf{x}); \mu_i^j(\mathbf{x}'), \Sigma_i^j(\mathbf{x}')) \, , \qquad (4)$$

and where the probability that template $\mathbf{c}_j^t$ is representative for the current object contour $\mathbf{c}_k$ in the image, is given by:

$$p(\mathbf{c}_j^t \mid \mathbf{c}_k) := \frac{\exp\left(-d_E(\mathbf{c}_j^t, \mathbf{c}_k)\right)}{\sum_{l=1}^{T} \exp\left(-d_E(\mathbf{c}_l^t, \mathbf{c}_k)\right)}$$

Hence, given the current image contour $\mathbf{c}_k$, parameters Θ_k comprise the mixture parameters for all templates, $\Theta_k = \left\{\pi_i^j(\mathbf{x}'), \mu_i^j(\mathbf{x}'), \Sigma_i^j(\mathbf{x}')\right\}_{i=1,2,3;\, j=1,\ldots,T}.$

4   Variational Inference

Having estimated parameters Θ_k given the image contour $\mathbf{c}_k$ for object O_k, we wish to update $\mathbf{c}_k$. This is accomplished by computing in parallel for all templates $\mathbf{c}_j^t$ the contour $\mathbf{c}$ minimizing the functional:

$$J(\mathbf{c};\mathbf{c}_j^t,\mathcal{O}) = J_d(\mathbf{c};\mathbf{c}_j^t,\mathcal{O}) + \alpha\, J_p(\mathbf{c};\mathbf{c}_j^t) \quad (5)$$

As usual in variational segmentation (cf. section 1), this functional comprises a data term and a prior. The prior is simply the matching functional (2):

$$J_p(\mathbf{c};\mathbf{c}_j^t) = d_E(\mathbf{c},\mathbf{c}_j^t)\,, \qquad (6)$$

whereas the data term has the form:

$$J_d(\mathbf{c};\mathbf{c}_j^t,\mathcal{O}) = -\oint \Big\{ \log p\big(I(\mathbf{c})\,|\,\mathbf{c}_j^t\big) + \\ \log p\big(I(\mathbf{c})\,|\,\mathcal{O}\setminus O_k\big) + \log p(\nabla I(\mathbf{c}))\Big\} \qquad (7)$$

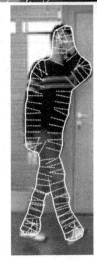

The first term of the integrand maximizes the probability that the intensity observed at $\mathbf{c}(s)$ matches the model associated with template $\mathbf{c}_j^t$ – see (4). The second term in (7), on the other hand, maximizes the probability that $I(\mathbf{c}(s))$ matches the model of another object, or the background – see (1). As a result, both terms together invoke segmentation through "region competition". Finally, the third term in (7) attracts $\mathbf{c}$ to edges, as is common in geodesic snake approaches and accounts for our prior belief that boundary contours are more probable at image edges. It has the form $-\log p(\nabla I(\mathbf{c})) = \frac{1}{1+|\nabla I(\mathbf{c})|}$. In our implementation, functional (5) is *globally optimized* over a region centered around $\mathbf{c}_k$, as indicated in Figure 4.

Fig. 4. Optimal updates of image contours are given by a deformation along the normal direction. We minimize the segmentation functional (5) through dynamic programming over a set of discrete putative contour locations (top). Intensity information is approximated locally by samples along inner normal directions of the current boundary (bottom).

5   Experiments and Discussion

In order to evaluate our novel combination of on-line object appearance models and statistical shape priors within the framework of variational segmentation, we processed an image sequence of 1400 frames containing four different persons entering and leaving the scene. This was deliberately done without any additional knowledge about object dynamics or elaborate scheme for tracking, with the exception of simple first-order Kalman predicting the bounding boxes of current object contours. Candidate regions were generated for regions which yielded local minima in the posterior probability of (1). New objects are automatically instantiated for these regions or existing objects re-instantiated if they have been absent. In subsequent frames we refine the contours of the objects using variational segmentation as described in section 4 followed by updates of the object and background intensity model as described in section 3.2 and [17].

We point out that not any tuning parameters are involved in our approach. Data-association is entirely accomplished by (1), and decisions are based on MAP-estimates. The algorithm automatically tracked the four humans in the sequence and due to the learned appearance information, recovers easily after occlusions or if an object leaves and reenters the scene. Several images of the sequence are shown in figure 5.

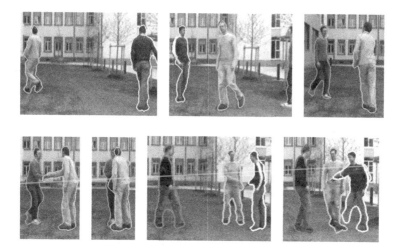

Fig. 5. Segmentation results. Shown are clipped frames 349, 519, 823, 842, 874, 1076, and 1091.

After processing the entire sequence we show in figure 6 images sampled from the learned intensity model for the four objects. The samples are generated by

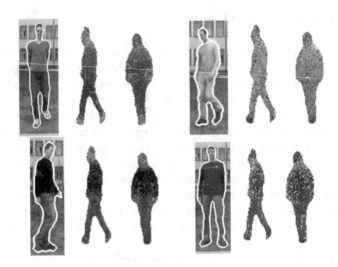

Fig. 6. Samples from the appearance model for four persons. Each triplet is: image from the sequence, sampled template 2 and 7.

choosing a template and sampling from the Gaussian mixture model at each pixel location. Overall we can see that the intensity information was correctly learned for the objects. A closer look also reveals that the multivariate nature of the intensity information due to clothes and viewpoint is captured by the mixture model: e.g. the white stripes on the shoulders of the person in the lower right appear in the sampled template images. Moreover probable locations for the hands can also be identified as the flesh-colored areas inside the regions, see e.g. template 2 of the person in the upper left.

6   Conclusion

We have presented a novel framework for scene analysis by the combination of offline and online object learning together with variational image segmentation. As we match shape and intensity information along the boundary we can efficiently solve for the global minimum of the correspondence problem using dynamic programming. This is a big advantage of 1D matchings that can not be transferred to the 2D case. We have found that for the case of human objects, the 2D problem is sufficiently well approximated by the 1D matching on the boundary and subsequent transformation to 2D using the correspondences.

In the future we want to augment our shape database to more objects. We will also investigate how shape information may be learned online.

References

1. R. Basri, L. Costa, D. Geiger, and D. Jacobs. Determining the similarity of deformable shapes. *Vision Res.*, 38:2365–2385, 1998.
2. M. Bergtholdt, D. Cremers, and C. Schnörr. *Mathematical Models in Computer Vision: The Handbook*, chapter Variational Segmentation with Shape Priors. Spring, 2005.
3. T. Chan and L. Vese. Active contours without edges. *IEEE Trans. Image Processing*, 10(2):266–277, 2001.
4. T. Chan and W. Zhu. Level set based shape prior segmentation. Technical Report 03-66, Computational Applied Mathematics, UCLA, Los Angeles, 2003.
5. Y. Chen, H.D. Tagare, S. Thiruvenkadam, F. Huang, D. Wilson, K.S. Gopinath, R.W. Briggs, and E.A. Geiser. Using prior shapes in geometric active contours in a variational framework. *Intl. J. of Computer Vision*, 50(3):315–328, 2002.
6. T. F. Cox and M. A. A. Cox. *Multidimensional Scaling*. Chapman & Hall, London, 2001.
7. D. Cremers, N. Sochen, and C. Schnörr. Towards recognition-based variational segmentation using shape priors and dynamic labeling. In L. Griffith, editor, *Int. Conf. on Scale Space Theories in Computer Vision*, volume 2695 of *LNCS*, pages 388–400, Isle of Skye, 2003. Springer.
8. D. Cremers, F. Tischhäuser, J. Weickert, and C. Schnörr. Diffusion Snakes: Introducing statistical shape knowledge into the Mumford–Shah functional. *Intl. J. of Computer Vision*, 50(3):295–313, 2002.
9. D. Gavrila. Multi-feature hierarchical template matching using distance transforms. In *Proc. of IEEE International Conference on Pattern Recognition*, pages 439–444. Brisbane, Australia, 1998.
10. D. Gavrila. Sensor-based pedestrian protection. In *IEEE Intelligent Systems*, volume 16, pages 77–81. 2001.
11. Matthias Heiler and Christoph Schnörr. Natural image statistics for natural image segmentation. *Intl. J. of Computer Vision*, 63(1):5–19, 2005.
12. S. Jehan-Besson, M. Barlaud, and G. Aubert. Dream^{2}s: Deformable regions driven by an eularian accurate minimization method for image and video segmentation. *Int. J. Computer Vision*, 53(1):45–70, 2003.
13. D. Mumford and J. Shah. Optimal approximations by piecewise smooth functions and associated variational problems. *Comm. Pure Appl. Math.*, 42:577–685, 1989.
14. N. Paragios and R. Deriche. Geodesic active regions and level set methods for supervised texture segmentation. *Intl. J. of Computer Vision*, 46(3):223–247, 2002.
15. T. Riklin-Raviv, N. Kiryati, and N. Sochen. Unlevel sets: Geometry and prior-based segmentation. In T. Pajdla and V. Hlavac, editors, *European Conf. on Computer Vision*, volume 3024 of *LNCS*, pages 50–61, Prague, 2004. Springer.
16. M. Rousson and N. Paragios. Shape priors for level set representations. In A. Heyden et al., editors, *Proc. of the Europ. Conf. on Comp. Vis.*, volume 2351 of *LNCS*, pages 78–92, Copenhagen, May 2002. Springer, Berlin.
17. C. Stauffer and W. E. L. Grimson. Adaptive background mixture models for real-time tracking. In *Proceedings of the IEEE Computer Science Conference on Computer Vision and Pattern Recognition (CVPR-99)*, pages 246–252, Los Alamitos, June 1999. IEEE.

18. A. Tsai, A. J. Yezzi, and A. S. Willsky. Curve evolution implementation of the Mumford-Shah functional for image segmentation, denoising, interpolation, and magnification. *IEEE Trans. on Image Processing*, 10(8):1169–1186, 2001.

19. L.A. Vese and T.F. Chan. A multiphase level set framework for image segmentation using the mumford and shah model. *Intl. J. of Computer Vision*, 50(3):271–293, 2002.

20. G. Wahba. *Spline models for observational data*. SIAM, Philadelphia, 1990.

21. J. Yang and J.S. Duncan. 3d image segmentation of deformable objects with joint shape-intensity prior models using level sets. *Medical Image Analysis*, 8(3):285–294, 2004.

22. S. C. Zhu and A. Yuille. Region competition: Unifying snakes, region growing, and Bayes/MDL for multiband image segmentation. *IEEE PAMI*, 18(9):884–900, 1996.

Over-Complete Wavelet Approximation of a Support Vector Machine for Efficient Classification

Matthias Rätsch[1], Sami Romdhani[1], Gerd Teschke[2], and Thomas Vetter[1]

[1] University of Basel, Computer Science Department,
Bernoullistrasse 16, CH - 4056 Basel, Switzerland
[2] University of Bremen, ZETEM, PF 33 04 40, D-28334 Bremen, Germany
{matthias.raetsch, sami.romdhani, thomas.vetter}@unibas.ch
teschke@math.uni-bremen.de

Abstract. In this paper, we present a novel algorithm for reducing the runtime computational complexity of a Support Vector Machine classifier. This is achieved by approximating the Support Vector Machine decision function by an over-complete Haar wavelet transformation. This provides a set of classifiers of increasing complexity that can be used in a cascaded fashion yielding excellent runtime performance. This over-complete transformation finds the optimal approximation of the Support Vectors by a set of rectangles with constant gray-level values (enabling an Integral Image based evaluation). A major feature of our training algorithm is that it is fast, simple and does not require complicated tuning by an expert in contrast to the Viola & Jones classifier. The paradigm of our method is that, instead of trying to estimate a classifier that is jointly accurate and fast (such as the Viola & Jones detector), we first build a classifier that is proven to have optimal generalization capabilities; the focus then becomes runtime efficiency while maintaining the classifier's optimal accuracy. We apply our algorithm to the problem of face detection in images but it can also be used for other image based classifications. We show that our algorithm provides, for a comparable accuracy, a 15 fold speed-up over the Reduced Support Vector Machine and a 530 fold speed-up over the Support Vector Machine, enabling face detection at 25 fps on a standard PC.

1   Introduction

Image based classification tasks are time consuming. For instance, detecting a specific object in an image, such as a face, is computationally expensive, as all the pixels of the image are potential object centres. Hence all the pixels must be classified.

Therefore, recently, more efficient methods have emerged based on a cascaded evaluation of hierarchical filters: image patches easy to discriminate are classified by a simple and fast filter, while patches that resemble the object of interest are classified by more involved and slower filters. In the area of face detection [11], cascaded based classification algorithms were introduced by Keren *et al.*[7], by Romdhani *et al.* [10] and by Viola and Jones [16]. The detector from Keren *et al.* [7] assumes that the negative examples (i.e. the non-faces) are modeled by a Boltzmann distribution and that they are smooth. This assumption could increase the number of false positive in presence of a

W. Kropatsch, R. Sablatnig, and A. Hanbury (Eds.): DAGM 2005, LNCS 3663, pp. 351–360, 2005.

cluttered background. Romdhani *et al.* [10] use a Cascaded Reduced Set Vectors (RSV) expansion of a Support Vector Machine (SVM) [15]. The speed bottleneck of [10] is that at least one convolution of a 20×20 filter has to be carried out on the full image, resulting in a computationally expensive evaluation of the kernel with an image patch. Kienzle *et al.* [8] present an improvement of this method, where the first (and only the first) RSV is approximated by a separable filter. Viola & Jones [16] use Haar-like oriented edge filters having a block like structure enabling a very fast evaluation by use of an Integral Image. These filters are weak, in the sense that their discrimination power is low. They are selected, among a finite set, by the Ada-boost algorithm that yields the ones with the best discrimination. A drawback of their approach is that it is not clear that the cascade achieves optimal generalization performances. Practically, the training proceeds by trial and error, and often, the number of filters per stage must be manually selected so that the false positive rate decreases smoothly. Another drawback of the method is that the set of available filters is limited and manually selected. Additionally, the training of the classifier is very slow, as every filter (and there are about 10^5 of them) is evaluated on the whole set of training examples and this is done every time a filter is added to a stage of the cascade.

In this paper, we present a novel efficient classification algorithm based on following features:

1. Use of an SVM classifier that is known to have optimal generalization capabilities.
2. To achieve high run-time efficiency we use a reduced set of Support Vector (RVM in [10]).
3. The high run-time efficiency is also obtained by a coarse-to-fine approximation of the classifier enabling a cascaded evaluation. For non-symmetric data (i.e. only few positives to many negatives) we achieve an early rejection of easy to discriminate vectors. The granularity of the accuracy of the approximation is set by the following parameters, which are automatically selected at detection time based on the image patch to be classified: (i) the number of Reduced Set Vector (RSV) used and (ii) the accuracy of the wavelet representation of these RSV's. This constitutes the major novelty of this paper. The trade-off between accuracy and speed is very continuous.
4. As the RSV's are approximated by a Haar wavelet transform, the Integral Image method is used for their evaluation, similarly to [16].
5. We use the over-complete wavelet theory to obtain the global optimum approximation of RSV's. As shown in Section 2.1.3.3, the over-complete wavelet theory provides an upper bound on the distance between the decision function of the RVM and of the proposed W-RSV. The proposed learning stage is fast, straightforward, automatic and does not require the manual selection of ad-hoc parameters, as opposed to the Viola and Jones method [16]. For example, the training time, on the data set mentioned in Section 3, was two hours which is a vast improvement over the Viola detector.

The novelty to [9] is 3. (ii) and 5.: The Simulated Annealing optimization using morphological filters is replaced by the over-complete wavelet transformation. The problems with the Simulated Annealing method is that it did not provide the global optimum of the RVM approximation in all cases and it was difficult to adjust the approximation accuracy. It should be noted that, in this work, we apply an over-complete wavelet transformation of the Reduced Support Vector Machine itself, and not of the input space as a pre-processing like [6,1].

Section 2 details our novel training algorithm that constructs a Wavelet Approximated Reduced Set Vectors expansion having a block-like structure. It is shown in Section 3 that the new expansion yields a comparable accuracy to the SVM while providing a significant speed-up.

2 Over-Complete Wavelet Approximated Support Vector Machine

Support Vector Machines (SVM), used as classifiers, are now well-known for their good generalisation capabilities. Their decision function has the following form: $y(\mathbf{x}) = \sum_k \alpha_i \cdot k(\mathbf{x}, \mathbf{x}_k) + b$, where $k(\cdot)$ is the kernel used. In order to improve the runtime performance [13] proposed to approximate the SVM by a Reduced Support Vector Machine (RVM), used with a cascaded evaluation in [10]. The RVM aims to approximate the Support Vectors, $\mathbf{x}_k$ by a *smaller* set of Reduces Set Vectors (RSV's), $\mathbf{z}_k$. During evaluation, most of the time is spent in kernel evaluations. In the case of the Gaussian kernel, $k(\mathbf{x}, \mathbf{z}_k) = \exp\left(\frac{-\|\mathbf{x} - \mathbf{z}_k\|^2}{2\,\sigma^2}\right)$, chosen here, the computational load is spent in evaluating the norm of the difference between a patch and a RSV. This norm can be expanded as follows: $\|\mathbf{x} - \mathbf{z}_k\|^2 = \mathbf{x}'\mathbf{x} - 2\mathbf{x}'\mathbf{z}_k + \mathbf{z}'_k\mathbf{z}_k$. As $\mathbf{z}_k$ is independent of the input image, it can be pre-computed. The sum of squares of the pixels of a patch of the input image, $\mathbf{x}'\mathbf{x}$ is efficiently computed using the Integral Image ([4,16]) of the squared pixel values of the input image. As a result, the computational load of this expression is determined by the term $2\mathbf{x}'\mathbf{z}_k$.

The novelty of this paper is the approximation the RSV's, $\mathbf{z}_k$, by a set of Wavelet Approximated Reduced Set Vectors (W-RSV), $\mathbf{u}_k$ that have a block-like structure, as seen in Figure 1. Then the term $2\mathbf{x}'\mathbf{u}_k$ can be evaluated very efficiently by use of the Integral Image. If $\mathbf{u}_k$ is an image patch with rectangles of constant (and optionally different) grey levels then the dot product is evaluated in constant time by the addition of four pixels of the Integral Image of the input image per rectangle and one multiplication per grey level value.

2.1 Learning Haar-Like Reduced Set Vectors Using OCWT

In contrast to other approaches ([6,1]), we do not use a wavelet transformation of the input images as a pre-processing at runtime. The novelty is that we apply the over-complete wavelet transformation at the learning stage. Our approach proposes a wavelet transformation of the Reduced Support Vector Machine itself as a means to speedup the runtime performance.

2.1.1 Wavelet-Shrinkage for Haar-Like Structured Reduced Set Vectors

In order to make full usage of the concept of Integral Images, it would be desirable to approximate the computed RSV's, $\mathbf{z}$, by block-wise structured images that are not too far off while keeping the number of rectangular regions with constant grey value much smaller than in $\mathbf{z}$. Mathematically speaking, we are searching for an approximation of a given image z by a piecewise block structured image u which is as sparse as possible. This optimization problem can be casted in the following variational form

$$\min_{\hat{u}} \left\{ \|\mathbf{z} - \hat{\mathbf{u}}\|_{L_2}^2 + 2\alpha |\hat{\mathbf{u}}|_{B_1^1(L_1)} \right\}, \tag{1}$$

where $B_1^1(L_1)$ denotes a particluar Besov semi–norm; for an overview we refer the reader to [14,12] and for a detailed discussion of the problem to [2]. The Besov (semi) norm of a given function can be expressed by means of its wavelet coefficients and, moreover, in two dimensions the Besov penalty is nothing else than a ℓ_1 constraint on the wavelet coefficients (promoting sparsity as required).

The minimization of (1) is easily obtained: Let $\{\psi_\lambda\}_{\lambda \in \Lambda}$ be the wavelet basis, where Λ is the double index over all grid points and all scalings. Then we may express z and û as follows: $\mathbf{z} = \sum_{\lambda \in \Lambda} z_\lambda \psi_\lambda$, $\hat{\mathbf{u}} = \sum_{\lambda \in \Lambda} \hat{u}_\lambda \psi_\lambda$, where $z_\lambda = \langle \mathbf{z}, \psi_\lambda \rangle$ and $\hat{u}_\lambda = \langle \hat{\mathbf{u}}, \psi_\lambda \rangle$ (here $\langle \cdot, \cdot \rangle$ stands for the inner product in the underlying Hilbert space). We may completely represent (1) by means of the associated wavelet coefficients,

$$\mathbf{u} = \arg \min_{\hat{u}} \sum_{\lambda \in \Lambda} \left\{ (z_\lambda - \hat{u}_\lambda)^2 + 2\alpha |\hat{u}_\lambda| \right\}. \tag{2}$$

Since the wavelet basis is linearly independent, we can minimize summand–wise and obtain the following explicit expression for the optimum u_λ, see, e.g. [5],

$$u_\lambda = S_\alpha(z_\lambda) = \text{sgn}(z_\lambda) \max\{|z_\lambda| - \alpha, 0\}, \tag{3}$$

where S_α is the soft–shrinkage operation with threshold α. Consequently, the optimum u is simply obtained by soft–shrinking the wavelet coefficients of z, i.e. $\mathbf{u} = \sum_{\lambda \in \Lambda} S_\alpha(z_\lambda) \psi_\lambda$.

2.1.2 Over-Complete Wavelet Transformation

Typically, a wavelet representation of an image is computed by fast discrete wavelet schemes. However, non–redundant representations and filtering very often creates artifacts in terms of undesirable oscillations or non–optimally represented details, which manifest themselves as ringing and edge blurring. For our purpose, it is essential to pick a representation that optimally meets the local image structure and is not restricted to a fixed grid (see Figure 1). The most promising method for adequately solving this kind of problem has its origin in translation invariance (the method of cycle spinning, see, e.g. [3]), i.e. representing the image by all possible shifted versions of the underlying (Haar) wavelet basis. But contrary to the idea of introducing redundancy by averaging over all possible representations of z, we aim to pick only that one which is optimally suited for our given image.

In order to give a rough sketch of this technique, assume that we are given an RSV z with $2^M \times 2^M$ pixel. Following the cycle–spinning approach, see again [3], we have to compute $2^{2(M+1-j_0)}$ different representations of z with respect to the $2^{2(M+1-j_0)}$ translates, s of the underlying wavelet basis. The scale j_0 denotes the coarsest resolution level of z. The family $\{\mathbf{z}^s\}_s$ generated this way serves now as our reservoir of possible wavelet representations of one single z. The best shift s^* is that one for which we have a minimal discrepancy to the SVM hyper-plane per operations for the kernel-evaluation. We evaluate all possible local shifts (in our case $s = 64$), hence the global optimum shift is guaranteed (see Section 2.1.4.4).

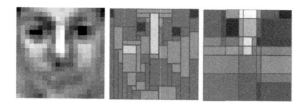

Fig. 1. Examples for Haar-like approximations of an RSV (*left*) using morphological filter (H-RSV [9], *middle*) and using an over-complete wavelet transformation (W-RSV, *right*). The OCWT representation meets optimally the local image structure. The ratio of the decreasing of the hyper-plane distance to the used operations (see Section 2.1.1.4) is more efficient for the W-RSV (0.73) than for the H-RSV (0.51).

2.1.3 Hyper-Plane Approximation by Wavelet Shrinkage

Once we approximate the Support Vectors of the SVM by the W-RSV's, the question arises whether the hyper-plane approximation $\Psi''_{N_z} = \sum_{i=1}^{N_z} \beta_i \Phi(\mathbf{u}_i)$ is close to $\Psi_{N_x} = \sum_{i=1}^{N_x} \alpha_i \Phi(\mathbf{x}_i)$, where $\Phi : \mathcal{X} \to F$, $\mathbf{x} \mapsto \Phi(\mathbf{x})$ is the map into the best discriminating hyper-space F. (The dot product in F is computed using a kernel function: $k(\mathbf{x}, \mathbf{x}') = \langle \Phi(\mathbf{x}), \Phi(\mathbf{x}') \rangle$ [15].) Indeed, we can demonstrate that the discrepancy between the W-RVM and the RVM is upper-bounded by the L_2 distance (which is minimised by (3) with a ℓ_1 constraint on the coefficients $\hat{u}_\lambda$) of the sparse approximation $\mathbf{u}_i$ of $\mathbf{z}_i$ (The derivation is omitted here for space reasons)(Note that the fact that the RVM ($\Psi'_{N_z} = \sum_{i=1}^{N_z} \beta_i \Phi(\mathbf{z}_i)$) minimises $\|\Psi'_{N_z} - \Psi_{N_x}\|$ is shown in [13].):

$$\|\Psi''_{N_z} - \Psi'_{N_z}\| \leq \sigma^{-1} \sum_{i=1}^{N_z} |\beta_i| \, \|\mathbf{z}_i - \mathbf{u}_i\|. \tag{4}$$

2.1.4 Algorithm for Generation of the W-RSV's

First, the RSV's, $\mathbf{z}_i$ are computed by minimising $\|\Psi'_{N_z} - \Psi_{N_x}\|^2$ (see [10]). Then, the W-RSV's, $\mathbf{u}_i^l$, of the RSV's, $\mathbf{z}_i$ ($i = 1, \ldots, N_z$) are computed using local best shift approximations at the level $l = 1$. The approximation at one level automatically selects the best shift and the number of wavelet basis used for this shift for all the $\mathbf{u}_i^l$, $i = 1, \ldots, N_z$. Once one level is computed, the residual of the previous level is approximated using the same procedure. The usage of the different approximation levels enables a smooth trade-off between accuracy and speed (see Section 2.2).

The approximation $\mathbf{u}_i^l$ of the RSV, $\mathbf{z}_i$, at the level l, is obtained by minimising the distance δ_i^l to the SVM hyper-plane with respect to β_i^l and $\mathbf{u}_i^l$:

$$\delta_i^l = \|\Psi_{i-1}^l - \beta_i^l \Phi(\mathbf{u}_i^l)\|^2, \text{ where } \Psi_{i-1}^l = \Psi_{N_z}^{l-1} - \sum_{k=1}^{i-1} \beta_k^l \Phi(\mathbf{u}_k^l), \tag{5}$$

where Ψ_{i-1}^l is the residual vector (in the feature space F) between the SVM and the classifier obtained using N_z RSV's for the levels 1 to $l - 1$, and using $i - 1$ RSV's for the level l. For the first level, this residual is the SVM itself: $\Psi_{N_z}^0 = \sum_{i=1}^{N_x} \alpha_i \Phi(\mathbf{x}_i)$. The

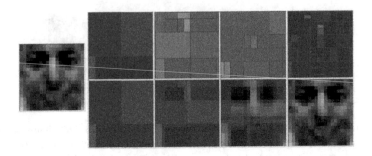

Fig. 2. Example of the approximation of a RSV (*left*), $\mathbf{z}_i$, by its W-RSV $\mathbf{u}_i^l$ at different approximation levels (*top row, left to right*: $l = 1, 2, 10, 19$). The *bottom row, (left to right)* shows the sum of the W-RSV's over the approximation levels: $\sum_{l=1}^n \mathbf{u}_i^l$ with $n = 1, 2, 10, 19$.

formal algorithm that provides the set of β_i^l and $\mathbf{u}_i^l$ for $i = 1, \ldots, N_z$ and $l = 1, \ldots, N_l$ follows:

1. Set $\Psi_{N_z}^0 = \sum_{i=1}^{N_z} \alpha_i \Phi(\mathbf{x}_i)$ and $\forall_{i=1,\ldots,N_z} : \mathbf{r}_i^1 = \mathbf{z}_i$, where $\mathbf{z}_i$ are the Reduced Set Vectors.

2. Start at the first approximation level $l = 1$.

3. Start with the first Reduced Set Vector $i = 1$.

4. Evaluate $\forall_s : \tilde{\mathbf{u}}^s = (W^s)^{-1} S_\alpha \left(W^s \mathbf{r}_i^l \right)$ where W^s is the wavelet decomposition and $(W^s)^{-1}$ the reconstruction with a shifted wavelet basis by the two dimensional shift $s \in \{1, 2, \ldots, 2^J\} \times \{1, 2, \ldots, 2^J\}$. For a 20×20 patch size a shift $J = 3$ is sufficient. S_α is the Shrinkage function with the sparsity parameter α (see Section 2.1.1.1 and 2.2).

5. Evaluate $\forall_s : \Delta_\delta^s = \delta_{i-1}^l - \delta_i^l$ where $\delta_0^l = \delta_{N_z}^{l-1}$ and the number of operations $\Delta_\omega^s = 4 * \# [\tilde{\mathbf{u}}^s] + v(\tilde{\mathbf{u}}^s)$ where $\# [\tilde{\mathbf{u}}^s]$ is the number of piecewise constant rectangles and $v(\tilde{\mathbf{u}}^s)$ the number of grey values of $\tilde{\mathbf{u}}^s$.

6. Select the best shift s^*, for which the ratio $\frac{\Delta_\delta^s}{\Delta_\omega^s}$ is maximum.

7. Set $\mathbf{u}_i^l = \tilde{\mathbf{u}}^{s^*}$ and save the rectangle structure for each approximation level of $\mathbf{u}_i^l$ separately. Then, the residual is updated: $\mathbf{r}_i^{l+1} = \mathbf{r}_i^l - \mathbf{u}_i^l$.

8. If $i \leq N_z$, increment i and proceed to step 4. If $i > N_z$ and $l \leq N_l$, increment l and proceed to step 3; else, stop.

Using this algorithm, we obtain for each RSV, $\mathbf{z}_i$, N_l levels of W-RSV's, $\mathbf{u}_i^l$ (see Figure 2 *top row*). The approximation level $l + 1$ of the W-RSV is not computed by a finer approximation of the original RSV, $\mathbf{z}_i$ (e.g. by increasing sparsity parameter α). Instead the algorithm achieves the approximation $\mathbf{u}_i^{l+1}$ from the residual $\mathbf{r}_i^{l+1} = \mathbf{z}_i - \sum_{h=1}^l \mathbf{u}_i^h$. Thus $\sum_{l=1}^{N_l} \mathbf{u}_i^l$ converge to $\mathbf{z}_i$ if $N_l \rightarrow \infty$ (see Figure 2 right column). We call it a local best shift method because the shift s^* is generally different for each approximation level. It is also noticed, that the rectangle structure of $\mathbf{u}_i^l$ is evaluated and stored during the training and applied at the classification process for each l separately because $\# \left[\sum_{h=1}^l \mathbf{u}_i^h \right] > \sum_{h=1}^l \# [\mathbf{u}_i^h]$. As seen in Figure 2 (*bottom row*) we obtain more rectangles, because the rectangles overlay by adding the approximations levels.

2.2   Detection Process

The classification function of the input patch $\mathbf{x}$ of the W-RVM, denoted by $y_i^l(\mathbf{x})$, using l levels and i RSV's at the level l is as follows:

$$
y_i^l(\mathbf{x}) = \text{sgn}\left(\sum_{h=1}^{l-1} \sum_{j=1}^{N_z^h} \beta_{h,j}^{l,i} k(\mathbf{x}, \mathbf{u}_j^h) + \sum_{j=1}^{i} \beta_{l,j}^{l,i} k(\mathbf{x}, \mathbf{u}_j^l) + b_i^l \right), \tag{6}
$$

where, N_z^h, for $h = 1, \dots, l-1$, denotes the number of RSV's used for the approximation of level h (see hereafter how to set N_z^h), b_i^l are the thresholds obtained automatically from an R.O.C. for a given accuracy. These thresholds are set to yield a given False Rejection Rate (FRR) so that the accuracy of the W-RVM is the same as the one of the full SVM (see [10] for details). The trade-off between FRR and FAR is the only parameter of our algorithm to be set by the user.

To achieve high run-time efficiency, we use a cascade of coarse-to-fine approximations of the SVM classifier. The aim is too reject as early as possible image parts that do not present the object of interest. This is performed by the following algorithm:

1. Start at the first approximation level $l = 1$.
2. Start with the first W-RSV, $\mathbf{u}_1^l$ at the level l.
3. Evaluate $y_i^l(\mathbf{x})$ for the input patch $\mathbf{x}$ using (6).
4. If $y_i^l < 0$ then the patch is classified as not being the object of interest. The evaluation stops.
5. If $i < N_z^l$, i is incremented and the algorithm proceeds to step 3; else if $l < N_l$, l is incremented and the algorithm proceeds to step 2; otherwise the full SVM is used to classify the patch.

When computing a RSV approximation of an SVM, it is not clear how many RSV's N_z should be computed (see [10]). This number of vectors may vary depending on the level of the approximation. This is why in Equation (6) the number of vectors used for the level h is denoted by N_z^h. The rationale of this dependency is that, at some point in the evaluation algorithm, it might be more efficient to increment l (and reset i), rather than to increment i. The best value of N_z^l is computed in an offline process using a validation dataset: N_z^l is set to the smallest i for which $\frac{\Delta_\omega(y_{i+1}^l)}{r(y_{i+1}^l)} > \frac{\Delta_\omega(y_1^{l+1})}{r(y_1^{l+1})}$, where $r(y_i^l)$ is the number of rejections of the negative examples obtained with i RSV's for the level l, and $\Delta_\omega(y_{i+1}^l)$ is the number of operations required to evaluate y_{i+1}^l (see Section 2.1.4).

By a similar evaluation the last used approximation level, N_l can be achieved. For this $N_l = l$ it is more efficient to classify the last few remaining patches by the SVM, instead of incrementing l. How many levels this are depends also on the sparsity parameter α of the OCWT. The smaller is α, the closer $\mathbf{u}_i^l$ is from $\mathbf{z}_i$ and the less approximation levels are required. However, the number of levels does not play a decisive role as the higher N_l, the sooner the evaluation process selects the next level, i.e. the less N_z^l. Therefore our proposed approach is not very sensitive to the parameter for setting the approximation accuracy (e.g. α), opposite to former methods using only one approximation level.

3   Experimental Results

We applied our novel over-complete wavelet approximated SVM to the task of face detection. The training set includes 3500, 20 × 20, face patches and 20000 non-face patches and, the validation set, 1000 face patches, and 100,000 non-face patches. The SVM computed on the training set yielded about 8000 Support Vectors that we approximated by $N_z = 90$ W-RSV's at $N_l = 5$ approximation levels by the method detailed in the previous section.

The first graph on Figure 3 plots the residual distance of the RVM (dashed line) and of the W-RVM (plain line) to the SVM (in terms of the distance $\Psi_{N_x} - \Psi_{N_z}''$) as a function of the number of vectors used, N_z. It can be seen that for a given accuracy more Wavelet Approximated Set Vectors are needed to approximate the SVM than for the RVM. However, as shown on the second plot, for a given computational load, the W-RVM rejects much more non-face patches than the RVM. This explains the improved run-time performances of the W-RVM. Additionally, it can be seen that the curve is more smooth for the W-RVM, hence a better trade-off between accuracy and speed can be obtained by the W-RVM.

Figure 4 shows the R.O.C.'s, computed on the validation set, of the SVM, the RVM and the W-RVM. It can be seen that the accuracies of the three classifiers are similar

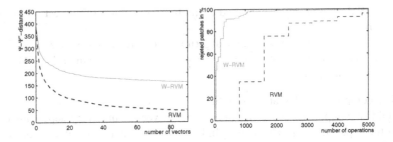

Fig. 3. *Left:* $\Psi_{N_x} - \Psi_{N_z}''$ distance as function of the number of vectors for the RVM (*dashed line*), and the W-RVM (*solid line*). *Right:* Percentage of rejected non-face patches as a function of the number of operations required.

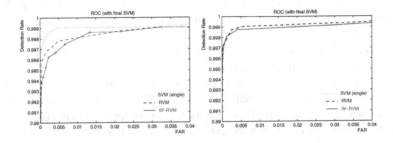

Fig. 4. R.O.C.'s for the SVM, the RVM and the W-RVM (*left*) without and (*right*) with the final SVM classification for the remaining patches. The FAR is related to non-face patches.

Table 1. Comparison of accuracy and speed improvement of the W-RVM to the RVM and SVM

method	FRR	FAR	time per patch
SVM	1.4%	0.002%	$787.34\mu s$
RVM	1.5%	0.001%	$22.51\mu s$
W-RVM	1.4%	0.002%	$1.48\mu s$

without (left plot) and almost equal with the final SVM classification for the remaining patches (right plot), see step 5. of the evaluation algorithm. Table 1 compares the accuracy and the average time required to evaluate the patches of the validation set. The speed-up over the former approach [9] is about a factor 2.5 ($3.85\mu s$). The novel W-RVM algorithms provides a significant speed-up (530-fold over the SVM and more than 15-fold over the RVM), for no substantial loss of accuracy.

We also proved the performance and detection accuracy under real life conditions in the "Institut für Techno- und Wirtschaftsmathematik" (ITWM) in Kaiserslautern. To demonstrate the fast and accurate detection algorithm, we implemented an application using a small webcam. Accurate face detection one obtained at 25 fps (on a Intel Pentium M Centrino 1600 CPU, at a resolution of 320x240, stepsize 1 pixel, 5 scales).

4 Conclusion

In this paper, we presented a novel efficient method for SVM classifications on image based vectors. We used an over-complete wavelet transformation of the Reduced Set Vectors. It was demonstrated on the task of face detection.

As opposed to the RVM, the sparseness of operations required for classification is not only controlled by the number of Reduced Set Vectors but also by the number of wavelets basis functions used to approximate a Reduced Set Vector. Hence, negative examples can be rejected with much fewer number of operations, making the run-time algorithm very efficient. Moreover, as the Haar wavelets are used, the SVM kernel may be evaluated extremely efficiently using Integral Images. The main advantage of this algorithm compared to other algorithm based on boosting, such as the Viola & Jones detector [16], is the fact that the training is much faster and does not require manual intervention.

References

1. G. Zikos C. Garcia and G. Tziritas. Face detection in color images using wavelet packet analysis. *IEEE Int. Conf. on Multimedia Computing and Systems*, 1999.
2. A. Cohen, R. DeVore, P. Petrushev, and H. Xu. Nonlinear Approximation and the Space $BV(\mathbb{R}^2)$. *American Journal of Mathematics*, (121):587–628, 1999.
3. R.R. Coifman and D. Donoho. Translation–invariant de–noising. in *Wavelets and Statistics, A. Antoniadis and G. Oppenheim*, eds., Springer–Verlag, New York, pages 125–150, 1995.
4. F. Crow. Summed-area tables for texture mapping. *In Proc. of SIGGRAPH*, 18(3):207 – 212, 1984.
5. I. Daubechies and G. Teschke. Variational image restoration by means of wavelets: simultaneous decomposition, deblurring and denoising. *Applied and Computational Harmonic Analysis*, 2005.

6. D.A. Karras. Improved defect detection in textile visual inspection using wavelet analysis and support vector machines. *International Journal on Graphics, Vision and Image Processing,* 2005.

7. D. Keren, M. Osadchy, and C. Gotsman. Antifaces: a novel, fast method for image detection. *IEEE Transactions on Pattern Analysis and Machine Intelligence,* 23:747–761, July 2001.

8. W. Kienzle, G. H. Bakir, M. O. Franz, and B. Schölkopf. Efficient approximations for support vector machines in object detection. *Proc. DAGM'04,* pages 54 – 61, 2005.

9. M. Rätsch, S. Romdhani, and T. Vetter. Efficient face detection by a cascaded support vector machine using haar-like features. *Proc. DAGM'04: 26th Pattern Recognition Symposium,* pages 62 – 70, 2005.

10. S. Romdhani, P. Torr, B. Schölkopf, and A. Blake. Computationally efficient face detection. In *Proceedings of the 8th International Conference on Computer Vision,* July 2001.

11. H. Rowley, S. Baluja, and T. Kanade. Neural network-based face detection. *PAMI,* 20:23–38, 1998.

12. H.-J. Schmeisser and H. Triebel. *Topics in Fourier Analysis and Function Spaces.* John Wiley and Sons, New York, 1987.

13. B. Schölkopf, S. Mika, C. Burges, P. Knirsch, K.-R. Müller, G. Rätsch, and A. Smola. Input space vs. feature space in kernel-based methods. *IEEE TNN,* 10(5):1000 – 1017, 1999.

14. H. Triebel. *Interpolation Theory, Function Spaces, Differential Operators.* Verlag der Wissenschaften, Berlin, 1978.

15. V. Vapnik. *Statistical Learning Theory.* Wiley, N.Y., 1998.

16. P. Viola and M. Jones. Rapid object detection using a boosted cascade of simple features. In *Proceedings IEEE Conf. on Computer Vision and Pattern Recognition,* 2001.

Regularization on Discrete Spaces

Dengyong Zhou and Bernhard Schölkopf

Max Planck Institute for Biological Cybernetics,
Spemannstr. 38, 72076 Tuebingen, Germany
{dengyong.zhou, bernhard.schoelkopf}@tuebingen.mpg.de

Abstract. We consider the classification problem on a finite set of objects. Some of them are labeled, and the task is to predict the labels of the remaining unlabeled ones. Such an estimation problem is generally referred to as transductive inference. It is well-known that many meaningful inductive or supervised methods can be derived from a regularization framework, which minimizes a loss function plus a regularization term. In the same spirit, we propose a general discrete regularization framework defined on finite object sets, which can be thought of as discrete analogue of classical regularization theory. A family of transductive inference schemes is then systemically derived from the framework, including our earlier algorithm for transductive inference, with which we obtained encouraging results on many practical classification problems. The discrete regularization framework is built on discrete analysis and geometry developed by ourselves, in which a number of discrete differential operators of various orders are constructed, which can be thought of as discrete analogues of their counterparts in the continuous case.

1 Introduction

Many real-world machine learning problems can be described as follows: given a set of objects $X = \{x_1, x_2, \ldots, x_l, x_{l+1}, \ldots, x_n\}$ from a domain of $\mathcal{X}$ (e.g., $\mathbb{R}^d$) of which the first l objects are labeled as $y_1, \ldots, y_l \in \mathcal{Y} = \{1, -1\}$, the goal is to predict the labels of remaining unlabeled objects indexed from $l + 1$ to n. If the objects to classify are totally unrelated to each other, we cannot make any prediction statistically better than random guessing. Hence we generally assume that there are pairwise relationships among data. A dataset endowed with pairwise relationships can be naturally thought of as a graph. In particular, if the pairwise relationships are symmetric, then the graph is undirected. Thus we consider learning on graphs.

Any supervised learning algorithm can be applied to this problem, by training a classifier $f : \mathcal{X} \to \mathcal{Y}$ on the set of pairs $\{(x_1, y_1), \ldots, (x_l, y_l)\}$, and then using the trained classifier f to predict the labels of the unlabeled objects. Following this approach, one will have estimated a classification function defined on the whole domain $\mathcal{X}$ before predicting the labels of the unlabeled objects. According to [8], estimating a classification function defined on the whole domain $\mathcal{X}$ is more complex than the original problem which only requires predicting the labels of the given unlabeled objects, and it is simpler to directly predict the labels of the

W. Kropatsch, R. Sablatnig, and A. Hanbury (Eds.): DAGM 2005, LNCS 3663, pp. 361–368, 2005.

given unlabeled objects. Therefore we consider estimating a discrete classification function which is defined on the given objects X only. Such an estimation problem is called *transductive inference* [8].

Many meaningful inductive methods can be derived from a regularization framework, which minimizes an empirical loss plus a regularization term. Inspired by this work, we develop a general discrete regularization framework defined on graphs, and then derive a family of transductive algorithms from the discrete regularization framework. This framework can be considered as discrete analogues of variational problems [2,3,5] and classical regularization [7,9]. The transductive inference algorithm which we proposed earlier [11] can be naturally derived from this framework, as can various new methods. Furthermore, to a certain extend, much existing work can be thought of in the framework of discrete regularization on graphs. The discrete regularization framework is built on discrete analysis and differential geometry on graphs developed by ourselves, in which a number of discrete differential operators of various orders are constructed. We follow the notation used in classical differential topology and geometry, which can be found in any standard textbook, e.g., see [6].

2   Discrete Analysis and Differential Geometry

2.1   Preliminaries

A graph $G = (V, E)$ consists of a finite set V, together with a subset $E \subseteq V \times V$. The elements of V are the *vertices* of the graph, and the elements of E are the *edges* of the graph. We say that an edge e is *incident* on vertex v if e starts from v. A *self-loop* is an edge which starts and ends at the same vertex. A *path* is a sequence of vertices $(v_1, v_2, \ldots, v_m)$ such that $[v_{i-1}, v_i]$ is an edge for all $1 < i \leq m$. A graph is *connected* when there is a path between any two vertices. A graph is *undirected* when the set of edges is *symmetric*, i.e., for each edge $[u, v] \in E$ we also have $[v, u] \in E$. In the following, the graphs are always assumed to be connected, undirected, and have no self-loops or multiple edges.

A graph is *weighted* when it is associated with a function $w : E \to \mathbb{R}_+$ which is symmetric, i.e. $w([u, v]) = w([v, u])$, for all $[u, v] \in E$. The *degree* function $d : V \to \mathbb{R}_+$ is defined to be $d(v) := \sum_{u \sim v} w([u, v])$, where $u \sim v$ denote the set of the vertices *adjacent with* v, i.e. $[u, v] \in E$. Let $\mathcal{H}(V)$ denote the Hilbert space of real-valued functions endowed with the usual inner product $\langle f, g \rangle_{\mathcal{H}(V)} := \sum_{v \in V} f(v)g(v)$, for all $f, g \in \mathcal{H}(V)$. Similarly define $\mathcal{H}(E)$. Note that function $h \in \mathcal{H}(E)$ have not to be symmetric. In other words, we do not require $h([u, v]) = h([v, u])$.

2.2   Gradient and Divergence Operators

In this section, we define the discrete gradient and divergence operators, which can be thought of as discrete analogues of their counterparts in the continuous case.

Definition 1. *The graph gradient is an operator* $\nabla : \mathcal{H}(V) \to \mathcal{H}(E)$ *defined by*

$$(\nabla \varphi)([u, v]) := \sqrt{\frac{w([u, v])}{g(v)}} \varphi(v) - \sqrt{\frac{w([u, v])}{g(u)}} \varphi(u), \text{ for all } [u, v] \in E. \quad (1)$$

The gradient measures the variation of a function on each edge. Clearly,

$$(\nabla \varphi)([u, v]) = -(\nabla \varphi)([v, u]), \quad (2)$$

i.e., $\nabla \varphi$ is skew-symmetric.

We may also define the graph gradient at each vertex. Given a function $\varphi \in \mathcal{H}(V)$ and a vertex v, the gradient of φ at v is defined by $\nabla \varphi(v) := \{(\nabla \varphi)([v, u]) | [v, u] \in E\}$. We also often denote $\nabla \varphi(v)$ by $\nabla_v \varphi$. Then the norm of the graph gradient $\nabla \varphi$ at vertex v is defined by

$$\|\nabla_v \varphi\| := \left(\sum_{u \sim v} (\nabla \varphi)^2 ([u, v]) \right)^{\frac{1}{2}},$$

and the *p-Dirichlet form* of the function φ by

$$S_p(\varphi) := \frac{1}{2} \sum_{v \in V} \|\nabla_v \varphi\|^p.$$

Intuitively, the norm of the graph gradient measures the roughness of a function around a vertex, and the p-Dirichlet form the roughness of a function over the graph. In addition, we define $\|\nabla \varphi([v, u])\| := \|\nabla_v \varphi\|$. Note that $\|\nabla \varphi\|$ is defined in the space $\mathcal{H}(E)$ as $\|\nabla \varphi\| = \langle \nabla \varphi, \nabla \varphi \rangle_{\mathcal{H}(E)}^{1/2}$.

Definition 2. *The graph divergence is an operator* div : $\mathcal{H}(E) \to \mathcal{H}(V)$ *which satisfies*

$$\langle \nabla \varphi, \psi \rangle_{\mathcal{H}(E)} = \langle \varphi, - \operatorname{div} \psi \rangle_{\mathcal{H}(V)}, \text{ for all } \varphi \in \mathcal{H}(V), \psi \in \mathcal{H}(E). \quad (3)$$

In other words, $-\operatorname{div}$ is defined to be the adjoint of the graph gradient. Eq.(3) can be thought of as discrete analogue of the Stokes' theorem [1]. Note that the inner products in the left and right sides of (3) are respectively in the spaces $\mathcal{H}(E)$ and $\mathcal{H}(V)$. We can show that the graph divergence can be computed by

$$(\operatorname{div} \psi)(v) = \sum_{u \sim v} \sqrt{\frac{w([u, v])}{g(v)}} \Big(\psi([v, u]) - \psi([u, v]) \Big). \quad (4)$$

Intuitively, the divergence measures the net outflow of function ψ at each vertex. Note that if ψ is symmetric, then $(\operatorname{div} \psi)(v) = 0$ for all $v \in V$.

---

[1] Given a compact Riemannian manifold (M, g) with a function $f \in C^\infty(M)$ and a vector field $X \in \mathcal{X}(M)$, it follows from the stokes' theorem that $\int_M \langle \nabla f, X \rangle = - \int_M (\operatorname{div} X) f$.

2.3 Laplace Operator

In this section, we introduce the graph Laplacian, which can be thought of as discrete analogue of the Laplace-Beltrami operator on Riemannian manifolds.

Definition 3. *The graph Laplacian is an operator* $\Delta : \mathcal{H}(V) \to \mathcal{H}(V)$ *defined by* [2]

$$\Delta\varphi := -\frac{1}{2}\operatorname{div}(\nabla\varphi). \tag{5}$$

Substituting (1) and (4) into (5), we have

$$(\Delta\varphi)(v) = \varphi(v) - \sum_{u \sim v} \frac{w([u,v])}{\sqrt{g(u)g(v)}}\varphi(u). \tag{6}$$

The graph Laplacian is a linear operator because both the gradient and divergence operators are linear. Furthermore, the graph Laplacian is self-adjoint:

$$\langle \Delta\varphi, \phi \rangle = \frac{1}{2}\langle -\operatorname{div}(\nabla\varphi), \phi \rangle = \frac{1}{2}\langle \nabla\varphi, \nabla\phi \rangle = \frac{1}{2}\langle \varphi, -\operatorname{div}(\nabla\phi)\rangle = \langle \varphi, \Delta\phi\rangle.$$

and positive semi-definite:

$$\langle \Delta\varphi, \varphi \rangle = \frac{1}{2}\langle -\operatorname{div}(\nabla\varphi), \varphi \rangle = \frac{1}{2}\langle \nabla\varphi, \nabla\varphi \rangle = S_2(\varphi) \geq 0. \tag{7}$$

It immediate follows from (7) that

Theorem 1. $2\Delta\varphi = D_\varphi S_2$.

Remark 1. Eq. (6) shows that our graph Laplacian defined by (5) is identical to the Laplace matrix in [1] defined to be $D^{-1/2}(D - W)D^{-1/2}$, where D is a diagonal matrix with $D(v, v) = g(v)$, and W is a matrix satisfying $W(u, v) = w([u, v])$ if $[u, v]$ is an edge and $W(u, v) = 0$ otherwise.

2.4 Curvature Operator

In this section, we introduce the graph curvature as discrete analogue of the curvature of a surface which is measured by the change in the unit normal.

Definition 4. *The graph curvature is an operator* $\kappa : \mathcal{H}(V) \to \mathcal{H}(V)$ *defined by*

$$\kappa\varphi := -\frac{1}{2}\operatorname{div}\left(\frac{\nabla\varphi}{\|\nabla\varphi\|}\right). \tag{8}$$

Substituting (1) and (4) into (8), we obtain

$$(\kappa\varphi)(v) = \frac{1}{2}\sum_{u \sim v} \frac{w([u,v])}{\sqrt{g(v)}}\left(\frac{1}{\|\nabla_u\varphi\|} + \frac{1}{\|\nabla_v\varphi\|}\right)\left(\frac{\varphi(v)}{\sqrt{g(v)}} - \frac{\varphi(u)}{\sqrt{g(u)}}\right). \tag{9}$$

Unlike the graph Laplacian (5), the graph curvature is a non-linear operator.

As Theorem 1, we can show that

Theorem 2. $\kappa\varphi = D_\varphi S_1$.

---

[2] The Laplace-Beltrami operator $\Delta : C^\infty(M) \to C^\infty(M)$ is defined to be $\Delta f = -\operatorname{div}(\nabla f)$. The additional factor $1/2$ in (5) is due to each edge being counted twice.

2.5 p-Laplacian Operator

In this section, we generalize the graph Laplacian and curvature to an operator, which can be thought of as discrete analogue of the p-Laplacian in the continuous case [3].

Definition 5. *The graph p-Laplacian is an operator* $\Delta_p : \mathcal{H}(V) \to \mathcal{H}(V)$ *defined by*

$$\Delta_p \varphi := -\frac{1}{2} \operatorname{div}(\|\nabla \varphi\|^{p-2} \nabla \varphi). \tag{10}$$

Clearly, $\Delta_1 = \kappa$, and $\Delta_2 = \Delta$. Substituting (1) and (4) into (10), we obtain

$$(\Delta_p \varphi)(v) = \frac{1}{2} \sum_{u \sim v} \frac{w([u,v])}{\sqrt{g(v)}} (\|\nabla_u \varphi\|^{p-2} + \|\nabla_v \varphi\|^{p-2}) \left(\frac{\varphi(v)}{\sqrt{g(v)}} - \frac{\varphi(u)}{\sqrt{g(u)}} \right), \tag{11}$$

which generalizes (6) and (9).

As before, it can be shown that

Theorem 3. $p\Delta_p \varphi = D_\varphi S_p.$

Remark 2. There is much literature on the p-Laplacian in the continuous case. We refer to [4] for a comprehensive study. There is also some work on discrete analogue of the p-Laplacian, e.g., see [10], where it is defined as

$$\Delta_p \varphi(v) = \frac{1}{g_p(v)} \sum_{u \sim v} w^{p-1}([u,v]) |\varphi(u) - \varphi(v)|^{p-1} \operatorname{sign}(\varphi(u) - \varphi(v)),$$

where $g_p(v) = \sum_{u \sim v} w^{p-1}([u,v])$ and $p \in [2, \infty[$. Note that $p = 1$ is not allowed.

3 Discrete Regularization Framework

Given a graph $G = (V, E)$ and a label set $\mathcal{Y} = \{1, -1\}$, the vertices v in a subset $S \subset V$ are labeled as $y(v) \in \mathcal{Y}$. The problem is to label the remaining unlabeled vertices, i.e., the vertices in the complement of S. Assume a classification function $f \in \mathcal{H}(V)$, which assigns a label $\operatorname{sign} f(v)$ to each vertex $v \in V$. Obviously, a good classification function should vary as slowly as possible between closely related vertices while changing the initial label assignment as little as possible. Define a function $y \in \mathcal{H}(V)$ with $y(v) = 1$ or -1 if vertex v is labeled as positive or negative respectively, and 0 if it is unlabeled. Thus we may consider the optimization problem

$$f^* = \operatorname*{argmin}_{f \in \mathcal{H}(V)} \{S_p(f) + \mu \|f - y\|^2\}, \tag{12}$$

where $\mu \in]0, \infty[$ is a parameter specifying the trade-off between the two competing terms. It is not hard to see the objective function is strictly convex, and hence by standard arguments in convex analysis the optimization problem has a unique solution.

3.1 Regularization with $p = 2$

When $p = 2$, it follows from Theorem 1 that

Theorem 4. *The solution of (12) satisfies that $\Delta f^* + \mu(f^* - y) = 0$.*

The equation in the theorem can be thought of as discrete analogue of the Euler-Lagrange equation. It is easy to see that we can obtain a closed form solution $f^* = \mu(\Delta + \mu I)^{-1} y$, where I denotes the identity operator. Define the function $c : E \to \mathbb{R}_+$ by

$$c([u, v]) = \frac{1}{1 + \mu} \frac{w([u, v])}{\sqrt{g(u)g(v)}}, \text{ if } u \neq v; \text{ and } c([v, v]) = \frac{\mu}{1 + \mu}. \tag{13}$$

We can show that the iteration

$$f^{(t+1)}(v) = \sum_{u \sim v} c([u, v]) f^{(t)}(v) + c([v, v]) y(v), \text{ for all } v \in V, \tag{14}$$

where t indicates the iteration step, converges to the closed from solution [11]. Note that the iterative result is independent of the setting of the initial value. The iteration can be thought of as discrete analogue of heat diffusion on Riemannian manifolds [2]. At every step, each node receives the values from its neighbors, which are weighed by the normalized pairwise relationships. At the same time, they also retain some fraction of their values. The relative amount by which these updates occur is specified by the coefficients defined in (13).

3.2 Regularization with $p = 1$

When $p = 1$, it follows from Theorem 2 that

Theorem 5. *The solution of (12) satisfies that $\kappa f^* + 2\mu(f^* - y) = 0$.*

As we have mentioned before, the curvature κ is a non-linear operator, and we are not aware of any closed form solution for this equation. However, we can construct an iterative algorithm to obtain the solution. Substituting (9) into the equation in the theorem, we have

$$\sum_{u \sim v} \frac{w([u, v])}{\sqrt{g(v)}} \left(\frac{1}{\|\nabla_u f^*\|} + \frac{1}{\|\nabla_v f^*\|} \right) \left(\frac{f^*(v)}{\sqrt{g(v)}} - \frac{f^*(u)}{\sqrt{g(u)}} \right) + 2\mu(f^*(v) - y(v)) = 0. \tag{15}$$

Define the function $m : E \to \mathbb{R}_+$ by

$$m([u, v]) = w([u, v]) \left(\frac{1}{\|\nabla_u f^*\|} + \frac{1}{\|\nabla_v f^*\|} \right). \tag{16}$$

Then

$$\sum_{u \sim v} \frac{m([u, v])}{\sqrt{g(v)}} \left(\frac{f^*(v)}{\sqrt{g(v)}} - \frac{f^*(u)}{\sqrt{g(u)}} \right) + 2\mu(f^*(v) - y(v)) = 0,$$

which can be transformed into

$$\left(\sum_{u\sim v}\frac{m([u,v])}{g(v)}+2\mu\right)f^*(v)=\sum_{u\sim v}\frac{m([u,v])}{\sqrt{g(u)g(v)}}f^*(u)+2\mu y(v).$$

Define the function $c:E\to\mathbb{R}_+$ by

$$c([u,v])=\frac{\dfrac{m([u,v])}{\sqrt{g(u)g(v)}}}{\sum_{u\sim v}\dfrac{m([u,v])}{g(v)}+2\mu},\quad\text{if }u\neq v;\text{ and }c([v,v])=\frac{2\mu}{\sum_{u\sim v}\dfrac{m([u,v])}{g(v)}+2\mu}.$$

(17)

Then

$$f^*(v)=\sum_{u\sim v}c([u,v])f^*(v)+c([v,v])y(v).\tag{18}$$

Thus we can use the iteration

$$f^{(t+1)}(v)=\sum_{u\sim v}c^{(t)}([u,v])f^{(t)}(v)+c^{(t)}([v,v])y(v),\text{ for all }v\in V\tag{19}$$

to obtain the solution, in which the coefficients $c^{(t)}$ are updated according to (17) and (16). This iterative result is independent of the setting of the initial value. Compared with the iterative algorithm (14) in the case of $p=2$, the coefficients in the present method are adaptively updated at each iteration, in addition to the function being updated.

3.3   Regularization with Arbitrary p

For arbitrary p, it follows from Theorem 3 that

Theorem 6. *The solution of (12) satisfies that $p\Delta_p f^*+2\mu(f^*-y)=0$.*

We can construct a similar iterative algorithm to obtain the solution. Specifically,

$$f^{(t+1)}(v)=\sum_{u\sim v}c^{(t)}([u,v])f^{(t)}(v)+c^{(t)}([v,v])y(v),\text{ for all }v\in V,\tag{20}$$

where

$$c^{(t)}([u,v])=\frac{\dfrac{m^{(t)}([u,v])}{\sqrt{g(u)g(v)}}}{\sum_{u\sim v}\dfrac{m^{(t)}([u,v])}{g(v)}+\dfrac{2\mu}{p}},\quad\text{if }u\neq v;\text{ and }c^{(t)}([v,v])=\frac{\dfrac{2\mu}{p}}{\sum_{u\sim v}\dfrac{m^{(t)}([u,v])}{g(v)}+\dfrac{2\mu}{p}},$$

(21)

and

$$m^{(t)}([u,v])=\frac{w([u,v])}{p}(\|\nabla_u f^{(t)}\|^{p-2}+\|\nabla_v f^{(t)}\|^{p-2}).\tag{22}$$

It is easy to see that the iterative algorithms in Sections 3.1 and 3.2 are the special cases of this algorithm with $p=2$ and $p=1$ respectively. Moreover, it is worth noticing that $p=2$ is a critical point.

4   Conclusions and Future Work

We have developed discrete analysis and geometry on graphs, and have constructed a general discrete regularization framework. A family of transductive inference algorithms was derived from the framework, including the algorithm we proposed earlier [11], which can substantially benefit from large amounts of available unlabeled data in many practical problems. There are many possible extensions to this work. One may consider defining discrete high-order differential operators, and then building a regularization framework that can penalize high-order derivatives. One may also develop a parallel framework on directed graphs [12], which model many real-world data structures, such as the World Wide Web. Finally, it is of interest to explore the properties of the graph p-Laplacian as the nonlinear extension of the usual graph Laplacian, since the latter has been intensively studied, and has many nice properties [1].

References

1. F. Chung. *Spectral Graph Theory*. Number 92 in CBMS-NSF Regional Conference Series in Mathematics. SIAM, 1997.
2. J. Eells and J.H. Sampson. Harmonic mappings of Riemannian manifolds. *American Journal of Mathematics*, 86:109–160, 1964.
3. R. Hardt and F.H. Lin. Mappings minimizing the L^p norm of the gradient. *Communications on Pure and Applied Mathematics*, 40:556–588, 1987.
4. J. Heinonen, T. Kilpeläinen, and O. Martio. *Nonlinear Potential Theory of Degenerate Elliptic Equations*. Oxford University Press, Oxford, 1993.
5. R. Jensen. Uniqueness of Lipschitz extensions: minimizing the sup-norm of the gradient. *Arch. Rat. Mech. Anal.*, 123(1):51–74, 1993.
6. J. Jost. *Riemannian Geometry and Geometric Analysis*. Springer-Verlag, Berlin-Heidelberg, third edition, 2002.
7. A.N. Tikhonov and V.Y. Arsenin. *Solutions of Ill-posed Problems*. W. H. Winston, Washington, DC, 1977.
8. V.N. Vapnik. *Statistical Learning Theory*. Wiley, NY, 1998.
9. G. Wahba. *Spline Models for Observational Data*. Number 59 in CBMS-NSF Regional Conference Series in Applied Mathematics. SIAM, 1990.
10. M. Yamasaki. Ideal boundary limit of discrete Dirichlet functions. *Hiroshima Math. J.*, 16(2):353–360, 1986.
11. D. Zhou, O. Bousquet, T.N. Lal, J. Weston, and B. Schölkopf. Learning with local and global consistency. In *Advances in Neural Information Processing Systems 16*. MIT Press, Cambridge, MA, 2004.
12. D. Zhou, B. Schölkopf, and T. Hofmann. Semi-supervised learning on directed graphs. In *Advances in Neural Information Processing Systems 17*. MIT Press, Cambridge, MA, 2005.

Recognition of 3D Objects by Learning from Correspondences in a Sequence of Unlabeled Training Images

Raimund Leitner[1] and Horst Bischof[2]

[1] Carinthian Tech Research AG, Villach, Austria
Raimund.Leitner@ctr.at, http://www.ctr.at
[2] University of Technology Graz, Institute for Computer Graphics, Austria
bischof@icg.tugraz.at, http://www.icg.tu-graz.ac.at

Abstract. This paper proposes an approach for the unsupervised learning of object models from local image feature correspondences. The object models are learned from an unlabeled sequence of training images showing one object after the other. The obtained object models enable the recognition of these objects in cluttered scenes, under occlusion, in-plane rotation and scale change. Maximally stable extremal regions are used as local image features and two different types of descriptors characterising the appearance and shape of the regions allow a robust matching. Experiments with real objects show the recognition performance of the presented approach under various conditions.

1 Introduction

A widely used approach in object recognition is to extract local viewpoint invariant features independently from test images and object models. An object is recognized, if a sufficient number of matches of the local features characterized by invariant descriptors can be found [9,5,6]. Robustness against clutter and occlusion comes from the use of local features, while affine invariant detectors and descriptors allow large viewpoint changes.

The recognition of 3D objects requires object models that contain multiple views of the object. The challenge is to obtain object models which comprise sufficient information for recognition of the object from *any* viewpoint covered by the training data. In this paper we consider a sequence of training images containing different views of several objects where we assume that consecutive training images show most of the time the same object (e.g. a full turn of object 1 is followed by a full turn of object 2). This type of training sequences can easily be gathered by still images from full turns of the objects to learn or by taking every n-th frame from a video sequence showing the important views of the objects of interest. The task addressed in this paper is to learn object models from such a training sequence and enable a recognition of the learned objects in cluttered environments, under occlusion, in-plane rotation and scale changes.

Most 3D object recognition approaches match the features of test images to all views present in the object model accepting that matches are dispersed

W. Kropatsch, R. Sablatnig, and A. Hanbury (Eds.): DAGM 2005, LNCS 3663, pp. 369–376, 2005.
© Springer-Verlag Berlin Heidelberg 2005

over similar views of the same object. If the view-dependent variation is integrated into a single feature model, additional robustness can be achieved because matches vote only for their object model and similar views can be disambiguated during a later step. Only a few recent works exploit correspondences between model views for this purpose [10,3,6].

Our approach to integrate the view-dependent variation into the object model is to track the features of each object through the training sequence and characterize them using two types of descriptors one for appearance and one for shape. During learning we construct an appearance and a shape model for the descriptors of each feature track. Using these feature models during the recognition stage has the advantage that each feature needs to be matched only once per object model regardless of how many model views the feature is visible in.

The remainder of the paper is structured as follows: section 2 briefly summarizes related work; the descriptors used and learning from correspondences are described in sections 3 and 4. Object recognition is discussed in section 5, while experimental results and the conclusion are given in section 6 and 7.

2   Related Work

Object recognition is an instance of the correspondence problem and there are many different approaches that use correspondences to learn object models and match the learned models to test images. For the sake of space only a few recent approaches are discussed.

The key to local object recognition are discriminative local features. Matas' maximally stable extremal regions (MSER) are based on the observation that for many images local segmentation is stable over a range of thresholds [11]. MSERs are regions that are stable for a range of binarization thresholds and possess a number of useful properties: they are inherently multi-scale as large and small regions are detected at the same time without the need to explicitly construct a scale-space and are closed under perspective image geometry and affine intensity transformations. Alternative local feature detectors are based on the multi-scale Harris detector [12], the extrema of difference of Gaussians [9] or multi-scale saliency [7].

These local features can be characterized by descriptors with different levels of invariance and discriminative power. The most popular descriptors focus on the local appearance: the SIFT features proposed by Lowe are based on gradient orientation histograms [9]. They have been sucessfully applied to image matching and object recognition. Another local descriptor are the differential invariants proposed by Schmid and Mohr [15] which are combinations of rotationally symmetric Gaussian derivatives. Baumberg used the second moment matrix to estimate a stretch and skew normalized frame for a reliable wide-baseline matching [1].

Some local feature detectors [11,7] provide not only the location but also a contour which can be used for a shape descriptor: assuming an interest region described by a set of contour points, the shape context is a two-dimensional

Fig. 1. MSER regions detected in two sample images of the training sequence differing by 10° viewing angle

histogram for each point with the log-distances and angles to all other points of the contour. Belongie showed that shape contexts can be successfully used for shape matching [2].

Local features characterized by descriptors are only half the way to object recognition, the other half are efficient methods to find correspondences and learn object models which then can be used to recognize objects in test images: Weber proposed an unsupervised approach for the recognition of objects from single views using a flexible set of rigid parts [16]. The joint probabilities of the part locations were estimated from part correspondences in the training data. An object is recognized by determining the most probable hypothesis given the estimated part locations. While that approach learned only the shape variation and fixed the part appearance, *a priori*, Fergus' approach learns appearance and shape variation simultaneously [4]. The object models are learned using expectation maximisation and allow a scale-invariant object class recognition of rigid and flexible objects. Ramanan and Forsyth proposed a method to learn, track and recognize objects (animals) from a video sequence exploiting temporal coherence using a color histogram based clustering and a kinematic model of rectangular regions [14]. Ferrari and van Gool proposed a method to obtain stable correspondences by grouping matches of planar or smoothly curved surfaces [5,6]. These groups are found by clustering matches that agree on the estimation of an local affine transformation between the two images. The result is an object recognition approach based on an elaborated scheme to eliminate conflicts between these groups.

3   Appearance and Shape Descriptors

We use MSER [11] to find locally distinctive regions. The maximally stable regions are extracted from the set of minimal and maximal regions by following conditions: (i) The regions must be larger than 15 pixels and smaller than 10% of the image area. (ii) The regions must survive at least 10% of the intensity range and their area has to be stable for at least 5% of the intensity range. Fig. 1 shows two sample images with the detected MSERs.

When matching with a single descriptor, false matches are inevitable and a validation of the matches (e.g. estimating the fundamental matrix) is required. To avoid any assumptions about the geometric transformation between the images, two descriptors are determined separately and false matches are rejected by accepting only consistent matches between both descriptors (see section 4). Consequently, the regions are characterised by two descriptors: (i) SIFT keys for appearance and (ii) shape context for shape.

3.1   Appearance Descriptor

Lowe's SIFT descriptor [9] uses orientation histograms to estimate the local orientation. The descriptor is formed from histograms of the local intensity gradients relative to the estimated local orientation. However, preliminary experiments showed that orientation histograms do not provide stable orientation estimates when used in conjunction with MSERs, hence we have used the principal axis of the MSER region as a rotation estimate. As the principal axis gives us only a direction, both orientations θ and $\theta + \pi$ are used during learning and recognition. Using SIFT keys and this orientation estimation provides stable matches as the descriptor matching in the results section shows (see section 6).

3.2   Shape Descriptor

The region's shape is modeled by a piecewise cubic spline of its contour. The spline allows a sampling to a fixed number of equally spaced boundary points. A good trade-off between descriptor complexity and discriminative power has been found empirically with 50 boundary points. The final shape descriptor is computed from the shape context [2] of these contour points using 5 distance and 12 orientation bins. These parameters are used throughout the paper.

4   Learning from Correspondences

The object models are learned from correspondences established between consecutive images of the training sequence. MSER [11] are used to find locally distinctive regions. The detected regions are characterized using SIFT keys for appearance and shape context for shape. Initial matches are found by matching the SIFT keys using the Euclidean distance and the shape contexts using the χ^2-distance [2].

Stable matches are determined by following scheme: An $n \times m$ matrix C_A indicates the mismatch between the appearance descriptors for a pair of consecutive training images (n regions in the first and m regions in the second image). Another matrix C_S is computed for the shape descriptor mismatch.

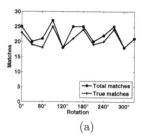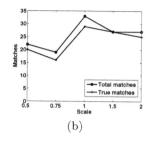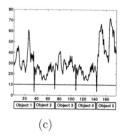

Fig. 2. Matching performance for in-plane rotation (a) and scale changes (b) for two images differing by $10°$ viewing angle. The number of matches between consecutive images for the training sequence showing five objects (c).

The matrix C_A is used as a cost matrix to find the optimal *appearance* assignment $\mathcal{A}_1$ between the regions of both images using the Munkres algorithm also called Hungarian method [8,13]. Analogously, using matrix C_S the optimal *shape* assignment $\mathcal{S}_1$ is determined. As it is inevitable that both assignments are contaminated by false matches, they do not agree on all matches. Accepting only matches present in both assignments efficiently suppresses false matches giving the consistent matches by $\mathcal{M}_1 = \mathcal{A}_1 \cap \mathcal{S}_1$.

The number of correct matches can be increased by the following idea: The probability that the correct match for a certain region is in the best three assignments is higher than that it is found by the best one. Consequently, we compute three *optimal* descriptor assignments by prohibiting the already taken matches (optimal assignment of the previous run) for the next run of the Munkres algorithm. Assuming that $\mathcal{A}_{tot}$ denotes all possible matches between the regions of two images and the first run of the Munkres algorithm determines the assignment $\mathcal{A}_1$ which causes the lowest costs regarding to C_A. By prohibiting the matches $\mathcal{A}_1$ for the next run of the Munkres algorithm, i.e. restricting the allowed matches to $\mathcal{A}_{tot} \backslash \mathcal{A}_1$, the second optimal assignment $\mathcal{A}_2$ is determined. Accordingly the k-th optimal assignment $\mathcal{A}_k$ is calculated by allowing only $\mathcal{A}_{tot} \backslash (\bigcup_{i=1}^{k-1} \mathcal{A}_i)$. By applying the same procedure to the shape descriptor matches, the final set of matches is found by $\mathcal{M}_n = (\bigcup_{i=1}^{n} \mathcal{A}_i) \cap (\bigcup_{i=1}^{n} \mathcal{S}_i)$. Empirical tests showed, that for most matching experiments $\mathcal{M}_3$ contains almost twice the number of correct matches and very few additional false matches compared to $\mathcal{M}_1$.

This matching procedure based on $\mathcal{M}_3$ is applied to the entire training sequence and provides stable correspondences between consecutive training images. Fig. 2 (c) shows the number of matches found between consecutive images of the training sequence of the five objects. It can be seen that where consecutive images show different objects the number of matches falls significantly. This effect is used to detect the locations in the training sequence where the objects change. Now, by using the correspondences of the regions of each object, these regions can be tracked through the object's training images and used to model the view dependent variation of the descriptors of each region.

The object models are learned by obtaining an appearance and a shape model for each region track: to characterize the region's appearance we use SIFT de-

scriptors with a 4x4 array of orientation histograms with 16 bins. The set of
SIFT descriptors of a region track are subjected to a PCA to obtain a SIFT-
eigenspace which models the view-dependent variation. We found that the first
three principal components of each region track's SIFT descriptor are sufficient
for a reliable recognition (see section 6). The set of shape contexts of each region
track is stored entirely in the object model because an eigenspace representation
gave poor results.

5   Object Recognition

Objects are recognised by matching the image regions to the model regions. The
shape contexts are matched, as in training, using the χ^2-distance. The SIFT
descriptors are projected onto the model's SIFT descriptor eigenspace and the
mean absolute reconstruction error is then used to rank the matches. Again the
best three assignments are determined separately for the appearance and shape
descriptors using the Munkres algorithm. Inconsistent matches are rejected by
determining the stable correspondences in $\mathcal{M}_3$ and, if a sufficient number of
regions of an object model are matched successfully in an image, then it is
assumed that the image shows this object.

Table 1. False positives and false negatives in percent for the different object recognition experiments focusing on cluttered scenes (cs), random in-plane rotation (rir),
scale change from 0.5 to 2.0 (s0.5, s0.8, s1.5, s2.0), occlusion from 20% to 50% (oc20,
oc30, oc40, oc50) and scenes showing several of the learned objects (mos)

Experiment	cs	rir	s0.5	s0.8	s1.5	s2.0	oc20	oc30	oc40	oc50	mos
False positives	4.6	7.8	0.0	8.3	9.7	1.4	3.2	2.6	2.3	2.9	8.9
False negatives	2.8	5.1	26.0	12.0	2.7	1.2	4.2	8.5	11.0	32.0	3.1
Recognition rate	92.6	87.1	74.0	79.7	87.6	84.8	92.6	88.9	86.7	65.1	88.0

6   Results

6.1   Descriptor Matching

The performance of the proposed matching is evaluated by the number of correct
matches identified for a number of matching experiments. Two sample images
of an object differing by 10° viewing angle are used for the evaluation, while
one image is subjected to in-plane rotations in 30° steps and to scale changes
between 0.5 and 2.0. Fig. 2 (a) shows the number of correct matches for in-plane
rotation and Fig. 2 (b) for scale change. One can see that the ratio of correct
matches remains stable for in-plane rotations and a scale change from 0.5 to 2.

6.2   Object Recognition

For the recognition experiments a dataset with images of five real objects (36
images per object at 10° increments) has been acquired. The dataset contains a

training sequence with 180 images and a different test sequence with 180 cluttered images. To our knowledge no publicly available dataset provides sufficient images for each object with black background (training) and cluttered scenes with one and several objects (testing). Our method is evaluated using the test sequence subjected to in-plane rotations, several levels of occlusion and scale changes. Tab. 1 shows the false positives, false negatives and the recognition rate for the different experiments focusing on cluttered scenes, random in-plane rotation, scale changes from 0.5 to 2, occlusion from 20% to 50% and scenes showing several of the learned objects. The recognition performance in cluttered environments is above 90% with false positives less than 3%. For scale changes from 0.5 to 2.0 the recognition rate remains above 74% and above 85% for occlusions up to 50%. Fig. 3 shows the recognition results in cluttered scenes with one and two objects and partial occlusion.

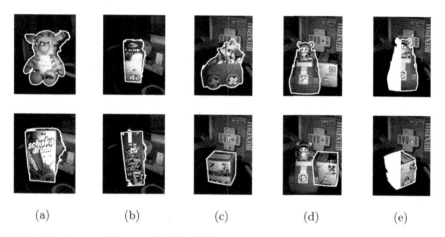

(a)   (b)   (c)   (d)   (e)

Fig. 3. Object recognition results for all five objects in cluttered scenes (a-c), the same object from two different view points (b), scenes with two objects (d) and partially occluded (e). The matched regions and the recognized objects are superimposed.

7   Conclusion

We have proposed an approach for 3D object recognition in cluttered scenes that is based on learning from an sequence of training images of several objects. The object models are learned without supervision from correspondences found in the training images. The proposed matching remains stable for in-plane rotations and scale changes from 0.5 to 2.0. The recognition performance in cluttered environments is above 90% with false positives less than 3%.

As a next step the spatial configuration of the detected regions will be modeled and included into the object model to verify or reject object hypotheses. This should increase the recognition performance and stability.

References

1. A. Baumberg. Reliable feature matching across widely separated views. In *CVPR*, pages 774–781, 2000.
2. S. Belongie and J. Malik. Matching with shape context. *IEEE Workshop on Content-based Access of Image and Video Libraries (CBAIVL-2000)*, 2000.
3. H. H. Bülthoff, C. Wallraven, and A. B. A. Graf. View-based dynamic object recognition based on human perception. In *ICPR*, pages 768–776. IEEE CS Press, 2002.
4. R. Fergus, P. Perona, and A. Zisserman. Object class recognition by unsupervised scale-invariant learning. In *Proceedings of the IEEE Conference on Computer Vision and Pattern Recognition*, volume 2, pages 264–271, June 2003.
5. V. Ferrari, T. Tuytelaars, and L. van Gool. Wide-baseline muliple-view correspondences. In *Proceeding of the IEEE Conference on Computer Vision and Pattern Recognition*, volume I, pages 718–728, June 2003.
6. V. Ferrari, T. Tuytelaars, and L. van Gool. Integrating multiple model views for object recognition. In *IEEE Computer Vision and Pattern Recognition (CVPR)*, volume II, pages 105–112, June 2004.
7. T. Kadir. *Scale, Saliency and Scene Description*. PhD thesis, University of Oxford, 2002.
8. H. W. Kuhn. The Hungarian method for the assignment problem. In *Naval Research Logistics Quarterly*, volume 2, pages 83–97, 1955.
9. D. G. Lowe. Object recognition from local scale-invariant features. In *Proc. Int. Conf. on Computer Vision ICCV, Corfu*, pages 1150–1157, 1999.
10. D. G. Lowe. Local feature view clustering for 3d object recognition. In *Proc. Int. Conf. on Computer Vision and Pattern Recognition CVPR*, 2001.
11. J. Matas, O. Chum, M. Urban, and Pajdla T. Robust wide baseline stereo from maximally stable extremal regions. In *Proc. BMVC*, pages 384–393, 2002.
12. Krystian Mikolajczyk and Cordelia Schmid. An affine invariant interest point detector. In *European Conference on Computer Vision*, pages 128–142. Springer, 2002. Copenhagen.
13. J. R. Munkres. Algorithms for the assignment and transportation problems. *SIAM* 5, pages 32–38, 1957.
14. D. Ramanan and D. A. Forsyth. Using temporal coherence to build models of animals. In *International Conference on Computer Vision (ICCV)*, Nice, October 2003.
15. C. Schmid and R. Mohr. Matching by local invariants. Rapport de Recherche N 2644, INRIA, 1995.
16. M. Weber, M. Welling, and P. Perona. Unsupervised learning of models for recognition. In *ECCV (1)*, pages 18–32, 2000.

Self-learning Segmentation and Classification of Cell-Nuclei in 3D Volumetric Data Using Voxel-Wise Gray Scale Invariants

Janis Fehr[1], Olaf Ronneberger[1], Haymo Kurz[2], and Hans Burkhardt[1]

[1] Albert-Ludwigs-Universität Freiburg, Institut für Informatik,
Lehrstuhl für Mustererkennung und Bildverarbeitung,
Georges-Koehler-Allee Geb. 052, 79110 Freiburg, Deutschland
fehr@informatik.uni-freiburg.de
http://lmb.informatik.uni-freiburg.de/
[2] Albert-Ludwigs-Universität Freiburg, Institut für Anatomie und Zell Biologie,
79104 Feiburg i.Br., Deutschland

Abstract. We introduce and discuss a new method for segmentation and classification of cells from 3D tissue probes. The anisotropic 3D volumetric data of fluorescent marked cell nuclei is recorded by a confocal laser scanning microscope (LSM). Voxel-wise gray scale features (see accompaning paper [1][2]), invariant towards 3D rotation of its neighborhood, are extracted from the original data by integrating over the 3D rotation group with non-linear kernels.

In an interactive process, support-vector machine models are trained for each cell type using user relevance feedback. With this reference database at hand, segmentation and classification can be achieved in one step, simply by classifying each voxel and performing a connected component labelling, automatically without further human interaction. This general approach easily allows adoption of other cell types or tissue structures just by adding new training samples and re-training the model. Experiments with datasets from chicken chorioallantoic membrane show encouraging results.

1 Introduction

In biological and medical research as well as in histopathologic diagnosis, the localization and classification of cells is an everyday business. A vast number of research techniques and treatment methods require detailed information on the amount, type, localization and state of cells in a given probe of tissue or dilution. Locating, classifying and analyzing cells is not a simple task, very time consuming, and in most cases a human expert is needed. The demand for automation is continuously growing with the large number of applications in biotechnology and medical research. But so far this problem is not satisfyingly solved in general. Although there are various methods around, which perform quite well for simple tasks like counting or the segmentation of cells in dilution, most problems are still subject to basic research.

W. Kropatsch, R. Sablatnig, and A. Hanbury (Eds.): DAGM 2005, LNCS 3663, pp. 377–384, 2005.
© Springer-Verlag Berlin Heidelberg 2005

Concerning the algorithms introduced in the literature so far, most of them suffer from the fact that they have been developed for one special purpose only and cannot be easily generalized to other cell types or tissues. Besides that, segmentation is often an unsolved problem as well, and many algorithms require manual interaction. We introduce a new general purpose algorithm using voxel-wise gray scale invariants([1][2]) for both, segmentation and classification of cells in 2D and 3D probes, and provide some first, promising experimental results. Motivated by the work of [3] and [4], gray scale invariants were very successfully applied to individual pollen recognition in [5] [6]. A major problem of cell classification in tissue probes is segmentation. In order to achieve good classification results, supervised-learning classifiers rely on proper segmented training samples and classification probes. Proper segmentation is hard to realize without higher semantic knowledge about the object to segment. But the use of a-priori knowledge or manual segmentation is not suited for a fully automatic general purpose approach.

For this reason we developed a self learning segmentation algorithm by use of gray scale invariants, which is capable of performing segmentation and classification in one step. Gray scale invariant features are extracted from the surrounding neighborhood of each pixel/voxel. In an interactive procedure, a support-vector machine model is trained. Once this model has been obtained for the requested types of cells, segmentation and classification can be performed automatically without any further human interaction.

This paper is structured as follows. Section 2 gives a brief introduction to voxel-wise gray scale invariants. In section 3 we introduce the actual segmentation using an interactive training method and support-vector machines. Finally, in section 4 we present some experimental results.

2   Voxel-Wise Gray Scale Invariants

Gray scale features, invariant towards Euclidean motion, using Haar-integration over the whole transformation group of an n-dimensional data set $\mathbf{X}$, are calculated as follows: [3] [5]

$$T[f](\mathbf{X}) := \int_G f(g\mathbf{X})dg \qquad (1)$$

where G denotes the transformation group, g one element of G, f a nonlinear kernel function and $g\mathbf{X}$ the transformed n-dimensional data set. If the kernel function f only depends on a few points of the image or volume, i.e., if we can rewrite $f(\mathbf{X})$ as $f\left(\mathbf{X}(\boldsymbol{x}_1), \mathbf{X}(\boldsymbol{x}_2), \mathbf{X}(\boldsymbol{x}_3), \ldots\right)$, where $\mathbf{X}(\boldsymbol{x}_i)$ is the gray value[1] at position $\boldsymbol{x}_i$ we only need to transform the kernel points $\boldsymbol{x}_1, \boldsymbol{x}_2, \boldsymbol{x}_3, \ldots$ accordingly, instead of the whole data set $\mathbf{X}$. This transformation of the kernel points is denoted as $s_g(\boldsymbol{x}_i)$, rewriting (1) as

---

[1] We use the term "gray value" even for color or other multi-channel data. In this case one "gray value" has multiple components.

$$T[f](\mathbf{X}) := \int_G f\Big(\mathbf{X}(s_g(\boldsymbol{x}_1)),\; \mathbf{X}(s_g(\boldsymbol{x}_2)),\; \mathbf{X}(s_g(\boldsymbol{x}_3)),\ldots\Big)\, dg\;. \qquad (2)$$

The direct evaluation of the integral (2) is usually too slow for real applications. [5] presented a fast calculation method (using FFTs) for a certain class of kernel-functions (so called separable two-point-kernel functions) of the form

$$f(\mathbf{X}) = f_a\Big(\mathbf{X}(\mathbf{0})\Big)\cdot f_b\Big(\mathbf{X}(\boldsymbol{q})\Big)$$

f_a, f_b : any nonlinear functions that transform the gray values   (3)
$\boldsymbol{q}$: span of the kernel function

Calculation of Voxel-Wise Gray Scale Invariants: The voxel-wise extraction of invariant features follows the same theory as above, restricting the transformation group to rotation. A major drawback of voxel-wise calculation with two-point-kernel functions is that the resulting features are not only invariant towards rotation, but also towards arbitrary permutation of neighboring gray values. To overcome this problem, we introduced a fast approximation using FFT and 3D *separable three-point-kernel functions* [2] of the type (see accompaning paper [1])

$$f(\mathbf{X}) = f_a\Big(\mathbf{X}(\mathbf{0})\Big)\cdot f_b\Big(\mathbf{X}(\boldsymbol{q}_1)\Big)\cdot f_c\Big(\mathbf{X}(\boldsymbol{q}_2)\Big) \qquad (4)$$

Multichannel Features: As illustrated in Fig. 1, biological probes are often stained with different fluorescent markers, which are recorded as multi channel datasets. Kernels of the form (4) can be evaluated over several channels, using the voxel-wise gray-scale representation of the recorded volumetric datasets $\mathbf{X}_\mathbf{v}$, where $\mathbf{X}_{\mathbf{v}_i}$ gives the gray-value for the i-th channel.

Kernel Functions: To increase separability, several features with different spans and non-linear mappings are combined to feature vectors for each voxel.

In the case of a compact transformation group, like rotation, any kernel function returning a scalar value may be used, because after parameterization, an integral with fixed borders (e.g., integration from 0 to 360 degrees) can be

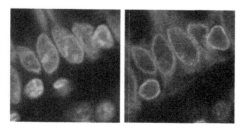

Fig. 1. By staining with different fluorescent markers and variation of the ecitation wave length, several data channels can be recorded from a single sample at once

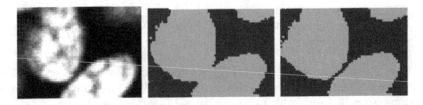

Fig. 2. From left to right: original data, classification of features without exponential kernels, classification with the same training samples but with some features calculated on the "inverse data"

found. For the later described segmentation we use simple non-linear functions like $f(\boldsymbol{v}) = v_i^2, v_i^3, v_i^4, \ldots or \sqrt{v_i}$ with spans from 2,4,8 up to 32. While small spans extract local object features (high frequencies), it is useful to have some larger spans covering the entire object (low frequencies). In addition, we perform Gaussian filtering previous to the non-linear mappings for increased local support [1][2]. For datasets with high valued object gray-values and low background values an additional problem arises: due to the nature of Haar-integration, the foreground values dominate the result of the voxel-wise features which leads to a reduced separability of the background close to objects. A solution is provided by calculating some features which are sensitive to the background. This can be achieved by use of an appropriate kernel function like:

$$f(\mathbf{X}) = \sqrt{\mathbf{X(0)}} \cdot e^{-\mathbf{X(q_1)}^2} \quad \text{two-point exponential kernel function} \qquad (5)$$

3   Segmentation

After the voxel-wise extraction of feature-vectors using two- and three-point kernels, a support-vector machine (SVM) [7][8] model is trained in an interactive

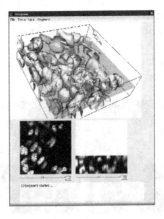

Fig. 3. Framework for interactive model training: xy-slices (bottom left) and yz-slices (bottom right) are moved through the volumetric dataset (top) and training samples are selected manually via "mouse clicks".

procedure over several iterations: First a small number of training samples (voxels) is manually selected for each class (Fig. 3). Second, a SVM model is trained based on the training feature-vectors. In the last step of one iteration, all voxels are classified against the previously trained model. After each iteration new training samples can be added in order to improve segmentation and classification results until the model reaches a "stable" state, e.g. the support-vectors do not change after adding new samples. In order to avoid overfitting and to find the

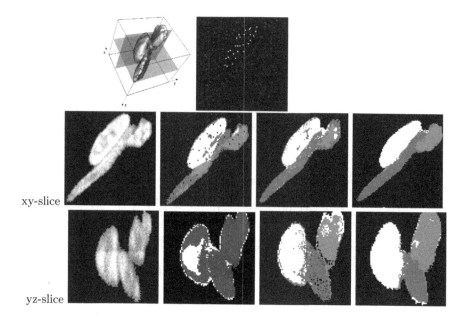

Fig. 4. The interactive training process - 1st row: 3D reconstruction of the original data, 311 training samples set for the first iteration of training. 2nd line - from left to right: section of xy-slice of original data as indicated in the 3D reconstruction, result after the first iteration (56 support vectors in model), result after 2nd iteration,result after the 3rd iteration (642 training samples, 129 support vectors in model). 3rd line: section of yz-slice of original data, results after 1st to 3rd iterations in yz-slice.

optimal SVM model, we perform a grid-search over SVM-kernel parameters and cost-function with cross-validation model selection in each training round. One of the major advantages of our approach is, that the obtained model can easily be extended with samples from other datasets and and even new classes, simply by executing additional training rounds. With the model at hand, objects in datasets which have been recorded under similar conditions (staining, excitation, etc.) can be segmented and classified fully automatically: voxel-wise features are extracted and classified. In a final step the labeled voxels are combined to closed objects by connected component labeling.

4   Experiments

In this section we present some experimental results and compare the performance of the previously described algorithms with a standard Watershed region growing approach.

Table 1. Overview of all used three- and two-pint gray-scale invariants of type $f(\mathbf{X}) = f_a(\mathbf{X}(0)) \cdot f_b(\mathbf{X}(q_1)) \cdot f_c(\mathbf{X}(q_2))$. q_α denotes the size of the scope, v_i the i-th channel.

	f_1	f_2	f_3	f_4	f_5	f_6	f_7	f_8
f_a	$X_{v_1}(0)$	$(X_{v_1}(0))^5$	$(X_{v_1}(0))^5$	$\sqrt{X_{v_1}(0)}$	$(X_{v_1}(0))^2$	$\sqrt{X_{v_1}(0)}$	$X_{v_1}(0)$	$(X_{v_1}(0))^2$
f_b	$X_{v_1}(0)$	$(X_{v_1}(q_2))^2$	$(X_{v_1}(q_2))^5$	$e^{(-X_{v_1}(q_4))^2}$	$(X_{v_1}(q_4))^5$	$\sqrt{X_{v_1}(q_4)}$	$X_{v_1}(q_4)$	$(X_{v_1}(q_8))^5$
f_c	-	$(X_{v_1}(q_2))^2$	-	-	$(X_{v_1}(q_4))^5$	$\sqrt{X_{v_1}(q_4)}$	$X_{v_1}(q_4)$	$(X_{v_1}(q_8))^5$

	f_{10}	f_{11}	f_{12}	f_{13}	f_{14}	f_{15}	f_{16}
f_a	$(X_{v_1}(0))^5$	$\sqrt{X_{v_1}}(0)$	$(X_{v_1}(0))^5$	$X_{v_1}(0)$	$e^{(-X_{v_1}(0))^2}$	$(X_{v_1}(0))^5$	$(X_{v_1}(0))^5$
f_b	$e^{-X_{v_1}(q_{16})}$	$\sqrt{X_{v_1}(q_{16})}$	$(X_{v_1}(q_{16}))^2$	$X_{v_2}(q_2)$	$e^{(-X_{v_2}(q_2))^2}$	$(X_{v_2}(q_2))^2$	$(X_{v_2}(q_2))^5$
f_c	-	$\sqrt{X_{v_1}(q_{16})}$	$(X_{v_1}(q_{16}))^2$	$X_{v_2}(q_2)$	$e^{(-X_{v_2}(q_2))^2}$	-	$(X_{v_2}(q_2))^5$

	f_{18}	f_{19}	f_{20}	f_{21}	f_{22}	f_{23}	f_{24}
f_a	$(X_{v_1}(0))^2$	$e^{(-X_{v_1}(0))^2}$	$(X_{v_1}(0))^5$	$(X_{v_1}(0))^2$	$\sqrt{X_{v_1}(0)}$	$(X_{v_1}(0))^5$	$(X_{v_1}(0))^5$
f_b	$(X_{v_2}(q_4))^5$	$e^{(-X_{v_2}(q_4))^2}$	$(X_{v_2}(q_4))^2$	$(X_{v_2}(q_8))^5$	$(X_{v_2}(q_8))^5$	$e^{-X_{v_2}(q_{16})}$	$(X_{v_2}(q_{16}))^2$
f_c	-	-	$(X_{v_2}(q_4))^2$	-	$(X_{v_2}(q_8))^5$	-	$(X_{v_2}(q_{16}))^2$

	f_{26}	f_{27}	f_{28}	f_{29}	f_{30}	f_{31}	f_{32}
f_a	$X_{v_2}(0)$	$e^{(-X_{v_2}(0))^2}$	$(X_{v_2}(0))^5$	$(X_{v_2}(0))^5$	$\sqrt{X_{v_2}(0)}$	$(X_{v_2}(0))^2$	$e^{(-X_{v_2}(0))^2}$
f_b	$X_{v_1}(q_2)$	$e^{(-X_{v_1}(q_2))^2}$	$(X_{v_1}(q_2))^2$	$(X_{v_1}(q_2))^5$	$e^{(-X_{v_1}(q_4))^2}$	$(X_{v_1}(q_4))^5$	$e^{(-X_{v_1}(q_4))^2}$
f_c	$X_{v_1}(q_2)$	$e^{(-X_{v_1}(q_2))^2}$	$(X_{v_1}(q_2))^5$	-	$e^{(-X_{v_1}(q_4))^2}$	-	-

Data: The experiments were performed on 3D volumetric data samples of chicken embryo chorioallantoic membrane (CAM) probes recorded by a confocal laser scanning microscope (LSM). The CAM is a widely used model for angiogenesis research. For angiogenesis research at cellular level, an automatic localization and identification of the different cell types is crucial. Understanding angiogenesis has been found key to treatment of many frequent diseases, including cancer and heart ischemia. The samples were prepared as described in [9][10] and treated with YoPro-1 and SMACy3 fluorescent markers.

Methods: A model was built performing the interactive training procedure on several training data sets. Other samples were classified against this model. As reference to our approach we performed seeded watershed segmentation with about one hundred manually set seeds for each cell. A median filter was applied prior to the watershed procedure. For this part we omitted the classification, since the classes were set manually.

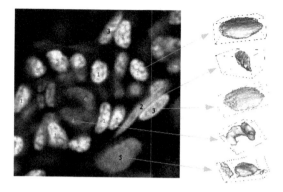

Fig. 5. Sample data, cross section of a capillary. Cell types with 3D reconstruction: 1. erythrocyte (**Ery**), 2. endothelial cell (**EC**), 3. pericyte (**PC**), 4. fibroblast (**FB**), 5. macrophage (**MΦ**).

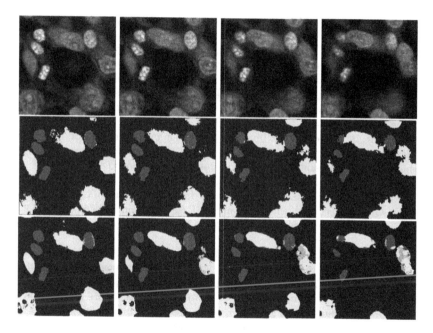

Fig. 6. Results of voxel-wise gray-scale invarinat segmentation in xy-slices. First line: raw data. Second line: watershed reference. Third line: results of our approach.

Fig. 7. Results of voxel-wise gray-scale invarinat segmentation in zy-slices. First line: two channels of raw data. Second line: watershed reference and results of our approach.

Results: For the experiment sown in (Fig. 6), the features in (Table 1) were used. Three-point kernels were restricted to have the points on one straight line and were approximated only by the first coefficient of the series [1].

Conclusion and Outlook. Our algorithm is able to automatically detect previously learned objects. Low fluorescent activity and strong intra cellular structures do not cause false or partial segmentation results. But still the low z-resolution is responsible for miss-classifications at object borders and some noise (Fig. 6). The rather simple approach of connected component labeling is the major drawback at this state - it is neither capable of suppressing small fractions of noise, nor splitting touching objects of the same class.

References

1. Ronneberger, O., Fehr, J., Burkhardt, H.: Voxel-wise gray scale invariants for simultaneous segmentation and classification. In: Pattern Recognition, Proceedings of the 27th DAGM Symposium, Vienna, Austria, Lecture Notes in Computer Science. (2005)
2. Ronneberger, O., Fehr, J., Burkhardt, H.: Voxel-wise gray scale invariants for simultaneous segmentation and classification – theory and application to cell-nuclei in 3d volumetric data. Internal report 2/05, IIF-LMB, University Freiburg (2005)
3. Schulz-Mirbach, H.: Invariant features for gray scale images. In Sagerer, G., Posch, S., Kummert, F., eds.: 17. DAGM - Symposium "Mustererkennung", Bielefeld, Reihe Informatik aktuell, Springer (1995) 1–14
4. Burkhardt, H., Siggelkow, S.: Invariant features in pattern recognition – fundamentals and applications. In Kotropoulos, C., Pitas, I., eds.: Nonlinear Model-Based Image/Video Processing and Analysis, John Wiley & Sons (2001) 269–307
5. Ronneberger, O., Burkhardt, H., Schultz, E.: General-purpose Object Recognition in 3D Volume Data Sets using Gray-Scale Invariants – Classification of Airborne Pollen-Grains Recorded with a Confocal Laser Scanning Microscope. In: Proceedings of the International Conference on Pattern Recognition, Quebec, Canada (2002)
6. Ronneberger, O., Schultz, E., Burkhardt, H.: Automated Pollen Recognition using 3D Volume Images from Fluorescence Microscopy. Aerobiologia **18** (2002) 107–115
7. Vapnik, V.N.: The nature of statistical learning theory. Springer (1995)
8. Ronneberger, O.: Libsvmtl - a support vector machine template library. download at: http://lmb.informatik.uni-freiburg.de/lmbsoft/libsvmtl/ (2004)
9. Kurz, H., et al.: Pericytes in experimental mda-mb231 tumor angiogenesis. Histochem Cell Biol (2002) 117:527–534
10. Kurz, H., et al.: Automatic classification of cell nuclei and cells during embryonic vascular development. Ann Anat 2005; 187 (Suppl): 130. (2005)

License Plate Character Segmentation Using Hidden Markov Chains

Vojtěch Franc and Václav Hlaváč

Center for Machine Perception, Department of Cybernetics,
Faculty of Electrical Engineering, Czech Technical University
{xfrancv, hlavac}@cmp.felk.cvut.cz
http://cmp.felk.cvut.cz

Abstract. We propose a method for segmentation of a line of characters in a noisy low resolution image of a car license plate. The Hidden Markov Chains are used to model a stochastic relation between an input image and a corresponding character segmentation. The segmentation problem is expressed as the maximum a posteriori estimation from a set of admissible segmentations. The proposed method exploits a specific prior knowledge available for the application at hand. Namely, the number of characters is known and its is also known that the characters can be segmented to sectors with equal but unknown width. The efficient algorithm for estimation based on dynamic programming is derived. The proposed method was successfully tested on data from a real life license plate recognition system.

1 Introduction

The segmentation of a line of characters is an important problem emerging in the license plate recognition (LPR) systems. The objective is to partition image into segments with isolated characters which serve as an input of the Optical Character Recognition (OCR) system. The problem is challenging due to noise in the image, low resolution, space marks, illumination changes, shadows and other artifacts present in real images (see Figure 1). Despite a large effort dedicated to the LPR systems a robust method for character segmentation remains to be an open problem.

Segmentation techniques of machine printed characters have been studied for a long time [2]. Common approaches to character segmentation specially designed for the LPR systems are based on the projection method [3], the Hough transform [7] and intensity thresholding with connected component analysis [5].

We approach the segmentation problem differently by using machine learning methods. In particular, we apply the Hidden Markov Chain (HMC) statistical model and the maximum a posteriori (MAP) estimation. The statistical model is learned from a training set of examples endowed with a ground truth segmentation provided by a user. The aim is to derive a method which mimics the user's segmentation and which exploits all the prior knowledge specific for

W. Kropatsch, R. Sablatnig, and A. Hanbury (Eds.): DAGM 2005, LNCS 3663, pp. 385–392, 2005.

the application at hand. Namely, we know the number of characters in the license plate in the Czech Republic and also that the characters can be segmented into sectors with the same but unknown width. We started from a segmentation method proposed in [4] which can be applied to find the maximum a posteriori set of beginnings of a specified number of characters. We extended this method in such sense that it exploits the knowledge about the equal width of the characters. We will demonstrate the positive effect of the exploited prior knowledge in the experiment performed on real life data. The proposed method is able to segment characters correctly even in images of a very poor quality. The error rate 3.3% was achieved on the testing set with 1000 examples captured by a real LPR system.

Fig. 1. Example of a car license plate and its ground truth segmentation provided by an user

The paper is organized as follows. The problem is defined in Section 2. Section 3 outlines two related approaches. The proposed segmentation method is described in Section 4. Section 5 gives experimental evaluation on real life data and Section 6 concludes the paper.

2   Task Definition

An input image is a sequence $x = (x_1, \ldots, x_n) \in \mathcal{X} \subset \mathbb{R}^{d \times n}$ of n column vectors each of which has d entries. The entries of each column vector are intensity values coded by real numbers from the interval $\langle 0, 255 \rangle$. The input image contains a line of $m \in \mathcal{N}$ characters (alphabets and numerals) which are assumed to be segmentable into sectors of equal width $w \in \mathcal{N}$. The number of characters m is known while their position in the image and their width w is unknown. A character position is an index i of an image column x_i corresponding to the beginning of the character. A segmentation of the input image x is a pair $(\mathcal{I}, w)$ where the set of indices $\mathcal{I} = \{i_1, \ldots, i_m\} \subset \{1, \ldots, n\}$ contains beginnings of m characters and w is their width. It is further assumed that $0 < i_1$, $i_q + w < i_{q+1}$, $\forall q \in \{1, \ldots, m-1\}$ and $i_m + w < n$, i.e., characters cannot overlap each other. The user provides a training set $\mathcal{T} = \{(x^1, \mathcal{I}^1, w^1), \ldots, (x^l, \mathcal{I}^l, w^l)\}$ of examples which contains triplets composed of an image x^j and a segmentation $(\mathcal{I}^j, w^j)$. The aim is to find a strategy which for a given image x returns the segmentation $(\mathcal{I}, w)$ as would be produced by the user.

2.1   Statistical Model

We decided to use the Hidden Markov Chain (HMC) model to describe a relation between the image x and its corresponding segmentation $(\mathcal{I}, w)$. To this end, we express the segmentation $(\mathcal{I}, w)$ as a sequence of labels $\boldsymbol{y} = (y_0, \ldots, y_n) \in \mathcal{Y} = \mathcal{L}^{n+1}$. We assume that the label y_i can attain value from a set $\mathcal{L} = \{0, 1, \ldots, w_{max}\}$ where w_{max} is the maximal possible character width. The symbol $\boldsymbol{y}(\mathcal{I}, w)$ denotes a sequence of labels $(y_0, y_1, \ldots, y_n)$ assigned to the segmentation $(\mathcal{I}, w)$ such that:

$$
y_i = \begin{cases} 1 & \text{if } i \in \mathcal{I}, \\ y_{i-1} + 1 & \text{if } y_{i-1} > 0 \text{ and } y_{i-1} + 1 \le w, \\ 0 & \text{otherwise.} \end{cases} \tag{1}
$$

The first label y_0 which has no corresponding image column is always set to 0. It plays no role in the segmentation but its presence eases the formal analysis. The label $y_i = 0$ means that the column x_i does not belong to any character. The label $y_i > 0$ means that x_i is the y_i-th column of a character. The upper part of Figure 2 shows an example of an input image $\boldsymbol{x}$ with two characters $m = 2$ of the width $w = 4$ and the corresponding labelling $\boldsymbol{y}$.

The formula (1) allows to represent the training set T by a new training set of sequences $T_{\mathcal{X}\mathcal{Y}} = \{(\boldsymbol{x}^1, \boldsymbol{y}^1), \ldots, (\boldsymbol{x}^l, \boldsymbol{y}^l)\}$ without loss of any information. A pair of sequences $(\boldsymbol{x}, \boldsymbol{y})$ is assumed to be a realization of a random process which is described by a joint probability distribution function

$$
p(\boldsymbol{x}, \boldsymbol{y}) = p(y_0) \prod_{i=1}^n p(x_i | y_i) p(y_i | y_{i-1}) . \tag{2}
$$

The formula (2) defines a distribution of the HMC model. It is assumed that the HMC model is determined by a discrete distribution $p(y_0)$, a discrete conditional distribution $p(y_i | y_{i-1})$ and a set of $|\mathcal{L}|$ multivariate distributions $p(x_i | y_i)$, $y_i \in \mathcal{L}$. All the distributions do not depend on the position i in the sequence. The bottom part of Figure 2 shows the HMC model and its states aligned with the corresponding image columns.

The parameters of the distributions were estimated from the training set $T_{\mathcal{X}\mathcal{Y}}$. The discrete distributions $p(y_0)$ and $p(y_i | y_{i-1})$ were estimated using the maximum-likelihood principle (e.g. [4]). The Parzen window density estimator [1] with isotropic Gaussian kernel was used to model the distributions $p(x_i | y_i)$, $y_i \in \mathcal{L}$. The kernel centers were found by the k-means algorithm. The kernel width and the number of kernels were determined using the cross-validation.

2.2   Maximum a Posteriori Estimation of Segmentation

The main aim is to find a most probable segmentation $(\mathcal{I}^*, w^*)$ given an input image $\boldsymbol{x}$. Each segmentation $(\mathcal{I}, w)$ can be equivalently expressed as a labelling $\boldsymbol{y}(\mathcal{I}, w)$ its construction is described by (1). On the other hand, not every labeling $\boldsymbol{y} \in \mathcal{Y}$ corresponds to a valid segmentation $(\mathcal{I}, w)$. The symbol $\mathcal{Y}_F = \{\boldsymbol{y}(\mathcal{I}, w) : \forall \mathcal{I}, \forall w\} \subset \mathcal{Y}$ denotes a set of all admissible labelings for which corresponding segmentations exist. The HMC model (2) can be used to evaluate a probability $p(\boldsymbol{x}, \boldsymbol{y})$ for given image $\boldsymbol{x}$ and its labeling $\boldsymbol{y}$. Thus the estimation of the most probable segmentation $(\mathcal{I}^*, w^*)$ can be seen as the search for the most

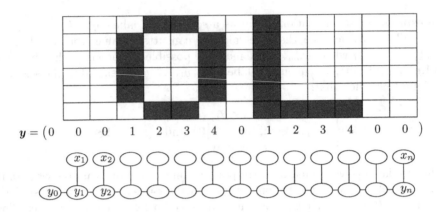

Fig. 2. Illustrative example of a license plate image aligned with the Hidden Markov Chain model

probable labelling $y(\mathcal{I}^*, w^*)$ which belongs to the set of admissible labelings $\mathcal{Y}_F$. We define the MAP estimation problem as the following optimization task

$$(\mathcal{I}^*, w^*) = \underset{y \in \mathcal{Y}_F}{\operatorname{argmax}} \, p(y|x) = \operatorname{argmax}_{\mathcal{I}} \max_{w} p(y(\mathcal{I}, w)|x) . \qquad (3)$$

It is seen that the task (3) cannot be solved directly by the Viterbi algorithm [6] which computes the MAP estimation of a sequence of labels but it searches through all possible sequences $\mathcal{Y}$. We started off by a segmentation method proposed in [4] which allows to find the most probable set of indices $\mathcal{I}$, however, the character width w is not regarded. The method is outlined in Section 3. We used the idea of the method to derive an algorithm which regards the character width w and solves precisely the task (3). The proposed algorithm will be described in Section 4.

3   Related Methods for Maximum a Posteriori Estimation

In this section we mention two related methods applicable for estimation of the sequence of labels and the segmentation. These methods are the Viterbi algorithm and the method for MAP estimation of segmentation described in [4]. We used both the methods in experimental comparison against the proposed approach (c.f. Section 5).

The first related methods is the Viterbi algorithm [6] which computes the maximum a posteriori (MAP) estimation of the sequence of labels

$$y^* = \underset{y \in \mathcal{Y}}{\operatorname{argmax}} \, p(x, y) , \qquad (4)$$

The symbol $x \in \mathcal{X}$ is the observed sequence and $y \in \mathcal{Y}$ is the unknown sequence of labels. Notice that the MAP sequence of labels y^* is selected from the set of all possible sequences $\mathcal{Y}$. Therefore, it can happen that the optimal sequence

y^* does not belong to the set of admissible sequences $\mathcal{Y}_F$. The task (4) can be solved efficiently by the dynamic programming. The computational complexity of the Viterbi algorithm scales with $O(n \cdot |\mathcal{L}|^2)$.

The second related method is the segmentation algorithm described in [4] which solves the following task. Let a set of indices $\mathcal{I} = \{i_1, i_2, \ldots, i_m\} \subset \{0, \ldots, n\}$ define a segmentation. The segmentation $\mathcal{I}$ defines a set of admissible sequences of labels $\mathcal{Y}(\mathcal{I})$. An admissible sequence $\boldsymbol{y} = (y_0, y_1, \ldots, y_n) \in \mathcal{Y}(\mathcal{I})$ satisfies $y_i = \sigma$, $i \in \mathcal{I}$ and $y_i \neq \sigma$, $i \notin \mathcal{I}$. In our application $\sigma = 1$, i.e., the set $\mathcal{I}$ contains beginnings of characters (indices of first columns). The probability that the true segmentation is $\mathcal{I}$ equals to the probability that the sequence $\boldsymbol{y}$ belongs to the set $\mathcal{Y}(\mathcal{I})$. The MAP estimation of the segmentation $\mathcal{I}$ is defined as

$$\mathcal{I}^* = \operatorname*{argmax}_{\mathcal{I}} \sum_{\boldsymbol{y} \in \mathcal{Y}(\mathcal{I})} p(\boldsymbol{y}|\boldsymbol{x}) = \operatorname*{argmax}_{\mathcal{I}} \sum_{\boldsymbol{y} \in \mathcal{Y}(\mathcal{I})} p(\boldsymbol{x}, \boldsymbol{y}) . \tag{5}$$

It is shown in [4] how to transform the task (5) into another one which is efficiently solvable by dynamic programming. The overall complexity of the method scales with $O(n^2 \cdot |\mathcal{L}|^2)$. The proposed extension of this algorithm which considers also the character width is a subject of the Section 4.

4   Proposed Method for Segmentation

Let a pair $(\mathcal{I}, w)$ define a segmentation where $\mathcal{I} = \{i_1, i_2, \ldots, i_m\} \subset \{0, \ldots, n\}$ is the set of indices and $w \in \mathcal{N}$ is character width. The indices $\mathcal{I}$ denote the beginnings of characters thus it must hold that $0 < i_1$, $i_q + w < i_{q+1}$, $\forall q \in \{1, \ldots, m-1\}$ and $i_m + w < n$, i.e., all the characters are completely visible and they must not overlap. A segmentation $(\mathcal{I}, w)$ can be expressed using (1) as a sequence of labels

$$\boldsymbol{y}(\mathcal{I}, w) = (0, a_1^{i_1-1}, b_{i_1}^{i_1+w-1}, a_{i_1+w}^{i_2-1}, b_{i_2}^{i_2+w-1}, \ldots, b_{i_m}^{i_m+w-1}, a_{i_m+w}^n) . \tag{6}$$

The subsequences $a_i^j = (0, 0, \ldots, 0)$ have all the labels equal to 0 and their width $j - i + 1$ varies from 0 (empty sequence) to $n - mw$, i.e., these subsequence corresponds to the gaps between the characters. The subsequences b_i^{i+w-1} have the identical form equal to $(1, 2, \ldots, w)$, i.e., these subsequences correspond to the characters. We define the MAP estimation of the segmentation $(\mathcal{I}, w)$ as

$$(\mathcal{I}^*, w^*) = \operatorname*{argmax}_{\mathcal{I}} \max_{w} p(\boldsymbol{y}(\mathcal{I}, w)|\boldsymbol{x}) = \operatorname*{argmax}_{\mathcal{I}} \max_{w} p(\boldsymbol{x}, \boldsymbol{y}(\mathcal{I}, w)) . \tag{7}$$

We will show that the optimization task (7) can be efficiently solved by dynamic programming.

Assuming the HMC model (2) allows to write

$$p(\boldsymbol{x}, \boldsymbol{y}(\mathcal{I}, w)) = \Phi(i_1) \left(\prod_{q=1}^{m-1} \Phi(i_q, i_{q+1}) \right) \Phi(i_m) ,$$

where

$$\Phi(i_1) = p(y_0)\, p(x_1^{i_1-1}, y_1^{i_1-1}|y_0)\, p(x_{i_1}^{i_1+w-1}, y_{i_1}^{i_1+w-1}|y_{i_1-1})$$

$$= p(y_0) \prod_{q=1}^{i_1-1} p(x_q|y_q)\, p(y_q|y_{q-1}) \prod_{r=1}^{i_1+w-1} p(x_r|y_r)\, p(y_r|y_{r-1})$$

$$\Phi(i,j) = p(x_{i+w}^{j-1}, y_{i+w}^{j-1}|y_{i+w-1})\, p(x_j^{j+w-1}, y_j^{j+w-1}|y_{j-1})$$

$$= \prod_{q=i+1}^{j-1} p(x_q|y_q)\, p(y_q|y_{q-1}) \prod_{r=j}^{j+w-1} p(x_r|y_r)\, p(y_r|y_{r-1})$$

$$\Phi(i_m) = p(x_{i_m+w}^{n}, y_{i_m+w}^{n}) = \prod_{q=i_m}^{n} p(x_q|y_q)\, p(y_q|y_{q-1})$$

The numbers Φ can be evaluated for a given image x and a sequence of labels $y(\mathcal{I}, w)$ given by (6). If $w \in \{1, \ldots, w_{max}\}$ is fixed then the most probable set of indices $\mathcal{I}^*(w)$ can be expressed as

$$\mathcal{I}^*(w) = \underset{i_1}{\operatorname{argmax}}\, \underset{i_2}{\operatorname{argmax}} \cdots \underset{i_m}{\operatorname{max}} \left(\Phi(i_1) \left(\prod_{q=1}^{m-1} \Phi(i_q, i_{q+1}) \right) \Phi(i_m) \right)$$

$$= \underset{i_1}{\operatorname{argmax}}\, \underset{i_2}{\operatorname{argmax}} \cdots \underset{i_m}{\operatorname{max}} \left(\log \Phi(i_1) + \sum_{q=1}^{m-1} \log \Phi(i_q, i_{q+1}) + \log \Phi(i_m) \right).$$

$$(8)$$

The indices must satisfy $0 < i_1$, $i_q + w < i_{q+1}$, $\forall q \in \{1, \ldots, m-1\}$ and $i_m + w < n$. It is easy to see that the task (8) can be already solved by dynamic programming. Finally, the desired MAP segmentation $(\mathcal{I}^*, w^*)$ defined by (7) is computed as

$$(\mathcal{I}^*, w^*) = \underset{w \in \{1, \ldots, w_{max}\}}{\operatorname{argmax}} \mathcal{I}^*(w).$$

The computation of the numbers Φ requires at most $O(n^2)$ operations. Dynamic programming which requires $O(n \cdot m)$ operations has to be performed $w_{max} = |\mathcal{L}| - 1$ times. Therefore the overall computation complexity is $O(n^2 \cdot |\mathcal{L}|)$.

5   Experiments

We tested the proposed method on data captured from a real recognition system for license plates used in the Czech Republic. We compared the following three methods for segmentation:

MAP-SEQ. The segmentation is computed from the MAP estimation of the sequence of labels obtained by the standard Viterbi algorithm (c.f. Section 3). Having the sequence y^* estimated the beginnings $\mathcal{I}$ and widths $\{w_1, \ldots, w_m\}$ are extracted.

MAP-I. The MAP estimation of set of m indices $\mathcal{I}^*$ is computed disregarding the character width (c.f. Section 3). To allow for comparison with other methods the character width was estimated as

$$w^* = \underset{w \in \{1,\dots,w_{max}\}}{\text{argmax}} \; p(y(\mathcal{I}^*, w), \boldsymbol{x}),$$

where $\mathcal{I}^*$ was fixed to the previously compute MAP estimate.

MAP-Iw. The most probable segmentation $(\mathcal{I}^*, w^*)$ computed by the proposed method (c.f. Section 4).

We used $l = 1570$ examples of images for the estimation of the HMC model. The number of 1000 examples was used for testing. The images were normalized to height $d = 14$ using the nearest neighbor rescaling. No other preprocessing was used. The number of image columns varied around $n = 190$. The license plates contained $m = 7$ characters.

Every tested segmentation method returned for each input image $\boldsymbol{x}$ a pair $(\mathcal{I}, w)$. Having the segmentation $(\mathcal{I}, w)$ the character centers $\{s_1, \dots, s_m\}$ can be computed as $s_q = i_q + \frac{w-1}{2}$, $\forall q \in \{1, \dots, m\}$. The ground truth centers $\{s_1^*, \dots, s_m^*\}$ can be determined likewise. The image was recognized to be correctly segmented if the estimated centers differed from the grounds truth centers by 20% of the ground truth character width w^* at most, i.e.,

$$\left| \left(i_q + \frac{w-1}{2} \right) - \left(i_q^* + \frac{w^*-1}{2} \right) \right| < 0.2 w^*, \quad \forall q \in \{1, \dots, m\},$$

must hold, where $(\mathcal{I}^*, w^*)$ is the ground truth segmentation.

We also measured the number of individual overlooked characters (false negative) and the number of individual false detected (false positives) characters. The total number of characters is $m = 7$ times higher then the number of images. The correctly segmented character is again such one its estimated center differs from the ground truth center by 20% of the ground truth character width w^* at most. Notice, that the false positives rate equals to the false negatives rate for the MAP-I and MAP-Iw methods because they are guaranteed to return the correct number of segmented characters unlike the MAP-SEQ method.

Table 1. Comparison of the segmentation algorithms

Method	Overlooked characters	False detected characters	Incorrect segmentations
MAP-SEQ	7.8%	3.7%	37.0%
MAP-I	0.9%	0.9%	6.1%
MAP-Iw	0.5%	0.5%	3.3%

Table 1 summarizes the results obtained. It is clear that the segmentation error decreases as the methods use more and more prior knowledge of the problem at hand. The MAP-SEQ gives the worst results. The MAP-I improves the segmentation considerably as it employs knowledge of the number of characters in the image. The proposed method reduces the error further as it fits best to the problem at hand, i.e., it employs knowledge of the number of characters as well as the fact that the characters are of the same width.

6   Conclusions

We proposed the method for segmentation of a line of characters in an image of a car license plate. The method uses the Hidden Markov Chains (HMC) for modeling the stochastic relation between an input image and its corresponding character segmentation. The segmentation is expressed as the maximum a posteriori estimation problem. The problem leads to the maximum a posteriori (MAP) estimation of a sequence of labels from a set of admissible sequences. An efficient algorithm to solve the problem based on dynamic programming was proposed. The method exploits a specific prior knowledge available for the application which helps to reduce the segmentation error considerably. The proposed method is able to segment characters correctly even in images of very poor quality. The method achieved an error rate 3.3% estimated on data captured by a real LPR system.

Acknowledgments

The authors were supported by the Austrian Ministry of Education under project CONEX GZ 45.535 and by the EC project IST-004176 COSPAL. The first author was support also by MSM 6840770013. The second author was also supported by GACR 102/03/0440.

References

1. R.O. Duda, P.E. Hart, and D.G. Stork. *Pattern classification.* John Wiley & Sons, 2nd edition, 2001.
2. Y. Lu. Machine printed characters segmentation - an overview. *Pattern Recognition,* 28(1):67–80, 1995.
3. F. Martin and D. Borges. Automatic car plate recognition using a partial segmentation algorithm. In *IASTED conference on Signal Processing, Pattern Recognition, and Applications (SPPRA),* 2003.
4. M.I. Schlesinger and V. Hlaváč. *Ten lectures on statistical and structural pattern recognition.* Kluwer Academic Publishers, 2002.
5. V. Shapiro and G. Gluhchev. Multinational license plate recognition system: Segmentation and classification. In *Proceedings of the 17th International Conference on Pattern Recognition,* volume 4, pages 352–355, 2004.
6. A.J. Viterbi. Error bounds for convolutional codes and an asymptotically optimal decoding algorithm. *IEEE Transations Information Theory,* 13:260–269, 1967.
7. Y. Zhang and C. Zhang. A new character segmentation algorithm for license plate. In *IEEE Intelligent Vehicles Symposium (IV2003). Columbus, USA,* June 2003.

Digital Subtraction CT Lung Perfusion Image Based on 3D Affine Registration

Helen Hong[1] and Jeongjin Lee[2]

[1] School of Electrical Engineering and Computer Science,
BK21: Information Technology, Seoul National University
hlhong@cse.snu.ac.kr
[2] School of Electrical Engineering and Computer Science, Seoul National University,
San 56-1 Shinlim 9-dong Kwanak-gu, Seoul 151-742, Korea
jjlee@cglab.snu.ac.kr

Abstract. We propose a fast and robust registration technique for accurately imaging lung perfusion and efficiently detecting pulmonary embolism in chest CT angiography. For the registration of a pair of CT scans, a proper geometrical transformation is found through the following steps: First, the initial registration using an optimal cube is performed for correcting the gross translational mismatch. Second, the initial alignment is refined by iterative surface registration. For fast and robust convergence of the distance measure to the optimal value, a 3D distance map is generated by the narrow-band distance propagation. Third, enhanced vessels are visualized by subtracting registered pre-contrast images from post-contrast images. To facilitate visualization of parenchymal enhancement, color-coded mapping and image fusion is used. Our method has been successfully applied to ten patients of pre- and post-contrast images in chest CT angiography. Experimental results show that the performance of our method is very promising compared with conventional method with the aspects of its visual inspection, accuracy and processing time.

1 Introduction

With the introduction of multi-detector row CT scanners providing high spatial and excellent contrast resolution for the pulmonary structures, the importance of computed tomography (CT) is increasing in the diagnosis of pulmonary embolism [1-3]. The basis of pulmonary embolism assessment on CT images is the direct visualization of contrast material within the pulmonary arteries. However, it provides only limited information on pulmonary perfusion since lung parenchymal attenuation changes as a result of the injection of contrast material are too faint to be identified on visual inspection of CT angiography images. If lung perfusion can be well visualized, CT may provide more accurate information on pulmonary embolism.

Several methods have been suggested for visualizing lung perfusion in CT angiography [4]. Herzog et al. [5-6] proposed an image post-processing algorithm for visualization of parenchymal attenuation in chest CT angiography, which divided into five steps: lung contour segmentation, vessel cutting, adaptive filtering, color-coding and overlay with the original images. However, the method has a limitation in the

W. Kropatsch, R. Sablatnig, and A. Hanbury (Eds.): DAGM 2005, LNCS 3663, pp. 393–400, 2005.
© Springer-Verlag Berlin Heidelberg 2005

direct visualization of emboli by CT angiography alone. Chung et al. [7] evaluated the value of CT perfusion image obtained by 2D mutual information-based registration and subtraction for the detection of pulmonary embolism. However, they evaluated their method using a porcine model under the limited conditions. The 2D registration has a limitation to accurately align three-dimensional anatomy. In addition, the processing time is about 40 seconds for single slice registration. Thus, it is difficult to be useful and acceptable technique for clinical applications in diagnosis of pulmonary embolism.

Current approaches still need more progress in computational efficiency and accuracy for detecting attenuation changes of pulmonary vessels in chest CT angiography. In this paper, we propose a fast and robust registration technique for accurately visualizing lung perfusion and efficiently detecting pulmonary embolism in chest CT angiography. Our method is composed of three steps. First, the gross translational mismatch is corrected by the optimal cube registration. This initial registration is refined by the iterative surface registration. To evaluate the distance measure between lung boundaries, a 3D distance map is generated by the narrow-band distance propagation, which drives fast and robust convergence to the optimal value. Finally, image subtraction is performed for visualizing enhanced vessels by contrast material. To facilitate visualization of parenchymal enhancement, color-coded mapping and image fusion is used. Experimental results show that our registration method aligns lung boundaries more accurate and much faster than the conventional one using a 3D distance map. Accurate and fast result of our method would be more useful for detecting pulmonary embolism.

The organization of the paper is as follows. In Section 2, we discuss how to correct the gross translational mismatch. Then we propose a narrow-band distance propagation to generate a 3D distance map and a distance measure to find an exact geometrical relationship in pre- and post-contrast images of CT angiography. In Section 3, experimental results show how our registration method accurately and rapidly aligns lung boundaries. This paper is concluded with brief discussion of the results in Section 4.

2   3D CT Lung Perfusion

Fig. 1 shows the pipeline of our method for 3D CT lung perfusion in pre- and post-contrast images of chest CT angiography. To find exact geometrical relationship between pre- and post-contrast images, one dataset is fixed as mask volume where other dataset is defined as contrast volume which is taken after injecting a contrast material to the mask volume. In order to extract the precise lung region borders, we apply the automatic segmentation method of Yim et al. [8] to our experimental datasets. Since our method is applied to the diagnosis of pulmonary embolism, we assume that each CT scan is almost acquired at the maximal inspiration and the dataset includes the thorax from the trachea to below the diaphragm. Based on this assumption and experience, we found that affine transformation would be sufficient for the registration of mask and contrast volumes.

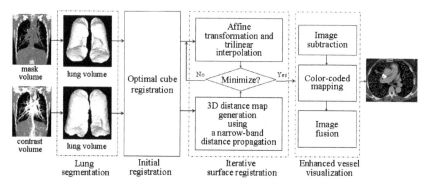

Fig. 1. The pipeline of proposed method for the 3D CT lung perfusion

2.1 Initial Registration Using an Optimal Cube

Although pre- and post-contrast images of chest CT angiography are acquired at the maximal inspiration, the position of lung boundaries between pre- and post-contrast images can be quite different according to the patient's unexpected respiration and small movement. For the efficient registration of such images, an initial gross correction method is usually applied. Several landmark-based registration techniques have been used for the initial gross correction. To achieve the initial alignment of lung boundaries, these landmark-based registrations require the detection of landmarks and point-to-point registration of corresponding landmarks. These processes much degrade the performance of the whole process.

To minimize the computation time and maximize the effectiveness of initial registration, we propose a simple method of global alignment using the circumscribed boundary of lungs. As shown in Fig. 2(a), a bounding volume, which includes left and right lung boundaries, is enlarged by a predefined distance d to be an optimal cube. The initial registration of two volumes is accomplished by aligning the centers of optimal cubes as shown in Fig. 2(b).

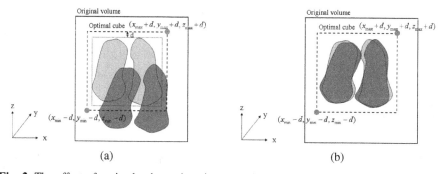

Fig. 2. The effect of optimal cube registration as an initial alignment (a) the generation of an optimal cube (b) after optimal cube registration

The processing time of initial registration using an optimal cube is dramatically reduced since it does not require any anatomical landmark detection. In addition, our method leads to robust convergence to the optimal value since the search space is limited near an optimal value.

2.2 Iterative Refinement Using Surface Registration

In a surface registration algorithm, the calculation of the distance from a surface boundary to a certain point can be done using a preprocessed distance map based on chamfer matching. Chamfer matching reduces the generation time of a distance map by an approximated distance transformation compared to a Euclidean distance transformation. However, the computation time of distance is still expensive by the two-step distance transformation of forward and backward masks. In particular, when the initial alignment almost corrects the gross translational mismatch, the generation of a 3D distance map of whole volume is unnecessary. From this observation, we propose the narrow-band distance propagation for the efficient generation of a 3D distance map.

To generate a 3D distance map, we approximate the global distance computation with repeated propagation of local distances within a small neighborhood. To approximate Euclidean distances, we consider 26-neighbor relations for 1-distance propagation as shown in Eq. (1). The distance value tells how far it is apart from a surface boundary point. The narrow-band distance propagation shown in Fig. 3 is applied to surface boundary points only in the contrast volume. We can generate a 3D distance map very fast since pixels are propagated only in the direction of increasing distances to the maximum neighborhood.

$$DP(i) = \min(\min_{j \in 26-neighbors(i)}(DP(j)+1), DP(i)) . \tag{1}$$

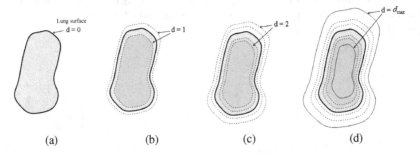

(a)   (b)   (c)   (d)

Fig. 3. The generation of the 3D distance map using our narrow-band distance propagation. (a) lung boundary in contrast volume (b) distance 1 propagation (c) distance 2 propagation (d) distance d_{max} propagation.

The distance measure in Eq. (2) is used to determine the degree of resemblance of lung boundaries of mask and contrast volume. The average of absolute distance difference, *AADD,* reaches the minimum when lung boundary points of mask and contrast volumes are aligned correctly. Since the search space of our distance measure is limited to the surrounding lung boundaries, the Powell's method is sufficient for evaluating *AADD* instead of using a more powerful optimization algorithm.

$$AADD = \frac{1}{N_{mask}} \sum_{i=0}^{N_{mask}-1} \left| D_{contrast}(i) - D_{mask}(i) \right| . \tag{2}$$

where $D_{mask}(i)$ and $D_{contrast}(i)$ is the distance value of mask volume and the distance value of the 3D distance map of contrast volume, respectively. We assume that $D_{mask}(i)$ are all set to 0. N_C is the total number of surface boundary points in mask volume.

2.3 Enhanced Vessel Visualization

A traditional approach for visualizing enhanced vessels after registration is to subtract registered mask volume from contrast volume. However, it is difficult to easily recognize the lung perfusion using just a traditional subtraction technique when lung parenchymal changes as a result of the injection of contrast material are too small. After subtraction, we apply color-coded mapping to only lung parenchyma and image fusion with original image.

To facilitate visualization of parenchymal enhancement, the subtraction image is mapped onto a spectral color scale, which is interactively controlled by modifying center and width of a spectral color. Then the resulting color-coded parenchymal images are overlaid onto the corresponding slice of contrast volume. For overlaying, all non-parenchymal pixels are replaced by the original pixels of the respective slice position and displayed in the usual CT gray-scale presentation.

3 Experimental Results

All our implementation and test were performed on an Intel Pentium IV PC containing 3.4 GHz and 2.0 GB of main memory. Our method has been applied to ten clinical datasets with pulmonary embolism, as described in Table 1, obtained from Siemens Sensation 16-channel multidetector row CT scanner. The image size of all experimental datasets is 512 x 512. The pre- and post-contrast images of chest CT angiography are acquired under the same image conditions excepting the injection of contrast material.

Table 1. Image conditions of experimental datasets

(mm)

Subject	Pixel size	Number of slices	Slice interval	Subject	Pixel size	Number of slices	Slice interval
1	0.60 x 0.60	258	1.5	6	0.69 x 0.69	221	1.5
2	0.61 x 0.61	175	1.5	7	0.60 x 0.60	207	1.5
3	0.68 x 0.68	174	1.5	8	0.64 x 0.64	420	0.75
4	0.77 x 0.77	209	1.5	9	0.59 x 0.59	214	1.5
5	0.58 x 0.58	183	1.5	10	0.63 x 0.63	181	1.5

The performance of our method is evaluated with the aspects of visual inspection, accuracy and total processing time. We show the results of visual inspection in Fig. 4

and 5. Fig. 4 shows two-dimensional comparison of a regular subtraction and our method in subject 10 with pulmonary embolism. Regular subtraction has artifacts and unwanted residuals within lung parenchyma as shown in Fig. 4(c). The result underlines the necessity of registration. The result of our method Fig. 4(d) is obtained by subtracting the post-contrast images to registered pre-contrast images. Contrary to the regular subtraction, the positional differences are aligned and enhanced vessels by contrast material are more distinguishable.

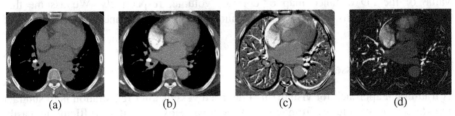

(a)   (b)   (c)   (d)

Fig. 4. The results of proposed method in chest CT angiography of subject 10 (a) pre-contrast image (b) post-contrast image (c) regular subtraction (d) proposed method

Fig. 5 shows the results of color-coded mapping and image fusion on post-contrast image. Segmental and subsegmental emboli are detected predominantly in the upper lobes of right lung as shown in Fig. 5(a) and (b). In Fig. 5(c) and (d), subsegmental emboli are detected in the lower lobes of left lung. We can easily recognize the occlusion of the corresponding segmental and subsegmental arteries as color-coded mapping and fusion.

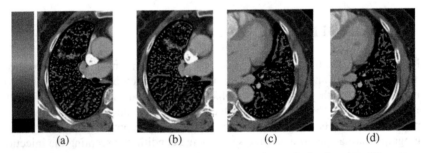

(a)   (b)   (c)   (d)

Fig. 5. The results of color-coded mapping and image fusion in subject 6

Fig. 6 shows how the error, the average of absolute distance difference (AADD), is reduced by the initial registration and subsequent iterative surface registration. Since the positional difference is almost aligned by the initial registration, iterative surface registration rapidly converge to the optimal position. In almost clinical datasets, the AADD errors are less than 0.6 voxels on optimal position.

Fig. 7 shows the results of our method of ten patients in comparison with chamfer matching-based registration. The average value of AADD error of our method (Method 1) and chamfer matching-based registration (Method 2) are same as 0.6 voxel. The total processing time is summarized in Table 2 where the execution time is

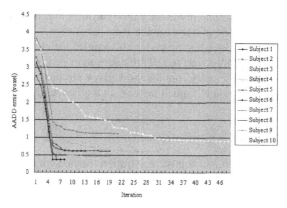

Fig. 6. The accuracy evaluation of corresponding lung boundaries using AADD error per iteration

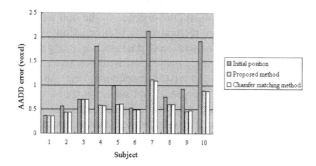

Fig. 7. The accuracy evaluation of corresponding lung boundaries using AADD error per subject

Table 2. The comparison of processing time for registration

(sec)

Subject #		Registration		Total processing time
		3D distance map generation	Distance measure & optimization	
1	Method 1	5.7	140.3	146.0
	Method 2	28.4	155.9	184.3
2	Method 1	3.1	70.9	74.0
	Method 2	18.9	80.8	99.7
3	Method 1	4.2	108.2	112.4
	Method 2	19.0	121.1	140.1
4	Method 1	3.5	85.5	89.0
	Method 2	22.7	97.2	119.9
5	Method 1	4.0	90.7	94.7
	Method 2	19.9	102.9	122.8
6	Method 1	4.8	127.0	131.8
	Method 2	24.0	143.6	167.6
7	Method 1	3.9	91.1	95.0
	Method 2	22.4	104.1	126.5
8	Method 1	7.1	198.1	205.2
	Method 2	45.5	223.7	269.2
9	Method 1	3.9	89.8	93.7
	Method 2	23.7	102.6	126.3
10	Method 1	3.8	77.5	81.3
	Method 2	19.6	91.4	111
Average	Method 1	4.4	107.9	112.3
	Method 2	24.4	122.3	146.7

measured for registration. The processing time for initial registration of our method is so small that it is included in 3D distance map generation step. The total processing time of our method is reduced compared with chamfer matching-based registration by the initial registration. Moreover, our 3D distance map generation time is much faster than that of Method 2. Finally, our method gives similar accuracy to the chamfer matching-based registration but much faster than the conventional one.

4   Conclusion

We have developed a fast and robust registration method for accurately imaging lung perfusion and efficiently detecting pulmonary embolism in pre- and post-contrast images of CT angiography. Using the optimal cube registration, the initial gross correction of lung boundaries can be done much fast and effective without detecting any anatomical landmarks. In the subsequent iterative surface registration, our distance measure using a 3D distance map generated by the narrow-band distance propagation allows rapid and robust convergence to the optimal value. Our enhanced vessel visualization makes the recognition of attenuation variations within lung parenchyma easily. Ten pairs of pre- and post-contrast images of CT angiography have been used for the performance evaluation with the aspects of visual inspection, accuracy and processing time. In visual inspection, we can easily recognize the occlusion of the corresponding segmental and subsegmental arteries. The registration error of our method is less than 0.6 voxel. In addition, our registration method is much faster than the chamfer matching-based registration. Accurate and fast result of our method can be successfully used to visualize pulmonary perfusion for the diagnosis of pulmonary embolism.

References

1. Schoepf, U.J., Costello, P., CT angiography for diagnosis of pulmonary embolism: state of the art, Radiology, Vol. 230 (2004) 329-337.
2. Patel, S., Kazerooni, E.A., Cascade, P.N., Pulmonary embolism: optimization of small pulmonary artery visualization at multi-detector row CT, Radiology, Vol. 227 (2003) 455-460.
3. Schoepf, U.J., Holzknecht, N., Helmberger, T.K. et al, Subsegmental pulmonary emboli: improved detection with thin-collimation multi-detector row spiral CT, Radiology, Vol. 222 (2002) 483-490.
4. Ko, J.P., Naidich, D.P., Computer-aided diagnosis and the evaluation of lung disease, Journal of Thoraic Imaging, Vol. 19, No. 3 (2004) 136-155.
5. Herzog, P., Wildberger, J.E., Niethammer, M et al., CT perfusion imaging of the lung in pulmonary embolism, Acad Radiol, Vol. 10 (2003) 1132-1146.
6. Wildberger, J.E., Schoepf, U.J., Mahnken, A.H., et al., Approaches to CT perfusion imaging in pulmonary embolism, Roentgenology (2005) 64-73.
7. Chung, M.J., Goo, J.M., Im, J.G., et al., CT perfusion image of the lung : value in the detection of pulmonary embolism in a porcine model, Investigative Radiology, Vol. 39, No. 10 (2004) 633-640.
8. Yim, Y., Hong, H., Shin, Y.G., Hybrid lung segmentation in chest CT images for computer-aided diagnosis, Proc. of HEALTHCOM 2005 (2005).

Combination of Tangent Distance and an Image Distortion Model for Appearance-Based Sign Language Recognition

Morteza Zahedi, Daniel Keysers, Thomas Deselaers, and Hermann Ney

Lehrstuhl für Informatik VI – Computer Science Department,
RWTH Aachen University – D-52056 Aachen, Germany
{zahedi, keysers, deselaers, ney}@informatik.rwth-aachen.de

Abstract. In this paper, we employ a zero-order local deformation model to model the visual variability of video streams of American sign language (ASL) words. We discuss two possible ways of combining the model with the tangent distance used to compensate for affine global transformations. The integration of the deformation model into our recognition system improves the error rate on a database of ASL words from 22.2% to 17.2%.

1 Introduction

In sign language recognition, as in other disciplines of pattern recognition, a considerable number of errors are due to the variability of the input signal. Each signer may utter a word differently, depending on his individual signing style or the predecessor and successor of the uttered word. Therefore, a large visual variability of utterances for each word exists. To model the variability of utterances, the tangent distance (TD) [1,2] and the image distortion model (IDM) [3,4] can be used to account for global and local variations, respectively.

The BOSTON50 database is a publicly available database in which the words are signed with high visual variability. In this paper we present experiments on this database using Hidden Markov Models (HMM) in a nearest neighbor manner. In [5] we have shown that the error rate using TD instead of the Euclidean distance in this setup is 22.2%.

Although tangent distance compensates for global affine transformations, it is sensitive to local image deformations. Therefore, we apply two different ways to combine the image distortion model with the tangent distance to compensate for local deformations. This combination enables the classifier to compensate for both local and global transformations. Using this combination, the error rate is considerably reduced from 22.2% to 17.2%, which is an improvement of 23 percent relative.

Our system is designed to recognize sign language words using appearance-based features extracted directly from standard cameras. This means that the system works without any explicit segmentation or tracking of the hands. Thus, the recognition can be expected to be more robust in cases where tracking and segmentation are difficult.

W. Kropatsch, R. Sablatnig, and A. Hanbury (Eds.): DAGM 2005, LNCS 3663, pp. 401–408, 2005.
© Springer-Verlag Berlin Heidelberg 2005

Fig. 1. The three signers as viewed from the two camera perspectives

Fig. 2. The topology of the employed HMM

2   Database and Extracted Features

The BOSTON50 database was created from the database of ASL sentences published by the National Center for Sign Language and Gesture Resources at Boston University[1]. It consists of 483 utterances of 50 American sign language words. The movies were recorded at 30 frames per second and the size of the frames is 195×165 pixels. The sentences were signed by three different signers, one man and two women. The signers were dressed differently. The frames of two cameras were used. One of the cameras shows a front view of the signer, the other one shows a side view. Sample images of the different views and the signers are shown in Figure 1. These two views are merged into one feature vector. According to the experiments reported in [6], the features of the front and side cameras are weighted with 0.38 and 0.62, respectively.

The feature vectors we have used consist of combinations of down-sampled original images which are multiplied by binary skin-intensity images and vertical and horizontal derivatives of these images. The images are down-scaled to 13×11 pixels and multiplied by a binary skin-intensity image. Afterwards, the derivatives are computed by applying Sobel filters. Thus, the feature vector x_t is between 143 and 3×143=429 dimensional. Note that the multiplication with the binary skin-intensity image is not an explicit segmentation step because it is a simple pixel-based transformation similar to e.g. Sobel filters.

3   Decision Process

The decision making of our system employs HMMs to recognize the sign language words. This approach is inspired by the success of the application of HMMs in speech recognition [7] and also most sign language recognition systems [8,9,10,11]. The recognition of sign language words is similar to spoken word recognition in the modelling of sequential samples. The topology of the HMM used is shown in Figure 2. There is a transition loop at each state and the maximum allowed transition distance is two, which means that one state, at most, can be skipped.

---

[1] http://www.bu.edu/asllrp/ncslgr.html

In [6] we presented a nearest neighbor approach using HMMs for recognition of sign language. The decision rule used to classify an observation sequence $x_1^T = x_1, \ldots, x_t, \ldots x_T$ in this approach is

$$r(x_1^T) = \arg\max_w \left\{ \max_{n=1,\ldots,N_w} \left\{ Pr\left(u_{wn} | x_1^T\right) \right\} \right\}$$

$$= \arg\max_w \left\{ \max_{n=1,\ldots,N_w} \left\{ Pr\left(u_{wn}\right) \cdot Pr\left(x_1^T | u_{wn}\right) \right\} \right\},$$

where u_{wn} is the n-th utterance of word w and $Pr(u_{wn})$ is the a-priori probability of an utterance, uniformly distributed, and can thus be neglected. $Pr\left(x_1^T | u_{wn}\right)$ is approximated using maximum approximation to be

$$Pr\left(x_1^T | u_{wn}\right) = \sum_{s_1^T} \left\{ \prod_{t=1}^{T} Pr(s_t | s_{t-1}, u_{wn}) \cdot Pr(x_t | s_t, u_{wn}) \right\}$$

$$\cong \max_{s_1^T} \left\{ \prod_{t=1}^{T} Pr(s_t | s_{t-1}, u_{wn}) \cdot Pr(x_t | s_t, u_{wn}) \right\}.$$

Here, the transition probability $Pr(s_t | s_{t-1}, u_{wn})$ is uniformly distributed, and the emission probability $Pr(x_t | s_t, u_{wn})$ is a Gaussian with $\mu_{s_t} = u_{wnt}$, and a diagonal covariance matrix with $\sigma_d^2 = \sigma^2 = 0.1$:

$$Pr(x_t | s_t, u_{wn}) = \frac{1}{\sqrt{2\pi\sigma^2}^D} \exp\left(-\frac{1}{2} \sum_{d=1}^{D} \frac{(x_{td} - \mu_{s_t d})^2}{\sigma^2} \right).$$

The feature vector x_t is a down-sampled image at time t. Therefore, the sum $\sum_{d=1}^{D} (x_{td} - \mu_{s_t d})^2 / \sigma^2$ is the distance between the observation image at time t and the prototype image μ_{s_t} of the state s_t that is scaled by the variances σ^2. This scaled distance can be replaced by other distance functions like the TD or IDM distance, which we introduce in the following section.

As the number of utterances in the database for each word is not large enough to have a separate training and test set, the experiments have been performed using leaving-one-out. That is, one observation is classified using all the other ones as training observations and this is repeated for all utterances from the database.

4   Invariant Distances

Because of the visual variability of utterances of each word, invariance of distance functions is an important aspect in sign language recognition. An invariant distance measure ideally takes into account transformations of the patterns, yielding small distances for patterns which differ by a transformation that does not change the class-membership. We briefly describe the *tangent distance* and the *image distortion model* which compensate for global and local transformations respectively.

Fig. 3. Example of first-order approximations of affine transformations. (Left to right: original image, ± horizontal translation, ± vertical translation, ±axis deformation, ± diagonal deformation, ± scale, ± rotation).

4.1   Overview of Tangent Distance

Let $\mu \in \mathbb{R}^D$ be a class specific prototype pattern, and $\mu(\alpha)$ denote a transformation of μ that depends on a parameter L-tuple $\alpha \in \mathbb{R}^L$. Here we assume that the transformation does not change class membership for small α. Now, the set of all transformed patterns is a manifold $\mathcal{M}_\mu = \{\mu(\alpha) \mid \alpha \in \mathbb{R}^L\} \subset \mathbb{R}^D$ in pattern space. The distance between two patterns can then be defined as the minimum distance between the pattern x_t and the manifold $\mathcal{M}_\mu$ of a class specific prototype pattern μ. However, the calculation of this distance is a hard non-linear optimization problem in general. The manifold can be approximated by a tangent subspace $\widehat{\mathcal{M}}_\mu$. The tangent vectors μ_l that span the subspace are the partial derivatives of $\mu(\alpha)$ with respect to α_l. Thus, a first-order approximation of $\mathcal{M}_\mu$ is obtained as

$$\widehat{\mathcal{M}}_\mu = \{\mu + \sum_{l=1}^{L} \alpha_l \mu_l \ : \ \alpha \in \mathbb{R}^L\} \subset \mathbb{R}^D.$$

The approximation is valid for small values of α, which is sufficient in many applications. All patterns depicted in Figure 3 lie in the same subspace and can therefore be represented by one prototype and the corresponding tangent vectors. Therefore, the tangent distance between the original image and any of these transformed images is zero, while the Euclidean distance is significantly greater than zero. Using the squared Euclidean norm, the TD is defined as

$$d_{TD}(x_t, \mu) = \min_{\alpha \in \mathbb{R}^L} \{||x_t - (\mu + \sum_{l=1}^{L} \alpha_l \mu_l)||^2\} \ .$$

A double-sided TD can also be defined, where both of the manifolds of the reference and observation are approximated.

4.2   Image Distortion Model

We briefly review an image distortion model that is able to compensate for local displacements. The efficiency of the model in handwritten character recognition is shown in [3]. In this model, to calculate the distance between the image frame x_t and the class-specific prototype image μ, instead of computing the squared

Fig. 4. Example of the image distortion model. (first row: original image and image pairs including the transformed image that results from the IDM distance (left) and artificially distorted image by displacement of the left hand of the signer (right); second row: difference images to the original image).

error between the pixels x_{ij} and μ_{ij}, we compute the minimum distance between x_{ij} and $\mu_{i'j'}$, where $(i', j') \in R_{ij}$, and R_{ij} is a certain neighborhood of (i, j). According to this definition, the invariant distance can be calculated by

$$d_{IDM}(x_t, \mu) = \sum_{ij} \min_{(i',j')\in R_{ij}} \{d(x_{ij}, \mu_{i'j'})\}.$$

The accuracy of the IDM depends on choosing a suitable R_{ij} which leaves the class-membership unchanged. If R_{ij} is too small, too few deformations can be compensated. If it is too large, deformations that change class membership are tolerated. In both cases, the error rate of the classifier will increase. To increase accuracy in finding the optimal displacement, local image context is used [3]. This leads to a mapping of edges to edges in the alignment. In informal experiments we found 7×7 sub images to be optimal. Therefore, the local distance $d(x_{ij}, \mu_{i'j'})$ between pixel x_{ij} and $\mu_{i'j'}$ is chosen to be

$$d(x_{ij}, \mu_{i'j'}) := \sum_{m=-3}^{3} \sum_{n=-3}^{3} ||x_{i+m,j+n} - \mu_{i'+m,j'+n}||^2.$$

Figure 4 shows the effect of the IDM. The figure consists of an image frame and three image pairs. Each image pair includes the transformed image that results from the IDM distance calculation (left) and an artificially distorted image (right). The difference from the original image is shown in the second row. The distorted image frames are created artificially by one pixel displacements of the left hand of the signer. The near-zero difference images for the left images of the pairs show that the IDM effectively compensates for the artificial distortion.

5   Combination of TD and IDM

To compensate for global and local variations simultaneously, we propose to combine TD and IDM. Here we apply two different methods for combination.

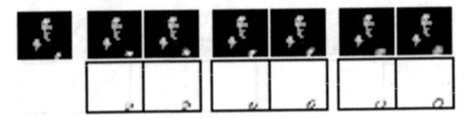

Fig. 5. Example of the first combination method. (first row: original image and image pairs including the transformed image that results from the combination method and distorted image by axis deformation, diagonal deformation and scaling of the left hand of the signer, second row: the difference image between the transformed or distorted image and the original image).

Method A: TD to compare sub images in IDM. In the IDM, only the displacement of the sub images is allowed. If we calculate the TD instead of the Euclidean distance $d(x_{ij}, \mu_{i',j'})$ between sub images, small affine transformations in the sub-images are considered. The image frames where only the left hand of the signer is distorted by axis deformation and where there is diagonal deformation and scaling of the left hand of the signer are shown in Figure 5. These distortions are tolerated by the proposed combination method, and the transformed images that result from the combination method are also shown. From the difference images, it can be seen that the method accounts for these transformations. Note that the distorted images are different from Figure 4.

Method B: IDM to compare TD-transformed images. Another possible way to combine the two invariant distances is the use of the TD before employing the image distortion model to find the closest image frames in the linear subspaces as proposed in [12]. We employ the one-sided tangent distance using the tangent vectors of the prototype image μ. The closest image frame in the subspace $\widehat{\mathcal{M}}_\mu$ to the observation image frame x_t is calculated by $\hat{\mu} = \mu + \sum_{l=1}^{L} \hat{\beta}_l \mu_l$ where

$$\hat{\beta} = \arg\min_{\beta}\left\{||x_t - (\mu + \sum_{l=1}^{L} \beta_l \mu_l)||^2\right\}, \qquad \beta \in \mathbb{R}^L.$$

Thus, $\hat{\mu}$ compensates for small global affine transformations. This $\hat{\mu}$ is then used in the IDM instead of μ. In this combination, we first account for global transformations and then for local deformations, yielding a distance function that is invariant with respect to global transformations and local deformations.

6   Experimental Results

In the experiments, we have used HMMs in a nearest neighbor manner, i.e. each training observation forms its own HMM, where variance is fixed globally. The achieved results for using the different distances are given in Table 1. It can be seen that both combination methods of TD and IDM improve the accuracy of the

Table 1. Error rates [%] of the classifier with different distances

Distance	Original image	Horizontal gradient	Vertical gradient	Horizontal & vertical gradients
TD [5]	22.2	22.8	23.4	21.3
IDM	21.9	21.5	24.6	23.4
IDM+TD (Method A)	**17.2**	18.8	18.2	18.4
IDM+TD (Method B)	20.3	21.1	21.5	20.9

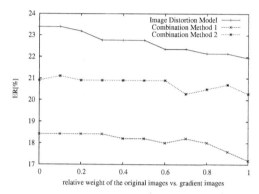

Fig. 6. Error rate of the system with respect to the gradient weight

classifier compared to using one of the invariant distances alone. Consistently, the best error rate is obtained with method A, which enables the classifier to model global transformations in the sub images of the image frames.

More experiments have been performed to investigate how to weigh the importance of the local sub images of the original image with respect to the gradient images. Figure 6 shows the error rate of the classifier using IDM and the two combination methods of TD and IDM depending on the relative weight of original images and derivatives. A relative weight of zero means that only gradient images are used. The graphs show that the best results are achieved when only the local sub images of the original images are used. The best error rate of 17.2% is obtained using combination method A, which is an improvement of 23% relative. About 65% of the remaining misclassified utterances of the data are due to very strong visual differences from the other utterances in the database, which means they are always different from all training utterances when classified.

Unfortunately, a direct comparison with results of other research groups is not possible here, because there are no results published on publicly available data so far and research groups working on sign language or gesture recognition usually use databases that were created within the group.

7   Conclusion

In this paper we have presented two different ways of combining IDM and TD in sign language recognition to account for visual variabilities. These methods allow for recognizing sequences with variations in position, orientation, or size of the hands or the head of the signer. The TD, accounting for global affine transformations, and the IDM, accounting for local deformation, complement each other and allow for compensating a combination of global and local transformations. The recognition results are consistently improved using the combined method.

In the future, we plan to use these methods on larger databases and in the recognition of continuous sign language.

References

1. P. Simard, Y. Le Cun, J. Denker. Efficient Pattern Recognition Using a New Transformation Distance. In *Advances in NIPS*, pp. 50–58, Morgan Kaufmann, 1993.
2. D. Keysers, W. Macherey, H. Ney, J. Dahmen. Adaptation in Statistical Pattern Recognition Using Tangent Vectors. In *TPAMI*, 26(2):269–274, Feb. 2004.
3. D. Keysers, C. Gollan, H. Ney. Local Context in Non-linear Deformation Models for Handwritten Character Recognition. In *ICPR*, vol. 4, pp. 511–514, Cambridge, UK, Aug. 2004.
4. P. Dreuw, D. Keysers, T. Deselaers, H. Ney. Gesture Recognition Using Image Comparison Methods. In *Gesture in Human-Computer Interaction and Simulation*, Vannes, France, May 2005. In press.
5. M. Zahedi, D. Keysers, H. Ney. Pronunciation Clustering and Modeling of Variability for Appearance-based Sign Language Recognition. In *Gesture in Human-Computer Interaction and Simulation*, Vannes, France, May 2005. In press.
6. M. Zahedi, D. Keysers, H. Ney. Appearance-based Recognition of Words in American Sign Language. In *Iberian Conf. on Pattern Recognition and Image Analysis*, Estoril, Portugal, June 2005. In press.
7. L.R. Rabiner. A Tutorial on Hidden Markov Models and Selected Applications in Speech Recognition. In *Proc. of the IEEE*, 77(2):267–296, Feb. 1989.
8. R. Bowden, D. Windridge, T. Kadir, A. Zisserman, M. Brady. A Linguistic Feature Vector for the Visual Interpretation of Sign Language. In *ECCV*, pp. 390–401, Prague, Czech Republic, May 2004.
9. B. Bauer, H. Hienz, K.F. Kraiss. Video-Based Continuous Sign Language Recognition Using Statistical Methods. In *ICPR*, pp. 463–466, Barcelona, Spain, Sep. 2000.
10. T. Starner, J. Weaver, A. Pentland. Real-Time American Sign Language Recognition Using Desk and Wearable Computer Based Video. In *TPAMI*, 20(12):1371–1375, Dec. 1998.
11. C. Vogler and D. Metaxas. Adapting Hidden Markov Models for ASL Recognition by Using Three-dimensional Computer Vision Methods. In *Proc. Int. Conf. on Systems, Man and Cybernetics*, pp. 156–161, Orlando, FL, Oct. 1997.
12. D. Keysers, J. Dahmen, H. Ney, B. Wein, and T.M. Lehmann Statistical Framework for Model-based Image Retrieval in Medical Applications In *Journal of Electronic Imaging* 12(1):59–68, Jan. 2003.

Volumetric Analysis of a Sinter Process in Time

Oliver Wirjadi[1], Andreas Jablonski[1], Katja Schladitz[1], and Michael Nöthe[2]

[1] Models and Algorithms in Image Processing,
Fraunhofer ITWM, Gottlieb-Daimler-Strasse, 67663 Kaiserslautern, Germany
{oliver.wirjadi, andreas.jablonski, katja.schladitz}@itwm.fraunhofer.de
[2] Institute for Materials Science, Department of Mechanical Engineering,
Technische Universität Dresden, 01062 Dresden, Germany
michael.noethe@mailbox.tu-dresden.de

Abstract. We present the first fully three dimensional analysis of the
sinter process of copper using particles of a realistic size. This has been
made possible through the use of μCT. A 3D image processing chain,
applied to each time step of this 4D dataset, followed by image registration and particle matching steps was used. This allows for the tracking
of individual particle motions during the sintering process, which gives
a large amount of information towards understanding this process.

1 Introduction

Sintering is a process of creating objects starting from a metal or ceramic particle
powder. The particles are filled in crucibles, usually some pressure is applied.
Then the particles are connected by heating the powder at temperatures below
the melting point of the material.

The growth of inter particle contacts during sintering and their rearrangement are well understood and can be observed in particle rows, 2D samples and
the surface of 3D samples. However, in 3D specimens a difference between measured and predicted shrinkage is observed. The discrepancy can be attributed
to cooperative material transport mechanisms like particle rotations and translations relative to neighboring particles, which can only be observed in 3D data
obtained from μCT.

Spherical copper powder (diameter 100–120μm) was filled into alumina crucibles and fixed in position by an initial sintering step. For each sintering stage,
a volume image of the specimen was taken using μCT (at room temperature).
Subsequently, the next sintering stage was prepared by heating the specimen
with a rate of 5K/min in a hydrogen atmosphere to the sintering temperature,
which was equal during all sintering steps. Holding time at sintering temperature
was doubled in each sintering step. This results in a series of 8 volume images,
each 903x903x721 voxels large with a voxel spacing of 5.4μm.

In earlier stages of this project, the sintering process was studied using morphological transformations together with measuring geometric characteristics of
the copper component [1] and a combination of the Euclidean distance transform
with Voronoi tessellations [2]. For the results see [3]. However, particles studied

W. Kropatsch, R. Sablatnig, and A. Hanbury (Eds.): DAGM 2005, LNCS 3663, pp. 409–416, 2005.

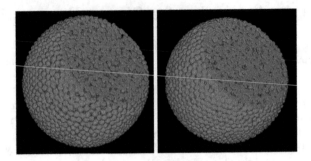

Fig. 1. Volume renderings of the dataset at beginning of the process and after 635 minutes. Note that the sinter balls are not contained in a sphere, but rather a cylinder with a half-spherical cap at the bottom. This view is from the bottom.

there were 1mm big, and therefore the numbers of observed particles were about 100. To finer powders (300μm), spectral methods were applied [4]. In the present series of images, sinter particles are much smaller (100μm) and the number of observed particles has increased to 10.000, the images require more than 500 Mb of memory in each of the seven time step. Therefore, segmentation is much more difficult and an efficient matching algorithm is crucial.

In this paper, we show how to combine several image processing steps to first segment the copper component and then the individual sinter particles in each stage. Particles are then registered and matched across time to study their behavior during the sinter process.

2   Segmentation

The segmentation process for this dataset consisted of a processing chain which was applied to each 3D dataset in the entire time chain. An example of the processing chain is shown in Fig. 2.1 for a part of one slice. Each step is a fully three dimensional algorithm. In order to track the individual balls' motion during the sinter process, we need to extract the centers of each ball. In a first step, we binarize the image. In a second step, the objects need to be separated in order to identify individual balls. We will write an image as $f(\mathbf{x}) \in \mathbb{N}$. In the following we will give details on each of the steps involved in this processing chain for segmentation.

2.1   Binarization

Since we wish to use the Euclidean distance transform on the results of this step later, special attention needs to be given to avoid holes within the foreground regions. Such holes would lead to false local maxima in the distance map, see Sec. 2.2.

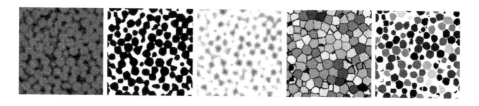

Fig. 2. Example for the segmentation processing chain, from left to right: Original image slice, binarization, Euclidean distance transformation (EDT) of the inverse binary image, watershed transformation of the inverse EDT image and labeled sinter balls.

Linear Filtering. To reduce the noise level and eliminate reconstruction artefacts in the data, we convolved with a Gaussian kernel. The standard deviation of the Gaussian was $\sigma = 2$ and the total support of the discretized mask was 13^3 voxels. We used a separable implementation to reduce computational complexity. Linear filters smooth across object edges. Degradation of edge information was not a problem in this work because of the two-step process proposed here, which views binarization and separation of sinter balls as separate tasks.

Adaptive Thresholding. The datasets have varying intensity levels through the image region, i.e. some areas of the dataset appear brighter than others. For that reason, the simplest possible binarization by global thresholding did not give useful results. We chose to use an adaptive thresholding described in [5] which thresholds each voxel relative to the mean value within a window. The local threshold at voxel $\mathbf{x}$ is given by

$$T(\mathbf{x}; c, W) = \text{Mean}_W \left[f(\mathbf{x}) \right] + c \cdot \sqrt{\text{Var}_W \left[f(\mathbf{x}) \right]}.$$

Mean_W and Var_W compute the empirical mean and variance, respectively, in a local window of user-defined size $(2W + 1)^3$ around the current voxel $\mathbf{x}$. The parameter c scales the threshold's distance from the mean. We binarized each time step using $c = -0.1$ and $W = 12$. The algorithm was implemented using a sliding window.

Opening. Morphological opening with an approximate ball as structuring element was performed in order to reconstruct some of the spherical structure that was lost in the previous steps.

2.2 Separation of Sinter Balls

Separation of the particles is necessary in order to compute the centers of the balls which we used for tracking the balls' movement, see Sec. 3. The method described here follows an example in P. Soille's book [6], where he argued that the Distance Transform was an appropriate segmentation function for overlapping blobs.

Euclidean Distance Transformation. In order to compute the separating planes between the sinter balls using the watershed algorithm, in a later stage, we first need to transform the binary image to a height map. Ideally, the ridges of that map should be the dividing planes between the cells occupied by the sinter balls. We define the Euclidean distance transform of a binary image as the distance of all background voxels to the closest foreground voxel. Due to this definition, we compute

$$f_{EDT}(\mathbf{x}) = \min_{\mathbf{x}' \in F} \left\{ \|\mathbf{x} - \mathbf{x}'\|^2 \right\}, \tag{1}$$

where $F = \{\mathbf{x} | \bar{f}(\mathbf{x}) = 1\}$ denotes the set of all foreground voxels in the inverted image $\bar{f}$.

To compute the exact Euclidean distance transformation in three dimensions, we follow the hybrid approach described in [7]. In that approach, an approximate raster-scanning distance transform and an error correction is computed yielding an exact EDT in two dimensional slices of the 3D dataset. A method due to Saito, which searches minimal distances along lines is used in the direction orthogonal to these slices. In [7], it is shown that this hybrid method's runtimes are below those of other exact 3D EDT methods for large data and compare favorably even with approximate 3D EDT algorithms.

Suppression of Local Maxima. The result from the previous step contains local maxima marking the centers of the sinter balls. These centers will be used as the starting point for a watershed transformation in the next section. One problem of the watershed method is that of oversegmentation. A possible strategy to avoid this is to eliminate the number of possible starting points. Thus, we suppressed local maxima in f_{EDT} by applying the h-maxima method from [6]. The h-maxima filter cuts all local maxima which stand out farther than h, here $h = 47$. See [6] for implementation details.

Watershed Segmentation. As a last step in the segmentation procedure, we apply the watershed transformation on the complement of the result from all previous steps, where local minima correspond to the centers of the sinter balls.

Watershed transformations, in two dimensions, have an appealing analogy of water rising in a topographic map. As water levels rise, water from different sources will meet at "watersheds", which will represent the separating lines between regions. The analogy of a topographic map does not hold anymore, in three dimensions, but the implementation of the method does not change. As described in [6], we sort the image voxels according to their grey value and process voxels in a first-in-first-out (FIFO) queue. By masking the result with the previous binarization, we get an image of labeled sinter particles.

3   Matching

To track the motion of every single ball over time, we have to find matching pairs. We first register the datasets and then match particles according to their distance.

3.1 Point Cloud Registration

Standard algorithms for geometric alignment of two point sets are the Iterative Closest Point Algorithm (ICP) and its variants [8]. Aside from runtime considerations for our large dataset (almost 10000 points), ICP is not applicable to our problem because we cannot provide pre-registered data, which is necessary for ICP. In our experiments, the specimen was removed from the tomograph several times, resulting in large rotations between images.

We propose an efficient registration method which can be seen as a generalized Hough transform [9], using the ball centers c_i which are computed as centroids of the segmented objects O_i. We assume that the movements of the balls have been sufficiently small so that there is still enough structure present to perform the registration.

The problem is then to register two 3D point sets A and B from two consecutive datasets at each of the seven time steps. Because of the experimental setting only one rotation angle θ (about the z-axis) and three translation parameters $(\mathbf{t} = (t_x, t_y, t_z)^T)$ have to be determined, i.e. we search for a rigid transformation. We define a translation invariant similarity measure $Sim(A, B)$ derived from the displacement histogram H between A and B.

$$H(q) = \#\{(\mathbf{x}, \mathbf{y}) | bin(\mathbf{x} - \mathbf{y}) = q, \mathbf{x} \in A, \mathbf{y} \in B\} \tag{2}$$

bin() maps the difference vectors to discrete indices of histogram bins. The similarity $Sim(A, B)$ for two point sets A and B is defined as the displacement histogram maximum over all possible pairs $(\mathbf{x}, \mathbf{y})$,

$$Sim(A, B) = \max_{\mathbf{x} \in A, \mathbf{y} \in B} (H(bin(\mathbf{x} - \mathbf{y}))). \tag{3}$$

This allows for the separation of the rotational and translational degrees of freedom so that essentially only a one dimensional search (over the angles) must be performed, which greatly facilitates the task. The correct registration angle θ_{reg} is computed as the angle corresponding to the rotation of B, $R_\theta(B)$, with the highest similarity to A, $\theta_{reg} = \operatorname{argmax} \{Sim(A, R_\theta(B))\}$. Fig. 3 shows clear global maxima in the angle and displacement histograms for one of the 7 steps.

After the registration angle has been determined, the translation vector can be directly estimated from the displacement histogram. To obtain translation estimates with increased accuracy we average over all translations corresponding to the histogram bin with maximum value, denoted by T_{max}.

$$\mathbf{t}_{reg} = \sum_{\mathbf{t} \in T_{max}} \mathbf{t} / \#(T_{max}) \tag{4}$$

3.2 Pair Matching

The weighted matching problem in a graph $G = (V, E)$ consists of finding a maximum subset of non-adjacent edges $M \subseteq E$ which minimizes $\sum_{e \in M} w(e)$, where $w(e)$ is the weight of an edge. Translated to our problem, we can model

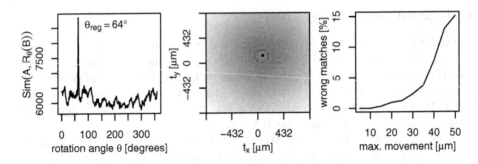

Fig. 3. *Left*: Similarity measure Sim over rotation angle. *Center*: The according displacement histogram, bin size 8×8 voxels in x and y direction. *Right*: Percentage of false matches of our matching heuristic for simulated increasing particle movements.

the (registered, "r") point sets as vertices in a bipartite graph, $V = A^r \cup B^r$, with edges E only between center points at two consecutive time steps. The weight function w assigns Euclidean distances to the edges. Note that we loose directional information by this choice of w. We assume correct registration and small particle movements.

Solution of this problem is possible in $O(n^3)$ steps using Edmond's algorithm. We did not apply that method for two reasons: (1) computation would take long and (2) minimizing the sum over all weights in the matching does not fit to our problem: We know that each particle will be found in its vicinity in the next registered time step. This constraint is not contained in the matching problem formulation. The heuristics recommended for use in [10] do not fit to our problem for the same reason plus the fact that the "Spiral Rack" heuristic, described there, relies on an arbitrary matching subroutine, which does not guarantee us to match corresponding pairs.

We use a deterministic greedy algorithm: In the first step all pairs are sorted according to their distance. Next, use all pairs in ascending oder to create the maximum number of possible unique assignments ignoring those pairs for which a better assignment has already been found.

This greedy algorithm is known to produce suboptimal results [10]. To estimate the error in our application, consider Fig. 3. For the right plot, we created a simulated set of 3000 packed points with a minimal distance of $100 \mu m$ using a force-bias algorithm [11]. We created uniformly distributed random shifts of this set, with maximal shift length indicated on the x-axis of this plot. Note that this shifted set does no longer represent particle centers. Our method's error is below 5% as long as the maximum movement is below 70% of the particles' radii. This is in line with our assumptions.

4   Interpretation

Here we show only few examples of possible measurements, while a full analysis of the data is currently under way. The result of the matching and registration yields the particle movements, see Fig. 4. After large initial movements, the movement amount drops and remains low. The rise in the plot can be attributed to the doubling of the sinter periods.

To investigate relative rotation, neighboring particles were detected by scanning the neighborhood in the labeld images. We searched for groups of three neighboring balls which were matched in two time consecutive steps and measured the angle between the outer particle centers. The difference angle $\Delta\alpha = \alpha(t+1) - \alpha(t)$ before and after a sintering stage is calculated and the maximum $\Delta\alpha$ of each sinter ball is taken. This gives a measure for the amount of relative movement that the balls perform with respect to each other. Correlation of this rotation measure with the movements described above is much weaker than reported in [3]. This indicates that the causal linkage between particle motion and rotation may not hold, anymore, for these smaller particles.

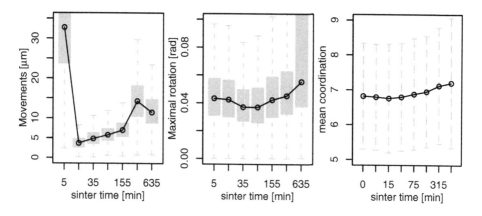

Fig. 4. Measurements after 5, 10, 20, 40, 80, 160 and 320 minutes. Left to right: Median movements of all matched balls in μm, median relative rotation angles (with boxplots) and mean coordination number (number of neighbors, with standard deviations).

The above described analysis also yields information on the number of neighbors connected by a sinter neck to a ball. The coordination number (number of neighbors) is also plotted in Fig. 4. There, we plot the mean instead of the median because the coordination number is discrete and small trends in the data cannot be observed as well in a discrete domain as in a continuous one. This result is consistent with our earlier work [3], where we observed fairly constant coordination numbers in all sintering stages.

The authors of [11] report a mean coordination number of 6.05 for random packings of equal spheres obtained by the force biased algorithm and with volume density 64%. Given the lower volume densities in our samples ($57 - 60\%$), the higher mean coordination number indicates clustering of the sinter particles. This means that there are large "gaps" persisting throughout the sintering. This finding has to be further examined.

5   Conclusions

Investigation of the sintering process using μCT combined with volume image analysis is possible, also for particle sizes close to those used in real sintering processes. The image processing methods described in this paper allow a wide variety of measurements and statistical analyses. Further steps of research are interpretation of the time series of volume images as a 4D image as well as analysis and modeling of the point process of the particle centers.

Acknowledgement

We would like to thank the ECKA Granulate GmbH & Co. KG for the supply of copper powder. We thank Axel Springhoff for fruitful discussions and excellent programming, Claudia Lautensack for the packing and the MAVI team at Fraunhofer ITWM for providing this toolbox. M. Nöthe and K. Schladitz acknowledge financial support by grants Pi 361/3-2 and Oh 59/5-1 of the German Research Foundation (DFG).

References

1. Nagel, W., Ohser, J., Pischang, K.: An integral-geometric approach for the Euler-Poincaré characteristic of spatial images. J. Microsc. **198** (2000) 54–62
2. Poniẑil, P.: Programms for image analysis of computer tomograph structures of sintered materials. http://fyzika.ft.utb.cz/ct/ (2002)
3. Nöthe, M., Pischang, K., Poniẑil, P., Kieback, B., Ohser, J.: Study of particle rearrangements during sintering processes by microfocus computer tomography (μct). In: Proc. World Congress PM2004 Powder Metallurgy, Vienna (2004)
4. Ohser, J., Schladitz, K., Koch, K., M.Nöthe: Diffraction by image processing and its application in materials science. Report 67, Fraunhofer ITWM, Kaiserslautern (2004)
5. Niblack, W.: An introduction to digital image processing. Prentice-Hall (1986)
6. Soille, P.: Morphological image analysis. Springer-Verlag (1999)
7. Cuisenaire, O.: Distance Transformations: Fast algorithms and applications to medical image processing. PhD thesis, Université catholique de Louvain (1998)
8. Chetverikov, D., Svirko, D., Stepanov, D., Krsek, P.: Shape matching: Similarity measures and algorithms. In: Proc. 16th International Conference on Pattern Recognition. Volume 3. (2002) 545–548
9. Ballard, D.: Generalizing the hough transform to detect arbitrary shapes. Pattern Recognition **13** (1981) 111–122
10. Avis, D.: A survey of heuristics for the weighted matching problem. Networks **13** (1983) 475–493
11. Bezrukov, A., Bargiel, M., Stoyan, D.: Spatial statistics for simulated packings of spheres. Image Anal. Stereol. **20** (2001) 203–206

Network Snakes-Supported Extraction
of Field Boundaries from Imagery

Matthias Butenuth and Christian Heipke

Institute of Photogrammetry and GeoInformation, University of Hannover,
Nienburger Str. 1, 30167 Hannover, Germany
{butenuth, heipke}@ipi.uni-hannover.de

Abstract. A fully automatic method to extract field boundaries from imagery is
described in this paper. The fields are represented together with additional prior
knowledge in the form of GIS-data in a semantic model. The approach consists
of two main steps: Firstly, a segmentation is carried out in a coarse scale
resulting in preliminary field boundaries. In a second step network snakes are
used to improve the geometrical correctness of the preliminary boundaries
taking into account topological constraints while exploiting the local image
information. Focussing on the network snakes and their specialties the results
demonstrate the potential of the proposed solution.

1 Introduction

Field boundaries have come to be objects of increasing interest during the last few
years. One application area are geo-scientific questions, for example the derivation of
potential wind erosion risk fields, which can be generated with field boundaries and
additional input information about the prevailing wind direction, wind shelters and
soil parameters [1]. Another area is the agricultural sector, where information about
field geometry is important for tasks concerning precision farming [2] or the
monitoring and control of subsidies, which are paid by the European Union to the
farmers.

   In the past, several investigations have been carried out regarding the automatic
extraction of man-made objects such as buildings or roads [3, 4]. Similarly, the
classification of vegetation areas in coarse scales [5] and investigations concerning
the extraction of trees [6] have been accomplished. In contrary, the extraction of field
boundaries from high resolution imagery is not in an advanced phase: a first approach
to update and refine topologically correct field boundaries by fusing raster-images and
vector-map data is presented in [7]. Focussing on the reconstruction of the geometry
and features of the land-use units, the acquisition of new boundaries is not discussed.
In [8] a so called region competition approach is described, which extracts field
boundaries from aerial images with a combination of region growing techniques and
snakes. To initialize the process, seed regions have to be defined manually, which is a
time and cost-intensive procedure. A technique for predicting missing field
boundaries from satellite images is presented in [9], using a comparison of modal land
cover and local variance. The approach involves manual post processing, because

W. Kropatsch, R. Sablatnig, and A. Hanbury (Eds.): DAGM 2005, LNCS 3663, pp. 417–424, 2005.
© Springer-Verlag Berlin Heidelberg 2005

only fields with a high likelihood of missing boundaries are identified, not field boundaries directly.

The goal of this paper is to highlight a fully automatic method to extract field boundaries from aerial imagery or high resolution satellite imagery. Consequently, the proposed strategy differs from the mentioned approaches: Initially, the integration of imagery and topographic GIS-data[1] in one semantic model is described to obtain an overview of the numerous relations between the objects to be extracted and the prior knowledge. Afterwards, the two main parts of the algorithm are explained in detail: At the beginning, a segmentation is carried out in a coarse scale resulting in preliminary field boundaries, which are topological correct but geometrical inaccurate. The following refinement is accomplished with network snakes, an enhanced approach of snakes (active contour models) [10] taking into account topological constraints of the initialization while exploiting the local image information. Only little work can be found in the literature concerning network snakes [11]. A main focus of this paper lies on network snakes with a special attention on the control of the nodal and end points of the snakes. The results demonstrate the potential of the proposed solution within the complex environment of vegetation. Finally, further work required is discussed in the conclusions.

2   Model and Strategy

In general, the recognition of objects with the help of image analysis methods starts with an integrated modelling of the objects of interest and the surrounding scene [12]. Furthermore, exploiting the context relations between different objects leads to an overall and holistic description, see for example [13]. The use of prior knowledge supporting object extraction can lead to better results as shown in [3]. These aspects are incorporated into the model for the extraction of field boundaries and are reflected in the resulting strategy of the proposed approach.

2.1   Semantic Model

Describing the integration of imagery and GIS-data in one semantic model is our starting point for object extraction, as highlighted in detail in [14]. The semantic model is differentiated into an object layer, a geometric and material part, as well as an image layer (cf. Fig. 1). The model is based on the assumption, that the used images imply an infrared (IR) channel and are generated in summer, when the vegetation is in an advanced period of growth.

The use of prior knowledge plays an important role, which is represented in the semantic model with an additional GIS-layer. Vector data of the ATKIS DLMBasis (German Authoritative Topographic-Cartographic Information System) is used, which is an object based digital landscape model of Germany: (1) Field boundaries are exclusively located in the open landscape, thus, further investigations are focussed to this area. The open landscape is not directly modelled in the ATKIS DLMBasis, this is why this information has to be derived by selecting all areas, which are not settlements, forests or water bodies. (2) Roads, railways, rivers, tree rows and hedges

---

[1] Topographic GIS-data include settlements, forests, roads, rivers etc., but not field boundaries.

can be used within the open landscape as prior knowledge: The locations of these GIS-objects are introduced as field boundaries in the semantic model with a direct relation from the GIS-layer to the real world (cf. Fig. 1). For example, the ATKIS-objects 3101 (road) and 3102 (path) are linked to the road of the real world and, thus, can be used as field boundaries (i.e. a road is a field boundary). Of course, the underlying assumption is based on correct GIS-objects. The modelling of all GIS-objects in the geometry and material layer together with the image layer is not of interest, because they do not have to be extracted from the imagery (depicted with dashed lines in Fig. 1). Nevertheless, additionally extracted objects which are not yet included in the GIS-database can be introduced at anytime.

The object to be extracted, the *field*, is divided in the semantic model in *field boundary* and *field area* in order to allow for different modelling in the layers: The field boundary is a 2D elongated vegetation boundary, which is formed as a straight line or edge in the image. The field area is a 2D vegetation region, which is a homogeneous region with a high NDVI (Normalized Difference Vegetation Index) value in the colour infrared (CIR) image.

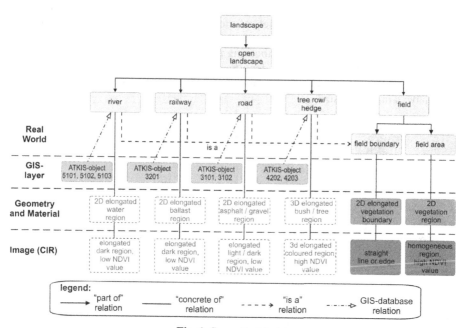

Fig. 1. Semantic Model

2.2 Strategy to Extract Field Boundaries

The general strategy for the extraction of field boundaries is derived from the modelled characteristics of the fields and their surrounding boundaries taking into account the realization of an automatic processing flow. Imagery and GIS-data are the input-data to initialize the process: First, the open landscape is derived from the GIS-data (cf. section 2.1). In addition, within the open landscape, regions of interest are selected using the roads, railways, rivers, tree rows and hedges as borderlines (cf. the thick black lines in Fig. 2 and 4). Consequently, the borderlines of the regions of interest are field boundaries, which are already fixed. The following image analysis methods are focused to field boundaries within the regions of interest.

The main approach extracting field boundaries within the regions of interest is divided into two parts: Firstly, a segmentation is carried out in a coarse scale ignoring small disturbing structures and thus exploiting the relative homogeneity of the vegetation within each field. The aim is to obtain a topological correct result, even if the geometrical correctness is not very high. Secondly, network snakes are used to improve the preliminary results. These two steps are described in detail in the next two sections.

3 Segmentation

In each region of interest a segmentation is carried out to exploit the modelled similar characteristics of each field. The border area is masked out due to disturbing heterogeneities, which are typical for fields and derogate the subsequent steps. As data source the RGB- and IR-channels of the images with a resolution of few meters are used to perform a multi-channel regiongrowing. The four channels give rise to a 4-dimensional feature vector: Neighbouring pixels are aggregated into the same field region, if the difference of their feature vectors does not exceed a predefined threshold. Also, in concert with the modelled constraints, the resulting field regions must have a minimum size.

Fig. 2. Exemplarily result of the segmentation: black lines are the borders of the regions of interest generated from the GIS-data, white lines are the preliminary field boundaries

The case of identical vegetation of neighbouring fields leads to missing boundaries, which is not yet taken into account: Accordingly, the standard deviation of the grey values in the image within a quadrate mask is computed. High values typically belong to field boundaries. Extracted lines [15] from the standard deviation image within only sufficiently large field regions are evaluated concerning length and straightness. Positive evaluated lines are used to split the initially generated field regions.

One result is shown in Fig. 2: borders of the regions of interest are depicted in black, preliminary field boundaries are depicted in white, the underlying and used imagery are IKONOS-data. The completeness and topological correctness is good, as a comparison with reference data has shown: only few boundaries are missing. Problems occur, when there are large heterogeneities within a field, in particular in grassland.

4 Network Snakes to Improve the Preliminary Field Boundaries

Snakes were originally introduced in [10] as a mid-level image analysis algorithm, which combines geometric and/or topologic constraints with the extraction of low-level features from images. A traditional snake is defined parametrically as [10, 11]

$$v(s,t) = (x(s,t), y(s,t)) ,$$
(1)

where s is the arc length, t the time, and x and y are the image coordinates of the 2D-curve.

The external energy (image energy) is defined as

$$E_I(v) = -\frac{1}{|v|} \int_0^{|v|} |\nabla I(v(s,t))| ds ,$$
(2)

where I represents the image, $|\nabla I(v(s,t))|$ is the gradient of the image at the coordinates $x(s)$ and $y(s)$ and $|v|$ is the total length of v. In practice, the external energy $E_I(v)$ is computed by integrating the gradient values $|\nabla I(v(s,t))|$ in precomputed gradient images along the line segments that connect the polygon vertices.

The internal energy is defined as

$$E_{v(s,t)} = \frac{1}{2} \left(\alpha(s) \cdot |v'(s,t)|^2 + \beta(s) \cdot |v''(s,t)|^2 \right),$$
(3)

where the arbitrary function $\alpha(s)$ controls the first-order term of the internal energy: the elasticity. Large values of $\alpha(s)$ let the contour becomes very straight between two points. The function $\beta(s)$ controls the second-order term: the rigidity. Large values of $\beta(s)$ let the contour becomes smooth, small values allow the generation of corners.

The total energy of the snake, to be minimized, is defined as $E_{snake} = E_{v(s,t)} + E_I(v)$. A minimum of the total energy can be derived by embedding the curve in a virtual viscous medium solving the equation

$$\frac{\partial E_{v(s,t)}}{\partial v(s,t)} + \kappa \frac{\partial E_I(v)}{\partial v(s,t)} + \gamma \frac{dv(s,t)}{dt} = 0 ,$$
(4)

where γ is the viscosity of the medium and κ is the weight between internal and external energy. After insertion of

$$\frac{\partial E_{v(s,t)}}{\partial v(s,t)} = A_{\alpha(s),\beta(s)}v(s,t) \quad \text{and} \quad \frac{dv(s,t)}{dt} = (v(s,t)-v(s,t-1)) \tag{5}$$

in equation 4 a final solution for the contour at point t depending on point t-1 can be computed:

$$V_{s,t} = (A+\gamma)^{-1}\left(\gamma V_{s,t-1} - \kappa\frac{\partial E_I(v)}{\partial v(s,t-1)}\right), \quad (I: \text{identity matrix}) \tag{6}$$

$V_{s,t}$ stands for either X or Y, the vectors of the x and y coordinates of the contour. A is a pentadiagonal matrix, which depends only on the functions $\alpha(s)$ and $\beta(s)$.

A main problem of snakes is the necessity to have an initialization close to the true boundary. Methods to increase the capture range of the image forces (e.g. pressure forces [16]) are not useful in our case, because there are lots of disturbing structures within the fields, which can cause an unwanted external energy and therefore a wrong result. Thus, only the local image information is of interest. As described in section 2, the result of the segmentation is used to initialize the processing (cf. Fig. 2 and 4a).

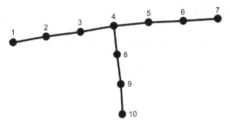

Fig. 3. Topology of a network snake

Most important is in addition to the good initialization the derivation of the *topology* of the initial contours (cf. Fig. 3 for an example). The global framework of the accomplished segmentation (cf. section 3) gives rise to a network of the preliminary field boundaries: Enhancing traditional snakes, network snakes are accessorily linked to each other in the *nodal points* (point 4 in Fig. 3) and thus interact during the processing. Similarly, the connection of the *end points* of the contours to the borders of the region of interest must be taken into account (point 1, 7 and 10 in Fig 3): In contrast to the nodal points, a movement of the end points is only allowed along the borders of the regions of interest. These topological constraints are considered, when filling the matrix A in equation 6 with the functions $\alpha(s)$ and $\beta(s)$, which are in our case taken to be constant.

5 Results

First results concerning the use of network snakes to extract field boundaries from IKONOS-images are shown in Fig. 4: Zooming to the lower right part of Fig. 2, one region of interest is selected to demonstrate the different steps during the processing. Fig. 4a shows the preliminary field boundaries after the segmentation, which are used to initialize the network snakes. The result of the network snake processing is depicted in Fig. 4b together with the initialization to demonstrate the movement of the snake. Fig. 4c shows the image superimposed with the result of the extracted field boundaries. The example demonstrates, that network snakes are a useful possibility to improve the geometrical correctness of topologically correct but geometrically inaccurate results.

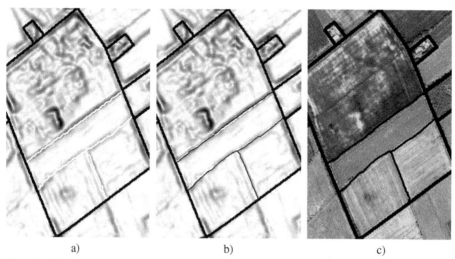

a)   b)   c)

Fig. 4. First result of the use of network snakes within one region of interest: a) initialization of the network snake superimposed to the absolute values of the gradients; b) initialization (white) and result after the movement of the snake (black); c) extracted field boundaries superimposed to the image.

6 Conclusions

A method to extract field boundaries fully automatically from imagery is presented in this paper. The objects of interest are represented with their surrounding scene and prior knowledge in the form of GIS-data in a semantic model. Derived from the modelled knowledge the initial step of our approach is the generation of regions of interest, thus, further investigations are only focussed to the field boundaries within these regions. The process is divided into two parts: First, a segmentation in a coarse scale gives a topological correct framework of the field boundaries. The inaccurate geometrical correctness is improved in a second step with network snakes, which use the local image information for a precise delineation taking into account the topological constraints. The presented results demonstrate the potential of the proposed solution in the complex environment of vegetation. Further work is required: The segmentation could be enhanced by a multi-resolution approach to stabilize the basic step of the strategy. In addition, a texture channel could be used to prevent wrong field boundaries, which occur, when there are large heterogeneities within a field and the predefined thresholds fail. The control of the network snakes could be improved by selecting variable values when filling the matrix A to increase the geometrical correctness furthermore.

Acknowledgements. This work is part of the programme GEOTECHNOLOGIEN funded by the Federal Ministry for Education and Research (BMBF) and the German Research Council (DFG) with the publication no. GEOTECH-173.

References

1. Thiermann, A., Sbresny, J., Schäfer, W.: GIS in WEELS - Wind Erosion on Light Soils. GeoInformatics, No. 5 (2002) 30-33

2. Anderson, J. E., Fischer, R. L., Deloach, S. R.: Remote Sensing and Precision Agriculture: Ready for Harvest or Still Maturing? Photogrammetric Engineering & Remote Sensing, Vol. 65, No. 10 (1999) 1118-1123

3. Baltsavias, E. P.: Object Extraction and Revision by Image Analysis Using Existing Geodata and Knowledge: Current Status and Steps towards Operational Systems. ISPRS Journal of Photogrammetry and Remote Sensing, Vol. 58, No. 3-4 (2004) 129-151

4. Mayer, H.: Automatic Object Extraction from Aerial Imagery - A Survey Focusing on Buildings. Computer Vision and Image Understanding, Vol. 74, No. 2 (1999) 138-149

5. Schowengerdt, R. A. (ed.): Remote Sensing, Models and Methods for Image Processing, 2nd edition. Academic Press, San Diego (1997)

6. Straub, B. M.: Automatische Extraktion von Bäumen aus Fernerkundungsdaten. Dissertation Reihe C, Deutsche Geodätische Kommission, München, No. 572 (2003) 99

7. Löcherbach, T.: Fusing Raster- and Vector-Data with Applications to Land-Use Mapping. Inaugural-Dissertation der Hohen Landwirtschaftlichen Fakultät der Universität Bonn, Bonn (1998) 107

8. Torre, M., Radeva, P.: Agricultural Field Extraction from Aerial Images Using a Region Competition Algorithm. International Archives of Photogrammetry and Remote Sensing, Amsterdam, Vol. XXXIII, No. B2 (2000) 889-896

9. Aplin, P., Atkinson, P. M.: Predicting Missing Field Boundaries to Increase Per-Field Classification Accuracy. Photogrammetric Engineering & Remote Sensing, Vol. 70, No. 1 (2004) 141-149

10. Kass, M., Witkin, A., Terzopoulus, D.: Snakes: Active Contour Models. International Journal of Computer Vision, Vol. 1 (1988) 321-331

11. Fua, P., Gruen, A., Li, H.: Optimization-Based Approaches to Feature Extraction from Aerial Images. Lecture notes of the 1998 International Summer School of the International Association of Geodesy on Data Analysis and the Statistical Foundations of Geomatics, Springer (1999)

12. Liedtke, C., Bückner, J., Pahl, M., Stahlhut, O.: Knowledge Based Systems for the Interpretation of Complex Scenes. Baltsavias Gruen v. Gool (eds), Automatic Extraction of Man-Made Objects from Aerial and Space Images III, A.A.Balkema Publishers, Ascona (2001) 3-12

13. Butenuth, M., Straub, B. M., Heipke, C., Willrich, F.: Tree Supported Road Extraction from Aerial Images Using Global and Local Context Knowledge. Crowley Piater Vincze Paletta (eds), Lecture Notes in Computer Science, Springer, Graz, Austria, LNCS 2626 (2003) 162-171

14. Butenuth, M.: Modelling the Extraction of Field Boundaries and Wind Erosion Obstacles from Aerial Imagery. International Archives of the Photogrammetry, Remote Sensing and Spatial Information Sciences, Istanbul, Vol. XXXV, No. B4 (2004) 1065-1070

15. Steger, C.: An unbiased detector of curvilinear structures. IEEE Transactions on Pattern Analysis and Machine Intelligence, Vol. 20, No. 2 (1998) 311-326

16. Cohen, L.: On active contour models and balloons. CVGIP: Image Understanding, Vol. 53, No. 2 (1991) 211-218

Structure Features for Content-Based Image Retrieval

Gerd Brunner[1] and Hans Burkhardt[1]

Institute for Pattern Recognition and Image Processing,
Computer Science Department, University of Freiburg, Georges-Koehler-Allee 052,
79110 Freiburg, Germany
{gbrunner, Hans.Burkhardt}@informatik.uni-freiburg.de

Abstract. The geometric structure of an image exhibits fundamental information. Various structure-based feature extraction methods have been developed and successfully applied to image processing problems. In this paper we introduce a geometric structure-based feature generation method, called line-structure recognition (LSR) and apply it to content-based image retrieval. The algorithm is adapted from line segment coherences, which incorporate inter-relational structure knowledge encoded by hierarchical agglomerative clustering, resulting in illumination, scale and rotation robust features. We have conducted comprehensive tests and analyzed the results in detail. The results have been obtained from a subset of 6000 images taken from the Corel image database. Moreover, we compared the performance of LSR with Gabor wavelet features.

1   Introduction

During the last years Content-Based Image Retrieval (CBIR) gained in importance and helped pushing research forward in different computer science disciplines. Despite of all undertaken endeavors there are still many unsolved problems left within CBIR. This paper describes line-structure recognition (LSR), a geometric structure-based feature extraction method and apply it to CBIR. Structure and/or shape-based features have been proven to be useful image features in CBIR. There are various approaches in the literature, dealing with shape and structure-based feature computation. In [1] the authors focused on color and shape information, where the shape attributes have been extracted from *significant* edges. The histogram of the edge directions was used to represent the shape attribute. The comparison of histograms was accomplished with the histogram intersection methods. [2] used various types of statistical feature vectors from the edges in non-segmented images. Decimated magnitude spectra of edge images, local edge-histogram-based features, including the co-occurrence matrix of edge directions have been used. The distribution of edge points orientations, combined with the normalized second moments, was taken as a feature vector by [3].

The method we propose exhibits relative context knowledge encoded from straight line segments. In a further step an adaptive hierarchical clustering al-

W. Kropatsch, R. Sablatnig, and A. Hanbury (Eds.): DAGM 2005, LNCS 3663, pp. 425–433, 2005.
© Springer-Verlag Berlin Heidelberg 2005

gorithm is applied, where after line segments of certain properties are grouped together, describing various spatial and geometrical arrangements.

2　Methodology

2.1　Line Segment Extraction

Before we can compute line segments it is necessary to generate edge maps from each image. We apply the well known Canny edge filter [4] to obtain edge images from all images of the database which we before converted to gray scale. Thus, we do not consider or use color information for our feature extraction. In a further step we link edge points together, resulting in straight line segments [5][6]. The set of line segments serves as ground truth features of our algorithm.

2.2　Distance Matrix

Euclidean distance geometry is the computation of point configurations by incorporation of inter-point distance relations. An Euclidean distance matrix (EDM) is a real $n \times n$ matrix D, of distance-square d_{ij}, between pairs of points from a table of M points; $\{y_k, k = 1...M\}$ in $\Re^n$;

$$D_{ij} = ||y_i - y_j||_2^2, \text{ where } || \cdot ||_2 \text{ is the 2-norm on } \Re^n. \tag{1}$$

An EDM D inherits all identities from the defining norm. Furthermore, D is an EDM if and only if the diagonal entries of D are all zero. The dimension of D is M^2, but only $M(M-1)/2$ elements of the matrix are unique. A complete description of all EDM properties and proofs may be found in [7]. Since the conventional approach of using points as input for the EDM does not fully describe the geometric structure of an image, we decided for an integrated approach. A more complete view of the geometrical image structure can be obtained by spatial and relative information primitives, like straight line segments. Thus, we construct 3 EDMs of the same size, with the following input data:

1. The image plane mid-point coordinates of each line segment.
2. The angles of each line segment with respect to the ordinate to obtain a rotation robust EDM.
3. The normalized line lengths of each line segment to gain scale robustness and avoid scaling problems.

Table 1. Range of EDM data

Feature	Range	Explanation
Angles (Φ)	$[-\pi, \pi]$	Angles between line segments
Lengths	$[0, 1]$	Differences of line segment lengths
Distances	$[0, 1]$	Scaled distances between mid-points of line segments

In a further step we combine all 3 EDMs into one by element-wise multiplication, i.e. having coded the structure interrelationships of an image in one matrix. Table 1 shortly summarizes the content of the EDM data settings. The final EDM serves as an input to an agglomerative hierarchical clustering analysis method, which is described in the next paragraph.

2.3   Clustering Line Segments

To group straight line segments into various clusters we apply hierarchical cluster analysis (HCA). Agglomerative hierarchical cluster analysis techniques characterize input data into partitions based on measured properties. The algorithm starts with each case (each line segment) in a separate cluster and then combines the clusters sequentially, reducing the number of clusters at each step until only one cluster remains (N cases involve N-1 clustering steps). The number of clusters is determined by the algorithm from the created dendrogram, which contains the inter-cluster distances. Note, the number of cluster need not be known before the computations start. This was an important reason for us to chose HCA, since the number of detected straight line segments varies from image to image.

Linkage is the criterion by which the clustering algorithm determines the actual distance between two clusters by defining single points that are associated with the clusters in question. There exist several linkage methods, frequently used are single, complete, average, centroid and ward linkage. During the pre-processing steps we reduced the number of line-segments. Thus, there are not many items left to be clustered, i.e. we expect clusters with few members. Since none of the methods performed significantly better we decided for single linkage, defined as follows:
$D_{kl} = min\ (dist(x_{ki}, y_{lj}))$; $k \in (1, ..., n_i)$, $l \in (1, ..., n_j)$, where n_i and n_j are the number of objects in cluster k and l, respectively. x_{ki} denotes the ith object in cluster k. Since we provide a special EDM to our HCA algorithm we are able to group line segments with respect to certain quantities into K clusters. The output of the HCA algorithm can be seen as a grouping of line segments under geometric constraints. For a better representation of the clustering output we create for each image a histogram of dimension 128, which depicts the geometrical structure of the input image. The dimension was obtained from experimental and feature space considerations, i.e. the histogram size reflects a tradeoff between a sufficient representation of the image characteristics and performance aspects.

3   Results

In this section we first describe the used image database and focus further on the comparison of LSR with Gabor wavelets. In the end we present results and analyze them in detail.

3.1   Data Description

We have conducted our experiments for reasons of comparison with the widely used Corel Image database [8] [9]. We have chosen 6000 random images consisting of 60 different classes. Each class contains 100 semantically similar images. We decided for this size to gain an optimal tradeoff between a representative image database size and keeping the manual validation of the results possible. It should be noted, that the class assignments of the images were performed by Corel. Although some images within a class possess a weak semantic similarity and thus, may distort the results, we did not modify the binning. Since we use 60 different image classes there are similar images within various classes, e.g. the classes *Boston* and New York contain mainly images of buildings.

Table 2. A comparison of the LSR and Gabor wavelet performance. The results for 6 random classes plus 2 image classes of our sample queries from Figures 2, 3, 4 and 5, are shown. The numbers indicate how many images within the first 10, 20 and 25 resulting images do not belong to the query image class, thus representing a mismatch. Note, that the numbers depict averaged values, i.e. each image of a class was used as a query. The mismatches were recorded and in the end averaged over all queries.

Features	LSR feat.			Gabor feat.		
within first	10	20	25	10	20	25
Monaco	0	2	4	7	16	20
Cloth	0	3	4	6	15	20
Waves	1	3	5	6	15	20
Shells	0	3	4	6	15	20
Building	0	0	0	6	16	20
Speed	1	4	6	6	15	20
Vineyard	0	3	5	7	16	20
WildlifeCats	1	3	4	5	13	27

Gabor Features We decided to compare our features with the well known Gabor functions, which are a set of oriented filters and have been very successfully applied to various CBIR problems [10] [11] [12]. In detail, Gabor wavelets capture energy at specific frequencies and directions. For a comprehensive study of Gabor wavelets we refer the interested reader to [13] [14]. We applied Gabor filters on various scales and under different orientations, obtaining a magnitude vector.

$$E(a,b) = \sum_x \sum_y |G_{ab}(x,y)|^2 , \tag{2}$$

where x, and y are the image dimensions and with $a = 1, 2, ...A$ and $b = 1, 2, ...B$, being the number of wavelet scales and number of orientations, respectively. In a consequent step we achieve rotation invariance by averaging the amplitude energy over the orientations for each scale. We extracted the Gabor features for the whole image database and stored them as histograms.

Similarity Measure For searching after similar images within a database, a measure, capturing the similarity between the query image feature vector and all feature vectors of a given database is necessary. The choice of the correct similarity measure stays an open discussion [15]. However, since our feature vectors are $\in \Re^n$ the usage of $\Re^n$ distance functions is reasonable. We found out that the histogram intersection measure, which is identical to the $L_1 - norm$ in case of normalized histograms, performed the best for our features. All following image retrieval results have been generated with the histogram intersection similarity measure. Note, that the measure returns values between $[0,1]$ with 1 as being identical with the query image feature vector.

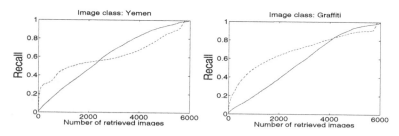

Fig. 1. Recall versus number of retrieved images plots, averaged over 100 queries of 2 random image classes. Left graph: Result for the class $Yemen$, where the dashed line was obtained by LSR and the solid line with the Gabor features. Right graph: Results for the class $Grafitti$ where the lines have the same meanings as in the left graph.

3.2   Evaluation and Discussion

For the evaluation of our algorithm we selected all image classes, resulting in 100 queries per class. From the resulting hitlist we consider each retrieved image out of the query image class as a match. For an objective performance evaluation we took every image out of the database as a query and computed the precision and recall. Finally, we averaged the results of all 100 queries for each class. Thus, we obtained a quantitative evaluation of the performance. Due to space limitations we show in Fig. 1 the averaged recall versus number of retrieved images plot for just two random classes, namely $Yemen$ and $Grafitti$. The left plot shows results for the image class $Yemen$ and the right one of the class $Grafitti$, where the dashed lines were created with our proposed method and the solid lines depict the results of the Gabor wavelets. It has to be stressed that a large number of relevant images was obtained by LSR already within the first 1% of all retrieved images. This gives it an clear advantage over the Gabor wavelets for the Corel image database.

Fig. 2. An exemplary random image search retrieved by our structure features, with the upper left image as the query image. One can see the 9 most similar images, where the similarity decreases from left to right, indicated by the numbers displayed above each image. Note, that all displayed images belong to the query image class.

Fig. 3. This figure shows the Gabor wavelet results generated with the query image out of Fig.2.

Since Fig. 1 shows the averaged overall performance for 2 random classes, but not an exemplary retrieval result, we visualize in Fig. 2 and Fig. 3 results from a randomly chosen query image. The results of Fig. 2 are obtained with our method, where the output in Fig. 3 was generated with Gabor wavelets for the same query image as in Fig. 2. It can be seen that both methods find the query image as most similar, first. Figure 2 shows that the structure information from our features capture enough discrimination ability to find leopards in very different surroundings and under different light conditions. Our features are quite robust against illumination changes and do not suffer too much from various background. This result illustrates the advantage of context knowledge we have built in our features, in contrary to the wavelet results. The wavelet results from Fig. 3 show images with similar textures as the query image but

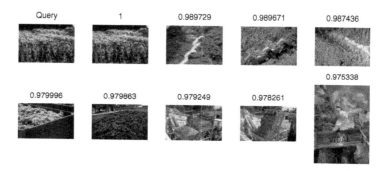

Fig. 4. Results produced with LSR features. The images are ranked in decreasing similarity order from left to the right. The numbers indicate the obtained similarity, where 1 means identical.

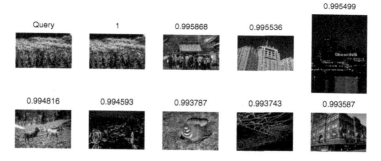

Fig. 5. Results obtained with Gabor features for the identical query image from Fig.4, with the same arrangement as in Fig.4.

only one image out of the first 9 retrieved images is from the $Wildlife - Cats$ class. For a more detailed validation we present another retrieval result with a random query image. Figure 4 and Fig. 5 possess the same query image but have been retrieved with LSR features and with wavelet features, respectively. Note, that all images displayed in Fig. 4 belong to query image class $Vineyard$. Moreover, we can see that the retrieved images are very similar in their appearance. A manual verification of this query revealed that the image class $Vineyard$ does not only contain outdoor images of vineyards but also indoor images of barrels, wine-glasses, people and bottles, thus, semantic similar images. However, our algorithm retrieved first all images from the class $Vineyard$ with similar structure. The results shown in Fig. 5 have been produced with the wavelet features describe earlier. It can be seen, that for the first 9 retrieved images the LSR feature clearly perform superiorly for this query image. Table 2 gives a more quantitative analysis of the query image classes depicted in Fig 2, 3, 4 and Fig. 5. We can see how many mismatched images, i.e. from a different class, are retrieved within the first 10, 20 and 25 results, respectively.

4   Conclusion

In this paper we have presented LSR, a generic structure-based feature computation method which we applied to CBIR. We have conducted a comprehensive evaluation and analysis of the results. The results have been obtained from a set of 6000 images taken out of the commonly used Corel image database. We have compared LSR with the well known and widely used Gabor wavelet energy feature approach. The results and their validation showed that generic structure information captured by LSR perform in the case of CBIR using Corels image database, significantly better than Gabor wavelets. The results show that our proposed method is robust against illumination changes and exhibit scale and rotation robustness too. The analysis revealed that our method is able to find similar geometrical structure of objects and scenes and thus, it is suitable for CBIR applications.

References

1. Jain, A., Vailaya, A.: Image retrieval using color and shape. Pattern Recognition **29(8)** (1996) 1233–1244
2. Brandt, S., Laaksonen, J., Oja, E.: Statistical shape features in content-based image retrieval. In: Proc. of 15th ICPR, Barcelona. (2000)
3. Zhu, W., Levinson, S.: Edge orientation-based multi-view object recognition. In: International Conference on Pattern Recognition (ICPR)-Vol. 1. (2000) 936–939
4. Canny, J.: A computational approach to edge detection. IEEE Transactions on Pattern Analysis and Machine Intelligence **8** (1986) 679–698
5. Pope, A., Lowe, D.: Vista: A software environment for computer vision research. In: CVPR94. (1994) 768–772
6. Kovesi, P.D.: Edges are not just steps. In: Proceedings of the Fifth Asian Conference on Computer Vision. (2002) 822–827 Melbourne.
7. Boyd, S., Vandenberghe, L.: Convex Optimization. Cambridge University Press (2004)
8. Wang, J.Z., Li, J., Wiederhold, G.: SIMPLIcity: Semantics-sensitive integrated matching for picture LIbraries. IEEE Transactions on Pattern Analysis and Machine Intelligence **23** (2001) 947–963
9. Li, J., Wang, J.Z.: Automatic linguistic indexing of pictures by a statistical modeling approach. IEEE Trans. Pattern Anal. Mach. Intell. **25** (2003) 1075–1088
10. Zhang, D.S., Wong, A., Indrawan, M., Lu, G.: Content-based image retrieval using gabor texture features. In: Proc. of First IEEE Pacific-Rim Conference on Multimedia (PCM'00),Sydney, Australia. (2000) 392–395
11. Wolf, C., Jolion, J.M., Kropatsch, W., Bischof, H.: Content based image retrieval using interest points and texture features. In: Proceedings of the ICPR2000, IEEE Computer Society (2000)
12. Tian, Q., Sebe, N., Loupias, E., Lew, M., Huang, T.: Content-based image retrieval using wavelet-based salient points. In: SPIE - Storage and Retrieval for Media Databases (EI28), San Jose, USA,. (2001) 425–436
13. Gabor, D.: Theory of communication. J. IEE (London), No. 26 (1946) 429–457

14. Daubechies, I.: The wavelet transform, time-frequency localization and signal analysis. IEEE Trans. Information Theory (1990)
15. Sebe, N., Lew, M., Huijsmans, N.: Towards optimal ranking metrics. IEEE Trans. on Pattern Analysis and Machine Intel. (PAMI) (2000) 1132–1143

Blind Background Subtraction in Dental Panoramic X-Ray Images: An Application Approach

Peter Michael Goebel[1,2], Nabil Ahmed Belbachir[1], and Michael Truppe[3]

[1] Vienna University of Technology, Institute of Computer Aided Automation,
Pattern Recognition and Image Processing Group, Austria
[2] fh-campus wien, Technical Project- and Processmanagement, Austria
[3] Karl Landsteiner Institute for Biotelematics, Danube University Krems, Austria

Abstract. Dental Panoramic X-ray images are images having complex content, because several layers of tissue, bone, fat, etc. are superimposed. Non-uniform illumination, stemming from the X-ray source, gives extra modulation to the image, which causes spatially varying X-ray photon density. The interaction of the X-ray photons with the density of matter causes spatially coherent varying noise contribution. Many algorithms exist to compensate background effects, by pixel based or global methods. However, if the image is contaminated by a non-negligible amount of noise, that is usually non-Gaussian, the methods cannot approximate the background efficiently. In this paper, a dedicated approach for background subtraction is presented, which operates blind, that means the separation of a set of independent signals from a set of mixed signals, with at least, only little a priori information about the nature of the signals, using the A-Trous multiresolution transform to alleviate this problem. The new method estimates the background bias from a reference scan, which is taken without a patient. The background values are rescaled by a polynomial compensation factor, given by mean square error criteria, thus subtracting the background will not produce additional artifacts in the image. The energy of the background estimate is subtracted from the energy of the mixture. The method is capable to remove spatially varying noise also, allocating an appropriate spatially noise estimate. This approach has been tested on 50 images from a database of panoramic X-ray images, where the results are cross validated by medical experts.

1 Introduction

Non-uniform illumination of any kind generates non-uniform background in an image. The term background comes from the usual classification of the image data into regions of interest and unwanted regions, referred foreground and background, respectively [13]. A number of different algorithms exist for removal of these effects, but if the image is contaminated by a non-negligible amount of noise, most of them are unable to give good results, especially, when the noise is non-Gaussian.

W. Kropatsch, R. Sablatnig, and A. Hanbury (Eds.): DAGM 2005, LNCS 3663, pp. 434–441, 2005.

1.1 Background Removal Methods

There exist Non-parametric [10], Pixel Based (like Kalman filtration [11] or Adaptive Thresholding [12]) and Global Methods, which generate the rules for the adaption of the background estimate from some measurable image attributes. Most approaches are preempt to images sequence analysis and detection of moving objects for surveillance use (see [6] and the references herein). A stationary, challenging task, is the reconstruction at forensic document examination [9].

A polynomial fit to a number of points associated with the background is appropriate when the non-uniformity is additive, and the resulting polynomial surface is subtracted from the whole image. For multiplicative non-uniformity, a correction image is generated, corresponding to the polynomial surface. The correction image has factors that represent the ratio of brightness between the non-uniform image and the uniform one and is applied to scale the original image values appropriately.

In [17] the background is defined to be the *bright* surrounding area of the X-ray film viewing box, where the X-ray film size is smaller than that viewing box. Thus the surrounding, bright white area has physiological influence on the detectability of contrast details in the darker X-ray film area [2]. The algorithm builds up a probabilistic model and cuts out the radiography by the biggest gradient at its border. The proposed, new approach is different in that it removes also unwanted modulation from the image of interest.

1.2 Basics of Panoramic Radiography

Dental Panoramic Radiography (DPR) is a technique where the entire dentition is projected onto a sensing device. The physics of such a radiographic process can be subdivided into X-ray source, interaction of the beam with matters and imaging of the surviving photons. Source and detector are in opposition, rotated around the patients head. The focal area of the X-ray beam describes a planar curve, which is standardized for the human teeth and jaws. The photon attenuation of each type of matter depends on its elementary and chemical composition as well as the beam. This effect is quantified by the linear mass attenuation coefficient μ, which gives the fraction of photons that are absorbed by unit thickness of matter [8], which varies by photoelectric absorption, coherent scatter, Compton scatter and the energy spectrum of the beam [1,4].

1.3 Image Degradation

The scattering of the photons due to their crossing of matter causes two effects: firstly an attenuation of the photon beam by different type or thickness of matter that excite the generation of the radiographic image; secondly scattered photons darken the film while carrying no useful information, because their path is randomly altered. Only photons absorbed by matter generate good image contrast. During a DPR scan of the entire dentition, the photon rate has to be increased, when the X-ray beam crosses bones from the spine region. Thus a multiplicative non-uniform illumination of the radio graph is caused, leading to additional, spurious modulation of the image.

In this work, a new approach to background subtraction, which is a process to correct an image for non-uniform background or non-uniform illumination is considered. The new approach takes a image without a patient as an estimate for the background. A model is given, which separates diagnostic information from background information and takes noise into consideration.

2   The Method Explained

As the geometry of the DPR system is fixed, a scan, taken without a patient can provide a good estimate for the background. Unfortunately, subtracting a background estimate directly from the diagnostic image usually increases the noise contribution in the difference image, because noise cannot be subtracted from noise in the spatial domain. Therefore, it is more convenient to perform this subtraction in another domain.

The A-Trous multiresolution transform [7] is used to form an undecimated, over complete representation, by decomposing the image into different contributions in several frequency bands and at different scales. The algorithm a-trous involves upsampling the filters (adding holes) at each scale instead of downsampling the signal. Upsampling the filters is accomplished by inserting 2^{J-k} zeros between each filter coefficient, where J is the highest level of decomposition, and k is the current level of decomposition. It requires more computations than the fast biorthogonal wavelet transform, but has the advantage of being translation invariant. Thus it is an overcomplete representation, which have been proven to be better for denoising purposes.

2.1   Image Model

The X-ray generator in Fig. 1 produces photons having Poisson count statistics; the arrival-time difference between successive Poisson counts is Gamma distributed; the photons, with intensity I_0, travel through collimator and filter to the patient. Thus, the intensity I_1 can be measured as it is proportional to the photon input energy to the patient. This photon energy interacts with the different layers of matter of the patient, therefore one can measure I_2 at the sensor. Formulating the physical situation of Fig. 1 in mathematical terms of linear attenuation coefficients leads to

$$I_2 = I_0 \cdot \underbrace{\exp(-\mu_{01}\,d_{01})}_{\substack{background\ scatter \\ \underbrace{}_{I_1}}} \cdot \underbrace{\exp(-\sum_{i=1}^{K}(\mu_i\,d_i))}_{diagnostic\ scatter} \qquad (1)$$

In (1) the intensity I_2 at the sensor is decomposed into the background part I_1, which is further attenuated by the diagnostic part. Photoelectric absorption and

Compton scattering, as the main contributors for scattering the beam, induce the contrast function of matter, which forms the image. Unfortunately they produce also an amount of non-negligible noise. The statistic is quite non-Gaussian.

In [4] the authors of this paper introduced a noise estimation model for DPR. It models the probabilities for scattering events and generates a scatter prior table, which is used together with a background and a diagnostic image to estimate the amount of scatter-glare. The spatially varying contribution of noise is modeled by locally Gaussian random variables $N(0,1)$, modulated by hidden factors ξ, representing the variance of every pixel in the image. Since the exposure time is long (about 14 seconds for an entire panoramic scan), photon counts get quite high, thus stressing the central limit theorem, one can argue that for each exponential term in (1) the contribution of noise is given by an additive term of locally Gaussian noise, scaled by a spatially dependent, hidden factor ξ. Therefore, modeling the images and contributions of noise leads to

$$\hat{Z}_{x,y}(I_2) = \underbrace{\underbrace{Z_{x,y}}_{image} + \underbrace{\xi_{x,y}^{(1)} N_{x,y}(0,\overline{\sigma})}_{noise}}_{diagnostic\ mixture} + \underbrace{\underbrace{B_{x,y}}_{illumination} + \underbrace{\xi_{x,y}^{(2)} N_{x,y}(0,\overline{\sigma})}_{noise}}_{background\ mixture} \quad (2)$$

In (2), $\hat{Z}_{x,y}$ is the output image, generated by I_2 following (1), decomposed into the diagnostic mixture and the background mixture. Both mixtures are subdivided into a deterministic part and an additive random part. As explained above, the random parts have locally Gaussian statistic with a scale factor $\xi^{(n)}$.

The estimate of the background mixture is taken with the same operating parameters as the patient scan, but without patient. Accordingly to (1) the effect of the non-uniform background illumination to the image I_2 is multiplicative. To alleviate this, one possible solution leads to a formulation of the image model in terms of transmittance, which considers the fraction of $\frac{I_2}{I_1}$ as the image of interest [5]. The present paper goes a different way in that I_1 is scaled accordingly to I_2, by a scale factor concerning mean square error fitting of two polynomials p_1, p_2 to I_1, I_2, respectively. Correction factors $F_k = \frac{p_2}{p_1}$ are then applied to gain

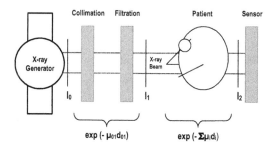

Fig. 1. Outline of the X-ray Physics

image $I'_1 = I_1 F_k$. Thus I'_1 can be subtracted, not introducing new artifacts, by the proposed method. The illumination correction by an evenness criteria can be applied after the background subtraction process.

As mentioned above, the subtraction of the background estimate is done in the multiresolution domain by a new shrinking method using the fractional ratio between the energies of the output image mixture and the background estimate.

2.2 Shrinking Method for the Wavelet Coefficients by Preservation of Energy

The idea is, that the energies of the contributions from the background illumination and the diagnostic information sum up to the mixture energy. Stressing Plancherel's Theorem [14] for non-orthogonal discrete wavelets and $M < \infty$ finite scales, using the $L^2(\Re)$ norm, yields to (3)

$$\|s\|^2 = C_E \underbrace{\sum_{i=0}^{M-1} \frac{1}{2^i} \|w_i\|^2}_{coefficients\ energy} + \underbrace{\frac{1}{2^M} \|r_M\|^2}_{resid.\ energy} \tag{3}$$

where $\int \|s\|^2$ is the signal energy in the spatial domain, w_i are the wavelet coefficients of the ith scale and r_M is the residual scale. The constant C_E in (3) is chosen for conservation of energy and is determined for M=1 and an input impulse function $s = \delta$, getting $\|s\| = 1$ (see [14] for more details).

Calculating the energies, using (3), for the background estimate (E_B), the output mixture image $(E_{\widehat{Z}})$ and making up the balance by the norm of the energies, leads to the energy of the diagnostic mixture (E_D) with background subtracted:

$$\left\|E_{D_{x,y}}\right\| = \left\|E_{\widehat{Z}_{x,y}}\right\| - \left\|E_{B_{x,y}}\right\| \tag{4}$$

From the reconstructed energy E_D, shrinkage weighting factors for $\left\|E_{\widehat{Z}_{x,y}}\right\| > 0$ are introduced, to be able to convey the result to the coefficients:

$$f_{D_{x,y}} = \frac{\left\|E_{D_{x,y}}\right\|}{\left\|E_{\widehat{Z}_{x,y}}\right\|} \tag{5}$$

The corrected coefficients are calculated now, by application of the shrinkage weights:

$$\breve{w}_{i_{x,y}} = w_{i_{x,y}} \cdot f_{D_{x,y}} \tag{6}$$

Then, the usually reconstruction of the A-Trous multiresolution transform yields to the reconstructed image I_R:

$$I_R = \sum_{i=0}^{M-1} \breve{w}_i + r_M \tag{7}$$

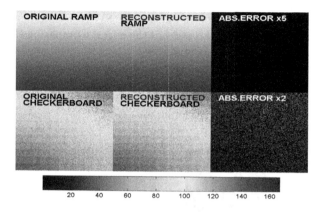

Fig. 2. The simulation: left originals, middle reconstructions, right errors

To take a simulation, consider an image with gently inclining gray levels, and another image, having a gray level checkerboard. From the checkerboard two images are produced, corrupted by two independent instances of Poisson noise. The original images, at the left in Fig.2 are added to form the mixture. As a cross validation, the proposed method reconstructs both, the gray ramp image and the checkerboard image, shown in the middle, from the one mixture. From this experiment it is obvious, the method properly distinguishes the two images, including the noise contribution of the gray checkerboard image. The reconstruction errors are shown at the right.

3   Analysis and Results

In this section results are shown in Fig.3 for a 12mm acrylic glass and a 5-layer test phantom in Fig.4 [Quart (Ltd.), Germany, 2004].

Fig.3-Top shows the background image, where one can see the non-uniformity of the X-ray illumination. Fig.3-Middle shows the acrylic glass phantom image as the diagnostic mixture. The non-uniformity goes into the diagnostic image. First the background estimate is registered with the diagnostic image [16] and the polynomial compensation applied, then both images are transformed into the multiresolution domain. The algorithm, explained in section 2 is applied, by using $M = 4$ scales and the standard triangle wavelet. Fig.3-Bottom shows the reconstruction after application of the method. At the bottom, one can see the non-uniformity of the illumination removed (Note: gray level's expanded for better view). For comparison, Fig.4 shows the result of a spatial background subtraction at a) and the result of the application of a standard stationary wavelet (SWT) denoising by a Daubechies wavelet db3, soft thresholding [3] at 3 scales in c). The original image is shown at quadrant b) and the result of the new method is found at d). It is obvious, that the spatial method in quadrant a) increases the noise contribution. The standard deviation of that image increases by a factor of around $\sqrt{2}$. The SWT method is given to compare the new method with a standard denoising method in c), thus the SWT method denoises all parts of the image and causes a slight blurring of the edges. Comparing the modulation transfer functions for frequencies of $2.5\frac{lines}{mm}$ give 53%, 21% and 44% for b), c) and d), respectively. Thus the proposed method has better preservation of high frequency information. The new method removes the noise in areas of lower Poisson counts (i.e. higher gray levels) and leave the noise at darker regions, where the diagnostic noise part is dominant (2).

 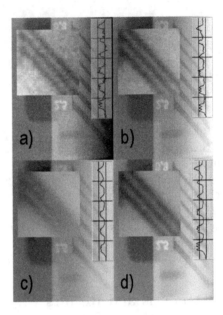

Fig. 3. Acrylic Test Phantom - Top: Background Image; Middle: Diagnostic Image; Bottom: Reconstruction Image (enhanced for a better detail view).

Fig. 4. The Comparison: a) spatially subtracted background estimate; b) the original image; c) db3 SWT denoised; d) result of the new method.

4   Conclusions

In this paper, a new method for the subtraction of background in dental panoramic X-ray, by shrinking the wavelet coefficients under the constraint of preservation of energy, is given. The energy of an image, representing a background estimate, taken without a patient, is subtracted from the diagnostic image in the multiresolution domain. The new method is compared to a spatial background subtraction method and a standard denoising method, in fact the results show improved quality in either case. Main purpose of the new background subtraction method is not in denoising, but it is shown, that the background noise part is properly removed, without any need to choose parameters for denoising, thus the method is non-parametric. As the method leave the part of noise unaffected, which is not found in the background, it can be the first stage of an improved denoising method, which considers the diagnostic noise part better. As proposed herein at first remove the background, then estimate a noise map of the remaining diagnostic noise and correct the factors (5) to remove the rest of the noise from the image.

References

1. Aird EGA. Basic Physics for Medical Imaging. Heinemann, Oxford, 1988
2. P. G. J. Barten. Physical model for the Contrast Sensitivity of the human eye. Proc. SPIE 1666, pp. 57-72 (1992)
3. D.L. Donoho. Denoising by Soft-thresholding. IEEE Trans. on Information Theory, **41**, pp.613-627, 1995
4. P. M. Goebel, A. N. Belbachir, M. Truppe. Noise estimation in panoramic X-ray images: An application analysis approach. *Workshop on Statist. Signal Proc., SSP05, Bordeaux, 17-20 July, 2005*
5. P. M. Goebel, A. N. Belbachir. Background Removal in Dental Panoramic X-ray Images by the A-Trous Multires. Trans. *to appear at ECCTD 2005, Cork, IE, 2005.*
6. D. Gutchessy, M. Trajkovicz, E. Cohen-Solalz, D. Lyonsz, A. K. Jain. A Background Model Initialization Algorithm for Video Surveillance. Proc. International Conference on Computer Vision, Vancouver,Canada, July 2001.
7. M. Holschneider, R. Kronland-Martinet, J. Morlet, and Ph. Tchamitchian. A real-time algorithm for signal analysis with help of the wavelet transform. Wavelets, Time-Frequency Methods and Phase Space, J. M. Combes, A. Grossmann, and Ph. Tchamitchian, Eds. Berlin: Springer, IPTI, 1989, pp. 286-297.
8. J. H. Hubbell, S. M. Seltzer Tables of X-Ray Mass Attenuation Coefficients and Mass Energy-Absorption Coefficients (version 1.4). NISTIR 5632, National Institute of Standards and Technology, Gaithersburg, MD (1995).
9. S. N Srihari and G. Leedham. A survey of computer methods in forensic document examination. Proc. Int. Graphonomics Soc. Conf., Scottsdale, USA, 2-5 Nov. 2003.
10. W. Long and Yee-Hong Yang. Stationary background generation: an alternative to the difference of two images. Pattern Recogn.,**23**(12):13511359, 1990.
11. C. Ridder, O. Munkelt, H. Kirchner. Adaptive Background Estimation and Foreground Detection using Kalman-Filtering. Proc. Int. Conf. on recent Advances in Mechatronics ICRAM'95, UNESCO Chair on Mechatronics, 193-199, 1995.
12. A. E. Savakis Adaptive document image thresholding using foreground and background clustering. 1998 Int. Conf. on Image Processing (ICIP '98) Oct. 04-07, 1998.
13. A. J. Shelley, N. L. Seed. Approaches to Static Background Identification and Removal. Journal of the Institution of Electrical Engineers, IEE, 1993.
14. M. J. Shensha. Discrete Inverses for Nonorthogonal Wavelet Transforms. IEEE Trans. on Signal Processing, vol.**44**, no. 4, pp. 798-807, April 1996.
15. T. M. Su and J. S. Hu. Background Removal in Vision Servo System Using Gaussian Mixture Model Framework. IEEE Proc. on Int. Conf. on Networking, Sensing and Control, Taipei, TW, 2004.
16. P. Thevenaz and M. Unser. A Pyramid Approach to Subpixel Registration Based on Intensity. IEEE Trans. on Image Processing, **7** No. 1., 27-41, 1998.
17. J. Zhang and H. K. Huang. Automatic Background Recognition and Removal (ABRR) in Computed Radiography Images. IEEE Trans. on Medical Imaging, Vol.**16**., No. 6., Dec. 1997.

Robust Head Detection and Tracking in Cluttered Workshop Environments Using GMM

Alexander Barth[1] and Rainer Herpers[1,2]

[1] Department of Computer Science, University of Applied Sciences Bonn-Rhein-Sieg,
Grantham-Allee 20, 53757 Sankt Augustin, Germany
[2] Department of Computer Science and Engineering, York University, Toronto,
Ontario, M3J 1P3, Canada

Abstract. A vision based head tracking approach is presented, combining foreground information with an elliptical head model based on the integration of gradient and skin-color information. The system has been developed to detect and robustly track a human head in cluttered workshop environments with changing illumination conditions. A foreground map based on *Gaussian Mixture Models* (GMM) is used to segment a person from the background and to eliminate unwanted background cues. To overcome known problems of adaptive background models, a *high-level feedback* module prevents regions of interest to become background over time. To obtain robust and reliable detection and tracking results, several extensions of the GMM update mechanism have been developed.

1 Introduction

The most characteristic and persistent feature of a human is the head. Compared to other body parts like arms or hands, head motion without moving the entire body is limited. Assuming a person standing or sitting in upright position, the head's location relative to the body can be predicted quite reliably.

Vision based head tracking systems have been established in many applications like in video conferencing, distance learning, video surveillance or in face detection systems used for biometric access control. Moreover, there are applications as interactive user interface in virtual environments or video games.

This contribution is part of a safety application developed at the German Berufsgenossenschaften (BG)-Institute for Occupational Safety and Health - BGIA. The task is to detect and track a person and his extremities operating a table saw in a wood workshop environment.

In [1], Birchfield introduced an elliptical 2D head model, combining gradient information and color histograms, to reliably track a human head. A drawback of his histogram based color module is a manual initialization step to train the systems skin color histogram without adaptation functionality. In cluttered environments, the gradient module can be distracted by strong background edges, since there is no discrimination between foreground and background. Furthermore, the presented work does only consider the tracking but not the initial localization of the head region. Therefore, without any extensive modifications

W. Kropatsch, R. Sablatnig, and A. Hanbury (Eds.): DAGM 2005, LNCS 3663, pp. 442–450, 2005.

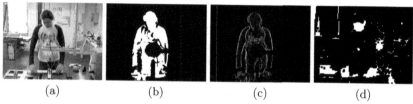

(a)   (b)   (c)   (d)

Fig. 1. Information used for tracking: (a) Input image (b) Foreground map (c) Gradient information (here vertical edges) (d) Skin-color map

this approach cannot solve the given tasks in our application. For that a pre-processing step and some extensions have been added to exclude background regions from further processing.

Segmenting a person from the background is a non trivial task. Potential image regions of persons are computed by evaluating an adaptive background model. A resulting foreground map (see Fig. 1b) provides clues where a head could be found. To detect a person's head, both edge and skin-color information is evaluated, as well as the characteristic elliptical outline. These information is merged into a single score indicating the probability of a possible head at a certain position. Meeting a certain threshold, the system starts tracking the head until the score falls short. If a head is found, the location of the person's body can be reliably estimated. The head and body region is then used to support as high-level feedback (HLF) for the background adaptation process, preserving a non-moving person from being faded into the background over time.

The foreground segmentation in this contribution is based on Gaussian Mixture Models (GMM) and was motivated by the work of Stauffer and Grimson [2]. Power and Schoonees [3] provide a deeper theoretical background on GMM and a more detailed description of a practical implementation. Porikli and Tuzel [4] introduced a mechanism to control the update frequency and intensity of the GMM based on global scene changes. Harville [5] emphasized the importance of HLF for background adaptation of per-pixel GMMs to overcome existing limits.

In the next section the extensions of the GMM-based foreground segmentation approach will be introduced. Subsequently the update mechanism and the integration of HLF into the detection and tracking process is presented. The computation of the different feature scores as needed for the head tracking is topic of chapter 4. At the end of this contribution the obtained results are discussed and conclusions are drawn.

2   GMM-Based Foreground Segmentation

Assuming a static camera setup, one common approach for object detection is to segment an image first into foreground and background regions based on a trained background model. Large changes from the background model are classified as foreground. One drawback of this approach is that both changes due to moving objects and those due to other changes in the scene, such as illumination changes or shadows, might be classified as foreground. To reduce the influence of illumination and to improve the robustness of the foreground segmentation, adaptive background update algorithms like [2] have been developed.

The main idea of the GMM-based background modeling approach is to represent a background pixel as a mixture of K Gaussian background models, weighting these models based on persistence and variance and classifying a pixel's status depending on the best match. If the persistence is high and the variance of a model low, it is more likely to correspond to background.

The decision whether a pixel is classified as background or foreground is based on a statistical interpretation. In this it is checked whether the pixel value is assigned to a certain confidence interval of a model or not. The result is a binary decision denoted as *foreground map* in the following. If a pixel does not match any of the K Gaussian models, the model with the least weight is replaced by a new model with the current pixel intensity as its mean value. Thus, in general it is possible that objects can be added dynamically to the background. Throughout our experiments $K = 3$ is used and was determined empirically.

3   Update Mechanism and High-Level Feedback

The background models are adapted by blending the current image values into the background. A learning coefficient $\alpha(p)$ controls the update intensity at pixel position p. It consists of a global learning rate α_{glb} as introduced in [4] and a new local learning rate component α_{loc}:

$$\alpha(p) = min\left(\alpha_{max}, (\alpha_{glb} + \alpha_{loc}(p)) \, e^{-\frac{(I(p)-\mu)^2}{\sigma^2}}\right) \qquad (1)$$

where $I(p)$ is the intensity and μ and σ^2 indicate the mean and variance of the Gaussian model to be updated at p. $\alpha(p)$ is limited to α_{max} with $0 < \alpha_{max} \leq 1$ ($\alpha_{max} = 0.8$ was used in our experiments). Additionally weighting the sum of α_{glb} and α_{loc} with respect to the quality of the match reduces the effect of overlapping models converging over time.

The underlying idea of the global component α_{glb} is to force an update, if there is a global scene change (e.g. illumination change). Without high-level knowledge of the scene and a semantic interpretation of foreground regions, the system can not distinguish efficiently and reliably between relevant and non-relevant information. The application of HLF causes the integration of the local component α_{loc}.

For that a binary *feedback map* is introduced to exclude parts of the scene from getting updated, i.e. a person which stopped moving can not be faded into the background. It is generated using both, the foreground map and the head tracking results. The idea is to cut out a region in the foreground map, which is likely to include the tracked person based on the head's position and underlying body proportions, as well as model knowledge of standard human body measures (*DIN 32 402, Part 2* [6]). However, in general foreground objects occlude parts of the background. If illumination changes significantly, only the background models apart of the occluded areas are updated. If a region is occluded for a longer time periode, the probability that its background models are not up-to-date anymore increases. Hence, once there is evidence that the foreground object has moved to another location, the former occluded region has to be updated much faster than other regions to compensate for the time of occlusion and to overcome the well known *ghost effect*. A foreground history stored with each pixel is used to compute the local learning rate α_{loc}:

$$\alpha_{loc}(p, t) = \frac{2\alpha_{max}}{1 + e^{-sH(p,t)}} - \alpha_{max} \tag{2}$$

where $H(p, t)$ is the number of consecutive frames in which a pixel has been foreground at time t, and s a parameter controlling the smoothness of this sigmoidal function.

4   Head Tracking

The head tracking is motivated by the work of Birchfield [1]. Our approach makes use of the underlying ellipse fitting concept, but extends the gradient module by knowledge of the foreground segmentation process and integrates a different color score for evaluation as explained in the following.

4.1   Gradient Score

The main idea of the gradient module is to detect the outline of a person's head and to find the best fitting ellipse with respect to the image intensity gradient. One option to adjust an ellipse by gradient information is to maximize the sum of gradient magnitude around the ellipse's perimeter. Here, a more sophisticated gradient score ϕ_g as shown in [1] is used, which considers not only the gradient magnitude, but also the gradient direction as

$$\phi_g(s) = \frac{1}{N_\sigma} \sum_{i=1}^{N_\sigma} |n_\sigma(i) \cdot g_s(i)| \tag{3}$$

with $s = (x, y, \sigma)$ indicating an ellipse's state and N_σ representing the number of outline pixels of that ellipse. $n_\sigma(i)$ is the unit normal vector to the ellipse with center position (x, y) and scale σ at pixel i, and $g_s(i) = (g_x(i), g_y(i))^T$ the gradient intensity at this pixel. '·' denotes dot product.

Test sequences have shown that in cluttered environments, without elimination of background edges, the ellipse fitting will prefer the strongest edge within its local neighborhood, regardless of whether it really originates from a head or not. To reduce the influence of distracting background edges, the binary foreground map is masking the gradient image, preserving only foreground edges before calculating ϕ_g.

4.2   Skin-Color Score

While the gradient score concentrates on the outline of the head, the skin-color score focuses on the inside. The color histogram approach used in [1] is replaced by a binary skin-color map (see Fig. 1 (d)) as introduced by Chai and Ngan [7]. This skin-color map can be calculated efficiently for each frame and overcomes the problems of the original approach.

In YCrCb color space, *skin-color* values are lying in a narrow and consistent range with respect to the chrominance component, independent of the luminance component. Further processing of the skin-color map can reduce the number of false positive and false negative skin-pixels. Since these steps did not noticeable perform better in our application, but increased the computation time significantly, they have been replaced by a simple morphological closing operation to fill small holes within skin blobs. An ellipse state is evaluated with respect to skin-color using the following score $\phi_c(s)$:

$$\phi_c(s) = \frac{N_{skin}(s)}{N_{non-skin}(s) + 1} \frac{N_{skin}(s)}{N_{max}} \tag{4}$$

with N_{skin} and $N_{non-skin}$ the number of skin or non-skin pixels within an ellipse represented by state s. N_{max} is the number of pixels of the maximum possible ellipse[1]. While the first factor in Eq. 4 represents the ratio of skin to non-skin pixels, the second factor supports large ellipses. A drawback of the skin-color map is that it does not take into account individual characteristics of a person's face. Thus, this approach is not able to distinguish between two persons. The integration of facial feature detection as in [8] would overcome these problems.

4.3   Initialization and Evaluation

An initial guess of the head's location is needed to start tracking. In our approach, the foreground module is evaluated to localize possible head positions. Assuming a person in upright position, the head can most likely be found at the upper third of the person's corresponding foreground blob. At each candidate position an ellipse fitting is performed and the position with maximum score is selected as starting point for later tracking.

Once the head tracker is initialized, the best fitting ellipse in the next frame within a certain search window around the previous position is chosen. Several ellipse locations and sizes relative to the previous ellipse state are tested. A total score Φ to be maximized is calculated as weighted sum of the scores ϕ_g and ϕ_c:

$$\Phi = w_g \phi_g(s_i) + w_c \phi_c(s_i), \tag{5}$$

with $i = \arg\max_j (w_g \phi_g(s_j) + w_c \phi_c(s_j))$. This means, the ellipse with state s_i reaches maximum score together in gradient and color. w_k, $k \in \{g, c\}$, are weighting coefficients, which are calculated as:

$$w_k = \frac{\Delta \phi_k}{\Delta \phi_g + \Delta \phi_c} \tag{6}$$

---

[1] To reduce computational costs, a minimum and maximum ellipse size is pre-defined.

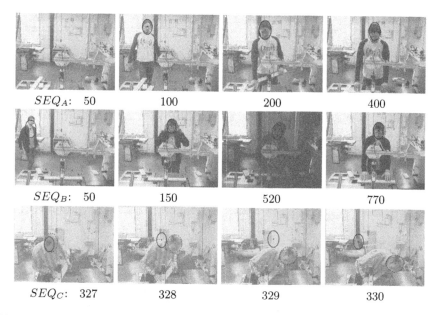

Fig. 2. Tracking results of sample sequences. Selected frames have been overlaid with both the tracking result (solid ellipse) and the ground truth head location (dashed ellipse). Image contrast has been reduced to emphasize the ellipses. SEQ_A is showing a sample sequence in which no person is visible in the first few frames. SEQ_B represents a sample sequence with drastic global illumination changes at frame 490 and 660. SEQ_C is showing fast movements of a person at low capture rates (3fps). The head region is lost (and recovered) several times due to the low capture rate.

where $\Delta\phi_g$ and $\Delta\phi_c$ are the difference of maximum and minimum score in gradient and color respectively. If the difference is large, the ellipse's state (i.e. position and scale) is more significant than if the distance is small. Thus, if one score yields almost equal values for every state or if one score fails at all (e.g. if contour or skin-color information is poor), the other automatically gets more influence. To reduce computational costs, ellipses of a fixed aspect ratio and assumed vertical orientation are considered, accepting lower tracking scores for rotated heads. An ellipse is considered as acceptable match, if the total score Φ meets a certain threshold. For more robustness, a hysteresis function is integrated into this thresholding process.

5   Experimental Results

The system has been successfully tested in different indoor environments which were focused on scenarios related to real workshop conditions showing quite complex and cluttered backgrounds. To yield realistic results, nothing has been changed manually in the background while processing. The wall at the back contains several strong edges and a window on the left side (daylight influence).

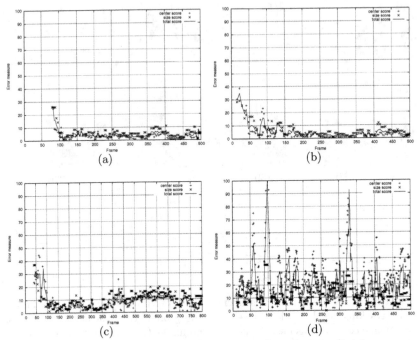

Fig. 3. Differences of the tracking results to ground truth data (total score, center score and size score), where the total score is $\varphi = 0.6\varphi_c + 0.4\varphi_s$. (a) SEQ_A (of Fig. 2) without any person in the visual field before frame 70. (b) SEQ_A time-shifted so that the operator is in the scene from the beginning. (c) SEQ_B showing drastic illumination changes at frame 490 and 660 and a slightly tilted head. (d) SEQ_C includes fast movements at a low capture rate (here 3 fps). The head region has been lost and recovered several times.

Under certain illumination conditions several parts in the scene look similar to skin color like wood or the color of the floor (see Fig. 1a,d).

The tracking results have been evaluated with respect to center position (*center score* φ_c) and size (*size score* φ_s) of the ellipse using manually acquired ground truth data as

$$\varphi_c = \left|\left|(x,y)_{gt}^T - (x,y)_{ht}^T\right|\right| , \qquad \varphi_s = \left|\left|(w,h)_{gt}^T - (w,h)_{ht}^T\right|\right| \qquad (7)$$

where $(x,y)_{gt}^T$ indicates the ellipse center of the ground truth and $(x,y)_{ht}^T$ of the headtracker (analog for φ_s with width w and height h).

Figure 2 and 3 show the results of some test sequences. SEQ_A is used to demonstrate the influence of well-initialized background models (see Fig. 3a,b). If a person is already in the scene at the beginning of the computation, the background models can not be set up correctly. However, if the person is moving only slightly, there is enough information to predict the head's location and track it robustly. The background models in combination with HLF are able to adapt misclassification due to missing initialization over time, forced by the local update learning rate. As a result of this observation, it was observed that the system is also able to continue tracking or at least to reinitialize on-the-fly even if the camera, assumed to be static, is accidentally moved. In SEQ_B there are changes in global illumination at frame 490 and 660. Fig. 3c shows that there is no significant change in the tracking results. Compared to SEQ_A, the difference between the head tracker and the ground truth is a bit higher. This is due to both, the ear protection the person is wearing altering the characteristic outline of the head, and the rotation of the head which is not considered so far. If the head movements are fast relative to the capturing rate the assumption that the difference of the head's location is limited in place and scale between two frames, does not hold (see SEQ_C in Fig. 2, third row). Thus, leading to poor tracking results as can be seen in Fig. 3d. These problems do not occur at higher frame rates (> 25 fps) and by applying appropriate model knowledge.

6   Conclusions

A vision based head tracking approach has been developed to serve as a model safety sensor in hazardous working areas. Motion, gradient and skin-color information have been combined and evaluated to realize a reliable and robust head region detection and tracking mechanism. Experiments have shown that the system is able to detect and track a human head in cluttered, real world workshop environments with changing illumination conditions. Although a static background is assumed, the system can adapt to new background situations. A time-consuming initialization or calibration step of the entire system is not necessary, however, better results can be achieved if background models can be trained without a person in the scene.

Acknowledgments. The work has been supported by the German Hauptverband der Berufsgenossenschaften (HVBG), Research Project FP 239, which is gratefully acknowledged.

References

1. Birchfield, S.: Elliptical head tracking using intensity gradients and color histograms. IEEE Conference on Computer Vision and Pattern Recognition (1998)
2. Stauffer, C., Grimson, W.E.L.: Adaptive background mixture models for real-time tracking. In: Proceedings of the IEEE Computer Science Conference on Computer Vision and Pattern Recognition (CVPR-99), Los Alamitos, IEEE (1999) 246–252
3. Power, P.W., Schoonees, J.A.: Understanding background mixture models for foreground segmentation. Imaging and Vision Computing (2002)
4. Porikli, F., Tuzel, O.: Human body tracking by adaptive background models and mean-shift analysis. Workshop on PETS (2003)
5. Harville, M.: A framework for high-level feedback to adaptive, per-pixel, mixture-of-gaussian background models. In Proc. of ECCV **3** (2002) 543–560

6. Juergens, H.W.: Erhebung anthropometrischer Maße zur Aktualisierung der DIN 33 402 - Teil 2 (2004) Schriftenreihe der BA für Arbeitsschutz und Arbeitsmedizin.
7. Chai, D., Ngan, K.N.: Face segmentation using skin color map in videophone applications. IEEE Transactions on Circuits and Systems for Video Technology 9 (1999) 551–564
8. Herpers, R., et al.: Savi: An actively controlled teleconferencing system. Image and Vision Computing **19(9)** (2001) 793–804

Stability and Local Feature Enhancement of Higher Order Nonlinear Diffusion Filtering

Stephan Didas, Joachim Weickert, and Bernhard Burgeth

Mathematical Image Analysis Group,
Faculty of Mathematics and Computer Science, Building 27,
Saarland University, 66041 Saarbrücken, Germany
{didas, weickert, burgeth}@mia.uni-saarland.de,
http://www.mia.uni-saarland.de

Abstract. This paper discusses the extension of nonlinear diffusion filters to higher derivative orders. While such processes can be useful in practice, their theoretical properties are only partly understood so far. We establish important results concerning L^2-stability and forward-backward diffusion properties which are related to well-posedness questions. Stability in the L^2-norm is proven for nonlinear diffusion filtering of arbitrary order. In the case of fourth order filtering, a qualitative description of the filtering behaviour in terms of forward and backward diffusion is given and compared to second order nonlinear diffusion. This description shows that *curvature enhancement* is possible with of fourth order nonlinear diffusion in contrast to second order filters where only edges can be enhanced.

1   Introduction

Nonlinear diffusion filtering is an established method for signal and image denoising and simplification. Starting with the pioneering work of Perona and Malik [1] in 1990, investigations have covered both the theoretical properties and the usefulness in practice of nonlinear diffusion filters and related variational methods [2,3,4,5,6,7]. With a whole spectrum of different diffusivities, the method produces smoothing effects as well as edge enhancement. The edge enhancement locally increases the first derivative and may also cause one of the major drawbacks of the method, the so-called *staircasing effect*: Regions with smooth grey value changes in the original signal or image can be turned into many segmentation-like regions. Fig. 1 (b.) shows a denoising example where this effect occurs. To circumvent these artifacts, higher derivative orders have been introduced in the diffusion process [8,9,10,11,12,13]. This allows a higher adaptivity to the local image structure and can yield piecewise linear regions. Several methods have been proposed which confirm the impression that higher order nonlinear diffusion is a very useful extension of the well-established second order methods in practice, see also Fig. 1 (c.). Unfortunately, not many theoretical properties have been established for higher-order smoothing so far.

W. Kropatsch, R. Sablatnig, and A. Hanbury (Eds.): DAGM 2005, LNCS 3663, pp. 451–458, 2005.
© Springer-Verlag Berlin Heidelberg 2005

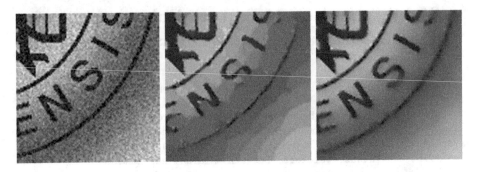

Fig. 1. (a.) *Left:* Initial noisy image. (b.) *Middle:* Second order Perona-Malik filtering. (c.) *Right:* Linear combination of second and fourth order Perona-Malik filtering.

In this paper we first consider stability properties of the higher order filtering methods. We mainly restrict ourselves to the one-dimensional case although some of the results can be carried over to higher dimensions. The main result presented here related to stability is that higher order nonlinear diffusion filtering is stable with respect to the L^2-norm. Furthermore we will see that there is an analogue to edge enhancement for fourth order nonlinear diffusion which will be called *curvature enhancement*. A closer look at various commonly used diffusivities shows that the behaviour for second and fourth order filtering is different but exhibits strong structural similarities.

This paper is organised as follows. Section 2 gives a short summary of useful properties of second order nonlinear diffusion related to this paper. In Section 3 we generalise the associated partial differential equation and its boundary conditions to higher orders and establish L^2-stability. The enhancement of local features is then discussed in Section 4 from a theoretical point of view. Section 5 displays some experiments confirming that fourth order forward and backward diffusion are practically observable effects. A summary of the main results concludes the paper with Section 6.

2   Second Order Nonlinear Diffusion

Let $f(x)$ denote a signal defined on an interval $[a, b]$. Second order nonlinear diffusion creates a filtered signal $u(x, t)$ as solution of the diffusion equation

$$\partial_t u = \partial_x \left(g \left((\partial_x u)^2 \right) \partial_x u \right) \tag{1}$$

with initial condition $u(x, 0) = f(x)$ for all $x \in [a, b]$. The velocity of diffusion is steered by the diffusivity function $g \geq 0$ depending on the square of the first derivative of the evolving signal u. Typical diffusivities g tend to 1 for small absolute values of their argument and are getting smaller for higher argument modulus. This speeds up the diffusion in almost flat regions of the signal and reduces the diffusion speed near edges. With an appropriate choice for the diffusivity g, piecewise constant filtering results are possible. We will have a closer look at some typical diffusivities in Section 4.3. To complete the PDE (1) usually homogeneous Neumann boundary conditions $\partial_x u(a) = \partial_x u(b) = 0$ are assumed. There are two reasons for the appearance of this type of boundary conditions: Firstly they can be physically motivated by the idea that the flux is zero at the image boundaries. That means no matter is entering or leaving the image during the filtering process. Secondly Neumann boundary conditions emerge in a natural way if one relates nonlinear diffusion filtering to regularisation and energy functional minimisation [14]. This approach starts with an energy functional of the form

$$E_1(u) = \int_a^b \left((u - f)^2 + \alpha \, \varphi \left((\partial_x u)^2 \right) \right) dx$$

with a penaliser φ and weight $\alpha > 0$ and searches for a minimiser u. The first term $(u - f)^2$ is minimal if u is close to the initial image f in the sense of the L^2-norm. The second term $\varphi((\partial_x u)^2)$ with $\varphi(0) = 0$ and $\varphi' \geq 0$ rewards signals whose first derivative is small, i. e. it rewards smoothness of the filtered signal. A necessary condition for a minimiser of E_1 is given by the elliptic Euler-Lagrange equation

$$\frac{u - f}{\alpha} = \partial_x \left(\varphi' \left((\partial_x u)^2 \right) \partial_x u \right) . \tag{2}$$

When no assumptions about the boundary behaviour are imposed, the derivation of the Euler-Lagrange equations leads to homogeneous Neumann boundary conditions. Interpreting the right-hand side of (2) as discretisation of a time derivative $\partial_t u$ and setting $g := \varphi'$, one ends up with the parabolic equation (1) with stopping time α. Later on we will see that this derivation helps us to find appropriate boundary conditions for the higher order diffusion filters, too. Stability in the L^2-norm and even a maximum-minimum principle belong to the properties which establish the good reputation of second order nonlinear diffusion methods [6].

3   Higher Order Nonlinear Diffusion

Higher order nonlinear diffusion filtering as considered in this paper is related to the equation

$$\partial_t u = (-1)^{m+1} \partial_x^m \left(g \left((\partial_x^m u)^2 \right) \partial_x^m u \right) \tag{3}$$

with initial condition $u(x,0) = f(x)$ for all $x \in [a, b]$. Since the highest derivative order appearing in (3) is $2m$, we will call the related process $2m$-th order nonlinear diffusion filtering. To determine appropriate boundary conditions we consider the derivation of (3) from the energy functional

$$E_m(u) = \int_a^b \left((u - f)^2 + \alpha \, \varphi \left((\partial_x^m u)^2 \right) \right) dx$$

following the train of thought of Section 2. A necessary condition for a minimiser u of this functional is given by the Euler-Lagrange equation

$$\frac{u - f}{\alpha} = (-1)^{m+1} \partial_x^m \left(g \left((\partial_x^m u)^2 \right) \partial_x^m u \right)$$

where we again set $g := \varphi'$. The corresponding natural boundary conditions are in this case

$$\partial_x^k \left(g \left((\partial_x^m u)^2 \right) \partial_x^m u \right) = 0 \quad \text{for } k \in \{0, \dots, m-1\} \tag{4}$$

for $x \in \{a, b\}$. We obtain m constraints at each boundary pixel as generalisation of the Neumann conditions for $m = 1$.

The subject of existence, uniqueness, and regularity of solutions will not be addressed in this paper. Usually a mollifier smoothing the argument of the diffusivity is required to obtain well-posedness [2,13]. Since the reasoning presented in this paper is independent of the presence of such a mollifier we omit it during the paper for simplicity. In the sequel we assume the existence, uniqueness and sufficient regularity of solutions. With these assumptions, the following proposition assures L^2-stability of the solutions:

Proposition 3.1. (L^2-Stability) *If a classical solution u of equation (3) exists which is continuously differentiable in the time variable t and $2m$ times continuously differentiable in the space variable $x \in [a, b]$, the L^2-norm of $u(\cdot, t)$ is monotonically decreasing with $t \geq 0$.*

Proof. Using the assumption that u satisfies (3) with the boundary conditions (4), integration by parts yields

$$\partial_t \left(\frac{1}{2} \int_a^b u^2 \, dx \right) = \int_a^b u \cdot (\partial_t u) \, dx$$

$$= (-1)^{m+1} \int_a^b u \cdot \partial_x^m \left(g \left((\partial_x^m u)^2 \right) \partial_x^m u \right) \, dx$$

$$= (-1)^{2m+1} \int_a^b (\partial_x^m u) \cdot g \left((\partial_x^m u)^2 \right) \cdot (\partial_x^m u) \, dx$$

$$+ \sum_{k=0}^{m-1} (-1)^{m-1-k} \left[(\partial_x^k u) \cdot \partial_x^{m-1-k} \left(g \left((\partial_x^m u)^2 \right) \partial_x^m u \right) \right]_a^b$$

$$= - \int_a^b g \left((\partial_x^m u)^2 \right) \cdot (\partial_x^m u)^2 \, dx \quad \leq \quad 0 \, .$$

This ensures that the L^2-norm of the solution may not increase with t.   □

This result guarantees that higher order nonlinear diffusion leads indeed to a simplification of the initial data.

4   Local Feature Enhancement

Though classical nonlinear diffusion simplifies signals or images, it may also enhance important local features such as edges. This section discusses higher order diffusion from this point of view.

4.1   Second Order Filtering and Edge Enhancement

To determine the possibility of edge enhancement for special diffusivities g one usually uses the the flux function $\Phi(s^2) := g(s^2)s$ to rewrite (1) yielding

$$\partial_t u = \Phi'\left((\partial_x u)^2\right)\partial_x^2 u = \left(2g'\left((\partial_x u)^2\right)(\partial_x u)^2 + g\left((\partial_x u)^2\right)\right)\partial_x^2 u \ .$$

In regions where $\Phi'((\partial_x u)^2) > 0$ this equation behaves like a forward diffusion equation while in regions with $\Phi'((\partial_x u)^2) < 0$ there is backward diffusion possible. In this regions with backward diffusion, an edge enhancing behaviour is plausible and can also be observed in practice [1].

4.2   Fourth Order Filtering

Now we take a closer look at the fourth order diffusion equation, i. e. we set $m = 2$ in (3) yielding

$$\partial_t u = -\partial_x^2\left(g\left((\partial_x^2 u)^2\right)\partial_x^2 u\right) \ .$$

We expand the right-hand side of this equation and rewrite it as

$$\partial_t u = -\left(2\left(\partial_x^3 u\right)^2 \Phi_1\left((\partial_x^2 u)^2\right)\right)\partial_x^2 u - \Phi_2\left((\partial_x^2 u)^2\right)\partial_x^4 u \qquad (5)$$

using $\Phi_1(s^2) := 2g''(s^2)s^2 + 3g'(s^2)$ and $\Phi_2(s^2) := 2g'(s^2)s^2 + g(s^2)$. Analogue to the second order case our argumentation is that (5) locally behaves similar to the linear equation $\partial_t u = -a\partial_x^2 u - b\partial_x^4 u$ if the signs of the factors a and b are equal to the signs of Φ_1 and Φ_2. For $\Phi_1((\partial_x^2 u)^2) < 0$ we expect some second order forward diffusion influence on the solution, whereas $\Phi_1((\partial_x^2 u)^2) > 0$ leads to second order backward diffusion. Vice versa, $\Phi_2((\partial_x^2 u)^2) > 0$ ensures fourth order forward diffusion, and $\Phi_2((\partial_x^2 u)^2) < 0$ fourth order backward diffusion. It should be mentioned that Φ_2 always coincides with the function Φ in the second order case presented in Section 4.1. Also for orders higher than four, the sign of this function determines the diffusion property (forward or backward) of the highest order term which implies a certain similarity in the behaviour of several filtering orders. The main difference is the argument: Φ depends on the squared m-th derivative for $2m$-th order filtering.

4.3   Application to Commonly Used Diffusivities

After showing the general approach for fourth order diffusion in the last section we now apply it to several diffusivities commonly used in practice to describe their characteristic behaviour. In the following the diffusivities are ordered according to their forward-backward diffusion properties:

– **Forward Diffusion:** The diffusivity related to the regularisation approach by Charbonnier et al. [3] is given by $g(s^2) = \left(1 + \frac{s^2}{\lambda^2}\right)^{-\frac{1}{2}}$ and is known to perform forward diffusion in the second order case. By computing

$$\Phi_1(s^2) = -\tfrac{3}{2\lambda^2}\left(1 + \tfrac{s^2}{\lambda^2}\right)^{-\frac{5}{2}} < 0 \quad \text{and} \quad \Phi_2(s^2) = \left(1 + \tfrac{s^2}{\lambda^2}\right)^{-\frac{3}{2}} > 0$$

we see that also the fourth order Charbonnier diffusion always performs forward diffusion. With the observation $(\varepsilon^2 + s^2)^{-\frac{1}{2}} = \varepsilon\left(1 + \frac{s^2}{\varepsilon^2}\right)^{-\frac{1}{2}}$ it is clear that regularised TV flow [15] behaves in the same way.
– **Boundary Case:** TV flow [5] comes from the diffusivity $g(s^2) = \frac{1}{|s|}$. At all points where the argument s is nonzero we have $\Phi_1(s^2) = \Phi_2(s^2) = 0$ which legitimates to consider TV flow as the boundary case between forward and backward diffusion.
– **Forward and Backward Diffusion:** The diffusivity $g(s^2) = \left(1 + \frac{s^2}{\lambda^2}\right)^{-1}$ proposed by Perona and Malik [1] leads to the conditions

$$\Phi_1(s^2) = \tfrac{1}{\lambda^4}\left(1 + \tfrac{s^2}{\lambda^2}\right)^{-3}(s^2 - 3\lambda^2) < 0 \quad \Longleftrightarrow \quad |s| < \sqrt{3}\lambda$$

$$\Phi_2(s^2) = \left(1 + \tfrac{s^2}{\lambda^2}\right)^{-2}\left(1 - \tfrac{s^2}{\lambda^2}\right) \quad > 0 \quad \Longleftrightarrow \quad |s| < \lambda .$$

This really displays the adaptive nature of this diffusivity: Depending on the parameter λ, the curvature $|\partial_x^2 u|$ leads to forward or backward diffusion. New to the fourth order case is the presence of two conditions and the possibility that only one of them holds, namely in regions where $\lambda < |\partial_x^2 u| < \sqrt{3}\lambda$. Similar conditions hold for the diffusivity $g(s^2) = \exp\left(-\frac{s^2}{2\lambda^2}\right)$ also proposed by Perona and Malik [1].
– **Backward Diffusion:** The balanced forward-backward diffusivity [4] defined by $g(s^2) = \frac{1}{s^2}$ leads to $\Phi_1(s^2) = s^{-4} > 0$ and $\Phi_2(s^2) = -s^{-2} < 0$ which implies that it always performs backward diffusion. As for total variation diffusivity we also suppose that the argument is nonzero here.

We conclude that even in the fourth order case there are diffusivities covering the whole spectrum from pure forward to pure backward diffusion.

5   Numerical Examples

After the theoretical description of fourth order diffusion, in this section we show results of Perona-Malik filtering in one dimension with different orders.

For $2m$-th order filtering with $g(s^2) = \left(1 + \frac{s^2}{\lambda^2}\right)^{-1}$ the parameter λ is chosen such that there are regions with $|\partial_x^m u| > \sqrt{3}\lambda$ where backward diffusion appears. Fig. 2 shows the initial signal and some filtering results. While second order filtering yields enhancement of edges, the fourth order filtering result tends to be piecewise linear with enhanced curvature at corner points. This observation for fourth order filtering is further affirmed by the almost piecewise constant derivative approximation of the filtering result also shown in Fig. 2.

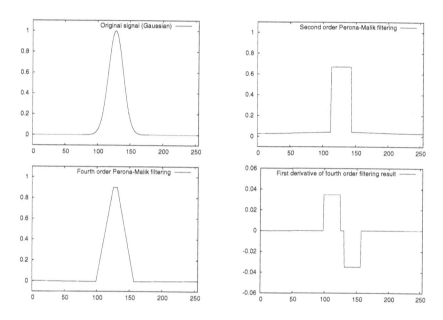

Fig. 2. *Top left:* Gaussian signal. *Top right:* Second order Perona-Malik filtering. *Bottom left:* Fourth order Perona-Malik filtering. *Bottom right:* First derivative of fourth order filtering result.

6   Conclusions

In this paper we have investigated theoretical properties of higher order nonlinear diffusion filters. For the first time we have presented stability considerations for a class of nonlinear diffusion filters related to variational methods. Furthermore, an argumentation in terms of forward and backward diffusion has been given which can be helpful to understand the behaviour of fourth order nonlinear diffusion filters. Numerical examples with one-dimensional data show that higher order filters can be used to enhance important data features. We have seen that in correspondence to the edge enhancement of second order diffusion, fourth order filters may act curvature enhancing, which is in accordance with the theoretical considerations presented in this paper.

A theoretical generalisation to orders higher than four and new practically usable diffusivities which are especially designed for higher orders are two questions of our ongoing research.

Acknowledgements. We gratefully acknowledge partly funding by the *Deutsche Forschungsgemeinschaft (DFG)*, project WE 2602/2-2.

References

1. Perona, P., Malik, J.: Scale space and edge detection using anisotropic diffusion. IEEE Transactions on Pattern Analysis and Machine Intelligence **12** (1990) 629–639
2. Catté, F., Loins, P.L., Morel, J.M., Coll, T.: Image selective smoothing and edge detection by nonlinear diffusion. SIAM Journal on Numerical Analysis **29** (1992) 182–193
3. Charbonnier, P., Blanc-Féraud, L., Aubert, G., Barlaud, M.: Deterministic edge-preserving regularization in computed imaging. IEEE Transactions on Image Processing **6** (1997) 298–311
4. Keeling, S.L., Stollberger, R.: Nonlinear anisotropic diffusion filtering for multiscale edge enhancement. Inverse Problems **18** (2002) 175–190
5. Andreu, F., Ballester, C., Caselles, V., Mazón, J.M.: Minimizing total variation flow. Differential and Integral Equations **14** (2001) 321–360
6. Weickert, J.: Anisotropic Diffusion in Image Processing. B. G. Teubner, Stuttgart (1998)
7. Aubert, G., Kornprobst, P.: Mathematical Problems in Image Processing: Partial Differential Equations and the Calculus of Variations. Volume 147 of Applied Mathematical Sciences. Springer, New York (2002)
8. You, Y.L., Kaveh, M.: Fourth-order partial differential equations for noise removal. IEEE Transactions on Image Processing **9** (2000) 1723–1730
9. Chan, T., Marquina, A., Mulet, P.: High-order total variation-based image restoration. SIAM Journal of Scientific Computing **22** (2000) 503–516
10. Lysaker, M., Lundervold, A., Tai, X.C.: Noise removal using fourth-order partial differential equation with applications to medical magnetic resonance images in space and time. IEEE Transactions on Image Processing **12** (2003) 1579–1590
11. Scherzer, O.: Denoising with higher order derivatives of bounded variation and an application to parameter estimation. Computing **60** (1998) 1–27
12. Tumblin, J., Turk, G.: LCIS: A boundary hierarchy for detail-preserving contrast reduction. In: SIGGRAPH '99: Proceedings of the 26th Annual Conference on Computer Graphics and Interactive Techniques, ACM Press/Addison-Wesley (1999) 83–90
13. Greer, J.B., Bertozzi, A.L.: H^1 solutions of a class of fourth order nonlinear equations for image processing. Discrete and Continuous Dynamical Systems **10** (2004) 349–368
14. Scherzer, O., Weickert, J.: Relations between regularization and diffusion filtering. Journal of Mathematical Imaging and Vision **12** (2000) 43–63
15. Feng, X., Prohl, A.: Analysis of total variation flow and its finite element approximations. ESAIM: Mathematical Modelling and Numerical Analysis **37** (2003) 533–556

Estimation of Geometric Entities and Operators from Uncertain Data*

Christian Perwass, Christian Gebken, and Gerald Sommer

Institut für Informatik, CAU Kiel,
Christian-Albrechts-Platz 4, 24118 Kiel, Germany
{chp, chg, gs}@ks.informatik.uni-kiel.de

Abstract. In this text we show how points, point pairs, lines, planes, circles, spheres, and rotation, translation and dilation operators and their uncertainty can be evaluated from uncertain data in a unified manner using the Geometric Algebra of conformal space. This extends previous work by Förstner et al. [3] from points, lines and planes to non-linear entities and operators, while keeping the linearity of the estimation method. We give a theoretical description of our approach and show the results of some synthetic experiments.

1 Introduction

In Computer Vision applications uncertain data occurs almost invariably. Appropriate methods to deal with this uncertainty do therefore play an important role. In this text we discuss the estimation of geometric entities and operators from uncertain data in a unified mathematical framework, namely Geometric Algebra. In particular, we will show that evaluating points, lines, planes, circle, spheres and their covariance matrices from a set of uncertain points can be done in much the same way as the evaluation of rotation, translation and dilation operators with corresponding covariance matrices. Using error propagation, further calculations can be performed with these uncertain entities, while keeping track of the uncertainty. This text builds on previous works by Förstner et al. [3] and Heuel [5] where uncertain points, lines and planes were treated in a unified manner. Perwass & Sommer previously discussed the linear estimation of rotation operators in Geometric Algebra [11], albeit without taking account of uncertainty. In [8] the description of uncertain circles and 2D-conics in Geometric Algebra was first discussed. The stratification of Euclidean, projective and affine spaces in Geometric Algebra, has been previously discussed in [12]. In this text, it is shown how the Geometric Algebra of the conformal space of 3D-Euclidean space can be used to deal with uncertain projective geometry and uncertain kinematics in a unified way. In particular, we will concentrate on the estimation of geometric entities and operators from uncertain data.

The structure of this text is as follows. First we give short introductions to Geometric Algebra, error propagation and the Gauss-Helmert model. Then we

---

* This work has been supported by DFG grant SO-320/2-3.

W. Kropatsch, R. Sablatnig, and A. Hanbury (Eds.): DAGM 2005, LNCS 3663, pp. 459–467, 2005.
© Springer-Verlag Berlin Heidelberg 2005

Table 1. Entities and their algebra basis. Note that the operators are multivectors of mixed grade

Entity	Grade	No.	Basis Elements
Point X	1	5	$e_1, e_2, e_3, e_\infty, e_o$
Point Pair $X \wedge Y$	2	10	$e_{23}, e_{31}, e_{12}, e_{1o}, e_{2o}, e_{3o}, e_{1\infty}, e_{2\infty}, e_{3\infty}, e_{o\infty}$
Line $X \wedge Y \wedge e_\infty$	3	6	$e_{23\infty}, e_{31\infty}, e_{12\infty}, e_{1o\infty}, e_{2o\infty}, e_{3o\infty}$
Circle $X \wedge Y \wedge Z$	3	10	$e_{23\infty}, e_{31\infty}, e_{12\infty}, e_{23o}, e_{31o}, e_{12o}, e_{1o\infty}, e_{2o\infty}, e_{3o\infty}, e_{123}$
Plane $X \wedge Y \wedge Z \wedge e_\infty$	4	4	$e_{123\infty}, e_{23o\infty}, e_{31o\infty}, e_{12o\infty}$
Sphere $X \wedge Y \wedge Z \wedge U$	4	5	$e_{123\infty}, e_{123o}, e_{23o\infty}, e_{31o\infty}, e_{12o\infty}$
Rotor R	0,2	4	$1, e_{23}, e_{31}, e_{12}$
Translator T	0,2	4	$1, e_{1\infty}, e_{2\infty}, e_{3\infty}$
Dilator D	0,2	2	$1, e_{o\infty}$
Motor RT	0,2,4	8	$1, e_{23}, e_{31}, e_{12}, e_{1\infty}, e_{2\infty}, e_{3\infty}, e_{123\infty}$
Gen. Rotor $T R \tilde{T}$	0,2	7	$1, e_{23}, e_{31}, e_{12}, e_{1\infty}, e_{2\infty}, e_{3\infty}$

combine these methods to show how the various objects can be estimated. We conclude the text with some synthetic experiments and conclusions.

2   Geometric Algebra

For a detailed introduction to Geometric Algebra see e.g. [10,4]. Here we can only give a short overview. Geometric Algebra is an associative, graded algebra, whereby the algebra product is called *geometric product*. The Geometric Algebra over a n-dimensional Euclidean vector space $\mathbb{R}^n$ has dimension 2^n and is denoted by $\mathbb{G}(\mathbb{R}^n)$ or simply $\mathbb{G}_n$. Elements of different grade of the algebra can be constructed through the *outer product* of linearly independent vectors. For example, if $\{a_i\} \in \mathbb{R}^n$ are a set of k linearly independent vectors, then $A_{\langle k \rangle} := a_1 \wedge \ldots \wedge a_k$ is an element of $\mathbb{G}_n$ of grade k, which is called a *blade*, where $\wedge$ denotes the outer product. A general element of the algebra, called *multivector*, can always be expressed as a linear combination of blades of possibly different grades. Blades can be used to represent geometric entities. To combine projective geometry and kinematics we need to consider the Geometric Algebra of the (projective) *conformal space* of 3D-Euclidean space (cf. [10]). The embedding function $\mathcal{K}$ is defined as $\mathcal{K} : x \in \mathbb{R}^3 \mapsto x + \frac{1}{2} x^2 e_\infty + e_o \in \mathbb{R}^{4,1}$. The basis of $\mathbb{R}^{4,1}$ can be written as $\{e_1, e_2, e_3, e_\infty, e_o\}$. The various geometric entities that can be represented by blades in $\mathbb{G}_{4,1}$ are shown in table 1. In this table $X, Y, Z, U, V \in \mathbb{R}^{4,1}$ are embeddings of points $x, y, z, u, v \in \mathbb{R}^3$, respectively, and the $e_{ij} \equiv e_i \wedge e_j$ etc. denote the algebra basis elements of an entity.

Apart from representing geometric entities by blades, it is also possible to define operators in Geometric Algebra. The class of operators we are particularly interested in are *versors*. A versor $V \in \mathbb{G}_n$ is a multivector that satisfies the following two conditions: $V\tilde{V} = 1$ and for any blade $A_{\langle k \rangle} \in \mathbb{G}_n$, $V A_{\langle k \rangle} \tilde{V}$ is also of grade k, i.e. a versor is *grade preserving*. The expression $\tilde{V}$ denotes the *reverse* of V. The reverse operation changes the sign of the constituent blade elements depending on their grade, which has an effect similar to complex conjugation in quaternions. The most interesting versors for our purposes in conformal space are rotation operators (rotors), translation operators (translators) and scaling operators (dilators).

If $\{E_i\}$ denotes the 2^n-dimensional algebra basis of $\mathbb{G}_n$, then a multivector $A \in \mathbb{G}_n$ can be written as $A = \mathsf{a}^i\, E_i$, where a^i denotes the ith component of a vector $\mathsf{a} \in \mathbb{R}^{2^n}$ and a sum over the repeated index i is implied. We will use this Einstein summation convention also in the following. If $B = \mathsf{b}^i\, E_i$ and $C = \mathsf{c}^i\, E_i$, then the components of C in the algebra equation $C = A \circ B$ can be evaluated via $\mathsf{c}^k = \mathsf{a}^i\, \mathsf{b}^j\, g^k{}_{ij}$. Here $\circ$ is a placeholder for an algebra product and $g^k{}_{ij} \in \mathbb{R}^{2^n \times 2^n \times 2^n}$ is a tensor encoding this product.

If we define the matrices $\mathsf{U}, \mathsf{V} \in \mathbb{R}^{2^n \times 2^n}$ as $\mathsf{U}(\mathsf{a}) := \alpha^i\, g^k{}_{ij}$ and $\mathsf{V}(\mathsf{b}) := \beta^j\, g^k{}_{ij}$, then $\mathsf{c} = \mathsf{U}(\mathsf{a})\, \mathsf{b} = \mathsf{V}(\mathsf{b})\, \mathsf{a}$. Therefore, we can define an isomorphism Φ, such that for $A, B \in \mathbb{G}_n$, $\Phi(A) \in \mathbb{R}^{2^n}$ and $\Phi(A \circ B) = \mathsf{U}(\Phi(A))\, \Phi(B) = \mathsf{V}(\Phi(B))\, \Phi(A)$, where $\circ$ is a placeholder for an algebra product. This isomorphism allows us to apply standard numerical algorithms to Geometric Algebra equations. We can also reduce the complexity of the equations considerably by only mapping those components of multivectors that are actually needed. In the following we therefore assume that Φ maps to the minimum number of components necessary.

3   Stochastic

In this section we give short descriptions of error propagation and the Gauss-Helmert model, which will be needed for the evaluation of multivectors from uncertain data. The *error propagation* we consider here is based on the assumption that the uncertainty of a (vector valued) measurement can be modeled by a Gaussian distribution. Hence, the probability density function of a random vector variable is fully described by a mean vector and a covariance matrix. Error propagation is a method to evaluate the mean and covariance of a function of random vector variables. In particular, this allows us to evaluate the mean and covariance of algebra products between multivector valued random variables. For a detailed introduction see [6,7].

For example, we have to apply error propagation to the embedding of Euclidean vectors in conformal space. Let $\underline{a} \in \mathbb{R}^3$ be a Euclidean random vector variable with covariance matrix $\Sigma_{a,a}$, and $\underline{A} \in \mathbb{R}^{4,1}$ be defined by $\underline{A} := \mathcal{K}(\underline{a})$. It may then be shown that $\bar{A} = \mathcal{E}[\mathcal{K}(\underline{a})] = \bar{a} + \frac{1}{2}\bar{a}^2\, e_\infty + e_o + \frac{1}{2}\mathrm{tr}(\Sigma_{a,a})\, e_\infty$. Typically the trace of $\Sigma_{a,a}$ is negligible, which leaves us with $\bar{A} = \mathcal{K}(\bar{a})$. If we denote the Jacobi matrix of $\mathcal{K}$ evaluated at $\bar{a}$ by $\mathsf{J}_\mathcal{K}(\bar{a})$, then the error propagation equation for the covariance matrix can be written as $\Sigma_{A,A} = \mathsf{J}_\mathcal{K}(\bar{a})\, \Sigma_{a,a}\, \mathsf{J}_\mathcal{K}^\mathsf{T}(\bar{a})$.

The *Gauss-Helmert* model was introduced by Helmert in 1872 as the general case of least squares adjustment. It is also called the *mixed model* [6]. The Gauss-Helmert model is a linear, stochastic model. The idea is to find the smallest adjustment to the data points, such that a valid parameter vector exists.

Mathematically this is expressed as follows. Given is a set of M data vectors $\{b_i\}$ with corresponding covariance matrices Σ_{b_i,b_i}. The goal is to find a parameter vector p, such that a given, vector valued constraint function g satisfies $g(b_i, p) = 0$ for all i. Furthermore, the set of valid parameter vectors is constraint by a function h, which has to satisfy $h(p) = 0$. Since the Gauss-Helmert model is linear, the functions g and h have to be linearized. For this purpose it is assumed that the true data point b_i is given by the current estimate $\hat{b}_i$ plus an adjustment Δb_i, and similarly for the parameter vector. That is, $b_i = \hat{b}_i + \Delta b$ and $p = \hat{p} + \Delta p$, which implies that an initial estimate of the parameter vector has to be known, before the Gauss-Helmert method can be applied. Substituting these expressions for b_i and p in the constraint equation $g(b_i, p) = 0$ and considering only its Taylor expansion up to first order results in $U_i \Delta p + V_i \Delta b_i = c_{g_i}$, where $U_i := (\partial_p g)(\hat{b}_i, \hat{p})$, $V_i := (\partial_{b_i} g)(\hat{b}_i, \hat{p})$ and $c_{g_i} := -g(\hat{b}_i, \hat{p})$. The constraint function h is linearized in a similar way leading to the constraint equation $H^T \Delta p = c_h$, where $H^T := (\partial_p h)(\hat{p})$ and $c_h := -h(\hat{p})$.

We now try to solve for Δb_i and Δp such that $\Delta b_i^T \Sigma_{b_i,b_i} \Delta b_i$ is minimized and the linearized constraint equations are satisfied for all i. This may be done using the method of Lagrange multipliers. This leads to the following equation system.

$$\begin{pmatrix} N & H \\ H^T & 0 \end{pmatrix} \begin{pmatrix} \Delta p \\ m \end{pmatrix} = \begin{pmatrix} c_n \\ c_h \end{pmatrix}, \tag{1}$$

where m is a Lagrange multiplier vector, $N := \sum_{i=1}^{M} U_i^T (V_i \Sigma_{b_i,b_i} V_i^T)^+ U_i$ and $c_n := \sum_{i=1}^{M} U_i^T (V_i \Sigma_{b_i,b_i} V_i^T)^+ c_{g_i}$. The vector Δp can be evaluated directly equation (1), while Δb_i has to be evaluated by substituting Δp into the equation

$$\Delta b_i = \Sigma_{b_i,b_i} V_i^T (V_i \Sigma_{b_i,b_i} V_i^T)^+ (c_{g_i} - U_i \Delta p). \tag{2}$$

The new estimates for b_i and p are then given by $\hat{p}' = \hat{p} + \Delta p$ and $\hat{b}_i' = \hat{b}_i + \Delta b_i$. If the constraint functions g and h are linear, then these new estimates are the best linear unbiased estimators for b_i and p, as is for example shown in [6,7]. If the constraint functions are not linear, then this is a step in an iterative estimation procedure.

4   Estimation of Multivectors

In this section we show how Geometric Algebra offers a unified framework to derive the constraint equations for geometrical problems, so that the Gauss-Helmert method can be applied. Since the standard algebra operations between multivectors can be mapped to bilinear functions, the estimation of all algebra elements is basically the same. This means in particular that operators as well as geometric entities are represented by vectors and their estimation is therefore very similar. In order to apply the Gauss-Helmert estimation, we need to define a constraint function that relates the parameter vector and the data vectors, as well as a constraint function for the parameter vector alone. Furthermore, we need to obtain an initial estimate of the parameter vector. Part of the constraints is that we only use those multivector components that can be non-zero in the particular elements we consider. For example, table 1 shows that for a line we only need to consider a subset of those components necessary for a circle, even though both are blades of grade 3.

Let $P \in \mathbb{G}_{4,1}$ represent the geometric entity that is to be estimated and $B_n \in \mathbb{G}_{4,1}$ the nth data point, then $g(B_n, P) = B_n \wedge P$, because $B_n \wedge P = 0$ if and only if B_n lies on P. Note that this constraint is only valid if B_n and/or P represents a point. For example, we could evaluate the best line (P) through a set of points (B_n), but also the best point (P) that lies on a set of lines (B_n). Mapping the g-constraint with Φ gives $\Phi(B_n \wedge P) = \mathsf{b}_n^i \, \mathsf{p}^j \, \mathsf{O}^k{}_{ij}$, where $\mathsf{O}^k{}_{ij}$ encodes the appropriate outer product.

The magnitude of $B_n \wedge P$ is only proportional to the Euclidean distance between a point B_n and the element represented by P, if P represents a point, line or plane. If P represents a point pair, circle or sphere, this is not the case, in general. However, the closer points lie to these entities, the better proportionality is satisfied. In 2D-Euclidean space the fitting of a circle P to a set of points $\{B_n\}$ with the constraint $B_n \wedge P = 0$, is equivalent to the well known algebraic fitting of circles [2]. However, $B_n \wedge P = 0$ is valid independent of the embedding dimension, which allows us to readily extract the algebraic constraint equations for circles in 3D-Euclidean space.

The constraints on P alone depend on the grade of P. If P is of grade 1 or 4, i.e. it represents a point, a plane or a sphere, then the only constraint is that the scale of P is fixed. This is needed, since we are working in a projective space and thus all scaled, non-zero versions of P represent the same geometric entity. If $\mathsf{p} = \Phi(P)$, then this constraint can be written as $h_1(\mathsf{p}) = \mathsf{p}^\mathsf{T} \mathsf{p} - 1$, such that $h_1(\mathsf{p}) = 0$ if $\|\mathsf{p}\| = 1$.

If P represents a point pair (grade 2), a line (grade 3) or a circle (grade 3), then there is an additional constraint that ensures that P is in fact a blade. Recall that a blade of grade k is the outer product of k vectors. However, if $k = 2$ or $k = 3$, *not* all linear combinations of the respective algebra basis elements form a blade. The constraints that ensure that P is a blade, are the Plücker constraints. In Geometric Algebra these constraints can be expressed by the equation $P \wedge P = 0$ if P is of grade 2 and $P^* \wedge P^* = 0$ if P is of grade 3, where P^* denotes the dual of P. The dual operation in Geometric Algebra is the geometric product with a constant element of the algebra (cf. [10]). Mapped with Φ we thus obtain the constraint equation $h_2(\mathsf{p}) = \Phi(P^* \wedge P^*) = \mathsf{p}^p \, \mathsf{p}^q \, \mathsf{D}^i{}_p \, \mathsf{D}^j{}_q \, \mathsf{O}^k{}_{ij}$, if P is of grade 3. Here $\mathsf{D}^i{}_p$ encodes the dual operation.

For versors $V \in \mathbb{G}_{4,1}$ the constraint functions are different. Suppose $A_n, B_n \in \mathbb{G}_{4,1}$ represent pairs of geometric entities of the same type. The problem now is to find the V that best satisfies $B_n = V A_n \tilde{V}$. Since $V \tilde{V} = 1$, this can also be written as $V A_n - B_n V = 0$. Hence, $g(B_n, V) = V A_n - B_n V$. The constraint function on V alone is $h(V) = V \tilde{V} - 1$, which is zero, if V is a versor. Mapping the latter constraint with Φ gives $g(\mathsf{b}_n, \mathsf{v}) = \Phi(V A_n - B_n V) = \mathsf{v}^i \, (\mathsf{a}_n^j \, \mathsf{G}^k{}_{ij} - \mathsf{b}_n^j \, \mathsf{G}^k{}_{ji})$, where $\mathsf{G}^k{}_{ij}$ encodes the appropriate geometric product. The h-constraint be-

Table 2. Jacobi matrices used in Gauss-Helmert estimation for different entities. A repeated index in a product implies summation over its range. The first index of a tensor denotes the row in matrix representation.

Entity	U_n	V	H_1^T	H_2^T
Point Pair	$b_n^i\, O^k{}_{ij}$	$p^j\, O^k{}_{ij}$	$2\, p^j$	$2\, p^j\, O^k{}_{ij}$
Line, Circle				$2\, p^q\, D^i{}_p\, D^j{}_q\, O^k{}_{ij}$
Point, Plane, Sphere				n/a
Versor	$a_n^j\, G^k{}_{ij} - b_n^j\, G^k{}_{ji}$	$-v^i\, G^k{}_{ji}$	$2\, v^q\, R^j{}_q\, G^k{}_{ij}$	n/a

comes $h(v) = \Phi(V\tilde{V} - 1) = v^i\, v^q\, R^j{}_q\, G^k{}_{ij} - w^k$, where $R^j{}_p$ encodes the reverse operation and w^k is zero everywhere apart from the entry representing the scalar component, which is unity.

Table 2 summarizes the Jacobi matrices of the constraint equations for the various entities, as needed in equation 1 in the Gauss-Helmert estimation. Matrices H_1^T and H_2^T have to be combined column-wise to result in H^T. These Jacobi matrices have to be evaluated for current estimates of the parameter and data vectors as described in section 3. The contractions of the algebra product tensors $O^k{}_{ij}$ and $G^k{}_{ij}$ with vectors can, for example, be evaluated with the software *CLUCalc* [9]. An initial estimate of the parameter vector, i.e. p or v, is given by the right null space that the respective set of U_n matrices have in common. This can be evaluated by finding the right null space of $U := \sum_n U_n^\mathsf{T} U_n$ using, for example, a singular value decomposition (SVD). Note that the matrices U_n and V for points, lines and planes as given in table 2 are equivalent to the matrices S, Π and Γ as defined by Förstner et al. in [3].

5   Experiments and Conclusions

To show the quality of the proposed estimation method of geometric entities and operators, we present two synthetic experiments. In the first experiment we fit 3D-circles to uncertain data points and in the second experiment we estimate general rotations between two 3D-point clouds.

To generate the uncertain data to which a circle is to be fitted, we first create a "true" circle C of radius one, oriented arbitrarily in 3D-space. We then randomly select N points $\{a_n \in \mathbb{R}^3\}$ on the true circle within a given angle range. For each of these points a covariance matrix Σ_{a_n,a_n} is generated randomly, within a certain range. For each of the a_n, Σ_{a_n,a_n} is used to generate a Gaussian distributed random error vector r_n. The data points $\{b_n\}$ with corresponding covariance matrices Σ_{b_n,b_n} are then given by $b_n = a_n + r_n$ and $\Sigma_{b_n,b_n} = \Sigma_{a_n,a_n}$. The standard deviation of the set $\{\|r_n\|\}$ will be denoted by σ_r. For each angle range, 30 sets of true points $\{a_n\}$ and for each of these sets, 40 sets of data points $\{b_n\}$ were generated.

A circle is then fitted to each of the data point sets. We will denote a circle estimate by $\hat{C}$ and the shortest vector between a true point a_n and

Table 3. Results of circle estimation for SVD method (SVD) and Gauss-Helmert method (GH)s

	Angle	$\bar{\Delta}_\Sigma$ ($\bar{\sigma}_\Sigma$)		$\bar{\Delta}_E$ ($\bar{\sigma}_E$)	
σ_r	Range	SVD	GH	SVD	GH
	10°	2.13 (0.90)	1.26 (0.52)	0.047 (0.015)	0.030 (0.009)
0.07	60°	1.20 (0.44)	0.92 (0.31)	0.033 (0.010)	0.028 (0.009)
	180°	1.38 (0.56)	0.97 (0.36)	0.030 (0.009)	0.025 (0.008)
	10°	2.17 (0.90)	1.15 (0.51)	0.100 (0.032)	0.057 (0.019)
0.15	60°	1.91 (0.99)	1.35 (0.68)	0.083 (0.033)	0.069 (0.028)
	180°	1.21 (0.44)	0.90 (0.30)	0.070 (0.022)	0.058 (0.018)

Table 4. Result of general rotation estimation for standard method (Std), SVD method (SVD) and Gauss-Helmert method (GH).

	$\bar{\Delta}_\Sigma$ ($\bar{\sigma}_\Sigma$)			$\bar{\Delta}_E$ ($\bar{\sigma}_E$)		
σ_r	Std	SVD	GH	Std	SVD	GH
0.09	1.44 (0.59)	1.47 (0.63)	0.68 (0.22)	0.037 (0.011)	0.037 (0.012)	0.024 (0.009)
0.18	1.47 (0.62)	1.53 (0.67)	0.72 (0.25)	0.078 (0.024)	0.079 (0.026)	0.052 (0.019)

$\hat{C}$ by d_n. For each $\hat{C}$ we then evaluate two quality measures: the Euclidean RMS distance $\delta_E := \sqrt{\sum_n d_n^T d_n / N}$ and the Mahalanobis RMS distance $\delta_\Sigma := \sqrt{\sum_n d_n^T \Sigma_{a_n,a_n}^{-1} d_n / N}$. The latter measure uses the covariance matrices as local metrics for the distance measure. δ_Σ is a unit-less value that is > 1, $= 1$ or < 1 if d_n lies outside, on or inside the standard deviation error ellipsoid represented by Σ_{a_n,a_n}. For each true point set, the mean and standard deviation of the δ_E and δ_Σ over all data point sets is denoted by Δ_E, σ_E and Δ_Σ, σ_Σ, respectively. Finally, we take the mean of the Δ_E, σ_E and Δ_Σ, σ_Σ over all true point sets, which are then denoted by $\bar{\Delta}_E$, $\bar{\sigma}_E$ and $\bar{\Delta}_\Sigma$, $\bar{\sigma}_\Sigma$. These quality measures are evaluated for the circle estimates by the SVD and the Gauss-Helmert (GH) method. In table 3 the results for different values of σ_r and different angle ranges is given. In all cases 10 data points are used.

It can be seen that for different levels of noise (σ_r) the Gauss-Helmert method always performs better in the mean quality and the mean standard deviation than the SVD method. It is also interesting to note that the Euclidean measure $\bar{\Delta}_E$ is approximately doubled when σ_r is doubled, while the "stochastic" measure $\bar{\Delta}_\Sigma$, only increases slightly. This is to be expected, since an increase in σ_r implies larger values in the Σ_{a_n,a_n}. Note that $\bar{\Delta}_\Sigma < 1$ implies that the estimated circle lies mostly inside the standard deviation ellipsoids of the true points.

For the evaluation of a general rotor, the "true" points $\{a_n\}$ are a cloud of Gaussian distributed points about the origin with standard deviation 0.8.

These points are then transformed by a "true" general rotation R. Given the set $\{a'_n\}$ of rotated true points, noise is added to generate the data points $\{b_n\}$ in just the same way as for the circle. For each of 40 sets of true points, 40 data point sets are generated and a general rotor $\hat{R}$ is estimated. Using $\hat{R}$ the true points are rotated to give $\{\hat{a}'_n\}$. The distance vectors $\{d_n\}$ are then defined as $d_n := a'_n - \hat{a}'_n$. From the $\{d_n\}$ the same quality measures as for the circle are evaluated. In table 4 we compare the results of the Gauss-Helmert (GH) method with the initial SVD estimate and a standard approach (Std) described in [1]. Since the quality measures did not give significantly different results for rotation angles between 3 and 160 degrees, the mean of the respective values over all rotation angles are shown in the table. The rotation axis always points along the z-axis and is moved one unit away from the origin along the x-axis. In all experiments 10 points are used. It can be seen that for different levels of noise (σ_r) the Gauss-Helmert method always performs significantly better in the mean quality and the mean standard deviation than the other two. Just as for the circle the Euclidean measure $\bar{\Delta}_E$ is approximately doubled when σ_r is doubled, while the "stochastic" measure $\bar{\Delta}_\Sigma$, only increases slightly. Note that $\bar{\Delta}_\Sigma < 1$ implies that the points $\{\hat{a}'_n\}$ lie mostly inside the standard deviation ellipsoids of the $\{a'_n\}$.

In conclusion it was shown by the synthetic experiments that accounting for the uncertainty in the data when estimating geometric and kinematic entities, does improve the results. Geometric Algebra offers a unifying framework where the constraints on geometric and kinematic entities can be expressed succinctly and dimension independently in such a way that linear estimation procedures may be applied. We believe that these properties can be of great value for many applications in Computer Vision.

References

1. K. S. Arun, T. S. Huang, and S. D. Blostein. Least-squares fitting of two 3-d point sets. *PAMI*, 9(5):698–700, 1987.
2. F.L. Bookstein. Fitting conic sections to scattered data. *Comp. Graph. Image Proc.*, 9:56–71, 1979.
3. W. Förstner, A. Brunn, and S. Heuel. Statistically testing uncertain geometric relations. In G. Sommer, N. Krüger, and C. Perwass, editors, *Mustererkennung 2000*, Informatik Aktuell, pages 17–26, Springer, Berlin, 2000.
4. D. Hestenes and G. Sobczyk. *Clifford Algebra to Geometric Calculus: A Unified Language for Mathematics and Physics*. Reidel, Dordrecht, 1984.
5. S. Heuel. *Uncertain Projective Geometry*, volume 3008 of *LNCS*. Springer, 2004.
6. K.-R. Koch. *Parameter Estimation and Hypothesis Testing in Linear Models*. Springer, 1997.
7. E.M. Mikhail and F. Ackermann. *Observations and Least Squares*. University Press of America, Lanham, MD20706, USA, 1976.
8. C. Perwass and W. Förstner. Uncertain geometry with circles, spheres and conics. In R. Klette, R. Kozera, L. Noakes, and J. Weickert, editors, *Geometric Properties from Incomplete Data*. Kluwer Academic Publ., to be publ. 2005.
9. C. Perwass, C. Gebken, and D. Grest. CLUCalc. http://www.clucalc.info/, 2004.

10. C. Perwass and D. Hildenbrand. Aspects of geometric algebra in Euclidean, projective and conformal space. Technical Report Number 0310, CAU Kiel, Institut für Informatik, September 2003.
11. C. Perwass and G. Sommer. Numerical evaluation of versors with Clifford algebra. In Leo Dorst, Chris Doran, and Joan Lasenby, editors, *Applications of Geometric Algebra in Computer Science and Engineering*, pages 341–349. Birkhäuser, 2002.
12. B. Rosenhahn and G. Sommer. Pose estimation in conformal geometric algebra, part I: The stratification of mathematical spaces. *Journal of Mathematical Imaging and Vision*, 22:27–48, 2005.

Wiener Channel Smoothing: Robust Wiener Filtering of Images*

Michael Felsberg

Linköping University, Computer Vision Laboratory,
SE-58183 Linköping, Sweden,
mfe@isy.liu.se, http://www.isy.liu.se/~mfe

Abstract. In this paper, we combine the well-established technique of Wiener filtering with an efficient method for robust smoothing: channel smoothing. The main parameters to choose in channel smoothing are the number of channels and the averaging filter. Whereas the number of channels has a natural lower bound given by the noise level and should for the sake of speed be as small as possible, the averaging filter is a less obvious choice. Based on the linear behavior of channel smoothing for inlier noise, we derive a Wiener filter applicable for averaging the channels of an image. We show in some experiments that our method compares favorable with established methods.

1   Introduction

Denoising of signals and images has always been an active area of research. For linear filtering, Wiener theory provides us with an optimal solution, cf. [1]. The restriction to linear filtering is however unsuitable for instationary signals and images, for instance at edges. Nonlinear denoising schemes which take care of instationarities are typically iterative methods or methods which embed the signal into higher dimensional spaces. To the former class belong all diffusion based methods, e.g., [2,3] and other variational methods as total variation and Mumford-Shah-based methods, see [4] for a comparison. To the class of n+1 dimensional embedding methods belong bilateral filtering [5] and the method of channel smoothing [6], which will be described and used further below. Furthermore, there exist also combinations of both, e.g. Beltrami flow [7] and mean-shift filtering [8]. Lately, we added a further method for directly solving an underlying robust problems [9], which however only works for 1D features.

The drawback of the non-linear schemes is the difficulty to decide when to stop the iterative process, how to choose the balance between proximity and smoothness, respectively the sizes of the kernels. Wiener theory does not apply in general, since the methods are highly non-linear. One new method which addresses this problem to some extent are the Kringing filters [10].

* This work has been supported by EC Grant IST-2003-004176 COSPAL. This paper does not represent the opinion of the European Community, and the European Community is not responsible for any use which may be made of its contents.

W. Kropatsch, R. Sablatnig, and A. Hanbury (Eds.): DAGM 2005, LNCS 3663, pp. 468–475, 2005.

In this paper we will exploit the locally linear behavior of channel smoothing to select appropriate smoothing kernels by Wiener filters. In order to make channel smoothing linear over the range of the noise, the channel width is selected based on an initial noise estimate according to [11].

As a result, all parameters of channel smoothing are automatically determined. Results and comparisons of this fully automatic method for denoising and inpainting are presented in a final section.

2   The Channel Representation

The channel representation is a particular information representation which applies local, smooth windows to the feature domain [12]. The representation is obtained from a finite set of *channel projection operators* F_n. These are applied to the signal values in a point-wise way to calculate the *channel values* $c_n(\mathbf{x})$:

$$c_n(\mathbf{x}) = F_n(f(\mathbf{x})) \qquad n = 1, \ldots, N , \tag{1}$$

where f is the signal and $\mathbf{x}$ is the spatial vector. Each signal value $f(\mathbf{x})$ is mapped to a vector $\mathbf{c}(\mathbf{x}) = (c_1(\mathbf{x}), \ldots, c_N(\mathbf{x}))$, the *channel vector* at $\mathbf{x}$. The components of $\mathbf{c}$ are called the *channels*. The set of all channel vectors, i.e., the vector valued function $\mathbf{c} : \mathbf{x} \mapsto \mathbf{c}(\mathbf{x})$, forms the *channel representation* of f. The channels of a signal can by themselves be considered as signals, i.e., the channel representation of a signal can be considered as a set of signals.

The projection operators can be of various form but we concentrate on quadratic splines, i.e.,

$$F_n(f) = B_2(f - n) , \tag{2}$$

where

$$B_2(f) = \begin{cases} \frac{3}{4} - f^2 & |f| \in [0, \frac{1}{2}) \\ \frac{1}{2}(\frac{3}{2} - |f|)^2 & |f| \in [\frac{1}{2}, \frac{3}{2}) \\ 0 & \text{otherwise.} \end{cases} \tag{3}$$

It has been shown that summing channel vectors of samples from a stochastic variable ξ results in a sampled kernel density estimate of the underlying distribution $p(\xi)$ [6]:

$$E\{\mathbf{c}\} = E\{[F_n(\xi)]\} = (B_2 * p)(n) . \tag{4}$$

The global maximum of p is the most probable value for ξ and for locally symmetric distributions, it is equivalent to the maximum of $B_2 * p$. The latter can be approximately extracted from the channel vector $\mathbf{c}$ using an implicit B-spline interpolation [6] resulting in an efficient semi-analytic method. The extraction of the maximum can therefore be considered as a functional inverse of the projection onto the channels. In what follows, we name the projection operation also *channel encoding* and the maximum extraction *channel decoding*.

Based on the previous considerations, the method of channel smoothing consists of three steps [6]:

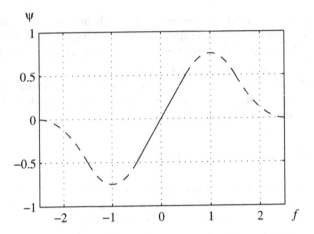

Fig. 1. Influence function of channel smoothing [6]

1. Encode the signal into channels,
2. Locally average each channel (-signal),
3. Decode the channel representation.

If the signal is perturbed by small scale noise relative to the distance between two neighbored channels, local averaging will reduce this noise. Large scale discontinuities remain unchanged. Outliers, i.e., point-wise, large scale deviations are removed. The signal is smoothed in a robust way.

The method has two parameters: the relative scale between the signal values and the channel positions n, i.e., the channel resolution, and the averaging kernel. These two parameters were up to now matter of manual selection, but in the subsequent section we will introduce an automated method based on Wiener theory.

It is of central importance for this derivation that the obtained effective *influence function* of channel smoothing [6] is piecewise linear in the interval $[-\frac{1}{2}; \frac{1}{2}]$, cf. Fig. 1. The influence function describes the change of the robust mean value if a new sample is added to the input set of the estimator. Linearity in $[-\frac{1}{2}; \frac{1}{2}]$ means that any value which is closer than one half to the mean value will be treated as in linear averaging. The decay of the influence function for large arguments leads to a suppression of outliers, since samples with a large distance to the robust mean have zero influence.

3   Wiener Channel Filters

The idea of Wiener channel filters is quite simple: If we assume that the noise stays within the linear interval of the influence function, we can simply apply the same filter as in the linear case, but the result will not suffer from the blurring of edges as in the linear case.

A necessary assumption for the derivations in the following steps is a signal model according to

$$f(\mathbf{x}) = s(\mathbf{x}) + n(\mathbf{x}) \ , \tag{5}$$

where s is the noise free signal and n is Gaussian white noise with variance σ_n^2. In order to assure that the noise stays within the linear interval, we have to select the channel resolution according to the noise level in the signal. More concretely, we choose the distance between the channels such that it covers the 2σ-interval of the noise distribution.

In practice we follow the noise-variance normalization procedure from [11] which estimates constant Gaussian noise variance σ_n^2 with a simple iterative approach based on a null-hypothesis test for a homogeneity function (here: gradient magnitude squared). In a second step, the signal is normalized such that the noise standard deviation becomes $\frac{1}{4}$ according to the requirement above. The normalized signal is then channel encoded with integer channel positions, i.e., the number of channels now depends on the relative noise level of the signal. Due to the rescaling before the encoding, the noise signal n falls nearly entirely into the support of one channel.

According to Wiener theory, the optimal linear filter for denoising f from independent noise is obtained through the autocorrelations of s and n [13]. Let $A_{gg}(\mathbf{x})$ denote the autocorrelation function of the signal g and its vectorization (by concatenation) by $\mathbf{r}_{gg}[k]$. The autocovariance matrix of g is then obtained as $\mathbf{R}_{gg}[k,l] = \mathbf{r}_{gg}[k-l]$. Using these notations, the optimal linear filter is defined as

$$\mathbf{h} = (\mathbf{R}_{ss} + \mathbf{R}_{nn})^{-1}\mathbf{r}_{ss} \ , \tag{6}$$

where $\mathbf{h}$ denotes the impulse response of the filter in vector form.

We do not want to go into details about varieties of Wiener filtering, but there are some particularities we have to mention:

- The autocorrelation of the noise-free signal is not know. Typically the filter is optimized for a whole class of images where (nearly) noise-free versions are available.
- If we only know slightly noisy signals, we can in good approximation estimate the optimal filter by replacing $\mathbf{r}_{ss}$ with the autocorrelation of the slightly noisy signals. This is only valid if the amount of noise in the image set is small compared to the noise in the present instance subject to denoising.
- In practice, we estimate $\mathbf{r}_{ss}$ and $\mathbf{R}_{ss}$ only once for a class of images. By the assumption of independent white noise, we obtain the optimal filter by setting the noise autocorrelation to an impulse with weight σ_n^2 ($\mathbf{r}_{nn} = \sigma_n^2\delta$).

Determining the optimal kernel allows us now to average the channels with a kernel that is optimal concerning denoising the stationary signal parts. After averaging the channels, we have different options to proceed, depending on the application. If we are interested in the denoised image itself, we apply the channel decoding. If we want to analyze the image, e.g. detect edges, it is not necessary to decode the image.

In what follows, we exploit that the averaged channel vector is an *approximation of the local probability density function* (4), which allows to estimate the local differential entropy of the image. We estimate the entropy by

$$\tilde{H}(\mathbf{x}) = - \sum_{n=1, c_n(\mathbf{x}) \neq 0}^{N} c_n(\mathbf{x}) \log c_n(\mathbf{x}) . \tag{7}$$

From (4) we get

$$E\{\tilde{H}\} = - \sum (B_2 * p)(n) \ln(B_2 * p)(n) \approx - \int (B_2 * p)(\xi) \ln(B_2 * p)(\xi) \, d\xi = H_{B_2 * p}.$$

The approximation of the integral by the sum becomes exact, if the term $(B_2 * p)(\xi) \ln(B_2 * p)(\xi)$ has zero Fourier coefficients for integer, non-zero multiples of 2π (i.e., no aliasing occurs). Due to the smoothing of the pdf with B_2, $H_{B_2 * p}$ itself is only an approximation to the true entropy H_p. In practice, the entropy is often estimated by a Parzen-window based approximation. However, this results in a poorer approximation, as we will show in the experiments.

4   Experiments

In the experiments we will focus on three aspects:

– Denoising of images
– Inpainting of images
– Edge detection by entropy

In the denoising experiment we compare our method with ordinary Wiener filtering. We added Gaussian white noise with different standard deviations and in some instances salt & pepper noise (1% density) to two test images, cf. Fig. 2. Both, linear Wiener filtering and Wiener channel filtering remove large parts of the Gaussian noise, but Wiener channel filtering preserves the edges and removes most of the salt & pepper noise. This becomes particularly visible in the difference images in Fig. 2. The different settings in the experiments and the obtained root mean square errors are listed in Tab. 1.

Table 1. Root mean square error comparison of linear Wiener filtering and Wiener channel smoothing.

test image	RMSE of test image	linear filtering	channel smoothing
house, $\sigma^2 = 10^{-3}$	0.032	0.024	0.019
house, $\sigma^2 = 5 \cdot 10^{-3}$	0.070	0.037	0.030
house, $\sigma^2 = 10^{-2}$	0.099	0.045	0.037
house, $\sigma^2 = 10^{-3}$, S&P 1%	0.063	0.036	0.023
cameraman, $\sigma^2 = 10^{-3}$	0.031	0.035	0.023
c.man, $\sigma^2 = 10^{-3}$, S&P 1%	0.063	0.044	0.023

Fig. 2. Denoising experiment. Row-wise from top left to bottom right: House image: original, noisy ($\sigma = 10^{-3}$, 1% Salt & Pepper noise), Wiener filtered, Wiener channel smoothed, difference between linear wiener filtering and Wiener channel smoothing (amplified by factor two); cameraman image: original, noisy ($\sigma = 10^{-3}$, 1% Salt & Pepper noise), Wiener filtered, Wiener channel smoothed, difference between linear wiener filtering and Wiener channel smoothing (amplified by factor two); randomly sampled house image image (25% samples, $\sigma = 10^{-3}$), inpainting result from normalized averaging.

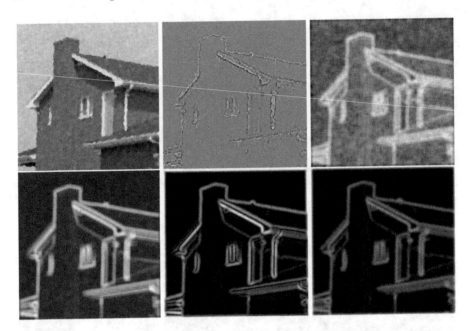

Fig. 3. Top from left to right: inpainting result from channel smoothing, difference between normalized averaging and channel smoothing; local entropy calculated from Matlab standard implementation. Bottom from left to right: entropy calculated from channel representation with same kernel as Matlab standard version (9x9 box filter), raw Canny response (Gaussian derivatives), and channel entropy with the same lowpass kernel as in the Canny filter ($\sigma = 3$).

In a second experiment, we compared the inpainting of channel smoothing and normalized averaging[1] [14], both with a Wiener kernel scaled according to the ratio of present pixels. We created a test image with 25% of the samples and $\sigma = 10^{-3}$, cf. Fig. 2. The results are illustrated in Fig. 2 and Fig. 3. Apparently, the two methods give similar results except for the edges which are better preserved by channel smoothing.

Finally, the edge detection by entropy is compared to the Canny detector [15] and histogram-based entropy computation (Matlab implementation). Whereas the Canny response (Gaussian derivatives) does not respond to lines, the entropy responds to any type of symmetry. Histogram-based entropy (Parzen window instead of B-spline) is more sensitive to noise. Furthermore, binary kernels as used in the Matlab entropy filtering lead to more blurring and a lower SNR.

Concerning the computational costs, channel based methods are 3-4 times slower than linear ones. The averaging itself takes about three times longer than the convolution in the linear case (channel encoding and averaging implemented in a combined look-up table). The channel decoding adds another linear term to

---

[1] We excluded linear filtering, which is basically incapable of performing inpainting.

the complexity. However, channel smoothing is at least one order of magnitude faster than diffusion filtering and other non-linear techniques, cf. [6].

5 Conclusion

Due to its local linearity, channel smoothing allows to combine non-linear smoothing with Wiener theory. The result is an efficient method with automatically adapted parameters for applications in the area of denoising, inpainting, and edge detection. Some variational methods as those described in [4] give probably better results, but they are by two orders slower that channel smoothing. Hence, for many time-critical applications, channel smoothing with automated parameter selection is a suitable approach.

References

1. Scharf, L.L.: Statistical Signal Processing: Detection, Estimation, and Time Series Analysis. Addison-Wesley New York (1990)
2. Perona, P., Malik, J.: Scale-space and edge detection using anisotropic diffusion. IEEE Trans. Pattern Analysis and Machine Intelligence **12** (1990) 629–639
3. Weickert, J.: Theoretical foundations of anisotropic diffusion in image processing. In: Computing, Suppl. 11. (1996) 221–236
4. Bar, L., Sochen, N., Kiryati, N.: Image deblurring in the presence of salt-and-pepper noise. In: Scale-Space 2005. LNCS, Springer Berlin (2005) 107–118
5. Tomasi, C., Manduchi, R.: Bilateral filtering for gray and color images. In: Proceedings of the 6th ICCV. (1998)
6. Felsberg, M., Forssén, P.E., Scharr, H.: Channel smoothing: Efficient robust smoothing of low-level signal features. IEEE Transactions on Pattern Analysis and Machine Intelligence (2005) accepted.
7. Sochen, N., Kimmel, R., Bruckstein, A.M.: Diffusions and confusions in signal and image processing. Journal of Mathematical Imaging and Vision **14** (2001) 237–244
8. Comaniciu, D., Meer, P.: Mean shift: A robust approach toward feature space analysis. IEEE Transactions on Pattern Analysis and Machine Intelligence **24** (2002) 603–619
9. Jonsson, E., Felsberg, M.: Efficient robust mean value computation of 1D features. In: Proceedings of the SSBA Symposium on Image Analysis. (2005)
10. Ruiz-Alzola, J., Alberola-López, C., Westin, C.F.: Kriging filters for multidimensional signal processing. Signal Processing **85** (2005) 413–439
11. Förstner, W.: Image preprocessing for feature extraction in digital intensity, color and range images. In: Proceedings of the International Summer School on Data Analysis and the Statistical Foundation of Geomatics. Lecture Notes on Earth Sciences, Springer (1998)
12. Granlund, G.H.: An Associative Perception-Action Structure Using a Localized Space Variant Information Representation. In: Proceedings of Algebraic Frames for the Perception-Action Cycle (AFPAC), Kiel, Germany (2000)
13. Papoulis, A.: Signal Analysis. McGraw-Hill (1977)
14. Granlund, G.H., Knutsson, H.: Signal Processing for Computer Vision. Kluwer Academic Publishers, Dordrecht (1995)
15. Canny, J.: A computational approach to edge detection. IEEE Transactions on Pattern Analysis and Machine Intelligence **8** (1986) 679–698

Signal and Noise Adapted Filters for Differential Motion Estimation

Kai Krajsek and Rudolf Mester

J. W. Goethe University, Frankfurt, Germany
Visual Sensorics and Information Processing Lab
{krajsek, mester}@vsi.cs.uni-frankfurt.de
http://www.vsi.cs.uni-frankfurt.de/

Abstract. Differential motion estimation in image sequences is based on measuring the orientation of local structures in spatio-temporal signal volumes. For this purpose, discrete filters which yield estimates of the local gradient are applied to the image sequence. Whereas previous approaches to filter optimization concentrate on the reduction of the systematical error of filters and motion models, the method presented in this paper is based on the statistical characteristics of the data. We present a method for adapting linear shift invariant filters to image sequences or whole classes of image sequences. We show how to simultaneously optimize derivative filters according to the systematical errors as well as to the statistical ones.

1 Introduction

Many methods have been developed to estimate the motion in image sequences. A class of methods delivering reliable estimates [1] are the differential motion estimators which contain a wide range of different algorithms [1,2,3]. All of them are based on approximation of derivatives on a discrete grid and it turns out that this approximation is an essential key point in order to achieve precise estimates [1,4]. Many different methods have been developed in the last decade trying to reduce the systematical approximation error of discrete derivative operators [5,6,7,8,9,10]. However, the fact that all real world images are with different extents corrupted by noise has been neglected by these methods. In extension to these approaches mentioned above we present derivative filters adapted to the statistical characteristics of the signal and the noise contained in it.

1.1 Differential Approaches to Motion Analysis

The general principle behind all differential approaches to motion estimation is that the conservation of some local image characteristic throughout its temporal evolution is reflected in terms of differential-geometric entities on the space-time signal $s(\boldsymbol{x})$, $\boldsymbol{x} = (x, y, t)^T$. In its simplest form, the assumed conservation of

W. Kropatsch, R. Sablatnig, and A. Hanbury (Eds.): DAGM 2005, LNCS 3663, pp. 476–484, 2005.
© Springer-Verlag Berlin Heidelberg 2005

brightness along the motion trajectory through space-time leads to the well-known brightness constancy constraint equation (BCCE), where $\partial s(\boldsymbol{x})/\partial \boldsymbol{r}$ denotes the directional derivative in direction $\boldsymbol{r}$, $|\boldsymbol{r}| = 1$ and $\boldsymbol{g}(\boldsymbol{x})$ is the gradient of the gray value signal $s(\boldsymbol{x})$:

$$\frac{\partial s(\boldsymbol{x})}{\partial \boldsymbol{r}} = 0 \quad \Leftrightarrow \quad \boldsymbol{g}^T(\boldsymbol{x}) \cdot \boldsymbol{r} = 0. \tag{1}$$

Since $\boldsymbol{g}^T(\boldsymbol{x}) \cdot \boldsymbol{r}$ is identical to the directional derivative of s in direction $\boldsymbol{r}$, the BCCE states that this derivative vanishes in the direction of motion. Since it is fundamentally impossible to solve for $\boldsymbol{r}$ by a single linear equation, additional constraints have to be considered. One way to cope with this so called *aperture problem* is to perform a weighted average of the residual term of multiple BCCE's in a local neighborhood V. Using a spatiotemporal weighting function $w(\boldsymbol{x})$ and the Euclidean metric this leads to the optimization problem [11]

$$\int_V w(\boldsymbol{x}) \left| \boldsymbol{g}^T(\boldsymbol{x}) \cdot \boldsymbol{r} \right|^2 \, d\boldsymbol{x} \longrightarrow \min$$

$$\Rightarrow \quad \boldsymbol{r}^T \mathbf{C}_g \boldsymbol{r} \longrightarrow \min \quad \text{with} \quad \mathbf{C}_g := \int_V w(\boldsymbol{x}) \boldsymbol{g}(\boldsymbol{x}) \boldsymbol{g}^T(\boldsymbol{x}) \, d\boldsymbol{x}.$$

The solution vector $\hat{\boldsymbol{r}}$ is the eigenvector corresponding to the minimum eigenvalue of the *structure tensor* $\mathbf{C}_g$ (cf. [12,13]) [1]. In order to calculate the structure tensor, the partial derivatives of the signal have to be computed at discrete grid points. The implementation of the discrete derivative operators itself is a formidable problem, even though some early authors [2] apparently disregarded the crucial importance of this point.

1.2   Discrete Derivative Operators

Since derivatives are only defined for continuous signals, an interpolation of the discrete signal $s(\boldsymbol{x}_n), n \in \{1, 2, ..., N\}$, $\boldsymbol{x}_n \in \mathbb{R}^3$ to the assumed underlying continuous signal $s(\boldsymbol{x})$ has to be performed [5] where $c(\boldsymbol{x})$ denotes the continuous interpolation kernel

$$\frac{\partial s(\boldsymbol{x})}{\partial \boldsymbol{r}} \bigg|_{\boldsymbol{x}_n} = \frac{\partial}{\partial \boldsymbol{r}} \left(\sum_j s(\boldsymbol{x}_j) c(\boldsymbol{x} - \boldsymbol{x}_j) \right) \bigg|_{\boldsymbol{x}_n} = \sum_j s(\boldsymbol{x}_j) \underbrace{\left(\frac{\partial}{\partial \boldsymbol{r}} c(\boldsymbol{x} - \boldsymbol{x}_j) \right) \bigg|_{\boldsymbol{x}_n}}_{d_{\boldsymbol{r}}(\boldsymbol{x}_n)} \tag{2}$$

The right hand side of eq. (2) is the convolution of the discrete signal $s(\boldsymbol{x}_n)$ with the sampled derivative of the interpolation kernel $d_{\boldsymbol{r}}(\boldsymbol{x}_n)$, the impulse response of the derivative filter $\frac{\partial s(\boldsymbol{x}_n)}{\partial \boldsymbol{r}} = s(\boldsymbol{x}_n) * d_{\boldsymbol{r}}(\boldsymbol{x}_n)$. Since an ideal discrete derivative filter $d_{\boldsymbol{r}}(\boldsymbol{x}_n)$ has an infinite number of coefficients ([14], p.128), an approximation

---

[1] This is the correct solution only in case that the noise contained in the gradient vectors $\boldsymbol{g}(\boldsymbol{x})$ is i.i.d. in all its components, and also between adjacent gradients.

$\tilde{d}_r(\boldsymbol{x}_n)$ has to be found. In an attempt to simultaneously perform the interpolation and some additional noise reduction by smoothing, often Gaussian functions are used as interpolation kernels $c(\boldsymbol{x})$ [13]. In the next section we show how to put such ad hoc approaches on solid theoretical grounds. Instead of choosing a Gaussian function in order to reduce assumed noise in high frequency regions, we derive a signal-and-noise adapted filter whose shape is determined by the actual statistical signal and noise characteristic.

2   The Signal and Noise Adapted Filter Approach

The signal and noise adapted (SNA)-filter approach is motivated by the fact that we can exchange the directional derivative filter $d_r(\boldsymbol{x}_n)$ in the BCCE by any other steerable filter $h_r(\boldsymbol{x}_n)$ which only nullifies the signal when applied in the direction of motion [15]. The shape of the frequency spectrum of any *rank 2*[2] signal is a plane K_r going through the origin of the Fourier space and its normal vector $\boldsymbol{n}$ points to the direction of motion $\boldsymbol{r}$ ([13],p.316). Thus, the transfer function [3] $H_r(\boldsymbol{f})$ has to be zero in that plane, but the shape of $H_r(\boldsymbol{f})$ outside of plane K_r can be chosen freely as long as it is not zero at all. If the impulse response $h_r(\boldsymbol{x}_n)$ shall be real-valued, the corresponding transfer function $H_r(\boldsymbol{f})$ has to be real and symmetric or imaginary and antisymmetric or a linear combination thereof. The additional degrees of freedom to design the shape outside K_r make it possible to consider the spectral characteristics of the signal and the noise which are encoded in the second order statistical moments in the filter design. In the following section the derivation of an optimal filter is shown which is a special case of the more general framework presented in [16] and for the special case of motion estimation in [17].

2.1   General Model of the Observed Signal

The general idea of the SNA-filter proposed first in [18] is to combine Wiener's theory of optimal filtering with a desired ideal impulse response. The term ideal, in this case, means that the filter is designed for noise free signal $s(\boldsymbol{x})$. But signals are always corrupted by noise. Our goal is now to adapt the ideal filter $h_r(\boldsymbol{x})$ to more realistic situations where signal is corrupted by noise. We model the observed image signal z at position i, j, k in a spatio-temporal block of dimension $N \times N \times N$ by the sum of the ideal (noise free) signal s and a noise term v: $z(i, j, k) = s(i, j, k) + v(i, j, k)$. For the subsequent steps, it is convenient to arrange the s, v, and z of the block in vectors $\boldsymbol{s} \in \mathbb{R}^M, \boldsymbol{v} \in \mathbb{R}^M$ and $\boldsymbol{z} \in \mathbb{R}^M$. The extraction of a single filter response value $\hat{g}$ thus be written as scalar product $\hat{g} = \boldsymbol{x}^T \boldsymbol{z}$ using a filter coefficient vector $\boldsymbol{x} \in \mathbb{R}^M$. The block diagram in fig. 1 provides a graphical representation of our model, and the corresponding equation for the actual filter output $\hat{g}$ reads:

$$\hat{g} = \boldsymbol{x}^T \boldsymbol{z} = \boldsymbol{x}^T (\boldsymbol{s} + \boldsymbol{v}) = \boldsymbol{x}^T \boldsymbol{s} + \boldsymbol{x}^T \boldsymbol{v} \,. \tag{3}$$

---

[2] The rank of a signal is defined by the rank of the corresponding structure tensor

[3] The Fourier transforms of functions are denoted here by capital letters.

Our task is to choose $\boldsymbol{x}^T$ in such a way that the filtered output $\hat{g}$ approximates, on an average, the desired output $g = \boldsymbol{h}^T\boldsymbol{s}$ for the error-free case as closely as possible. The next step is to define the statistical properties of the signal and the noise processes, respectively. Let the noise vector $\boldsymbol{v} \in \mathbb{R}^N$ be a zero-mean random vector with covariance matrix $\mathsf{E}\left[\boldsymbol{v}\boldsymbol{v}^T\right] = \mathbf{C}_v$ (which is in this case equal to its correlation matrix $\mathbf{R}_v$). Furthermore, we assume that the process which has generated the signal $\boldsymbol{s} \in \mathbb{R}^N$ can be described by the expectation $\mathsf{E}\left[\boldsymbol{s}\right] = \boldsymbol{m}_s$ of the signal vector, and an autocorrelation matrix $\mathsf{E}\left[\boldsymbol{s}\boldsymbol{s}^T\right] = \mathbf{R}_s$. Our last assumption is that noise and signal are uncorrelated $\mathsf{E}\left[\boldsymbol{s}\boldsymbol{v}^T\right] = 0$.

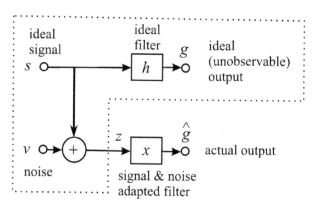

Fig. 1. Block diagram of the filter design scenario (unobservable entities in the dashed frame)

2.2   Designing the Optimized Filter

Knowing these first and second order statistical moments for both the noise as well as the signal allows the derivation of the optimum filter $\boldsymbol{x}$. For this purpose, we define the approximation error $e := \hat{g} - g$ between the ideal output g and the actual output $\hat{g}$. The expected squared error Q as a function of the vector $\boldsymbol{x}$ can be computed from the second order statistical moments:

$$Q(\boldsymbol{x}) = \mathsf{E}\left[e^2\right] = \mathsf{E}\left[\hat{g}^2\right] - 2\mathsf{E}\left[g\hat{g}\right] + \mathsf{E}\left[g^2\right]$$
$$= \boldsymbol{h}^T\mathbf{R}_s\boldsymbol{h} - 2\boldsymbol{x}^T\mathbf{R}_s\boldsymbol{h} + \boldsymbol{x}^T(\mathbf{R}_s^T + \mathbf{R}_v)\boldsymbol{x}$$

We see that a minimum mean squared error (MMSE) estimator can now be designed. We set the derivative $\partial Q(\boldsymbol{x})/\partial\boldsymbol{x}$ to $\mathbf{0}$ and after solving for $\boldsymbol{x}$ we obtain

$$\boldsymbol{x} = \underbrace{(\mathbf{R}_s^T + \mathbf{R}_v)^{-1}\mathbf{R}_s}_{\mathbf{M}}\,\boldsymbol{h} = \mathbf{M}\boldsymbol{h}\;. \tag{4}$$

Thus, the desired SNA-filter is obtained by a matrix vector multiplication. The ideal filter designed for the ideal noise free case is multiplied with a matrix $\mathbf{M}$ composed out of the correlation matrices of signal and noise. In principle, this result is a direct consequence of the Gauss-Markov theorem.

3 Designed Filter Sets

With the framework presented in section 2 we are able to find for each linear shift invariant filter h a corresponding noise resistent filter operator x which takes into account the 2nd order statistics. In order to obtain optimal results also for low signal to noise ratios, h should be already optimized for the noise free case. We use filters optimized by the methods of SCHARR [7] and SIMONCELLI [5]. The methods of ELAD ET AL.[9] and ROBINSON and MILANFAR [10] use prior information about the true velocity range which is not guaranteed to be available in all applications. If this information is available it should be used to adapt the filter to it. However, our approach is already adapted to the motion range reflected in the autocorrelation function of the image sequence which can easily be estimated. For reasons of comparison, we also optimize the $5 \times 5 \times 5$ Sobel operator, which is clearly a non-suitable operator for high-precision motion estimation.

In general, we cannot assume any direction of motion to be more important than others. In practice we are faced with the problem of estimating the correlation function of the statistical process from a limited number of signal samples. Estimation the necessary acf (needed for $\mathbf{R}_s$) of a given image sequence is prob-

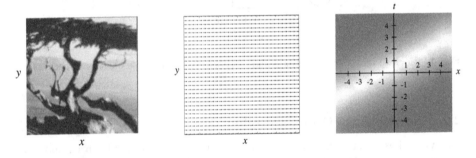

Fig. 2. Translating tree: Left: One frame of the image sequence. Middle: True motion field. Right: Slice through the corresponding autocorrelation function showing a clear structure in direction of motion r.

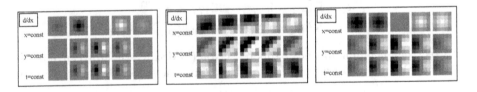

Fig. 3. Left: Original SCHARR derivative filter; Middle: SCHARR derivative SNA-filter according to the covariance structure of the translating tree sequence; Right: SCHARR derivative SNA-filter according to the symmetrized covariance structure of the translating tree sequence. The filter masks are shown for t=constant (upper row), y=constant (middle row) and t=constant (lower row).

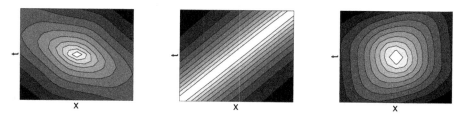

Fig. 4. Contour Plots of a slice through the 3D ACF; left: Yosemite sequence; middle: translating tree; right: diverging tree

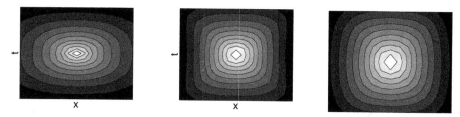

Fig. 5. Contour plots of a slide through the 3D symmetrized ACF; left: Yosemite sequence; middle: translating tree; right: diverging tree

lematic in that *temporal* position of the acf will in general be very strongly determined by the current flow field, thus yielding an over-adaption to just the sequence at hand. In order to illustrate this issue, let us regard the influence of measured autocorrelation function (acf) on SNA-filters. In fig. 3 the original SCHARR filter (left, for details about this filter we refer to [7]) and the SNA SCHARR filter (middle) optimized for the translating tree sequence (fig. 2, left) for $S/N=0$ dB, are depicted. The structure of the autocorrelation function (shown in fig. 2, right) with the maximum being aligned with the direction of motion, is reflected in the filter masks leading to a rotation in the impulse responses of the partial derivatives. The partial derivative operator does not point along the corresponding principal axes any more but is adjusted towards the direction of motion r. This is caused by the optimization procedure described by equation 4. The matrix $\mathbf{M}$ rotates the filter such that the filter output is on average as close as possible to the output of the ideal filter applied to the ideal signal as long as we regard only this sequence, or if the acf of the given sequence(s) is typical for all potential input sequences.

The key to avoid over-adaptation to the preference motion direction of given sequences is to virtually rotate the sequence in the x-y plane. This can equivalently also be done by rotating the measured acf. We average the estimated autocorrelation matrix over all possible directions of motion r whereas the absolute value of the velocity is kept constant. Thus, we eliminate any direction preference and the optimized filter mask does not induce any bias. The absolute value of the velocity is still encoded in the averaged autocorrelation matrix. Fig. 4 shows some examples of such symmetrized autocorrelation functions. The corresponding optimized filters are shown in fig. 3 (right).

4   Experimental Results

In this section, we present examples which show the performance of our optimization method. For the test we use three image sequences, together with the true optical flow: 'Yosemite' (without clouds) 'diverging tree' and 'translating tree' sequences[4]. The optical flow has been estimated with the tensor based

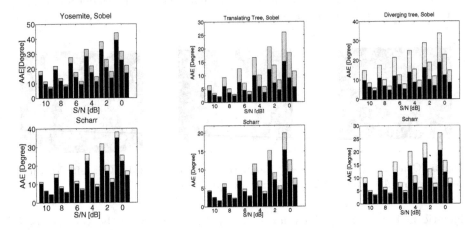

Fig. 6. Bar plots of the average angular error (AAE) vs. the signal to noise (S/N) ratio. For every S/N ratio the AAE for three different densities is depicted: From left to right: 86%, 64% and 43%. The gray bar denotes the AAE with the original, the black ones the AAE with the optimized filters. Note that the experiment is performed at rather bad S/N ratio in range 10 dB to 0 dB.

method described in section 1.1. For all experiments, an averaging volume of size $11 \times 11 \times 11$ and filters of size $5 \times 5 \times 5$ are applied. For the weighting function $w(\boldsymbol{x})$, we chose a sampled Gaussian function with width $\sigma = 8$ (in pixels) in all directions. For performance evaluation, the average angular error (AAE) [1] is computed. The AAE is computed by taking the average over 1000 trials with individual noise realization. In order to achieve a fair comparison between the different filters but also between different signal-to-noise ratios S/N, we compute all AAEs for three different but fixed densities [5] determined by applying the *total coherence measure* and the *spatial coherence measure* [13]. We optimized the SCHARR, SIMONCELLI and the Sobel filter for every individual signal to noise ratio S/N in a range from 10 dB to 0 dB (for i. i. d. noise). We then applied

---

[4] The diverging and translating tree sequence has been taken from Barron's web-site and the Yosemite sequence from *http://www.cs.brown.edu/people/black/images.html*

[5] The density of an optical flow field is defined as the percentage of estimated flow vectors which have been used for computing the AAE with respect to all estimated flow vectors.

both the original SIMONCELLI, SCHARR and the $5 \times 5 \times 5$ Sobel filter and its corresponding SNA-filters.

As expected and shown in fig. 6, the SNA-filters yield a better performance than the original non-adapted filters in case the image sequence being corrupted by noise for all types of ideal filters (the SIMONCELLI filter performs equivalently to the SCHARR filter, thus only the performance of the latter is shown in the figures). The highest performance increase could be gained by optimizing the Sobel filter. But also the performance of the SCHARR filter is increased by optimizing it to the corresponding images sequence. In the case of the translating tree and diverging tree sequences, the difference between the optimized Sobel and optimized SCHARR filter decreases for lower signal to noise ratio. We can conclude that for these cases the optimum shape of the filter is mainly determined by the signal and noise characteristics, whereas for higher signal to noise ratios the systematical optimization plays a greater role.

5   Summary and Conclusion

We have presented a method for designing derivative filters for motion estimation which are optimized according to the characteristics of signal and noise. Our filter adapts to the characteristics in spatial and temporal direction which is implicitly reflected in correlation structure of the image sequence. The SNA-filter design is completely automatic without the need of any assumption on the flow field characteristics as opposed to previous approaches [9,10]. All information necessary for the filter design can be obtained from measurable data. In order to design filters which are universally applicable, we averaged the autocorrelation matrix over all possible directions while keeping the absolute value of the velocity constant. Thus this method still encodes the absolute value of the velocity in the covariance structure and optimizes the filter according to it. The combination of these filters with the structure tensor approach showed a significant gain in motion estimation when applied to noisy image sequences.

This work has been funded by DFG SPP1114.

References

1. Barron, J.L., Fleet, D.J., Beauchemin, S.S.: Performance of optical flow techniques. Int. Journal of Computer Vision **12** (1994) 43–77
2. Horn, B., Schunck, B.: Determining optical flow. Artificial Intelligence **17** (1981) 185–204
3. Lucas, B., Kanade, T.: An iterative image registration technique with an application to stereo vision. In: Proc. Seventh International Joint Conference on Artificial Intelligence, Vancouver, Canada (August 1981) 674–679
4. Simoncelli, E.P.: Distributed Analysis and Representation of Visual Motion. PhD thesis, Massachusetts Institut of Technology, USA (1993)
5. Simoncelli, E.P.: Design of multi-dimensional derivative filters. In: Intern. Conf. on Image Processing, Austin TX (1994)

6. Knutsson, H., Andersson, M.: Optimization of sequential filters. Technical Report LiTH-ISY-R-1797, Computer Vision Laboratory, Linköping University, S-581 83 Linköping, Sweden (1995)
7. Scharr, H., Körkel, S., Jähne, B.: Numerische Isotropieoptimierung von FIR-Filtern mittels Querglättung. In: Mustererkennung 1997 (Proc. DAGM 1997), Springer Verlag (1997)
8. Knutsson, H., Andersson, M.: Multiple space filter design. In: Proc. SSAB Swedish Symposium on Image Analysis, Göteborg, Sweden (1998)
9. Elad, M., Teo, P., Hel-Or, Y.: Optimal filters for gradient-based motion estimation. In: Proc. Intern. Conf. on Computer Vision (ICCV'99). (1999)
10. Robinson, D., Milanfar, P.: Fundamental performance limits in image registration. IEEE Transactions on Image Processing **13** (2004)
11. Mester, R.: A new view at differential and tensor-based motion estimation schemes. In Michaelis, B., ed.: Pattern Recognition 2003. Lecture Notes in Computer Science, Magdeburg, Germany, Springer Verlag (2003)
12. Bigün, J., Granlund, G.H.: Optimal orientation detection of linear symmetry. In: First International Conference on Computer Vision, ICCV, Washington, DC., IEEE Computer Society Press (1987) 433–438
13. Haussecker, H., Spies, H.: Motion. In Handbook of Computer Vision and Applications (1999) 310–396
14. Jähne, B., Scharr, H., Körkel, S.: Principles of filter design. In Handbook of Computer Vision and Applications (1999) 125–153
15. Mester, R.: On the mathematical structure of direction and motion estimation. In: Workshop on Physics in Signal and Image Processing, Grenoble, France (2003)
16. Mühlich, M., Mester, R.: A statistical unification of image interpolation, error concealment, and source-adapted filter design. In: Proc. Sixth IEEE Southwest Symposium on Image Analysis and Interpretation, Lake Tahoe, NV/U.S.A. (2004)
17. Krajsek, K., Mester, R.: Wiener-optimized discrete filters for differential motion estimation. In: Complex Motion, 1.Int. Workshop, Günzburg, Oct.2004. Volume 3417 of Lecture Notes in Computer Science., Springer Verlag (2005)
18. Mester, R.: A system-theoretical view on local motion estimation. In: Proc. IEEE SouthWest Symposium on Image Analysis and Interpretation, Santa Fé (NM), IEEE Computer Society (2002)

Variational Deblurring of Images with Uncertain and Spatially Variant Blurs

Martin Welk[1], David Theis[2], and Joachim Weickert[1]

[1] Mathematical Image Analysis Group,
Faculty of Mathematics and Computer Science, Bldg. 27,
Saarland University, 66041 Saarbrücken, Germany
{welk,weickert}@mia.uni-saarland.de
http://www.mia.uni-saarland.de

[2] Department of Mathematics, Faculty of Mathematics and Computer Science,
Bldg. 36, Saarland University, PO box 151150, 66041 Saarbrücken, Germany
theis@num.uni-sb.de
http://www.num.uni-sb.de/iam/schusterPE.php

Abstract. We consider the problem of deblurring images which have been blurred by different reasons during image acquisition. We propose a variational approach admitting spatially variant and irregularly shaped point-spread functions. By involving robust data terms, it achieves a high robustness particularly with respect to imprecisions in the estimation of the point-spread function. A good restoration of image features is ensured by using non-convex regularisers and a strategy of reducing the regularisation weight. Experiments with irregular spatially invariant as well as with spatially variant point-spread functions demonstrate the good quality of the method as well as its stability under noise.

Keywords: deblurring, variational method, robust data terms.

1   Introduction

Blurring of images in the process of acquisition appears in many application contexts. Reasons include defocussing as well as camera and object motion during exposition. Besides that, optical imperfection of the lens system also causes blurring. Ubiquity of these image degradation makes deblurring a problem of outstanding importance in image processing.

Often the blurring can be captured by convolution of a sharp image with some kernel, or point-spread function (PSF), which does not depend on the location within the image. Typical cases where such *spatially invariant* blur occurs are translatory motion of the camera, and defocussing if all objects are at equal depth. However, in many important cases the PSF changes between different locations in the image, i.e. one has a *spatially variant* blur. Even rotations of the camera for static scenes lead to spatially variant blur.

Assume first we have spatially invariant blur with known PSF. One relatively simple approach to deblurring is then to multiply the Fourier transform of the blurred image

W. Kropatsch, R. Sablatnig, and A. Hanbury (Eds.): DAGM 2005, LNCS 3663, pp. 485–492, 2005.

by the reciprocal $\hat{h}^{-1}$ of the Fourier transform of the kernel h. Refinement of this idea by suitable treatment of such frequencies for which $\hat{h}$ is close to zero leads to classical linear deblurring filters like pseudoinverse filtering and Wiener filtering [21,10]. Limitations of this approach are its restriction to spatially invariant blur as well as characteristic oscillatory artifacts which cannot be avoided by linear methods [3].

The variational deblurring approach is able to reduce these artifacts. A rich literature exists on variational deblurring in the case of spatially invariant PSF. The choice of suitable regularisation terms ensures that important structures in the image like edges are restored in good quality. In this paper, we will extend the variational approach to a slightly more general form which also covers spatially variant blurs.

It is worth noting that many papers on deblurring show only synthetic tests where the degraded image is obtained by blurring a sharp image with a known PSF. In application contexts, however, the PSF will mostly not be known exactly. In some cases, such as optical errors, it can be measured fairly precise in calibration procedures. In other cases a-priori knowledge restricts the variety of possible kernels, e.g. in defocussing where typically cylindrical kernels occur. Sometimes no restricting assumptions of this kind hold.

As a remedy for this deficient knowledge on the PSF, one can consider blind deconvolution which estimates a convolution kernel and sharp image at the same time. Variational blind deconvolution methods can be found e.g. in [22,9]. For the ill-posedness of the deblurring problem, however, it is desirable to introduce as much a-priori information as one can have into the deblurring process. The approach we present here is a non-blind deconvolution method which is tolerant to imprecision in the kernel to a higher degree than previous ones. In fact, it allows a reasonable deblurring of images which are degraded by natural sources of blur and for which we do principally not know a precise PSF or a sharp ground-truth image. The PSFs in our experiments are just approximated to a modest precision from manually selected image features.

The key to this enhanced robustness is to employ in the variational ansatz *robust data terms* which made their first appearance in a deblurring context in the paper by Bar et al. [2]. Robust data terms are motivated by robust statistics [13,11] and have been introduced in computer vision particularly in motion detection [5,6,12,16,8]. Important theoretical results were contributed by Nikolova [19].

Our paper is organised as follows. In Sec. 2 we derive the gradient descent PDE with robust data terms and spatially invariant PSF. Subsection 2.2 is devoted to specific problems of the selection of the regularisation weight and treatment of boundaries. Experiments are presented in Sec. 3. We end with conclusions in Sec. 4.

Related Work. The deblurring problem has played a role in computer vision research over a considerable time. A great variety of approaches have been undertaken. Blind and non-blind variational deconvolution with total variation regularisation has been considered in [15] as well as in [9] and [1], the latter in combination with a segmentation approach. A blind deconvolution approach with more general regulariser is found in [22]. Bar et al. [2] introduced robust data terms into this field. Bertero et al. [4] contributed results on existence, uniqueness and stability of solutions for variational problems of this type.

Deconvolution with spatially variant PSF has been studied mainly within discrete frameworks such as [17,18,14].

2   Variational Deblurring with Spatially Variant PSF

2.1   Basic Model with Robust Data Terms

A general PSF has the form $H(y,x)$ where y, x denote locations in the sharp and degraded images, respectively. The sharp image g and degraded image f are then connected via

$$f(x) = \int_\Omega g(y) \, H(y,x) \, \mathrm{d}y + n(x)$$

where $\Omega \subset \mathbb{R}^2$ is the image domain, and n denotes noise. Given some approximation u for g, we have the *residual error*

$$R_{f,H}[u](x) := f(x) - \int_\Omega u(y) \, H(y,x) \, \mathrm{d}x \ .$$

Variational deblurring of the image f is achieved by minimising the functional

$$E(u) = \int_\Omega \left(\Phi((R_{f,H}[u])^2) + \alpha \Psi(|\nabla u|^2) \right) \mathrm{d}x \tag{1}$$

where Φ and Ψ are monotonically increasing functions from $\mathbb{R}_0^+$ to $\mathbb{R}$. The first summand in the integrand is the *data term* which favours images u with small residual error. The second summand, called *regulariser*, enforces smoothness of the image. The strength of its influence is determined by the *regularisation weight* $\alpha > 0$. If the function Φ increases for $s \to \infty$ slower than $\Phi(s^2) = s^2$, one speaks of a *robust data term* since in this case large residual errors are given less influence on the value of $E(u)$ than with the quadratic error term. One typical choice is the regularised L^1-norm $\Phi(s^2) = \sqrt{s^2 + \beta^2}$ with $\beta > 0$.

Robust data terms have been introduced in a deblurring context only recently by Bar et al. [2]. In the regularisation term, (regularised) total variation $\Psi(s^2) = \sqrt{s^2 + \varepsilon^2}$ (with small positive ε) has already been preferred over the quadratic Tikhonov regulariser $\Psi(s^2) = s^2$ for a long time because of their better ability to preserve sharp edges in the image. The non-convex Perona–Malik regulariser $\Psi(s^2) = (1 + s^2/\lambda^2)^{-1}$ has been considered in [20]. Here, $\lambda > 0$ is a contrast parameter which determines above which steepness edges are enhanced in the gradient descent process.

A gradient descent equation for (1) reads

$$\partial_t u = \alpha \, \mathrm{div}(\Psi'(|\nabla u|^2) \, \nabla u) - \int_\Omega \Phi'((R_{f,H}[u])^2)(y) \cdot R_{f,H}[u](y) H(y,x) \, \mathrm{d}y \tag{2}$$

which can be evaluated numerically in the simplest case by an explicit scheme. A speed-up could be achieved by using more efficient semi-implicit schemes.

2.2 Boundary Treatment and Parameter Choice

Notice that when writing spatially invariant blur as convolution, problems occur at the boundaries where the blur transfers information from inside the image to outside and vice versa. Our formalism with a general PSF $H(y, x)$ with two location arguments removes these difficulties since only locations within the image occur. Transfer of image information from inside to outside is neglected while the reverse transfer can be considered as part of the noise.

To be able to choose appropriately the parameter α, we must be aware of the double function of the regularisation in deblurring. On one side, deblurring is a highly ill-posed problem such that regularisation is needed to suppress noise. This entails that in the presence of strong noise α should be chosen larger. On the other side, even in a noise-free setting the regularisation term has the function to suppress certain oscillatory perturbations in the filtered image which are not detected by the data term.

The latter aspect generally leads to a much larger α than the pure noise suppression. However, such strong regularisation introduces an unwanted smearing of structures into the filtered image. In [20] a continuation strategy has been proposed which consists in starting with large α and repeating the gradient descent several times with successively decreasing α. In each decrement step, the previously reached steady state serves as initialisation. This method combines a good suppression of oscillation with sharp restoration of image structures. A similar continuation strategy had been proposed in a different context in [7]. We will use this continuation strategy also here. Here, the initial level of α is primarily adapted to the suppression of oscillations while the final level of α depends on the noise intensity.

3 Experiments

In our tests, we used the gradient descent PDE (2) with the robust data term $\Phi(s^2) = \sqrt{s^2 + \beta^2}$ (except for the non-robust case in Fig. 1 (c)). Tieing up with [20] we chose a Perona–Malik regulariser in all cases. With our present implementation based on an explicit scheme, computation times range from 15 to 90 minutes on standard PCs for the images shown in this paper.

Our first experiment, Fig. 1, shows a photograph of Paris at dusk blurred by camera movement during the exposition, with three enlarged detail views. The resulting PSF is fairly irregular. For the deblurring process, it was assumed to be spatially invariant. The PSF then was approximated by clipping the image of an isolated light source from the lower part of the river region. Clearly, the estimation of the convolution kernel from such an approximate impulse response induces an imprecision. Further, a closer look at the blurred image reveals that the assumption of spatially invariant blur does not perfectly capture the situation since impulse responses in opposite corners of the image are of slightly different shape. In the case of non-robust variational deblurring it was therefore necessary to choose a large diffusion weight which caused most finer structures in the image to be smoothed away. Nevertheless, street lights are still restored inaccurately, as they are accompanied by shadows and echo images. Street lights far from the river region are badly restored because of the PSF inaccuracy.

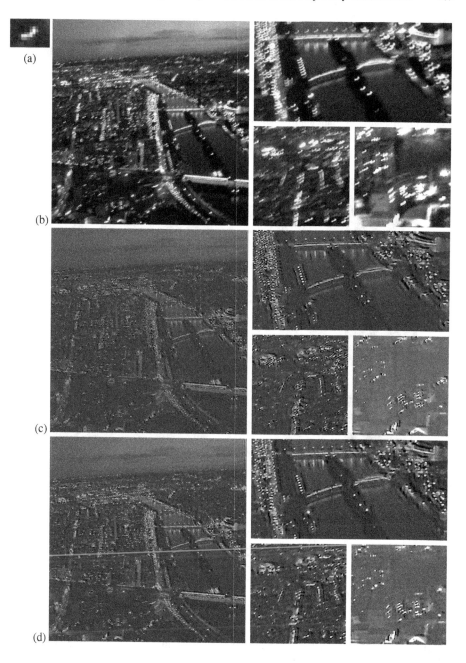

Fig. 1. (a) Spatially invariant, irregularly shaped approximate PSF for deconvolution (enlarged). –
(b) Paris at dusk from Eiffel tower, blurred by camera movement during exposition. Complete image (480×480) and three detail views. Grey-values in lower right detail view have been linearly rescaled. – **(c)** Restoration by variational deblurring with non-robust data term and Perona–Malik regulariser, $\lambda = 15$, $\alpha = 0.1$. – **(d)** Same with robust data term, $\lambda = 15$, $\alpha = 0.02$.

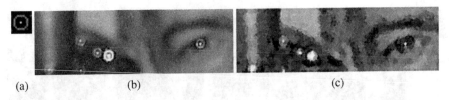

Fig. 2. (a) Spatially invariant approximate PSF (enlarged). – **(b)** Blurred photograph (clipping). – **(c)** Variational deblurring with robust data terms, Perona–Malik regularisation ($\lambda = 40$) and continuation strategy (4 levels with $\alpha = 0.06, 0.03, 0.015, 0.0075$).

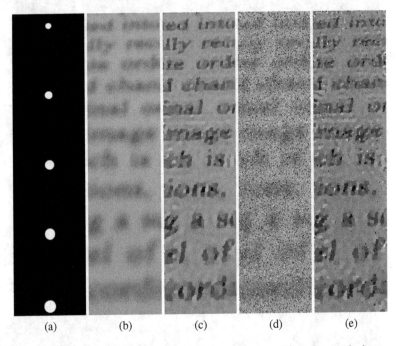

    (a)   (b)   (c)   (d)   (e)

Fig. 3. (a) Spatially variant defocussing PSF (correct size). – **(b)** Defocussed photograph of printed text. – **(c)** Restored by variational deblurring with robust data term and Perona–Malik regulariser ($\lambda = 5$), using continuation strategy (2 levels with $\alpha = 0.03$ and $\alpha = 0.003$). – **(d)** Defocussed photograph with 30 % uniform noise. – **(e)** Restored by variational deblurring with robust data term and Perona–Malik regulariser ($\lambda = 5$), using continuation strategy (2 levels with $\alpha = 0.03$ and $\alpha = 0.015$).

    Robust deblurring, in contrast, can cope with the PSF imprecision much better. A smaller diffusion weight has been chosen such that more structures like streets and buildings are recovered. Shadows and double images near the street lights do hardly occur. Even in the lower left part of the image where the PSF's shape deviates much from that in the river region favourable sharpness is achieved.

    Secondly, we show a detail from a photograph where defocussing together with possible optical errors have introduced a ring-like blur, Fig. 2. The PSF has again been distilled from an approximate impulse response in the image. Obviously it is only a rough estimate. Moreover the image contains many half-tones. The filtered image displays a trend towards steepened contrasts but besides that reveals a sharpening of small structures and highlights.

In our last experiment, Fig. 3, a piece of printed text was photographed from small distance without appropriate focussing. The distance between lens and object varied widely, leading to a stronger defocussing in the lower than in the upper part of the image. Theoretical considerations show that defocussing PSFs are well approximated by cylindrical functions. For defocussing we used therefore a cylindrical PSF whose diameter varies linearly from 5 at the top edge to 10.5 at the bottom edge.

To demonstrate also the robustness of the proposed deblurring method with respect to noise, we replaced 30 % of all pixels by uniform noise. Noise of such intensity is not typically encountered in application data that the method is intended for, so we had to resort to artificial image degradation at this single point. Restoration using our variational method still works well. One difference is that the continuation strategy must stop reducing the diffusion weight α at a larger value now, in order to remove the over-smoothing at the initial large α while preserving the noise suppression by regularisation.

We stress that although we used in Fig. 3 a special PSF shape where effectively only one parameter – the diameter – controls the spatial variation, our deblurring PDE itself is not restricted to such a setting. Indeed it can cope with arbitrarily given $H(y, x)$.

4   Conclusions and Ongoing Work

We have proposed a general energy-minimising approach to image deblurring which allows to treat spatially variant blurs and includes the robust data terms which have first been used in this context by Bar et al. [2]. We used a non-convex regulariser of Perona–Malik type. By employing also the continuation strategy for the regularisation weight that was previously developed in [20], we have obtained a performant method. Experiments demonstrate that image blurs of fairly general shape and different types which emerged during image acquisition could be reverted by this method.

Ongoing work aims at the development of methods to automatise the detection of point-spread functions as well as improved representation of more general types of spatially variant PSFs.

References

1. L. Bar, N. Sochen, N. Kiryati. Variational pairing of image segmentation and blind restoration. In T. Pajdla, J. Matas, editors, *Computer Vision – ECCV 2004*, vol. 3022 of *Lecture Notes in Computer Science*, pages 166–177, Berlin, 2004, Springer
2. L. Bar, N. Sochen, N. Kiryati. Image deblurring in the presence of salt-and-pepper noise. In R. Kimmel, N. Sochen, J. Weickert, editors, *Scale Space and PDE Methods in Computer Vision*, vol. 3459 of *Lecture Notes in Computer Science*, pages 107–118, Berlin, 2005, Springer
3. M. Bertero and P. Boccacci. *Introduction to Inverse Problems in Imaging*. IoP Publishing, Bristol, 1998.
4. M. Bertero, T. A. Poggio, and V. Torre. Ill-posed problems in early vision. *Proceedings of the IEEE*, 76(8):869–889, Aug. 1988.

5. M. J. Black and P. Anandan. Robust dynamic motion estimation over time. In *Proc. 1991 IEEE Computer Society Conference on Computer Vision and Pattern Recognition*, pages 292–302, Maui, HI, June 1991. IEEE Computer Society Press.
6. M. J. Black and P. Anandan. The robust estimation of multiple motions: parametric and piecewise smooth flow fields. *Computer Vision and Image Understanding*, 63(1):75–104, Jan. 1996.
7. A. Blake and A. Zisserman. *Visual Reconstruction*. MIT Press, Cambridge, MA, 1987.
8. T. Brox, A. Bruhn, N. Papenberg, and J. Weickert. High accuracy optical flow estimation based on a theory for warping. In T. Pajdla and J. Matas, editors, *Computer Vision – ECCV 2004, Part IV*, volume 3024 of *Lecture Notes in Computer Science*, pages 25–36. Springer, Berlin, 2004.
9. T. F. Chan and C. K. Wong. Total variation blind deconvolution. *IEEE Transactions on Image Processing*, 7:370–375, 1998.
10. R. C. Gonzalez and R. E. Woods. *Digital Image Processing*. Addison–Wesley, Reading, second edition, 2002.
11. F. R. Hampel, E. M. Ronchetti, P. J. Rousseeuw, and W. A. Stahel. *Robust Statistics: The Approach Based on Influence Functions*. MIT Press, Cambridge, MA, 1986.
12. W. Hinterberger, O. Scherzer, C. Schnörr, and J. Weickert. Analysis of optical flow models in the framework of calculus of variations. *Numerical Functional Analysis and Optimization*, 23(1/2):69–89, May 2002.
13. P. J. Huber. *Robust Statistics*. Wiley, New York, 1981.
14. J. Kamm and J. G. Nagy. Kronecker product and SVD approximations in image restoration. *Linear Algebra and Applications*, 284:177–192, 1998
15. A. Marquina, S. Osher. A new time dependent model based on level set motion for nonlinear deblurring and noise removal. In M. Nielsen, P. Johansen, O. F. Olsen, and J. Weickert, editors, *Scale-Space Theories in Computer Vision*, volume 1682 of *Lecture Notes in Computer Science*, pages 429–434. Springer, Berlin, 1999.
16. E. Mémin and P. Pérez. Hierarchical estimation and segmentation of dense motion fields. *International Journal of Computer Vision*, 46(2):129–155, 2002.
17. J. G. Nagy and D. P. O'Leary. Fast iterative image restoration with a spatially varying PSF. In F. T. Luk, ed., *Advanced Signal Processing Algorithms, Architectures, and Implementations IV*, vol. 3162, pages 388–399, 1997
18. J. G. Nagy and D. P. O'Leary. Restoring images degraded by spatially-variant blur. *SIAM Journal on Scientific Computing*, 19, 1063–1082, 1998
19. M. Nikolova. Minimizers of cost-functions involving nonsmooth data-fidelity terms. Application to the processing of outliers. *SIAM Journal on Numerical Analysis* 40(3):965–994, 2002.
20. M. Welk, D. Theis, T. Brox, J. Weickert. PDE-based deconvolution with forward-backward diffusivities and diffusion tensors. In R. Kimmel, N. Sochen, J. Weickert, editors, *Scale Space and PDE Methods in Computer Vision*, vol. 3459 of *Lecture Notes in Computer Science*, pages 585–597, Berlin, 2005, Springer
21. N. Wiener. *Extrapolation, Interpolation and Smoothing of Stationary Time Series with Engineering Applications*. Cambridge (Mass.), 1949, The MIT Press
22. Y.-L. You and M. Kaveh. Anisotropic blind image restoration. In *Proc. 1996 IEEE International Conference on Image Processing*, volume 2, pages 461–464, Lausanne, Switzerland, Sept. 1996.

Energy Tensors: Quadratic, Phase Invariant Image Operators*

Michael Felsberg and Erik Jonsson

Linköping University,
Computer Vision Laboratory,
SE-58183 Linköping, Sweden

Abstract. In this paper we briefly review a not so well known quadratic, phase invariant image processing operator, the energy operator, and describe its tensor-valued generalization, the energy tensor. We present relations to the real-valued and the complex valued energy operators and discuss properties of the three operators. We then focus on the discrete implementation for estimating the tensor based on Teager's algorithm and frame theory. The kernels of the real-valued and the tensor-valued operators are formally derived. In a simple experiment we compare the energy tensor to other operators for orientation estimation. The paper is concluded with a short outlook to future work.

1 Introduction

Quadratic image processing operators are an important extension of linear systems theory for various purposes, as e.g. corner detection [1,2,3]. Phase-based approaches are an important field when it comes to intensity invariant processing and feature detection, see e.g. quadrature filters [4], phase-based disparity and motion estimation [5], and phase congruency for edge detection [6].

Although the phase-based techniques are based on the Hilbert transform and are therefore supposed to be linear, the extraction of the phase and the computation of phase invariant features requires non-linear operations as modulus or arcustangent. This essential non-linearity gives rise to the field of non-linear phase invariant operators: If we use non-linear operations anyway, there is little reason to restrict our basis filters to linear operators.

One of the most popular operators in context of quadratic, phase invariant signal processing is the energy operator [7,8], which bears its name because it responds with the energy of a single oscillation. For images, this operator can be extended in various ways: as a real-valued operator [9], as a complex-valued operator [10], or as a tensor-valued operator [11], the energy tensor. The latter can be further generalized to higher order derivatives in terms of the gradient energy tensor [12].

---

* This work has been supported by EC Grant IST-2002-002013 MATRIS and by EC Grant IST-2003-004176 COSPAL. However, this paper does not necessarily represent the opinion of the European Community, and the European Community is not responsible for any use which may be made of its contents.

W. Kropatsch, R. Sablatnig, and A. Hanbury (Eds.): DAGM 2005, LNCS 3663, pp. 493–500, 2005.
© Springer-Verlag Berlin Heidelberg 2005

The purpose of this paper is to investigate the background of the energy-operator-like approaches more in detail. In particular we will derive some relations between the operators and their kernels, i.e., those functions which map to zero. In most theoretic considerations we will stick to the continuous case, but we will also propose an algorithm for discrete signals.

2   Energy-Operator-Like Operators

2.1   Definitions

According to [9], the energy operator is defined for continuous 1D signals $s(t)$ as

$$\Psi_1[s(t)] = [\dot{s}(t)]^2 - s(t)\ddot{s}(t) . \tag{1}$$

The real-valued energy operator for continuous 2D signals $s(\mathbf{x})$, $\mathbf{x} = [x\ y]^T$, is defined as [9]

$$\Psi_r[s(\mathbf{x})] = [s_x(\mathbf{x})]^2 - s(\mathbf{x})s_{xx}(\mathbf{x}) + [s_y(\mathbf{x})]^2 - s(\mathbf{x})s_{yy}(\mathbf{x}) . \tag{2}$$

The complex-valued energy operator for continuous 2D signals is defined as [10]

$$\Psi_c[s(\mathbf{x})] = [D\{s\}(\mathbf{x})]^2 - s(\mathbf{x})D^2\{s\}(\mathbf{x}) , \tag{3}$$

where $D\{\cdot\} = \frac{\partial}{\partial x} + i\frac{\partial}{\partial y}$. The tensor-valued energy operator, the energy tensor, is defined as [11]

$$\Psi_t[s(\mathbf{x})] = [\nabla s(\mathbf{x})][\nabla s(\mathbf{x})]^T - s(\mathbf{x})\mathbf{H}s(\mathbf{x}) , \tag{4}$$

where $\nabla s = [s_x\ s_y]^T$ and $\mathbf{H} = \nabla\nabla^T$.

2.2   Basic Relations

Obviously, the operators (2)-(4) are direct generalizations of (1) since all are of the same structure. However, the three different generalizations also show some mutual dependencies. The real-valued 2D operator consists simply of the 1D operator applied to both coordinates and summed up. Furthermore, it is obtained as the trace of (4):

$$\Psi_r[s(\mathbf{x})] = \text{trace}\{\Psi_t[s(\mathbf{x})]\} , \tag{5}$$

i.e., it is equal to the sum of the eigenvalues of Ψ_t. Following the proof in [13], the complex-valued operator corresponds to the double-angle representation of Ψ_t. More concrete: if $\mathbf{n} = [n_1\ n_2]^T$ denotes the eigenvector corresponding to the larger eigenvalue λ_1 of Ψ_t and if we decompose the tensor-valued operator as

$$\Psi_t[s(\mathbf{x})] = \lambda_1\mathbf{n}\mathbf{n}^T + \lambda_2\mathbf{n}^\perp\mathbf{n}^{\perp T} = \begin{bmatrix} \Psi_{11} & \Psi_{12} \\ \Psi_{12} & \Psi_{22} \end{bmatrix} , \tag{6}$$

we obtain the complex-valued operator as

$$\Psi_c = (\lambda_1 - \lambda_2)(n_1 + in_2)^2 = \Psi_{11} - \Psi_{22} + i2\Psi_{12} . \tag{7}$$

To draw a parallel to better known operators, the three energy operators have the same mutual dependencies as gradient magnitude squared, complex gradient squared ($[D\{s\}]^2$), and outer product of gradients.

2.3   Basic Properties

As stated in [9] for the 1D case and the real-valued 2D case, all energy operators share the property

$$\Psi[s_1 s_2] = s_1^2 \Psi[s_2] + s_2^2 \Psi[s_1] \ . \tag{8}$$

Due to the fact that the real-valued and the complex-valued operators can be derived from the tensor-valued one, it is sufficient to show (8) for Ψ_t.

Proof.

$$
\begin{aligned}
\Psi_t[s_1 s_2] &= [\nabla(s_1 s_2)][\nabla(s_1 s_2)]^T - (s_1 s_2)\mathbf{H}(s_1 s_2) \\
&= [s_2 \nabla s_1 + s_1 \nabla s_2][s_2 \nabla s_1 + s_1 \nabla s_2]^T - (s_1 s_2)\nabla[s_2 \nabla s_1 + s_1 \nabla s_2]^T \\
&= s_1^2 [\nabla s_2][\nabla s_2]^T + s_2^2 [\nabla s_1][\nabla s_1]^T + (s_1 s_2)([\nabla s_1][\nabla s_2]^T + [\nabla s_2][\nabla s_1]^T) \\
&\quad -(s_1 s_2)([\nabla s_2][\nabla s_1]^T + [\nabla s_1][\nabla s_2]^T) - (s_1 s_2)(s_2 \mathbf{H} s_1 + s_1 \mathbf{H} s_2) \\
&= s_1^2 \Psi_t[s_2] + s_2^2 \Psi_t[s_1] \ .
\end{aligned}
$$

As also stated in [9] for the 1D case and the real-valued 2D case, all energy operators respond identically zero to exponential signals:

$$\Psi[A\exp(ax + by)] = 0 \ , \tag{9}$$

where A, a, $b \in \mathbb{C}$. With the same argument as above it is sufficient to show (9) for Ψ_t.

Proof. Let $s(\mathbf{x}) = A\exp(ax + by)$.

$$\Psi_t[s] = \begin{bmatrix} a \\ b \end{bmatrix} s \begin{bmatrix} a & b \end{bmatrix} s - s \begin{bmatrix} aa & ab \\ ab & bb \end{bmatrix} s = 0 \ .$$

As mentioned above, the energy operator bears its name because of the fact that it tracks the energy of a single oscialltion. For general signals however, positivity of the 'energy' operators is not always given. In [14] the authors give a proof for a necessary and sufficient condition for positivity: The logarithm of the signal magnitude must be concave between every two consecutive zeros of the signal. The relation to the signal logarithm will be considered in more detail further below.

3   Discrete Implementation of the Energy Tensor

3.1   Teager's Algorithm

Teager's algorithm [7] is a very efficient way to compute the energy operator in 1D. The discrete 1D energy operator is computed as

$$\Psi_1[s_k] = s_k^2 - s_{k+1}s_{k-1} \ . \tag{10}$$

Teager's algorithm can also be used for the real-valued 2D operator by adding the results of the algorithm in x- and y-direction [9]. For the 2D complex-valued and tensor-valued operator, the implementation based on central differences or modified Sobel operators [15] is straightforward. This changes if one tries to use differences of neighbored samples in order to end up with a 3×3 operator.

3.2   A 2D Teager's Algorithm

It is straightforward that we can apply the 1D algorithm in four different directions:

$$t_1[s_{k,l}] = s_{k,l}^2 - s_{k+1,l}s_{k-1,l} \tag{11}$$

$$t_2[s_{k,l}] = s_{k,l}^2 - s_{k+1,l+1}s_{k-1,l-1} \tag{12}$$

$$t_3[s_{k,l}] = s_{k,l}^2 - s_{k,l+1}s_{k,l-1} \tag{13}$$

$$t_4[s_{k,l}] = s_{k,l}^2 - s_{k-1,l+1}s_{k+1,l-1} \; . \tag{14}$$

These four responses can be combined to a tensor in a similar way as described for the quadrature filter in [4].

As a first step, we consider the series expansion of the four responses for a pure oscillation with frequency vector $[u \; v]^T$:

$$T_1 \propto \sin^2 u = cu^2 + \mathcal{O}(u^4) \tag{15}$$

$$T_2 \propto \sin^2(u+v) = c(u+v)^2 + \mathcal{O}((u+v)^4) \tag{16}$$

$$T_3 \propto \sin^2 v = cv^2 + \mathcal{O}(v^4) \tag{17}$$

$$T_4 \propto \sin^2(u-v) = c(u-v)^2 + \mathcal{O}((u-v)^4), \tag{18}$$

i.e., the four responses correspond to the frame tensors

$$B_1 = \begin{bmatrix} 1 & 0 \\ 0 & 0 \end{bmatrix} \qquad B_2 = \begin{bmatrix} 1 & 1 \\ 1 & 1 \end{bmatrix} \tag{19}$$

$$B_3 = \begin{bmatrix} 0 & 0 \\ 0 & 1 \end{bmatrix} \qquad B_4 = \begin{bmatrix} 1 & -1 \\ -1 & 1 \end{bmatrix} \; . \tag{20}$$

The dual frame with minimum norm is obtained as [16]

$$\tilde{B}_1 = \begin{bmatrix} 0.6 & 0 \\ 0 & -0.4 \end{bmatrix} \qquad \tilde{B}_2 = \begin{bmatrix} 0.2 & 0.25 \\ 0.25 & 0.2 \end{bmatrix} \tag{21}$$

$$\tilde{B}_3 = \begin{bmatrix} -0.4 & 0 \\ 0 & 0.6 \end{bmatrix} \qquad \tilde{B}_4 = \begin{bmatrix} 0.2 & -0.25 \\ -0.25 & 0.2 \end{bmatrix} \; . \tag{22}$$

We can therefore compute the discrete energy tensor as

$$\Psi_t[s_{k,l}] = \sum_{n=1}^{4} t_n[s_{k,l}]\tilde{B}_n \; . \tag{23}$$

Note that the quadratic term is the same in (11–14), so that we can speed-up the calculation by setting

$$t'_n[s_{k,l}] = t_n[s_{k,l}] - s_{k,l}^2 \tag{24}$$

and

$$\Psi_t[s_{k,l}] = s_{k,l}^2 \begin{bmatrix} 0.6 & 0 \\ 0 & 0.6 \end{bmatrix} + \sum_{n=1}^{4} t'_n[s_{k,l}]\tilde{B}_n \; . \tag{25}$$

3.3   Regularization

As pointed out in [11], images typically contain local DC components which cause problems for energy operators [7]. Since we are interested in a simple operator, more advanced methods for suppressing DC components are out of scope and we stick to a simple 3×3 bandpass which subtracts the DC component from the signal.

4   Kernels of Energy Operators

In this section we derive the kernels of the energy operators. Since the operators are quadratic expression of second order derivatives, the equation

$$\Psi[s] = 0 \tag{26}$$

is not at all simple to solve. We start with the 1D case.

4.1   Kernel of the 1D Operator

We start with the observation that

$$\Psi_1[s(t)] = -s(t)^2 \frac{d}{dt} \frac{\dot{s}(t)}{s(t)} \ . \tag{27}$$

Assuming that $s(t) \neq 0$, we therefore get instead of (26)

$$\dot{s}(t) = a\, s(t) \tag{28}$$

for a suitable constant $a \in \mathbb{C}$. As it is well known, the solution to this equation is $s(t) = A \exp(at)$, and assuming s being continuous, (9) is not only sufficient but also necessary to obtain $\Psi_1 = 0$.

Remembering the undergraduate math lessons one might come up with the quick-and-dirty solution of (28), namely to 'multiply' with dt and to integrate. As a result, one obtains the logarithm of $s(t)$, which directly leads to the positivity statement in [14]:

$$\Psi_1[s(t)] = -s(t)^2 \frac{d^2}{dt^2} \log(|s(t)|) \ . \tag{29}$$

4.2   Kernel of the Tensor-Valued Operator

We will now show that the 2D separable exponential (9) is the kernel of the tensor-valued operator $\Psi_t[s(\mathbf{x})]$. At the end of Sect. 2.3 we have already shown that (9) is in the kernel of Ψ_t.

What is left to show is that all functions in the kernel of Ψ_t are of the form (9). The two diagonal elements of the tensor require $s(x, \cdot) = A \exp(ax)$ respectively $s(\cdot, y) = A \exp(by)$. Hence, all functions in the kernel of Ψ_t are of the form (9).

4.3   Kernel of the 2D Real-Valued Operator

The class of real-valued functions where Ψ_r becomes zero can be extended beyond (9). In particular, the real-valued operator Ψ_r becomes zero for and only for

$$|s(\mathbf{x})| = \exp(u(x + iy)) \; , \tag{30}$$

where $u(x + iy)$ is a harmonic function.

Proof. Likewise as in the 1D case, we assume $s \neq 0$ and

$$0 = \frac{\Psi_t}{s^2} = \nabla^T \frac{\nabla s}{s} = \Delta \log(|s(\mathbf{x})|) \; , \tag{31}$$

where $\Delta = \nabla^T \nabla$ denotes the Laplacian. The constraint (31) means that $\log(|s(\mathbf{x})|)$ is harmonic. Hence, $|s|$ must be the exponential of a harmonic function.

Note that u might be generated as the real part of an analytic function [17]. Furthermore, negative s are obtained by adding $i\pi$ to u.

5   Experiments

In this section we show some experiments which relate the performance of the energy tensor to other operators for orientation estimation. In this context it is important to notice that the energy tensor does not only estimate the local orientation but also the local coherence, i.e., it provides a full structure tensor from a 3×3 region.

We therefore compared the pure energy tensor with the standard gradient operator from Matlab and an improved 3×3 Sobel operator [15]. Since it is also common to use regularized operators, we compared the regularized energy tensor (Gaussian post-filtering with $\sigma^2 = 1$, size 7×7) with a comparable Gabor filter set and the structure tensor (same Gaussian post-filter).

The signal which is used in the experiment is a 2D Chirp-like signal with Gaussian noise (29dB SNR), cf. Fig. 5. The orientation error was calculated according to [16] as

$$\Delta\theta = \cos^{-1}\left(\sqrt{\sum \cos^2(\theta_m(\mathbf{x}) - \theta_t(\mathbf{x}))}\right) \; , \tag{32}$$

where θ_m and θ_t indicate the estimated orientation and the ground truth, respectively. The results are plotted in Fig. 5 as functions of the radius, which is reciprocal to the frequency.

Obviously, the energy tensor outperforms the other approaches for the 3×3 filter size. For 9×9 filters, it is still much better than the Gabor filter, but slightly worse than the structure tensor. The slightly poorer performance is caused by the approximation error for the calculation of the dual frame, resulting in a small bias for orientations which are no multiple of $\pi/4$.

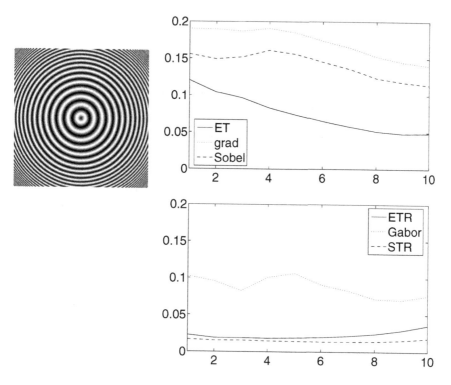

Fig. 1. Left: Test image with 29 dB SNR. Right: Orientation error (in radians) depending on the radius aka frequency. Top: 3×3 operators: ET (energy tensor), grad (Matlab gradient), Sobel. Bottom: 9×9 operators: ETR (regularized ET), Gabor, STR (structure tensor).

6 Outlook

The energy operator can easily be extended to higher dimensions. Both, the continuous operator and the nD Teager's algorithm are straightforward to generalize. What might turn out to be more complicated are the kernels of the discrete operators and the higher dimensional continuous operators as well as the kernel of the complex operator.

For practical applications real-time implementations of the 2D and 3D Teager's algorithm are planned. Experimental comparisons for several applications as corner detection and optical flow estimation will be done.

Acknowledgment

We would like to thank our colleague Klas Nordberg for the discussions about kernels.

References

1. Förstner, W., Gülch, E.: A fast operator for detection and precise location of distinct points, corners and centres of circular features. In: ISPRS Intercommission Workshop, Interlaken. (1987) 149–155
2. Bigün, J., Granlund, G.H.: Optimal orientation detection of linear symmetry. In: Proceedings of the IEEE First International Conference on Computer Vision, London, Great Britain (1987) 433–438
3. Harris, C.G., Stephens, M.: A combined corner and edge detector. In: 4th Alvey Vision Conference. (1988) 147–151
4. Granlund, G.H., Knutsson, H.: Signal Processing for Computer Vision. Kluwer Academic Publishers, Dordrecht (1995)
5. Jähne, B.: Digital Image Processing. Springer, Berlin (2002)
6. Kovesi, P.: Image features from phase information. Videre: Journal of Computer Vision Research 1 (1999)
7. Kaiser, J.F.: On a simple algorithm to calculate the 'energy' of a signal. In: Proc. IEEE Int'l. Conf. Acoust., Speech, Signal Processing, Albuquerque, New Mexico (1990) 381–384
8. Potamianos, A., Maragos, P.: A comparison of the energy operator and the Hilbert transform approach to signal and speech demodulation. Signal Processing 37 (1994) 95–120
9. Maragos, P., Bovik, A.C., Quartieri, J.F.: A multi-dimensional energy operator for image processing. In: SPIE Conference on Visual Communications and Image Processing, Boston, MA (1992) 177–186
10. Larkin, K.G., Oldfield, M.A., Bone, D.J.: Demodulation and phase estimation of two-dimensional patterns. Australian patent AU 200110005 A1 (2001)
11. Felsberg, M., Granlund, G.: POI detection using channel clustering and the 2D energy tensor. In: 26. DAGM Symposium Mustererkennung, Tübingen. (2004)
12. Felsberg, M., Köthe, U.: Get: The connection between monogenic scale-space and gaussian derivatives. In: Proc. Scale Space Conference. (2005)
13. Bigün, J., Granlund, G.H., Wiklund, J.: Multidimensional orientation estimation with applications to texture analysis and optical flow. IEEE Transactions on Pattern Analysis and Machine Intelligence 13 (1991) 775–790
14. Bovik, A.C., Maragos, P.: Conditions for positivity of an energy operator. IEEE Transactions on Signal Processing 42 (1994) 469–471
15. Weickert, J., Scharr, H.: A scheme for coherence-enhancing diffusion filtering with optimized rotation invariance. Journal of Visual Communication and Image Representation, Special Issue On Partial Differential Equations In Image Processing, Computer Vision, And Computer Graphics (2002) 103–118
16. Knutsson, H., Andersson, M.: Robust N-dimensional orientation estimation using quadrature filters and tensor whitening. In: Proceedings of IEEE International Conference on Acoustics, Speech, & Signal Processing, Adelaide, Australia, IEEE (1994)
17. Burg, K., Haf, H., Wille, F.: Höhere Mathematik für Ingenieure, Band IV Vektoranalysis und Funktionentheorie. Teubner Stuttgart (1994)

Object Categorization and the Need for Many-to-Many Matching

Sven Dickinson[1], Ali Shokoufandeh[2], Yakov Keselman[3],
Fatih Demirci[2], and Diego Macrini[1]

[1] Department of Computer Science, University of Toronto
[2] Department of Computer Science, Drexel University
[3] School of CTI, DePaul University

Abstract. Object recognition systems have their roots in the AI community, and originally addressed the problem of object categorization. These early systems, however, were limited by their inability to bridge the representational gap between low-level image features and high-level object models, hindered by the assumption of one-to-one correspondence between image and model features. Over the next thirty years, the mainstream recognition community moved steadily in the direction of exemplar recognition while narrowing the representational gap. The community is now returning to the categorization problem, and faces the same representational gap as its predecessors did. We review the evolution of object recognition systems and argue that bridging this representational gap requires an ability to match image and model features many-to-many. We review three formulations of the many-to-many matching problem as applied to model acquisition and object recognition.

1 Introduction

The evolution of object recognition over the past thirty years has witnessed a shift from shape-based category recognition to appearance-based exemplar recognition. As seen in Figure 1, early object recognition systems modeled object categories as collections of high-level, volumetric parts, such as generalized cylinders. These models represented intuitive, parts-based abstractions of objects that offered invariance to minor shape deformations, part articulation, and occlusion (due to the locality of the representation). Unfortunately, the vision community lacked the tools to recover such shape abstractions from real images of real objects, leaving a representational gap that remains a challenge to this day. Instead, category-level object recognition systems were presented with images of simple, textureless objects in which image features, such as edges, mapped directly to the surface discontinuities and occluding boundaries of the abstract parts comprising categorical models. In effect, the representational gap was artificially eliminated by bringing the images closer to the models. However, the simplistic nature of the resulting scenes left many unsatisfied.

The 1980's witnessed a movement toward geometric CAD models that captured the exact geometry of an object. Rather than defining object categories,

W. Kropatsch, R. Sablatnig, and A. Hanbury (Eds.): DAGM 2005, LNCS 3663, pp. 501–510, 2005.

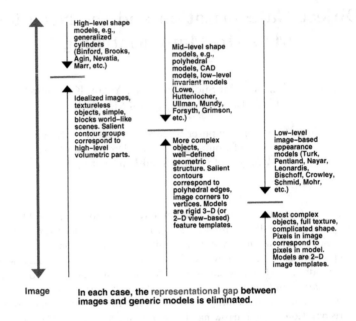

Image   In each case, the representational gap **between** images and generic models is eliminated.

Fig. 1. Evolution of object recognition. In each period, the representational gap was avoided by either bringing the images closer to the models, bringing the models closer to the images, or both. Figure taken from [3], copyright IEEE, 2005.

such models were effectively 3-D shape templates of object exemplars. Once again, simple image features, such as edges, mapped directly to surface discontinuities and occluding boundaries of the model. This time, however, the representational gap was artificially eliminated by bringing the models closer to the image. Although the models were not categorical, they could be used to recognize object exemplars in real images, provided that a detailed geometric model could be acquired and that the imaged objects were textureless. These two restrictions meant that not only did a user have to construct or acquire a faithful 3-D geometric model of the object, the object had to be smoothly shaded, resulting yet again in an unrealistic recognition setting.

The 1990's saw a significant shift in object recognition philosophy from object-centered modeling and recognition to viewer-centered modeling and recognition. Whereas object-centered systems recognize 3-D models from 2-D images, viewer-centered systems modeled an object as a set of 2-D views, thereby reducing "3-D from 2-D" recognition to simple 2-D recognition, at the cost of having to store/match potentially many views. Within the viewer-centered framework, the same representational gap exists between low-level image features and categorical, view-based models. Instead of bridging this gap, the community eliminated the gap by bringing the models even closer to the image, storing the actual images of an object exemplar as its (appearance-based) model views. This paradigm gained tremendous popularity, as 3-D object modeling was no longer required and an object could have arbitrarily complex structure and surface texture. An object database could be constructed by simply placing an object on a turntable and spinning it in front of a camera to acquire a dense set of views.

For the first time, real images of real objects could be recognized. However, it is important to note that through this evolution, the recognition community redefined the recognition problem from category recognition (the predominant goal of recognition systems in the 70's/80's) to exemplar recognition. In each of the three periods above, the difficult problem of image abstraction, i.e., bridging the representational gap by mapping low-level image features to high-level shape primitives, was avoided by either moving the images up or moving the models down. Underlying this movement is a fundamental assumption that for every salient image feature (e.g., region, line, pixel, pixel neighborhood, etc.) there exists a corresponding salient model feature. However, due to noise, segmentation errors, articulation, scale difference, within-class variation, etc., a feature in one image may correspond to a collection of features in another image.

The community is now beginning to return to its categorization roots, armed with new machine learning techniques and invariant image features. But the one-to-one feature correspondence assumption remains, and today's models still tend to encode the appearance (i.e., discriminating texture) of specific exemplars rather than the prototypical shapes of object categories. Hence, two exemplars with different texture/appearance that belong to the same shape category will have little in common with respect to their low-level image structure (e.g., neighborhood-encoded interest points or image patches). The success of object categorization depends on solving two problems. First, we must strive to recover the coarse, high-level shape features that define the prototypical shape of an object, with such features representing abstractions/groupings of low-level image features. Second, we must relax the restrictive, one-to-one correspondence assumption and develop mechanisms for matching image features *many-to-many*.

In this paper, we review three formulations of the many-to-many matching problem and its application to both shape category acquisition and recognition. We assume that an image can be processed to yield a structured collection of image features, conveniently represented as a graph whose nodes encode attributed features and whose edges encode feature relations. In each formulation, one-to-one feature (i.e., one-to-one node) correspondence between exemplars in a given category may not exist at the level of extracted features, but may exist at the level of groups of features. This sets up an intractable many-to-many graph matching problem, for which approximation methods must be sought. Each formulation takes a different approach to the problem, and we review preliminary progress on each front.

2   Model Abstraction from Examples

Our first formulation of many-to-many matching addresses the problem of trying to recover a structural model from a set of exemplars belonging to a known

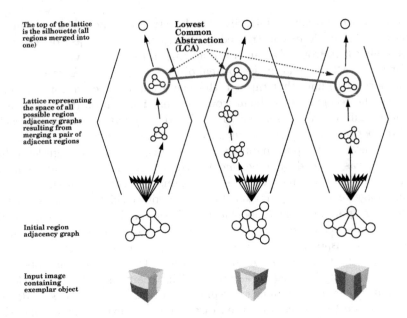

The top of the lattice is the silhouette (all regions merged into one)

Lowest Common Abstraction (LCA)

Lattice representing the space of all possible region adjacency graphs resulting from merging a pair of adjacent regions

Initial region adjacency graph

Input image containing exemplar object

Fig. 2. The Lowest Common Abstraction (LCA) of a set of input exemplars (blocks). In this case, the LCA of the three input exemplars would be the canonical view of the block, in which three surfaces are visible. Figure taken from [3], copyright IEEE, 2005.

class. Consider the simple example shown in Figure 2, in which three different exemplar images are presented to the system, each region segmented to yield a region adjacency graph. Although the structure of the input graphs may be different – in fact, not a single one-to-one node (feature) correspondence may exist between the input exemplar graphs – the exemplars are similar at a higher level of abstraction. If we consider the space of all possible graphs formed by merging two adjacent regions, then each input exemplar gives rise to a lattice of region adjacency graphs, representing all possible region groupings. Finding a model abstraction that best accounts for the input exemplars consists of finding the most complex (maximum cardinality equals most informative) graph that lies in the intersection of the lattices. Since more complex abstraction graphs are lower in the lattice, we call this graph the *lowest common abstraction* (LCA), representing a category-level, view-based description of one view class; additional view classes are acquired by rotating each of the exemplars and repeating the process. Note that the LCA may not be unique.

The above formulation is intractable, for neither the lattices nor their intersection can be realistically generated. Instead, we first narrow the scope of the problem by finding the lowest common abstraction of two lattices, and exploit the fact that we know one member of the intersection lattice, namely the silhouette. As shown in Figure 3, we work top-down from the silhouette, searching for a pair of cuts, one per graph, in the two exemplars' region adjacency graphs,

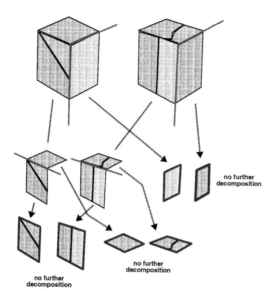

Fig. 3. Finding the lowest common abstraction between two exemplars through a coordinated, recursive decomposition of their silhouettes. Figure taken from [3], copyright IEEE, 2005.

such that corresponding shapes (each cut yields two shapes) and their relations are similar. When a successful cut is found, the corresponding shapes represent a many-to-many matching of component regions.

The process continues recursively down the intersection lattice until no further decomposition is possible. The union of primitive shapes forms the LCA of the two graphs. This procedure is applied to all pairs of input exemplar graphs, leading to a weak approximation of the intersection lattice for all inputs. Finally, we search this approximation for the global lowest common abstraction. Figure 4 shows the LCA computed for three different coffee cup exemplars and the resulting intersection lattice; the computed global LCA is highlighted in orange and represents a good abstraction of the cup, including a handle, body, top, and hole (which it can't distinguish from a surface). Details of the algorithm can be found in [3].

3   Matching Structural Abstractions

The previous formulation of categorical model acquisition from examples searched for abstractions (groupings) of regions (features) that were similar in shape and common to many input lattices. The intractable complexity of the resulting many-to-many graph matching problem led to an effective approximation method that yielded matching abstractions among pairs. However, the abstractions were still graphs, and isomorphism had to be effectively computed. One way of reducing the complexity of graph matching in the presence of noise

Fig. 4. Computed LCA (orange border) of 3 examples. From a set of three region adjacency graphs representing the appearance of three different cup exemplars, the algorithm extracts the salient surfaces of the cup, including the body, inside surface (ellipse at top), handle, and hole (indistinguishable from a real surface). Figure taken from [3], copyright IEEE, 2005.

(spurious nodes and edges), occlusion (both extraneous and missing structure), and minor deformation (leading to graphs of different size) is not to match the graphs themselves but rather low-dimensional vector abstractions of the graphs, each of which encodes the "shape" of a subgraph. Drawing on the domain of spectral graph theory, we have developed a low-dimensional abstraction of directed acyclic graph structure that is robust to noise and perturbation yet rich enough to distinguish structural differences between graphs. It assigns a "structural signature" vector to each node, encoding the "shape" of the underlying subgraph rooted at that node. In a hierarchical structure, where nodes reflect a coarse-to-fine feature decomposition, these vectors provide us with a powerful tool for coarse-to-fine object recognition.

Our vector abstraction of graph structure is a function of the magnitudes of the eigenvalues of a directed graph's underlying adjacency matrix. The eigenvalues encode the degree distribution of the graph and are provably robust to minor perturbation of the graph. Moreover, the dimensionality of the resulting vectors is bounded by the maximum branching factor of the graph

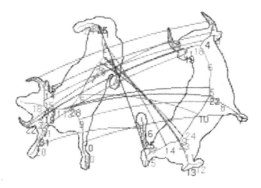

Fig. 5. Part correspondences in two Shock Graphs. Each colored branch in the shape's skeleton represents a node in the shape's hierarchical shock graph. Node correspondences are shown, with correspondences at coarser levels of the hierarchy implicitly defining many-to-many correspondences among substructures at finer levels.

and not by the number of nodes in the graph. Not only do these structural signature vectors offer an effective mechanism for rapid indexing from large databases of graphs [7], but they offer a mechanism for matching graph abstractions [8,6,5]. If the vectors computed for two nodes of two directed acyclic graphs are similar, then their underlying subgraphs have similar structure, i.e., the collection of nodes forming the subgraph rooted at a node in one graph matches a collection of nodes forming the subgraph rooted at a node in a second graph, effectively yielding a many-to-many node (and structure) correspondence. Figure 5 indicates the part correspondence computed for two silhouettes, each represented using a *shock graph* [8], a qualitative decomposition of a silhouette's medial axis structure in terms of a vocabulary of qualitatively defined parts.

4 Structural Matching as Weighted Point Matching

Our first problem formulation could be seen as computing a set of many-to-many node correspondences across a set of input graphs. However, the graphs were known to belong to the same class, i.e., isomorphic at some level of abstraction. Our second problem formulation was more general in that it computed correspondences between nodes whose underlying (rooted) subgraphs have similar structure. The vector abstraction of graph structure implicitly defined a many-to-many matching of the underlying nodes without explicitly computing node correspondences. In this section, we look at the most general formulation of the many-to-many matching problem. Specifically, how do we match two graphs whose structure may be different (as in our first problem) but which may not belong to the same class (as in our second problem)?

Many-to-many graph matching is intractable, for any subset of nodes in one graph may correspond to any subset of nodes in the other graph. Our approach,

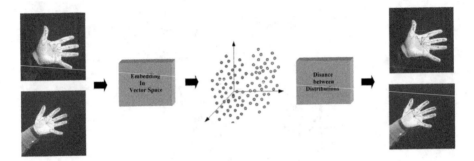

Fig. 6. Many-to-Many Graph Matching as Weighted Geometric Point Matching. Two graphs to be matched are embedded with low distortion into a low-dimensional Euclidean space, the two weighted sets of points are matched many-to-many using the Earth Mover's Distance (EMD) algorithm, and the solution defines a many-to-many node correspondence in the original graphs.

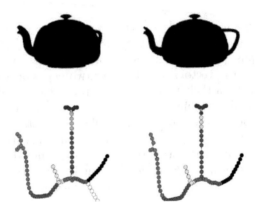

Fig. 7. Many-to-Many Graph Matching Applied to Skeleton Graphs. Corresponding groups of nodes (whose cardinalities may be different) are colored the same, with white nodes unmatched. Figure taken from [4], copyright IEEE, 2003.

depicted in Figure 6, transforms the many-to-many graph matching problem into a domain in which many-to-many matching is easier. Specifically, in working with edge-weighted, attributed graphs, each node maps to a point in a low-dimensional geometric space, with the node's attributes mapping to a mass vector assigned to the point. The structure of the graph is effectively mapped (embedded) into the geometric space by ensuring that the shortest path distances (along graph edges, summing edge weights) between pairs of nodes in the original graph are preserved (with low distortion) as Euclidean distances between their corresponding points in the transformed space; the edges of the graph are effectively discarded.

The above graph embedding framework allows us to translate our original many-to-many graph matching problem to a many-to-many point matching

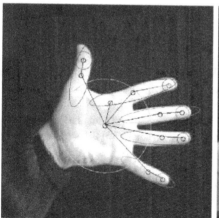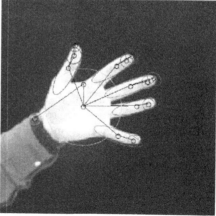

Fig. 8. Many-to-Many Graph Matching Applied to Blob Graphs. Many-to-many feature correspondences have been colored the same. Corresponding groups of nodes (whose cardinalities may be different) are colored the same. Figure taken from [2] (pg. 332), copyright, Springer, 2004, used with kind permission of Springer Science and Business Media.

problem. If we let one graph's points (embedded nodes) be represented as piles of dirt, each of whose volume is proportional to the node's mass, and the other graph's points be represented as holes, each of whose volume is proportional to the node's mass, the many-to-many weighted point matching problem can be formulated as finding the assignment of dirt to holes that minimizes the work required to move the dirt. The Earth Mover's Distance (EMD) algorithm [1] provides an efficient solution, allowing a pile of dirt to be spread across multiple holes and allowing a hole to receive dirt from multiple piles. Moreover, the computed flows between piles and holes can be translated back to the original problem, yielding a many-to-many node correspondence between the original graphs. Details can be found in [4,2].

Figures 7 and 8 illustrate two example domains in which we have successfully applied the approach. In Figure 7, we compute many-to-many node correspondences between two silhouettes represented as skeleton graphs, in which nodes represent medial axis points, edge weights represent Euclidean distances between connected points, and node masses represent the radii of the maximally inscribed circles. The algorithm computes the many-to-many correspondence shown below the silhouettes, with corresponding points colored similarly. In Figure 8, we compute many-to-many node correspondences between two hand images represented as hierarchical blob and ridge decompositions [6]; note that the number of blobs used to model the fingers or palm differs between the two decompositions. The algorithm computes the many-to-many correspondences indicated by the similar coloring.

5   Conclusions

The within-class shape and appearance variation of many object categories precludes recognition strategies that assume a one-to-one correspondence between low-level image features, for it is only at higher levels of abstraction that similarity or correspondence may exist. Image abstraction is an open problem, and it's not clear what form image abstractions should take or how to compute them. In one part of this paper, we review a particular graph (structural description) abstraction and apply it to matching structural descriptions. In a second part of this paper, we use the fact that two objects belong to the same category to help search for a common abstraction. In the final part of the paper, we map structural descriptions to be matched into a geometric space in which rules (i.e., edge weights) for abstracting/grouping features in graph space can be exploited by computationally tractable strategies (e.g., EMD) in geometric space to find corresponding abstractions. Each of these formulations effectively addresses the underlying problem of many-to-many object matching, an important challenge to categorization systems.

References

1. S. D. Cohen and L. J. Guibas. The earth mover's distance under transformation sets. In *Proceedings, 7th ICCV*, Kerkyra, Greece, 1999.
2. M. Demirci, A. Shokoufandeh, S. Dickinson, Y. Keselman, , and L. Bretzner. Many-to-many feature matching using spherical coding of directed graphs. In *Proceedings, ECCV*, Prague, 2004.
3. Y. Keselman and S. Dickinson. Generic model abstraction from examples. *IEEE PAMI*, 27(7), 2005.
4. Y. Keselman, A. Shokoufandeh, M. Demirci, , and S. Dickinson. Many-to-many graph matching via metric embedding. In *Proceedings, IEEE CVPR*, Madison, WI, 2003.
5. D. Macrini, A. Shokoufandeh, S. Dickinson, K. Siddiqi, and S. Zucker. View-based 3-D object recognition using shock graphs. In *Proceedings, Internal Conference on Pattern Recognition*, pages 24–28, Quebec City, August 2002.
6. A. Shokoufandeh, S. Dickinson, C. Jönsson, L. Bretzner, and T. Lindeberg. The representation and matching of qualitative shape at multiple scales. In *Proceedings, ECCV 2002*, pages 759–772, Copenhagen, 2002.
7. A. Shokoufandeh, D. Macrini, S. Dickinson, K. Siddiqi, , and S. Zucker. Indexing hierarchical structures using graph spectra. *IEEE PAMI*, 27(7), 2005.
8. K. Siddiqi, A. Shokoufandeh, S. Dickinson, and S. Zucker. Shock graphs and shape matching. *International Journal of Computer Vision*, 30:1–24, 1999.

Author Index

Lecture Notes in Computer Science

For information about Vols. 1–3554

please contact your bookseller or Springer